The Evolution of Walt Whitman

THE EVOLUTION OF

Walt Whitman

AN EXPANDED EDITION

By Roger Asselineau

Foreword by Ed Folsom

University of Iowa Press

Iowa City

University of Iowa Press, Iowa City 52242
Copyright © 1999 by the University of Iowa Press
All rights reserved
Printed in the United States of America
http://www.uiowa.edu/~uipress

Printed on acid-free paper
Library of Congress Cataloging-in-Publication Data
Asselineau, Roger.
The evolution of Walt Whitman / by Roger Asselineau; foreword by Ed Folsom.—An
expanded ed.
p.   cm.
Originally published: Belknap Press of Harvard University Press, 1960–1962.
Contents: The creation of a personality—The creation of a book.
ISBN 0-87745-682-8 (paper)
1. Whitman, Walt, 1819–1892.   2. Poets, American—
19th century—Biography.   I. Title.
PS3231.A833   1999
811'.3—dc21
[B]   99-33533
99 00 01 02 03 P 5 4 3 2 1

The Belknap Press of Harvard University Press originally published *The Evolution
of Walt Whitman: The Creation of a Personality* in 1960, followed by *The Evolution
of Walt Whitman: The Creation of a Book* in 1962.

To the memory of my parents and Paule, my wife

CONTENTS

FOREWORD

By Ed Folsom

This reprinting of Roger Asselineau's classic critical work is a culminating moment in the University of Iowa Press's ongoing commitment to Whitman scholarship. In the late 1980s, when I began to work with the University of Iowa Press to gather a group of outstanding books about Walt Whitman, one goal was to mingle the several active generations of Whitman scholars. I wanted—through the process of review, through collections of essays, and through the publishing of books by both established and beginning critics—to bring promising young scholars into contact with the still-active group of senior scholars who had written the standard biographies, edited the definitive collections of texts, and written the criticism that had opened the field of modern Whitman studies.

The first book in the informal Iowa series was by one of the venerable senior scholars, Edwin Haviland Miller, who had collected and edited Whitman's correspondence and had written the first detailed psychological study of Whitman. For the Iowa series, he produced *Walt Whitman's "Song of Myself": A Mosaic of Interpretations* (1989), in which he culled over a century of commentary on Whitman's great poem and offered a kind of variorum of criticism on the poem, joining recent controversial interpretations with established standard readings. Miller also produced for Iowa the first selected volume of Whitman's letters, *Selected Letters of Walt Whitman* (1990). Then, as the centennial of Whitman's death approached in 1992, Robert K. Martin gathered a collection of essays under the title *The Con-*

tinuing Presence of Walt Whitman: The Life after the Life
(1992), bringing together distinguished poets and critics from
several generations to discuss Whitman's influence, especially
on the homosexual tradition in American literature. My own
collection, Walt Whitman: The Centennial Essays (1994), put
three generations of Whitman scholars in conversation with
each other, including the distinguished senior group of Gay
Wilson Allen, Roger Asselineau, C. Carroll Hollis, and James E.
Miller Jr. Allen and Asselineau reappeared in Walt Whitman
and the World (1995), which I edited with Gay Allen and for
which Roger Asselineau compiled the sections on Whitman's
impact on French, Belgian, Portuguese, and Italian cultures.
The Iowa Whitman series continued to explore Whitman's international impact with Walter Grünzweig's groundbreaking
Constructing the German Walt Whitman (1995), and recently
Joann P. Krieg's invaluable Whitman Chronology (1998) joined
the cluster.

   Roger Asselineau's book underscores and forwards the goal
of the Iowa series, which has from its beginnings sought to
remind readers of the complex weave of the traditions of Whitman scholarship. The reprinting of Asselineau's magisterial
work of criticism makes it available again to younger scholars
and perpetuates a proud tradition in the Whitman scholarly
community, where different generations of scholars have collaborated rather than competed with each other. The new
Iowa edition of The Evolution of Walt Whitman should now
occupy a prominent place on any scholar's shelf of Whitman
criticism. It is a publication that is at once retrospective and
prospective, taking us back to the origins of modern Whitman
scholarship at the same time that it continues to influence
emerging scholarship.

   To call a critical work "magisterial" today probably sounds
naive or at least quaint, but it is the right adjective for Asselineau's book. It is one of those massive critical accomplish-

ments not uncommon in the 1950s but unlike anything we see today. From the beginning and throughout its seven hundred–plus pages, the book speaks with authority on a vast range of topics. Whitman's mysticism, his poetry of the body, his metaphysics, his ethics, his aesthetics, his sexuality, his patriotism, his ideas of democracy, his racial attitudes, his relation to America's emerging capitalism, his style, his language, his prosody—they are all here, and they are all dealt with directly, clearly, and intelligently. Remarkably, most of the discussions still seem fresh and relevant, and that is in part because they have been so influential—as we read contemporary criticism on Whitman, we continually hear echoes of Asselineau's acumen. Asselineau's individual chapters have been the seedbeds for subsequent criticism, and we can trace the evolution (to use Asselineau's key trope) of this book into hundreds of critical studies over the past four decades. His psychological examination of Whitman, for example, stands behind later studies by Edwin Haviland Miller, Stephen Black, and David Cavitch, while his subtle melding of the poetry and the life influences Jerome Loving's recent critical biography of the poet. Asselineau's ideas certainly have been developed and altered, sometimes in surprising ways, but few have been overturned. Reading *Evolution* today, we experience the uncanny sense that we are once again present at the very origins of contemporary Whitman scholarship.

Asselineau's book, as its title suggests, insists on viewing Whitman's life and work as an "evolution." It inaugurated the study of *Leaves of Grass* as a changing, altering, lifelong work in progress, and it marked the end of the habit of talking about *Leaves* as if it were a single unified book. Asselineau saw Whitman's poetry "not as a body of static data, but as a constantly changing continuum whose evolution must be carefully observed." Throughout *Evolution*, Asselineau places himself in the role of the "observer," analyzing Whitman's development with a kind of scientific detachment, coolly judging the poems, both good and bad. But behind this objective persona burns the soul of a risk-taker who was willing to rewrite Whitman studies by bravely proposing what was then a controversial biographical source for Whitman's art. While most American critics were dissembling or circumventing or euphemizing, Asselineau cut to the chase: Whitman's "most difficult battle," he writes, was "with his wild homosexual desires, which never left him at peace and constantly menaced his balance." In other words, his homosexuality—and his conflicting desires both to express it and hide it—was the very source of much of his poetry.

Asselineau's book, then, was in large part responsible for moving the discussion of Whitman firmly into the realm of the physical. Unlike the earliest generation of Whitman critics— hagiographers who saw his poetry as a new religion—Asselineau grounded Whitman's poetry in the poet's body and sexuality. From his frank acceptance of Whitman's homosexuality to his depiction of Whitman's relationships with Peter Doyle and Harry Stafford to his view of the poetry itself as a result of repressed sexual urges, Asselineau constructed a Whitman who was a more *sexual* figure than any of the versions of Whitman that were then operative in America. Whitman, Asselineau writes, "makes the sexual organ the center of the world" and considers "coitus as a mode of knowledge." Whitman's "curious pansexualism," Asselineau asserts, led to "a hyperesthesia of all the senses, particularly that of touch": "He appears constantly to feel the need of rubbing himself, in his imagination, against things and against people . . . [and] so frantic is his joy and intense his happiness that one continually has the impression of a vigor that nothing can check and of an insolent health—a 'reckless health,' as he himself calls it."

While Asselineau's diction now marks his book as definitely

pre-Stonewall—he refers to Whitman's homosexuality as an "abnormal desire"—his understanding of the importance of Whitman's "love of comrades" anticipates the insights of many of the best recent commentators on Whitman's sexuality. Asselineau's chapter on "the poetry of the body" and his tracking of Whitman's "quiet labor of self-censorship" leads directly to M. Jimmie Killingsworth's *Whitman's Poetry of the Body* (1989). His suggestion that Whitman's third edition of *Leaves*, in which the "Calamus" poems first appeared, resulted from "a great passion for a man about whom nothing is known" and his assertion that Whitman's homosexuality remained at the center of his work for his whole career anticipate the work of critics like Robert K. Martin, Charley Shively, Michael Moon, Byrne Fone, and Gary Schmidgall, all of whom would disagree with Asselineau's characterization of Whitman's "sick soul," but all of whom nonetheless owe a great deal to Asselineau's insights about how Whitman's gay encounters made him "drunk with love," an intoxication and exhilaration that generated his most powerful poetry. And Asselineau's discussion of how Whitman's "love of comrades . . . blossoms out into love of mankind and becomes synonymous with universal brotherhood" stands behind Betsy Erkkila's recent work on the nature of what she calls Whitman's "homosexual republic."

It would in fact be easy to chart a critical genealogy in which *Evolution* is the common great-grandparent of a wide variety of Whitman scholarship from the late 1960s to the present. I think many younger students and scholars will be startled to see how much of our current understanding of Whitman Asselineau had already managed to articulate nearly a half century ago. To read this book is to be reminded that extraordinary works of criticism never exist in and of themselves. They initiate debates and dialogues and extended responses and get written into talks and articles and books. Their ideas develop and alter, reoccur and recombine. Asselineau's book, in tracking Whitman's evolution, set in motion its *own* evolution. Put this new Iowa edition on your bookshelf to the left of all the Whitman criticism that has been published since 1965: the books to its right now comprise the evolution of *The Evolution of Walt Whitman.*

The Evolution of Walt Whitman

INTRODUCTION

On this occasion of the reprinting of *The Evolution of Walt Whitman*—forty-five years after its first appearance in French and nearly forty years after its translation into English—the appropriate moment has arrived for me to reminisce about my sixty-year journey with Walt Whitman. It was not as easy as one might think for a young Frenchman to discover Whitman in France in the late 1930s. True, Léon Bazalgette's biography of Whitman had appeared in 1908, followed the next year by his complete translation of *Leaves of Grass* and ten years later by Whitman's *Oeuvres Choisies*, translated by Jules Laforgue, Louis Fabulet, Francis Vielé-Griffin, and no less a writer than André Gide. But during my secondary studies in Latin, Greek, and philosophy (plus English, of course), Whitman was never mentioned (nor, for that matter, was Gide, for in those days the only good writer was a dead writer, and French literature stopped with the last year of the nineteenth century).

After my baccalaureat, however, I decided to take a degree in English and become a teacher of English. I thought classical studies were too bookish, and the study of English would give me a chance to meet people and travel abroad. So I took a degree in English at the Sorbonne (*licence ès lettres*) and studied English literature from Beowulf to Virginia Woolf, but not to Thomas Wolfe, for no American author was ever mentioned. The curriculum was exclusively English. There were a few courses in American literature, but they were optional and did not count toward a degree. Very few students took them, and there were hardly any students of English in them. I did take them, however, during my MA year, for the writing of my thesis, "The Pantheistic Elements in Wordsworth's Poetry," left me some leisure. There were only three books on the syllabus: *Tom Sawyer* (not *Huckleberry Finn*, of course, for fear Huck's dialect should corrupt our English), Edwin Arlington Robinson's *Cavender's House* (which I thought rather tedious), and Edith Wharton's *Hudson River Bracketed* (because she lived in France, I suppose). It was rather poor fare, and I must confess that, except for Mark Twain, I was not too much impressed by this first contact with American literature.

I took my *agrégation* in English in 1938, after spending a year in England, where I taught French in a small public school (Canford School, near Wimborne, in Dorset) to improve my spoken English. Of the twelve authors on the syllabus, there was not a single American writer, unless T. S. Eliot is counted as one, but *Murder in the Cathedral*, which was on the syllabus, can hardly be considered a specifically American play.

After I obtained my *agrégation*, I was appointed to the lycée in Havre and taught (British) English there for a year. By that time, the sky was beginning to darken in Europe, but after Munich we had a year's respite. At Havre, I could not help thinking of America. I lived in an apartment that looked out on the entrance to the harbor. From my window I could see the transatlantic liners sail in and out, and I dreamed of traveling on one of them someday. I was determined sooner or later to go to America. In the meantime, I thoroughly studied *The American Language* by H. L. Mencken to prepare myself for the linguistic discovery of the United States.

But this could not take place in the immediate future. War with Germany broke out in the fall of 1939. I was drafted and spent one year in the French army and narrowly escaped being taken prisoner. During the German occupation, the atmosphere was stifling. France had become a huge prison camp, and traveling was impossible. This exacerbated my wanderlust, which I had not yet been able to satisfy. I decided that, as soon as the war was over, I would travel at last to my heart's content. I needed a good reason for it. So I made up my mind to work for a doctorate in American literature—a rather rash decision, since I knew practically nothing about it.

However, I did not want my doctoral dissertation to be an imposition, a purely academic exercise on some dull topic leading to dryasdust scholarship. I loved poetry, the poetry of Wordsworth in particular. I tried therefore to find an American poet who would somehow remind me of him and would have the same mystical leanings. The solution to my problem was Walt Whitman. I discovered him by chance while skimming through a textbook for secondary schools entitled *The Spirit of the Age*, edited by Germain d'Hangest Sr. I don't have it anymore and don't remember what poems were quoted, but I was immediately struck by their extraordinary appearance. Instead of being printed from left to right, as is the rule, the poems were printed from the bottom to the top of the page, so that the lines were vertical instead of horizontal and thus sprawled on each page as comfortably as in the 1855 quarto edition of *Leaves of Grass* (which, of course, I did not know yet). It was an arresting sight, and I was not disappointed when I read them. They called up immense open spaces and gave an impression of strength and irrepressible dynamism. They were only samples, but I was conquered.

The information about Whitman that I found in *A History of English Literature* by Arthur Compton-Rickett (which, despite its title, treated American literature) confirmed my impression. Without taking the trouble to look further into the matter, I called on Professor Louis Cazamian, whom I knew and admired, and told him of my desire to write a dissertation on Whitman. My innocence was such that I did not even know that a fellow countryman, Jean Catel, had already written two dissertations on Whitman. The major one was entitled "Walt Whitman: la naissance du poete" (1929), and the minor one was more technical and bore the title "Rythme et langage dans la 1ère édition des 'Leaves of Grass,' 1855" (1930). In those days, when doctoral candidates were few and there remained numerous authors to study, there was not supposed to be more than one dissertation per author. Fortunately, Louis Cazamian thought that Catel's dissertations did not block the way (since they did not cover the whole field), and he welcomed with enthusiasm my project of writing on the entire life and career of Whitman. I then had to obtain the approval of Professor Charles Cestre, who was *the* professor of American literature at the Sorbonne. I was unknown to him, but, as he was about to retire and Louis Cazamian recommended me, he accepted my project—with resignation.

By then (1942) I had a topic but still no copy of *Leaves of Grass* on which to work. Luckily, the United States had not yet entered the war, and Shakespeare and Company was still open. I thus could buy the last copy that Sylvia Beach had in stock, without suspecting that she owned some Whitman manuscripts and had known Catel and published in *Le Navire d'Argent* the text of *The Eighteenth Presidency,* which Amy Lowell had helped him find in a Boston bookshop.

Now at last I was the proud owner of a copy of *Leaves of Grass,* but it was a very imperfect copy. It was the old Everyman's Library edition of *Leaves of Grass—Part I and Democratic Vistas,* first published in 1912. It stopped with "By Blue Ontario's Shore" and "Reversals"; to make up for what was missing, it offered the complete text of *Democratic Vistas.* The editor was Horace Traubel, who gave a very partial image of Whitman and saw him as, above all, a prophet of democracy and a radical. I was very inadequately equipped, but, circumstances being what they were, I considered myself very fortunate. Whenever I had some spare time, during the long summer vacations in particular, I read and reread "Part I" of *Leaves of Grass* and tried to extract from the poems all that they contained implicitly as well as explicitly. I squeezed them to the last drop and took hundreds of pages of notes.

I taught in lycées in Beauvais and Paris after I was evacuated from Havre on account of the almost daily British air raids. But I had other responsibilities, too, for, with a group of friends and colleagues, I helped Allied airmen, who had parachuted over France when their planes were brought down, to hide and afterward escape, returning to England by way of the Pyrenees at first and by way of Brittany later. I thus became acquainted with a varied assortment of Americans: WASPs from New England and New York, Poles from the Midwest, Irishmen, southerners, etc. It was very much like reading one of Whitman's catalogs, but it was more dangerous, and I was eventually arrested by the German police in February 1944 and tried by a court martial of the German air force, which condemned me to death. This could very well have been the end of my (still-born) dissertation, but the sentence was not carried out. I stayed in jail at Fresnes, near Paris, until August 1944, when I was liberated by my jailers during the truce negotiated by the French resistance forces, one week before the arrival of the Allied forces.

I was saved, but my dissertation had been delayed by several months, for I could neither read nor write while I was in jail. Actually, the project remained practically at a standstill until the end of the war in Europe. But when the war stopped, I obtained an American Field Service Fellowship and left for the United States as soon as I possibly could, on a Liberty ship carrying American troops back home. I landed in Boston. My destination was Harvard. It was like being in paradise after what I had gone through. The nightmare was over. I was at last in a position to work seriously and steadily and to explore the Whitman continent I had discovered almost accidentally several years before.

Harvard was an ideal place for such an undertaking. The English Department was doing pioneering work in the field of American studies and included such distinguished Americanists as Kenneth Murdock, Perry Miller (just back from the war and at the top of his form), Howard Mumford Jones, and, above all, F. O. Matthiessen, whose *American Renaissance* had appeared only a few years before in 1941. The first two were supposed to be my supervisors, but actually they left me full liberty to work as I chose, and I spent all my time in the Widener Library. I had stack privileges and a stall in the stacks (an unheard-of privilege in France) next to the American literature shelves. I had, at my elbow so to speak, all the documents I needed. In those pre-Xerox days, I frantically copied pages and pages of books and articles, which I thought I might need in France later. This was not mere mechanical compilation, however, for I had already prepared a detailed plan of my dissertation. I had a priori divided my subject into chapters and subchapters, and I had a folder full of blank sheets of paper at the top of which I had written all my chapter and subchapter headings. In proportion as I collected materials, I sorted them out and assigned places to them in my plan. My blank pages thus were gradually filled, and I sometimes had to add new ones, for I constantly found new matter and new ideas. It was a kind of organic growth within each chapter; it was not anarchic and random but predetermined and regulated.

That was a very exciting time, full of unexpected occurrences. For one thing, I found in the Houghton Library a rich repository of original documents on Whitman, and then I made the acquaintance of Clifton J. Furness, who had published some of them in his *Walt Whitman Workshop* (1928). By a curious coincidence, he lived only two or three blocks from Perkins Hall, where I had been given a room. I met him several times, and we had some interesting conversations about our common hero, whose biography he was trying to write. Unfortunately, he died only a few months after our first encounter.

By another coincidence, it was at that time (the beginning of 1946) that Gay Wilson Allen's *Walt Whitman Handbook* appeared. It was the best available overall study, the best guidebook to the territory I was exploring. I immediately bought it, devoured it, and digested it, and shortly afterward I made the acquaintance of its author. He then lived close to New York, in Leonia, New Jersey, and it happened that I spent all my vacations in Teaneck about a mile from his house. I called him up and he invited me to visit him. He and his wife, Eve, received me very warmly and became lifelong friends.

Exploring the Whitman continent takes time. After a year at Harvard there still remained terrae incognitae to visit before returning to France if I wanted my documentation to be complete. I decided to stay another year in America, but this time I was an instructor in French in the Romance Language Department at Harvard, and I had much less time to devote to my research. I was able, however, to visit Duke University during the summer vacation and to work for three weeks in the Trent Collection, then presided over by Ellen Frances Frey, who had compiled an admirable catalog of it, published the year before in 1945. During the academic year, I also managed to visit the Whitman Collection of the University of Pennsylvania in Philadelphia. There Sculley Bradley took me to Timber Creek and, of course, I went on a pilgrimage to Mickle Street in Camden and to Whitman's tomb in Harleigh Cemetery. My most thrilling experience and the climax of all my explorations occurred while I was working in the Manuscript Division of the Library of Congress, when I suddenly realized that I had found what I thought was the definitive and incontrovertible proof of Whitman's (at least potential) homosexuality. When I examined a scrap of paper belonging to Manuscript Notebook 9, dating from 1868 to 1870, I noticed that in the sentence "But pursue her no more," "her" had been erased and above the letter "e" the dot of an "i" was very clearly visible. It was this detail that attracted my attention first; looking more closely, I could very clearly read "him" under "her," which was added later to camouflage the masculine pronoun—a correction that Emory Holloway failed to indicate (and perhaps to notice) when he published this document in *The Uncollected Poetry and Prose of Walt Whitman*, though he noted other substitutions. This discovery, to my mind, confirmed and justified a homosexual interpretation of "Calamus" and other poems and shed new light on certain dubious aspects of Whitman's life. Though nearly all critics of Whitman (and more particularly Emory Holloway) had fought shy of this issue until then and done their best to hush it up, I saw no reason for doing so. I knew *Corydon*, Gide's apology for homosexuality, and did not regard this sexual preference as a taint liable to detract from the value of Whitman's poetry. I was delighted with my discovery and did not hesitate to put at the head of my chapter on his sex life the unambiguous epigraph "The Love that dare not speak its name," which I borrowed from Lord Alfred Douglas. As early as 1949, interpreting three unpublished letters addressed to Whitman (two of which had been given to me by Holloway), I showed that, when boasting of having a French mistress in Washington, he was merely trying to hide his predilection (*Modern Language Quarterly*, March 1949, pp. 91–95). Holloway rather resented this use of these letters.

I completed my research by visiting the Beinecke Library of Yale University, the Saunders Collection of Brown University, and the Berg Collection of the New York Public Library. When I returned to France in September 1947, I had all the materials I needed to write my dissertation. I once more taught in a Parisian lycée at first, but as the Sorbonne was short of Americanists (there was just Professor Maurice Le Breton, who had succeeded Professor Cestre), I was appointed "assistant," that is, instructor in English, in 1949. This was a promotion, but no matter for rejoicing, for it was rather a curse in disguise. I was submerged with work and, contrary to what I expected, had no time to write. So I applied for and obtained a Smith-Mundt grant and spent the year 1950–1951 in the United States, at Harvard once more. This time I was completely free, and I finished the first draft of my dissertation by the summer of 1951 as well as the research I had to do for my minor dissertation, "The Literary Reputation of Mark Twain after His Death."

When I returned to France, I was immediately appointed assistant professor in American literature at the University of Clermont-Ferrand. Despite this handicap, I succeeded in having my dissertation typed and approved by Professor Le Breton (who was my supervisor by now) and in completing my minor dissertation by the end of 1952; in January 1953, I defended both dissertations at the Sorbonne. Thus things went quickly at the end. Thanks to a generous grant from the Ministry of Education, the record of my long exploration of the Whitman continent was published in 1954 under the title of *L'Evolution de Walt Whitman*. It was a fat volume of 569 pages.

Despite its bulk and daunting appearance, it was well received and obtained good reviews, notably in the *Figaro Littéraire* by Jean Guéhenno. It had the honor of the front page, and it caused a minor Whitman revival in France. It was even reviewed in an obscure anarchist sheet called *L'Unique* by one Louis Armand. But in the United States, it caused little stir, though there were two long and enthusiastic reviews by Sculley Bradley. French having ceased to be a universal language, American Americanists could not be expected to read from cover to cover a French book of over five hundred pages. In its original language, the impact of my book in the United States was bound to be limited. But Kenneth Murdock and other friends at Harvard convinced the Harvard University Press that they must publish a translation of it, and I agreed to translate it. I did so with the cooperation of American colleagues who happened to be teaching in my university (I was by then professor of American literature at the University of Lyon): Richard P. Adams and Burton L. Cooper. The book appeared in two volumes: the first in 1960 as *The Evolution of Walt Whitman*, with a subtitle, *The Creation of a Personality*, and the second in 1962, subtitled *The Creation of a Book*. Now, with this new Iowa edition, the two volumes are once again joined into one.

With the generous support of Gay Wilson Allen (whose own critical biography of Whitman, *The Solitary Singer,* had appeared in 1955), my *Evolution* became one of the standard books on Whitman. I am not blind, however, to its limitations. If I were to write such a book now, I would no doubt proceed differently. As Seymour Betsky pointed out in *English Studies* ("Whose Walt Whitman? French Scholar and American Critics," 1966), my method tends to overintellectualize Whitman's poetry and to emphasize his ideas to the detriment of what took place in the inmost recesses of his soul. Charles Cestre made much the same point when he accused me of ignoring Whitman's lyricism (about which he had himself written an article). But no book of criticism can be all-inclusive, of course. If I had focused my study on Whitman's lyricism and on the dark forces that impelled him, I would have neglected other aspects of his work which, to my mind, were well worth examining.

Despite the proliferation of biographies and books of criticism about Whitman in the last forty years, I do not believe that the main outlines of Whitman's life and work have substantially changed since the first publication of *The Evolution of Walt Whitman*: my depiction of his physiognomy is still recognizable. Some of the poet's features have perhaps been more clearly or more strongly delineated, but nothing of essential importance has been added. Certainly, his homosexuality has been a topic of increasing concern, but I treated that aspect of his life unambiguously in the chapter I entitled "Sex Life: 'The Love that dare not speak its name.'" This aspect of my work can now be described as pioneering, though it was unfortunately ignored by most biographers and critics for many years, perhaps because I placed it in the second volume, viewing his homosexuality as one of the main themes of *Leaves of*

Grass, rather than in the first volume, which focused on the life. I thought such placement would allow me to treat his sexuality more fully—to see it as having aesthetic as well as biographical implications—but maybe some biographers never read that far into *Evolution*.

During the four decades that separate me from the time I wrote this book, I have found no reason to change my view of Whitman or my interpretation of *Leaves of Grass*. Under the influence of Gaston Bachelard's theories about the influences of the four elements on poetic imagination, I have added only one thing to my *Evolution*: an essay on Whitman's water imagery, that element whose presence he felt even in "liquid trees." Instead of writing more criticism on Whitman, I turned to translating his poetry. Because of the revival of interest in Whitman's poetry in France—a revival in which my *Evolution* played some part—a French publisher asked me to translate a selection from *Leaves of Grass*, though three translations were already available; but Léon Bazalgette's was awkward, that of Gide and his group was too fragmentary, and that of Pierre Messiaen too grossly incorrect at times. I accepted the invitation with enthusiasm and thought I could do the job easily since I knew Whitman from A to Z. Actually, it turned out to be a very difficult task, for the translator always discovers unsuspected depths and mysteries when trying to replace English words with French ones, but I found the result quite rewarding. The intensity of Whitman's poetry is such that the reader can feel its radiations through the leaden screen of the translation. That is how I felt, at least, and my translation, published by Les Belles Lettres in 1956, was twice reprinted in the form of a bilingual edition (in 1972 and 1989), preceded by a critical introduction, and it has been quite popular with students ever since.

Today, at the end of the millennium, I still feel as strongly as ever the impact of Whitman's poetry, which the Italian essayist Giovanni Papini described so aptly in a sentence I never tire of quoting: "I, a Tuscan, an Italian, a Latin, have not felt what poetry really means through Vergil or Dante, still less through Petrarch and Tasso . . . , but through the childish enumerations and impassioned incantations of the kindly harvester of *Leaves of Grass*" (*Ritratti Stranieri,* 1932). I must confess, however, that I have undergone a certain evolution of my own, and I now tend more and more to neglect or ignore Whitman's democratic message and to prefer instead the transcendentalist poet who tirelessly tried to find an answer to the child's unanswerable question: "What is the grass?" (*not* "What is capitalism?"). I find myself today more attracted to his attempts to found a personal religion—the metaphysical contents of his poetry, his weltanschauung, have lost none of their appeal, largely because they are less self-assured and more discreet than his political program.

This is why I gave Whitman pride of place in my book *The Transcendentalist Constant in American Literature* (1980). His transcendentalism, it seems to me, may well be the response to that thirst for a new faith, for a metaphysical certainty, which so many people nowadays experience—according to another prophet of our times, André Malraux—after the undermining of Christianity by science in the nineteenth century. Whitman's *Leaves of Grass,* in this respect, still seem as green as ever. My hope is that I have contributed to their greenness as I have attempted in my own way to answer the question we go on asking: "What is the grass?"

Bibliographic Note

So much has been written on Whitman, especially in the last four decades, that it is now necessary to consult specialized bibliographies, which can serve as guides to the extraordinary range of commentary that is available. The bibliography that accompanies *Evolution* is obviously hopelessly out of date.

The reader should consult the following useful bibliographic sources.

Ed Folsom, "Walt Whitman: A Current Bibliography," in each issue of the *Walt Whitman Quarterly Review* and available online at http://www.uiowa.edu~wwqr

Scott Giantvalley, *Walt Whitman, 1838–1939: A Reference Guide* (Boston: G. K. Hall, 1981)

Donald D. Kummings, *Walt Whitman, 1940–1975: A Reference Guide* (Boston: G. K. Hall, 1982)

Joel Myerson, *Walt Whitman: A Descriptive Bibliography* (Pittsburgh: University of Pittsburgh Press, 1992)

Another invaluable digest of information about Whitman's work and work about Whitman is J. R. LeMaster and Donald D. Kummings, eds., *Walt Whitman: An Encyclopedia* (New York: Garland, 1998).

THE EVOLUTION OF
WALT WHITMAN
THE CREATION OF
A PERSONALITY

FOREWORD

THE French edition of this book having been warmly received in English-speaking countries and several reviewers having expressed the wish that it should be translated,* I have tried to satisfy their demands, and this is the result of my efforts. But I would never have carried out such a task without the help of Professor Richard P. Adams of Tulane University, who, during his stay in France as a Fulbright lecturer in 1959–60, worked with me on the translation with untiring devotion. I wish also to express my thanks to the Director and to the Syndics of the Harvard University Press, and more particularly to Professor Kenneth B. Murdock, for undertaking to publish an American edition of my book in spite of its length and bulkiness. They have shown admirable understanding.

As a matter of fact, *L'Evolution de Walt Whitman* is such a long book that it has seemed preferable to publish it in two volumes in the United States. But this dichotomy needs a few words of explanation. The first volume is practically a biography of Walt Whitman, whereas the second volume will be devoted to a critical study of his works. Such a division has fallen into disrepute. Yet, it offers undeniable advantages. It enables a critic to cover the whole field much more thoroughly than a so-called critical biography which in practice results in a loosely knit biography marred by inadequate critical dis-

* Gay W. Allen in *Etudes Anglaises,* October 1954; Sculley Bradley in *Modern Language Notes,* December 1955; and an anonymous reviewer in the *Times Literary Supplement,* January 27, 1956.

quisitions. I have preferred to follow the old pattern and treat the man and his works separately in order to give to each part its due.

Let me also add that, as Whitman scholars have been more active than ever since the French edition of this work appeared six years ago, I have brought the documentation of my notes up to date and corrected a few minor errors in the text.

When I undertook to write *L'Evolution de Walt Whitman,* there already existed a French doctoral dissertation on the author of *Leaves of Grass: Walt Whitman: la Naissance du Poète* by Jean Catel. But that work, so rich in original insight, studies only Whitman's youth and ends with the first edition of *Leaves of Grass,* and ignores the fact that nine other editions followed and that Whitman for the remaining thirty-seven years of his life did not cease to alter, to correct, and to enrich his book. Thus it seemed to me that there was room for a second work devoted to the growth of *Leaves of Grass* after its sudden birth in 1855.

Two authors had the same idea before: Frederik Schyberg, a Danish critic, and Gay Wilson Allen, Professor of English at New York University. Schyberg's *Walt Whitman* appeared in 1933, but since few Whitman scholars understand Danish, it was necessary to wait for Gay Wilson Allen's *Walt Whitman Handbook* (1946), which gave a summary of it, to know the general scope of that remarkable thesis. Finally, in 1951, the Columbia University Press published an English translation of it, done by Evie Allison Allen, and so the work became accessible to all. One finds there a penetrating study of the successive editions of *Leaves of Grass.* Thanks to a precise and close analysis of the poems and their variations, Schyberg brings out the true personality of Whitman, which so many of his biographers had, up to then, misunderstood, and he illumines the dramatic character of a grave crisis through which Whitman passed between 1855 and 1860. Gay W. Allen followed the same method and came to the same conclusions in his *Walt Whitman Handbook*. But, realizing the weaknesses of the analytic and chronological approach of the Danish critic, he tried, in a section of his work entitled "Fundamental Ideas," to go beyond the biographical to the critical level and to synthetize what the study of the variations revealed. Unfortunately, having too little space at his disposal, he could only begin that study. My debt to these two predecessors is naturally considerable. Thanks to them I have been able to push my analyses farther and to explore more minutely a domain which they had already pioneered.

An American Field Service Fellowship and a Smith-Mundt grant have permitted me to make two visits of a year each to the United States and to do my research there. I should like to express my gratitude to those organizations and I wish equally to thank Harvard University, where I worked under the expert guidance of Professors Kenneth B. Murdock and Perry Miller and which always opened wide to me the doors of its libraries. I must also give my thanks to the librarians of the universities of Pennsylvania, Yale, Brown, Columbia, and Duke and to the curators of the Berg Collection of the New York Public Library and of the Rare Book Division of the Library of Congress. Thanks to their generosity I have had access to original documents, some of which, still unpublished, were, with their permission, for the first time printed in the French edition of this book.

I cannot end this foreword without recalling the memory of Jean Catel, my French predecessor, who, during the German Occupation, at a time when I had no document whatever at my disposal, opened his library to me and lent me his books with that kindness and total disinterestedness that none of his friends can forget.

When the idea of beginning this study came to me, I was encouraged by Professors Louis Cazamian and Charles Cestre.

But I would especially like to express my gratitude to Professor Maurice LeBreton of the Sorbonne who directed my thesis with as much sympathy as competence. In the course of my stays in the United States I had the occasion to meet the most eminent Whitman specialists, the late Joseph C. Furness, Sculley Bradley, Emory Holloway, who were all very gracious to me, and, especially, I made the acquaintance of Professor Gay W. Allen, who did not hesitate to put his notes and his books at my disposal and with whom, in his charming house in New Jersey, I many times spent long hours discussing Whitman. He has been more than a guide for me, he has been a friend.

Before concluding, I must not forget to acknowledge my debt to Mrs. James E. Duffy of the Editorial Department of the Harvard University Press who, with admirable thoroughness, has prepared my typescript for the printer.

April 1960   R. A.

CONTENTS

THE EVOLUTION OF
WALT WHITMAN

THE CREATION OF
A PERSONALITY

INTRODUCTION

*I charge you forever reject those who would
expound me, for I cannot expound myself . . .*
("Myself and Mine," line 27.)

THE idea of writing this book came to me during the
gloomiest years of the German Occupation of France. Nothing
could have been more natural at that time, when every Frenchman was a prisoner in his own country, than to try to escape
from that world of concentration camps into the vast spaces
of Whitman's universe where all is liberty and promise of
happiness. To avoid moral suffocation it was necessary to find,
in spite of an intolerable situation, some ground for hope and
for a renewal of faith in mankind. Whitman, in this respect,
was an ideal source of inspiration. Invaluable lessons of tenacious energy could be drawn from his *Leaves of Grass,* in
which with patient strength he overcame his anxieties and
doubts and repelled their repeated attacks over the years. The
presence of evil within him and around him never broke his
spirit. His faith and enthusiasm always brought him through.
But this invincible optimism was the result of a continual
struggle, and thus the serenity of his old age was a victory
over anguish. This is revealed by an attentive reading of his
works, as I shall try to show. The subject was in the air at
the time. As early as 1940, Jean Guéhenno wrote in his *Jour-*

nal, after commenting on the constantly enriched text of Montaigne's *Essays:*

> I know only one other book which in the same way has grown, ripened, matured along with its author: Whitman's *Leaves of Grass.* And it is no accident that both use almost the same formula:
> "Whoever takes my book in his hands takes a man."

At a distance of four centuries, the same individualistic zeal impelled them, drier and more intellectual in Montaigne, in Whitman, more generous and, as it were, in harmony with a new freedom, a new world in which the individual need not develop himself at the expense of others, but together with others, realizing that he benefits himself by becoming more fraternal.[1]

So I propose to study Walt Whitman's evolution from 1855 to his death. But why that initial date? Is it not arbitrary to set such a time limit to the inquiry? True, it is artificial, but it was imposed by the very nature of the subject. Why go back before 1855 to try to explain the birth of *Leaves of Grass?* The attempt would be doomed to failure. Nothing in the life of the author justifies any prediction of the sudden blossoming of such a strange masterpiece and nothing justifies any *a posteriori* deduction of its necessity. It seems wiser therefore to renounce the idea of clearing up the mystery and to attempt a humbler and more fruitful approach: a study of the years after 1855 during which the poet at last became himself and developed harmoniously rather than those in which he was still unsuccessfully searching for himself. Whitman, for that matter, was plainly aware of this superiority — at least so far as he was concerned — of middle age over youth, as is shown by this fragment found among his papers after his death:

> Between the ages of thirty-five and eighty may be the perfection and realization of moral life; rising above the previous periods in all that makes a person better, healthier, happier, more command-

ing, more beloved and more a realisee of love. The mind matured, the senses in full activity, the digestion even, the voice firm, the walk untired, the arms and chest sinewy and imposing, the hip joints flexible, the hands capable of many things, the complexion and blood pure, the breath sweet, the procreative power ever ready in man and the womb power in woman, the inward organs all sweetly performing their offices — during those years the universe presents its riches, its strength, its beauty, to be parts of a man, a woman. Then the body is ripe and the soul also and all the shows of nature attained and the production of thought in books.[2]

"At the age of thirty-five," he said; now in 1855 he was thirty-six. He was obviously thinking of himself.

Accordingly my purpose is to follow the growth of *Leaves of Grass* through the successive editions and not to attack the insoluble problem of its genesis. This course seems all the more appropriate since the youth of Whitman has already been thoroughly and carefully studied by Jean Catel in his *Walt Whitman: La Naissance du poète* (1929).

To be sure, it will often be necessary to go back in time before the limit which I have assigned. However unexpected the appearance of *Leaves of Grass,* it did not spring fully armed from the brow of its author. Certain themes had been sketched in the course of the preceding years in newspaper articles, in stories, and in a few poems written along conventional patterns. The recapitulation of certain aspects of Whitman's career before 1855 will then compensate for the artificiality of the break I have made in his development.

But is it proper to speak of the evolution of Whitman? I will try to show that it is and to describe the process. If the subject has never been treated exhaustively, it has often been touched on by critics, particularly by William Sloane Kennedy, Oscar Lovell Triggs, Floyd Stovall, Frederik Schyberg, Irving C. Story, and Gay Wilson Allen. I will have occasion to examine their theses and discuss their conclusions. At the moment, I wish merely to call attention to the difficulty of the subject, which results from the complexity of the revisions that Whitman made in *Leaves of Grass* and the scarcity of biographical documents. We must not forget that this unique collection was the object of his constant care throughout his poetic career and that in the course of thirty-seven years he brought out ten different editions. Moreover each edition not only contained new poems, but the old ones had been corrected, cut, and enriched; sometimes titles and punctuation had been changed and the arrangement of poems completely upset. The problem is to explain these changes and throw light on the obscurities of the poems, which are generally more allusive than explicit, with the help of what little we know about Whitman's life and personality. Paradoxically, this exuberant poet of comradeship was an extremely secretive man, and the passionate dithyrambs of his friends give us very little information about him. In a way, he is almost as mysterious as Shakespeare — no wonder he savored the mystery that surrounds the personality of Shakespeare and is still the despair of commentators. Since his own work was essentially lyric, its obscurity is even more troublesome, and it is important that we do our best to dissipate it. Unfortunately, the critic finds himself in the position of a paleontologist who, with only a few fossils, must try to reconstruct the whole evolution of the animal kingdom.

What is the best method to overcome these difficulties? In the absence of any critical edition of *Leaves of Grass,* I have had to collate the texts of the successive editions in order to determine each time the additions and the structural changes. At the same time I have had to study the variants, that is to say, the corrections made to previously printed poems.[3] Of course, I have also made full use of the facts of Whitman's biography and of the history of the time in order to interpret the results of the analysis correctly and to define their mean-

ing more accurately. Sometimes, however, the process was reversed: a careful study of the text and its development over
the years permitted a clarification of certain obscure biographical points.

Naturally, this procedure calls for extreme prudence. I
have been particularly careful not to read the early editions
in the light of what I knew about the later ones. I have also
been careful not to draw hasty conclusions from the examination of variant readings. A correction might very well be a
matter of form and not the indication of a new attitude. An
addition does not necessarily represent a new orientation of
thought. It may merely fill a gap or supply an omission. I have
constantly kept these various possibilities in mind and have
tried to avoid the errors they might have occasioned.

My purpose was not to write a biography of Whitman or a
chapter in the history of American literature, but rather to
perform the critical task of bringing out the meaning of
Leaves of Grass by continually confronting it with its own
successive aspects and with Whitman's other works, as well
as with what we know of the author and his time. It seemed
to me that this study would promote a better understanding
of *Leaves of Grass* and a deeper penetration into the mind of
its author. The book is too often studied as a unit and critics
tend to forget that it represents forty years of assiduous ex-
perimentation, that Whitman was thirty years old when he
began, and that he was an old man when he stopped. They also
forget that during the same period of time the United States
made the transition from a rural to an industrial civilization
after a terrible civil war. Whitman's book is therefore the
fruit of a long life and the mirror of a crucial period of
American history.[4] To use another image, it is not a plain of
uniform nature and origin, but a plateau where layers of
different geological periods have been brought to the surface
by various upheavals and later eroded. It is true that Whit-

man wanted us to consider only the final result, that is to say, the text of 1892. He said so in a note prefixed to the "deathbed" edition:

As there are now several editions of L. of G., different texts and dates, I wish to say that I prefer and recommend this present one, complete, for future printing, if there should be any; a copy and fac-simile, indeed, of the text of these 438 pages.[5]

And Horace L. Traubel reports that he once said:

So far as you may have anything to do with it I place upon you the injunction that whatever may be added to the *Leaves* shall be supplementary, avowed as such, leaving the book complete as I left it, consecutive to the point I left off, marking always an unmistakable, deep down, unobliteratable division line. In the long run the world will do as it pleases with the book. I am determined to have the world know what I was pleased to do.[6]

Surely he has a right to try to impose a version to which he did his best to give a definitive structure, but we also have a right, which he recognized, to prefer a different approach, to try to rediscover behind the completed façade which he has left us the living presence of the author who slowly built up this work.

Here a problem arises: had Whitman conceived the definitive plan of *Leaves of Grass* as it appeared in the "deathbed" edition before 1855? He said so in 1881. For, when the 1881 edition was published, he declared to a Boston reporter:

It is now, I believe, twenty-six years since I began to work upon the structure; and this edition will complete the design which I had in mind when I began to write. The whole affair is like one of those old architectural edifices, some of which were hundreds of years in building, and the designer of which had the whole idea in mind from the first. His plans are pretty ambitious, and as means or time permits, he adds part after part, perhaps at quite wide intervals. To a casual observer it looks in the course of its construction odd enough. Only after the whole is completed one catches the idea which inspired the designer, in whose mind the relation of each part to the whole had existed all along. That is the way it has been with my book. It has been twenty-six years building. There have been seven different hitches at it. Seven different times have parts of the edifice been constructed sometimes in Brooklyn, sometimes in Washington, sometimes in Boston, and at other places. The book has been built partially in every part of the United States. And this edition is the completed edifice.[7]

As early as 1876 he had stated in an interview with one J.B.S. of the New York *World*: "I set out with a design as thoroughly considered as an architect's plan for a cathedral." [8]

What do these assertions mean? At first glance they are at least surprising. The book gives the impression, not of having developed harmoniously over the years, but of having undergone a series of Protean metamorphoses. A quick look at the different editions is enough to show this. The text of 1855 is a river of lava. Some of the poems in it, particularly the one which later became "Song of Myself," are interminable. They are not differentiated by titles, they are all indiscriminately called "Leaves of Grass." In 1856 the work was enriched with a large number of short pieces, and this time all the poems had titles. But it is only in 1860 that we find the first attempt at organization; most of the short poems now are grouped in sections with titles, but within each section, the poems lose their individuality; instead of titles they bear only numbers, as one numbers the panels of a frame house before taking it to pieces and moving it to another location. In 1867 the aspect of the book once more changed completely. Titles reappeared, each poem had its own, but now the sections in their turn lost their individuality. Except for "Children of Adam" and "Calamus" they were undifferentiated and all called "Leaves of Grass"; a partial return to the uniformity of the first edition. In 1871 the poems devoted to the Civil War were finally incorporated in the book. They formed three groups interpolated among the existing sections, thus introducing an element of diversity and also giving the collection a sort of skeleton. The edition of 1876 consisted for its part of two volumes, but the first merely reproduced the edition of 1871. For the new poems were not yet part and parcel of *Leaves of Grass* proper. They were relegated to the second volume and mingled with pieces of prose. It was only in 1881 that they were allowed a place in the collection. Is it not altogether remarkable that from 1867, that is to say, precisely from the time Whitman tried to give his book a little order, he was unable immediately to incorporate the poems which he wrote? If he had really had a plan in mind, it would have been easy for him to find a place for each of them. Even if we concede that the Civil War surprised him and upset his projects, how can we explain his failure to include in *Leaves of Grass* the poems which in 1876 he was constrained to keep apart provisionally in the miscellaneous volume entitled *Two Rivulets*? Why, moreover, did he not announce his design in the 1855 preface? And, if he had a plan from the beginning, why is it that he continued until 1881 to change the order and the titles of the various poems? Why did his book begin to be organized only in 1860 (and even then not tightly)? As a matter of fact, in 1857, commenting in a letter on the 1860 edition which was almost ready, he made this very revealing statement:

It is, I know Well enough, that *that* must be the *true Leaves of Grass* — and I think it has an aspect of completeness, and makes its case clearer. — The old poems are all retained. — The difference is in the new character given to the mass, by the additions.[9]

According to this, he had as early as 1857 the impression that the edifice was finished. But can we even speak of an edifice? He was so reluctant to give his work an architectural aspect that he used a word as little suggestive of order and harmony as "mass" to describe the material of the volume to come. Besides, he made no allusion to any changes in structure; the difference he found between the two volumes was mainly quantitative; if the new edition was to produce a different impression, it would not be owing to a different arrangement, but to added material.

Several years later, on May 31, 1861, to be precise, he noted in the rough draft of a preface which he never had occasion to publish: "The paths to the house are made — but where is the house itself? At most only indicated or touched." [10] Could he say more frankly that there was no order in the work which he thus submitted to the reader and that he had not followed any plan? However he went on in these terms: "Nevertheless, as while we live some dream will play its part, I keep it in my plan of work ahead to yet fill up these *Whisperings*, (if I live & have luck) somehow proportionate to their original design." [11]

Thus, at the very time when he seemed to recognize that there was no trace of a plan in his *Leaves of Grass,* once more he asserted that he had one in his head. What precisely did he mean by "plan"? The interview which he gave in 1876 to the New York *World,* from which I have already cited a passage, may be of some help. For here he said among other things:

I set out to illustrate, without any flinching, actual humanity. I proposed to myself a series of compositions which should depict the physical, emotional, moral, intellectual and spiritual nature of a man.

— That man being yourself?

— That man for purposes of illustration, being myself . . . You can see I had first to deal with the physical, the corporal, the amative business — that part of our nature which is developed so strongly between the ages of 22 and 35. It is that part of my endeavor which caused most of the harsh criticism, and prevented candid examination of the ensuing stages of the design.[12]

We may compare this declaration with the one he made the same year in the Preface to *Two Rivulets*:

It was originally my intention, after chanting in *Leaves of Grass* the songs of the Body and Existence, to then compose a further, equally needed Volume, based on those convictions of perpetuity and conservation which, enveloping all precedents, make the unseen Soul govern absolutely at last. I meant, while in a sort continuing the theme of my first chants, to shift the slides, and exhibit the problem and paradox of the same ardent and fully appointed Personality entering the sphere of the re- sistless gravitation of Spiritual Law, and with cheerful face esti- mating Death, not at all as the cessation, but as somehow what I feel it must be, the entrance upon by far the greatest part of existence, and something that Life is at least as much for, as it is for itself. . .

Meanwhile, not entirely to give the go-by to my original plan, and far more to avoid a mark'd hiatus in it, than to entirely fulfil it, I end my books with thoughts, or radiations from thoughts, on Death, Immortality, and a free entrance into the Spiritual world. In those thoughts, in a sort, I make the first steps or studies toward the mighty theme, from the point of view necessitated by my foregoing poems, and by Modern Science. In them I also seek to set the key-stone to my Democracy's enduring arch.[13]

It is clear then that if Whitman had a plan in mind from the beginning, it was a singularly vague one — not a detailed and rigorous scheme with logical articulations clearly marked, but only two or three very general ideas which he proposed to develop. In other words, from the beginning, he knew where he was going and what he wanted, what great themes he was going to treat: the body, then the spiritual life, and then, by a natural progression, death and immortality, and finally, man no longer alone but in society, which for him was, of course, a democratic society. But he had no idea of the way in which he was to organize this rich material and compose his book. Only the goal toward which he was head- ing was fixed; the ways which he would take to attain it

changed constantly, as his gropings and the frequent revisions
he made in his poems indicate. In fact he admitted in the
Preface of 1872:

When I commenced, years ago, elaborating the plan of my
poems, and continued turning over that plan, and shifting it in
my mind through many years, (from the age of twenty-eight to
thirty-five,) experimenting much, and writing and abandoning
much, one deep purpose underlay the others, and has underlain
it and its execution ever since — and that has been the Religious
purpose. Amid many changes, and a formulation taking far different shape from what I had first supposed, this basic purpose
has never been departed from in the composition of my verses.[14]

It would therefore be more proper to speak of germs than
of a plan. The word "plan" implies an architectural structure.
But, as the evidence given above has shown, and as the detailed study of the different editions will prove, *Leaves of
Grass* was not really constructed. Whitman allowed his book
to grow within his mind little by little with an organic and
almost vegetable growth. (In this sense the title of his book
was particularly happy.) He did not intervene except to preserve a certain cohesion, a unity more organic than logical,
which he defined himself in the "Notes on the Meaning and
Intention of *Leaves of Grass*" published after his death by
Richard Maurice Bucke: "My poems when complete should
be *a unity*, in the same sense that the earth is, or that the
human body, (senses, soul, head, trunk, feet, blood, viscera,
man-root, eyes, hair) or that a perfect musical composition
is." [15]

Or again, as John Burroughs said in his *Notes on Walt
Whitman, Leaves of Grass* is "a series of growths, or strata,
rising or starting out from a settled foundation or centre and
expanding in successive accumulations." [16]

This comparison with the formation of a tree trunk is perhaps a little stiff, but at least it takes account of the instinc-

tive, non-logical character of the development of *Leaves of Grass*. On the contrary, Oscar L. Triggs misses the point badly when he maintains that "*Leaves of Grass* has a marked tectonic quality. The author, like an architect, drew his plans, and the poem, like a cathedral long in building, slowly advanced to fulfilment. Each poem was designed and written with reference to its place in an ideal edifice." [17] Nothing could be more false, as we have seen. Such order as can be found in the later editions was imposed from the outside; it represents an intervention posterior to the act of creation.

At the beginning, then, Whitman had no plan; only a group of fairly general themes. It could hardly have been otherwise, given the subject which he had chosen. He was trying to express the inexpressible, an impossible task, never-ending, always to be resumed. He wanted his poems joyously to proclaim their "tidings old, yet ever new, untranslatable." [18]

He set off bravely in search of a new *Weltanschauung* that would be in harmony with the needs of his democratic and scientific century:

. . . it is imperatively and ever to be borne in mind that *Leaves of Grass* entire is not to be construed as an intellectual or scholastic effort or Poem mainly, but more as a radical utterance out of the abysms of the Soul, the Emotions and the Physique — an utterance adjusted to, perhaps born of, Democracy and Modern Science. . .[19]

Though from no definite plan at the time, I see now that I have unconsciously sought by indirections at least as much as directions, to express the whirls and rapid growth and intensity of the United States, the prevailing tendency and events of the Nineteenth Century, and largely the spirit of the whole current World, my time. . .[20]

Therefore he was only gradually aware of all the implications of his work:

. . . I set out with the intention also of indicating or hinting some point-characteristics which I since see (though I did not then, at least not definitely) were bases and object-urgings toward those "Leaves" from the first.[21]

This was hardly a rational process, or one that could be defined in rational terms. However, his subject being otherwise impossible to grasp, it was the only method that offered itself to him. Anyhow, he did not believe that anyone could ever succeed in pressing more closely into the mystery which lies at the heart of things:

The best poetic utterance, after all, can merely hint, or remind, often very indirectly, or at distant removes. Aught of real perfection, or the solution of any deep problem, or any completed statement of the moral, the true, the beautiful, eludes the greatest, deftest poet — flies away like an always uncaught bird.[22]

Though the fowler in the course of successive editions tried to tighten the meshes of his net, he could never succeed in catching the bird.

Consequently, because of the fleeting nature of the subject and the peculiar progress of a way of thinking that proceeded by successive approximations, *Leaves of Grass* was slowly shaped by the interaction of two different processes, the one of instinctive growth and the other of rational and deliberate construction. As a result, the evolution of the work is difficult to trace in detail, as can be shown by the following example: in the edition of 1871 Whitman achieved with "Passage to India" a serenity and a mastery of himself he had never evinced before. Nevertheless this change had been announced as early as 1865–66 by a short poem ending with these lines:

Ah think not you finally triumph, my real self has
    yet to come forth,
It shall yet march forth o'ermastering, till all lies be-
    neath me,
It shall yet stand up the soldier of ultimate victory.[23]

Thus a theme which appears at a given moment generally has its origin in a previous edition where it existed only as a germ. But the germ has invisibly developed in the interval and suddenly comes to light. It seems to be new, but it has been there for several years abiding its time. Whitman described this germination himself in one of his poems, "Unseen Buds." [24]

However, this slow, tenacious, and apparently regular evolution was actually interrupted by crises in the life of the poet. He himself compared his existence to a long sea voyage in the course of which the ship seemed several times about to sink: ". . . some lengthen'd ship-voyage, wherein more than once the last hour had apparently arrived, and we seem'd certainly going down — yet reaching port in a sufficient way through all discomfitures at last. . ." [25]

There was no exaggeration in that; as we shall see, each new edition marked a victory and was the resolution of a spiritual crisis. Accordingly I must precede my critical study with a biographical introduction in which I shall disentangle the complex relations that linked his life with his work. For if his life determined his work, his work in turn had an influence on his life. He tried to embody himself in *Leaves of Grass,* he hoped that his book would be inseparable from himself, that the one would be impossible to distinguish from the other.

> Camerado, this is no book,
> Who touches this touches a man. . .

he said at the end of "Songs of Parting." [26] His subject was first of all himself: "I celebrate myself, and sing myself. . ." he proclaimed in 1855 at the beginning of "Song of Myself"; [27] or, as he explained in 1888 in "A Backward Glance o'er Travel'd Roads":

"Leaves of Grass" indeed (I cannot too often reiterate) has

mainly been the outcropping of my own emotional and other personal nature — an attempt, from first to last, to put *a Person,* a human being (myself, in the latter half of the Nineteenth Century, in America,) freely, fully and truly on record. I could not find any similar personal record in current literature that satisfied me.[28]

But he dreamed of himself as a prophet of a new evangel and it was in that aspect that he portrayed himself; therefore it was necessary for him to try to resemble his own portrait if he wanted it to be a good likeness. He was obliged to shape both his life and his work at once. And he was very clearly aware of the duality of the task which he had imposed on himself, if we may believe what he said in a review of the first edition of *Leaves of Grass* that he himself wrote for the Brooklyn *Daily Times*: "First be yourself what you would show in your poem. . ." [29] Accordingly he was led to treat his life as a work of art, to make of his life and his book two parallel, always superimposable creations:

> On, on the same, ye jocund twain!
> My life and recitative, containing birth, youth, mid-
>   age years,
> Fitful as motley-tongues of flame, inseparably twined
>   and merged in one — combining all,
> My single soul. . .[30]

This is why W. B. Yeats in *A Vision* takes Whitman as an example of what he calls "an artificial personality." [31]

In order to resemble the mythical personage of the book, the one Whitman wanted to be but was not, he was often obliged to distort the facts somewhat. In particular, in his first edition, he completely suppressed his past as a journalist and a man of letters and passed himself off as an uneducated but inspired carpenter, as a "rough." [32] Is it then necessary to accuse him of duplicity and imposture, to reproach him for his "pose" as Esther Shephard has done? [33] This would be to misconceive the complexity of the problem. When Whitman made such affirmations, he was perfectly sincere. He really identi-fied himself in imagination with the man he wanted to be. To a certain extent he became the ideal being of whom he dreamed and thus lived the part he had written for himself. He was so firmly persuaded of his own absolute sincerity that he made complete frankness one of the criteria for the recognition of great poets: "The great poets are . . . to be known by the absence in them of tricks and by the justifica-tion of perfect personal candor." [34]

There is no justification for speaking of a "pose" in the case of Whitman, for that would be to take up again the whole problem of sincerity and to affirm with J. P. Sartre that "a man is never anything but an imposture," [35] or with Valéry that "every work of art is a fake." [36] Let us say, then, quite simply that Whitman wanted to create a book and that in so doing he has created himself. His whole life was changed by his decision, thus illustrating Oscar Wilde's para-dox that nature imitates art. He was tormented, unstable, storm-tossed; [37] his work allowed him to recover his equi-librium and achieve serenity. His poetry saved him. By its means he gradually escaped the dark and stormy chaos where he had been floundering and emerged in an orderly, peace-ful universe where light overcame dark.[38]

These considerations explain why I have divided this work into two main parts, one a biographical introduction devoted to the "Creation of a Personality," the other a critical study in which I shall try to analyze the "Creation of a Book" and to examine the evolution of the great themes of *Leaves of Grass* and the development of Whitman's art.

CHAPTER I

YOUTH — THE UNSUCCESSFUL QUEST

B EFORE arriving at the crucial years which saw the birth of *Leaves of Grass,* it will be well to examine briefly the youth of the poet in order to bring out certain elements which will contribute to a better understanding of his work — and project an indirect light upon it, clarifying some of its aspects, without, however, fully explaining it or determining with certainty the reasons for its extraordinary emergence. For, though we can follow the how of things, their why will escape us. True, we shall establish a certain number of causal relations to account for the more superficial aspects of the work, but the underlying cause will remain obscure; only the study of its later development will allow us to catch glimpses of that.

Walter Whitman was born at West Hills, a small country hamlet on Long Island, on May 31, 1819. (Walt Whitman was not to be born until some thirty-five years later at the same time as *Leaves of Grass.*) Through his mother, he was descended from Welsh Quaker sailors and Dutch farmers; through his father, from colonists of English origin.[1] Later, it was his Dutch ancestors whom he mentioned with greater pleasure, attributing to them some of the virtues of which he was most proud: his physical strength and perfect health, his taste for cleanliness, his moral seriousness, and a tenacity which at times amounted almost to stubbornness.[2] But he probably owed something also to his English ancestors, his mystic idealism for instance. He belonged therefore to a class of simple rural people of plain manners, whose rough life he described later in magazine articles and in his memoirs.[3] All of his early childhood was spent in the country. Soon, however, his father sold the farm at West Hills (which still exists hardly changed), and moved to Brooklyn, probably in the hope of making a better living by practicing the trade of carpentering. The father, also named Walter, was a rather enigmatic person; an admirer of Thomas Paine and Elias Hicks, a subscriber to the *Free Inquirer* of Frances Wright, he seems to have had a hard, self-contained, independent character,[4] accommodating himself poorly to the ground rules of a mercantile society. A mediocre and dissatisfied farmer, he apparently succeeded no better as a builder of frame-houses in Brooklyn. Whitman's family was continually forced to abandon too heavily mortgaged houses.[5] Whitman was probably thinking of him when he described:

> The father, strong, self-sufficient, manly, mean, anger'd, unjust,
> The blow, the quick loud word, the tight bargain, the crafty lure. . .[6]

Hardly a flattering portrait, but, as he himself admitted,[7] Whitman preferred the women in his family. Still some of the traits of his own character may be seen in this uncongenial father: his instability, his relative indifference to worldly success, and his taste for independence.

In those days Brooklyn was not yet connected by bridges to New York; it was only an overgrown village and young Whitman continued to lead there the fairly rural life he has described in *Specimen Days*.[8] A seaside existence, too, marked by frequent fishing or bathing parties on the coast and long solitary walks on the immense deserted beaches.[9] One can imagine him silently absorbing the beauty of the countryside and all the sights it offered his eager eyes. He must have been somewhat like that child whose experiences he has recorded in one of his poems:

> The early lilacs became part of this child,
> And grass and white and red morning-glories, and
> white and red clover, and the song of the phoebe-
> bird,
> And the Third-month lambs and the sow's pink-faint
> litter, and the mare's foal and the cow's calf,
> And the noisy brood of the barnyard or by the mire of
> the pond-side,
> And the fish suspending themselves so curiously below
> there, and the beautiful curious liquid,
> And the water-plants with their graceful flat heads, all
> became part of him.
> The field-sprouts of Fourth-month and Fifth-month
> became part of him,
> Winter-grain sprouts and those of the light-yellow corn,
> and the esculent roots of the garden,
> And the apple-trees cover'd with blossoms and the fruit
> afterward, and wood-berries, and the commonest
> weeds by the road,
> And the old drunkard staggering home from the out-
> house of the tavern whence he had lately risen,
> And the schoolmistress that pass'd on her way to the
> school,
> And the friendly boys that pass'd, and the quarrelsome
> boys,
> And the tidy and fresh-cheek'd girls, and the barefoot
> negro boy and girl,
> And all the changes of city and country wherever he
> went.[10]

We may imagine him also barefoot at night on the shore of the sea, his hair blown by the wind, listening by moonlight to the sad song of the mockingbird like the child he describes in "Out of the Cradle Endlessly Rocking." [11]

These joys, however, were not unmixed, for he also had to go to school. But this bondage was short, for he stopped at the age of eleven,[12] with no regret if we may believe "Beginning My Studies." [13] This was the only formal education he ever received. In 1830, his parents, finding his upkeep a burden (he was the second of seven children),[14] placed him as an errand boy with a lawyer, then with a doctor. But young Whitman loved to read, and fortunately his first employer encouraged him by giving him a subscription to a circulating library. He was then able to plunge with delight into the *Arabian Nights* and the novels of Walter Scott. For the rest of his life he had a special affection for Scott, for the ballads as well as the fiction.[15]

A more important event in his education was his entry into journalism. It was, to be sure, by the back door, since he began very modestly as an apprentice-typesetter for the *Long Island Patriot* in Brooklyn, which then had about five hundred subscribers. Nevertheless this humble beginning was very important for Whitman.[16] He learned several things that were later useful to him, for in years to come each new edition of *Leaves of Grass* was planned not only poetically but also typographically. He attached the greatest importance to page make-up, to punctuation, to the choice of type. Once he even sacrificed nine verses to preserve a blank space, because, he said, he did not love his lines enough to let them spoil the effect of a page.[17] He always closely supervised the work of his printers, and when at the end of his life he could no longer go out, he sent them very detailed instructions in writing.

On the other hand, at that time when American journalism in the small towns was still a craft and not yet an industry, the workmen were not specialized and could be at the same time typographers and journalists.[18] Whitman's fellow-employees accordingly taught him writing as well as typesetting. We should also remember that the editorial room of a small-town newspaper was an ideal post of observation; there he could observe life and obtain a working knowledge of politics. There was in fact little news in these small papers. Most of the articles were devoted to political questions and campaign propaganda. He also had occasion to learn the history of his city and his country. An old printer on the *Patriot* had taken part in the Revolutionary War and had seen General Washington, and Whitman listened with fascination to his reminiscences.[19] Several of his historical poems are probably poetic transpositions of the stories of old Hartshorne.

Thus, between the ages of twelve and sixteen, Whitman worked for various papers in Brooklyn and New York, for he was soon drawn to New York, where he lived from May 1835 to May 1836.[20] When he described the misadventures of Franklin Evans, his temperance hero in search of a room in New York, he probably used recollections from this period of his life.[21] He no doubt preferred New York to Brooklyn because he was already a devotee of the theater,[22] and there was no theater in Brooklyn, then a suburban town of 30,000 inhabitants.[23] We may wonder why he did not stay in New York. The reason is apparently that he lost his job, like the hero of "The Shadow and the Light of a Young Man's Soul," [24] as a result of the great fire which ravaged the city in 1835 and caused serious unemployment for several months.

He was therefore forced to return to Long Island and this time completely changed his occupation. He became a schoolmaster for nearly five years from 1836 to 1841, but he did not lead a completely sedentary life, for he taught in seven different schools and for several months was the sole publisher of a newspaper.

After a solid year of city life he thus found himself again in the country, for he taught in small village schools [25] and boarded in the homes of the farmers. This gave him a chance to mix more closely than he ever had before in the life of the country people on Long Island. He took part in their holidays if not in their work and joined them in fishing parties and boating excursions.[26] They accepted him as one of themselves. And yet he was already different, even in his methods of teaching. In particular, he did not believe in corporal punishment and refused to whip his students as much out of respect for humanity as out of his distaste for violence. He even wrote a very melodramatic story, "Death in a School-Room," to show the terrible dangers children might run from the brutality of a teacher.[27] He also disapproved of mechanical methods of teaching. His ideal, as he expressed it several years later in the Brooklyn *Eagle*,[28] was a good head rather than a full one. He tried above all to awaken his pupils' intelligence. Even at this time he wanted his disciples to be independent of their master and even to surpass him.[29]

He had at this period a well-established reputation as a shameless idler [30] and an incorrigible dreamer, if we are to believe the testimony of Mrs. Orvetta Hall Brenton, at whose stepmother's home in Jamaica he boarded for some time.[31] No doubt, like all adolescents, he was dreaming of the glorious future which awaited him. Since in his case some of these dreams came true, they are worth examining. We know the content of some, thanks to a series of articles he published in the *Long Island Democrat* in 1840. We find this in particular among his youthful effusions:

I think that if I should make pretensions to be a philosopher, and should determine to edify the world with what would add to the number of those sage and ingenious theories which do already so much abound, I would compose a wonderful and ponderous book. Therein should be treated on, the nature and peculiarities of men, the diversity of their characters, the means of improving their state, and the proper mode of governing nations. . . Nobody, I hope, will accuse me of conceit in these opinions of my own capacity for doing great things. In good truth, I think the world suffers from this much-bepraised modesty. Who should be a better judge of a man's talents than the man himself? I see no reason why we should let our lights shine under bushels. Yes: I *would* write a book! And who shall say that it might not be a very pretty book? Who knows but that I might do something very respectable? [32]

Evidently he already had in mind the project he undertook fifteen years later; however, the notion of the great book which he would write was still extremely vague; he speaks of a work in prose and was probably thinking of some political treatise, for at that time he was much interested in politics. This interest was natural since he had been initiated into it in the printing and editorial rooms of Brooklyn and New York. During the fall of 1840 he took an active part in the electoral campaign in Queens County [33] and made himself conspicuous in his zeal and a certain talent in public speaking; for on July 29, 1841, he was invited by the bosses of Tammany Hall to speak at New York before some ten thousand people.[34] He was only twenty-two, and it looked as if he had a brilliant career ahead of him. However he did not persist in this course. Probably his indolent temperament prompted him to abandon so absorbing an occupation, and it is likely also that he was too idealistic to be satisfied for long with the dirty work of local politics.

This period of his life was very full and in *Specimen Days* he emphasized its importance. It was especially rich in various human contacts, particularly when he was boarding with the parents of his students at their farms.[35] He also took advantage of the leisure his profession granted him for reading and beginning to write. From 1838 to 1841, he contributed to the *Long Island Democrat* a series of ten articles under the general title of "Sun-Down Papers — From the Desk of a Schoolmaster" [36] and also several poems.[37] He wanted to write, but the result of his efforts was still mediocre. The articles were naïve and artless, and the poems were unoriginal treatments of conventional feelings about death and the vanity of earthly glory. Their form was traditional and awkward. Nothing suggested the future author of *Leaves of Grass* except the frequency with which he recurred to the theme of death.

His need to write — or perhaps, more simply, his taste for journalism — was so strong that for eight or ten months he abandoned teaching completely and devoted all his time to a small biweekly, the *Long Islander*, which he edited, printed, and delivered himself. This adventure lasted from June 1838 to the spring of 1839.[38] Whitman, it seems, soon became tired of this much too regular work. The paper appeared at longer and longer intervals and finally stopped completely: a good example of his lack of perseverance in all the enterprises which require business sense; a proof also that he was able on occasion to shake his indolence and take the initiative. But at this time he was not only trying to express himself in writing, he was also training himself in the art of speaking. This effort began several years before he took an active part in political campaigns. When he was teaching school at Smithtown in 1837 he belonged to a debating society of which he even became secretary, and the minutes of the debates, which survive, show that he was one of the most eloquent members of this rural forum.[39] It was a symptom both of intellectual curiosity and of his constant desire to express himself and communicate with others.

Another striking trait of his youth which may be inferred from all this was his extreme love of independence. He left home when he was only fourteen and without any help or much education succeeded in establishing himself respectably outside his family. This must have been something of a wrench, for he was very attached to his brothers and sisters and he passionately loved his mother. It looks almost as if he were running away, and he probably was. Most of his biographers have painted his family in tender and idyllic tones, but recent investigations have revealed a much less attractive reality.[40] The elder Walter Whitman was, as we have already seen, a hasty and violent man, soured by failure, somber and morose. The mother was perfect in Whitman's eyes and he adored her, but she was often ill and, being illiterate, could not understand his ambitions. Edward, his youngest brother, born in 1835, was a congenital idiot, and the oldest, Jesse, was syphilitic and was to die in an insane asylum. Andrew, who was probably also infected, tried to forget his troubles by drinking and soon became a habitual drunkard. He later married a woman not much better than himself. After he died of tuberculosis or cancer of the throat, his widow sent their children out to beg in the streets and herself became a prostitute. Hannah, one of the sisters, after her marriage, became neurasthenic and probably showed signs of instability even during Whitman's youth. No wonder that he felt the need to escape and this flight for a time was his salvation.

In May of 1841 he ran away still farther and established himself once more in New York.[41] He threw himself wholeheartedly into the whirl of city life to make up for the long rustic interlude. His career was now as uncertain, if not as varied, as it had been in Long Island. He began as a typesetter for the *New World* and in 1842 worked as a reporter for various democratic papers, the *Aurora*, the *Sun*, the *Tattler*. In 1843 he was on the staff of the *Statesman*, a biweekly, and contributed at the same time to the *Democratic Review*.[42] The following year he campaigned in the *Democrat* for Silas Wright, a radical Democrat.[43] These continual shifts do not necessarily indicate his instability. They were due as much to the journalistic conditions of the time as to his own temperament. In this fast-growing city, newspapers started up and died with astonishing rapidity. Their polemic character made them extremely vulnerable to the reverses of politics. At any rate, the speed with which Whitman found a new job whenever he lost one shows that he was well thought of. Unfortunately nothing has survived of what he wrote in these ephemeral sheets, and we know this period of his life only by what he said of it later. There is also, to be sure, the description left by William Cauldwell, one of his colleagues on the *Aurora*:

> He was tall and graceful in appearance, neat in attire, and possessed a very pleasing and impressive eye and a cheerful, happy-looking countenance. He usually wore a frock-coat and a high hat, carried a small cane, and the lapel of his coat was almost invariably ornamented with a boutonnière.[44]

This description corresponds closely to the way Whitman looks in a daguerreotype apparently taken at about that time and which can still be seen today at his house in Camden.[45]

He had become very different from the country schoolmaster of a short time before or the editor-printer of the *Long Islander* who made the round of his subscribers in a cart. He was now almost a dandy. The change was complete. Instead of being in love with the open air and vast spaces, he seemed now to dream only of walks on Broadway, of cafés and theaters. He was transformed into a city-man and the crowd was his element. In 1846 he returned to Brooklyn as chief editor of the *Eagle* and he kept the job for two years, but every day after work he took the ferry early in the afternoon and passed the rest of the day in New York. He was interested in everything: the art exhibits, the new Egyptian museum, the theater, the opera, the fires, the movement of ships in the harbor, and above all, the countless crowds in the streets. His favorite pastime was to ride the Broadway omnibus seated beside the driver, gossiping familiarly with him or declaiming verses which were lost in the noise,[46] or observing with untiring interest the flood of humanity on the sidewalks which later inspired him to write the poem "Faces."[47]

He hoarded sensations, noted attitudes, gestures, cries, and

odors, and later poured them all out in long catalogues in the
first edition of *Leaves of Grass*. These loungings were not a
loss of time. They enriched him, allowed him to add to his
collection of picturesque sketches and develop the sense, which
was so strong in him, of the unanimous life of a great city, of
what he later called humanity "en-masse."

What part he himself took in that life cannot be known.
Was he simply a spectator or did he participate intensely?
There is no reliable information on this point. According to
Burroughs,

> Through this period (1840–1855), without entering into par-
> ticulars, it is enough to say that he sounded all experiences of life,
> with all their passions, pleasures and abandonments. He was
> young, in perfect bodily condition, and had the city of New
> York and its ample opportunities around him.

And he adds:

> I trace this period in some of the poems of "Children of Adam"
> and occasionally in other parts of his book, including "Calamus." [48]

Perhaps; but these are, as we shall see, only conjectures. The
Whitman of this period escapes our grasp. He was already
pregnant with his masterpiece, but nothing as yet in what he
wrote or did gave any indication of it.

There was nothing exceptional in his editorials for the
Brooklyn *Daily Eagle*.[49] They were honest articles, good journalism and nothing more. They do contain ideas that later
appeared in *Leaves of Grass*, but they were written in a sloppy
style without force or distinction, rather in the tone, as Canby
suggests,[50] of a talk on the radio. They are familiar asides to
the reader, not cries sounded "over the roofs of the world." [51]
Even the titles are flat and characterless. For example, he
wrote an editorial with the banal title "Morbid Appetite for
Money," [52] whereas he stigmatized the same vice with much

more vigor in *Leaves of Grass* as "the mania of owning things," in which his scorn and anger come through.[53]

If we compare his description of a New York fire in the Brooklyn *Eagle* [54] with its evocation in "Song of Myself," [55] we can hardly believe that the two are the work of the same author. The first was written by an idler gaping at the crowd and the firemen, afraid of tripping over the hoses, by a reporter short of copy who filled his article with commonplaces on human misfortune and with moral platitudes such as this:

> And those crumbled ashes! what comforts were entombed there — what memories of affection and brotherhood — what preparation, never to be consummated — what hopes, never to see their own fruition — fell down as the walls fell down, and were crushed as they were crushed! [56]

There is no personal emotion in all this, only conventional phrases and sentimental banalities that do not involve the author's feelings. On the contrary, the poet who wrote "Song of Myself" was fully involved, he was at the center of the drama, he was the fireman buried in the debris, he was the fireman's comrades who feverishly dug to free him, he was the silent crowd who waited and trembled for him. Instead of the curious and detached idler recording all the details of some scene of the street, he intensely lived through a personal tragedy, he participated profoundly and succeeded in making us participate also. It may be symptomatic that the journalist used the past and the poet the present tense. The one reports and the other re-creates. The same comparison can be made between his descriptions of the Brooklyn ferry. The journalist in search of anecdotes amused himself watching people run when the bell rang for departure and good-naturedly mocked his contemporaries' habitual hurry. He gossiped familiarly with his "gentle reader," for, he said, "we like that time-honoured phrase." [57] He was still far from being the poet who, crossing the ferry, meditated on himself and on the future of the world, addressing all men and all women in all times.[58]

Nevertheless the journalist was the same man as the poet, and the editorial writer of the Brooklyn *Eagle* survived in the author of *Leaves of Grass*, which Emerson called "a combination of the *Baghavat-Gita* and the *New York Herald*." [59] The poet, in fact, owed something to the journalist: he often has the same familiarity and simplicity of expression. It is apparent that he has worked in editorial rooms and that this experience has freed him from the mannerisms and affectations which marred his early stories. He avoids literary effects, conventional expressions, and poetic clichés. Above all, journalism opened his mind. The young countryman of Long Island, the provincial Brooklynite, has had a revelation in New York of the immensity of his country and the world. It was probably there that he acquired that cosmic sense which characterizes his poetry and at the same time his lively feeling for the grandeur and the tremendous future of the United States. His political and social views were equally enlarged; many opinions of the chief editor of the Brooklyn *Eagle* are to be found in *Leaves of Grass*.

He kept his job for two years. It was the first time that he had remained so long in the same place. According to some reports [60] the paper lost subscribers during his editorship, and therefore the proprietor, one Isaac Van Anden, took the first opportunity to relieve himself of an unpopular editor. The occasion presented itself early in 1848. The Mexican War was about to end and the problem of the extension of slavery to the territories was posed with new sharpness. Whitman was not an abolitionist, but he wanted the West to be colonized only by free men who would not have to fear the competition of cheap slave labor. He became therefore a "free-soiler," that is, a Democrat who much to the horror of the Southern Democrats advocated the prohibition of slavery in the territories. Such a policy might have led to a schism in the Democratic camp. For this reason the conservatives in the party did their best to prevent the movement from developing, and that is probably why, according to some, Van Anden demanded that Whitman stop sustaining the free-soilers. But Whitman apparently refused and was dismissed in January 1848.[61]

If so, he lost his job — a job which he must have liked since he remained in it so long — for refusing to compromise on a question of principles: a fine case of disinterestedness and an early manifestation of an obstinacy of which he gave many further proofs. It was probably the only reason for his rupture with Van Anden, who, in all likelihood, would not have waited two years to get rid of him if his direction of the paper had been as disastrous as some biographers have thought. The theory of a political disagreement seems the best explanation of his sudden departure.[62]

At any rate, he had no difficulty in finding a new position. There had been some talk of his becoming editor of a barn-burner paper in Brooklyn,[63] but the project never materialized, probably for lack of funds. However, there was no need for Whitman to be disappointed, for in February, in the lobby of a New York theater, he met one McClure, who was part-owner of a New Orleans paper and who after a quarter-hour's conversation hired Whitman as an assistant editor and gave him an advance of two hundred dollars. This promised well, but in fact the paper, called the *Crescent*, did not yet exist and did not begin to appear until March. However, McClure, who had come North to procure the necessary equipment, had plenty of money at his disposal and success seemed sure.[64] Of course there was no question of Whitman's writing editorials. His free-soil articles would have been somewhat out of place in a southern newspaper. McClure needed a reporter, and more important, a journalist able to select and rewrite, as the custom was, articles from northern newspapers. He must have been delighted to have found a man with the experience of Whitman who for two years had competently directed the largest journal in a city of 60,000 inhabitants.

Thus, on February 11, 1848, Whitman left Brooklyn with his younger brother Jeff on his way to New Orleans. He was twenty-nine years old, but it was the first time that he had made so long a journey. It took him two weeks: the train went only as far as Cumberland, Maryland, and from there he had to take a stage-coach to Wheeling, from which point steamboats descended the Ohio and then the Mississippi. This trip must have been a revelation for Whitman, yet the account of it which he has left is rather dull. He did publish in the first three issues of the *Crescent* his notes on the stretch from Baltimore to Cairo. But they were extremely prosaic. He carefully recorded the prices of tickets and meals, but the descriptions were sketchy and prosaic and the picturesque details scarce.[65] He had not been insensible to the beauties of the countryside, for he deplored the fact that no American painter had yet turned it to account. In a way, he was already indicating his own program in this passage: an American artist, instead of trying to copy or imitate his European predecessors, should make an effort to express what was characteristic of his own country in an original way.[66] However, he had been sometimes disappointed. The Ohio in particular struck him as having been overpraised. This great river with its muddy water was decidedly unworthy of the poems which had been devoted to it.[67] But, if the landscape did not come up to his expectations, he was nevertheless favorably impressed by the quality of the men whom he met on the way: ". . . I was by no means prepared for the sterling vein of common sense that seemed to pervade them — even the roughest shod and roughest clad of all."[68]

This first contact with the West accordingly confirmed the hopes he had conceived before visiting it.[69] Moreover he was pleased with the prosperity of the region, the abundance which seemed to reign everywhere. His experience on this trip, even though it does not appear in the plain and dry notes which he published, must have reinforced his faith in democracy and in the future of the United States.

He was also sensitive to the beauty and grandeur of the Mississippi, which inspired him to write "The Mississippi at Midnight," but these stilted quatrains were still far from *Leaves of Grass*. The images were as conventional as stage props and only one stanza in which two present participles echo each other in an effort to suggest the incessant flow of the river and of life feebly foretells what was to come.[70]

But, if the West impressed him, New Orleans enchanted him. The climate, the vegetation, the people, the customs were all new to him and filled him with wonder. He never tired of walking through the town during the ample free time which his work on the *Crescent* allowed him. He found there an easy way of living unknown in New York and Brooklyn, and above all, it showed him a richer and healthier sensual life, unfettered by puritanism. He expanded in this freer atmosphere. A few years before he had hardly dared to speak of women, because, he said, "it behoves a modest personage like myself not to speak upon a class of beings of whose nature, habits, notions, and ways he has not been able to gather any knowledge, either by experience or observation."[71] He now devoted a whole article to Miss Dusky Grisette, a quadroon who sold flowers every evening in the open air close to where he lived. Her beauty and her charming smile delighted him.[72] In his old age he still spoke with admiration of the New Orleans octoroons, "women with splendid bodies — no bustles, no corsets, no enormities of any sort: large, luminous rich eyes: face a rich olive: habits indolent, yet not lazy as we define laziness North: fascinating, magnetic, sexual, ignorant, illiterate: always more than pretty — 'pretty' is too weak a word to apply to them."[73]

He was also pleased with the French quarter. He liked to walk in its narrow streets with their strange-looking houses and to hear the people around him speaking a language that he did not understand. He felt as if he had been transported into the Old World. He tried, through what he saw, to imagine Europe and its curious customs. He went, for instance, to the St. Louis Cathedral on Maundy Thursday, and although he had been reared in the simplicity and austerity of the Quaker faith, he never thought of criticizing the somewhat theatrical pomp of the catholic liturgy. On the contrary, he was struck by the fervor of the worshipers and immediately understood the underlying meaning of the bizarre ceremonies, namely that beauty might be an important aspect of religion.[74] This shows the openness of his mind and foretells the universal sympathy he was to proclaim in *Leaves of Grass*.

The taste for French and Spanish words with which he later sprinkled his poems probably also originated from this period. They were already appearing in his articles for the *Crescent*.[75] Even if he later borrowed from books the ones used in *Leaves of Grass*, they nonetheless had a sentimental value which dated back to his walks through the picturesque streets of New Orleans.

His visit to Louisiana was thus marked essentially by the discovery of a Latin culture of which he probably had no previous knowledge and of a semitropical vegetation, the splendor of which he celebrated several years later with nostalgia.[76] According to some biographers, he also had at this time a touching and almost tragic love affair. Henry Bryan Binns was the first to circulate this strange and tenacious myth by reporting in his biography that Whitman had had a liaison in New Orleans with a woman from a higher social rank than his own. He even said boldly that a child was born of this union, perhaps several children, but that, because of family opposition, Whitman was unable to marry the one he loved and even formally to recognize his children.[77] Binns unfortunately was unable to give any proof of this romantic tale, for it was nothing but a conjecture which he applied to a set of imprecise and hardly verifiable facts. The most plausible of the documents he invoked was the reply that Whitman later made to John Addington Symonds, who had urged him to clarify the meaning and scope of "Calamus." Whitman — and we will have occasion to return to this point — evaded the question with this avowal: "My life, young manhood, mid-age, times South, etc., have been jolly bodily, and doubtless open to criticism. Tho' unmarried I have had six children — two are dead — one living, Southern grandchild, fine boy, writes to me occasionally — circumstances (connected with their fortune and benefit) have separated me from intimate relations." [78]

He also alluded several times in talking with Horace Traubel — very vaguely however — to his illegitimate children,[79] but we shall see later what was behind this impudent falsehood which was apparently intended to camouflage one whole aspect of his life. At any rate, none of this evidence lends any credibility to the tale imagined by Binns. The hypothesis was certainly tempting, the more so as Binns supposed that the mysterious lady was a high-born Creole, romantic, sensual, noble, and passionate, who "opened the gates for him and showed him himself in the divine mirror of her love." [80]

Léon Bazalgette with his usual enthusiasm devoted one whole chapter of his biography to this pretty story under the enticing title of "Vers le sud et vers l'amour de la femme." [81] Even Basil de Selincourt let himself be seduced by this myth, and worse still, Emory Holloway, after successfully resisting the temptation in the preface to his edition of Whitman's uncollected papers,[82] succumbed in his turn when he wrote his biography.[83]

Another argument invoked by the partisans of this romance

is that Whitman did not really begin to be himself until after his return from New Orleans. They claim that the shock of this great passion suddenly made of him the poet that we know. I shall have to return to this question, but my purpose for the moment is only to indicate roughly the established exterior facts which marked Whitman's life up to the appearance of his masterpiece. It must be noted at this point that the earliest verses which he wrote in the manner of *Leaves of Grass* (that we know of) are found in a manuscript notebook dated 1847 — that is to say, a year before his departure for the South.[84] The love-affair hypothesis accordingly explains nothing and loses its *raison d'être*.

It seemed very convenient, though, because it furnished an explanation not only for the sudden birth of Whitman's genius but also for his hasty departure from New Orleans after a stay of exactly three months. But here again we can do very well without it. The facts explain themselves. Whitman recorded them in a notebook which has survived, and there is no reason to doubt the truth of his account since this memorandum was not intended for publication. According to him, after a time, Hayes and McClure, the proprietors of the *Crescent*, began to show a singular coldness toward him and an ungracious reluctance to discuss the politics of the paper with him. He became haughty in his turn, and finally, when they refused him an advance to which he thought he had a right, he offered his resignation, which they accepted.[85] He seems to have been surprised at their eagerness to get rid of him; [86] he was probably unprepared to lose so quickly a remunerative job in which he had hoped to make savings in order to buy a small farm on Long Island.[87] However, he made a virtue of necessity and decided to leave New Orleans at once. The reason for his departure was therefore purely professional and not at all sentimental. In all probability he was forced to leave not because of his work, but because of his political opinions. The articles he selected or rewrote for the paper must to some extent have reflected his convictions as a free-soiler, whether he so intended or not.[88] Hence, no doubt, the unwillingness of Hayes and McClure to discuss with him the policy of the *Crescent* as soon as they became aware of his intransigence. They very likely expected more flexibility on his part. Accordingly, when he asked for an advance, they may have refused it under the pretext that the two hundred dollars McClure had given him in New York was to be considered not as a payment for the expenses of the trip but as an initial advance on his salary. If they had wanted to keep him, they would have been more generous. Whitman must have realized this and preferred to leave — but not without regret, as is shown by the parenthesis added in pencil to his notes in which he referred to "some objections on the part of me."

Jean Catel speaks of Whitman's nostalgia and of his desire to return to his family.[89] This, I think, is an exaggeration. Certainly Whitman intended to return to Long Island, but not so soon. He had no intention of living permanently in the South, but for the moment it attracted him strongly. New Orleans had conquered him at once, and he enjoyed his work there. Nothing in either his personal journal or in what he published later suggests that he was in any hurry to leave. To speak of his nostalgia is to attribute to him the feelings of his brother Jeff, who did want to return as quickly as possible.[90] This is understandable since Jeff was only fifteen and was away from home for the first time. He felt very far from his family — all the more so since in those days a letter took several weeks to go from Brooklyn to New Orleans. The brothers were there for a whole month without receiving any mail.[91] Whitman recorded this fact in his notebook, but without any undue emotion. The theory of home-sickness does not seem to hold in his case, and the only possible reason for his sudden departure therefore must be simply and solely a disagreement with the owners of the paper, apparently on political grounds. This is a rather prosaic and matter-of-fact account which lacks the charm of Binns's romantic fable and which unfortunately offers no ready-made explanation for the genesis of *Leaves of Grass*, but it has the advantage of leaving the field clear for an unprejudiced study of the problem.

Whitman returned to Brooklyn, but without haste by way of the Great Lakes, Chicago, Buffalo, Niagara Falls, and Albany. Leaving New Orleans on May 26, he did not get home until June 15.[92] This leisurely progress does not seem to indicate an overwhelming nostalgia. It is rather the normal conduct of a man who has lost his job, but who is not greatly worried, knowing that he will easily find another.

And that is in fact what happened. By September he had again become chief editor of a Brooklyn free-soil paper, the *Freeman*, which had just been started by the wing of the Democratic Party with which Whitman was in sympathy. There was therefore no break in his career at this particular time. It was as if he had never left home. Apparently nothing in his life had changed, which is another indication that the supposed crisis of New Orleans very probably occurred only in the imagination of over-romantic biographers.

A year later, on September 11, 1849, Whitman resigned from the *Freeman*, and his farewell article to his readers vituperated the Old Hunkers, the conservatives of the Democratic Party.[93] He blamed them for the disunity of the Democrats and for their failure to live up to the hopes he had placed in them during his youth.[94] In fact it seems that at this time he did experience a rather serious political crisis. The exasperation shown by his resignation and by his farewell article apparently grew, for he was soon writing a whole series of political poems in an extremely violent tone. The first of these appeared on March 2, 1850, in Bryant's *Evening Post*, the "Song for Certain Congressmen," a brutal satire written under the pressure of indignation caused by the Compromise of Clay and the attitude of Webster.[95] The next was "Blood-Money," which Horace Greeley published in the New York *Tribune Supplement* on March 22 and which appeared again on April 30 in the New York *Evening Post*.[96] This was the cry of pain and anger of his idealism in revolt against the cowardice of the politicians who had allowed the Fugitive Slave Law to pass. The impetuosity of his inspiration on this occasion was such that the traditional poetic molds broke under the pressure and he used for the first time a kind of free verse which, in a rudimentary way, suggests the rhythm of *Leaves of Grass*. He must have felt that this experiment was a success, for two months later he used the new mode of expression to proclaim in "Resurgemus" his hatred of tyranny and his sympathy for the revolutionary movements of 1848 in Europe.[97] He had now found his voice. This poem was in fact the first of the *Leaves of Grass* and was included in the 1855 edition. All that Whitman needed to do in order to fit it in was to change the typography. In the version of 1850 the poem looks a little meager on the page, but two or three verses together made a line of the desired length in 1855.

Thus the signs multiplied. The masterpiece was on the way. The first rumblings of the coming eruption could already be heard. Let us try to discover what was going on in Whitman's mind without having recourse as yet to *Leaves of Grass*.

At the time of his return from New Orleans in 1848, as we have seen, nothing was changed. He was still a political journalist, and he took an active part in electoral campaigns. The Brooklyn *Freeman*, of which he was chief editor, reported that he was a member of the general committee of the free-soil faction in Ward 7. He was evidently the most influential member because his name was at the top of the list.[98] In August he had been sent by the Brooklyn free-soilers with a delegation of fourteen others to the party convention at Buffalo, where he spoke in favor of Martin Van Buren.[99] It was an exciting time. Everywhere, it seemed, the cause of liberty and democracy was triumphant. In all of Europe insurrectionist movements had been victorious, and tyrants had been overthrown or forced to make concessions to their subjects. In America free-soilers, full of illusions about the idealism of the people, hoped to win in the approaching presidential elections. Unfortunately disappointments soon multiplied. To begin with, Van Buren was not even nominated, and it was General Zachary Taylor, the Whig candidate, who won because of the schism in the Democratic Party. As a result of this defeat many free-soil politicians, feeling that the cause was lost, deserted to the right wing of the Democratic Party, doubtless to Whitman's great disgust. The free-soil minority quickly fell apart.

What was Whitman to do? He could not follow the opportunists and return to Democratic orthodoxy. He was too proud to recant and too much convinced of the justice of the cause to which he was devoted. We can see in this connection why several months earlier he had left the Brooklyn *Eagle* in a huff and why it had been impossible for him to remain longer in New Orleans on a paper that printed along with his articles announcements of slave auctions or descriptions of fugitive Negroes such as Dickens quotes in his *American Notes.*[100] Since there was no question of his becoming a Whig, he found himself without a party, completely left out. In the following months his disgust must have grown as the Dough-Faces increased their concessions to the advocates of slavery and of its extension. His feelings during these crucial years are expressed not only in his 1840 poems, but also in a short prose piece, "Origins of Attempted Secession," which he later reprinted in *Specimen Days.*[101] Even though some of its pages were written long after the period we are examining, they seem to have preserved all of the violent disgust which he had

felt at that time.[102] He castigated the delegates to the Democratic convention with a force and virulence unusual for him.
For twenty-five lines he throws insults at them, revealing the
strength of his anger and hatred against those whom he held
responsible for the collapse of all his dreams of peace and
harmonious progress.[103] He had good reasons for this grudge,
for his darkest forebodings were soon to be realized.

On March 7, 1850, Daniel Webster made his famous speech
in support of Clay's compromise resolutions, and in September
the Compromise was adopted by Congress. The federal authorities were henceforth required to pursue fugitive slaves in the
North and return them to their masters. Many conscientious
people rebelled because all citizens, whether they liked it or
not, found themselves accomplices of the slave-owners of the
South. There was a surge of indignation throughout the North.
It was on this occasion that Whittier wrote "Ichabod" and
described Daniel Webster's "bright soul" being "driven, fiend-
goaded down the endless dark." [104] The gentle Emerson, who
was not yet an abolitionist, noted in his Journal shortly after
Webster's speech: "He has brought down . . . the free and
Christian State of Massachusetts to the Cannibal level." And
a little later, when the Fugitive Slave Law was passed, his
despair knew no bounds.[105] The intractable Thoreau, though
not yet an abolitionist either, had dissociated himself a year
earlier from a government which he considered unjust by
refusing to pay his poll tax and writing his essay on "Civil
Disobedience," for which he had passed a night in the Concord
jail. When the crisis came, his resistance, passive before,
became active and he declared himself an ardent abolitionist.[106]

Whitman therefore was not the only one who suffered during this trying period. But, unlike Thoreau, he passed from
action to inaction. Profoundly discouraged by the opportunism
of the politicians, undoubtedly disappointed also by the voters'
indifference to the ideas which were dear to him, he gave up

active politics for good. He was never again seen on a platform
among those

> Terrific screamers of Freedom,
> Who roar and bawl and get hot i' the face. . .[107]

He had been "wounded in the house of friends" [108] and had
now realized his mistake. He had not reckoned with the love
of money. He had thought all men were devoted to his ideal,
but most men apparently wanted only material goods and
nothing really touched their hearts without at the same time
touching their pockets.[109] He had kept for a long time the
illusions formed in his youth, but now his eyes were finally
opened — a painful awakening. And yet, at the height of his
pain and anger, he did not lose all hope. Let others despair of
liberty, he never would.[110] The present was disappointing, so
he took refuge in the future. In so doing he was not running
away from reality, he was merely trying to nourish his faith
with the image of its ultimate triumph. He was not a dilettante
who evaded the present, but a visionary who defied it. He now
knew the ugliness of reality, yet he did not condemn it. He
courageously accepted it as it was. He did not try to beautify
it or to forget its flaws and turpitudes, but he was not resigned.
He protested, he revolted.

This was the result of the first crisis through which he
passed — at least the first that we know of. He did not suc-
cumb; he surmounted it and emerged stronger and more sure
of himself. He was now a different man from the sentimental
and rather naïve dreamer he had formerly been, and different
from everybody else too. He knew it, and therefore detached
himself from the world in which he had developed thus far
and which had seemed to give him complete satisfaction. Not
only did he renounce active politics, but he almost completely
abandoned journalism. After his resignation from the *Freeman*,
his career is difficult to follow; documents are lacking. We

know only that he contributed to various newspapers in Brooklyn and New York. In May and June of 1850, for instance, he wrote a series of articles entitled "Paragraph Sketches of Brooklynites" for the Brooklyn *Daily Advertizer*, a Whig paper (apparently he had become indifferent to political labels).[111] The following year he published in the same paper an article recommending that the city authorities undertake the construction of new water-works.[112] The subject is a little surprising, but Whitman had always been interested in such matters of health.[113] What is more surprising is that he maintained this interest during the time when he was working on *Leaves of Grass*. But this detail clearly shows that in spite of the crisis of 1850 there was no cleavage in his career and that there never would be. The journalist would always continue to co-exist with the poet and the poet would never be indifferent to the fate of his city. He was not exaggerating when he declared in *Leaves of Grass*:

> This is the city and I am one of the citizens;
> Whatever interests the rest interests me. . . . politics,
>   churches, newspapers, schools,
> Benevolent societies, improvements, banks, tariffs,
>   steamships, factories, markets,
> Stocks and stores and real estate and personal estate.[114]

He demonstrated this interest in 1854 when he protested vigorously against the decision of the Brooklyn City Council to prohibit the running of street-cars and to force the closing of restaurants on Sunday in order to compel everyone willy nilly to observe the Sabbath. On this occasion he stated a principle which he was soon to proclaim in his poems: the representatives of the people must never forget that they are only representatives and that their duty is to act in the interest of all, not to tyrannize. The duty of the citizen, on the other hand, is not to obey but to make his will respected.[115]

Probably the most interesting piece that he wrote during

this period was his essay on "Art and Artists" which he read before the Brooklyn Art Union on March 31, 1851.[116] In this he raised, as an artist, the same protest that he had launched as a politician in "Blood-Money" against the materialism of the American people and their worship of the dollar. But it is evident that he had now found his way. It did not matter to him if others thought of nothing but running after honors and money; he preferred to be like that idler who lived in Persia hundreds and hundreds of years before and who replied when they asked him what he was good for: "to perceive [the] beauty [of this rose] and to smell its perfume." [117]

As a matter of fact this was not altogether his ideal. He did not want such an extreme detachment. He wanted to keep in touch with the rest of humanity, to share the life of the people, fighting along with them against their oppressors and guiding them in their struggle for liberty. The example he proposed was Socrates and, greater than Socrates, Christ.[118] The artist, according to him, should be the champion of the people and the advocate of the rights of man. That being so, there would be no divorce between art and society. Art would ennoble and sanctify the society that received it.[119] These ideas calmly expressed were those which would be developed more passionately in the 1855 Preface to *Leaves of Grass*.

This was his position after the crisis of 1850 when he was about to throw himself into his great poetic venture. On the one hand, he had a profound desire to live aside from the people and their base preoccupations in order to devote himself entirely to the contemplation of the world's beauty. On the other hand, he wanted to remain committed and to share the destiny of the society and the nation to which he belonged in spite of their unworthiness. In other ways also his life at that time showed his oscillations between the two extremes. As we have seen, he had not lost all contact with his contemporaries. If he no longer took part directly in their conflicts, he did intervene from time to time with newspaper articles. But for the most part he recoiled. He stayed with his family and made his living as a carpenter, working with his father and his brothers:[120] a strange and sudden change of direction. It is hard to say why he chose this trade. He never said himself. No doubt it was an easy way to supply his needs and protect his independence without having to mix in the political struggles with which he was disgusted. It seems to me that we need not see in this any profound desire to sink into the mass of the people or any mystic urge to identify himself with the proletariat by adopting the costume of a laborer and working with his hands, as his hagiographers, especially O'Connor, have supposed.[121] He was no Tolstoy and in any case such changes of status were not unusual in mid-nineteenth-century America. Society was neither very stable nor very stratified and no opprobrium attached to manual labor. It was therefore quite natural for Whitman to escape from the dilemma which his abandonment of journalism had placed him in by becoming a carpenter and thus helping his father whose health was declining (he died in 1855). True, he might have gone back to his old trade and taken a printer's job, but this would have been too close to the situation from which he wished to escape, and after the collapse of all his hopes he probably wanted a complete change of atmosphere.

At any rate, in practice, this solution proved to be ideal. Working with his family he could be at ease and, according to his fancy, either handle the plane and the hammer or step aside in order to dream. If we may believe his brother George, "he would lie abed late, and after getting up would write a few hours if he took the notion — perhaps would go off the rest of the day. We were all at work — all except Walt." [122]

Evidently he was not a very regular worker nor very strongly persuaded of the nobility of the craft he had chosen by chance and as an easy way out. But he probably soon realized how he could turn it to advantage — or rather, to describe the process in a somewhat less objective way, his imagination soon surrounded this prosaic occupation with a poetic halo. He wanted to be a poet of the people, a prophet of democracy, and here he was, dressed like a man of the people and apparently living by the labor of his hands. It was a fortunate coincidence. Circumstances had done away with the young dandy in the impeccable frock-coat who some years earlier had strolled down Broadway with a flower in his lapel and a cane in his hand. In his place was now a worker in canvas trousers and shirt sleeves whose open collar "ne se referma jamais plus, pas même dans la bière où il ful couché," as Bazalgette says with his usual romantic bombast.[123] So he appears in the engraved portrait on the frontispiece of the first edition of *Leaves of Grass*. He resembled then, without trying to at first, later consciously and intentionally perhaps, the man whom he wanted to be. Or it may be that the image of the man whom he wanted to be was formed in his mind under the influence of the man whom, without really intending it, he had already to some extent become. At any rate the work and the personality were taking shape together. The book he was writing in the ample leisure time allowed by his work as an amateur carpenter was subtly changing him. He modeled himself on his book and his book in its turn reflected him. It was a slow growth with many complex exchanges which we can guess at, but which it is impossible for lack of documentation to follow in detail or completely reconstruct. Only the result of this evolution has reached us, and it is toward this that we must now turn our attention.

But first let me recapitulate. We have followed Whitman from his childhood, we have observed his beginnings in journalism and literature, we have learned of his faith in democracy, his angry disappointments, his gropings for a poetic form and an individual style, but we will find it very difficult to

arrive at a judgment of value on this early phase of his literary
career. We cannot help recognizing that nothing which he
had written was better than mediocre. The thinking is often
dull and banal and the form undistinguished. No one would
ever have exhumed his occasional poems or his newspaper
articles if he had not later become the author of a masterpiece.
Even his stories, which before 1855 would have been his most
likely claim to fame, showed no originality though they had
enabled him at an early age to see his name listed in the
synopsis of the *Democratic Review* among those of Longfellow,
Hawthorne, and Thoreau. He had been a good pupil, sometimes of Poe as in "The Angel of Tears," [124] sometimes of
Fenimore Cooper or Hawthorne.[125] With great acumen Jean
Catel has read in these stories confessions and thoughts which
foretell Whitman's masterpiece, but, if they were examined
outside the context of *Leaves of Grass*, none of these writings
would have any interest. In themselves they are of no value;
they mean something only in relation to what followed them.
They precede, but they do not really foretell. They are only
the dawn, not the sunrise.

And yet, for several years, an obscure process of germination
had been going on — even though no outward sign had appeared. A face had been forming behind the mask of the
journalist and of the man of letters — the face of a poet. In
Leaves of Grass we will discover a new man to whom poetry
had granted the power at last to become himself.

CHAPTER II

THE 1855 EDITION — BIRTH OF A POET

ON or about July 4, 1855, there appeared simultaneous-ly in New York and Brooklyn a strange book entitled *Leaves of Grass*. Even its dimensions were unusual, for it was a quarto similar to those of the Elizabethan period. The cover was no less startling, not because of its deep green color, but because of its curious ornamentation. On the front and the back, which were identical, the title stood out in letters of gold. They were no ordinary letters. On close examination, they appeared to be alive, not merely inert characters, but plants with innumer-able roots and leaves. The rest of the cover was similarly decorated with leaves and flowers.[1] Such a harmonious match-ing of the color and the decoration with the title gave notice that this was an exceptional work and a labor of love.[2] But whose? On the cover there was no author's name;[3] nor did it appear on the title page, which gave only this information: *Leaves of Grass*, New York, 1855. Not even a publisher's name. It was necessary to turn the page in order to find in very small print the name of Walter Whitman in the copyright notice. But even this was not the true signature of the work. Whitman had not wanted to be a name, but a presence; he wished to be a man rather than an author, and had therefore placed his portrait at the beginning of the book facing the title page.[4] Here we meet again the Brooklyn carpenter whom we have just left. He has not dressed up to meet his reader. He is wearing his everyday canvas trousers and workman's shirt. He has not even bothered to put on a necktie and the open collar reveals his undershirt. However he has kept his hat on his head, because he uncovers for no one.[5] He does not pose as a thinker. He stands before us in all simplicity, one hand in his pocket, the other on his hip, but not at all in a defiant attitude, for his eyes are those of a dreamer who looks without seeing. He certainly does not see his reader.

For a man who wanted to be so simple and easy the name of Walter is still a little too pretentious, so he renounces it. He uses it here only in the copyright notice. He does not want this barrier between him and us, and on page 29 of the book he presents himself by his nickname: Walt Whitman. Walter Whitman, the journalist, whom we have known thus far is dead; he is replaced henceforth by Walt Whitman, the poet, born on the fourth of July 1855.

As a matter of fact this birth had been in preparation for a long time, though no one knew it. For several years Whitman had been jotting in the little notebooks he always carried in his pockets germs and even long fragments of poems. One of these notebooks at least has survived — there may have been others before — carrying the date 1847. Whitman had therefore begun to use it during the time when he was chief editor of the Brooklyn *Eagle*; but, since the various changes of address he has recorded in it show that he was still using it in 1848, nothing proves that he had begun to write the long passage which foretells "Song of Myself" before his return from New Orleans.[6] The initial date of the gestation period cannot be fixed, but one thing is certain: the process was so slow and so secret that the unexpected appearance of *Leaves of Grass* in 1855 seems an inexplicable miracle. The fact that we are now aware of the beginnings of the book seven or eight years earlier does not change the problem. The mystery remains unsolved. Nothing can explain why, suddenly — or little by little — the idea occurred to this very ordinary journalist, this writer of mediocre accomplishment, to break with all his habits of expression — which were also those of his contemporaries and predecessors — and try to write as no one had ever written before on life and death, on God and men. The difficulty of the problem has stimulated the ingenuity of the critics and various theories have been advanced.

One of these hypotheses which is purely biographical I have already mentioned in passing, that which was invented by Binns [7] and taken up by Bazalgette,[8] Basil de Selincourt,[9] and Emory Holloway.[10] According to them, the explanation is simple: Whitman had in New Orleans the revelation of love; he was overwhelmed by it, and the shock transformed him. A simple journalist when he left New York, he returned four months later a poet of genius — a marvellous metamorphosis from caterpillar to butterfly. Unfortunately we cannot accept this tale. The evidence does not support it and his notebook of 1847–48 indicates that the change may have begun before he visited the South.[11]

The mystic hypothesis formulated by Maurice Bucke is more attractive.[12] According to him, there is not only a difference of degree, but a difference of kind between the pre-1855 Whitman and the author of *Leaves of Grass*. Whereas most authors develop by a gradual and regular evolution, the career of Whitman is marked by a sharp break, a sudden mutation. The man suddenly changed into a Titan. Bucke explains the mystery by comparing the case of Whitman to those of Buddha, St. Paul, and Mohammed.[13] Like them he had a vision. His soul was filled with joy and ineffable peace, and this ecstasy was accompanied by an illumination. He had the revelation of the presence of God in the world, of the immortality of the soul, of the continuity of creation, and of the universal brotherhood of all living things. This ecstasy marked him forever and was the first sign of the appearance in him of a new faculty which Bucke calls "cosmic consciousness" and which is more commonly designated as mysticism. Bucke estimates that Whitman had this revelation in June 1853 as he was entering his thirty-fifth year [14] and supports this hypothesis by referring to the passage in the 1855 edition of *Leaves of Grass* where the ecstasy is described.[15]

According to Bucke, this initial ecstasy was a consecration, and all of Whitman's works flowed from it. This extraordinary ability to see the spiritual reality behind material appearances never completely died in Whitman. To the very end, in spite of illness and old age, it remained alive. It can still be felt in "Prayer of Columbus" in 1874–75,[16] in "Now Precedent Songs Farewell" in 1888,[17] and even in one of the very last poems, "To the Sunset Breeze." [18] No doubt there is a relation between Whitman's mystical sense and his poetic activity, but this parallelism or coincidence in itself explains nothing. It replaces one mystery by another. To say that Whitman's genius was born of his mysticism does not solve the problem of its sudden appearance. Even if the principle of equivalence which Bucke invokes was just, it would be necessary to carry his analysis further and define more precisely what is meant by "cosmic consciousness." And in any case it would still be impossible to penetrate the mystery of the first ecstasy. Why did it happen in 1853 and not some other year? What spark suddenly set off the explosive mixture which had gradually accumulated in him? Such questions are probably unanswerable. Where mysticism is concerned we can only describe the how of things; the why always evades us. There is also another aspect of the problem that the mystical hypothesis does not account for: the transmutation of the vision into poetry, the reason why Whitman felt the need of translating his revelations poetically instead of merely experiencing them.

Other critics have thought that they could say with certainty

what caused this sudden explosion, notably Edward Hungerford.[19] According to him, everything can easily be explained.
Whitman hesitated, not knowing which way to go; he doubted
himself, and this doubt paralyzed him. He was suddenly re-
leased when in July 1849 he had himself examined by a
famous New York phrenologist, Lorenzo Niles Fowler.[20] Phrenology was then a very popular fad and Whitman partook of
the general infatuation. He was persuaded that a skillful
specialist could infallibly read the character and aptitudes of
an individual by feeling the bumps of his head.[21] In 1888 he
still believed it.[22] Experience, he thought, had confirmed his
faith. Now Fowler had found in Whitman a remarkable subject whose amativeness, philoprogetiveness, adhesiveness, in-
habitiveness, alimentiveness, self-esteem, and sublimity were
all equally prominent. And Whitman was so well pleased
with his "rugged phrenology" [23] that he took every occasion
to publicize it. He published it in a footnote to an article he
wrote for the Brooklyn *Times* reviewing his own *Leaves of
Grass* and reprinted it in some prospectuses of the 1855 edition
and again in *Leaves-Droppings* in 1856 and finally in *Leaves
of Grass Imprints* in 1860.[24] It is probable then, as Hungerford supposes, that his self-esteem was profoundly affected.
He had great projects in hand,[25] but he was not sure that he
had the qualities needed to carry them out, and here was
science bringing the strength of its authority to the support
of his ambitions. In a moment all his doubts vanished. After
Fowler's conclusions, he felt that success was sure. To use
the terms of Haniel Long, who has adopted Hungerford's
hypothesis, phrenology became a "spring of courage" for
Whitman.[26] It catalogued and recognized all of his traits, and
though it warned him against his indolence, it gave him an
exalted idea of his powers and especially of his mental balance
and moral health. He now considered himself as a type of
perfect humanity and threw himself joyously forward.[27] He

probably recognized himself in this cutting from a phrenological journal which was found among his papers:

Good taste consists in the appropriate manifestations of each
and all of the faculties in their proper season and degree; and
this can only take place from persons in whom there is no tendency for any one of them unduly to assume the mastery. When
such a mind is prompted by some high theme to its fullest action,
each organ contributes to the emotion of the moment and words
are uttered in such condensed meaning, that a single sentence
will touch every fibre of the heart, or, what is the same thing,
arouse every faculty of the hearer. The power is known as Inspiration, and the medium in which it is conveyed is called
Poetry.[28]

Such a passage must have been a source of great exaltation
to Whitman. Certainly the moral support that Fowler's examination gave him cannot be denied, but its importance
should not be exaggerated. It cannot be assigned a decisive
role or even a predominant influence in his development. It
was only one factor among many others. In particular, the
intellectual encounters he happened to make during these crucial years must be taken into account.

The most important was probably that of Ralph Waldo
Emerson. Haniel Long mentioned it,[29] but earlier it had been
the subject of a lively controversy prompted by the contradictory declarations of Whitman himself. For, after addressing
Emerson as "Master" half a dozen times in the open letter appended to the 1856 edition of *Leaves of Grass*,[30] Whitman later
recanted. In 1867, through the medium of Burroughs' *Notes on
Walt Whitman as Poet and Person*, he let it be known that

up to the time he published the quarto edition [of 1855] . . .
[he] had never read the Essays or Poems of Mr. Emerson at all.
This is positively true. In the summer following that publication,
he first became acquainted with the Essays, in this wise: He was
frequently in the habit of going down to the sea-shore at Coney
Island, and spending the day bathing in the surf and rambling

along the shore, or lounging on the sand; and on one of these excursions he put a volume of Emerson into the little basket containing his dinner, and his towel. There, for the first [time], he
read "Nature", &c. Soon, on similar excursions, the two other
volumes followed. Two years still elapsed, however, and after his
second edition was issued, before he read Mr. E.'s poems.[31]

In *Specimen Days*, in 1882, speaking this time for himself,
he mentioned offhand the reading which he might have done
in Emerson during his youth, but pretended not to attach
much importance to it:

The reminiscence that years ago I began like most youngsters
to have a touch (though it came late, and was only on the surface) of Emerson-on-the-brain — that I read his writings reverently, and address'd him in print as "Master", and for a month
or so thought of him as such — I retain not only with composure,
but positive satisfaction. I have noticed that most young people
of eager minds pass through this stage of exercise.[32]

Several years later, in 1887, in a letter to W. S. Kennedy,
he was absolutely categorical:

It is of no importance whether I had read Emerson before
starting L of G or not. The fact happens to be positively that I
had *not*.[33]

Thus, after proclaiming himself a fervent disciple in 1856,
he later denied any influence and his hagiographers took full
advantage of the opportunity to maintain that he owed nothing to anyone.[34] In fact, the open letter of 1856 does not prove
much. It might very well have been motivated by mere opportunism and desire for publicity.[35] But in 1902 John T. Trowbridge threw in a new piece of evidence, and the bases of the
problem were completely changed. Whitman, he claimed, had
made some sensational revelations to him in 1860, while staying in Boston to supervise the printing of the third edition of
Leaves of Grass. One Sunday, in the course of a long conver-

sation, he told the story of his life and spoke of Emerson in the following manner:

I was extremely interested to know how far the influence of our greatest writer had been felt in the making of a book which, without being at all imitative, was pitched in the very highest key of self-reliance. . . Whitman talked frankly on the subject, that day on Prospect Hill, and told how he became acquainted with Emerson's writings. He was at work as a carpenter (his father's trade before him) in Brooklyn, building with his own hands and on his own account small and very plain houses for laboring men; as soon as one was finished and sold, beginning another, — houses of two or three rooms. This was in 1854; he was then thirty-five years old. He lived at home with his mother; going off to his work in the morning and returning at night, carrying his dinner pail like any common laborer. Along with his pail he usually carried a book, between which and his solitary meal he would divide his nooning. Once the book chanced to be a volume of Emerson; and from that time he took with him no other writer. . .

He freely admitted that he could never have written his poems if he had not first "come to himself," and that Emerson helped him to "find himself." I asked him if he thought he would have come to himself without that help. He said, "Yes, but it would have taken longer." And he used this characteristic expression: "I was simmering, simmering, simmering; Emerson brought me to a boil" . . .

I make this statement thus explicit because a question of profound personal and literary interest is involved, and because it is claimed by some of the later friends of Whitman that he wrote his first Leaves of Grass before he had read Emerson. When they urge his own authority for their contention, I can only reply that he told me distinctly the contrary, when his memory was fresher.[36]

This looks like the answer to the problem. We wanted to know what spark set fire to the powder and here Trowbridge shows it to us. But, should we believe his testimony? He claims to remember the conversation of that day vividly in all its details;[37] but, after all, the meeting took place forty years earlier, and we might well doubt the exactness of his memory. However, he is probably right, for we know from the Brooklyn *Eagle* that Whitman had read Emerson before 1855. In the issue for December 15, 1847, Whitman quoted a whole paragraph from one of the "inimitable lectures" of Ralph Waldo Emerson.[38] Moreover, he was certainly interested in everything Emerson wrote, for reviews of Emerson's books were found among his papers, dating back to 1847 and carefully annotated in his own hand.[39] Besides, as a contributor to the *Democratic Review*, he could hardly have ignored the long articles on Emerson in that magazine.[40] Whitman not only went through the published works, but he had also heard some of Emerson's lectures in New York. In *Good-Bye My Fancy* he reports that he had been present at antislavery meetings addressed by Wendell Phillips, Emerson, and others, and that he had heard in a room at the Athenaeum on Broadway "two or three addresses by R. W. Emerson." [41] He remembered this occasion vividly enough to evoke later in a poem not published during his lifetime the figure of Emerson speaking from a platform: "And there, tall and slender, stands Ralph Waldo Emerson, of New England, at the lecturer's desk, lecturing . . ." [42]

From all this we may conclude that Whitman knew the writings of Emerson at least second-hand from 1847 at the latest and that he read them with enthusiasm as he admits in the passage from *Specimen Days* quoted above.[43] But we see no trace of the lightning-stroke mentioned by Trowbridge which would explain everything. On the contrary, if Emerson's ideas and philosophy were familiar to him for so long, it is very unlikely that they suddenly overwhelmed him in 1854 and were then imposed on him with the force of an unexpected revelation. It seems therefore that Emerson was one of the many influences which helped Whitman find himself rather than the spark that made it possible for him to achieve at one stroke the synthesis of hitherto inert elements.

Many another scholar discovering in his turn one of these influences has thought that he had finally found the key to the mystery. Fred Manning Smith has thus tried to explain everything by the influence of Carlyle.[44] He points out that if it is true that Whitman had read very little Emerson before 1855, he might very well have felt the impress of Carlyle, with whom after all Emerson had much in common. The transcendentalist themes and phraseology which are found in *Leaves of Grass* consequently might come, not from the poems and essays of the Sage of Concord, but directly from the works of his Scottish predecessor. Whitman had published in the Brooklyn *Eagle* reviews of several books of Carlyle, *Sartor Resartus, Heroes and Hero-Worship,* and *Past and Present.*[45] He could very well have found in *Heroes and Hero-Worship* the idea of becoming a poet-prophet and of giving the world a new Bible.[46] He merely followed the example of Mohammed, Luther, and Knox.[47] His poems often evoke ecstatic states which suggest that he was visited by the same kind of inspiration as, according to Carlyle, was Odin.[48] His writing of poems in free verse which he calls "chants" brings to mind Carlyle's remarks in his chapter on "The Hero as Poet" that "all passionate language does of itself become musical . . ." and that "Rhyme that had no inward necessity to be rhymed; — it ought to have told us plainly, without any jingle, what it was aiming at." [49]

Like the heroes of Carlyle, Whitman prefers Nature to Art, which has always seemed to him to be marred by artifice.[50] And again, like them, he embraces all men in the same fraternal love. Like Mohammed, he is the "equalizer" of men.[51] And, like Knox and Luther, he refuses to bow his head to worldly powers. For him all men are equal. He despises wealth and practices the trade of carpentry instead of making a brilliant career in journalism, as if prompted by this passage in which Carlyle praises poverty:

On the whole one is weary of hearing about the omnipotence of money. I will say rather that, for a genuine man, it is no evil to be poor; that there ought to be Literary Men poor, — to show whether they are genuine or not.[52]

Moreover, this notion of the man of letters, of the "Literatus," as Whitman says, strongly resembles the ideas that Carlyle expresses in his chapter on "The Hero as Man of Letters." [53] In the same way as Carlyle he believes that all religions are true, that they all in their time have expressed a part of the essential verity, but that the poet must go beyond them.[54] Finally, the world which our senses perceive was for Carlyle the permanent proof of the presence of God beyond material appearances.[55] This is the very source of Whitman's poetic wonder. Certainly there is no lack of correspondences between the two writers. F. M. Smith in his second article is able to devote one whole page to a double-column list of striking analogies between *Leaves of Grass* and *Sartor Resartus*.[56] From all this he concludes that Carlyle was at least as much a master of Whitman as Emerson was. However he does not go quite so far as in his first article. At the end of his inquiry he is content to maintain, taking up Trowbridge's image, that if Emerson had brought Whitman to a boil, it was certainly Carlyle who began to make him simmer.[57] Thus, in spite of the great hopes which he had conceived for his hypothesis at the beginning, he is forced to recognize that it is impossible to demonstrate more than a diffuse and very distant influence. This is not at all the sudden illumination, the heavy and decisive shock which in itself would allow us to explain satisfactorily the unexpected appearance of *Leaves of Grass*. The work of Carlyle is only one of the sources on which Whitman drew; it was not at all the direct, immediate cause of his conversion.

In her book entitled *Walt Whitman's Pose*, Esther Shephard has unfortunately failed to show the same moderation as F. M. Smith.[58] Overjoyed at having caught Whitman in the act of imitating, she undertakes to demonstrate that *Leaves of Grass* is nothing but a shameless plagiarism from the works of George Sand and that even Whitman's attitude was copied from that of certain heroes of the French novelist and is therefore nothing but a pose. According to her, the source of *Leaves of Grass* is quite simply the epilogue of *La Comtesse de Rudolstadt,* which Whitman could have read in a translation by Francis G. Shaw.[59] There is, in fact, in this novel a "rhapsode vagabond" dressed as a peasant or a worker,[60] who, during a mystic trance, composes "the most magnificent poem that can be conceived." [61]

This mysterious personage is at the same time a poet and a prophet,[62] a magus and a philosopher,[63] whom Spartacus, the revolutionary and the man of action, consults with respect as an oracle. Like Whitman in the 1855 edition of *Leaves of Grass* he wants to be anonymous: "My name is *man,* and I am nothing more than any other man." [64] It is the soul of the whole of humanity that speaks through him.[65] He interprets all the religions of the past and brings out what is living and true in them, for he believes in the continuity of human history and in progress.[66] In this evolution each has his part, however humble: no effort is vain; nothing is lost. [67] Is not that precisely what Whitman proclaims in his "Song of Prudence"? [68] To the poet-prophet everything is beautiful — life, nature, humanity. The only evil is tyranny, which goes against nature and ignores the fact that all men are born brothers in freedom and equality.[69] Surely all this is remarkably similar to certain themes in *Leaves of Grass,* and therefore Esther Shephard concludes that Whitman was inspired, not by a transcendentalist mysticism, but by very conscious and carefully concealed borrowings from the work of George Sand.[70] She is indignant to find him writing in the 1855 Preface: "The great poets are also to be known by the absence in them of tricks and by the justification of perfect personal candor." [71]

Why then did he conceal his sources? she demands. Why did he never mention *The Companion of the Tour of France*, which he had reviewed in the Brooklyn *Eagle* in 1847 [72] and which must have influenced him? In this volume George Sand had told the story of a young carpenter, as handsome and noble as Christ, who worked with his father but used his leisure to read and talk about art. Although he dressed as a laborer, he was always impeccably clean. One day he experienced an ecstasy — like Whitman — and, when he was moved, he spoke with such eloquence that his friends saw him as a potentially great orator or writer.[73]

The analogy is certainly striking. But, even if we admit that Whitman, giving way to a somewhat puerile desire to identify himself with a fictional hero, sometimes modeled his dress and behavior on the Count of Rudolstadt and Pierre Huguenin, the Companion of the Tour of France, is that sufficient to explain the birth of his masterpiece? It seems unlikely, for it is not possible to find anything more than very vague suggestions in these verbose novels, and these suggestions probably did no more than confirm tendencies already present and living in him. Many of the analogies that Esther Shephard points out are in fact more apparent than real. In spite of what she says the ecstasy of Pierre Huguenin has nothing in common with the rapture that Whitman describes in "Song of Myself." [74] The resemblance is purely superficial. The trance into which the Count of Rudolstadt falls when questioned by Spartacus is of a totally different kind.[75] It permits him to prophesy, to express his ideas and dreams with passion and eloquence. It illustrates in general the romantic concept of inspiration, but this was not at all in practice Whitman's method of composition. With him the ecstasy was the source of inspiration. It put him in a state of poetic grace, but it was not immediately translated into poetry. It preceded the poem instead of accompanying it and creating it on the spot, as in the case of George

Sand's "rhapsode vagabond." On this point at least Whitman differs notably from his model. As for the philosophical and social ideas of these heroes whom Esther Shephard accuses him of copying, he could equally well have found them in the works of Carlyle and Emerson. They were not the exclusive property of George Sand. They were in the air, and Whitman may certainly be forgiven if he forgot where he found them.[76] A possibility remains that Pierre Huguenin and the Count of Rudolstadt inspired Whitman's attitude at the time of his return from New Orleans. Their example gave him the courage to become what he had dreamed of being. He may have felt less lonely in their company and less abnormal. These precedents were reassuring. Others had taken before him the way which he wanted to follow — fictional heroes, it is true, but that fact did not deter him. It seemed quite natural for him to try to become a poet-prophet like the Count of Rudolstadt and, to begin with, to make his living as a carpenter in the manner of Pierre Huguenin and of his own father. The fact that his own father was also a carpenter probably appeared to him as a striking and portentous coincidence.

This is in fact the limit of George Sand's influence. It seems almost certain that she helped and encouraged Whitman in fashioning the curious personality which he was trying to develop during the years from 1850 to 1855 in order to bring his life into harmony with his work. Perhaps she also suggested some of the ideas he took up in his poems, but this is by no means certain. At any rate it is clear that she did not provide the great and decisive shock which critics are looking for and which would by itself explain the birth of *Leaves of Grass*.[77]

Esther Shephard's hypothesis thus proves on analysis to be as disappointing as the others. The most reasonable conclusion would probably be a confession of failure. Jean Catel is close to this when, at the end of his book, he formulates his theory of the "I" in Whitman's poetry. He rejects both the hypothesis of mysticism and that of a sexual awakening in New Orleans; according to him, Walt Whitman was merely a misfit; he had thus far encountered nothing but disappointments and finally, tired of the continuous struggle, he retreated to an interior world where he was the sovereign creator, where his "I" was master and this "I" imposed itself on him to the point that he forgot the existence of the discontented journalist, of the loveless young man that he had been until then.[78] Artistic creation was for him a compensation, a making up for the deficiencies of life. This is a penetrating interpretation. Gay Wilson Allen has taken it up and expressed it with vigor in his *Walt Whitman Handbook*.[79] But the attempt to explain a work by reference to the slow and mysterious and almost undefinable operations of the unconscious amounts to a renunciation of the effort to discover the origin of the *fiat* which gave it birth.

Thus all the hypotheses that have been suggested for the origin of *Leaves of Grass* prove equally unsatisfactory. Their number alone shows the complexity of the problem. Their defect is precisely their failure to recognize this complexity. Each of these theories is too partial and accounts for only one aspect of the question. Each of these critics imagines that he has discovered Ariadne's thread, but one thread is not enough, for there is really a cluster of causes. The most reasonable course is perhaps to refrain from attacking this difficult problem and frankly admit to an inability to penetrate the mystery. To use the image of Whitman in his conversation with Trowbridge,[80] he simmered from 1847 to 1855, but no one knows what finally brought him to a boil. He probably did not know himself. His mind at that time might be described as a supersaturated solution very rich in elements borrowed from life and from books: childhood dreams, adolescent disturbances, ecstasies, memories of Long Island, scenes of Brooklyn and New York, unsettling impressions of New Orleans, recollections of Carlyle, Emerson, and George Sand. All this was probably full of eddies, but it remained amorphous until a sudden crystallization occurred. This crystallization is as inexplicable as that of the glycerine sent to Russia in a barrel which was found solidified at the end of the journey. No one ever knew how this first specimen of solid glycerine came into the world. The birth of *Leaves of Grass* is an enigma of the same kind. No one has discovered the crystal which served as a "germ," and probably no one ever will.

It might be tempting to examine the notebooks that Emory Holloway has published,[81] some of which go back to 1847–48, in the hope of discovering the secret there, but they contain nothing that is not more clearly and more forcefully set forth in *Leaves of Grass*. These documents are interesting only because they permit us to attribute an earlier date to the thoughts and feelings Whitman expressed in his poems. The only remaining possibility is to examine the work itself as it was revealed to Whitman's contemporaries in 1855.

The earliest version of *Leaves of Grass* is different from the others not only in format, but also in form. One of its peculiarities is that an important role is played by prose. Of the ninety-five quarto pages, the Preface alone takes ten, printed in very small type. At first glance the work appears to be twofold and consist of a prose manifesto and a collection of poems. But in the reading, the differences diminish; for in the unusual prose of the Preface, there are hardly any subordinate constructions. Whitman proceeds by series of independent clauses, by the juxtaposition of affirmations which he makes no attempt either to prove by logic or to integrate into a well-constructed whole. He is content to affirm. This is the reason for the peculiar punctuation that he uses both in the Preface and in the poems. Instead of commas and semicolons, we find only points of suspension varying in number from two to eight.[82] He uses them to indicate the rhythm of the sentences and to mark the places where the reader, if he were reading aloud, would need to take breath. This is the normal concern of a poet or an orator. He does not try to convince by argument, but rather to affect emotionally. He wants his text to be an incantation or a rhapsody. Therefore his prose is very close to his verse. It looks as if he had not had time to versify the ideas of the Preface. As we shall see, it required only a rapid revision in the following year to turn this long piece of prose into the poem later called "By Blue Ontario's Shore." [83] And the book thus gained at once in richness and homogeneity.

Here we see the essential character of the first edition, which is its lack of finish. It is very close to the primitive magma. It has the appearance of a flow of lava which nothing could stop and which has remained formless. The twelve poems the book contains are part of the same amorphous mass. Outwardly nothing distinguishes one from another. To be sure, they are separated by double horizontal lines, but this typographical device is not sufficient to give them any individuality. They have no titles and must be considered indiscriminately as "Leaves of Grass." The 1855 edition is undoubtedly the least organized of any. Thus it is not surprising that the poems do not entirely fulfill the promise of the Preface. The subject of the Preface is mainly America and democracy, whereas in the poems these themes are hardly touched upon.[84] In the Preface the accent is on politics; in the poems it is on metaphysics. The poet had not yet completely absorbed the political journalist, or rather, since the political journalist would never completely disappear, the poet was not yet able to transmute into poetry the political ideal with which he was pregnant and of which he had been aware since the crisis of 1850.[85]

The *Leaves of Grass* of 1855 is then a heterogeneous and rather poorly constructed book. The composition is more musical than architectural, but the content is already extremely rich. The title itself is worth dwelling on. Why did Whitman

call the book *Leaves of Grass* instead of "Blades of Grass"? [86]
He evidently wanted this play on words. These "leaves" would
be at the same time the leaves of his book and those of the
grass. Thus the work would be a bunch of leaves consisting of
poems which were already written when he gathered them,
as he was soon to explain in "Spontaneous Me":

> And this bunch pluck'd at random from myself,
> It has done its work — I toss it carelessly to fall where
>   it may. [87]

Others — Fanny Fern in particular — had already played
on the word, [88] but with Whitman it was no longer a banal
pun designed to make the reader smile; it was the expression
of a symbolic relationship suggesting mystical correspondences.
These pages, these "leaves," are both himself and his work
since he incorporates himself in the book:

> Camerado, this is no book,
> Who touches this touches a man. [89]

But at the same time they are actual leaves, not only the leaves
of graminaceous plants, but the leaves of any herbaceous
plants, as is shown by the designs on the cover. [90] These *Leaves
of Grass* therefore include the poet and his song and all the
vegetation which covers the earth. He has chosen grass, the
anonymous mass of herbaceous plants, because it symbolizes
for him the universal presence of life, not only in space, [91]
but also in time, even beyond death:

> This is the grass that grows wherever the land is and
>   the water is . . . [92]

> And it means, Sprouting alike in broad zones and
>   narrow zones,
> Growing among black folks as among white,
> Kanuck, Tuckahoe, Congressman, Cuff, I give them
>   the same, I receive them the same . . . [93]

Tenderly will I use you curling grass,
It may be you transpire from the breasts of young men,
It may be if I had known them I would have loved
them,

. . . . .
The smallest sprout shows there is really no death . . .[94]

Thus *Leaves of Grass* represents the universal brotherhood of
all living things permeated in all places and times by the same
immortal burning force. The title admirably characterizes this
book and fairly sums up one of its essential themes, the eternal
cycle of life.[95]

Since the book purports to be above all a man, let us look
for the man who hides behind these strange *Leaves of Grass*.
To be sure, when the book is opened, he does not hide at all;
on the contrary he sings himself and celebrates himself [96] and
he presents us several times in "Song of Myself" with his full-
length portrait. He introduces himself as a man of the people:

Walt Whitman, an American, one of the roughs, a kosmos,
Disorderly fleshy and sensual. . . . eating drinking
and breeding,
No sentimentalist. . . . no stander above men and
women or apart from them. . . . no more modest
than immodest.[97]

He wished first of all to give an impression of physical vigor.
The image he tries to impose is that of a laborer, solidly built,
proud of his strength and of his carnal appetites, whose sensual
instincts are not paralyzed by any inhibition. He is no "gentleman" distant and reserved. He wears no mask. He gives free
rein to his emotions; he is not ashamed of the needs of his
body and, above all, he does not stand apart from the other
people; he is, as he loudly proclaims, a part of the mass.

These are the two aspects of his personality that he seems
to value most: a vigorous animality and a highly developed

sense of human brotherhood. He returns to them constantly. "The friendly and flowing savage"[98] he describes a little farther along is no other than himself. There is so much force in him and so much love for his fellow-men that all feel irresistibly drawn toward him as if his body radiated a secret magnetism:

> Wherever he goes men and women accept and desire him,
> They desire he should like them and touch them and speak to them and stay with them.[99]
> He has the passkey of hearts . . . to him the response of the prying of hands on the knobs.
> His welcome is universal . . .
> . . . the mechanics take him for a mechanic,
> And the soldiers suppose him to be a captain. . . . and the sailors that he has followed the sea,
> And the authors take him for an author. . . . and the artists for an artist,
> And the laborers perceive he could labor with them and love them . . .[100]

He makes common cause with all the oppressed; [101] no social barrier stops him:

> To the drudge of the cottonfields or emptier of privies I lean. . . . on his right cheek I put the family kiss . . .[102]

He moves through life and among men with sovereign ease. He is "not different" and fraternizes with everyone. He is not embarrassed with anyone and no one is embarrassed with him. He lives democracy. Wherever he goes, equality and fraternity are immediately realized, thanks to his wonderful faculty of speaking with the first to come without reserve or constraint and of giving himself entirely to each one.

If he is not at all a "gentleman," he is no more an intellectual. He exalts physical power and life in the open air. He

avoids libraries and prefers the rude, bronzed, bearded face
of the vagabond always on the go to the smooth-shaven face
of the city man:

> I tramp a perpetual journey,
> My signs are a rain-proof coat and good shoes and a
>   staff cut in the woods;
> I lead no man to a dinner-table or library or exchange
>   . . .[103]

He passionately loves the countryside and sometimes takes
part in the work of the fields — as a dilettante, for he is more
a spectator than an actor. Nothing pleases him more than to
return to the farmyard lying on a wagon-load of hay, or to
roll in the dried grass stored in the mow.[104] He takes part in
fishing parties and spends whole days at the seaside digging
clams,[105] or he wanders alone in the woods and gazes after the
wild ducks who fly away at his approach.[106] He is

> . . . enamoured of growing outdoors,
> Of men that live among cattle or taste of the ocean or
>   woods,
> Of the builders and steerers of ships, of the wielders
>   of axes and mauls, of the drivers of horses . . .[107]

He needs the open spaces of the American countryside in
order to feel at ease and breathe freely. His vigorous body needs
air and movement. In this sense he retains the tastes of the
country boy which he had acquired in his childhood at West
Hills. He is fully aware of this background and in one of the
last poems of the book he describes his youthful wonder before
the ever-new beauty of all things that struck him as a child.[108]

This is the portrait of the artist by himself which emerges
from the 1855 edition of *Leaves of Grass*, his "Me myself" [109]
insofar as it is possible to disentangle it from the mystical
metamorphoses which it underwent in imagination while he
was writing "Song of Myself." He wanted first of all to appear

as an apostle of democracy and as an uncultured man filled
with masculine force and a powerful animality. He was especially proud of his "perfect health," [110] of his "reckless
health." [111] He gave an impression of firmness and complete
confidence in himself bordering on arrogance. He chanted at
the top of his lungs his joy in living and in creating, and his
nonchalance, it seems, was the sign of a perfect physical and
moral equilibrium.

At least that was the image which he wished to impose on
us, but a more attentive reading of "Song of Myself" brings
out strange dissonances. First of all there is the admission that
he had not always possessed the faith and the certitude which
now prompted his exultant optimism:

> Backward I see in my own days where I sweated
>   through fog with linguists and contenders . . .[112]

> Down-hearted doubters, dull and excluded,
> Frivolous sullen moping angry affected disheartened
>   atheistical,
> I know every one of you, and know the unspoken in-
>   terrogatories,
> By experience I know them.[113]

> Be at peace bloody flukes of doubters and sullen mopers,
> I take my place among you as much as among any.[114]

Moreover, when he thought of the suffering of the oppressed
and of all those who were ill and about to die, he still sometimes paled and trembled:

> Agonies are one of my changes of garments . . .[115]

> I am less the jolly one there, and more the silent one
>   with sweat on my twitching lips.[116]

So he was not simply the happy extrovert of his portrait.
His exuberance concealed agonies and secret doubts. His personality was less simple than he wanted his reader to think,

less normal. That was to be expected. The mystical overtones of "Song of Myself" and the extreme sensuality of some passages indicated an exceptional temperament.[117] For, surprisingly, as soon as Whitman stops talking directly about himself, the hearty, superficial man of the people of the self-portraits gives way to the dreamy poet of the frontispiece who looks without seeing, his gaze lost in the clouds:

> Apart from the pulling and hauling stands what I am,
> Stands amused, complacent, compassionating, idle, unitary,
> Looks down, is erect, bends an arm on an impalpable certain rest,
> Looks with its sidecurved head curious what will come next,
> Both in and out of the game, and watching and wondering at it.[118]

Other passages permit this analysis to be pushed still further. In a notebook which he used about 1848–49 the following reflections are found:

> I am not glad to-night. Gloom has gathered round me like a mantle, tightly folded.
> The oppression of my heart is not fitful and has no pangs; but a torpor like that of some stagnant pool.
> Yet I know not why I should be sad.
> Around me are my brother men, merry and jovial . . .
> No dear one is in danger, and health shelter and food are vouchsafed me.
> O, Nature! impartial, and perfect in imperfection
> Every precious gift to man is linked with a curse — and each pollution has some sparkle from heaven.
> The mind, raised upward, then holds communion with angels and its reach overtops heaven; yet then it stays in the meshes of the world too and is stung by a hundred serpents every day . . .
> Thus it comes that I am not glad to-night.–

I feel cramped here in these coarse walls of flesh.
The soul disdains its [incomplete]
O Mystery of Death, I pant for the time when I shall
    solve you! [119]

We do not have enough information for a diagnosis of this
incurable sadness which he suffered on occasional evenings
and could not exorcise,[120] but we now know with certainty
that there were discordant elements at the heart of his exuberant optimism and his triumphant health. We suspect that
the joy which uplifts his poems has a secret corollary in moments of depression that, he claims, are without cause. It is
clear that he had never learned to analyze himself, for he
indicates in passing, without realizing it, two very plausible
reasons: the presence of evil in the world and the weakness of
the flesh. These probably account for some of his melancholy
and echo the crisis described in the preceding chapter which
caused him to withdraw from the world into himself. The
crisis persisted. He was not completely cured. In spite of his
assurance and his apparent equilibrium, he had not yet attained the serenity of faith. His personality still contained
elements of instability disquieting for the future.[121]

This analysis shows at any rate that there was a wide gap
between the image of himself which he tried to impose on us
and the person whom the documents permit us to reconstruct
and whose character we can infer from the poems. The jolly
fellow of the official portrait was actually very unstable, passing back and forth between exaltation and gloom. The man of
the people who claimed that he had never sat on a platform
among the notables forgot the political speeches he had made
when he had fought in the ranks of the Democratic Party and
the free-soil faction.[122] By his account he had never associated
with men of letters or read any books.[123] He ignored his contributions to the *Democratic Review* and all the book reviews
that he had published in the various newspapers on which he

had worked. He never even breathed a word of his journalistic career.[124] One would think by his testimony that he had spent his life in the fields.

Does this mean that he was deliberately trying to deceive us? Probably not, for the portrait includes a number of authentic features. In any case, as we have already noticed, the working clothes which he was now wearing were not a disguise put on for the occasion.[125] He had adopted this costume about 1850 when he decided to change his way of life, to break with his past and renounce the world with all its pomp and circumstance in order to devote himself entirely to his ideal.[126] He took the vow of poverty and that alone is sufficient evidence of his sincerity. There is no justification for reproaching him with the fact that he did not altogether resemble his portrait. He had described the kind of person he wanted to be rather than the one he really was. We will see how he kept on trying to approximate more and more closely the model he had set for himself. There is certainly no reason for accusing him of charlatanism. He had no intention of deceiving; he was attempting rather to impose a new personality on himself.

He wanted to become manful, expansive, and normal, and he began by claiming that he already had these qualities. He wanted to play in real life the role he had given himself in his book. He was, however, obscurely aware of the distance that still separated the dream from the reality. He wrote in one of his notebooks in 1848 or 1849: "I cannot understand the mystery, but I am always conscious of myself as two — as my soul and I: and I reckon it is the same with all men and women." [127] He was evidently more naïve than deceptive, less the player than the man incapable of seeing clearly what passed within himself.

His contemporaries, naturally, were somewhat disconcerted by this book which pretended to be a man and by this strange man who wanted so much to identify himself with his book.

Many critics reacted violently, some to the point of gratuitous insults. For example, R. W. Griswold wrote slanderously in the New York *Criterion*: ". . . it is impossible to imagine how any man's fancy could have conceived such a mass of stupid filth, unless he were possessed of the soul of a sentimental donkey that had died of disappointed love." [128] And the critic of the Boston *Intelligencer*, after citing this edifying passage, saw fit to add on his own account: ". . . the author should be kicked from all decent society as below the level of the brute. There is neither wit nor method in this disjointed babbling, and it seems to us he must be some escaped lunatic, raving in pitiable delirium." [129]

Those who condescended to give reasons for their judgment made in general two main accusations: lack of art in the form and obscenity in the contents. What the reviewer in the London *Critic* said was typical of the reproaches commonly made:

> But what claim has this Walt Whitman . . . to be considered a poet at all? We grant freely enough that he has a strong relish for nature and freedom, just as an animal has; nay, further, that his crude mind is capable of appreciating some of nature's beauties; but it by no means follows that, because nature is excellent, therefore art is contemptible. Walt Whitman is as unacquainted with art, as a hog is with mathematics. His poems — we must call them so for convenience . . . are innocent of rhythm, and resemble nothing so much as the war-cry of the Red Indians . . . Or rather perhaps, this Walt Whitman reminds us of Caliban flinging down his logs, and setting himself to write a poem . . . [130]

After these amiable remarks, the reviewer went on to the second complaint:

> The depth of his indecencies will be the grave of his fame, or ought to be if all proper feeling is not extinct . . . we who are not prudish, emphatically declare that the man who wrote page 79 of the *Leaves of Grass* deserves nothing so richly as the public executioner's whip.[131]

In conclusion he slyly quoted the line, "I talk wildly . . . I have lost my wits," which he affected to take literally as a confession. Another gratuitous insult.

The London *Examiner*, equally shocked by the formal deficiencies, paid particular attention to the long catalogues which Whitman loved: "Three-fourths of Walt Whitman's book is poetry as catalogues of auctioneers are poems. . ." [132] Likewise the *Crayon* in New York: ". . . according to Walt Whitman's theory, the greatest poet is he who performs the office of camera to the world, merely reflecting what he sees — art is merely reproduction." [133] Although this critic admitted that Whitman had a certain power, he concluded with an unfavorable verdict: "With a wonderful vigor of thought and intensity of perception, a power, indeed, not often found, *Leaves of Grass* has no ideality, no concentration, no purpose — it is barbarous, undisciplined, like the poetry of a half civilized people. . ." [134]

The critic of the London *Leader* mainly complained that "The poem is written in wild, irregular, unrhymed, almost unmetrical 'lengths' . . . by no means seductive to English ears. . ." And, like the others, he condemned the lack of modesty:

. . . much . . . seems to us purely fantastical and preposterous; much . . . appears to our muddy vision gratuitously prosaic, needlessly plain-speaking, disgusting without purpose, and singular without result. There are so many evidences of a noble soul in Whitman's pages that we regret these aberrations, which only have the effect of discrediting what is genuine by the show of something false; and especially do we deplore the unnecessary openness with which he reveals to us matters which ought rather to remain in sacred silence.[135]

The New York *Times* protested similarly in an otherwise favorable article: "If . . . to roam like a drunken satyr, with inflamed blood, through every field of lascivious thought . . .

is to be a Kosmos then indeed we cede to Mr. Walt Whitman his arrogated title. Like the priests of Belus, he wreathes around his brow the emblems of the Phallic worship." [136]

The gross violence of some of these articles was not, however, the general rule. Even the most hostile critics were often courteous and even occasionally mingled praise with blame. The publication of *Leaves of Grass* did not provoke a universal outcry. On the contrary a surprising number of reviews were, if not enthusiastic, at least frankly sympathetic.

One of the most favorable was that of Charles Eliot Norton, published anonymously in *Putnam's Monthly Magazine* for September 1855. He praised "this gross yet elevated, this superficial yet profound, this preposterous yet somehow fascinating book." It was, he said,

a mixture of Yankee transcendentalism and New York rowdyism, and, what must be surprising to both these elements, they here seem to fuse and combine with the most perfect harmony . . . there is an original perception of nature, a manly brawn, and an epic directness in our new poet, which belong to no other adept of the transcendental school.

To be sure, he made some reservations, such as: "the introduction of terms, never before heard or seen, and of slang expressions, often renders an otherwise striking passage altogether laughable." But in general the book thrilled him, as his conclusion shows: "Precisely what a kosmos is, we hope Walt Whitman will take early occasion to inform the impatient public." [137]

Edward Everett Hale in the *North American Review* was equally fascinated by the naturalness and vigor of this new poetry: ". . . one reads and enjoys the freshness, simplicity, and reality of what he reads, just as the tired man, lying on the ground, lying on the hillside in summer, enjoys the leaves of grass around him,– enjoys the shadow,– enjoys the flecks of sunshine,– not for what they 'suggest to him', but for what they are." [138]

The *Christian Spiritualist*, which had been founded by a group of Swedenborgians, welcomed *Leaves of Grass* with enthusiasm and recommended it as containing — without the author's knowledge — echoes of the Master's doctrines. The reviewer was apparently so pleased with these correspondences that he easily pardoned the obscenities and unreservedly praised the style, which hardly anyone had dared to do thus far:

His style is everywhere graphic and strong, and he sings many things before untouched in prose or rhyme, in an idiom that is neither prose nor rhyme, nor yet orthodox blank verse. But it serves his purpose well. He wears his strange garb, cut and made by himself, as gracefully as a South American cavalier his poncho . . .

A "remarkable volume," he concluded.[139]

These commendations were pale beside the hymn of praise intoned by Fanny Fern in the New York *Ledger: "Leaves of Grass* thou art unspeakably delicious, after the forced, stiff, Parnassian exotics for which our admiration had been vainly challenged. Walt Whitman, the effeminate world needed thee. . ." This tone pervaded the whole article. She even absolved Whitman of the accusation of grossness and sensuality which had been brought against him: "My moral constitution may be hopelessly tainted or — too sound to be tainted, as the critic wills, but I confess that I extract no poison from these "Leaves" — to me they have brought only healing. Let him who can do so shroud the eyes of the nursing babe lest it should see its mother's breast. . ." [140]

And this was not an isolated article. Others could be cited, particularly that of William Howitt in the London *Dispatch*. The English critic, less impulsive than Fanny Fern, was able to praise Whitman's peculiar style with intelligence and analyze it with finesse:

> They [these poems] are destitute of rhyme, measure of feet and the like — every condition under which poetry is generally understood to exist, being absent; but in their strength of expression, their fervor, hearty wholesomeness, their originality, mannerism, and freshness, one finds in them a singular harmony and flow, as if by reading they gradually formed themselves into melody, and adopted characteristics peculiar and appropriate to themselves alone.

He predicted for Whitman a great and lasting success: "He will soon make his way into the confidence of his readers, and his poems in time will become a pregnant text-book, out of which quotations as sterling as the minted gold will be taken. . ." [141]

The reviews in the *Monthly Gazette*,[142] the *National Intelligencer*,[143] and the Brooklyn *Daily Eagle* [144] were also flattering. On the whole, then, in spite of the cries of anger and indignation of part of the press, the critical reception was favorable. This, it must be added, was the impression, from a distance, of the commentator in the London *Critic* who wrote:

> We should have passed over this book, *Leaves of Grass*, with indignant contempt, had not some few Transatlantic critics attempted to "fix" this Walt Whitman as the poet who shall give a new and independent literature to America — who shall form a race of poets as Banquo's issue formed a line of kings.[145]

The English critic in writing these lines may have been thinking of the extremely enthusiastic and almost dithyrambic articles which had appeared in the Brooklyn *Daily Times*, the *American Phrenological Journal*, and the *United States Review*,[146] but Whitman himself was the author of these. His desire to achieve a great success in publishing *Leaves of Grass* was such that he had neglected no means of drawing public attention to his book. Apparently dissatisfied with the reviews it had received, he undertook to compose a certain number himself for anonymous publication in friendly periodicals. The ruse was promptly uncovered, and Whitman was sharply criticized for the indelicacy of this procedure.[147] Certainly such methods were inelegant and bordered on dishonesty, but it should be remembered that Whitman had no publisher or publicity agent and that he had to do the necessary advertising himself. He did what he could. And, besides, as he pointed out, he was not the first to do so. Leigh Hunt following Spenser's example had also reviewed his own poems.[148] Whitman was then in very good company; however, he did not have the excuse which he later claimed: that he had been obliged to write these articles to defend himself against the insults of his enemies and to clear up misunderstandings.[149] He tried to establish this legend in his old age, but as we have seen, it is not founded on fact.[150]

There is another legend which ought to be destroyed, that of the commercial failure of the first edition. It was also invented by Whitman. In 1886 he declared in an interview published by the Brooklyn *Eagle*: "The edition was 1,000 copies — the ordinary edition of new books in those days. But there wasn't a single copy sold, not a single copy. I couldn't even give them all away. Many of them were returned to me with insulting letters." [151] A little later he repeated this story to Horace Traubel, and, when Traubel incredulously demanded what had become of all these copies, he replied, "It is a mystery: the books scattered, somehow, somewhere, God knows, to the four corners of the earth . . ." [152] — a most evasive reply and indeed a contradiction of his first assertion. He was forced to admit that the first edition had disappeared and that not a single copy remained in his possession. This is, in fact, the conclusion toward which all the pertinent evidence leads.

First of all, it must be granted that *Leaves of Grass* was

printed in an edition of 1,000 copies. There is no reason to doubt Whitman's word on that point. It was, as he said, the usual number for a first edition at the time. In 1836 Emerson's first book, *Nature*, had been issued in only 500 copies, which had taken thirteen years to sell. And in 1849 only 2,000 copies of *Walden* were printed.[153] It is true, however, that the first edition of *Leaves of Grass* was not immediately sold out. Ralph Adimari,[154] studying the advertisements that Fowler and Wells, who handled the book, placed in the New York *Tribune* has been able to show that there were three successive issues — which is confirmed by an examination of the copies still in existence.[155] The first and handsomest, with gilding on the cover, was put on sale from July 6 to the end of September for two dollars — which was a very high price for the time (*Hiawatha* sold for only one dollar and *The Scarlet Letter* for seventy-five cents). Most of the surviving copies are of this issue. After September 26, the price was cut in half and the cover lost part of its gilding; this was the second issue.[156] Then on November 24 and 25 Fowler and Wells announced the sale of paper-covered copies for seventy-five cents — which constituted the third issue. In spite of this the sales must have dropped; for, on February 18 of the following year, Fowler and Wells ran the following announcement in the *Tribune*: "Walt Whitman's Poems — *Leaves of Grass* — This work was not stereotyped; a few copies only remain, after which it will be out of print." This announcement continued until March 1.

It seems unlikely that this last announcement can have been a mere publicity trick. If the book had failed to sell, Fowler and Wells would hardly have spent so much money on advertising. Adimari has calculated that these announcements in the *Tribune* cost them $84.30. They were too commercialminded to risk so much without being sure of getting their money back. It would seem, then, that *Leaves of Grass* had a fair success with the critics and the public. On this point, the best testimony is not that of Whitman in his last years, but that of the young author proud of the victory which he had just won and which he proclaimed in his open letter to Emerson in 1856: "I printed a thousand copies and they readily sold." [157] If the public and critical reaction had been what he later described, he could hardly have had the courage to continue. Yet, in less than a year, as we shall see, his book was to double in size. Such an intensive output would be difficult to explain if the 1855 edition had been a failure. It was to some extent the demand which encouraged the supply.

Whitman, it is true, might have done without this success, for, shortly after the appearance of *Leaves of Grass*, he had received an encouragement beside which all the others faded: Emerson had sent him an enthusiastic letter that had gone straight to his heart and that must have aroused boundless hopes. Emerson had said:

I greet you at the beginning of a great career . . . I find [your book] the most extraordinary piece of wit and wisdom that America has yet contributed . . . I have great joy of it. I find incomparable things said incomparably well, as they must be . . .[158]

The Master, in other words, had recognized the ideal American poet whose coming he had looked for and predicted.[159] Whitman could not help being stimulated by such a warm tribute. He had not perhaps achieved the triumph he had hoped for,[160] but he had at least obtained enough of a victory to preserve all his confidence in himself and all his faith in the genuineness of his inspiration. All that he had to do was to persevere, to respond to Emerson's letter and the encouragements of the critics with an even richer and more vigorous work. That was what he did. Several months later a second edition appeared.

CHAPTER III

THE 1856 EDITION

IN June of 1856 [1] there appeared in Brooklyn and New York a small sextodecimo of nearly four hundred pages entitled *Leaves of Grass*. The thin quarto of 1855 had thus undergone a curious metamorphosis. On the outside, except for the color, the two books were completely different. Not only was the format greatly reduced, but also the cover had lost a large part of its ornamentation. The vegetation which had flourished there had almost completely disappeared; there remained only some small floral motifs confined to the four corners. Similarly the letters of the title had lost their former luxuriance; they were no longer half-letters, half-plants, but large thin characters without life or mystery. The backstrip had also become much simpler. *Leaves of Grass* was repeated there, and discreetly recalling the mystic interlacings of the 1855 title, the *a* of "Grass" extended itself into a leaf and the last leg of the *m* of "Whitman" was adorned with a clover leaf. For this was by far the greatest innovation: the name of the author, which had been so carefully hidden in the first edition, now followed the title as on any other book.

This, then, was no longer an anonymous pamphlet presented in such a way as to intrigue and arouse curiosity, but an ordinary commercial edition, economically and plainly bound, signed by an author already known to the public. Moreover, the book sold for only one dollar instead of two, which confirmed this impression. It was no longer the work of an amateur published at his own expense. Although their names were not on the title page, the publication this time had been undertaken by Fowler and Wells,[2] who, having acted as distributors of the first edition, performed the same function for this one, as is shown by the fact that the last page was used for their advertisements.[3]

The commercial character of this second edition also appeared in another detail. On the backstrip, in letters of gold, one of the most flattering sentences in Emerson's letter was reproduced: "I greet you at the beginning of a great career." [4] This advertising was in doubtful taste,[5] though it would not surprise a modern reader accustomed to the highly colored dust-jackets of today's popular novels.

When the book was opened, the reader found as the frontispiece the same portrait used in the 1855 volume, and the title page, also recalling the preceding edition, did not carry the name of the author. But this omission was no longer significant since his name now appeared on the backstrip. Curiously enough, on the next page, in the copyright notice, the first name was no longer Walter as in 1855, but Walt. He was consistent this time: Walter was really dead.

Leafing through the book, the reader would be struck by a notable difference between it and the first edition. The book was now organized — there was even a table of contents — and the poems were differentiated and classified. Each of them had been given a title and a number. It is true that these titles were rather monotonous and singularly lacking in distinction — they all contained the word "poem" — and these poems were merely juxtaposed rather than really grouped, as we shall see; but one thing is certain, they no longer gave the impression of a continuous tide that had characterized the 1855 edition.[6] The composition of the pages, moreover, had also changed. With the reduced format, the long verses had lost their amplitude and the punctuation had become more conventional. The points of suspension had disappeared; commas and semicolons had replaced them. Decidedly *Leaves of Grass* had been vulgarized. In appearance at least it was a book like any other.

However, it was considerably enriched. It had contained only twelve poems in 1855; the table of contents listed thirty-two this time, and they occupied about 340 pages. None attained the exceptional length of the first poem, which had now become "Poem of Walt Whitman, an American." But the fact remains that the work had nearly doubled in size, a sure sign of vigor and fecundity.

If the presentation showed a certain number of concessions to the public, the text nevertheless remained equally novel and bold. Whitman had even introduced a new theme, the sexual theme which in 1855 had been hardly sketched and which he now developed extensively. There had previously been allusions and occasional images, but now he had written whole poems on this subject: "Poem of Women" (later "Unfolded out of the Folds"), "Poem of the Body" (later "I Sing the Body Electric"),[7] "Poem of Procreation" (later "A Woman Waits for Me"), "Bunch Poem" (later "Spontaneous Me").[8] Moreover, he proclaimed in his reply to Emerson's letter his intention of celebrating henceforth, with complete freedom and without reserve, all that pertained to the sexual life:

I say that the body of a man or woman, the main matter, is so far quite unexpressed in poems; but that the body is to be expressed, and sex is. Of bards for These States, if it come to a question, it is whether they shall celebrate in poems the eternal decency of the amativeness of Nature, the motherhood of all, or whether they shall be the bards of the fashionable delusion of the inherent nastiness of sex, and of the feeble and querulous modesty of deprivation. This is important in poems, because the whole of the other expressions of a nation are but flanges out of its great poems. To me, henceforth, that theory of any thing, no matter what, stagnates in its vitals, cowardly and rotten, while it cannot publicly accept, and publicly name, with specific words, the things on which all existence, all souls, all realization, all decency, all health, all that is worth being here for, all of woman and of man, all beauty, all purity, all sweetness, all friendship, all strength, all life, all immortality depend. The courageous soul, for a year or two to come, may be proved by faith in sex, and by disdaining concessions.[9]

It appears from the warmth of the tone that this topic was close to his heart, even though he had not breathed a word of it in the 1855 Preface and nothing in any of his previous writings had given any hint of it. He had, it would seem, suddenly decided to reveal this secret aspect of his personality. The enterprise required a certain amount of courage in the face of the extreme prudishness which at that time characterized American society. As the last sentence indicates, Whitman expected resistance and protests. However, in spite of that, he considered it his duty to go ahead and make the most complete frankness in sexual matters a basic aspect of his message,[10] for reasons which we will try to specify later.

Another new theme, or at least one to which he gave a new emphasis, for it already existed as a germ,[11] was that of the journey. He devoted an entire poem to it, "Poem of the Road," [12] one of the longest in the collection, in which he sang of a strange and purely symbolic *Wanderlust* (since his return from New Orleans he had not left New York). This journey on the open road to which he invited his reader was first of all a renunciation of the comforts of routine and conformity, an uprooting similar to that which he had effected for himself when he had decided to abandon his journalistic career in order to consecrate himself to his poetry. Thus, he discovered an aspect of himself that he had hardly alluded to before, and he erected his own spiritual adventure into a general rule of conduct. But he added something else. With this theme of the journey was mingled and associated the theme of the universe contemplated in its totality or in its perpetual becoming. This was the subject not only of the "Poem of the Road," but also of the "Sun-Down Poem" (later "Crossing Brooklyn Ferry"); [13] for, in order to perceive the total becoming of the world, one need not get away from Brooklyn or Manhattan. The eternal ebb and flow of life were visible to any who could see. It was enough to look at the water, the passing boats, and the crowds of people. Whitman had feasted his eyes on these every day, and it was probably for that reason that he could issue his fervent invitation to the journey without being aware of any inconsistency with his own sedentary habits. He traversed the infinities of space and time without moving. He had succeeded in uprooting himself on the spot, but, if others wished to do so, they would first have to depart. For himself he had achieved a higher liberty than could be obtained by motion in space, which is the most elementary form of liberty; he was now able to evoke cosmic visions merely by taking the ferry to New York; he did not even need, in order to place himself in a state of grace, to catalogue for pages and pages everything that was happening in the world, as he had recently done in "Song of Myself." [14]

However, side by side with the mystic and visionary poet, there was still the rowdy Walt in love with publicity, who the year before had hesitated at nothing in order to launch his book. The quotation from Emerson's letter which he had put on the backstrip of his volume was a sufficient symptom. But there was more: the complete text of this letter was printed in an appendix,[15] and Whitman answered it with a long twelve-page proclamation that served as a postscript to the book. The tone was extremely declamatory, — at least at the outset:

. . . these thirty-two Poems I stereotype, to print several thousand copies of. I much enjoy making poems . . . the work of

my life is making poems. I keep on till I make a hundred, and
then several hundred — perhaps a thousand. The way is clear
to me. A few years, and the average annual call for my Poems is
ten or twenty thousand copies — more, quite likely. Why should
I hurry or compromise? [16]

Apparently the success of the first edition had intoxicated
him with delusions of grandeur. But the naïveté of his swagger
should not be allowed to obscure the value of this manifesto
which has been too often underestimated, perhaps because
bibliophiles for sentimental reasons place a high value only
on the 1855 edition. This reply to Emerson is a document of
equal importance with the 1855 Preface. First of all, he
stated the reasons why he intended henceforth to celebrate
sex in all frankness. Then he took up again the problem,
which he had attacked in the 1855 Preface, of the relations
between the poet and the public; but, this time, he adopted a
less subjective point of view. Instead of trying to define the
American poet of the future as he conceived him, he now
attempted rather to define the conditions of his success and
the qualities which, in his opinion, the American public
should have. It was now less a matter of the poet than of the
nation. Whereas in the 1855 Preface the constantly recurring
words had been "the poet," "the great poet," the keynote of
this letter was "These States," "America." The new manifesto
was less personal and much more national. He advocated, in
short, a less egocentric and more democratic poetry. He was
less "Myself" and more the "Bard of Democracy." Another
detail shows the same tendency: the 1855 Preface had completely disappeared; it had been converted into poems,[17] the
most important of which was significantly entitled "Poem of
Many in One," [18] in which he celebrated the mystic participation of everyone in democracy. In the following edition, he
placed this poem at the head of his "Chants Democratic." [19]
The center of interest was therefore shifting. Nevertheless he

still exalted the individual who remained an end in himself and not a means. It is clear that he was passing gradually from his initial subjectivism into his faith in democracy simply by generalizing his own experience.[20]

It is evident from all this that the version of 1856 was in many respects richer than that of 1855. It emphasized several of the deeper preoccupations of Whitman which could only be glimpsed a year earlier, such as his concern with sex. It vigorously developed the theme of the journey, which inspired one of his finest poems, the future "Song of the Open Road." It brought into full development his cosmic poetry, which instead of being monotonously analytic achieved a powerful synthetic form in the poem that later became "Crossing Brooklyn Ferry." And, finally, it definitely initiated a purification of his previous egotism, which henceforth shifted more and more toward a passionate affirmation of his faith in democracy.

It seems therefore that Malcolm Cowley is mistaken when he says:

Some of the pure intensity of emotion that produced the first edition was carried over into the 20 new poems of the second, in 1856; but by then Whitman was less visionary and more calculating in his methods. If these new poems have one quality in common, it is that whether good or bad they are all inflated. One feels in reading them that Whitman had some kinship with the manufacturers and promoters of his busy era. Having created a new poetic personality — in the same way that a businessman might acquire a new invention — he was determined to exploit it and, as we can see from his notebooks, to produce more and bigger poems each year, like a thriving factory . . . but all of them, even the best, are padded out with lists of things seen or done, things merely read about, anatomical details and geographical names.[21]

But we have already noted that the 1856 edition, on the contrary, marks a definite enrichment of the material, if not by a complete change, at least by a more profound treatment of certain themes; and, in the form, it is not inferior, for the 1855 edition already contained some very long catalogues which weighed it down considerably.[22] There is no reason therefore to consider the first edition superior to the second.

By far the most interesting poem — or at least the most revealing — in the 1856 edition happens to be one of the last in the collection, the "Poem of the Propositions of Nakedness" (later called "Respondez," which disappeared from *Leaves of Grass* after 1876).[23] Its tone is bitterly ironic in contrast to the exuberant and joyful lyricism of the other poems. It recalls "A Boston Ballad," [24] but the subject is infinitely greater. The title is Carlylean: it concerns the tearing away of appearances, which, like clothes, cover and conceal the essential reality, in order to show the real in all its nakedness.[25] But the method that Whitman used was strictly his own. He sought, by means of a long series of fiats which in the end reach blasphemy,[26] to provoke in the reader a reaction of revolt, not against the speaker of the blasphemy, but against the present condition of things; for the reader could not fail to realize before long that these were not really blasphemies, that Whitman, in fact, was only evoking reality in all its ugliness in order to arouse disgust, because he was disgusted himself. He had good reasons. The world in which we live has its seamy side. Evil triumphs.[27] "Infidels" — that is to say, unbelievers, those who have neither ideal nor love — impose their law on the rest of mankind.[28] And they seem to be justified, for men think neither of themselves (by that Whitman means that they do not think of their essential identity), nor of the death which will nevertheless prolong their lives to infinity.[29] They repress love and live in the dark.[30] They prefer respectability to life, appearances to reality.[31] It is a desperate scene. Everywhere the wicked triumph over the good, and indeed one looks in vain for the good. To make things worse, democracy, which might have saved humanity, has not succeeded in building in the United States the ideal society of which Whitman among many others had dreamed. There are still castes and differences between men. Liberty is not yet everyone's inalienable right.[32] Worse still, some men are sold like cattle. In the country which should be a model, slavery is not yet abolished.[33]

The long enumeration of Whitman's complaints continues thus for several pages. With bitter humor he describes things as they are and pretends to believe that they are as they should be. He goes even further by calling for things which exist already — and thus introduces irony. He seems tormented and unable fully to express the pain and impotent rage which smoulder in him (for this poem is extremely awkward and that is probably one of the reasons why he suppressed it in 1881). Here at any rate is a denial of the cry of joy which he utters in "Poem of the Heart of the Son of Manhattan Island": "And who has been happiest? O I think it is I — I think no one was ever happier than I. . ." [34]

How could he have been as happy as he pretended with all these causes for sadness? Wherever he turned he found only occasions for suffering. On the metaphysical plane, he was troubled by the predominance of evil in the world; on the moral plane, he was shocked by the apathy and worthlessness of most men, seduced by the vanity of appearances, insensitive to the dazzling realities of life and love; and finally, on the political plane, the United States inflicted a cruel disappointment on him by betraying the cause of democracy.

Here again are some of the symptoms that we had detected in the 1855 edition. The crisis had not yet ended, the wound had not closed. Apparently he was reconciled with the world, but in his inmost heart there still was the same indignation, and the spectacle of evil in all its forms continued to obsess and afflict him. He himself participated in the universal corruption and in the misery of mankind:

> It is not you alone who know what it is to be evil,
> I am he who knew what it was to be evil,
> I too knitted the old knot of contrariety,
> Blabbed, blushed, resented, lied, stole, grudged,
> Had guile, anger, lust, hot wishes I dared not speak,
> Was wayward, vain, greedy, shallow, sly, a solitary
>   committer, a coward, a malignant person,
> The wolf, the snake, the hog, not wanting in me,
> The cheating look, the frivolous word, the adulterous
>   wish, not wanting. . .[35]

A strange confession, which is certainly not mere rhetoric, but rather a sincere avowal and a lyrical confirmation of the moral indignation and satirical sarcasms of "Respondez." Instead of scourging others, he castigates himself, but again we find the same obsession with evil and the same torments of an unquiet soul. Moreover, in spite of his habitual assurance, he admits that he has known moments of doubt and despair when it has seemed to him that his work was ridiculous and worthless. There could hardly be a better proof of his secret instability. This passionate optimist was haunted by the idea of evil. This arrogant Walt Whitman trying to impose his faith on the rest of the world was sometimes doubtful of himself and his mission.

But these hesitations and these painful uncertainties, which in any case occupy only a very minor place in the book, probably escaped his contemporaries, judging by the reviews that appeared in periodicals at the time. As in 1855, what mainly struck the critics was the impression of "manly vigor" and "brawny health" that emerged from the book.[36] And in general the reaction of the press seems to have been the same as in the preceding year, in spite of the somewhat different character of the new edition. The positions were unchanged. The Puritans, of course, again protested with utmost violence against the indecency of the work. The critic of the Boston *Christian Examiner*, for instance, wrote:

. . . in point of style, the book is an impertinence towards the English language; and in point of sentiment, an affront upon the recognized morality of respectable people. Both its language and thought seem to have just broken out of Bedlam . . . he has no objection to any persons whatever, unless they wear good clothes, or keep themselves tidy . . . an ithyphallic audacity that insults what is most sacred and decent among men.[37]

But curiously, in spite of the augmented importance of the sexual theme in the second edition, those who liked Whitman continued to offer their praise and encouragement. The New York *Times*, for example, printed these flattering comments:

Still, this man has brave stuff in him. He is truly astonishing. The originality of his philosophy is of little account . . . In manner only can we be novel, and truly Mr. Whitman is novelty itself. Since the greater portion of this review was written, we confess to having been attracted again and again to *Leaves of Grass*. It has a singular electric attraction . . . We look forward with curious anticipation to Mr. Walt Whitman's future works.[38]

The review in the Boston *Times* was more subtle and included some reservations, but recognized nevertheless the exceptional value of the book.[39]

Again, in spite of some attacks, the critical reception was far from discouraging. But, however flattering the praises which were occasionally offered, this was not yet the immense success that Whitman had dreamed of. Though several lines from *Leaves of Grass* had been quoted by way of preface in a collection of tales and sketches as early as 1856,[40] Whitman had had higher hopes for his book, if we may believe the ambitious declarations of his open letter to Emerson.

It is possible, however, that he had resigned himself to a

more modest success. Certain scattered allusions in the new poems seem to indicate that he had accepted the idea of being only a precursor:

> I am willing to wait to be understood by the growth of
> the taste of myself . . .[41]

> Say on, sayers!
> Delve! mould! pile the words of the earth!
> Work on, age after age, nothing is to be lost,
> It may have to wait long, but it will certainly come in
> use,
> When the materials are all prepared, the architects shall
> appear.
> I swear to you the architects shall appear without fail!
> I announce them and lead them! [42]

In any case, the triumph on which perhaps he had counted in spite of these prudent reservations never materialized. The second edition was no more successful commercially than the first. Even if it was stereotyped, as he claimed, it was probably not printed in more than a thousand copies, and sales were slow.[43] But he was prepared for this; his readings had informed him of similar failures; he knew that Wordsworth, for instance, had had to wait many years for recognition by the public.[44] So he bravely continued his work, persevering in the way which he had chosen, refusing to be discouraged by disappointments.

CHAPTER IV

NEW UNCERTAINTIES:
CONTEMPLATION OR ACTION?
JOURNALISM OR POETRY?

FOR an impression of the way Whitman lived at the time of the second edition of *Leaves of Grass*, some very good evidence is offered by Bronson Alcott in his report of the visit which he made to him in Brooklyn at the end of 1856:

> He receives us kindly, yet awkwardly [Alcott was accompanied by Thoreau], and takes us up two narrow flights of stairs to sit or stand as we might in his attic study — also the bed-chamber of himself and his feeble brother, the pressure of whose bodies was still apparent in the unmade bed standing in one corner, and the vessel scarcely hidden underneath. A few books were piled disorderly over the mantelpiece, and some characteristic pictures — a Hercules, a Bacchus, and a satyr — were pasted, unframed, upon the rude wall . . .

> He took occasion to inform us . . . of his bathing daily through the mid-winter; said he rode sometimes a-top of an omnibus up and down Broadway from morning till night beside the driver, and dined afterwards with the whipsters, frequented the opera during the season, and "lived to make pomes", and for nothing else particularly.

> He had told me on my former visit of his being a house-builder, but I learned from his mother that his brother was the house-builder, and not Walt, who, she said, had no business but going

out and coming in to eat, drink, write and sleep. And she told how all the common folks loved him. He had his faults, she knew, and was not a perfect man, but means us to understand that she thought him an extraordinary son of a fond mother.[1]

This unpremeditated page tells us many things — first of all, Whitman's total indifference to his environment. (This was one of the constants of his life and explains in particular how he was able to spend his old age in Camden without suffering from the ugliness of that industrial city with its dirt and smoke.) He had no need for beautiful surroundings: the sordid attic [2] shared with an infirm brother sufficed him. He lived there in disorder and discomfort, but he did not care. He was a Bohemian — and a stay-at-home at the same time, so much so that at the age of thirty-seven he had not yet completely detached himself from his family — which is rather a remarkable fact. The situation had its advantages. Though he lived at home, he enjoyed complete freedom of movement and everyone respected his independence. Free of material cares, he was able to consecrate himself entirely to his work and to follow his dreams without the risk of being brutally recalled to reality by material considerations.

However, he did not live in an artificial vacuum. He was indifferent to beauty, but he needed to be surrounded by some human warmth, and this was not lacking in Brooklyn. He had the affection of his mother and the friendship of ordinary people: his neighbors, the men he met on the street and with whom he took the ferry to New York, and the omnibus drivers on Broadway.[3] He had really become the democratic poet, the friend of all, whom he had evoked in the self-portraits of his 1855 edition, as Alcott's testimony shows.

But, above all, Alcott tells us that Whitman, at the end of 1856, had practically ceased to work as a carpenter. We already know that he had never been very industrious in pursuing this trade,[4] but it seems that now he had completely given up earning his living by manual labor. Is it necessary to conclude that he was living as a parasite on his family? Although it is impossible to know what *modus vivendi* he had come to with his relatives, such an eventuality seems improbable because later on he regularly sent small sums of money to his mother and contributed to the support of Edward, his infirm brother. He had a strong sense of family solidarity. It is much more reasonable to suppose that he lived on his savings and on the income from the sales of *Leaves of Grass*. Unfortunately, since the book sold poorly, this inaction could not last for ever. Sooner or later his lack of money [5] would inevitably force him, if not completely to renounce a life of contemplation, at least to seek some kind of work which would enable him to supply his material needs and still remain faithful to his ideal. Probably for this reason he thought very seriously of becoming an orator. It might be the best solution.[6] He would travel through the country giving lectures, spreading the message of his poems everywhere and at the same time making his living. This attractive idea had occurred to him even before he had found himself again obliged to work for a living. In his open letter to Emerson he had already declared:

Other work I have set for myself to do, to meet people and The States face to face, to confront them with an American rude tongue . . . In poems or in speeches I say the word or two that has got to be said, adhere to the body, step with the countless common footsteps, and remind every man and woman of something.[7]

Some months later, disappointed by the public reception of his book, he had recompensed himself in imagination by dreaming that he might some day become a great orator, the champion and supreme arbiter of American democracy:

The strong thought-impression or conviction that the straight, broad, open, well-marked true vista before, or course of public teacher, "wander-speaker", — by powerful words, orations, ut-

tered with copiousness and decision, with all the aid of art, also
the natural flowing vocal luxuriance of oratory. That the mightiest
rule over America could be thus — as for instance, on occasion,
at Washington, to be, launching from public room, at the opening of the session of Congress — perhaps launching at the President, leading persons, Congressmen, or Judges of the Supreme
Court. That to dart hither and thither, as some great emergency
might demand — the greatest champion America ever could
know, yet holding no office or emolument whatever, — but first
in the esteem of men and women. Not to direct eyes or thoughts
to any of the usual avenues, as of official appointment, or to get
such anyway. To put all those aside for good. But always to keep
up living interest in public questions — and *always to hold the
ear of the people.*[8]

This great prophet, this hero of the people, though he was
not named, was no other than himself and it was to himself
that these recommendations were addressed. For a long time,
moreover, he had cherished the dream of influencing his contemporaries through the medium of speech because it always
gives an impression of direct contact and tremendous power.
Journalism was only a poor substitute. In 1837, as an obscure
country school-master on Long Island, he had already launched
himself in public speaking, taking an active part in the meetings of the Smithtown debating society.[9] Later, but when still
very young, he had had occasion to speak in political meetings
before large audiences — [10] though we do not know with what
success. In any case, in 1855, he still thought of becoming a
great political orator. In one of the reviews of *Leaves of Grass*
which he himself wrote, he said: "Doubtless in the scheme
this man has built for himself, the writing of poems is but a
proportionate part of the whole. . . In politics he could
enter with the freedom and reality he shows in poetry." [11]

He had made preparations for this career; according to his
brother George, he had composed " 'barrels' of lectures," [12]
and among his papers many notes have been found which

prove that he had often reflected on the art of oratory and on the techniques of lecturing, and had already assembled materials for these future speeches.[13] He had not limited himself to politics. He had attacked all the subjects that interested him, particularly art, literature, and above all, religion.[14] He wanted, in short, to take up in a simpler, more direct, and explicit form some of the essential themes of his poems. This would have been one way of familiarizing the public with his thinking and of imparting to it a taste for his poetry. For, according to him, every poet had himself to create his public if he wished to be appreciated or even merely accepted.[15] His oratorical activity would thus have been a supplement to his poetic creation and his speeches would have been more than a mere source of income. Eloquence and poetry would have been two parallel modes of expression: "Henceforth two co-expressions. They expand, amicable from common sources, but each with individual stamps by itself. First POEMS, *Leaves of Grass*, as of INTUITIONS. . . Second, Lectures, or Reasoning. . ."[16]

In addition he contemplated publishing his lectures in the form of a book that would be a sort of companion-piece to *Leaves of Grass*,[17] and it seems that his project of becoming a lecturer or an orator (for he continually confused the two ideas)[18] developed as the failure of *Leaves of Grass* became more apparent and his need for money more pressing.[19] Thus in 1858 he thought of undertaking a lecture tour throughout the United States, particularly in the West and South, and into Canada. In this way he would be able to live on his fees and on the income from the sale of his printed lectures.[20]

But this fine project was never realized, probably because it was easier to dream about it[21] than to put it into execution, and perhaps also because Whitman, although he delighted in imagining the triumph which he would obtain as an orator, knew very well that in practice he would inevitably fail. His voice was too weak, his delivery monotonous; he lacked fire; he would never be able to move an audience — as was proved later when he gave commemorative addresses on the death of Lincoln. He was therefore constrained to resign himself again to being a mere journalist.

In May 1857 he became in fact the editor-in-chief of the Brooklyn *Daily Times*.[22] His experimental period had apparently ended. He had given up carpentry.[23] It is true that the portraits of this period still show him dressed as a laborer. He had not resumed the costume of the dandy, but he bowed for the time being to bourgeois taste and consented to wear a necktie.[24] Since the editorials in the *Daily Times* were not signed, it is impossible to tell exactly when he took office. However, it seems almost certain that his first regular contribution was dated the first of May 1857.[25]

The *Daily Times* was the youngest and most important of the Brooklyn newspapers. It had come to the fore after very humble beginnings, thanks to the skill of its proprietors and also to its political neutrality.[26] The fact that the direction of such a paper was confided to Whitman proves that its owners had complete faith in his competence. Moreover, a glance through *I Sit and Look Out*, in which the articles he wrote at this time have been collected, shows that he acquitted himself creditably. In his editorials he attacked the most various subjects, from Washington's birthday [27] to liquor legislation [28] by way of the education of teachers.[29] A comparison of these articles with those written nine years earlier for the Brooklyn *Eagle* shows how much he had matured in the interval. He no longer had the same illusions. Previously, he had violently opposed capital punishment; [30] now he admitted that it was a necessary evil.[31] He knew more of life. He had lost his former youthful naïveté and his belief in utopias. On occasion he even made fun of overenthusiastic reformers — though he recognized their importance as forerunners.[32] His earlier absolute idealism had given way to a somewhat disillusioned realism. He condemned the blind fanaticism of those who wanted to impose temperance on the rest of the nation.[33] This was far from the conventional clichés of *Franklin Evans*; he even went so far as to propose the supervision of prostitution which he did not believe could be suppressed.[34] Generally speaking he was hostile to any radical measure. He had realized that human nature could not be changed by decree and that progress could be made only as the result of a slow and gradual evolution,[35] depending not on a reform of society but on the moral improvement of individuals.[36] Even his patriotism was shaken. Formerly so proud of his country, he now denounced the anarchical taste for violence in some of his compatriots — [37] which Dickens had so severely criticized in *American Notes*. Ten years earlier, Whitman had been an enthusiastic partisan of the Mexican War,[38] but now he came out in the *Daily Times* against the imperialistic visions of those who would have liked to see the United States annex the South American republics.[39]

This apparent eclipse of his faith in man and his country was probably due to a new political crisis which he had just gone through and which had begun in 1856. In that year, the presidential campaign had been particularly violent. In 1854, under Franklin Pierce's administration, the Democrats led by Douglas denounced the Missouri Compromise and authorized the introduction of slavery into the Territory of Kansas, and this measure provoked the immediate indignation of all those in the North who were opposed to slavery, or even, more simply, to its extension into the new territories of the West. In 1856 the dissatisfied politicians organized a new party, the Republican Party, which proposed to bring Kansas into the Union as a free state. Their candidate for the presidency was John C. Frémont, the famous explorer. The old parties chose professional politicians as their candidates. The Whigs named Millard Fillmore, who had served as President from 1850 to

1853 after the death of Zachary Taylor, and the Democrats nominated James Buchanan. Whitman, apparently as much revolted by the tergiversations and compromises of the two traditional parties as he had been in 1850, cried out his indignation and rage in an unusually violent pamphlet: *The Eighteenth Presidency.*[40] He addressed himself "to each young man in the Nation, North, South, East, and West"; to "mechanics, farmers, sailors, etc.," who "constitute some six millions of the inhabitants of These States"; to "merchants, lawyers, doctors, teachers and priests," whom he opposed to the 350 owners of slaves and to the handful of corrupt politicians who managed to govern the country without taking account of its profound aspirations.[41] He began by proclaiming his faith and absolute confidence in the honesty and genius of the people:

There is more rude and undeveloped bravery, friendship, conscientiousness, clear-sightedness, and practical genius for any scope of action, even the broadest and highest, now among the American mechanics and young men, than in all the official persons in These States, legislative, executive, judicial, military, and naval, and more than among all the literary persons. I would be much pleased to see some heroic, shrewd, fully-informed, healthy-bodied, middle-aged, beard-faced American blacksmith or boatman come down from the West across the Alleghanies and walk into the Presidency, dressed in a clean suit of working attire, and with the tan all over his face, breast and arms; I would certainly vote for that sort of man, possessing the due requirements before any other candidate.[42]

After this measured and almost solemn preamble, he hastened to the attack. Carried away by anger, he could hardly control himself; he let go more and more insults: "traitors . . . prostitutes . . . dough-faces, office-vermin, kept-editors. . ."[43] And shortly after, for a whole page,[44] he heaped abuse on his enemies the politicians, some of it gratuitous ("body-snatchers"), some probably deserved. He was disheartened by the mediocrity of Buchanan and Fillmore,[45] and he called for a "Redeemer President" who would be the representative of all and not just of some. It seemed to him that Frémont might play this role.[46] In any case, he felt that slavery had to be abolished at whatever cost, lest it abolish the liberties of the people.[47] Such was the essential message of this passionate pamphlet — generous and fervent when it addressed the American people, full of hate and contempt when it scourged those who had betrayed the democratic ideal. Its language was firm and bare; he had instinctively adopted a clear and energetic polemic style that contrasted vividly with the habitual imprecision of the prose he had been writing at this period — the prose of the 1855 Preface, for example, or of the open letter to Emerson or of his projected lectures. He seems to have been tense and fully in control of himself (except, of course, in the several passages where he indulged in insults); but under this contained vehemence, an unshakable conviction can be felt. Moreover, the last paragraph was a tranquil affirmation of his faith in the continued progress of humanity and in the final victory of democracy. The argument expanded, it was not a matter only of the United States but of the destiny of mankind and of the struggle for liberty which was raging throughout the world:

Freedom against slavery is not issuing here alone, but is issuing everywhere. The horizon rises, it divides, I perceive, for a more august drama than any of the past . . . Everything indicates unparalleled reforms. . . Never was justice so mighty amid injustice; never did the idea of equality erect itself so haughty and uncompromising amid inequality, as today. . . Never was the representative man more energetic, more like a god than today. . . What whispers are these running through the eastern Continents, and crossing the Atlantic and Pacific? What historic denouements are these we are approaching? On all sides tyrants tremble, crowns are unsteady, the human race restive, on the watch for some better era, some divine war. . .[48]

A cosmic vision of the future of humanity in which the pamphleteer rejoined the poet.

It is clear that in spite of the severe disappointments that Whitman had experienced in 1850, his faith in democracy had remained intact. He saw a new crisis coming, and he wanted to speak his mind and to play an active part. He longed to join the fray. He was again tempted to action, but he stopped short of actual intervention. He did not really act, he contented himself with dreaming that he acted — or was about to act. For this violent pamphlet, which might have had a certain influence and created a great stir, was not published. He prepared it with the greatest care and went so far as to set it in type in order to print some proofs, but at the last moment he refrained from having it published himself. He abandoned to others the responsibility of diffusing it. Just before the conclusion he inserted this appeal:

To the editors of the independent press, and to rich persons. Circulate and reprint this Voice of mine for the workingmen's sake. I hereby permit and invite any rich person, anywhere, to stereotype it, or reproduce it in any form, to deluge the cities of The States with it, North, South, East and West.[49]

Apparently he hoped that someone else would publish his pamphlet. It is not even known whether he sent any copies to the newspapers. At any rate, no one seems to have read it during Whitman's lifetime, and if two specimens had not been found among his papers, nothing would be known today of his velleity of intervening in the electoral campaign of 1856.

Could this powerlessness to act have been caused by a lack of practical ability? Did he not know how to set about publishing his diatribe? Or was it a lack of courage, a fear of making enemies? It is possible, but not probable. He had already given proof of his courage by making no concessions to his detractors in the second edition of *Leaves of Grass*. Whatever the cause, there was a strange failure in this, which is the more difficult to understand since the passionate tone of the pamphlet indicates a wholehearted adhesion to the cause which he extolled.

There can be no doubt of his sincerity, for otherwise how can the bitter realism and the disillusioned skepticism of some of his editorials in the *Daily Times* be explained, except on the ground of the pain that the defeat of Frémont must have given him? Reality had once again inflicted a harsh reproof to the incorrigible dreamer. It must have been heartbreaking for him to be obliged once more to postpone the realization of his ideal. It seems likely that he experienced, at least temporarily, some disgust for the blindness of the majority of his fellow-countrymen and some fear for the immediate future. Cruelly disappointed in his dearest hopes, he could do nothing except retire for a time into his tent. And so he did — which accounts for the neutrality of his articles in the Brooklyn *Daily Times.* He deliberately kept away from the party battles, the senselessness of which he had realized. This is the line of conduct he laid out for himself in a short poem written at this time, "To the States. To identify the 16th, 17th or 18th Presidentiad." [50] He was speaking here of his disillusionment and his decision to withdraw for a time until the American people should awake from their torpor:

> Are those really Congressmen? are those the great
>   Judges? is that the President?
> Then I will sleep awhile yet, for I see that these States
>   sleep, for reasons;
> (With gathering murk, with muttering thunder and
>   lambent shoots we all duly awake,
> South, North, East, West, inland and seaboard, we will
>   surely awake.) [51]

But this painful political crisis had by no means extinguished the poet in him. A few months later, he wrote in his journal:

The Great Construction of the New Bible. Not to be diverted

from the principal object — the main life work — the three
hundred and sixty-five. — It ought to be ready in 1859 (June
'57).[52]

This passage refers of course to *Leaves of Grass*. He had not
stopped working at it. Even while he trembled for the future
of democracy, his poetic activity was not diminished, for, on
June 20, 1857 (when he had been editor of the *Daily Times*
for nearly two months), he wrote to a friend:

> Fowler and Wells are bad persons for me. — They retard my
> book very much. — It is worse than ever. — I wish now to bring
> out a third edition. — I have now a *hundred* poems ready (the
> last edition had thirty-two.) — and shall endeavor to make an
> arrangement with some publisher here to take the plates from
> F.&W. and make the additions needed, and so bring out the third
> edition. — F.&W. are very willing to give up the plates — they
> want the thing off their hands. — In the forthcoming Vol. I
> shall have, as I said, a hundred poems, and no other matter but
> poems — (no letters to or from Emerson — no Notices or any
> thing of that sort.) — It is, I know Well enough, that *that* must
> be the *true Leaves of Grass*.[53]

So in the space of about a year he had composed some
seventy poems. His creative power was still as great — at
least quantitatively — as at the time when he had been preparing the first edition. Since 1855, in spite of setbacks and disappointments, the flow of his poems had been uninterrupted.
It looked as if he were immune to the influence of exterior
events. Although he became excited over the political battles of
these crucial years, and to some extent participated in them —
more as a dreamer than as a man of action — in his innermost
being something escaped the vicissitudes of life and resisted
all the assaults of experience. He hoped and despaired by turns,
but at the center of himself, the poet looked out, an imperturbable spectator whose faith in mankind and in his own
destiny could not be shaken by any contradictory experience.

One might also ask why he did not publish a new edition of his poems in 1857, but the reason was probably that his efforts to find a publisher interested in the venture did not succeed. He was therefore obliged to remain a journalist and to write mediocre editorials in the Brooklyn *Daily Times*. He was, in short, living a double life; for no reader of his articles could have suspected that their author was a poet. Nothing in their style or their language recalls *Leaves of Grass*, and only on rare occasions can a parallelism between his journalistic productions and his poems be discovered.[54]

Apparently this kind of existence suited him, for he remained with the *Daily Times* for nearly two years. The job of chief editor required no great expense of physical energy, and it evidently allowed him a great deal of leisure. As he had done when he was editing the Brooklyn *Eagle*, he passed his time running about New York whenever he had a free moment. He had taken up again with his friends, the omnibus drivers, and rode along Fifth Avenue or Broadway, seated beside them, watching the innumerable crowds on the sidewalks and half lost in his dreams:

A fine warmish afternoon — and Broadway in the full flow of its Gulf Stream of fashion. . . Omnibuses! — There they go incessantly — the Broadway line, Yellow Bird, Twenty-Third Street. . . Everything appertaining to them is a study. — One man appears to think so at any rate — Do you mind him, as the driver of the handsome Fifth Avenue pulls up casting at the lounger a friendly and inquiring glance, as much as to say, come take a ride, Walt Whitman? For none other than Walt is it who in response turns off from the pave, and seizes the handle, swings himself up with spring and elastic motion, and lights on the off-handside of the stage, with his hip held by the rod as quietly as a hawk swoops to its nest.

That man is the subject for the whole of this week's Plaza Sketch — that pet and pride of the Broadway stage-drivers.

As onward speeds the stage, mark his nonchalant air, seated

aslant and quite at home — Our million-hued, ever-changing
panorama of Broadway moves steadily down; he, going up, sees
it all, as in a kind of half-dream. — Mark the salutes of four out
of each five of the drivers, downward bound; — salutes which he
silently returns in the same manner — the raised arm, and the
upright hand.[55]

When he had enough of such promenading, he took refuge
at Pfaff's. This famous Swiss restaurant on Broadway was at
that time the favorite haunt of literary Bohemia in New York.
In particular Whitman found there Henry Clapp, founder of
the *Saturday Press*, who became one of his more faithful allies
and who lost no occasion to praise him in his review at the
expense of Longfellow, whom he detested.[56] There he also met
William Winter, Clapp's assistant, a Bostonian and an admirer
of Longfellow — with whom Whitman got along less well —
and Ada Clare, nicknamed Queen of Bohemia, a rich adven-
turess who had come back from Paris with the ambition of re-
creating in New York the atmosphere of the Latin Quarter.[57]
William Dean Howells, who visited Pfaff's in 1860, tells how
Whitman on seeing him

leaned back in his chair and reached out his great hand to [him]
as if he were going to give it to [him] for good and all. He had a
fine head, with a cloud of Jovian hair upon it, and a branching
beard and moustache, gentle eyes that looked most kindly into
[his], and seemed to wish the linking which [he] instantly
gave him, though [they] hardly passed a word, and [their]
acquaintance was summed up in that glance and the grasp of his
mighty fist upon [his] hand.[58]

Two details stand out: Whitman's Olympian majesty and his
taciturnity. He never really mingled with the New York
Bohemians. He was there as a spectator. Instead of taking part
in the conversation, he preferred to look on in silence or to
think about the Broadway crowds whose uninterrupted flood
passed a few yards away:

> The curious appearance of the faces — the glimpse
> first caught of the eyes and expressions as they flit
> along,
> O You phantoms! oft I pause, yearning to arrest some
> one of you!
> Oft I doubt your reality whether you are real — I sus-
> pect all is but a pageant.[59]

The problem of the reality of the exterior world preoccupied him more than the remarks exchanged around him. His curiosity was metaphysical rather than psychological. Therefore he never became a regular member of the group. "My own greatest pleasure at Pfaff's," he declared to Traubel, "was to look on — to see, talk little, absorb. I never was a great discusser, anyway — never. I was much better satisfied to listen to a fight than take part in it." [60]

This aloofness is characteristic of his attitude toward life. He wrote in a sketch for a poem dating from this time:

> But that shadow, my likeness, that goes to and fro
> seeking a livelihood, chattering, chaffering,
> I often find myself standing and looking at it where it
> flits —
> That likeness of me, but never substantially me.[61]

During this whole period, his life was in general extremely calm, he worked in the morning for his paper and idled all afternoon. But in 1859, toward the end of June, he lost his job as chief editor of the Brooklyn *Times*. The exact circumstances are not known,[62] but very probably it was because he had written two articles which must have provoked the anger of the clergy of the town. On June 20, the columns of his paper contained an article on "A Delicate Subject," namely, prostitution, a tabooed topic which he should never have brought up, especially since he declared himself in favor of a realistic solution of the problem and hoped that the authorities would recognize the existence of prostitution in New York instead of hypocritically pretending that there was no such thing.[63] The second article, two days later, discussed celibacy. "Can All Marry?" he asked, and he took occasion frankly to dilate on the dangers of sexual repression.[64] It seems probable that after this, because of the indignation of some of his readers, Whitman was obliged to resign or that the proprietor of the paper found it necessary to part company with him. Anyhow, he was again unemployed, and on June 29, he wrote in one of his notebooks: "It is now time to *stir* first for *Money* enough, *to live and provide for* M——. *To Stir* — first write stories and get out of this Slough." [65]

Who was this mysterious M——? Emory Holloway has proposed several explanations. Perhaps it was his mother, or his sister Mary? But why did he not write out the name in full? Or it may have been some mistress, perhaps the woman he had loved in New Orleans.[66] Canby believes that it must have been his mother, whom he had supported since the death of his father in 1855.[67] It is impossible to arrive at any certainty here. We are coming into a very obscure period in Whitman's life. There is at this time a gap in the recollections which he had recorded in *Specimen Days*,[68] and no notebook has been found among his papers to fill in the hiatus.[69] We can only make conjectures. It seems almost certain, however, that during this time he went through a severe moral crisis. The two articles that caused his resignation or dismissal from the Brooklyn *Times* were perhaps symptoms of it. Sexual problems were beginning to trouble him to the point that he could not refrain from discussing them in his editorials in spite of the reprobation which he was sure to encounter.[70] He was to treat them poetically with still more boldness in the 1860 edition of his book.[71] Moreover this edition shows unequivocal traces of a painful emotional disappointment. It seems that he experienced in 1858–59 (the exact date is uncertain) a great passion for a man about whom nothing is known, not even his name.[72] This passion was so violent and so exclusive that it superseded everything that concerned him previously. He was in love, nothing else mattered:

> . . . now take notice, land of the prairies, land of the
>   south savannas, Ohio's land,
> Take notice Kanuck woods — and you Lake Huron —
>   and all that with you roll toward Niagara — and
>   you Niagara also,
> And you, Californian mountains, — That you each
>   and all find somebody else to be your singer of songs,
> For I can be your singer of songs no longer — One who
>   loves me is jealous of me, and withdraws me from
>   all but love,
> With the rest I dispense — I sever from what I thought
>   would suffice me — it is now empty and tasteless to
>   me,
> I heed knowledge, and the grandeur of The States, and
>   the example of heroes, no more,
> I am indifferent to my own songs — I will go with him
>   I love,
> It is to be enough for us that we are together — We
>   never separate again.[73]

Drunk with love, he experienced moments of extraordinary exaltation in which his usual apathy completely disappeared. Normally a stay-at-home, he now dreamed of setting out with the one he loved on the open road of which he had formerly sung platonically in the 1856 *Leaves of Grass* — at least if it is possible to believe the following poem composed at this time, which probably reflects the feelings that he then experienced:

> We two boys together clinging,
> One the other never leaving,
> Up and down the roads going — North and South
>   excursions making,
> Power enjoying — elbows stretching — fingers clutch-
>   ing,

Armed and fearless — eating, drinking, sleeping, loving,
No law less than ourselves owning — sailing, soldier-
ing, thieving, threatening,
Misers, menials, priests alarming — air breathing,
water drinking, on the turf or the sea-beach dancing,
With birds singing — With fishes swimming — With
trees branching and leafing,
Cities wrenching, ease scorning, statutes mocking,
feebleness chasing,
Fulfilling our foray.[74]

But this great love was probably not returned, and soon
Whitman found himself alone, abandoned by his loved one
and broken-hearted.

Hours continuing long, sore and heavy-hearted,
Hours of dusk, when I withdraw to a lonesome and
unfrequented spot, seating myself, leaning my face
in my hands,
Hours sleepless, deep in the night, when I go forth,
speeding swiftly the country roads, or through the
city streets, or pacing miles and miles, stifling plain-
tive cries;
Hours discouraged, distracted — for the one I cannot
content myself without, soon I saw him content himself without me;
Hours when I am forgotten, (O weeks and months are
passing, but I believe I am never to forget!)
Sullen and suffering hours! (I am ashamed — but it is
useless — I am what I am;)
Hours of my torment — I wonder if other men ever
have the like, out of the like feelings?
Is there even one other like me — distracted — his
friend, his lover lost to him?
Is he too as I am now? Does he still rise in the morning,
dejected, thinking who is lost to him? and at night,
awaking, think who is lost?
Does he too harbor his friendship silent and endless?
harbor his anguish and passion?

> Does some stray reminder, or the casual mention of a
> name, bring the fit back upon him, taciturn and
> deprest?
> Does he see himself reflected in me? In these hours,
> does he see the face of his hours reflected.[75]

This remarkably poignant cry of pain seems to come from the
depth of his being. He moans like a wounded animal. His
suffering was still so keen in 1860 that he could not refrain
from giving it a place in his book, but the confession was too
intimate, the revelation too compromising; therefore in the
next edition he suppressed this poem and also the preceding
one. The terrible despair he had experienced was probably
rendered still more painful by an awareness of his singularity
— of his inversion of which I will speak again. He was to
some extent ashamed of it and did not dare to complain or to
confess as much as he would have liked:

> Sullen and suffering hours! (I am ashamed — but it is
> useless — I am what I am;)
> . . . I wonder if other men ever have the like, out of
> the like feelings?

In this connection it is possible to understand the quality
of despair of certain poems of the 1860 edition, notably "A
Word Out of the Sea," [76] the extremely personal overtones of
which he later tried to minimize. There was this admission in
particular:

> O throes!
> O you demon, singing by yourself — projecting me.[77]

Clearly the bird weeping for the loss of its companion was the
poet himself and the major theme of the fragment was originally abandonment, not death.[78] "My love soothes not me,"
says the bird, and thinking it sees its mate, it cries: "Hither,
my love! Here I am! Here! . . . Do not be decoyed else-

where!" [79] And it is the abandoned poet, not the child, the fictitious witness of a tragedy of nature, who exclaims:

O a word! O what is my destination?
O I fear it is henceforth chaos!
O how joys, dreads, convolutions, human shapes, and
all shapes, spring as from graves around me!
O phantoms! you cover all the land, and all the sea!
O I cannot see in the dimness whether you smile or
frown upon me;
O vapor, a look, a word! O well-beloved!
O you dear women's and men's phantoms! [80]

This macabre evocation provides a measure of Whitman's dismay when he suddenly found himself alone once more after having loved so deeply. It also accounts for the despair of "As I Ebb'd with the Ocean of Life," [81] whose topic is the desolation and vanity of life and in which he inaugurates the theme of the shipwreck resumed more tragically in "Thoughts." In his pain he almost goes so far as to doubt the immortality of the soul:

Are souls drown'd and destroy'd so?
Is only matter triumphant? [82]

Life itself became suspect to him, and he was obsessed with the idea of death, the tragic irreversibility of which weighed on his mind now that he had suffered the experience of separation. He could see nothing but graves around him, but he searched them in vain; nowhere could he find the body of the one he loved. Death was dissolution and annihilation, and the dust of the dead was mingled with the living:

Of him I love day and night, I dreamed I heard he was
dead,
And I dreamed I went where they had buried him I
love — but he was not in that place,
And I dreamed I wandered, searching among burial-
places, to find him,

And I found that every place was a burial-place,
The houses full of life were equally full of death,
    (This house is now,)
The streets, the shipping, the places of amusement, the
    Chicago, Boston, Philadelphia, the Mannahatta, were
    as full of the dead as of the living,
And fuller, O vastly fuller, of the dead than of the
    living. . .
And if the memorials of the dead were put up in-
    differently everywhere, even in the room where I
    eat or sleep, I should be satisfied,
And if the corpse of any one I love, or if my own corpse,
    be duly rendered to powder, and poured in the sea,
    I shall be satisfied,
Or if it be distributed to the winds, I shall be satisfied.[83]

Nevertheless there were moments when he could not believe that separation in space or time could be permanent. It sometimes seemed to him that his friend was again by his side, but the phantom, alas, soon vanished away:

I thought I was not alone here by the shore,
But the one I thought was with me, as now I walk by
    the shore,
As I lean and look through the glimmering light — that
    one has utterly disappeared,
And those appear that perplex me.[84]

His grief was so keen that at the age of forty he anticipated nothing more from life. He could only say "so long" to his readers and die:

It appears to me I am dying. . .
Dear friend, whoever you are, here, take this kiss,
I give it especially to you — Do not forget me,
I feel like one who has done his work — I progress on,
The unknown sphere, more real than I dreamed, more
    direct, darts awakening rays about me — *So Long!*

Remember my words — I love you — I depart from
   materials,
I am as one disembodied, triumphant, dead.[85]

And it is probably his own face that he describes in this profoundly melancholy little poem:

What weeping face is that looking from the window?
Why does it stream those sorrowful tears?
Is it for some burial place, vast and dry?
Is it to wet the soil of graves? [86]

In 1855 he had exclaimed in his joy before the spectacle of the universe:

It is not chaos or death. . . . it is form and union
   and plan. . . . it is eternal life. . . . it is happiness.[87]

Now he commented, sad and disillusioned:

. . . O what is my destination?
O I fear it is henceforth chaos! [88]

His former exuberant and triumphant pantheism had given way, as Frederik Schyberg notes,[89] to a desperate pantheism — at least in his moments of depression, for it seems to me that Schyberg exaggerates the morbid character of the 1860 edition. According to him, after the emotional crisis that had brought Whitman to the brink of suicide (which is probable, though not demonstrable), Whitman had led in New York a life of debauchery from which he did not succeed in extricating himself until 1861, at the outbreak of the Civil War.[90] But in that case how can the publication of the 1860 edition be explained? The mere existence of this edition would seem to prove that Whitman had by that time regained his equilibrium, otherwise how could he have found the courage to publish a new version of his book? Moreover the tranquil tone of the letters he wrote from Boston during that year [91] permit no doubt that he had recovered his serenity. Once again he had triumphed over his despair. In spite of his anguish and doubts, he had resumed his creative work and art had saved his life. The 1860 *Leaves of Grass* is the indication and the proof of this new victory over himself. The words with which he concludes:

> . . . I depart from materials,
> I am as one disembodied, triumphant, dead [92]

are not those of a defeated or desperate man.

CHAPTER V

THE 1860 EDITION

THE 1860 edition of *Leaves of Grass* represented for Whitman a double victory, for not only did he emerge successfully from a lacerating crisis, but again he won an unexpected victory over circumstances. For the first time his book had been brought out by a publisher and not by himself. This was a dream which he had cherished for a long time, but which he had not yet realized.[1] In December 1859, however, his luck had begun to turn; he had succeeded in publishing a poem, "A Child's Reminiscence," in the New York *Saturday Press* edited by his friend Henry Clapp.[2] It was shortly after this that the young Boston publishers, Thayer and Eldridge, agreed to bring out a new edition of his book.[3] In the following March, Whitman was in Boston supervising the composition and printing of his volume with the care and competence one would expect from a former typographer. He spent three months there, and as his proofreading left him plenty of leisure, he took the opportunity to see the sights.[4] For example, he went to hear Father Taylor, a former seaman, who preached in a vigorous and picturesque language, at once familiar and Biblical, whose eloquence was greatly appreciated by Whitman. Every time, he tells us, Father Taylor's prayers moved him to tears.[5] He also attended the trial of Frank Sanborn, who was being prosecuted for complicity in John Brown's raid on Harper's Ferry. He was one of a group of abolitionists ready to intervene if the judge decided to surrender Sanborn to the federal authorities.[6] He made many friends during this visit, notably C. W. Eldridge, one of his publishers, with whom he maintained friendly relations for the rest of his life. It was probably owing to Eldridge that "Bardic Symbols" (later "As I Ebb'd with the Ocean of Life") was published in April in the *Atlantic Monthly*, then edited by W. D. Howells.[7] The poem appeared anonymously, as was the custom in that magazine, but Whitman's style was easily recognizable. Eldridge also introduced him to William D. O'Connor, whose anti-slavery novel, *Harrington*, he was publishing at the time. Later, O'Connor became one of the most fanatical champions of *Leaves of Grass*. Whitman became equally friendly with John T. Trowbridge, who has left an account of their relations.[8] It is remarkable that none of those with whom he became acquainted noticed anything abnormal in him. On the contrary, they were all impressed by his physical vigor and his perfect equilibrium. Apparently he had completely recovered.

His book appeared at the end of June. It was a thick, strongly bound duodecimo of 456 pages.[9] As in the earlier editions, the name of the author was not given on the title page.[10] In order to find it, the reader had to refer to a copyright notice on the second page or to the title of the second poem, proudly called "Walt Whitman." (In 1856 this poem, which had been the introductory piece in the 1855 edition, was already entitled "A Poem of Walt Whitman, an American.")

As in 1855, he used his portrait instead of his name. He wanted his reader to see him not as an abstract entity, but as a living reality, a presence. Therefore, we find facing the title page a steel-engraving by S. A. Schoff after a portrait by Charles Hine. This time it was no longer the nonchalant and somewhat affected workingman of 1855, but the dreaming face of an artist or of a prophet. The vague and distant look remained, but the visage had aged. It gave the impression now of a fully matured man. His forehead was wrinkled. The beard and the abundant hair looked gray — and in fact they were. Whitman had become gray very early. Only the eyebrows were still brown. He was no longer in shirt sleeves as in 1855. He wore a coat, but the collar of his white shirt was still wide open. He had made one further concession, however: he had negligently tied a cravat round his neck, with the knot hanging low on his breast.

The vegetable motifs that had decorated the previous editions had completely disappeared. They were recalled only by the tendrils which prolonged the *L* and the *a*'s of *Leaves of Grass* on the cover and in all the letters of *Grass* on the title page. The color of the binding had also changed. Some of the copies were green, the rest were reddish-brown. Otherwise vegetable symbolism tended to be replaced by other themes in the decoration. The front cover showed the globe with the two Americas resting on clouds, and the back cover showed the sun rising — or setting — on the sea, and these motifs were repeated several times inside the book, as if to emphasize the cosmic character of the poet's inspiration. On the spine appeared a butterfly perched on a hand. It was also to be found on the last page and was meant to suggest the "magnetism" of Whitman, to which even the insects were susceptible. It made him comparable to Buddha or St. Francis of Assisi. Perhaps this butterfly also represented the soul, the "psyche" of the Ancient Greeks.[11]

The 1860 edition contained 154 poems, of which 122 were new, for the 1856 edition had included thirty-two. As he had announced in June 1857 that he had a hundred poems ready,[12] he must have composed some fifty poems since then — that is to say, probably all of "Calamus" and the greater part of "Children of Adam." [13]

A striking aspect of the book is its structure. Whereas in

1856 the poems were all placed on the same level and numbered in sequence from 1 to 32, Whitman had tried this time
to introduce an order and a hierarchy into his work. Ap-
propriately, the first poem, entitled "Proto-Leaf," presents the
author and announces the essential themes: Love, Religion,
and Democracy.[14] Then came "Walt Whitman," which had
been placed at the beginning in the first two editions and
which like "Proto-Leaf" is essentially an introduction. It was
followed by a group of poems collectively entitled "Chants
Democratic and Native American" and differentiated only by
numbers. This is one of the characteristics of the new presentation, for there were several other similar groups: "Leaves
of Grass" (which was thus at the same time the title of the
whole book and of one of its parts), "Enfans d' Adam;"
"Calamus," and "Messenger Leaves." Among these groups,
which were still in a nebulous state, Whitman intercalated
clearly individualized poems that were given titles — "Salut
au Monde," "Poem of Joys," "A Word out of the Sea," *et
cetera*, down to "So Long!" which, being a farewell poem, very
naturally brought the book to a close. For the first time, then,
Whitman tried to impose an architectonic structure on his
work. In the table of contents his intention is clear. He had
even had the section titles printed in boldface type, as if he
wanted to make them the pillars upon which the rest of the
edifice would stand. And there is a remarkably close correspondence between them and the themes announced in "Proto-
Leaf." The "Chants Democratic" develop the theme of democracy, "Leaves of Grass" that of religion (God, death, evil,
nature), "Enfans d'Adam" and "Calamus" two aspects of love.
In "Messenger Leaves" the intention is less clear, but it seems
probable that Whitman wanted to present himself as a new
Messiah: the three principal themes are here repeated and
regrouped.

Thus, although *Leaves of Grass* had hardly any structure

yet, the poems now followed a plan, the main lines of which were clear and immediately perceptible. The form of the book had become much more vigorous. It had been musical in the first two versions; this time it was more architectural. The themes formerly had been mingled and interlaced; they were now separated and distinguished. Compared to this, the previous editions were incoherent. Whitman recognized this fact himself when he announced:

We are able to declare that there will also soon crop out the true *Leaves of Grass*, the fuller-grown work of which the former two issues were the inchoates — this forthcoming one, far, very far ahead of them in quality, quantity, and in supple lyric exuberance. . . Walt Whitman, for his own purpose, slowly trying his hand at the edifice, the structure he has undertaken, has lazily loafed on, letting each part have time to set, — evidently building not so much with reference to any part itself, considered alone, but more with reference to the ensemble, — always bearing in mind the combination of the whole, to fully justify the parts when finished.[15]

He wanted this volume to be a finished work, self-sufficient and clear to all: "It is, I know well enough, that *that* must be the *true Leaves of Grass* — and I think it has an aspect of completeness and makes its case clearer." [16] If he had disappeared or stopped writing at that time — these were eventualities which he envisaged in "Leaves of Grass n°20" [17] and in "So Long!" [18] — no matter, he had formulated his essential message, his Bible was written.[19]

But the presentation was not the only novelty in this edition. This third version of *Leaves of Grass* had a different character from the others. The essential themes were those found already in the text of 1856, but they were expressed with more vigor. The disposition and structure of the book gave them an emphasis they had not possessed before. And, moreover, their relative importance had changed. The accent was placed on

democracy since the "Chants Democratic" came at the beginning, just after the introductory poems, and occupied
nearly ninety pages of the book — comprising by far the
longest group of poems. Previously *Leaves of Grass* had been
much more personal. Its subject had been the poet in his
relation with the universe. The center of interest had now
shifted. The poet had partly given place to the prophet, as
can be seen in "Proto-Leaf" and in the embryonic "Messenger
Leaves." At the same time, however, a very personal theme —
and one which was generally considered taboo — had acquired
a new importance along with the democratic theme: that of
physical love or of sex. It had been announced as early as
1855:

> Through me forbidden voices,
> Voices of sexes and lusts. . . . voices veiled, and I
>   remove the veil,
> Voices indecent by me clarified and transfigured.[20]

The fifth poem of that collection, besides, had already treated
it to some extent.[21] In 1856 this theme recurred more in-
sistently. Three new poems scattered through the book were
devoted to it: "Poem of Women," "Poem of Procreation," and
"Bunch-Poem." [22] But in 1860, as if Whitman could no longer
contain himself,[23] two whole groups of poems, "Enfans
d'Adam" and "Calamus," chanted the violent joys of love with
a crudity that prompted Thoreau to say: "It is as if the beasts
spoke." [24] "Enfans d'Adam" celebrates the love of woman and
"Calamus," more obscurely, but with greater force and tenderness, homosexual love. Whitman seems to have put together "Enfans d'Adam" after "Calamus" both to counter-
balance [25] and to camouflage the abnormal character of his
instincts. Dr. Bucke discovered the following note among his
papers: "A string of poems, (short etc.) embodying the amative
love of woman — the same as Live Oak Leaves [such was

originally the title of "Calamus"] do the passion of friendship
for man." [26]

"Calamus," then, was an echo of the great emotional crisis
which he had just gone through [27] and which would otherwise be unknown. None of the biographical documents establish the date or the circumstances, but there can be no
mistake: the tone of "Calamus" is so vehement, so passionate,
that it leaves no possible doubt of the sincerity of this confession. We shall have occasion to return later to this delicate
problem. The internal evidence of the work is enough for the
time being. Up to this point Whitman's sexual desires had
been very vague, as if they had not yet found their object. In
1855 he was still exclusively preoccupied with the troubled
emotions of adolescence:

> I have perceived that to be with those I like is enough,
> To stop in company with the rest at evening is enough,
> To be surrounded by beautiful curious breathing laugh-
>   ing flesh is enough,
> To pass among them. . to touch any one. . . . to rest
>   my arm ever so lightly round his or her neck for a
>   moment. . . . what is this then?
> I do not ask any more delight. . . . I swim in it as in
>   a sea.[28]

The following year he had loudly celebrated the duty and
joys of procreation in "Poem of Procreation," [29] but he had
declared at the same time in "Bunch-Poem":

> The greed that eats in me day and night with hungry
>   gnaw, till I saturate what shall produce boys to fill
>   my place when I am through. . .[30]

If we are to believe this statement, he had not yet encountered the ideal woman who could give him children
worthy of him and his line. Where he had written "A Woman
Waits for Me," [31] it would be more correct to read "I Wait for

a Woman." His early poems clearly show his disquietude and
the torments his sexual nature caused him. In 1860, on the
contrary, he had found himself. True, he had expanded the
"Poem of Procreation," which later became "Enfans d'Adam,"
but he did so from a sense of duty; his heart was elsewhere.
He had in the meantime suddenly discovered what his body
was longing for. It seems probable that a brief homosexual
affair had given him a revelation of love and also of the abnormal character of his desires.[32] Hence the passionate vehemence and at the same time the reserve of "Calamus," and
his desire, already clear, to reconcile this theme with that of
democracy.

Although these admissions were veiled, they touched nonetheless on a subject that had never before been treated with
so much frankness, and it required great courage — or an
extremely pressing need for confession — for Whitman to
dare to celebrate these forbidden desires and joys. In spite of
the fact that he had already been criticized for obscenity in
his two previous editions, he still persisted in the course he
had chosen. This stubbornness clearly shows the importance
which he attached to the sexual theme. He himself tells us
how, during February of 1860, while he was supervising the
printing of his book in Boston, Emerson, in the course of a
long conversation tried to dissuade him from publishing
"Enfans d'Adam":

> More precious than gold to me that dissertation — it afforded
> me, ever after, this strange and paradoxical lesson; each point of
> Emerson's statement was unanswerable, no judge's charge ever
> more complete or convincing, I could never hear the points better
> put — and then I felt down in my soul the clear and unmistakable
> conviction to disobey all, and pursue my own way. "What have
> you to say to such things?" said Emerson, pausing in conclusion.
> "Only that while I can't answer them at all, I feel more settled
> than ever to adhere to my own theory, and exemplify it," was my
> candid response. Whereupon we went and had a good dinner.[33]

Another theme which also gained in importance was that of life in the great cities. The germs of this can be found in the 1855 *Leaves of Grass*, but now the theme had grown. Whitman was already the "lover of populous pavements, dweller in Mannahatta my city," [34] as he proclaimed in 1867. And perhaps he insisted more than ever before on the theme of America:

> You bards of ages hence! when you refer to me, mind
>   not so much my poems,
> Nor speak of me that I prophesied of The States, and led
>   them the way of their glories. . .[35]

> And then, to enclose all, it came to me to strike up the
>   songs of the New World.[36]

Moreover, the full title of "Chants Democratic" is "Chants Democratic and Native American." [37] And in "Proto-Leaf" Whitman devoted some forty lines to the immensity and wealth of his country.

This new edition therefore presents a subtler and more complex image of the poet himself than the previous ones. The shadows were deeper, the relief sharper. To be sure, he was still "free, fresh, savage, fluent, luxuriant, self-content, fond of persons and places," [38] but he also was the one who loved to step aside to "muse and meditate in some deep recess, far from the clank of crowds . . . rapt and happy." [39]

"Rapt"? — perhaps, but "happy"? That seems doubtful since he sometimes thought of giving up his writing, not because he was discouraged by the indifference of the public, but because, having dreamed of being the poet of ideal democracy, he regarded the results obtained thus far with despair:

> So far, and so far, and on toward the end,
> Singing what is sung in this book, from the irresistible
>   impulses of me;
> But whether I continue beyond this book, to maturity,

> Whether I shall dart forth the true rays, the ones that
>   wait unfired,
> (Did you think the sun was shining its brightest?
> No — it has not yet fully risen;)
> Whether I shall complete what is here started,
> Whether I shall attain my own height, to justify these,
>   yet unfinished,
> Whether I shall make THE POEM OF THE NEW
>   WORLD, transcending all others — depends, rich
>   persons, upon you,
> Depends, whoever you are now filling the current Presi-
>   dentiad, upon you,
> Upon you, Governor, Mayor, Congressman,
> And you, contemporary America.[40]

He was not at all sure that this passionate appeal would be
heard. He despaired to the point of saying good-by to his
reader in "So Long!" [41] Above all, he trembled for the Union.
If it should be broken through the fault of a few, what would
become of American democracy or of democracy anywhere?
It would be the collapse of his dreams and the death of all his
hopes:

> O, as I walk'd the beach, I heard the mournful notes
>   foreboding a tempest — the low, oft-repeated shriek
>   of the diver, the long-lived loon;
> O I heard, and yet hear, angry thunder; — O you
>   sailors!
> O ships! make quick preparation!
> O from his masterful sweep, the warning cry of the
>   eagle!
> (Give way there all! It is useless! Give up your spoils;)
> O sarcasms! Propositions! (O if the whole world should
>   prove indeed a sham, a sell!)
> O I believe there is nothing real but America and free-
>   dom!
> O to sternly reject all except Democracy!
> O imperator! O who dare confront you and me?
> O to promulgate our own! O to build for that which
>   builds for mankind! [42]

Although he exclaimed a little later in the same poem:

O Libertad! O compact! O union impossible to dissever!

he nevertheless feared a secession of the southern states:

And I will make a song that there shall be comity by
day and by night between all The States, and between any two of them,
And I will make a song of the organic bargains of These
States — And a shrill song of curses on him who
would dissever the Union;
And I will make a song for the ears of the President,
full of weapons with menacing points,
And behind the weapons countless dissatisfied faces.[43]

The following poem has been found in one of his notebooks:

Why now I shall know whether there is anything in
you, Libertad,
I shall see how much you can stand
Perhaps I shall see the crash — is all then lost?
What then? Have those thrones there stood so long?
Does the Queen of England represent a thousand years?
And the Queen of Spain a thousand years?
And you
Welcome the storm — welcome the trial — let the
waves
Why now I shall see what the old ship is made of
Any body can sail with a fair wind or a smooth sea
Come now we will see what stuff you are made of Ship
of Libertad
Let others tremble and turn pale — let them? [sic]
I want to see what? [sic] before I die
I welcome this menace, I welcome thee with joy Ship
of Libertad
Blow mad winds!
Rage, boil, vex, yawn wide, yeasty waves
Crash away
Tug at the planks, make them groan — fall around,
black clouds of death

Ship of the world — ship of Humanity — Ship of the
ages? Ship that circlest the world
Ship of the hope of the world — Ship of promise.[44]

But these were only muffled echoes of the severe crisis he
had undergone in 1856–57; [45] in spite of these fears, he had
confidence in the future. A few selfish and petty-minded
politicians might indulge in underhand intrigues and, for a
time, deceive the people, but sooner or later people would see
through these deceptions and impose their will. Democracy
would triumph:

Thought
Of public opinion
Of a calm and cool fiat, sooner or later, (How impas-
sive! How certain and final!)
Of the President with pale face asking secretly to him-
self, *What will the people say at last?*
Of the frivolous Judge — Of the corrupt Congressman,
Governor, Mayor — Of such as these, standing help-
less and exposed.
Of the New World — Of the Democracies, resplend-
ent, en-masse,
Of the conformity of politics, armies, navies, to them
and to me,
Of the shining sun by them — Of the inherent light,
greater than the rest. . ." [46]

Of these years I sing — how they pass through con-
vulsed pains, as through parturitions. . .
Of how many hold despairingly yet to the models departed, caste, myths, obedience, compulsion, and to
infidelity;
How few see the arrived models, the Athletes, The
States — or see freedom or spirituality — or hold
any faith in results,
(But I see the Athletes — and I see the results glorious
and inevitable — and they again leading to other
results;) [47]

> . . . of seeds dropping into the ground — of birth. . .
>   of the growth of a mightier race than any yet. . .
> Of cities yet unsurveyed and unsuspected. . .
> Of immense spiritual results. . .[48]

In order to proclaim his faith and emphasize his credo, Whitman gathered together, as we have seen, all his poems inspired by democracy under the title of "Chants Democratic." He even went so far as to date all the historical events, including the publication of his book,[49] from the year 1776, which had the same importance to him as the Hegira to a Mohammedan. He regarded it as the beginning of a new era for humanity, the promise of a millennium.

But the gravity of the political situation was not his only torment, there were many other reasons for distress. The dangers menacing democracy were after all only one aspect among many of an infinitely greater problem, the problem of evil. In one of the purely political poems which we have just quoted, he declared: "America. . . illustrates evil as well as good," [50] and it was this omnipresence of evil in creation and in himself which obsessed him. Already in 1856 this thought had disturbed him,[51] but it returned now with greater insistence than ever:

> I own that I have been sly, thievish, mean, a prevaricator, greedy, derelict,
> And I own that I remain so yet.
> What foul thought but I think it — or have in me the stuff out of which it is thought. . .
> Beneath this face that appears so impassive, hell's tides continually run,
> Lusts and wickedness are acceptable to me,
> I walk with delinquents with passionate love,
> I feel I am of them — I belong to those convicts and prostitutes myself,
> And henceforth I will not deny them — for how can I deny myself.[52]

> This is curious, and may not be realized immediately —
>   But it must be realized;
> I feel in myself that I represent falsehood equally with
>   the rest,
> And that the universe does . . .
> And henceforth I will go celebrate anything I see or am,
>   and sing and laugh, and deny nothing.[53]

He suffered from it, but apparently resigned himself to it:

> I sit and look out upon all the sorrows of the world,
>   and upon all oppression and shame [then follows a
>   rather long list of the ills of humanity]. . .
> All these — All the meanness and agony without end,
>   I sitting, look out upon,
> See, hear, and am silent.[54]

But whence came this keen perception of evil and this apparently new sense of guilt? Its origin seems to have been almost physiological: the uneasiness and remorse that follow the sexual act:

> I hear secret convulsive sobs from young men, at anguish
>   with themselves, remorseful after deeds done.[55]

This is probably an echo of the intense emotional crisis which had tortured him a little earlier and which had perhaps revealed to him how abnormal his instincts were. He was ashamed of himself. He suffered because he was different from others:

> Who is now reading this?
> May-be one is now reading this who knows some wrong-
>   doing of my past life. . .
> Or may-be one who is puzzled at me.
> As if I were not puzzled at myself!
> Or as if I never deride myself! (O conscience-struck!
>   O self-convicted!) [56]

The relation between his obsession with evil and his sexual life is evident here. It accounts for the sadness and reticence of many passages in "Calamus," the modest tone of which is surprising after the triumphant proclamations of "Enfans d'Adam." [57] He felt so depressed at times that he longed for death. Thus far, only life had counted for him, and death had been merely a distant prospect, an abstraction, a conception of the mind. Now, on the contrary, life was of little importance; death seemed lovely and sweet:

> Yet you are very beautiful to me, you faint-tinged roots
> — you make me think of Death,
> Death is beautiful from you — (what indeed is beautiful, except Death and Love?). . .
> Death or life I am then indifferent — my Soul declines to prefer. . .) [58]

Sometimes he even surrendered himself to death, and as in "As the Time Draws Nigh" or in "So Long!" he calmly and almost indifferently envisaged his approaching end. [59]

This seems a strange passivity and a surprising sadness in a poet who had lately been singing the joy of life at the top of his voice. Should we conclude that he had sunk into pessimism and that he was tired of life? That would be an extremely simplistic interpretation of the 1860 *Leaves of Grass*. For these melancholy and resigned strains coincide with paeans of victory such as "Proto-Leaf" [60] and the "Poem of Joys" [61] in which resounds the same gladness as in "Song of Myself." Moreover, the tenth poem in the group entitled "Leaves of Grass" is no different in tone from those which precede or follow it, and which were present in the earlier editions:

> It is ended — I dally no more,
> After to-day I inure myself to run, leap, swim, wrestle, fight,
> To stand the cold or heat — to take good aim with a gun — to manage horses — to beget superb children,
> To speak readily and clearly — to feel at home among common people.

> And to hold my own in terrible positions, on land and
> sea. . .
> After me, vista!
> O I see life is not short, but immeasurably long,
> I henceforth tread the world, chaste, temperate, an
> early riser, a gymnast, a steady grower,
> Every hour the semen of centuries — and still of cen-
> turies.[62]

The crisis was definitely ended. He felt in himself now an excess of energy [63] that he wished to expend; he longed for a more active life; he launched himself confidently into the future; the idea of death no longer disturbed him; he looked forward to eternity.

It seems then that Schyberg — and after him Gay W. Allen [64] — have greatly exaggerated the pessimism of the 1860 edition. Certainly Whitman in his moments of despair some-times had the impression that his *Leaves of Grass* were nothing but a handful of "dead leaves," [65] but he did not let himself be discouraged for long (otherwise how could he have so quickly prepared this new edition?); soon the "leaves of grass" became green again:

> Tomb-leaves, body-leaves, growing up above me, above
> death,
> Perennial roots, tall leaves — O the winter shall not
> freeze you, delicate leaves,
> Every year shall you bloom again.[66]
>
> . . . these are not to be pensive leaves, but leaves of
> joy. . .[67]

Malcolm Cowley makes the same mistake [68] when he undertakes to show that the "word unsaid" [69] by means of which Whitman in 1855 promised to explain the world had become in 1860 the word "death" in "A Word Out of the Sea." [70] But this is to underestimate the importance of "Poem of Joys"; it ends with these lines which (probably not by accident) immediately precede "A Word Out of the Sea":

O to have my life henceforth my poem of joys!
To dance, clap hands, exult, shout, skip, leap, roll on,
    float on,
An athlete — full of rich words — full of joys.[71]

Besides, although the mockingbird in "A Word Out of the Sea" sends forth his desperate cry, in "Proto-Leaf," at the very beginning of the book, Whitman describes the same bird "inflating his throat and joyfully singing." [72] Even if he wrote "Proto-Leaf" before "A Word Out of the Sea," as all the evidence indicates, the fact that he let it stand in 1860 is sufficient assurance that he had overcome his pessimism of 1859. Neither did he try to diminish the impression of infinite happiness that emerges in many of the "Calamus" poems,[73] a happiness which was at the same time a blossoming and a relief since it sprang from the profound satisfaction of his instincts at last free and in possession of the object for which they had been so long and vainly searching.[74] He made no effort either to conceal the signs of the optimism that he had attained in the fulness of his joy when, during his homosexual liaison, he had had the belated revelation of love; all the metaphysical problems that had previously been torturing him had suddenly been resolved:

I cannot answer the question of appearances, or that of
    identity beyond the grave,
But I walk or sit indifferent — I am satisfied,
He ahold of my hand has completely satisfied me.[75]

And this serene certainty survived the terrible disappointment which the liaison brought him: betrayed by one lover, he extended his love to all the potential lovers whom the world held in store,[76] and not only to them, but to the entire universe:

Sometimes with one I love, I fill myself with rage, for
    fear I effuse unreturned love;
But now I think there is no unreturned love — the pay
    is certain, one way or another,

> Doubtless I could not have perceived the universe, or
> written one of my poems, if I had not freely given
> myself to comrades, to love.[77]

By celebrating in this way the love that he had experienced,
he generalized his emotions and at the same time purified and
transcended them. It was not a matter now of the great passion that had torn him, but a very pure and noble transport
which brought men together and which would assure the unity
of his country and later of the world. In short, he proposed to
support democracy on a universal web of homosexual friendships — giving it in this way an indestructible physiological
basis [78] (we shall have occasion to return to this point). In his
usual fashion he trusted in the future. The present disappointed
him, but the future, he felt sure, would justify him by realizing his dream of a universal love among men. What had been
an abnormal liaison became, by virtue of this sublimation, the
point of departure for a great democratic utopia. The hope
born of his songs and the songs born of this hope had saved
him. By the time he published the 1860 edition he had recovered; the wound had healed and he was able to proclaim in
the closing poem of "Calamus":

> Full of life, sweet-blooded, compact, visible,
> I, forty years old the Eighty-third Year of The
> States. . .[79]

The trials and disappointments he had experienced did not
matter to him. After his pains and sufferings he had attained
a perfect serenity:

> O Soul, we have positively appeared — that is enough.[80]
>
> Quicksand years that whirl me I know not whither,
> Your schemes, politics, fail, lines give way, substances
> mock and elude me,
> Only the theme I sing, the great and strong-possess'd
> soul, eludes not,

One's-self must never give way — that is the final substance — that out of all is sure,
Out of politics, triumphs, battles, life, what at last
  finally remains?
When shows break up what but One's-Self is sure.[81]

He was henceforth "imperturbe"; contingencies no longer
affected him:

Me imperturbe,
Me standing at ease in Nature,
Master of all, or mistress of all — aplomb in the midst
  of irrational things,
Imbued as they — passive, receptive, silent as they,
Finding my occupation, poverty, notoriety, foibles,
  crimes, less important than I thought. . .
Me, wherever my life is to be lived, O to be self-bal-
  anced for contingencies!
O to confront night, storms, hunger, ridicule, accidents,
  rebuffs, as the trees and animals do.[82]

Accordingly, he found it easy to resign himself to the public's lack of enthusiasm. It is true that his book showed — provisionally — the marks of moments of bitterness, [83] but it also
included poems in which he renewed the optimism of his
1856 "Sun-Down Poem" [84] and affirmed his faith in the ap-
preciation of future generations.[85] He knew that the great
innovators had always been misunderstood by their contemporaries. Besides, he had not altogether renounced his hope
of achieving immediate recognition. The East misunderstood
him, but perhaps he would be triumphantly welcomed in the
West as soon as his work was known there. The pioneers, he
thought, were pure of heart and despised money.[86] He had
faith in them.

But there is another aspect of the 1860 edition which even
more emphatically shows his recovered equilibrium: in the
whole group of partly new poems entitled "Messenger

Leaves," [87] he presented himself as a Messiah and Redeemer.
Here it looks as if, having cured himself, he now felt able to
liberate and cure others. Not content with being a poet, he
wanted to be a prophet and equal to Christ, whom he called
his "dear brother" and his "comrade." [88] They would go through
the world together, bringing to all men the same message of
pity and consolation. For his part, he addressed himself more
particularly for the moment "To One Shortly to Die" [89] or "To
a Common Prostitute." [90] He had long had this ambition in
an embryonic form,[91] but what had so far been a vague and
confused aspiration now became a categorical assertion. He
described himself as a savior. He seems really to have had a
great power, a reservoir of spiritual energy on which anyone
might draw. He even proposed to found a new religion that
would synthetize and surpass all others:

> I too, following many, and followed by many, inaugu-
>   rate a Religion — I too go to the wars,
> It may be I am destined to utter the loudest cries there-
>   of, the conqueror's shouts,
> They may rise from me yet, and soar above everything.[92]
>
> . . . now a third religion I give. . . I include the
>   antique two. . . I include the divine Jew, and the
>   Greek sage. . . More still — that which is not con-
>   science, but against it — that which is not the Soul,
>   I include
> These, and whatever exists, I include — I surround all,
>   and dare not make a single exception.[93]

In other words, democracy would be his religion.

These pretensions might appear exorbitant, but they probably seemed quite natural to him. Thanks to the power that
was in him, he had succeeded in emerging from the abyss of
despair into which he had fallen. By his example and his
songs he could help those who were too weak to save themselves.[94]

In spite of these exalted virtues, the critical reception of the 1860 *Leaves of Grass* was substantially the same as that which had greeted the preceding editions. It was easy to make jokes at Whitman's expense. Many reviewers did so.[95] Thus the author of a review published by the *Southern Field and Fireside*:

Five years ago we recollect to have seen the first edition of it, and to have made up our mind that if it did not proceed from a lunatic, it was designed as a solemn hoax upon the public. The extravagance of the style, the beastliness of the sentiments. . . its frequent indecency of language, all suggested Bedlam. The bizarre appearance of the book also indicated a crazy origin. The page, about half the size of our own, was printed in type as large as a playbill, the presswork seemed to have been done with a sledge-hammer. . . he can perceive no difference between Bacon and a Berkshire pig. . . Among the Heenan-ities of the day, his verse may find admirers, but with all the votaries of a pure literature, he must be greeted with a "Procul, procul, este profani!" [96]

Here again were the usual reproaches: indecency, obscurity, and lack of art and rhythm. The critic who reviewed "A Child's Reminiscence" in the Cincinnati *Commercial* gave a good summary of these complaints in the following passage:

. . . we grieve to say he revived last week, and although somewhat changed, changed very little for the better. We do not find so much that is offensive, but we do find a vast amount of irreclaimable drivel and inexplicable nonsense. . . It ["A Word Out of the Sea"] has neither rhythm nor melody, rhyme nor reason, metre nor sense.[97]

But luckily for Whitman, not all the critics shared that opinion. A certain number of favorable articles appeared — notably in the Brooklyn papers where he still had friends [98] and in the New York press.[99] Henry P. Leland in the Philadelphia *City Item* recognized him as undoubtedly a poetic genius:

He is the Consuelo for the poor man, the friendless, the outcast. . . in spite of a belief that poetry can only be appreciated by the few, he goes in for giving it to the "oi polloi". . . There are two thousand roses to a drachm of the otto, there are untold thousands of poems in this duodecimo. . .[100]

So, in spite of the violent attacks of which he was always the object, Whitman was beginning to be appreciated. The critic in the London *Saturday Review* realized the fact with surprise and was further astonished that a book which he had condemned four years before appeared in such a handsome edition: "It is startling to find such a poet acquiring popularity in a country where piano-legs wear frilled trousers. . ." [101]

In fact, Whitman had become popular — in a relative but quite real way. According to Burroughs, several thousand copies of the 1860 edition were sold.[102] The figure is open to doubt, for the evidence on which it was founded is not known; still it is certain that the book achieved a very decent success.[103] Unfortunately, when the Civil War broke out, Thayer and Eldridge, some of whose assets were frozen in the South, suddenly found themselves deprived of part of their capital and went bankrupt. Their equipment, their stock, and their plates were sold at auction. That was the end of the first commercial edition of *Leaves of Grass*. And so Whitman lost the only chance he had had to reach a large public. He found himself again thrown back on his own resources, and he had to wait twenty years before finding another commercial publisher for his book.[104]

CHAPTER VI

THE WOUND DRESSER

IT is probable that after his return from Boston in June 1860 Whitman resumed his indolent existence and divided his time between Brooklyn, where he continued to live with his family, and New York, where he rejoined his friends at Pfaff's. But we know absolutely nothing for certain concerning this period of his life. He says nothing about it in *Specimen Days,* and we are reduced to conjectures. One thing, however, seems sure: he had no regular employment. Rather than submit to the daily servitude of a job, he preferred to live poorly on the income from the sale of his poems. He preferred complete independence to security and comfort. Yet, he would probably have been glad to accept the help of a patron in order to be able to consecrate himself entirely to his work without any concern for the future. He had declared in one of the poems of the 1860 edition:

> Whether I shall make THE POEM OF THE NEW
>   WORLD, transcending all others — depends, rich persons,
>   upon you,
> Depends, whoever you are now filling the current Presi-
>   dentiad, upon you,
> Upon you, Governor, Mayor, Congressman,
> And you, contemporary America.[1]

So long as he was free to create, it mattered little to him

whether his patron was a rich man or a politician. He would
not have felt at all humiliated by this apparent dependence:

> What you give me, I cheerfully accept,
> A little sustenance, a hut and garden, a little money —
>   these as a rendez-vous with my poems,
> A traveller's lodging and breakfast as I journey through
>   The States — Why should I be ashamed to own
>   such gifts? Why to advertise for them?
> For I myself am not one who bestows nothing upon
>   man and woman,
> For I know that what I bestow upon any man or
>   woman, is no less than the entrance to all the gifts
>   of the universe.[2]

Unfortunately this appeal went unheard; Whitman found
no William Calvert on his road, and he would perhaps have
continued to share the rather artificial Bohemian life of New
York if the war had not wrenched him out of it. On April 12,
1861, less than a year after his return from Boston, the federal
troops who occupied Fort Sumter in Charleston harbor were
bombarded by Confederate batteries and surrendered two
days later. Whitman recounts in *Specimen Days* with what
emotion he heard the news in New York on April 13.[3] The
event was not unexpected. For several years the trial of force
between the two camps seemed imminent and almost inevitable. Whitman, because of his hatred for dishonorable compromises, had sometimes almost wanted it. But now that the
time had come, he felt profoundly shaken and upset. On April
18, he jotted in one of his private notebooks:

I have this hour, this day resolved to inaugurate a sweet, clean-
blooded body by ignoring all drinks but water and pure milk —
and all fat meats, late suppers — a great body — a purged,
cleansed, spiritualized invigorated body.[4]

This strange resolution looks like the program of an ascetic who proposes to do penance in order to redeem the sins of mankind. At the deepest level, without ostentation, Whitman, it seems, associated himself with his contemporaries and intended secretly to participate in their trial.

However, by a curious contradiction, there was no immediate change in his life. To be sure, he renounced the joys of nature in order to devote himself to New York and participate more intensely than ever in the life of Manhattan, but he continued nevertheless shamelessly to enjoy all the pleasures which a great city has to offer:

> Keep your splendid silent sun;
> Keep your woods, O Nature, and the quiet places by the woods;
> Keep your fields of clover and timothy, and your corn-fields and orchards;
> Keep the blossoming buckwheat fields, where the Ninth-month bees hum;
> Give me faces and streets! give me these phantoms incessant and endless along the trottoirs!
> Give me interminable eyes! give me women! give me comrades and lovers by the thousand!
> Let me see new ones every day! let me hold new ones by the hand every day!
> Give me such shows! give me the streets of Manhattan!
> . . . . .
> O such for me! O an intense life! O full to repletion, and varied!
> The life of the theater, bar-room, huge hotel, for me!
> The saloon of the steamer! the crowded excursion for me! the torch-light procession!
> The dense brigade, bound for the war, with high piled military wagons following. . .[5]

Thus he thought about the war, but it was only one preoccupation among many others, and he seems to have been remarkably attracted by the "comrades and lovers" whom he encountered on the sidewalks and in the bars. His private notebooks confirm this impression; we find indications such as these:

> Victor Smith — Evening June 30 '62 — met a man who introduced himself to me as V. Smith — in the government employ on the Pacific Coast . . . Afternoon July 3rd in front of Hospital Broadway Aaron B. Cohn — talk with — he was from Fort Edward Institute — appears to be 19 years old — fresh and affectionate young man. . . William Robinson, Brooklyn lad (Socratic nose) Aug. 16 — driving on 23rd St. is going to enlist — said he would enlist with me in two minutes.[6]

Strange encounters to which we will have occasion to refer again. However that may be, it is clear by now that, for all his ascetic resolutions, Whitman continued to lead a carefree life. The only notable change that can be seen in his existence is that he ceased to be completely unemployed and became active again in journalism. He was probably constrained to this by circumstances, the failure of his publishers having suddenly deprived him of the income from the sale of *Leaves of Grass*.

Contrary to what might be expected, instead of writing about the war, he published in the Brooklyn *Standard* [7] a series of twenty-five articles on the past and present of the city — a form of escape literature which would seem remarkably inappropriate in such a historic context. It may be said in his defense that perhaps he could find nothing better to do. He needed money, and he was probably forced to accept the assignment. The series was nothing but a pot-boiler which he never mentioned afterwards, although the copyright was in his name, which was rare at that time for such articles. On the other hand, if he was able to choose his own topic, his natural indolence must have prompted him to take the easy way out, for he had written about Brooklyn several years before in the Brooklyn *Daily Times*,[8] and he would merely have to draw on his memory or his notes.

Nevertheless, in spite of the inappropriateness of these articles, Whitman was not unaware of the war. At the time of the disaster at Bull Run on July 21, 1861, and during the several days when everything seemed lost,[9] he found himself brusquely recalled to reality. The shock was so brutal that he ceased for several months to work on his "Brooklyniana." It is true that once the alarm had passed, he resumed his routine, and nothing in his articles reflected the grave events occurring at the time. In fact, his chronicle became a reportage and gave him a pretext to revisit the small villages of Long Island which he had known in his youth and to take part in a fishing party at Montauk Point.[10] But he may have foreseen the more and more tragic turn that the war would take and the role that he himself would come to play in it. This happy excursion was in some ways a pilgrimage and a farewell visit to the countryside which he had loved so much.

It may seem surprising, however, that after having celebrated the departure of the troops for the front with so much enthusiasm and patriotic fervor in several of his poems,[11] he did not sign up himself in a New York regiment. Certain critics have accused him of cowardice and inconsistency on this ground. But this is to forget that Whitman was forty-two years old; the average age of volunteers was a great deal less, especially at the beginning of the war.[12] And it is remarkable that none of his contemporaries thought of blaming him for this supposed defection and that it never occurred to any of his enemies to use it against him. Besides his age, there were many other reasons for his abstention: First of all, his temperament, which had always made him avoid action; his stay-at-home tastes; his placid disposition; and his natural horror of violence, reinforced by his Quaker education. It is hard to imagine him as a warrior, even though, on principle, he was heartily in sympathy with those who fought for the Union.

His true vocation was to sing and celebrate the Union and the indissoluble compact which bound the various states together:

> From Paumanok starting, I fly like a bird,
> Around and around to soar, to sing, the idea of all. . .
> To sing first, (to the tap of the war-drum, if need be,)
> The idea of all — of the western world, one and insepa-
>   rable,
> And then the song of each member of These States.[13]

In 1855 he had already defined the role of the poet in wartime: "In war he is the most deadly force of the war. . . Who recruits him recruits horse and foot . . . he fetches parks of artillery the best that engineer ever saw . . . he can make every word he speaks draw blood." [14]

His family situation must also be considered. His father was dead. Two of his brothers, Eddie and Jesse, were unable to support themselves. George, ten years his junior, had left among the first volunteers. Another of his brothers, Andrew, was drafted a little later. Whitman therefore found himself, with Jeff, the only support of all the women and children remaining in the Portland Street house. Hence his uneasiness in 1863 at the possibility that Jeff might be drafted in his turn,[15] or that he himself might be drafted too.[16] And yet, for a moment in 1864 he thought of volunteering and confided to his mother: "The war must be carried on, and I could willingly go myself in the ranks if I thought it would profit more than at present, and I don't know sometimes but I shall as it is." [17]

In any case, up to the end of 1862, he continued to lead a quiet existence in New York — quite comparable to that which most Americans of his age had in the two world wars. He was far from the theater of operation. He certainly followed the war news with eagerness, but however great his power of sympathy may have been, the fighting could only have been for him an unreal abstraction that did not deeply affect him. War cannot be imagined, it must be seen. He soon had occasion to see it.

On December 13, 1862, he heard that his brother George had been seriously wounded during an attack, and without hesitation, he took the train for the South to try to find him. He stopped first for two days at Washington, where he thought George had already been brought. And during those two days he searched feverishly in all the hospitals in the city without success. Very fortunately, a few hours after his arrival, he met William O'Connor whose acquaintance he had made in Boston and who was now employed in the Lighthouse Bureau. Without O'Connor's help he would have been much embarrassed, for he had been robbed of his wallet in Philadelphia, while changing trains, and had no money.[18] Thanks to him, Whitman was able to learn where his brother was and to continue his journey, furnished with papers and the necessary cash. On December 19 he arrived at Falmouth, Virginia, on the left bank of the Rappahannock River, where the 51st New York Regiment, to which his brother belonged, was bivouacking.[19] George, whose wound was less serious than had been feared, was already out of danger. Walt's presence was therefore superfluous, but he nevertheless remained at Falmouth until the end of the month, spending about eight days on the front-lines with the troops. It was an unforgettable adventure. He shared the hard life of the soldiers, subsisting like them on salt pork and sea biscuits and sleeping in the mud and snow, rolled up in a blanket. And, above all, for the first time, he saw the war close up, in all its horror. He did not actually participate in any fighting, but he did see some of the immediate results. He visited the improvised hospital where the more serious cases were treated. Outside, at the foot of a tree, was a pile of feet, legs, arms, and hands freshly amputated and waiting for a cart to take them away.[20] He saw even more horrible things: the wounded being cared for at the dressing-stations, often lying on the ground under tents. He was immediately overcome by a great pity for all these young soldiers who were suffering so atrociously and some of whom seized on him convulsively and constrained him to stay beside them for hours.[21] By his own testimony, on one occasion, he even helped the stretcher-bearers to remove the dead from the battle-field and to give first-aid to the wounded during a truce.[22]

This accidental encounter with the war changed the course of his life. At the end of December he left Falmouth with a convoy of wounded soldiers whose sufferings he tried to relieve during the trip,[23] and instead of returning home to Brooklyn, he established himself in Washington in order to remain close to his beloved soldiers. From then until the end of the war, he was to pass as much time as possible in the military hospitals. The letters that he wrote to his family and friends and the pages of *Specimen Days* that he devoted to this period allow us to follow him in his charitable rounds.[24] Although he sometimes helped the doctors and nurses to change bandages, he was never, in a literal sense, a "wound-dresser," as Bucke called him.[25] Nevertheless this title suited him perfectly; for, if he did not attend the wounds of the body, he brought to the wounded or sick soldiers something which was as necessary to their recovery as medical care, but for which the regulations had not provided: the comfort of a loving presence, the sweetness of an almost maternal affection, the delicate attentions of an ingenious kindness. He had already rehearsed this role in the New York hospitals where he had often visited sick omnibus drivers.[26] He fulfilled it with perfect tact. He tried to explain it in these terms in a letter:

The work of the army hospital visitor is indeed a trade, an art, requiring both experience and natural gifts, and the greatest judgment. A large number of the visitors to the hospitals do no

good at all, while many do harm. The surgeons have great trouble
from them. . . there are always some poor fellows, in the crises
of sickness or wounds, that imperatively need perfect quiet —
not to be talked to by strangers. Few realize that it is not the mere
giving of gifts that does good; it is the proper adaptation. Nothing
is of any avail among the soldiers except conscientious personal
investigation of cases, each for itself; with sharp critical faculties,
but in the fullest spirit of human sympathy and boundless love.
The men feel such love more than anything else. I have met very
few persons who realize the importance of humoring the yearn-
ings for love and friendship of these American young men, pros-
trated by sickness and wounds.

To many of the wounded and sick, especially the youngsters,
there is something in personal love, caresses, and the magnetic
flood of sympathy and friendship, that does, in its way, more good
than all the medicine in the world. . . Many will think this
merely sentimentalism, but I know it is the most solid of facts.
I believe that even the moving around among the men, or through
the ward, of a hearty, healthy, clean, strong, generous-souled
person, man or woman, full of humanity and love, sending out
invisible, constant currents thereof, does immense good to the
sick and wounded.[27]

These are the principles that he put into practice. He went
from bed to bed, distributing oranges, lemons, sugar, jam,
preserved fruit, tobacco (which the soldiers rarely had, for
none of the welfare workers sent by the various churches
brought any to them),[28] and even small sums of money which
permitted them to buy some comforts. But, above all, he paused
at the bedside of one or another to listen to their stories. He
was passionately interested in the fate of each one [29] and recorded in his notebooks the more remarkable cases.[30] Many
of the young soldiers felt abandoned and deprived of affection,
and he performed the function of a family and gave them
back the will to live. He had for them, it seemed,[31] a fatherly
affection, and some of them called him "Uncle" [32] or even "Pa."
He wrote letters for them to their mothers or their wives:

"When eligible, I encourage the men to write, and myself, when called upon, write all sorts of letters for them (including love letters, very tender ones)." [33]

Sometimes also he read them passages from the Bible [34] or poems — but never his own, a surprising abnegation for a poet.[35] To those who were too ill to listen or to speak, he offered his silent presence, the presence of a body which from the first days of the war he had consecrated to purity and health.[36] He remained at their bedside for hours if necessary. Thus took place a mysterious transfusion of strength. It was as if his serenity and health were contagious; at his contact the wounded regained hope. He gave them the desire to recover. In short, he was the mystical healer whom he had described in the first edition of *Leaves of Grass*:

> To any one dying. . . . thither I speed and twist the
>   knob of the door,
> Turn the bedclothes toward the foot of the bed,
> Let the physician and the priest go home.
> I seize the descending man. . . . I raise him with
>   resistless will.
> O despairer, here is my neck,
> By God! you shall not go down! Hang your whole weight
>   upon me.
> I dilate you with tremendous breath. . . . I buoy you
>   up;
> Every room of the house do I fill with an armed
>   force. . . . lovers of me, bafflers of graves:
> Sleep! I and they keep guard all night;
> Not doubt, not decease shall dare to lay finger upon you,
> I have embraced you, and henceforth possess you to
>   myself,
> And when you rise in the morning you will find what I
>   tell you is so.
> I am he bringing help for the sick as they pant on their
>   backs.[37]

Once more then nature imitated art and his life conformed

to his work. He was becoming more and more that which he had dreamed of being in 1855. At any rate, one thing is certain: his presence and care sometimes worked miracles. Doctors themselves were obliged to admit it,[38] and in a letter to his mother, he told the story of a cure which he had effected in 1865 after several days' battle with death:

One soldier brought here about fifteen days ago, very low with typhoid fever, Livingston Brooks, Co. B. 17th Penn. Cavalry, I have particularly stuck to, as I found him to be in what appeared to be a dying condition, from negligence and a horrible journey of about forty miles, bad roads and fast driving; and then, after he got here, as he is a simple country boy, very shy and silent, and made no complaint, they neglected him. . . I called the doctor's atttention to him, shook up the nurses, had him bathed in spirits, gave him lumps of ice, and ice to his head; he had a fearful bursting pain in his head, and his body was like fire. He was very quiet, a very sensible boy, old fashioned; he did not want to die and I had to lie to him without stint, for he thought I knew everything, and I always put in of course that what I told him was exactly the truth and that if he got dangerous I would tell him and not conceal it. The rule is to remove bad fever patients out from the main wards to a tent by themselves, and the doctor told me he would have to be removed. I broke it gently to him, but the poor boy got it immediately in his head that he was marked with death, and was to be removed on that account. It had a great effect upon him, and although I told the truth this time it did not have as good a result as my former fibs. I persuaded the doctor to let him remain. For three days he lay just about an even chance, go or stay, with a little leaning toward the first. But, mother, to make a long story short, he is now out of immediate danger. He has been perfectly rational throughout — begins to taste a little food (for a week he ate nothing; I had to compel him to take a quarter of an orange now and then), and I will say, whether any-one calls it pride or not, that if he *does* get up and around again it's me that saved his life.[39]

By the power of patience and tenderness he had in fact succeeded in tipping the balance toward the side of life. And he saved the lives of many sick and wounded soldiers in the same way:

Mother, [he wrote a few months later,] I have real pride in telling you that I have the consciousness of saving quite a number of lives by saving them from giving up — and being a good deal with them; the men say it is so, and the doctors say it is so — and I will candidly confess I can see it is true, though I say it of myself.[40]

It was above all to his marvellous health that Whitman attributed these miraculous results. In a letter of 1863 he said:

I believe I weigh about 200, and as to my face, (so scarlet,) and my beard and neck, they are terrible to behold. I fancy the reason I am able to do some good in the hospitals among the poor languishing and wounded boys, is, that I am so large and well — indeed like a great wild buffalo, with much hair.[41]

He felt full of strength, and yet, knowing how unhealthy his existence in the pestilential atmosphere of the hospitals was, he began, after several months, to take better care of himself:

I keep about as stout as ever, and the past five or six days, I have felt wonderful well, indeed never did I feel better. . . I generally go to the hospitals from twelve to four — and then again from six to nine; some days I only go in the middle of the day or evening, not both — and then when I feel somewhat opprest, I skip over a day, or make perhaps a light call only, as I had several cautions by the doctors, who tell me that one must beware of continuing too steady and long in the air and influences of the hospitals. I find the caution a wise one.[42]

His uneasiness and these warnings were justified, for, in June, he began to complain for the first time of symptoms of illness: "Mother, I have had quite an attack of sore throat and distress in my head for some days past, up to last night, but today I feel nearly all right again." [43] In October this concern had been forgotten and he boasted of his excellent health as if nothing had happened:

I feel so tremendously well myself — I will have to come and show myself to you, I think — I am so fat, good appetite, out considerably in the open air, and all red and tanned worse than ever. You see, therefore, that my life amid these sad and death-stricken hospitals has not told at all badly upon me, for I am this fall so running over with health I feel as if I ought to go on, on that account, working among all who are deprived of it.[44]

The following month, however, he left his wounded friends and did not return for several weeks.[45] Ostensibly, he went in order to vote at Brooklyn, but he was apparently very glad of this relief, for he remained until December 2 and took advantage of his visit to attend the opera and the theater,[46] of which pleasures he had been deprived for a year. But, however greatly he may have been tempted to indulge again in this careless life, he did not give way. The memory of those he had left in the hospitals pursued him:

I do not think [he wrote to one of them] one night has passed in New York or Brooklyn when I have been at the theatre or opera or afterward to some supper party or carousal made by the young fellows for me, but what amid the play and the singing I would perhaps think of you, — and the same at the gayest supper-party of men where all was fun and noise and laughing and drinking, of a dozen young men and I among them I would see your face before me. . . and my amusement or drink would be all turned to nothing. . .[47]

Therefore he returned to Washington. Two months later he left again for Culpeper, Virginia, with a paymaster, Major Hapgood, for whom he was working as a clerk. Again he found himself very near the front, but the sector was fairly calm; [48] the troops were in winter quarters and no action was under way. He tried however, in talking with the men, to learn as much as possible about their life; for, he said, "I can never cease to crave more and more knowledge of actual soldier's life and be among them as much as possible." [49] But this second visit to Virginia was very brief and less dramatic than the first. Perhaps also Whitman had become more accustomed to the horrors of war.

By March he had resumed his visits to the Washington hospitals, apparently always in excellent health,[50] but in June he felt very depressed:

> Mother, if this campaign was not in progress I should not stop here, as it is now beginning to tell a little upon me, so many bad wounds, many putrefied, and all kinds of dreadful ones, I have been rather too much with. . .[51]

A few days later, he complained of headaches and fits of dizziness,[52] and since the symptons instead of abating became worse,[53] he was obliged on the advice of doctors to return to his family in Brooklyn for a rest. He remained there from the end of June to the middle of January 1865. However, thanks to the rest and the change of climate, he recovered quickly. He was even able during these six months to work on his *Drum-Taps* and prepare them for publication.[54]

For all that, he did not interrupt his visits to the wounded. He still went regularly to the military hospitals in Brooklyn and New York.[55] And after his return to Washington he resumed his charitable rounds as if nothing had happened. Even peace did not immediately put an end to his voluntary service. Until April 1867 he was still going almost every Sunday to see the invalids who remained in the hospitals of the capital.[56] He himself had apparently completely recovered, but the symptoms which he had noticed during these last few years were the advanced signs of the stroke of paralysis which he suffered in 1873.

But how did he make his living during his stay in Washington? And how, without any regular income, could he afford his charities to the soldiers in the hospitals? The fact is that the money which he distributed or which he used to buy small

gifts was furnished for the most part by friends who wanted
to help him relieve the misery of the wounded.[57] But he had
to make his own living also, and therefore he had to look for
work. He found some quickly, thanks to Eldridge, his former
Boston publisher, also in difficulty, who served as deputy-pay-
master to Major Hapgood. Whitman was hired as part-time
assistant. He worked three or four hours a day copying payrolls
and earned enough to support himself without giving up his
freedom of movement.[58] From time to time he also sent articles
to New York or Brooklyn newspapers,[59] which brought him
a little money. But all this did not amount to much. He would
have liked to earn a great deal more in order to be able to
help the wounded without the support of others and at the
same time relieve the needs of his relatives by purchasing a
small farm for them on Long Island.[60] To make these fine
dreams come true, he thought for a time of undertaking one of
the lecture tours he had had in mind since 1856, but he quickly
gave it up, probably realizing that circumstances were less
favorable than ever and that his project would have no chance
of success.[61] He also cherished for some time the hope of
publishing a book of memories of the war, but he was probably
unable to find a publisher interested in the venture.[62]

During this period in any case he could have found a more
lucrative employment in some government office through the
agency of influential friends such as Emerson,[63] but he preferred the humbler tasks which left him more freedom
to dispose of his time as he wished. Instead of trying to increase
his income, it probably seemed to him worthier of a free man
to simplify his life, like Thoreau, and reduce his wants.[64]
During the war years he lived very cheaply, almost in destitution. At first, he rented a small room in the same house as the
O'Connors for seven dollars a month and took his meals with
them — free of charge, for the O'Connors refused to let him
pay, although they did allow him after a time to provide some

of the food at his own expense.[65] J. T. Trowbridge, who paid him a visit during this time, has left a description of his lodgings:

> Walt led the way up those dreary stairs, partly in darkness, found the keyhole of a door which he unlocked and opened, scratched a match, and welcomed us to his garret.

> Garret it literally was, containing hardly more furniture than a bed, a cheap pine table, and a little stove in which there was no fire. A window was open and it was a December night. But Walt, clearing a chair or two of their litter of newspapers, invited us to sit down and stop awhile, with as simple and sweet hospitality as if he had been offering us the luxuries of the great mansion across the square. . . Two mornings after this I went by appointment to call on Walt in his garret. . . he was cutting slices of bread from a baker's loaf with a jackknife, getting them ready for toasting. The smallest of tin-kettles simmering on the stove, a bowl and spoon, and a covered tin cup used as a teapot comprised with the aforesaid useful jackknife his entire outfit of visible housekeeping utensils. His sugar-bowl was a brown paper-bag. His butter plate was another piece of brown paper, the same coarse wrapping in which he had brought home his modest lump from the corner grocery.[66]

He moved several times,[67] but he always took a room as miserable as the first in order to save as much money as possible for the wounded and perhaps also in order to remain faithful to the ascetic vow he had made at the beginning of the war.[68] He suffered however. He suffocated during the humid, stifling summers that prevail in Washington, and he complained sometimes in his letters,[69] but he held out until the end and never occupied more comfortable quarters. He had always lived in an attic in Brooklyn in the home of his family,[70] so it was not as much of a trial as Trowbridge may have thought. It remains true nevertheless that he could have lived more comfortably if he had wished, and that he deliberately chose poverty.[71]

Such was his life during the Civil War — seen from the outside. We must now try to determine what effects all these events had on his personality and works.

When war broke out in 1861, Whitman immediately chanted his joy and enthusiasm. It was the end of the revolting compromises. The war would cut at one stroke the Gordian knot of the political intrigues. He rejoiced; all the plots of the Democrats in league with the slave-merchants of the South would be thwarted. They had tried to impose their will on the mass of the nation, but these events had silenced them. Now the people had the floor, and not their corrupt representatives. Selfish plotters had tried to put the country to sleep and sell its soul to preserve a senseless peace, but, at the first cannon shots fired on Fort Sumter, the country had awakened. Its soul had been saved. All the doubts which had tortured Whitman were dissipated when he saw how enthusiastically the volunteers responded to the government's appeal.[72] Carried away by the same patriotic fervor as all these young men, he set himself to vindicate the war:

> Long, too long, O land,
> Traveling roads all even and peaceful, you learn'd from
>   joys and prosperity only;
> But now, ah now, to learn from crises of anguish —
>   advancing, grappling with direst fate, and recoiling
>   not;
> And now to conceive, and show to the world, what your
>   children en-masse really are;
> (For who except myself has yet conceived what your
>   children en-masse really are?) [73]

He now felt that events were justifying him; he had been right. The masses were not enamoured of peace at any price as the politicians had maintained and believed.[74] They accepted the trial. The "too long" which escaped him in the first line marks his impatience at the delay which he had been obliged to endure. According to him, peace was not always best for a country, for it was in war that a nation took form and consciousness and the true character of a people revealed itself.[75] A strangely idealistic conception.

In another poem, entitled "1861," he celebrated war because it was for him the synonym of energy, of manly vigor and generous spirit.[76] He refused to sing the sweetness of a debilitating peace;[77] he meant to consecrate himself from now on to the war. No matter to him if it lasted months or years, it was a virile undertaking.[78] He considered it as a fresh and joyous adventure:

> And ever the sound of the cannon, far or near, (rousing, even in dreams, a devilish exultation, and all the old mad joy, in the depths of my soul;) [79]

At the time he was acquainted only with that aspect of war, not having seen it at close range. He had made no progress since 1860 when he sang in "Poem of Joys":

> O the joys of the soldier!
> To feel the presence of a brave general! to feel his sympathy!
> To behold his calmness! to be warmed in the rays of his smile!
> To go to battle! to hear the bugles play; and the drums beat!
> To hear the artillery! to see the glittering of the bayonets and musket-barrels in the sun!
> To see men fall and die and not complain!
> To taste the savage taste of blood! to be so devilish!
> To gloat over the wounds and deaths of the enemy.[80]

He was soon to have occasion "to see men fall and die and not complain" with very different feelings, but for the moment, absorbed in his dream of glory and heroic death, he wanted total war. Everyone should renounce his peaceful occupations and take part in the struggle. No one had the right to remain behind when the drums beat.[81] He earnestly called for the mobilization of all men old enough to bear arms — without any exception, for thus the nation would cease to be an abstraction and become a living reality.[82]

In "Song of the Banner at Daybreak" — which may have been written before the outbreak of the war, but which he revised for inclusion in *Drum-Taps* [83] — he contrasted peace with war; the father represents the love of peace and material riches, whereas the child, the banner, and the poet embody an opposing aspiration to the ideal that Whitman defined as "out of reach, an idea only, yet furiously fought for, risking bloody death. . ." [84] In short, then, he did not glorify all wars, or war in general, but this particular one which involved an ideal — his ideal, the cause of democracy which he had always placed above everything else. It was for him, as we say today, an ideological war. He heard Liberty,[85] armed Liberty,[86] and Democracy advancing in a sound of thunder,[87] and he indissolubly linked the government at Washington, the cause of the North, with the cause of democracy. Above all, the Union must be saved. For, if the links uniting the various members of the federation should be broken, it would be the end of democracy in the world; the United States, henceforth disunited, would be too weak to defend itself against attacks from without and nowhere else would democracy be able to triumph over tyranny. So he exalted the Union because it had become for him a sacred and mystical notion to which everything, if necessary, must be sacrificed:

> See the Identity formed out of thirty-eight spacious and
> haughty States, (and many more to come,). . .[88]

The parenthesis is important, he attached less importance to the political bonds that united the thirty-eight states in a single federation than to the promise of future grandeur of which that unity was the pledge. What mattered was the profound unity of this new race on the way to a glorious destiny. This is the theme of "Pioneers! O Pioneers!" which originally was part of *Drum-Taps* and which he later detached in order to give it a more general significance. Originally the poem was an appeal for unity in the name of the great tasks that awaited the whole American nation without distinction by states, North or South:

> From Nebraska, from Arkansas,
> Central inland race are we, from Missouri, with the
>   continental blood intervein'd;
> All the hands of comrades clasping, all the Southern,
>   all the Northern,
>   Pioneers! O pioneers! [89]

This war, the purpose of which was to save the Union, was therefore indispensable to the future of the nation, and by way of consequence, to the progress of the whole human race of which the American people were the vanguard: "We, the youthful sinewy races, all the rest on us depend." [90] and Whitman, who was a pioneer among the pioneers in the vanguard of the American nation, could not but throw himself wholeheartedly into the conflict — at least in imagination.

That was his first reaction; but, at the touch of harsh reality, his illusions were quickly dissipated; his idealistic concepts of a sacred and redeeming war collapsed as soon as he had a close view of the horrors with which it was inevitably accompanied, and he quickly passed from enthusiasm to disillusion: [91]

> Arous'd and angry, I'd thought to beat the alarum, and
>   urge relentless war,
> But soon my fingers fail'd me, my face droop'd and I
>   resign'd myself,
> To sit by the wounded and soothe them, or silently
>   watch the dead. [92]

One day, during a visit to friends, he became angry and began to pace the floor and cry out: "I say stop this war, this

horrible massacre of men!" [93] and no opposing argument could
make him give in. A little later, on September 8, 1863, he
wrote to his mother: "Mother, one's heart grows sick of war,
after all, when you see what it really is; every once in a while
I feel so horrified and disgusted — it seems to me like a great
slaughter-house and the men mutually butchering each
other." [94]

So, from then on, instead of celebrating the exaltation of
the volunteers going into combat, he chanted his infinite pity
for the young men whose death made him think of Christ on
the cross,[95] or the sufferings of the wounded who had been
operated on near the front-lines [96] and of the dying on the
battlefields.[97] Instead of glorifying the drunken excitement of
the fighting, he described the poignant pain of the families
when the terrible news arrived of the death of a son.[98] He no
longer exalted the proud bearing and discipline of the troops,
he criticized the officers and condemned their class-feeling
and lack of democratic spirit.[99]

This complete reversal was caused not only by the spectacle
of the evils engendered by the war, but was also the fruit of
the terrible disappointment which he had experienced when,
contrary to his expectation, the Confederate armies at first
inflicted defeat after defeat on the armies of the Union. After
the first battle of Bull Run in July 1861 he recorded his discouragement and despair:

The dream of humanity, the vaunted Union, we thought so
strong, so impregnable — lo! it seems already smash'd like a China
plate. . . the hour was one of the three or four of those crises
we had then and afterward, during the fluctuations of four years,
when human eyes appear'd at least just as likely to see the last
breath of the Union as to see it continue.[100]

> Year that trembled and reel'd beneath me!
> Your summer wind was warm enough — yet the air I
>   breathed froze me:

> A thick gloom fell through the sunshine and darken'd
>   me;
> Must I change my triumphant songs? said I to myself;
> Must I indeed learn to chant the cold dirges of the
>   baffled?
> And sullen hymns of defeat? [101]

This would have been unendurable for Whitman if it had meant that the North would lose the war; it would have been the ruin of his great democratic dream and the destruction of his faith.

But this crisis did not last long. His faith in democracy was so firmly anchored that he could never altogether despair of final victory. At the very moment when he was assailed by doubts he affirmed the necessity of pursuing the war. In the letter to his mother which has just been quoted he continued immediately in these terms: "I feel how impossible it appears . . . to retire from this contest, until we have carried our points." He was himself perfectly aware of the inconsistency of his position and he was troubled by it: "It is cruel to be so tossed from pillar to post in one's judgment." [102]

But little by little the agony this harrowing crisis caused him subsided, and a year later he was able to write to his mother: "After first Fredericksburg [December 1862] I felt discouraged myself, and doubted whether our rulers could carry on the war — but that has passed away. The war must be carried on. . ." [103] The victories won in the interval had revived his courage and renewed his hope. In the spring of 1863, he declared to a young friend: ". . . but for all our bad success at Charleston and even if we fail for a while elsewhere I believe this Union will conquer in the end as sure as there's a God in heaven. This country can't be broken up by Jeff Davis and all his damned crew." [104]

This assurance quickly hardened him and extinguished all the pity which he had felt up to that time. He became accus-

tomed to the idea that the sacrifice of human lives was necessary to secure the victory of democracy. When the draft riots
broke out in New York in July 1863, he was at first prejudiced
in favor of the demonstrators,[105] but soon, recognizing his
error, he declared himself in favor of vigorous government
action to crush the resistance of the disloyal.[106] Although he
had lately mourned the death of young soldiers in "Vigil
Strange I Kept on the Field One Night" and in "A Sight in
Camp in the Daybreak Gray and Dim," [107] he was now resigned; for the young soldiers were not really dead, they survived in the trees and the grass and in the aromas exhaled by
the soil which would perfume the air for ages and ages.[108] This
pantheistic vision of the eternal cycle of life reconciled him to
the horror of the present. Besides, it seemed to him that he
heard above the carnage a prophetic voice announcing the final
triumph of the love of comrades and the reconciliation of the
states in liberty and equality.[109] He tended — and he would
tend more and more — to see only the happy consequences of
this war [110] and, if not to close his eyes on the sufferings which
it had brought, at least to accord them only a relative importance. He thus recovered little by little, not without struggles
and hesitations, the serene optimism expressed in certain
poems of the 1860 edition.[111]

After the war, true, he did not forget the dead; he celebrated
their heroism and their sacrifice,[112] but he preferred the splendor of the future to the sorrow of the past. His optimism knew
no bounds: [113]

> Years of the unperform'd! your horizon rises. . .
> I see not America only — I see not only Liberty's
>   nation, but other nations preparing. . .
> I see Freedom, completely arm'd, and victorious, and
>   very haughty, with Law by her side. . .[114]

Borders would disappear; thanks to the steamship and the

telegraph, distances would be abolished. The world would achieve unity and universal democracy:

> Are all nations communing? is there going to be but one
> heart to the globe?. . .
> Years prophetical! the space ahead as I walk, as I vainly
> try to pierce it, is full of phantoms; . . .
> The perform'd America and Europe grow dim, retiring
> in shadow before me,
> The unperform'd, more gigantic than ever, advance,
> advance upon me.[114]

He dreamed and prophesied of the infinite potentialities of human grandeur. The war had confirmed and reinforced his faith in the average man: "Never was average man, his soul, more energetic, more like a God." [114] He had witnessed the courage of the soldiers who freely accepted their trials [115] and bravely confronted death in the hospitals. It was this, above all, which impressed him:

> To me the points illustrating the latent personal character and eligibilities of these States, in the two or three millions of American young and middle-aged men, North and South, embodied in those armies — and especially the one-third or one-fourth of their number stricken by wounds or disease at some time in the course of the contest — were of more significance even than the political interests. (As so much of a race depends on how it faces death and how it stands personal anguish and sickness. . .) [116]
>
> Those three years [spent in the hospitals] I consider the greatest privilege and satisfaction. . . and, of course, the most profound lesson of my life. . . It has given me my most fervent view of the true *ensemble* and extent of the *States*.[117]

But it was necessary first, in order that this dream of universal democracy [118] might come true, that the North and the South forget their fratricidal struggles. Therefore he launched an appeal for reconciliation at the end of his *Sequel to Drum-Taps*.[119] During the war, in spite of his hatred for the Copperheads [120] and his profound antislavery convictions, he had never had anything but pity and sympathy for the Confederate soldiers. In the hospitals he had cared for them with as much devotion as for the others.[121] They had, after all, the same essentially American qualities as the soldiers of the federal armies, [122] and they were equally heroic: "Was one side so brave? the other was equally brave." [123] And had they not been reconciled by death? [124] It is therefore easy to understand his pain and his concern when Lincoln was assassinated by a fanatical southerner. What would happen? Would the North in anger and despair indulge in bloody reprisals? Such acts would be the end of the Union. Fortunately, there were none, and Whitman exulted. This was another proof of the political maturity of the American people:

We must own to a feeling of pride that the hand of summary vengeance was stayed under such an ordeal of wrath, and justice allowed to work out her own unfailing purposes. Surely the calm hour of reflection, following on the first heat of passion, marked us pre-eminently as a self-governing people.[125]

Thus, at the end of war, after a period of disillusion, doubt, and despair, he recovered the fervor by which he had been carried away in 1861, but this was mingled with sadness at the memory of the sufferings he had witnessed and shared vicariously. In short, his evolution had followed a Hegelian pattern: thesis, antithesis, synthesis; and he was probably aware of such a threefold movement when he constructed about this time three of the sides of his "Square Deific." [126] We shall return to this topic later.

Drum-Taps appeared in New York in November 1865 as a pamphlet of seventy-two pages printed, like *Leaves of Grass*, at the author's expense.[127] It contained fifty-three poems, none of which had previously been published. Although there is no way of dating them precisely, these poems clearly were composed throughout the duration of the war, and some of them must have been written even before the outbreak of hostilities. One feels this in reading them, and we have tried to reconstruct their chronological order as accurately as possible in describing Whitman's development during these tragic years.[128] Besides, we do know that, even before his departure for Washington in 1862, Whitman had among his papers a small notebook entitled "Drum-Taps." Writing to his mother on March 31, 1863, he asked her to take the greatest care of it [129] (and this is a further proof of the profound interest which in spite of appearances he had in the war at that time). He tried very early to publish it. A year later, on April 10, 1864, he announced to his mother: "I want to come on in a month and try to print my *Drum-Taps*. I think it may be a success pecuniarily, too." [130] Trowbridge had already tried, vainly, to find a publisher for it in Boston.[131] Whitman was no more successful and finally, as usual, had to resign himself to being his own publisher.

He felt, however, that he had made great progress since his latest edition of *Leaves of Grass*:

It is in my opinion superior to *Leaves of Grass* — certainly more perfect as a work of art, being adjusted in all its proportions, & its passion having the indispensable merit that though to the ordinary reader let loose with wildest abandon, the true artist can see it is yet under control.[132]

And he was very proud of the discipline he had succeeded in imposing on himself:

But I am perhaps mainly satisfied with *Drum-Taps* because it delivers my ambition of the task that has haunted me, namely, to express in a poem (& in the way I like, which is not at all by directly stating it) the pending action of this *Time & Land we swim in*, with all their large conflicting fluctuations of despair & hope, the shiftings, masses, & the whirl & deafening din, (yet over all, as by invisible hand, a definite purport and idea). . .[133]

To be sure the material was less subjective and easier to handle; [134] however, according to him, *Drum-Taps* was also superior to *Leaves of Grass* in another way: the style was purer and less heavy.

I see I have said I consider *Drum-Taps* superior to *Leaves of Grass*. I probably mean as a piece of art, & from the more simple and winning nature of the subject, & also because I have in it succeeded to my satisfaction in removing all superfluity from it, verbal superfluity I mean, I delight to make a poem where I feel clear that not a word but is indispensable part thereof & of my meaning.[135]

He was right in that this feeling for conciseness and economy of means was something new in his work. But the formal simplicity was largely owing, as he realized, to the simplicity of the subject, since most of the poems were descriptive and anecdotal.[136] In spite of what he said, the direct method of expression used in *Drum-Taps* naturally resulted in a clarity which the indirect suggestions of his earlier poems could not attain. But it remains to be seen whether this was a progress, as he seems to have thought, or an impoverishment and a loss of power. This can only be shown by his later development. It seems in any case that he became more and more resigned to the idea of making concessions to the public. He even thought of expurgating *Leaves of Grass*:

Drum-Taps has none of the perturbations of *Leaves of Grass*. I am satisfied with *Leaves of Grass*. . . but there are a few things I shall carefully eliminate in the next issue, & a few more I shall considerably change.[137]

He did not go quite so far as to repudiate his great work, but he seems now to have regretted some of the things which had hampered its sale. He retained them out of stubbornness and for the sake of the past, but it is clear that he was not quite the same man as he had been:

Still *Leaves of Grass* is dear to me, always dearest to me, as my first born, as daughter of my life's first hopes, doubts, & the putting in form of those days' efforts & aspirations — true, I see now, with some things in it I should not put in if I were to write now, but yet I shall certainly let them stand, even if but for proofs of phases passed away.[138]

We shall see how far in 1867 he pushed his expurgation of *Leaves of Grass* and to what extent he remained faithful to himself.

Most copies of *Drum-Taps* included under the same cover another small booklet of twenty-four pages entitled "When Lilacs Last in the Door-Yard Bloom'd and Other Pieces," dated Washington, 1865–66. This collection is more commonly referred to by its subtitle "Sequel to Drum-Taps," which also appeared at the top of each page.[139] It is a natural extension of *Drum Taps*. When Lincoln was assassinated, Whitman was in Brooklyn supervising the printing of *Drum-Taps*. The war had just ended; it was early spring and the lilacs were in bloom in the yard of the family home; joy was everywhere. But when he heard the shocking news, he was overcome. For him Lincoln was more than the savior of the Union, he was a friendly and familiar presence; for though they had never met, Whitman had often had occasion to see him in Washington.[140] In the first intensity of pain, he wrote a short poem, "Hush'd Be the Camps To-Day," commemorating the martyred President's funeral at Springfield,[141] and he held up the printing of *Drum-Taps* to include it, probably in the place of another poem of equal length. On his return to Washington, his friend Peter Doyle, who had witnessed the assassination at the Ford Theater, told him the story of what he had seen. It was probably then that Whitman composed "When Lilacs Last in the Door-Yard Bloom'd." [142] This long and moving threnody is generally regarded by critics as Whitman's masterpiece.[143] In it he demonstrates the greatness of his art in a very personal way. On the whole, he repeated the formula he had used in 1860 for "Out of the Cradle Endlessly Rocking." The poem is first of all a symphony of interlacing musical and symbolic themes, but the pattern is simpler than that of 1860 and shows greater mastery — though, perhaps, less power.

It was now too late to include "When Lilacs Last. . ." in *Drum-Taps*, the printing of which was in progress, if not completed, at New York. Whitman was therefore obliged to have the poem printed separately in Washington. He took advantage of the occasion to put a certain number of other poems in with it. Some, such as "I Heard You, Solemn-Sweet Pipes of the Organ," "Not My Enemies Ever Invade Me," "O Me! O Life!" and "Ah Poverties, Wincings and Sulky Retreats," [144] were essentially personal and, later, either disappeared from *Leaves of Grass* or were transferred to sections other than "Drum-Taps." Whitman probably included them for good measure, but it seems likely that they had been written much earlier and that they referred to the emotional crisis of 1859–60.[145] The others, however, concerned the end of the war and did belong to *Drum-Taps*. At any rate they remained in *Leaves of Grass* under that title, which shows the fundamental unity of the two books — with the exception of "O Captain! My Captain!" [146] which commemorates Lincoln and was later put in a separate group with "When Lilacs Last. . ." The case of "Chanting the Square Deific" [147] is a little peculiar, and we shall take it up later.

Whitman had hoped that *Drum-Taps* would sell rapidly and bring him some money.[148] Unfortunately we do not know to what extent this hope was realized, but there is no doubt that the book was much better received than *Leaves of Grass*.[149] Critics in fact were sometimes embarrassed at having to recommend a book by Whitman after having treated him so rudely up to that time. George William Curtis, for instance, in *Harper's* apologized in these terms for mentioning him at the same time as Tennyson and Jean Ingelow:

> If any reader is appalled by seeing that name in so choice a society, let us not argue the matter, nor express any opinion, but ask whether there is no poetry in this wail upon the death of Lincoln and in the Song of the Drum.[150]

Whitman's friends multiplied their efforts in the reviews and the newspapers to dissipate such prejudices, especially William O'Connor, who became his acknowledged champion and boldly broke lances with all assailants in the columns of the New York *Times* and the *Round Table*.[151] John Burroughs, a friend of more recent date, less fiery and more judicious, wrote articles for the *Boston Commonwealth* and *Galaxy*, in which with a more discerning enthusiasm he praised Whitman for being a difficult poet who made no concessions to the public — a judgment which, as we have seen, was beginning to be less true:

> . . . let it be understood we are dealing with one of the most tyrannical and exacting of bards — one who steadfastly refuses to be read in any but his own spirit. It is only after repeated readings and turning to him again and again that the atmosphere he breathes is reached. . . The poem may disappoint on the first perusal. The treatment of the subject is so unusual, so unlike the direct and prosy style to which our ears have been educated — that it seems to want method and purpose.[152]

In this concert of praises there were, however, two discords: the articles of W. D. Howells and Henry James. Howells recognized that on this occasion the poet could not be accused of obscenity, but he still reproached him for a lack of art:

> . . . there is no indecent thing in *Drum-Taps*. The artistic method of the poet remains, however, the same, and we must think it mistaken. . . it is unspeakably inartistic. On this ac-

count it is a failure. . . Art cannot greatly employ itself with things in embryo. . . *Expression* will always suggest; but mere *suggestion* in art is unworthy of existence, vexes the heart and shall not live. . . There are such rich possibilities in the man that it is lamentable to contemplate his error of theory. . . A man's greatness is good for nothing folded up in him, and if emitted in barbaric yawps, it is not more filling than Ossian or the east wind.[153]

Howells in spite of the prejudices owing to his education seems to have felt a certain sympathy for Whitman. It was otherwise with Henry James, for whom "it [had] been a melancholy task to read this book." [154] He too condemned the lack of art, but his analysis went further than that of Howells. Art for him was not only a matter of technique, it was also a way of life, a discipline which governed the artist as well as his art and implied a lucid awareness of himself and others. Surely there was nothing of this sort in Whitman, whose lack of restraint James found repelling:

We find a medley of extravagances and commonplaces. We find art, measure, grace, sense sneered at on every page, and nothing positive given us in their stead. To be positive one must have something to say; to be positive requires reason, labor and art; and art requires, above all things, a suppression of one's self, a subordination of one's self to an idea. . . It is not enough to be rude, lugubrious and grim. You must also be serious. You must forget yourself in your ideas. Your personal qualities — the vigor of your temperament, the manly independence of your nature, the tenderness of your heart — these facts are impertinent.[155]

Thus, even the severest critics no longer complained of anything except Whitman's lack of form. But in spite of this greater sympathy, no one seems to have seen what constituted the real value and originality of *Drum-Taps*. The image of war which emerged from it was quite unconventional, though. The opening poems were warlike enough, praising warfare as a fine and noble adventure,[156] and Whitman sometimes celebrated acts of heroism in the best tradition of epic poetry, as in "The Centenarian's Story" and "I Saw Old General at Bay." [157] He also sang the glory of battles and the beauty of troops on the march,[158] but in general, in spite of his vibrant call to arms and his cries of triumph, the tone of the book is melancholy, as he knew perfectly well himself.[159] This is because, as we have seen,[160] after his first contact with the realities of war he had been, if not repelled (once begun, the conflict could not be stopped), at least profoundly moved by the martyrdom of the young soldiers, by what Wilfred Owen was later to call "the pity of War." [161] He was, in short, the first poet of modern war as we know it, the war of masses, of large-scale massacres, where heroism has become anonymous and courage more passive than active, the individual having lost all independence and initiative. Whitman was thus the first and the only poet of his time who dared to do what we call the debunking of war.[162] Herman Melville, in his *Battle-Pieces*, in spite of his sense of evil and original sin, in spite of his great sympathy for Confederate soldiers (as men, for he detested their cause as much as Whitman did), offers only weak stories of individual acts of heroism.[163] Lacking personal experience, he could not vividly imagine the terrible sufferings of the hundreds of thousands of wounded and sick. He was therefore reduced to treating the war in the traditional epic fashion. In *Drum-Taps*, on the contrary, Whitman removed the poetry of war from the epic and infused it with the more human and subjective tones of lyric poetry. Instead of celebrating heroes and supermen, he described the sufferings of ordinary men.

Even though more lyric than epic, it is remarkable that *Drum-Taps* at first occupied a place apart in Whitman's work. For the time being it did not occur to him to include the poems in *Leaves of Grass*. So he made them into a separate volume which he believed would always remain distinct from the other poems.[164] It was only gradually that he decided to incorporate them in *Leaves of Grass*. In the fourth edition in 1867, they were relegated to an appendix. It was not until 1871 that he succeeded in fitting them into the body of the book, but even then they formed a distinct group (or rather three groups), and in the definitive edition, they are still almost all grouped together. Moreover, as O. L. Triggs has noted, unlike the rest of *Leaves of Grass*, *Drum-Taps* remained almost completely unrevised.[165] The arrangement changed, but the original text underwent few alterations, as if Whitman feared that in revising his war poems he might weaken them. It seems that he particularly wanted to preserve the primitive character of these poems. One has the impression, in short, that he was never entirely able to assimilate the extraordinary adventure and tragic trial which the Civil War had been for him. When *Drum-Taps* first appeared, he was still dazed by his emotions and could not as yet absorb such exceptional experiences or integrate such new and overwhelming feelings into the web of his life. These circumstances explain the autonomy he gave at first to *Drum-Taps*. The war was an intrusion which he had not foreseen and which compelled him to modify the organization of *Leaves of Grass*. Even if he had a plan in mind at the beginning, the irruption of war into his work forced him to change it.

The Civil War, then, exercised on his life and on his poetic career a considerable influence, the importance of which he further exaggerated later on. In 1888, casting "a backward glance o'er travel'd roads," he went so far as to declare:

It is certain, I say, that, although I had made a start before, only from the occurrence of the Secession War, and what it show'd me as by flashes of lightning, with the emotional depths it sounded and arous'd (of course, I don't mean in my own heart only, I saw it just as plain in others, in millions) — that only from the strong flare and provocation of that war's sights and scenes the final reasons-for-being of an autochthonic and passionate song definitely came forth. . .

I went down to the war fields of Virginia (end of 1862), lived thenceforward in camp — saw great battles. . . Without those three or four years and the experiences they gave, *Leaves of Grass* would not now be existing.[166]

The exaggeration is striking. With the passage of time he had almost succeeded in persuading himself that he had taken part in the great battles of the Civil War, or at least that he had witnessed them, although the most he had actually seen — and that at a distance — was a few skirmishes.[167] As to the statement that *Leaves of Grass* could not have existed without the War of Secession, if we take it literally, it is absurd, since most of the poems in *Leaves of Grass* were written before 1860. It should be interpreted as meaning that without the impetus of the war his career would have ended, and he would have had nothing further to say. At the end of the 1860 edition he had indeed made his farewell to his readers.[168] Nevertheless, even in this restricted sense, there is still a patent exaggeration; for when the 1860 edition appeared, he had already surmounted the crisis which had inspired the pessimistic poems written during that period.[169] The war had not caused him to find himself, since his poetic birth took place in 1855; and neither had it saved him, since he had saved himself at least twice before 1862; but it had consolidated the victories which he had won by definitively confirming his reasons for belief in and hope for mankind. For he knew now that the human character was essentially made up of heroism and love. He had seen the proof of this in the hospitals. Evil was only accidental.[170] Thus reassured, he lived henceforth with the conviction that his democratic ideal was attainable. It was no longer for him a utopian dream, but a certainty founded on facts that he had been able to verify daily during more than three years.

But that was not all. The years he had passed in the hospitals had brought him other revelations, more precious still. He had served an apprenticeship there to brotherhood and friendship. Up to that time he led a very solitary existence. True, he lived with his family, but none of them could understand him, and he came and went among them without really living in the same world.[171] In New York, he had many acquaintances among the journalists and comrades among the omnibus drivers, but no real friends. His rides along Broadway on the roofs of coaches symbolize the solitude in which he lived in the midst of the noisy crowds of the great city.[172] At Pfaff's he was equally isolated. He sat there among the rest, affable and smiling, but as far away from them as if he had lived on another planet.[173] In Washington everything changed; he was finally able to step outside himself and fraternize with the wounded and the sick without fear of scandal. He was at last permitted to lavish every day the treasures of unused affection which had accumulated in him and to lay the foundations of that democracy of comrades of which he had dreamed for ten years.[174] He expanded in the new atmosphere. He became for the first time, it seems, capable of friendship, and it was then that he linked himself with William O'Connor and his wife Ellen, with John Burroughs, and on a different level, with Peter Doyle. From then on, he ceased to be alone in life. In addition to his mother, he had his friends. Even when he was separated from them, he wrote to them very simple letters, very direct, without ornaments, the only purpose of which was to maintain relations. He also wrote for several years to some of the soldiers whom he had known in Washington.[175] This correspondence, part of which has survived, shows how precious these friendships were to him in permitting him to escape from his original solitude. Thanks to his young comrades of the hospitals, and to his new friends, he participated more fully in the life of his contemporaries and mingled more effectively than before in the society of his time.

The war was responsible for another change: his sensuality, at least in appearance, subsided. He was less tormented by his homosexual leanings, which his visits to the hospitals permitted him to satisfy in part without incurring social disapproval or even suspicion. His vocation as "wound-dresser" was certainly not a pose. He was undoubtedly motivated by charity, but, unconsciously at least, he was also moved by his desire and his need to be among young men. He experienced not only pity for them, but a tremendous affection, and he was happy because it seemed to him that this affection was reciprocated. He had the very strong impression that these young soldiers, like himself, needed manly affection — [176] a reassuring discovery since it furnished proof that his instincts were more normal than he had thought. Having dreamed of "the comrade's long-dwelling kiss" in the City of the Future,[177] he now had occasion every day to kiss the wounded who were eager for affection and caresses:

> Lots of them have grown to expect, as I leave at night, that we should kiss each other, sometimes quite a number; I have to go round. There is very little petting in a soldier's life in the field, but . . . I know what is in their hearts, always waiting, though they may be unconscious of it themselves.[178]

So, again, nature imitated art and his life was modeled on his work. At any rate, these marks of affection, innocent as they may have seemed, indicated the violent desires he was obliged to repress:

> O beloved race in all! O my breast aches with tender love for all. . .[179]

> These and more I dress with impassive hand — (yet deep in my breast a fire, a burning flame.) [180]

> How good they look as they tramp down to the river, sweaty, with their guns on their shoulders!

How I love them! how I could hug them, with their
brown faces and their clothes and knapsacks cover'd
with dust.[181]

It was, then, their beauty which moved him. When he
described the nation mourning its dead, he made it say in
its prayer to the earth: "My dead absorb — my young men's
beautiful bodies absorb. . ." [182] Curiously enough, the adjective "beautiful" later disappeared, as if Whitman had been
afraid of betraying his secret thoughts. In fact, these very
discreet avowals revealed his sensual stirrings. We shall have
occasion later to examine further the nature of these amorous
instincts and to determine how far he let them go. One thing
seems certain: he did not at this time do anything which
society would disapprove. He was sometimes tempted to enter
into more intimate relations with some of the soldiers, but
his dreams of peaceful domestic life with them never came
true.[183] He learned to content himself with much less; a pressure of the hand, an exchange of kisses, or even a mere loving
look were enough to satisfy him.[184] Moreover, it seems that,
without any sensual satisfaction during the war years, his
homosexual passion was gradually purified and idealized. His
troubled desires were succeeded by an ardent but ethereal
and completely Platonic emotion:

I have been and am now, thinking so of you, dear young man,
and of your love, or more rightly speaking, our love for each
other — so curious, so sweet, I say so *religious* — We met there
in the Hospitals — how little we have been together — seems to
me we ought to be some together every day of our lives — I don't
care about talking, or amusement — but just to be together, and
work together, or go off in the open air together.[185]

Such were, in all likelihood, the sentiments which he wished
to express in one of the most mysterious poems of *Drum-Taps*,
"Out of the Rolling Ocean the Crowd":

"Out of the rolling ocean, the crowd, came a drop gently
to me,
Whispering, *I love you, before long I die,*
I have travel'd a long way, merely to look on you, to
touch you,
For I could not die till I once look'd on you,
For I fear'd I might afterward lose you.
Now we have met, we have look'd, we are safe;
Return in peace to the ocean my love;
I too am part of that ocean, my love — we are not so
much separated;
Behold the great rondure — the cohesion of all, how
perfect!
But as for me, for you, the irresistible sea is to separate
us,
As for an hour carrying us diverse — yet cannot carry
us diverse for ever;
Be not impatient — a little space — know you, I salute
the air, the ocean and the land,
Every day, at sundown, for your dear sake, my love.[186]

Thus, by a strange transmutation, doubtless under the influence of his pity for the young wounded soldiers, his homosexual feelings were sublimated during these three years, and
transformed into a mystical kind of love, so pure of all carnal
desire that he could sometimes speak of it in terms of paternal
or fraternal love.[187] The war permitted him in some degree
to realize that democracy of comrades founded on "manly love"
which he had announced in 1860 [188] and for which he always
longed, although he knew that its realization would encounter
innumerable difficulties:

. . . Dear camerado! I confess I have urged you onward with me, and still urge you, without the least
idea what is our destination,
Or whether we shall be victorious, or utterly quell'd
and defeated.[189]

The war also had another effect on Whitman. It brought

about his final reconciliation with death. Already in 1860, in "Out of the Cradle Endlessly Rocking," he had celebrated the sweetness of "the low and delicious word death." [190] But death, in spite of this acceptance in principle, was still associated at this time with the angry moans of the sea [191] and with the infinitely dolorous theme of the separation of two loving creatures. For all its promises it concealed an obscure menace, since, who knows, it might be nothing but chaos.[192] In 1865 it had lost its tragic halo; it was the certainty of peace and repose. It brought deliverance and redemption instead of chaos and despair:

> Come lovely and soothing Death. . .
> Approach, encompassing Death — strong Deliveress!
> When it is so — when thou hast taken them, I joyously
>   sing the dead,
> Lost in the loving, floating ocean of thee,
> Laved in the flood of thy bliss, O Death,[193]

sings the bird from a distance at the time of Lincoln's funeral, because, in the interval, Whitman had lived familiarly with death. In the hospitals he had seen so many young soldiers meet it so bravely that it no longer had either horror or mystery for him: [194]

> For I have seen many wounded soldiers die,
> After dread suffering — have seen their lives pass off
>   with smiles. . .[195]

This then, what frightened us so long. Why, it is put to flight with ignominy — a mere stuffed scarecrow of the fields. Oh death, where is thy sting? Oh grave, where is thy victory? [196]

Those who die, no longer suffer. Death was a deliverance in those days. It freed thousands and thousands of young men. It was those who remained, the living, who suffered.[197]

The joy with which Whitman had welcomed peace and the victory of democracy and the serenity with which he regarded

death were therefore tempered with sadness, even though
he now almost preferred the repose of death to the life he had
so passionately loved before. This was undoubtedly a sign of
lassitude, probably due to the accumulated physical fatigue
from the long months in the hospitals and also to the moral
distaste aroused by all the horrors and turpitudes which he had
witnessed [198] and which are perhaps echoed in "O Me! O Life!"
— unless that poem was written before the war.[199] The elegy
on Lincoln, besides, includes a casual admission of his nervous-
ness and restlessness at this time: ". . . something I know
not what kept me from sleep." [200]

So the same battle between doubt and hope went on. He
wavered endlessly between suffering and serenity, but once
more he emerged victorious — thanks to his art. He was
perfectly aware of it himself, since he said to the fraternal
bird who sang sorrowfully in the distance:

> . . . well dear brother I know,
> If thou wast not granted to sing thou wouldst surely
> die.[201]

He knew that his victory was precarious and that the
battle would have to be continually renewed. Peace, he foresaw, would be another struggle. So he gathered his forces in
the expectation of new trials to come:

> Weave in! weave in, my hardy life!. . .
> We know not what the use, O life! nor know the aim,
>   the end — nor really aught we know;
> But know the work, the need goes on, and shall go on —
>   the death-envelop'd march of peace as well as war,
>   goes on;
> For great campaigns of peace the same, the wiry threads
>   to weave;
> We know not why or what, yet weave, forever weave.[202]

CHAPTER VII

HAPPY BUREAUCRAT AND
TORMENTED POET

ONE day, during the war, a New York newspaper correspondent named Swinton, finding Whitman on time for an
appointment, exclaimed: "Well, Walt, I have known you
dozens of years, and made hundreds of appointments with
you, but this is the first time that I ever knew you to keep one.
I thought that I saw signs of decay." [1]

This is the general impression which the evidence gives of
Whitman at the end of the war. He had never before been
settled but had continually changed from one paper, and
even from one profession, to another; now, on the contrary,
he had installed himself in Washington, and he did not leave
it until he was forced to do so by illness in 1873, after a stay
of nearly ten years. Besides, he had even renounced his independence and consented to become a civil servant. The vagabond always ready to take the open road now resigned himself
to the monotonous routine of a clerk's life in an office. At first
glance, this appears a strange downfall.

In January 1863, soon after his return from Falmouth, he
had sought a job in the government service in order to make
a living; [2] but his efforts were unsuccessful and he soon became tired of waiting in antechambers. So he contented
himself with the modest position of part-time assistant that

Major Hapgood had offered him. But at the end of the war, vigorously supported by J. Hubley Ashton, Assistant Attorney General, whose acquaintance he had made at the home of the O'Connors, and by Assistant Secretary W. T. Otto of the Department of the Interior, he obtained a clerkship in the Indian Bureau at a salary of twelve hundred dollars a year.[3] He amply deserved it, as the poet of *Drum-Taps* and the indefatigable wound-dresser, the two claims that he had advanced in support of his request — taking care at the same time not to mention *Leaves of Grass*.[4] If James Harlan, the Secretary of the Interior, had known him as the author of that book, Whitman would probably never have obtained the position. Harlan was a narrow and fanatical Methodist who could live only in an atmosphere of virtue and purity. Unfortunately, through some zealous employee, he soon learned that Whitman had written an indecent book. In June 1865, to make certain, he searched the suspect's desk after office hours and seized a copy of *Leaves of Grass* which he found there.[5] What he read in it must have horrified him, for the next day Whitman was dismissed without explanation.[6] Ashton quickly intervened and protested against this unjustified dismissal of his protégé, who, strangely enough, had been promoted the month before.[7] But Harlan was inflexible and claimed that it was impossible for him to keep such an immoral author among his subordinates. He would resign rather than reconsider his decision. Ashton gave up the attempt and found a job for Whitman in the Department of the Interior.

The incident was closed and the crisis resolved without damage to Whitman, but the ebullient and generous O'Connor, always ready to fly to the help of the weak and the oppressed, did not take that view. In his opinion, Harlan had shown a criminal intolerance in persecuting a poet and deserved to be punished. In a few weeks, Whitman's fearless champion composed a virulent and lyrical pamphlet attacking Harlan and lauding the author of *Leaves of Grass. The Good Gray Poet* [8] is a masterpiece of its kind.[9] O'Connor gave free rein to his virtuosity in invective and hyperbole. He represented Whitman as a superman equal, if not superior, to Homer, Shakespeare, Dante, and Christ and acclaimed *Leaves of Grass* as one of the world's great books. At the same time, with a great deal of skill, he praised Whitman for having tried to found a specifically American literature completely free from all European influence, and in taking this line, he was sure to gain sympathy for Whitman. Besides, in representing Whitman's dismissal as an infringement on freedom of thought and a manifestation of obscurantism, he further enlarged the argument and made his hero a martyr whom every liberal in the land would feel bound to support.

For these reasons the pamphlet created a certain stir when it was published in 1866.[10] It helped to draw attention to *Drum-Taps* and their *Sequel*, which appeared about the same time. It was favorably mentioned in the reviews,[11] and it gave rise to a current of sympathy for Whitman. Even those who found O'Connor's dithyrambic eulogies exaggerated were obliged to respect the work Whitman had done in the hospitals and to recognize the value of his war poems. It was impossible henceforth to ignore him or to abuse him as certain critics had done before the war. The obscene author of *Leaves of Grass* had now become "the Good Gray Poet." He was no longer merely a poet but a legendary personage.

While O'Connor stormed, Whitman took things easy.[12] His work in the office was not exacting and left him a great deal of leisure.[13] Theoretically, his working day began at nine o'clock and finished at four, but he always came late in the morning after having gossiped with his friends for a long time at breakfast,[14] and he generally left early in the afternoon.[15] Thus he had long evenings to himself, which he spent idling, chatting, or reading. When he wished to read after dinner, he returned to his office and there, comfortably installed, warmed, and lighted at government expense, he devoured the books of the departmental library.[16] Moreover, it is probable that even during working hours he occupied himself more with literary than with governmental matters.[17] Bureaucratic customs were then much easier than they are today, and his career as a civil servant in no way hampered his activity as a writer. He was in fact given a leave of absence whenever he wanted one in order to supervise the printing of his books. Thus it was that in April 1865 (only three months after his appointment and one month after his first promotion) he was in Brooklyn preparing *Drum-Taps* for publication.[18] And he obtained the same favor each time he had a book to publish.[19] This did not prevent his advancement, since in November 1866 he was promoted to the status of third class with a salary of sixteen hundred dollars a year.[20] He had never been so rich before.[21] He began to live less frugally and moved to a somewhat more comfortable boardinghouse at the corner of M and Twelfth Streets.[22] He occupied an attic as usual, but in his letters to his mother, he repeatedly praised the abundant food.[23] His tastes were decidedly becoming more bourgeois.

What a difference indeed between the untidy Whitman of 1855 and the well-behaved, conventional personage whose image he now tried to convey to his English readers through the medium of Moncure D. Conway and William Rossetti:

. . . personally the author of *Leaves of Grass* is in no sense or sort whatever the "rough," the "eccentric," "vagabond," or queer person that the commentators (always bound for the intensest possible statement,) persist in making him. He has moved and moves still along the path of his life's happenings and fortunes, as they befall or have befallen him, with entire serenity and decorum, never defiant even to the conventions, always bodily sweet and fresh, dressed plainly and cleanly, a gait and demeanor of antique simplicity, cheerful and smiling, performing carefully all his domestic, social and municipal obligations, his demonstrative nature toned very low but eloquent enough of eye, posture and expression, using only moderate words, and offering to the world, in himself, an American Personality and real Democratic Presence, that not only the best old Hindu, Greek and Roman worthies would have at once responded to, but which the most cultured European from court or academy would likewise on meeting to-day, see and own without demur.[24]

He had come a long way in ten years, from the superb arrogance with which in the 1855 Preface he had affirmed the superiority of America and of American poets,[25] an arrogance which perhaps arose from an obscure feeling of inferiority. But now American democracy had emerged victorious from a terrible struggle and no one could doubt its solidity. He no longer needed to shout its praises, he could be content to affirm them quietly. Similarly he no longer needed to call attention to himself by means of eccentric clothing or revolutionary appeals. He had succeeded in compelling recognition; he could now afford to give up the "rough," the vagabond of the "Song of the Open Road" who had never existed anyhow, except metaphorically. He shed the personality which he had once wanted to embody (which he had perhaps believed he did embody), but which had never really been his. The more conventional portrait of himself that he presented in 1866 placed the accent on equilibrium and serenity rather than on passion and dynamism.[26] A trait of the earlier portrait remained however: perfect physical health. It was unfortunately the most illusory.

In fact, during the summer of 1866, the symptoms which had bothered him during the war recurred: fits of dizziness, violent headaches, and insomnia.[27] He complained of them constantly in his letters to his mother. Over the years his condition, instead of improving, grew worse. In 1869 he had several attacks of this mysterious illness, each of which lasted three or four days and left him prostrate and powerless.[28] The heat overcame him. He who had once taken sunbaths on the Long Island beaches was now obliged to walk with a parasol in the summer.[29] In 1870 he felt better, but for several weeks his sight failed so rapidly that he had to wear spectacles for reading and writing.[30] In 1872, after several months of good health, his apparently causeless maladies recurred [31] and worried him so much that he made a will and sent it to his brother George, telling him not to be alarmed, but not to laugh either.[32]

His presentiments were in fact well founded. On January 23, 1873,[33] as he was quietly reading a novel by Bulwer-Lytton before a good fire in his office, he suddenly felt ill and hurried home as fast as he could. When he woke up next morning he realized that his left side was paralyzed. He had had a stroke during the night.[34] The poet of perfect health had suddenly become an invalid. After having emerged from so many psychological crises, he was now brought low — defeated by his own body.

There has been much speculation concerning the causes of this sudden physical collapse. For Whitman and his friends, the explanation was simple: he had lost his health in the military hospitals during the war; overwork and continual strain had finally broken his resistance to the infections to which he was exposed. They recalled also that he had had blood poisoning from a cut on the hand by the scalpel of a surgeon during an operation,[35] and they did not wonder that he had finally succumbed. Accordingly this paralytic attack became for Whitman a new claim to glory. It made a martyr of him and a victim of the war which he had extolled. He wrote of it proudly in the Preface to the 2nd Annex of *Leaves of Grass* in 1891.[36] But soon after his death, the iconoclasts began to express their doubts. In March 1892, Thomas Wentworth Higginson, to the indignation of Whitman's admirers, advanced the hypothesis that his stroke was probably caused not by his heroic conduct in the hospitals, but by the irregularities of his sexual life.[37] And several years later, the German critic Eduard Bertz, comparing Whitman's case to that of Nietzsche, inquired whether this attack was not the result of a hereditary taint.[38] There was no lack of arguments in favor of such an explanation. Edward (Eddie), his youngest brother, was feeble-minded, subject to epileptic fits, and paralyzed on the left side (perhaps as a result of a difficult delivery and a violent attack of scarlet fever); Jesse, his oldest brother, was syphilitic and died insane in an asylum (but his insanity may have been due to a fall or to a blow on the head); another brother, Andrew, died at the age of thirty-seven from cancer or tuberculosis of the throat; his younger sister, Hannah, was a neurotic, incapable of keeping house and also had a paralytic attack in 1892; finally, one of his brothers had died six months after birth.[39] Certainly, the picture is dark, but it should be pointed out that Mary and George Whitman both led perfectly normal lives and died, like their mother, at an advanced age. So there is nothing to prove, even if there was actually a taint in the family, that Walt Whitman was affected. Moreover, a physician, Dr. J. C. Trent, who analyzed Whitman's case in 1948,[40] withholds his opinion and seems to lean toward the hypothesis of a stroke due to hypertension.[41] This diagnosis by a practitioner acquainted with recent medical theories is also confirmed by the opinion of John Burroughs who knew Whitman well.

In any case, whatever the cause of his illness, the uneventful life Whitman had thus far led in Washington was brutally interrupted. Had he been truly happy during the years following the intoxication of victory and the joy of renewed peace? It seems not. He had been very lonely and his solitude had weighed upon him. "As to me, I lead rather a dull life here. . . I do not associate much with the department clerks, yet many appear to be good fellows enough," he wrote in 1866 to a young soldier whom he had known in the hospitals.[42] Two years later, he expressed himself in almost the same terms: "I am leading a quiet monotonous life, working a few hours every day very moderately. Have plenty of books to read but few acquaintances. I spend my evenings mostly in the office." [43]

This is a long way from the vigorous and happy vagabond that he had imagined himself to be in 1855 and that he had presented in his self-portrait, the friend of all whose friendship all had sought as if drawn by his secret magnetism.[44] There were no more wounded soldiers to visit and to comfort.[45] Peace had left a great emptiness which nothing came to fill. Now he was no longer living with the O'Connors, he saw them infrequently. He was able to visit John Burroughs only on Sundays.[46] He therefore felt terribly isolated — in spite of the friendship of Peter Doyle — and he was sometimes at the point of tears. It was at this time that he wrote the poignant little poem entitled "Tears," one of the few new poems of the 1867 edition:

> Tears! tears! tears!
> In the night, in solitude, tears,
> On the white shore dripping, dripping, suck'd in by the
> sand,
> Tears, not a star shining, all dark and desolate,
> Moist tears from the eyes of a muffled head;
> O who is that ghost? that form in the dark, with tears?
> What shapeless lump is that, bent, crouch'd there on
> the sand?
> Streaming tears, sobbing tears, throes, choked with
> wild cries;
> O storm, embodied, rising, careering with swift steps
> along the beach!
> O wild and dismal night storm, with wind — O belch-
> ing and desperate!
> O shade so sedate and decorous by day, with calm
> countenance and regulated pace,

But away at night as you fly, none looking, — O then
the unloosen'd ocean,
Of tears! tears! tears! [47]

Who is this tragic phantom if not himself, a model employee
by day and a desperate man at night when he found himself
alone? The serenity which he had attained at the end of the
war was thus, it seems, once more endangered. In appearance,
as always, he gave an impression of perfect balance,[48] but in
the depth of his mind a tempest raged. He was passing through
a new crisis.

It is true that very little is known about his emotional life
at this time. According to Emory Holloway, in his introduction to the *Uncollected Poetry and Prose of Walt Whitman,*[49]
and Frances Winwar, in her fictional biography,[50] Whitman
had been torn by an unhappy passion for a married woman,
Mrs. Juliette H. Beach, in whose honor he had written "Out
of the Cradle Endlessly Rocking." But Clifton J. Furness has
proved that this romantic story is totally unfounded,[51] and
Holloway himself later recanted; the biography of Whitman
which he published in 1926, several years after his *Uncollected
Poetry and Prose,* makes no mention of Juliette Beach.[52] All
that we know for certain is that Whitman was again obsessed
by ambiguous sexual desires which he tried to suppress. One
of his private notebooks, dated July 15, 1870, furnishes evidence of his secret troubles:

. . . fancying what does not really exist in another, but is all
the time in myself alone — utterly deluded & cheated by *myself*
& my own weakness — REMEMBER WERE I AM MOST WEAK, &
most lacking. Yet always preserve a kind spirit & demeanor to 16.
But PURSUE HER NO MORE. . .

It is IMPERATIVE, that I obviate & remove myself (&
my orbit) *at all hazards* [away from] this *incessant
enormous* & . . . . PERTURBATION

To GIVE UP ABSOLUTELY & *for good, from this present hour,* [all] this FEVERISH, FLUCTUATING, *useless undignified pursuit of* 164 — *too long, (much too long)* persevered in, — so humiliating — *it must come at last* & had better come now — *(It cannot possibly be a success)*

LET THERE FROM THIS HOUR BE NO FALTERING, . . NO GETTING . . . at all henceforth, (NOT ONCE, *under any circumstances)* — *avoid seeing her, or meeting her, or any talk or explanations* — or ANY MEETING WHATEVER, FROM THIS HOUR FORTH, FOR LIFE.[53]

This curious resolution recalls the one that he made at the beginning of the Civil War,[54] but it is much more revealing and its tone much more urgent. It is not a matter of sobriety, but of continence. It shows to what degree his feelings were agitated by sexual desires. He felt disabled. He was no longer master of himself and felt ashamed. In his poems he had sung the joys of the flesh and celebrated the sexual act; now he blushed for his desires. The "child of Adam" had been driven from the earthly paradise and had discovered shame. To what should this change be attributed? Probably to the loss of vitality which we have already noted. His appetites were less ardent, his instincts less imperious, and he controlled them more easily. Formerly their violence had frightened him too,[55] but they were too powerful then and their force carried him away. Now he curbed them, or at least he tried to do so; for the struggle was long and difficult, and he was constantly tossed between his desires and the denials which he endeavored to impose on them. Apparently a sedentary bureaucrat, he was actually the young helmsman who prudently steered through dangerous reefs a ship that threatened at any moment to sink:

Aboard, at the ship's helm,
A young steersman, steering with care.
A bell through fog on a sea-coast dolefully ringing,
An ocean-bell — O a warning bell, rock'd by the waves.
O you give good notice indeed, you bell by the sea-
    reefs ringing,
Ringing, ringing, to warn the ship from its wreck-place.
For, as on the alert, O steersman, you mind the bell's
    admonition,
The bows turn, — the freighted ship, tacking, speeds
    away under her gray sails,
The beautiful and noble ship, with all her precious
    wealth, speeds away gaily and safe.
But O the ship, the immortal ship! O ship aboard the
    ship!
O ship of the body — ship of the soul — voyaging,
    voyaging, voyaging. [56]

But what was the danger that menaced him and that he
must at all costs escape? A close examination of the manuscript
of this resolution reveals it. The cause of these troubles was
not a woman, but a man. All the masculine pronouns of the
text have been erased and replaced by their feminine equivalent, but under the superscription they can still be very clearly
seen.[57] There can be no doubt: Whitman deliberately camou-
flaged his private notes. Moreover, one of the pages is missing,
and it was probably Whitman himself who tore it out,[58] finding
his admission too compromising. If he feared the judgment of
posterity to this extent, how much more must he have feared
the scandal that would have broken out if anyone had known
the true nature of his passion. This would explain the panic
that seems to have seized him and his frantic efforts to smother
such dangerous tendencies.

Besides the shame which this inadmissible instinct [59] caused
him, there was the fear that he could not succeed in his amorous attempt; "useless, undignified pursuit . . . it cannot pos-

sibly be a success," he noted. Since the failure of his love affair in 1859–60, he feared rebuff. In short, he was afraid of life and very far now from the attitude of defiance he glorified in "One Hour to Madness and Joy": "To court destruction with taunts, with invitations." [60] The time of madness had apparently passed. His vitality had obviously decreased.

He had, of course, gone through similar crises in the past. In the edition of 1865–66 in particular there is a poem dealing with exactly the same struggles and the same agonies:

> Ah poverties, wincings, and sulky retreats!
> Ah you foes that in conflict have overcome me!
> (For what is my life, or any man's life, but a conflict
>   with foes — the old, the incessant war?)
> You degradations — you tussle with passions and
>   appetites;
> You smarts from dissatisfied friendships, (ah wounds,
>   the sharpest of all;)
> You toil of painful and choked articulations — you
>   meannesses;
> You shallow tongue-talks at tables, (my tongue the
>   shallowest of any;)
> You broken resolutions, you racking angers, you
>   smothered ennuis. . .[61]

We find the same disappointed love, the same efforts to control himself in the notebook of 1870 and in the poem. The same disgust with himself and the others is pushed to the point of a condemnation of the innocent pleasures of conversation.[62] There is the same revulsion from love. He had already depicted himself in a poem of the same period as "utterly abject, grovelling on the ground" before the one he loved.[63] Whether these poems were written during the war, or as is more likely, in 1860–61,[64] it is clear that whatever was tormenting him recurred at regular intervals and seized on him periodically. But each time, with a prodigious effort of will, he succeeded in freeing himself. His notebook of 1870 shows him appealing to the stoicism of Epictetus and the wisdom of Heine to help him through the crisis [65] and hoping eventually to live in full harmony with nature and to attain the age of Merlin "strong & wise & beautiful at 100 years old." [66]

Once again he succeeded effectively in controlling himself and regaining his equilibrium. Yet nothing in his behavior seems to have indicated that his serenity was menaced at this time. These struggles and this distress were all internal. Outwardly they did not appear. Peter Doyle, the young Irish streetcar conductor whose acquaintance Whitman had made in 1866 [67] and who may have been the cause of his despair, probably suspected nothing. We have the letter which Whitman wrote to him from Brooklyn on July 30, 1870, only two weeks after recording his resolutions in his notebook; its tone is calm, it gives the impression of an unclouded friendship.[68] Whitman had apparently succeeded in repressing and sublimating the passion that was torturing him.

The edition of *Leaves of Grass* which came out in 1871–72 confirms both his moral recovery and his physical fatigue. The new poems show him tired of life and of its perpetual struggles. He would have like to escape from his body and launch himself with his soul in search of God, a God almost transcendent to the creation, but in whom he could lose himself and find rest and peace. All this is symbolically suggested in "Passage to India":

> Passage — immediate passage! the blood burns in my
>   veins!
> Away, O soul! hoist instantly the anchor! . . .
> Have we not grovell'd here long enough, eating and
>   drinking like mere brutes? . . .
> Sail forth! steer for the deep waters only!
> Reckless, O soul, exploring, I with thee, and thou with
>   me. . .

> O my brave soul!
> O farther, farther sail!
> O daring joy, but safe! Are they not all the seas of God?
> O farther, farther, farther sail! [69]

The same joyful certainty of an immortal happiness after death is expressed in "On the Beach at Night," which, over the intervening years, answers the despair of "As I Ebb'd with the Ocean of Life" and renews with more human warmth the pantheistic affirmation of "On the Beach at Night Alone":

> Something there is more immortal than the stars, . .
> Something that shall endure longer even than lustrous
>   Jupiter,
> Longer than sun, or any revolving satellite,
> Or the radiant sisters, the Pleiades. [70]

When the lilacs bloomed in the spring, he no longer thought of Lincoln or his former sorrow; he wished to go away, to lose himself, to leave this world:

> Thou, Soul, unloosen'd — the restlessness after I know
>   not what;
> Come! let us lag here no longer — let us be up and
>   away!
> O for another world! O if one could but fly like a bird!
> O to escape — to sail forth, as in a ship!
> To glide with thee, O Soul, o'er all, in all, as a ship
>   o'er the waters! [71]

To the problems posed by his body he had thus finally found a spiritual solution. He wanted to separate himself from matter and to die. In this connection, the new passage which he inserted in the "Poem of Joys" (later entitled "Song of Joys") is quite revealing:

> Yet, O my soul supreme!
> Know'st thou the joys of pensive thought?
> Joys of the free and lonesome heart — the tender,
>   gloomy heart?

Joy of the solitary walk — the spirit bowed yet proud —
   the suffering and the struggle?
The agonistic throes, the ecstasies — joys of solemn
   musings, day or night?
Joys of the thought of Death — the great spheres Time
   and Space?
Prophetic joys of better, loftier love's ideals — the
   Divine Wife — the sweet, eternal, perfect Comrade?
Joys all thine own, undying one — joys worthy of thee,
   O Soul.[72]

The poem is still quivering from the battles Whitman had fought with his instincts during the preceding years. He had had to wrestle like an athlete in the arena, but happiness had finally escaped him. He was lonely and depressed, but his spirit was indomitable ("the spirit bowed yet proud"). He had no reason to despair after all. Later, after his death, he would have the consolation of knowing, in a nobler form, the love which had been refused him on earth, an ideal, imperishable love. His poems henceforth would build a bridge between life and death,[73] between the world of matter where he had suffered and the infinite spaces where his soul would have the revelation of the highest spiritual joys.

Whereas in 1860 he had stood on the beach and listened with fear to the moaning of the sea, he now imagined himself sailing far from shore in the supreme adventure of death. The image of embarkation and departure on the high seas haunted him. As early as 1867, in "Aboard at a Ship's Helm," [74] he had braved the dangers of the ocean, but his ship had stayed close to shore; now, on the contrary, he threw himself out to sea toward India and farther than India. Joy accompanied him on his quest ("Joy, Shipmate, Joy"),[75] and he said a last farewell to the land: "Now Finale to the Shore." [76]

The untold want, by life and land ne'er granted,
Now, Voyager, sail thou forth, to seek and find.[77]

So he prepared to depart with his soul, ". . . accepting, exulting in Death, in its turn, the same as life." [78]

With exultation, he said; with resignation too. He realized himself that his powers had diminished. He no longer felt the same urge to write and to create as when his imperious vocation had made him renounce any temporal occupation. He probably also felt the approach of the death which in a few months was to strike its first blow and leave him half-paralyzed. He had even made his will.[79] It seemed to him that his life and work were ended. As in 1860 he said farewell to his reader:

> One song, America, before I go.[80]

However, once again, he underestimated his energy and his will to live.

But, before proceeding, we must examine more closely the works produced during this period of trouble and crises. In 1867, less than two years after *Drum-Taps,* a new edition of *Leaves of Grass* came out, the fourth, very different in appearance from that of 1860.[81] Its binding was remarkably sober: the boards were without decoration, the corners and backstrip were of black leather, and only the title, *Leaves of Grass,* and "Ed'n 1867" appeared on the latter. No author's name. The title page was equally plain: "Leaves of Grass — New York, 1867." The author's name appeared only in the copyright notice and at the head of the poem later called "Song of Myself," but which in 1860 had already carried the title "Walt Whitman." There was thus a return to the relative anonymity of the first edition, but for the first time, the author's portrait was missing. The appearance of the book was on the whole rather poor; the paper was mediocre and the number of variants in details of binding seems to indicate that copies were bound as orders came in. It is probable that Whitman, who this time no longer had a publisher as in 1860, was having difficulty in financing the publication of a book of over 400 pages. This, in fact, represented a heavy investment. The work included not only *Leaves of Grass* proper, but *Drum-Taps* and *Sequel to Drum-Taps,* and, in some copies, "Songs before Parting," each with its own pagination and each printed separately on different kinds of paper.[82] These appendices were not yet assimilated into *Leaves of Grass.* They were only superimposed, but Whitman's intention was clearly to attach them to the main body. Besides, "Songs before Parting" were also called "Leaves of Grass"; in Whitman's mind they were therefore already part and parcel of *Leaves of Grass.* It is not clear why he had detached them, for they do not include a single poem which had not already appeared in the 1860 volume. Perhaps he had intended at some time to reject them. At any rate, there is no way of explaining the reasons for this wavering in Whitman's plan.

As for *Leaves of Grass* proper, the organization had changed, as the table of contents immediately shows. Moreover, all the poems now had titles, and not, as they often had in 1860, mere numbers. However, almost all of them had been published in the earlier edition. There were only seven new ones:[83] "Inscriptions,"[84] "The Runner,"[85] "Tears! Tears! Tears!"[86] "Aboard at a Ship's Helm,"[87] "When I Read the Book,"[88] "The City Dead-House,"[89] and "Leaflets."[90]

They are all very short and, with the exception of the third and fourth which we already have had occasion to examine, they are rather trivial. The originality of the 1867 edition does not reside in these almost negligible additions, but in the revisions undergone by the old poems, the meaning and character of which were often considerably altered. The war had not only inspired *Drum-Taps,* it had also had repercussions on *Leaves of Grass.* In the first lines of "Starting from Paumanok," which as in 1860 opened the book, Whitman now mentioned among his imaginary avatars "a soldier camp'd or carrying [his] knapsack and gun,"[91] and throughout the

book he took the same meticulous care to bring his poems up
to date by introducing allusions to the recent past and by suppressing all references to slavery.[92] But this was not all; the
war, as we have seen, had fortified his faith in democracy
and accordingly he celebrated it with renewed fervor. "As I
Sat Alone by Blue Ontario's Shore," which in 1860 had exalted
above all the role of the poet-prophet of democracy (that is,
his own role),[93] now celebrated the Democracy of which the
prophet was the poet. The emphasis this time is placed on
democracy rather than on the poet.[94] He added whole paragraphs [95] in which he chanted the victory of the "great Idea,"
of democracy with its marvellous inventions and its armies
on the march.[96] There could be no question now of its "defections"; [97] he was entirely reassured about its future. The
inspiration of the poems is thus more frankly democratic and
less exclusively personal, more plainly political and less preoccupied, at least in principle, with poetic expression. Whereas in 1856 he wanted only "to speak beautiful words," in 1867
he aspired, or so he claimed, "to sing the songs of the great
Idea." [98]

However (this was an unexpected consequence of his exaltation), having become more modest about himself, he now
showed an outrageous arrogance about everything concerning
his country. His patriotism sometimes takes the form of a
challenge to the rest of the world, as in these two lines:

> We stand self-pois'd in the middle, branching thence
>   over the world,
> From Missouri, Nebraska, or Kansas, laughing attacks
>   to scorn.[99]

And at other times it takes the form of a narrow and scornful nationalism, as in this tirade:

> America isolated I sing;
> I say that works made here in the spirit of other lands,
>   are so much poison to These States.

> How dare these insects assume to write poems for
> America?
> For our armies, and the offspring following the
> armies.[100]

Later, in 1881, realizing that such haughty isolationism was in contradiction with his aspirations to universality, he suppressed this awkward passage.

On the personal level, the 1867 edition also presented some new aspects, of a rather negative character to be sure. Several poems of "Calamus" which contained intimate and hardly disguised confessions were now excluded from the book. Among these were Number 8, in which he proclaimed his great love for a man ("Long I thought that knowledge alone would suffice"); Number 9 ("Hours continuing long sore and heavy-hearted"), in which he lamented his lover's desertion; and Number 16 ("Who is now reading this?") in which he deplored his abnormal instincts.[101] There were in these poems too many transparent allusions to the emotional crisis he had undergone just before the war. He probably suppressed them out of prudence, but perhaps also because his feelings had changed in the interval. These confessions corresponded to a stage which he may have thought he had passed, since he had to some extent succeeded in sublimating his homosexual instincts in the course of his visits to the hospitals. Besides, the suppressions are not limited to these three poems. Here and there, even outside of "Calamus" and "Children of Adam" [102] where the more sensual pieces were concentrated, he discreetly eliminated a certain number of inessential sexual allusions; in "Song of Myself," for instance, where he canceled such verses as:

> We hurt each other as the bridegroom and bride hurt
> each other.[103]

Or:

> The most they offer for mankind and eternity less than
> a spirit of my own seminal wet.[104]

He had already begun this work of expurgation in the edition of 1860,[105] but the changes were very few; in 1867 the tendency was confirmed and amplified. Was this a denial of one part of himself? It seems not, since "Calamus" and "Children of Adam" remained almost unchanged. Perhaps he sometimes regretted his former aggressive frankness, but he was much too stubborn to erase the past and disavow what he had been. In 1860 he had refused to give way to Emerson's exhortations and he was now bound by that refusal. It seems in any case that in 1867 he endeavored to suppress whatever might have been too morbid in his book and that he wanted once again, as in the first two editions, to place the accent on the poet-prophet rather than on the lover.[106]

This partial submission to the exigencies of conventional morality which the 1867 *Leaves of Grass* reveals explains how the English edition of the book came to be published. A volume entitled *Poems by Walt Whitman* appeared in 1868 in London, under the imprint of J. C. Hotten and selected and edited by W. M. Rossetti.[107] The book contained none of the poems which at the time of their publication had brought down on Whitman so many reproaches and insults. In the classification adopted by Rossetti, there were no groups entitled "Calamus" or "Children of Adam"; from these two sections he kept only four poems, the most innocent and least sensual of all.[108] The problem of an expurgated edition had been posed from the moment that the question of publishing *Leaves of Grass* in England came up. Moncure D. Conway, whom Whitman had asked to sound out the publishers,[109] wrote to O'Connor that Swinburne, W. M. Rossetti, and J. C. Hotten were agreed that publication of the complete text was impossible. The publisher would immediately be prosecuted. Whitman, who very much wanted to be published in Great Britain, was rather easily persuaded to make the necessary concessions. On November 1, 1867, he wrote to Conway:

My feeling and attitude about a volume of selections from my *Leaves* by Mr. Rossetti, for London publication, are simply passive ones, yet with decided satisfaction that if the job is to be done, it is to be by such hands. . . I have no objection to his substituting other words — leaving it all to his own tact — for "onanist", "father-stuff", &c. &c. Briefly, I hereby empower him (since that is the pivotal affair and since he has the kindness to shape his action so much by my wishes — and since, indeed, the sovereignty of the responsibility is not mine in the case) to make verbal changes of that sort wherever, for reasons sufficient for him, he decides that they are indispensible.[110]

Thus he fully accepted the principle of changes such as those which he himself in 1867 had made in the 1860 text. But two months later he became panicky and felt that he had gone too far. He wrote directly to W. M. Rossetti this time to try to withdraw the authorization which he had given:

I hasten to write you that the authorization in my letter of Nov. 1st to Mr. Conway, for you, to make verbal alterations, substitute words, &c. was meant to be construed as an answer to the case presented in Mr. Conway's letter of Oct. 12. Mr. Conway stated the case of a volume of selections, in which it had been decided that the poems reprinted in London should appear verbatim, and asking my authority to change certain words in the preface to first edition of poems, &c. . . . I penned that authorization, and did not feel to set limits to it. But abstractly, and standing alone, and not read in connection with Mr. C.'s letter of Oct. 12, I see now it is far too loose, and needs distinct guarding. I cannot and will not consent, of my own volition, to countenance an expurgated edition of my pieces. I have steadily refused to do so here in my own country, even under seductive offers, and must not do so in another country. . . And now, my friend, having set myself right, in that matter, I proceed to say, on the other hand, for you and for Mr. Hotten, that if, before the arrival of this letter, you have practically invested in and accomplished, or partially accomplished, any plan, even contrary to this letter, I do not expect you to abandon it, at loss of outlay, but shall *bona fide* consider you blameless if you let go on and be carried out as you may have arranged. It is the question of the authorization of an expurgated edition proceeding from me that deepest engages me.[111]

It is clear that the outcome of this intervention mattered little to him and that he was ready to accept any conditions in order that the book might appear. He was really concerned only with the question of principle and wanted at all cost to avoid seeming to authorize the publication of an expurgated edition. He went so far as to add: "It would be better, in any introduction, to make no allusion to me as authorizing, or not prohibiting; &c." [112]

Finally, it *was* an expurgated edition that appeared, but Rossetti alone was responsible for it; Whitman had saved face. He would certainly have preferred that the complete 1867 text be published, but he had every reason to be satisfied with this partial victory, since without any cost to his self-esteem or any concession on his part, his collection had been relieved of the more compromising poems which would have limited its distribution in England as they had done in the United States. What is more, in his preface, Rossetti openly sided with Whitman against the absurd prudery of the public — though at the same time, to be sure, he condemned the sexual poems for aesthetic reasons. Not eager to acquire the reputation of a new Bowdler he had at any rate refused to mutilate a single poem. He had preferred to omit completely all those at which a delicate reader might have had to blush, and he was thus able to claim with some appearance of justice that his edition was not strictly speaking expurgated, but rather abridged.[113] However, this subtle distinction did not satisfy Whitman for long. In 1871 he attacked the problem again and tried to find another publisher who would agree to print the complete version, but F. S. Ellis, whom he had approached, shied off invoking exactly the same reasons as Conway.[114] The only edition of his poems to appear in England during his lifetime was therefore that of Rossetti, which in his old age he could not help referring to with bitterness and regret, forgetting the success it had achieved and the friendships it had brought him.[115]

But Whitman had other things on his mind besides these literary preoccupations. Political questions continued to interest and even to torment him. In 1867 he published in *Galaxy* an essay entitled "Democracy," in which he tried to refute the objections that Carlyle had raised against democratic principles in *Shooting Niagara*.[116] The following year he published in the same review an essay on what he called "Personalism," that is, on his conception of the relations between the individual and society in a democracy.[117] Finally, in 1871, he returned to the same problems in a small pamphlet of some eighty pages entitled *Democratic Vistas*.[118] This title was particularly well chosen; his gaze was turned away from the present and lost itself in the infinite perspectives of the future:

> The boundless vista and the horizon far and dim are
> all here. . .[119]

He was once more disappointed by reality, and this was precisely the reason why he felt the need of solemnly reaffirming his faith in democracy. Before the war, he had already had some doubts, but the heroism of the soldiers had dissipated them. Unfortunately, once the war was over, during the period of Reconstruction, corruption was more manifest than ever and politicians happily gave themselves up to it. Whitman had no illusions on this point. In *Democratic Vistas*, with ruthless lucidity, he unveiled all the hidden vices of American society and left out none of its turpitudes.[120] Carlyle himself had not been more pitiless. But, whereas Carlyle concluded that democracy was impossible, Whitman proclaimed that these flaws were accidental and that some day all would be well. He did not give up his dream; he only postponed its realization to a later time, and by that means, avoided pessimism and despair. This bold extrapolation enabled him to calm his fears and gracefully resolve the political problem which had again begun to trouble him. *Democratic Vistas* thus replied to certain cries of pain which had escaped him in the 1871 edition of *Leaves of Grass*. For instance:

> (Stifled, O days! O lands! in every public and private corruption!
> Smother'd in thievery, impotence, shamelessness, mountain-high;
> Brazen effrontery, scheming, rolling like ocean's waves around and upon you, O my days! my lands!
> For not even those thunderstorms, nor fiercest lightnings of the war, have purified the atmosphere;) [121]

Logic as well as chronology leads us now to a discussion of the fifth edition of *Leaves of Grass*,[122] which appeared the same year as *Democratic Vistas,* in 1871.[123] Like the 1867 edition, it lacked cohesion and consistency. Some copies consisted only of *Leaves of Grass* proper; others contained, besides *Leaves of Grass*, an annex called "Passage to India," with independent pagination, which however was also entitled "Leaves of Grass." [124] In some copies, there was also a second annex, "After All Not to Create Only," [125] which had already been published separately as a small pamphlet of twenty-four pages. The physical appearance of the book was again mediocre; it had a green cloth binding on the spine of which was stamped *Leaves of Grass — Complete —* and nothing else. The place and date were given on the title page: Washington, D.C., 1871, or 1872,[126] for there were two printings of this edition a year apart; but since they are identical, we will not distinguish them. As in some of the previous editions, the name of the author appeared only in the copyright notice. And, as in 1867, there was no portrait, perhaps again for reasons of economy, but the paper was of better quality.

Although the external appearance of the book was not much changed, the contents had undergone certain modifications. In the first place, the work of expurgation had quietly continued. For instance, this particularly disturbing verse of a "Song of Joys" disappeared from a passage which was to be completely suppressed in 1881: "O of men — of women toward me as I pass — The memory of only one look — the boy lingering and waiting." [127] The short poem entitled "To You" was also removed.[128]

But there were more important changes. This edition shows that the memory of the war was still haunting Whitman. He kept thinking about it. *Drum-Taps*, which in 1867 still remained outside the main body of the work, were now definitively incorporated and mingled in *Leaves of Grass*.[129] Not only that, but he had written new poems on the subject of the war. He had not forgotten those who had taken part in it, as is shown by "Adieu to a Soldier." [130] He still heard the "echoes of camps with all the different bugle-calls," the "sounds from distant guns with galloping cavalry." [131] He evoked again

> the sobs of women, the wounded groaning in agony,
> The hiss and crackle of flame, the blacken'd ruins, the
>   embers of cities,
> The dirge and desolation of mankind.[132]

And he anathematized war and its devastations:

> Away with themes of war! away with war itself!
> Hence from my shuddering sight to never more return
>   that show of blacken'd, mutilated corpses!
> The hell unpent and raid of blood, fit for wild tigers or
>   for lop-tongued wolves, not reasoning men. . .[133]

But he did not consistently maintain this purely negative attitude, which was merely a return to the pessimism of the darkest hours of 1863. He also celebrated the greatness of the Union which the war had saved, and he preached the reconciliation of the North and South.[134] This was nothing new, but

this time, he went much further. He no longer treated the war
from a local or national point of view; he gave it a universal
value. Instead of being a mere accident, it became an eternal
symbol; for he considered it now as an episode in the perpetual
struggle that humanity must carry on for liberty and the
triumph of democracy, for the "good old cause":

> To thee, old Cause!
> Thou peerless, passionate, good cause!
> Thou stern, remorseless, sweet Idea!
> Deathless throughout the ages, races, lands!
> After a strange, sad war — great war for thee,
> (I think all war through time was really fought, and
>   ever will be really fought, for thee;)
> These chants for thee — the eternal march of thee.[135]

He now saw life itself as a struggle and a continual war:

> I . . . sing war — and a longer and greater one than
>   any,
> . . . The field the world;
> For life and death, for the Body, and for the eternal
>   Soul. . .[136]

This is the underlying reason for the integration of *Drum-
Taps* into *Leaves of Grass*. Whitman now considered war —
war in general and not only the Civil War, war no longer in
its military form, but as an act of violent revolt — as a form of
human progress, as an aspect of life; and as such it became one
of the essential themes of his book. Accordingly he entitled
one of the new sections, "Marches Now the War is Over" [137]
and included in it some of the poems formerly in *Drum-Taps*.
After the war, the forward march was resumed, or rather
continued.

While this important transmutation was going on, the democratic character of *Leaves of Grass*, already strongly marked
in 1867,[138] was further accentuated, as is seen at the beginning
of the book if one compares the introductory poem, "One's

Self I Sing," with its original version, entitled "Inscription" in 1867. He considerably attenuated its individualism:

> Small is the theme of the following Chant, yet the greatest — namely ONE'S SELF — that wondrous thing, a simple, separate person. That, for the use of the New World, I sing.

became in 1871:

> One's self I sing, a simple separate person. . .[139]

And the last line in which he had tried to establish a personal and almost physical contact, man to man, with the reader was dropped.[140] The essential ideas are the same in the two versions, but in 1871 the accent was clearly on man "en-masse"; the separate man, the individual, had, by comparison, almost disappeared. This was no accident. Whitman was fully aware of the new orientation of his work as is shown by this passage from the 1872 Preface:

> *Leaves of Grass* already published, is, in its intentions, the song of a great composite *Democratic Individual*, male or female. And following on and amplifying the same purpose, I suppose I have in my mind to run through the chants of this Volume, (if ever completed,) the thread-voice, more or less audible, of an aggregated, inseparable, unprecedented, vast, composite, electric *Democratic Nationality*.[141]

It was probably to strengthen this voice that he regrouped a certain number of poems under the title of "Songs of Insurrection" [142] and wrote by way of introduction some unusually violent lines:

> Still though the one I sing,
> (One, yet of contradictions made,) I dedicate to Nationality,
> I leave in him revolt, (O latent right of insurrection! O quenchless, indispensable fire!) [143]

This glorification of revolt can be explained by reference to the historical context. The edition of 1871–72 appeared in the midst of the "Gilded Age." [144] Taking advantage of the unprecedented prosperity of the United States after the Civil War, employers engaged in a shameless exploitation of their workers, who had no legal protection whatever. Whitman was aware of it, and it disturbed him, as is shown by this note which he seems at one time to have considered publishing as an introduction to his "Songs of Insurrection":

Not only are These States the born offspring of Revolt against mere overweening authority — but seeing ahead for Them in the future, a long, long reign of Peace with all the growths, corruptions and tyrannies & formalisms of Obedience, (accumulating, vast folds, strata, from the rankness of continued prosperity and the more and more insidious grip of capital) I feel to raise a note of caution (perhaps unneeded alarm) that the ideas of the following cluster will always be needed, that it may be worth while to keep well up, & vital, such ideas and verses as the following. [145]

Thus the nascent social problem was already beginning to trouble him. He was apparently thinking less and less of himself and more and more of the human society of which he was a member. This is far from the subjectivism of *Leaves of Grass* in 1855 — or even in 1860. The starting-point is no longer himself, but frequently an event outside himself. Several of the new poems are occasional. This is a new aspect in the development of *Leaves of Grass*, but one which was to grow in importance in the years to come. For example the long poem entitled "After All Not to Create Only" was composed expressly to be read during the inaugural ceremony of the 40th Annual Exhibition in New York at the invitation of the sponsors. [146] "Passage to India," though its inspiration was personal, was written on the occasion of the opening of the Suez Canal, the completion of the North American railroad, and the laying of the Atlantic marine cable. [147] "Brother of All, with Generous Hand" was a tribute to the memory of a philanthropist, George Peabody,[148] and "The Singer in Prison" commemorated a concert given by the soprano, Parepa Rosa, at Sing-Sing.[149] "A Carol of Harvest for 1867" [150] was also an occasional poem, as the title indicates.[151]

"As a Strong Bird on Pinions Free." [152] must also be added to this list, since Whitman, on the invitation of a group of students, was to read it at the Dartmouth College Commencement on June 26, 1872. He had written the poem especially for the occasion, and he published it separately in 1872 [153] with several others composed since the publication of the 1871 edition.[154] Among these was another occasional piece, "O Star of France," particularly moving to the French since it expressed his pity and admiration for France at the time of her defeat by Prussia.[155]

From the frequency of such poems one might ask oneself whether it was a question of a voluntarily more democratic poetry or whether the inspiration of the poet was declining. Apparently Whitman himself was aware of a certain loss of power, for he wrote in the preface to "As a Strong Bird on Pinions Free": ". . . the present and any future pieces from me are really but the surplusage forming after that Volume [*Leaves of Grass*] or the wake eddying behind it. . . it may be that mere habit has got dominion of me, when there is no real need of saying anything further. . ." [156]

He no longer had the health or the vigor of old; he was tired. Sometimes, as we have seen, he even felt death approaching.[157] But, in general, he did not let himself be discouraged,[158] and in his preface, after having expressed his fears concerning the value of his present inspiration, he announced his decision to continue writing on new themes and particularly on the prodigious development of contemporary America: "I have the ambition of devoting yet a few years to poetic composition. . . . The mighty present age! To absorb, and express in poetry any thing of it. . ." [159]

Thus, in spite of his fatigue and of the decline of his inspiration, he did not lose heart. The old fighter was not yet vanquished. To the personal crisis which he went through in the course of these postwar years and to the political crisis which the country was undergoing, he opposed the same tenacious will to live, the same steadfast faith in the future. The personal optimism of "In Cabin'd Ships at Sea" is matched by the political optimism of "One Song, America, before I Go."

> One song, America, before I go. . .
> For thee — the Future.
> Belief I sing — and Preparation;
> As Life and Nature are not great with reference to the
>   Present only,
> But greater still from what is to come. . .[160]

echoes:

> In cabin'd ships at sea,
> The boundless blue on every side expanding. . .
> Or some lone bark buoy'd on the dense marine,
> Where joyous full of faith, spreading white sails,
> She cleaves the ether mid the sparkle and the foam of
>   day. . .
> Here not the land, firm land, alone appears. . .
> We feel the long pulsation, ebb and flow of endless
>   motion. . .
> The boundless vista and the horizon far and dim are
>   all here. . .
> Then falter not O book, fulfil your destiny. . .
> You too as a lone bark cleaving the ether, purpos'd I
>   know not whither, yet ever full of faith. . .[161]

In both cases the solution of the crisis is the same: Whitman took refuge in the future, or more precisely — for it was not a question of cowardly flight, but of a journey toward something — he threw himself with impatient fervor forward in the direction of his destiny and that of his country.

This was the nature of his work during the period of Reconstruction, but how was it received? Immediately after the

war, his good works in the hospitals had earned him the
respect of everyone, while the scandal of his dismissal by
Harlan and the violent campaign conducted in his favor by
O'Connor had given him a certain notoriety. *Drum-Taps* had
been praised by the critics. He thought for a time that he was
about to receive the recognition he felt he deserved. During a
visit in 1867 to F. P. Church, the editor of *Galaxy*, he had the
impression that he was being given special consideration, as if
he were regarded as one of the great forces in American
literature:

. . . the Galaxy folks have received and treated me with
welcome warmth and respect. . . The indirect and inferential
of his tone and words in speaking to me would have satisfied your
highest requirements — they evidently meant that in his opinion
I was, or was soon to be, "one of the great powers." [162]

Following this interview he was able to publish his two
articles on democracy [163] in *Galaxy*; and Church had earlier
published "A Carol of Harvest for 1867." [164] It was the first
time since his contributions to the *Democratic Review* that
he had succeeded in publishing anything in a magazine. His
joy was understandable. He must have thought that the
quarantine in which he had been placed by the *literati* was at
an end.[165]

When the 1867 edition appeared, the reviews were again
favorable. There were still a few sullen critics to renew the
habitual reproach of obscenity — such as the reviewer of the
Round Table who compared "To a Common Prostitute" with
a licentious poem by Catullus — [166] but in general they preferred not to dwell on that aspect of his inspiration or on his
lack of art; but tried rather, like the reviewer in *The Nation*,
to emphasize his democratic message, which indicates that
they were aware of the change of direction in his work and
that they appreciated it.[167] This approval can easily be explained. The Civil War had brought the victory of the demo-

cratic North over the aristocratic South, and the North, as a result of the conflict, had become more clearly aware of the meaning and value of its civilization. In short, Whitman had in this respect merely followed the general development of his country — or more precisely, since in spite of his pessimism in 1859–60 his faith in democracy had always been strong — the war had prepared his country for a better understanding of his political doctrine.

However, in spite of the increased understanding of the critics and the larger public thus drawn to his work, he still did not obtain the triumphant success of which he had dreamed. And, paradoxically, it was not in the United States, the chosen land of democracy, but in England, a country which he had hitherto regarded as feudal, that he found at this time his most fervent admirers.[168] On July 6, 1867, W. M. Rossetti published in the London *Chronicle* an enthusiastic article in which he described *Leaves of Grass* as the poetical masterpiece of the century.[169] This compliment must have been particularly pleasing to Whitman, for Rossetti attributed to his poetry all the artistic qualities that most of the American critics had denied him. When the English edition of *Leaves of Grass* appeared a few months later, it was enthusiastically welcomed by the press, and Whitman was profoundly moved: ". . . it flushed my friends and myself too, like a sun dash, brief, hot, and dazzling," [170] he wrote to Hotten, his publisher, with reference to a review in the London *Morning Star*. He had already expressed his gratitude to Conway:

Indeed, my dear friend, I may here confess to you that to be accepted by these young men of England, and treated with highest courtesy and even honor, touches me deeply. In my own country, so far, — from the press, and from authoritative quarters, I have received but one long tirade of impudence, mockery, and scurrilous jeers. Only since the English recognition have the skies here lighted up a little.[171]

Here he darkened the picture somewhat, for "the press . . .

and authoritative quarters," had never, as we have again and again noticed, been unanimous in condemning his poetic experiments. It is true that his public had never been large, and that he had sometimes been violently attacked, but the connoisseurs from 1855 on had supported and encouraged him. His complaints were therefore exaggerated, but during his remaining years we will encounter other manifestations of this strange self-pity, an after-effect of his wounded pride.

Whitman had some reason to be proud of the success he had achieved in England, for as soon as Rossetti's selected *Poems* appeared, a strong movement in his favor sprang up in English literary circles. Writers as different as Robert Buchanan [172] and Swinburne [173] took up his cause. Soon afterwards, Alfred Austin, in his book on contemporary poetry, devoted a whole chapter to him under the title of "The Poetry of the Future." [174] Mrs. Herbert Gilchrist, seeing in *Leaves of Grass* a declaration of love to the world in general and to herself in particular, published in May 1870 in the *Boston Radical* "A Woman's Estimate of Walt Whitman," a passionate and unreserved tribute. Its principal merit in Whitman's eyes was probably that it absolved him of the charge of obscenity. She had written:

> Nor do I sympathize with those who grumble at the unexpected words that turn up now and then. . . If the thing a word stands for exists by divine appointment (and what does not so exist?), the word need never be ashamed of itself.[175]

Most of the American critics had condemned him either for his lack of art or for his grossness, and now Rossetti and Mrs. Gilchrist in turn justified him on both counts. It must have been a pleasant balm for his wounded self-esteem. He was so delighted with this unexpected succour that he immediately arranged to have these articles distributed to the American newspapers and magazines.[176]

Also his fame began to extend beyond the frontiers of the

English-speaking world. In 1868, Ferdinand Freiligrath published three articles accompanied by translations in the *Augsburger Allgemeine Zeitung*.[177] In France, as early as 1868, Amédée Pichot spoke of him in the *Revue Britannique*[178] and a few years later Mme Bentzon presented him to the general public in the *Revue des Deux Mondes* under the somewhat ironic title, "Un Poète Américain, Walt Whitman: Muscle and Pluck Forever."[179] Emile Blémont devoted several pages to him in his *Renaissance Littéraire et Artistique*.[180] He was even discussed in Denmark, where Rudolf Schmidt saw him as the bard of American democracy.[181]

All these articles were very encouraging to Whitman; he had them translated and he circulated them as widely as he could.[182] He probably regarded them as a means of persuading the American public that outside the United States he was considered as the spokesman and representative of America.[183] And, in many ways, the victories which he had enjoyed in Europe consoled him for the relative indifference of his fellow-countrymen. He needed this comfort. It was at this time that he wrote "My Legacy," in which, comparing his own life to that of a rich businessman, he concluded with a rather bitter resignation under the apparent idealism:

> But I my life surveying,
> With nothing to show, to devise, from its idle years,
> Nor houses nor land — nor tokens of gems or gold for
>   my friends,
> Only these Souvenirs of Democracy.[184]

Still, even in America, he also had warm admirers, particularly his friend John Burroughs who, in 1867, published his *Notes on Walt Whitman as Poet and Person*,[185] an apologetic work in which Whitman collaborated shamelessly, for it has been demonstrated that he wrote the first few chapters himself.[186] William O'Connor, who had already shown his mettle in *The Good Gray Poet*, went even further. In 1868, in a story entitled *The Carpenter*, he presented Christ as having the physical and moral traits of Whitman.[187] In this instance apologetics had turned to hagiography.

Thus, in spite of the temporal failure which he lamented in "My Legacy," Whitman had no reason for despair. Since the war his position had greatly improved. The "good gray poet" had acquired a universal esteem, and from this time on it was impossible to treat him with contempt. Some critics regarded him as the greatest poet or one of the greatest poets of the century. To some fanatics he appeared as a saint or a prophet, as the equal of Christ or Buddha. In the space of a few years his renown had become international.

Moreover, the 1871 edition of *Leaves of Grass* sold well, and Whitman congratulated himself on this fact in a letter to Peter Doyle in July of the same year: "I am doing well, both in health and *business prospects* here — my book is doing first rate — so everything is lovely." [188]

The book succeeded so well that he issued a second printing the following year. In Great Britain this new edition attracted the attention of an academic critic, Edward Dowden, who devoted an entire essay to it.[189] Whitman was very pleased with this tribute. He appreciated its measured but in general very flattering tone.[190]

This notoriety however still fell short of true fame. As John C. Dent noted in an essay on "America and Her Literature":

It is within the bounds of probability that Walt Whitman will be compelled to pass through quite as fiery an ordeal in America as erewhile fell to the lot of Wordsworth in England; but, if so, we here beg to record our sincere conviction that the ultimate result in his case will be the same as was that in the case of Wordsworth.[191]

But, before undergoing this trial, Whitman was to experience another, a more cruel one, that of illness and suffering.

CHAPTER VIII

THE HEROIC INVALID (1873–1876)

ON January 23, 1873, Whitman woke up paralyzed on the left side and threatened with death if another attack should occur. But instead of sinking into despair, he accepted the tragic situation,[1] and without complaining or lamenting, clung with all his strength to what life remained in him. Slowly, very slowly, he recovered. He was attended by one of the best physicians in Washington, Dr. W. B. Drinkard, who treated him according to the newest methods with electricity.[2] In a few weeks, his improvement was evident; and at the end of March he went back to his office, but he was still unable to work regularly. Then bad news came from Camden. His mother, who was now living with George, was very ill. Although he was hardly in a condition to travel, Whitman went to her bedside at once on May 20. Three days later his mother was dead, and he was plunged into intense grief. In August he wrote to Peter Doyle: ". . . it is the great cloud of my life — nothing that ever happened before has had such an effect on me. . ."[3]

And, in 1875, when he published the sixth edition of *Leaves of Grass*, he was still thinking of her:

I occupy myself arranging these pages for publication, still envelopt in thoughts of the death two years since of my dear Mother, the most perfect and magnetic character, the rarest combination of practical, moral and spiritual, and the least selfish, of all and any I have ever known — and by me O so much the most deeply loved. . .[4]

This loss was all the more cruel as it came only a few weeks after the death of his sister-in-law, Martha, for whom he always had a great deal of affection.[5]

Destiny seemed set against him: 1873 was for him a terrible year. Still he kept up his courage. Ten days after his mother's death, he returned to Washington [6] and discharged his duties as well as he could, though he was still under medical care. But, in June, when hot weather came, he was obliged to ask for two months' leave. He hoped to find rest and fresh air on the New Jersey coast, but he fell ill on the way, at Philadelphia, and had to take refuge with George at Camden.[7] Thus he was led by chance to the city where he was to reside until his death.

In spite of this relapse, probably caused by his family losses, he again recovered little by little. His slow progress can be followed in the letters that he regularly sent to Peter Doyle. In July, the headaches from which he had been suffering abated and became less frequent.[8] He had good hope of regaining his health, but he sometimes thought of death with great courage and complete resignation.[9] In September, he began to feel much better. His strength was returning. He was thought to be suffering from cerebral anaemia, and this diagnosis reassured him: his life was not in danger, all that he needed was patience. He took no medicine, but he was careful to guard against any excess.[10] Although he moved only with difficulty, he refused to let himself go and went out as often as he could, even as far as Philadelphia.[11] But sometimes the slow pace of his progress discouraged him, and the frequency with which he noticed announcements of deaths due to paralytic attacks in the newspapers troubled him.[12] He went so far as to make a new will.[13] Still he never lost hope.[14] His courage was steadfast and his morale high. He suffered most from loneliness, although he lived with his brother, and his sister-in-law took very good care of him. He missed his Washington friends. He knew no one at Camden as yet and was so lonesome at times that he felt the need of a dog to keep him company.[15]

The setting must also have been depressing. Camden was, and still is, to a large extent a gray, dirty, industrial suburb. He could not but feel severely deprived after having known the nobly designed avenues of Washington, the vibrant life of New York, and the open spaces of Long Island. Yet he did not complain and seems to have accepted the situation calmly. In this, his natural passivity was a great help. Instead of worrying and chafing, he bore the trial calmly. When his brother moved to Stevens Street, not far from the railroad track, Whitman, as usual, took possession of the attic in the new house [16] and spent his time watching the trains go by.[17] Perhaps it was at this time that he wrote "To a Locomotive in Winter," [18] which shows that he quickly became aware of the powerful beauty of steam-engines, which none of the poets of his time had as yet been able to see. Thus he succeeded in escaping the apparent ugliness of his surroundings.

But he soon had other reasons for uneasiness. When he found himself unable to resume his duties in Washington, he obtained permission to hire a substitute, one Walter Godey. After paying Godey's salary, he still had enough money to live on. But this arrangement could not last for ever. At the end of a year, in July 1874, though Whitman had tried an appeal to the President, the post which he occupied was abolished,[19] and he suddenly found himself without resources.

True, he was not condemned to absolute poverty, for he had some savings; but deprived from then on of any steady income, he could not help being worried about the future, even though, in the letter announcing this bad news to Peter Doyle, he pretended to be indifferent.[20]

Interminable illness, spiritual isolation and lack of sympathy, ugliness of the surroundings in which he was obliged to live, financial insecurity — the picture was gloomy. "Ah, the physical shatter and troubled spirit of me the last three years!" he exclaimed in *Specimen Days*.[21] And it was at that time that he wrote "Prayer of Columbus," [22] in which he identified himself with the "Great Admiral" "near the close of his indomitable and pious life," when in Jamaica in 1503 "death seem'd daily imminent." [23]

Like Christopher Columbus, he was "a batter'd, wreck'd old man," "sicken'd and nigh to death," "sore" and with a "heavy heart"; [24] and the prayer that Columbus offered up to God was undoubtedly his own:

Thou knowest the prayers and vigils of my youth,
Thou knowest my mandhood's solemn and visionary
    meditations,
Thou knowest how before I commenced I devoted all to
    come to Thee,
Thou knowest I have in age ratified all those vows and
    strictly kept them,
Thou knowest I have not once lost nor faith nor ecstasy
    in Thee. . .[24]

Whitman was forgetting his moments of doubt and his crises of despair, as he had the right to do since he had always surmounted them. And, once more, his faith sustained him; he reaffirmed it emphatically:

The urge, the ardor, the unconquerable will,
The potent, felt, interior command, stronger than
    words,
A message from the Heavens whispering to me in sleep,
These sped me on.[25]

He too, though his body betrayed him, though his hands and limbs were powerless and his brain was tortured, clung to God as his supreme and only certainty.[26] It was not only Whitman who was identified with Columbus, but Columbus who was confused with Whitman, since he is decribed as "old, poor and paralyzed," [27] which in reality he was not.

At the same time, Whitman identified himself with a great sequoia being cut down by lumberjacks, and he said farewell to the world:

> Farewell my brethren,
> Farewell O earth and sky, farewell ye neighboring waters,
> My time has ended, my term has come.[28]

He felt death coming, but it did not matter, he was ready to disappear since he would survive in the "race" he would leave behind and whose triumph was assured:

> . . . a superber race. . .
> For them we abdicate, in them ourselves. . .[29]

This certainty of animistic survival reassured him. The errors that had formerly tormented him were only "passing errors, perturbations of the surface." [30]

Thus, in 1874, one year only after his paralytic attack, he had regained his equilibrium and his serenity. He had emerged victorious from the terrible trial imposed on him by his illness. Though he wrote in 1875, "O how different the moral atmosphere amid which I now revise this Volume [*Two Rivulets*], from the jocund influences surrounding the growth and advent of *Leaves of Grass*," [31] the danger had been left behind and the crisis ended several months earlier. Suffering, in any case, is soon forgotten, and in writing these lines he greatly exaggerated the joy out of which his work had grown; for, as we have seen, each single edition of *Leaves of Grass* had been born of pain rather than of happiness.

His renewed optimism was not for himself alone; it extended equally to politics, in which nevertheless occasions for worry and despair were not lacking. It was the period of the Crédit Mobilier frauds, the Salary Grab, the Sanborn contracts, and the Whisky Ring. Political circles seemed hopelessly corrupt.[32] But Whitman preferred to ignore these turpitudes:

> Nay, tell me not to-day the publish'd shame,
> Read not to-day the journal's crowded page,
> The merciless reports still branding forehead after fore-
> head,
> The guilty column following guilty column.[33]

The poem in which he thus expressed his discouragement was not incorporated into *Leaves of Grass* during his lifetime; he published it in *Lippincott's Magazine* for March 5, 1873, and then put it out of his mind and his work. It is now found only in the posthumous section entitled "Old Age Echoes." All these scandals were to him merely temporary accidents, ripples on the surface; the deeper water was pure and tranquil; these blemishes did not affect the truth or the essential validity of democracy:

> Your million untold manly healthy lives, or East or
> West, city or country,
> Your noiseless mothers, sisters, wives, unconscious of
> their good. . .
> (Plunging to these as a determin'd diver down the deep
> hidden waters,)
> These, these to-day I brood upon — all else refusing,
> these will I con. . .[34]

In March 1874 he wrote in the same vein to Mrs. O'Connor:

Nelly, your last letter is very blue, mainly about political and public degradation. Sumner's death and inferior men etc. being rampant etc. I look on all such states of things exactly as I look on a cloudy and evil state of weather, or a fog, or a long sulk meteorological — it is a natural result of things, a growth of something deeper, has its uses and will hasten to exhaust itself and yield to something better.[35]

And, during the same period, in an article for the New York *Graphic*, he could claim, this time without restriction:

The present! Our great Centennial of 1 8 7 6 nigher and nigher at hand — the abandonment, by tacit consent, of dead issues — the general readjustment and rehabilitation, at least by intention and beginning, South and North, to the exigencies of the Present and Future — the momentous nebulae left by the convulsions of the previous thirty years definitely considered and settled by the re-election of General Grant — the Twenty-second Presidentiad well-sped on its course — the inevitable unfolding and developments of the tremendous complexity we call the United States. . .[36]

In this context the optimistic conclusion of the "Song of the Reedwood Tree" is not surprising:

Fresh come, to a new world indeed, yet long prepared,
I see the genius of the modern, child of the real and
    ideal,
Clearing the ground for broad humanity, the true
    America, heir of the past so grand,
To build a grander future.[37]

What gave him confidence above all was that it seemed to him on reflection that the worst was over:

Within my time the United States have emerged from nebulous vagueness and suspense, to full orbic, (though varied,) decision. . . and are henceforth to enter upon their real history — the way being now (i.e. since the result of the Secession War,) clear'd of death-threatening impedimenta.[38]

Reasoning by analogy in one of his poems,[39] he compared his country to a thrush which transformed the loathsome worms that nourished it into songs of ecstatic joy. For him comparison was synonymous with reason: the United States would also some day transform the meannesses and the scandals which for the moment its citizens fed on into harmony and beauty. Then their "joyous trills" would "fill the world."

This grandiose future which awaited America reassured him concerning his own destiny and that of his work:

Shadowy vast shapes smile through the air and sky,
And on the distant waves sail countless ships,
And anthems in new tongues I hear saluting me.[40]

Thus, oppressed by illness, confined to Camden and to the present by his paralysis, he consoled himself by imagining his coming apotheosis in a radiant future. It was an effective consolation, since it freed him from the worry which his health and the political situation might otherwise have caused.

At the end of 1875, in spite of his occasional uneasiness,[41] he was feeling distinctly better. He was able to undertake, in the company of John Burroughs, a three-week trip to Washington and to Baltimore, where he attended the reburial of Poe's remains.[42] In the spring, he felt restless and planned other trips; he even declared himself ready to go to England.[43]

As usual, however, the clearest sign of his recovery was the publication of a new edition of *Leaves of Grass*, the sixth, which he called the "Centennial Edition," in honor of the centennial of the United States for which he was waiting with so much impatience in 1874. The new edition was ready by the end of 1875 [44] and appeared in 1876; of course, at the author's expense. It consisted of two volumes priced at ten dollars. The first volume was merely a reprint of the fifth edition. Only the second volume included new pieces, and curiously, it was not entitled *Leaves of Grass*, but *Two Rivulets*. It was made up of several pamphlets with separate pagination: first, "Two Rivulets" proper, which consisted of a preface and a collection of new poems accompanied by prose passages printed as notes to the poems; then "Democratic Vistas," a reprint of the 1871 text; four poems under the title "Centennial Songs," three of which were new; "As a Strong Bird on Pinions Free," a mere reprint; "Memoranda during the War," previously printed in the New York *Graphic*; and finally "Passage to India," which had appeared in 1871–72 as an appendix to *Leaves of Grass*.[45]

This volume was therefore truly a "melange," as Whitman said.[46] But what did the title mean? *Two Rivulets,* as he explained in various places,[47] referred first to the duality of form, since he sometimes used prose and sometimes poetry; and also, more important, to the duality of the subject, since the prose notes were devoted to politics, that is, to the actual, and the poems to immortality or the ideal. In short, the prose was objective and the poetry subjective.

The most striking aspect of the new poems was the importance attributed to death. It dominated the volume, and Whitman knew it. He recognized the fact in the Preface.[48] Whereas in *Leaves of Grass* the accent was placed on life and the body,[49] here he was obsessed by the thought of death and immortality. In this connection, the placing of "Passage to India" is symptomatic. In 1872 he had added it almost fortuitously as an appendix to the rest of *Leaves of Grass;* this time, he deliberately made it his farewell song to the reader and the conclusion of his two volumes. Certainly, as we have often noticed, death had always been an important theme in his work — he was perfectly aware of it himself — [50] but it is nonetheless true that this was the first time he had purposely given it so much emphasis.

This preoccupation is also related to a more general tendency. He was detaching himself more and more from the actual, from the material, in order to devote himself exclusively to the spiritual. This tendency to spiritualization is particularly marked in the poem with the curious title "Eidólons" where objects are replaced by their eternal archetypes. Evanescent material appearances give way to the true reality which is spiritual.[51] The ideal triumphs over the real. Instead of celebrating the vigor and magnificent nonchalance of the oxen as in 1855, Whitman now reserved his admiration for the old farmer who dominates them with all the spiritual force which is in him.[52]

In the ideal world in which he was now living, he was no longer as sensitive as before to the ugliness of reality. Thus, in "Song of the Universal," he eliminated the problem of evil by giving it a Hegelian solution:

> In spiral routes by long detours
> (As a much-tacking ship upon the sea,)
> For it the partial to the permanent flowing,
> For it the real to the ideal tends.[53]

This process of idealization was general and even affected politics:

Has not the time come, indeed, in the development of the New World, when its Politics should ascend into atmospheres and regions hitherto unknown — (far, far different from the miserable business that of late and current years passes under that name) — and take rank with Science, Philosophy and Art?. . .[54]

He similarly idealized his whole past life. He remembered only the moments of happiness: "the jocund influences surrounding the growth and advent of *Leaves of Grass*." [55] He neglected to speak of the painful crises through which he had passed, and he may really have forgotten them, unless he was making a distant allusion to them in "Out from Behind This Mask":

> (Tragedies, sorrows, laughter, tears — O heaven!
> The passionate teeming plays this curtain hid!). . .
> This film of Satan's seething pit. . .[56]

This idealization particularly affected the "adhesiveness" which Whitman had celebrated in "Calamus" and the purely sexual significance of which we have noted. That which had originally been, as he himself recognized, an "irresistible and deadly urge" became now a "never-satisfied appetite for sympathy," a "boundless offering of sympathy" and "universal democratic comradeship." [57] Thus he belatedly took cognizance

in 1876 of the transformation which we have seen in his
personality since the period of the Civil War. In the same
way "Calamus," which had been at first an expression of his
own Self, now acquired an essentially political meaning that
it certainly had not had before.

Besides, important as they are in my purpose as emotional
expressions for humanity, the special meaning of the *Calamus*
cluster of *Leaves of Grass*. . . mainly resides in its Political
significance. . .[58]

Thus Whitman changed the whole character of the book
by emphasizing the importance of the theme of democracy at
the expense of the theme of individuality. He tried to make
his work seem more impersonal and less egoistic than it had
been in the beginning by attributing to some of his earlier
poems a significance that properly belonged only to his most
recent writings.

In addition, as the Preface of *Two Rivulets* shows, he was
becoming more clearly aware of the basic premises of *Leaves
of Grass*. In particular he distinguished two themes on which
he had not previously passed judgment, science and industry,
even though he had long ago included them in his poems.
He was now, he claimed, "joyfully accepting Modern Science,
and loyally following it without the slightest hesitation," [59] and
on occasion he drew his inspiration from the great industrial
expositions, "the majestic outgrowths of the Modern Spirit
and Practice." [60]

Such were in 1876 the new characteristics of Whitman's
book, but the fact is that the new material in *Two Rivulets*
was meager. There were only seventeen new poems (most of
them, besides, were very short) since 1872, that is to say, in
four years, though he had no longer to spend his time making
a living. His productiveness had greatly declined. His illness,
although he had conquered it, had weighed on him heavily;

he found it very difficult now to do any creative work; he hardly
did more than revise and rearrange what he had already
written. But, at least, he did not renounce anything that he
had done — a proof that he remained essentially himself.
Upon rereading his book, he declared himself well pleased:

> Ere closing the book, what pride! what joy, to find them,
> Standing so well the test of death and night! [61]

And, we might add, of illness and suffering.

His fatigue — already apparent in 1871–72 — was betrayed in particular, as in the preceding edition, by the frequency
of occasional poems. There are two in *Two Rivulets*: "Spain,
1873–'74" [62] and "An Old Man's Thought of School," [63] which
was read at Camden on October 31, 1874, at the inauguration
of a public school. "Centennial Songs" contained another,
much more important, "Song of the Universal," which Whitman composed for the Tufts College Commencement in June
1874.[64] He was, of course, unable to attend; he could only
send the poem, which was read for him.[65]

Another symptom of the decline of his creative power is
the increasingly intellectual tone of his poems. "Eidólons" is
characteristic of his new manner. He no longer concerned
himself now with the concrete details which swarmed in
"Song of Myself"; he preferred to philosophize. His instinctive
pantheism has become a kind of dessicated Hegelianism. This
intellectualization can be seen also in the suddenly increased
proportion of prose in his work. In the second volume of the
Centennial Edition it almost smothered the poetry, and in
the section entitled "Two Rivulets" it even intrudes into the
poems in the form of footnotes running parallel to the poetic
text, but unrelated to it.

The two volumes of the Centennial Edition appeared at
the beginning of March 1876. As usual, Whitman, incorrigibly
optimistic, hoped that they would sell well and that the

profits would permit him to repair his finances and even to buy a small house where he would be completely independent.[66] It seemed to him that the occasion was propitious and that people would celebrate the centenary of the American Republic by purchasing the works of the spokesman of democracy. Unfortunately, the Centennial Edition was very coolly received by American critics. They no longer insulted him — since the Civil War the fashion had changed — but they affected to treat him with contempt as a second-rate poet. This was the tone, for instance, of the review in *The Hour,* though it was in general favorable enough: "No doubt he overrates himself, and his friends overrate him. But still the man has a touch of something uncommonly like poetic fire." [67] A few weeks later, Charles F. Richardson expressed almost the same opinion in the New York *Independent*: "His gold is very bright; but its tiny nuggets are embedded in disproportionate masses of earth and organic matter . . . He is a poet of the second rank among American bards . . ." [68]

This reception must have discouraged Whitman somewhat. In an anonymous article printed by the *West Jersey Press,* May 24, 1876 — which, if he did not write it himself, he at least inspired — he complained not bitterly, but sadly of having been the victim of a veritable conspiracy of silence:

Down to the present time, and to this hour, not one leading author of the United States (Whitman says grimly he is "getting to be rather proud of it") is friendly in either a personal or professional mode to *Leaves of Grass* or Whitman himself. Will it not prove a pretty page of the history of our literature a couple of decades hence, that in 1874-5 Emerson, Bryant and Whittier each made great Omnibus-gatherings of all the current poets and poetry — putting in such as Nora Perry and Charles Gayler and carefully leaving Walt Whitman out? Not a magazine in America — not a single well-established literary journal — will to-day, on the usual terms, accept and issue his productions. Not a publisher will bring out his book (which to this hour has never been really published at all). . .[69]

The facts which he mentioned were generally correct. Although the 1860 edition of *Leaves of Grass* had been issued by a publisher, the venture, as we have seen, had turned out badly because of the Civil War. Also, *Harper's Monthly* in 1874 had accepted the "Song of the Redwood Tree" and "Prayer of Columbus," [70] but these favors had not lasted; the editors had soon rejected his contributions like the others. The only periodical which had offered Whitman the hospitality of its columns during this period had been the New York *Graphic*, [71] but it was a daily newspaper with no prestige and the consolation was slight.

This was the situation when, unexpectedly, Robert Buchanan, having read in the London *Athenaeum* [72] the article of the *West Jersey Press* of January 26, 1876, published in the London *Daily News* for March 13, in the form of a letter to the editor, a violent attack against American writers who, in his opinion, were guilty of neglecting the greatest poet of the United States and even of conspiring against him. He compared them to a flock of crows harrying an old eagle.[73] These insulting insinuations raised a general outcry in the American press. On March 28 (the London papers at the time took two weeks to get to the United States), Bayard Taylor and G. W. Smalley protested in the New York *Tribune* against the subscription which was being taken up in England for Whitman, claiming that he had no need of financial assistance. On March 30 and April 12 Bayard Taylor renewed his attack, even going so far as to revive against Whitman the old charge of obscenity. Naturally, Whitman's friends did not remain inactive. On April 13, Burroughs came to his defense in a long letter which occupied an entire column of the *Tribune*. Then, on April 22, O'Connor in his turn came into the lists, striking at Whitman's enemies with an article of two columns, to which Taylor replied in the same issue.[74] The battle then spread and was soon raging in other papers. The New York *Herald*, after having published on April 1 an article by John Swinton which described Whitman's poverty and called on the public to help him, contained the next day an anonymous protest, the author of which, though praising Whitman for his faith in democracy, condemned his "naked nastiness" and concluded, "even Mr. Buchanan will admit that in a country where women can read, it would be hard to circulate his prophet." [75] This attack was the more perfidious in that it pretended to be impartial. During the same month, an equally hostile article was published in *Scribner's* by J. G. Holland, to whom Charles A. Dana replied on April 28 in the New York *Sun,* defending Whitman against "Tupper Holland," as he ironically called him.[76]

It appears from all this that even in the United States, Whitman had about as many friends as he had enemies, since whenever he was attacked, someone rose in his defense. Moreover, though some of the critics tended to dig up forgotten grievances which might adversely have affected the sale of *Leaves of Grass,* this controversy had on the whole the good effect of drawing public attention to Whitman and his work. It was, in short, good publicity. However, it was chiefly in England that his book sold, thanks to the exertions of Buchanan and Rossetti.[77] Many subscribers came to his aid by sending two or three times the price of his two volumes, among them Lord Houghton, Edward Dowden, Tennyson, Ruskin, Edmund Gosse, George Saintsbury, and Ford Madox Brown.[78] The literary and artistic élite of Great Britain gave him financial and moral support, and his reputation spread as far as Australia.[79] It was a powerful encouragement for him. As he later declared to Traubel:

I was down, down, physically down, my outlook was clouded: the appearance of that English group was like a flash out of heaven. . .[80]

Those blessed gales from the British Isles probably (certainly) saved me.[81]

Even his health was favorably influenced. The pleasure of this unexpected success must have stimulated his system and accelerated his recovery. In December, he was able to write to Peter Doyle: "I certainly am feeling better this winter, more strength to hold out, walking or like, than for nearly now four years — bad enough yet, but still *decidedly better* . . ." [82] He could now face the future with confidence. The clouds which had darkened the horizon were gone; new victories were on the way.

CHAPTER IX

NEW VICTORIES (1876–1882)

IN September 1876, someone arrived in Philadelphia, who, if Whitman had been prepared, would have changed the course of his life. This person was his great English admirer, Mrs. Anne Gilchrist. When she first read *Leaves of Grass* in 1869 she had been immediately overcome. In the distracted cry of the mockingbird from Alabama seeking his lost mate, she had heard the voice of Whitman, and being a warm-hearted widow, she felt capable of filling the painful emptiness in the poet's life.[1] It seemed to her that *Leaves of Grass* was a call, a love-letter, and she was soon passionately in love with Whitman even though she had not met him. Her modesty and her respect for the conventions prompted her at first to maintain a certain reserve. She had to content herself with singing the praises of *Leaves of Grass*,[2] but it was not the work that attracted her so much as the man, and after several months she gave way and sent him an impassioned letter expressly offering him her love. Whitman, much embarrassed by this gift for which he had no use, kept silent, probably hoping that the flame would die out for lack of fuel. But Mrs. Gilchrist, extremely worried at receiving no answer, sent him a second letter, and this time he was forced to write to her; he could no longer leave her in doubt. Therefore he addressed to her on November 3, 1871, a very brief note which was

actually nothing but a friendly acknowledgment. This calculated coolness was not enough to discourage Mrs. Gilchrist;
she continued to send long, passionate letters to which Whitman replied from time to time with a few lines informing her
of the progress of his work and inquiring after the health of
her children, which was a way of reminding her that she owed
her first duty to them. In August 1873, however, after his
paralytic attack, he committed an error. He sent her a ring
which he had worn on his finger for a number of years.[3] He
was at that time very ill and sometimes wondered whether
he was not going to die. It was therefore natural enough for
him to offer her a remembrance, but the symbolic significance
of a ring was not without its dangers.

Mrs. Gilchrist, imagining that all her hopes were now
justified, began to speak of traveling to the United States.
Whitman turned a deaf ear, but she refused to give up her
project and, one day, early in 1876, she informed him that
all her preparations had been made and that she was coming
to Philadelphia with her three youngest children. This change
of scene, she said, would be greatly beneficial to her son
Herbert, a painter, and would permit her daughter Beatrice to
pursue in the United States the medical studies which she
could not undertake in England.[4] Whitman immediately advised her strongly against such a move and asked her not to
make a final decision yet — to await his arrival in London, at
which time they could discuss the matter. To dissuade her he
went so far as to speak slightingly of the United States.[5] But
nothing could stop Mrs. Gilchrist, and six months later she
was in Philadelphia. No one knows how the encounter went.
But one thing is certain: Whitman must have demonstrated
admirable tact since he remained the friend of this woman
whose dream he had failed to realize. As long as the Gilchrists
remained in Philadelphia, he regularly visited their home,
even for several days at a time.[6] But he refused to let himself

be adopted; he successfully resisted the temptation to settle down and remained the incorrigible Bohemian which he had always been. His independence had been seriously threatened, but he emerged victorious from the battle.

He was too fond of solitude ever to live permanently with another person. This characteristic immediately struck Edward Carpenter, who met him for the first time during this period at Mrs. Gilchrist's: "I have seldom known anyone who, though so cordial and near to others, detached and withdrew himself at times more decisively than he did, or who on the whole spent more time in solitude." [7] He needed the company of others, but solitude was equally necessary to him; hence his taste for the attics in which he had lived in boarding-houses and in the homes of his parents and of his brother. During the years he spent in his brother's house, he probably suffered as much from the impossibility of being sufficiently alone as from the lack of friends. He therefore escaped from Camden for weeks at a time as soon as his health allowed him to travel again. He took refuge not far away at Timber Creek, on the small farm of the Staffords, whose son Harry, a printer, he had become acquainted with in Philadelphia. Beginning in 1876 he went there regularly every summer and sometimes from early spring until autumn. In *Specimen Days* he has left an account — or rather a description, since nothing ever happened there — of his visits to this enchanting spot, among trees and flowers, in the company of birds and insects.[8] His notes are entirely spontaneous, for he recorded them in notebooks which he carried with him on these walks.[9] They are still full of country odors, the rustling of leaves, the cries of quail, and the buzzing of bees. Days passed peacefully while he watched the clouds go by and listened to the song of the cicadas.[10] He relaxed deliciously, enjoying to the full his newly recovered health. The only important events were the passing of migratory birds or an encounter with a saucy squirrel coming down from a tree to get a close look at him.[11] All these fascinating sights brought back his childhood from beyond the long years which he had spent in cities. Not being a professional naturalist, he did not observe them with the same precise care as his friend John Burroughs, but rather tried to absorb the "vital influences" with which they were loaded.[12] He abandoned himself to the pleasure of feeling nature live around him. It revived and stimulated his own vitality:

> After you have exhausted what there is in business, politics, conviviality, love, and so on — have found that none of these finally satisfy, or permanently wear — what remains? Nature remains; to bring out from their torpid recesses, the affinities of a man or woman with the open air, the trees, fields, the changes of seasons — the sun by day and the stars of heaven by night.[13]

He tried to be like his favorite poplar which, instead of trying to *seem,* was content with *being.*[14] It was probably at this time that he wrote the short poem entitled "Supplement Hours," published posthumously in "Old Age Echoes":

> Sane, random, negligent hours,
> Sane, easy, culminating hours,
> After the flush, the Indian Summer of my life,
> Away from Books — away from Art — the lesson
>   learn'd, pass'd o'er,
> Soothing, bathing, merging all — the sane, magnetic,
> Now for the day and night themselves — the open air,
> Now for the fields, the seasons, insects, trees — the
>   rain and snow,
> Where wild bees flitting hum,
> Or August mulleins grow, or winter's snowflakes fall,
> Or stars in the skies roll round —
> The silent sun and stars.[15]

But he was not content to lead a purely vegetative or contemplative life at Timber Creek, he also tried to shake off the torpor of his body and to reawaken the limbs deadened by paralysis. He exercised every day by wrestling with the trees. His favorite partner was a young hickory sapling with which he amused himself by bending the trunk and pulling with all his strength, but without roughness or jerkiness. The combat lasted about an hour and, after each round, he stopped to take a deep breath. During his walks, he similarly tested his returning vigor on low branches or saplings, along his way. It seemed to him that thanks to these "natural gymnasia" his benumbed muscles acquired the elasticity and robustness of the young trees and that the same clear sap circulated in his veins.[16]

In addition to these exercises, he had instituted a whole system of natural therapy based on sunbaths, mud-baths and nakedness, which he practiced in a well-hidden little dell, not far from the Stafford farm. The direct contact of his body with the sand, air, and water restored his vigor and made him a new man.[17]

The salutary effects of this treatment quickly made themselves felt. He was no longer a wreck stranded on the shore and slowly rotting. In 1877 he began to travel once more. He had been invited to New York by J. H. Johnston, a rich jeweler of his acquaintance, and his wife, and in March he spent several weeks with them. It was a triumphal time.[18] Receptions were given in his honor at the Liberal Club, at the Portfolio, and at the Palette Club. During one of the dinners, he delivered a speech on the question of feminism and recited some lines by Henri Murger.[19] These honors and entertainments probably did him as much good as his visits to Timber Creek. He needed warmth and sympathy in which to expand. So he visited the Johnstons again the following year on the occasion of W. C. Bryant's funeral.[20] Again he stayed in New York for nearly a month, during which he made an excursion to West Point and on up the Hudson to Esopus, where he called on his old friend John Burroughs at his country house. There he spent three delightful days, which he has recorded in *Specimen Days*.[21] On his return, he stopped again in New York. He never grew tired of the spectacle of this immense city, "bubbling and whirling and moving like its own environment of waters." [22]

He saw in this harmonious conglomerate life the best proof "of successful Democracy and of the solution of that paradox, the eligibility of the free and fully developed individual with the paramount aggregate." [23] He was an example of it himself. The "Mannahatta" which he had celebrated in 1856 had now welcomed him as a prodigal son. The New York *Tribune,* which had so often attacked him, now opened its columns to him.[24] He had been received as a celebrity, a satisfaction he highly appreciated.[25]

In 1879, his appetite for travel whetted by all these trips, he not only returned to New York [26] in order to give his first lecture on the death of Lincoln,[27] and to Esopus,[28] but he also undertook in September the longest journey of his life, traveling as far west as Colorado. He accompanied Colonel John W. Forney in order to participate in the celebration of the twenty-fifth anniversary of Kansas.[29] He went by way of Pittsburgh, Columbus, Indianapolis, and St. Louis, marveling as much at the comfort of the Pullman cars and the speed of the trains as at the wealth and immensity of the land.[30] On September 13, after a three days' journey, he arrived at Kansas City and went from there to Lawrence, where the ceremony was to take place; but he was so well entertained by the Mayor, John P. Usher, the Secretary of the Interior in Lincoln's administration, that he never got to the meeting at which he was supposed to speak. He was apparently not aware that he was expected to read a poem and had not prepared one. To make up for it, he wrote a message to the people of Kansas, which is reproduced in *Specimen Days*.[31] He then visited Topeka, the state capital, and pushing farther west, arrived at Denver on September 20. The Rocky Mountains attracted him, and he made an excursion to Pueblo, from where he was able to see Pike's Peak.[32] The Rockies did not disappoint him. These enormous piles of fantastic shapes, he thought, emanated "a beauty, terror, power, more than Dante or Angelo ever knew." [33] It seemed to him that he had found there the "law" and justification of his own poems. They had the same plenitude, the same total absence of art.[34] It was at this time that he wrote "Italian Music in Dakota," [35] "Spirit that Form'd this Scene," [36] and "The Prairie States," [37] which he was to publish in the 1881 edition of *Leaves of Grass*. Three rather slight poems were not much to show for such an impressive journey. His strength had returned, but his creative faculty was still benumbed.

On the way back, he stopped at Sterling, Kansas, to visit a Civil War veteran whom he had nursed in a Washington hospital and who had invited him to stay with him for the winter. The memory of the "wound-dresser" still lived. But Whitman continued on his way, and after a brief stay at Kansas City, arrived at St. Louis at the beginning of October. He intended to spend some time there with his brother Jeff and he stayed for three months. He was, in fact, forced by illness to prolong his visit; besides, he probably found himself short of money. As usual, he resigned himself easily to circumstances beyond his control and explored with lively interest the city where "American electricity" went so well, he thought, with "German phlegm." [38] He visited factories, schools, and slaughterhouses; he was interviewed for the local papers,[39] and he did not return to Camden until the beginning of January 1880.

He did not remain there long. In the middle of February, he went to Timber Creek for several weeks,[40] and on June 3 he was on his way to Canada to visit one of his admirers, Dr. R. M. Bucke, director of the insane asylum at London, Ontario.

On the way, he was able to see Niagara Falls from the train, and he remembered it always afterwards.[41] At the end of the trip he found himself ill again — [42] these frequent relapses show that, although he had recovered to some extent, he had not regained his former triumphant health. However, he was very well cared for, and three weeks later he was well enough to accompany his host on a long boat trip from Toronto to Quebec and even farther, since they went up the Saguenay as far as Chicoutimi.[43] They came back the same way, and in September Whitman returned to Camden with his head full of new impressions, but his work was not much richer for them. From this long trip he brought back only a thin notebook,[43] which furnished material for a few pages in *Specimen Days* [44] but not a single poem. Although more than once, as his travel notes show, he had been moved or interested, he had not felt the need to create. The sterility already evident on the occasion of his western journey was growing worse. Canada, in any case, had nothing new to offer him. The scenery was not essentially different from that of the United States, and he was not prepared by training or experience to appreciate the peculiarities of Canadian life. In the British part of the country he saw only militarism and in the French region nothing but stagnation and superstition.

All these journeys were undertaken in response to invitations, which proves that he did not lack friends or admirers, and he was warmly welcomed wherever he went. Every year large audiences attended his lecture on Lincoln to show their sympathy for him. Younger men regarded him as a master, among them Joaquin Miller, who wrote a poem in his honor in 1877,[45] and Edward Carpenter, who made a special trip to the United States to see him. Camden was beginning to attract pilgrims. Among other visitors he received Dr. Bucke in 1877 [46] and Longfellow in 1878.[47] The homage thus rendered by the author of "Evangeline" amounted to a consecration and moved him deeply. For, however great his confidence in his own genius, he did not find it displeasing to be treated as an equal by one of the most famous of the Harvard professors.

Yet, Whitman was not satisfied. In an interview for a St. Louis newspaper during his western trip, he complained (on behalf of the young, but actually it was his own grievance which he was airing) that the publishing houses and the reviews were controlled by "fossils," "old fogies" like Holland and "fops" like Howells.[48] Indeed he had some ground for irritation. In spite of the success of *Leaves of Grass* in England and even in America he had never succeeded in getting his articles or his poems accepted by the reviews. He complained bitterly of it in a letter to W. S. Kennedy:

. . . Did I tell you my last piece (poem) was rejected by the *Century* (R. W. Gilder). I have now been shut off by *all* the magazines here and the *Nineteenth Century* in England — and feel like closing house as poem writer — (you know a fellow doesn't make brooms or shoes if nobody will have 'em). . .[49]

And in 1880, he noted in his Canadian diary:

Received back to-day the MS. of the little piece of "A Summer Invocation," which I had sent to H.'s [*Harper's*] magazine. The editor said he returned it because his readers wouldn't understand any meaning to it. . .[50]

The principal reason for all these rejections was simply Whitman's reputation for indecency, as this letter from J. G. Holland, the editor of *Scribner's Monthly,* shows:

I have read Stedman's paper. His treatment of Whitman's indecency is excellent, and the old wretch can no longer defend it. Without any plea for morality and purely on artistic grounds, he demolishes all the old man's defenses and leaves him without any apology for adhering to his early smut. I shall find no fault with the rest, that is, I do not criticize it, though I cannot help feeling that Whitman does not in any measure deserve the great attention we are giving him. . . I am only troubled — in regard to this paper — by the thought that we are helping to bolster a reputation that has no legitimate basis on which to stand.[51]

Holland's uneasiness was not unjustified, for according to some people,[52] Stedman's article, which was very favorable in spite of its many reservations,[53] helped to bring Whitman to the attention of James R. Osgood and Company of Boston. However, it is more likely that Whitman's visit to that city in 1881 had something to do with the offer which Osgood made him for the publication of *Leaves of Grass*. For it was in Boston that Whitman gave his lecture on the death of Lincoln that year,[54] and he spent a full week there. The day after his talk, he returned the visit which Longfellow had made to him at Camden, and he was very cordially received.[55] He went to see Quincy Shaw's collection of Millet's paintings and remained to contemplate them for hours. The elemental strength of "The Sower" vividly impressed him, and all of Millet's somber, rought-cut peasants helped him to gain a better understanding of France.[56] On Sunday, April 17, he stood meditating in Memorial Hall at Cambridge before the long list of Harvard students killed in the Civil War.[57] After sixteen years, the memory of the war still haunted him. His stay in Boston thus was uneventful, but it drew attention to him. The Massachusetts newspapers reported his smallest movements and praised his lecture in enthusiastic reviews.[57] Osgood must have thought this sterling publicity, and, in any event, a poet who was a friend of Longfellow must certainly be a respectable author and a good investment.

However, the publisher's offer did not come immediately, and Whitman had time to return to Camden and spend a vacation at Timber Creek.[58] A few weeks later, toward the end of July, he went with Dr. Bucke to revisit the places where he had spent his childhood and youth on Long Island. He returned to Long Branch and Far Rockaway, where he bathed and walked naked on the beach, reciting poetry as of old.[59] Later they went as far as West Hills to have a look at Whitman's birthplace and at the cemetery where his ancestors lay.[60] It was not a melancholy pilgrimage, but it shows that he was living more and more in the past. On the way back, he stopped for several days in New York, where he also searched out his old haunts. He visited Pfaff, with whom he called up memories of the good old days before the Civil War and all the friends now dead or scattered.[61]

In spite of his premature old age and his relative lack of success, Whitman did not give way to sadness or despair, but braced himself against them. As he declared later to Traubel: " . . . it stiffens a fellow up to be told all around that he is not wanted, that his room is better than his company, that he has a good heart — that he can nurse soldiers but can't write poetry." [62] Deep in his own mind he persisted in the belief that he was right and that the future would justify him; and the improvement which he had observed in his position during the preceding years inclined him to optimism. As a reporter wrote in the Boston *Herald* in April 1881:

Walt Whitman has in times past been perhaps more ignorantly than wilfully misunderstood, but time brings about its revenges, and his present position goes to prove that, let a man be true to himself, however he defies the world, the world will come at last to respect him for his loyalty.[63]

It must have seemed to him that his patience was finally being rewarded when he learned through John Boyle O'Reilly that James R. Osgood and Company wanted to bring out a definitive edition of *Leaves of Grass*.[64] Of course, he accepted the offer at once, but he generously warned the publishers that "the sexuality odes about which the original row was started and kept up so long are all retained and must go in the same as ever." [65] They asked for a look at the text and were apparently not scandalized by Whitman's audacities for they accepted his conditions and promised him 12.5 per cent royalties.

In August, Whitman was in Boston again to supervise the printing of his new edition.[66] He remained for more than two months and enjoyed the visit very much. He saw Joaquin Miller almost every day and met various New England celebrities such as Longfellow, who came to see him again, O. W. Holmes, and Henry James, Sr.[67] But his greatest pleasure was to be invited to dinner at Emerson's during a visit with F. B. Sanborn at Concord.[68] The venerable philosopher, now seventy-eight years old, had completely lost his memory. He was almost incapable of taking part in a conversation and did not recognize Whitman. But physically he was still well preserved and his smiling presence was a source of great happiness to the poet of *Leaves of Grass.*

From the start, the Osgood edition had a very remarkable success. It sold about 2,000 copies during the winter of 1881–82,[69] and Whitman had reason to think that it was the end of his troubles and that he had finally succeeded. Unfortunately, on March 1, 1882, acting on a complaint of the Society for the Prevention of Vice, Oliver Stevens, District Attorney of Massachusetts, gave notice to the publisher that if he did not withdraw *Leaves of Grass* from circulation he would be prosecuted for printing and selling obscene literature.[70] Whitman was immediately informed, and not wanting to lose the support of an influential publisher, he offered to make concessions:

I am not afraid of the District Attorney's threat — it quite certainly could not amount to anything — but I want you to be satisfied, to continue as publishers of the book, (I had already thought favorably of some such brief cancellation). Yes, under the circumstances I am willing to make a revision and cancellation in the pages alluded to — wouldn't be more than half a dozen any how — perhaps indeed about ten lines to be left out & a half dozen words or phrases.[71]

But the District Attorney, upon being consulted, furnished a list of offensive passages [72] which included in addition to scattered lines three whole poems: "A Woman Waits for Me," "The Dalliance of the Eagles," and "To a Common Prostitute." This time, Whitman refused to give way: "The list whole and several is rejected by me, and will not be thought of under any circumstances." [73] The only concessions he offered were those he had already proposed: "I mail you with this a copy of *L of G*, with the not numerous, but fully effective changes and cancellations I thought of making: See pages 84 88 89 90 . . . The whole thing would not involve an expense of more than from 5 to $10." [73]

Thus he would have consented discreetly to censor the volume himself, but the poems which Stevens asked him to sacrifice seemed to him indispensable and irreproachable. So he felt that he had to hold fast and issue the revised volume in spite of the threat of prosecution: "My proposition is that we at once make the revision here indicated, & go on with the regular issue of the book. If then any further move is made by the District Attorney and his backer — as of course there is somebody behind it all — they will only burn their own fingers, & very badly." [74] But the publishers, wishing to avoid scandal at any price were unwilling to run this risk and suggested a compromise solution: to suppress the two most daring poems, "A Woman Waits for Me" and "To a Common Prostitute." [75] Whitman made no reply. They sent him a telegram requesting one. His answer was a refusal. [76]

At this point, the publishers had either to risk prosecution or capitulate and stop the sale of *Leaves of Grass*. Osgood, who was eminently respectable and did not want his name associated in the newspapers with a case involving obscene literature, preferred to give up without a fight. [77] Whitman therefore found himself again obliged to undertake the publication of his own book, which, undiscouraged, he did at once. He consoled himself by saying: "I tickle myself with the thought how it may be said years hence that at any rate no book on earth ever had such a history." [78]

Osgood having surrendered the plates of the Boston edition, Whitman made arrangements with a Camden printer to put on sale another edition exactly like the former one.[79] But the burden was too heavy for him and he soon concluded an agreement with Rees Welsh and Company of Philadelphia to publish the book. This was not a very happy choice. Several printings were quickly sold,[80] but Rees Welsh and Company printed some vulgar and ridiculous advertisements which offended Whitman's admirers.[81] As soon as he could Whitman chose another firm and had the good luck this time to find David McKay, who was to remain his publisher until his death.[82]

On the whole, Whitman had accepted Osgood's capitulation very philosophically. He had not protested against the action of the Boston District Attorney. Rather than rebelling and opposing the attack, he had preferred to shift his ground. He was stubborn, but not at all aggressive. The main thing for him was to publish *Leaves of Grass,* and as long as he succeeded, he did not care how it was done. Moreover he did not need to fight his own battle. As soon at it was known that Stevens had suppressed his book, a violent controversy broke out in the newspapers, many of which immediately supported him on the ground of freedom of thought.[83] The faithful O'Connor was of course in the front rank of his defenders, sending letter after letter to the New York *Tribune.*[84] The Reverend Mr. Morrow, a Methodist preacher in Philadelphia, supported him with equal fervor and vigorously opposed the suppression of *Leaves of Grass* in Pennsylvania.[85] But the most fanatical supporters of Whitman were the free-thinkers. Several groups in Massachusetts campaigned energetically for him, notably George Chainey, a former Baptist minister who had lost his faith and who preached free-thought every Sunday afternoon in Paine Memorial Hall in Boston. He devoted a lecture and an entire number of his journal, *This World*, to the defense of *Leaves of Grass* and particularly "To a Common Prostitute," which he quoted in its entirety. His audacity got him into trouble. The Boston postmaster refused to accept this issue of his journal on grounds of obscenity. It took an intervention by Robert Ingersoll with James H. Marr, Acting First Postmaster at Washington, to lift the embargo.[86]

Benjamin Tucker, too, launched a resounding challenge to Stevens and all the professional defenders of virtue by offering in *Liberty* to sell the proscribed book to anyone who wanted to buy it.[87] His enflamed prose suggests a thirst for martyrdom; however, he was not arrested. This good fortune came to Ezra Heywood of Princeton, Massachusetts, who published a small free-thought paper, *The Word*. Like Chainey he had printed the texts of "To a Common Prostitute" and "A Woman Waits for Me" in an issue of his periodical. Stevens had him arrested on the complaint of Anthony Comstock, Secretary of the Society for the Prevention of Vice. But when the case came to trial, Heywood was acquitted — much to Whitman's delight. "So Anthony Comstock retires with his tail intensely curved inwards," he wrote to O'Connor.[88] However, the campaign of the free-thinkers caused Whitman some discomfort. He did not want to be associated with them because he disapproved of the excesses of some of them who went so far as to advocate the practice of free-love. Therefore he kept aloof from all their activities. He even confided his doubts and hesitations to the fiery O'Connor, who was troubled with no such scruples:

As to the vehement action of the Free religious and lover folk, in their conventions, papers, &c. in my favor — and even proceedings like those of Heywood — I see nothing better for myself or friends to do than quietly stand aside & let it go on. . . I got a letter from Dr. Channing asking me to lecture in the Tilton sisters' course this winter in Boston — but I cannot lecture at present — besides I shall certainly not do anything to identify myself specially with free love.[89]

He was a poet, not a doctrinaire. It was enough for him at this time to be the author of *Leaves of Grass*. He no longer wanted to revolutionize the world. The sage of Camden had neither the enthusiasm nor the optimism of the carpenter-bard of 1855.

But what sort of book was it which had raised such a tempest of protest and such equally fanatical devotion? The fact is that the 1881 edition of *Leaves of Grass* differed little from its predecessors, at least as regards the text. As the reviewer for the *Critic* remarked.

The two volumes called *Leaves of Grass* and *The Two Rivulets* which he had printed and himself sold at Camden, N.J., are now issued in one, under the former title, without special accretion of new work, but not without a good deal of re-arrangement in the sequence of the poems. Pieces that were evidently written later and intended to be eventually put under Leaves of Grass, now find their place; some that apparently did well enough where they were have been shifted to other departments. On the whole, however, the changes have been in the direction of greater clearness as regards their relation to the sub-titles. It is not apparent, however, that the new book is greatly superior to the old in typography, although undeniably the fault of the privately printed volumes, a variation in types used, is no longer met with. The margins are narrower, and the look of the page more common-place.[90]

This uniformity and simplicity were intentional. Whitman wanted his book to have a Quakerish quality.[91] Since the war he had not tried to make an impression with the originality of his bindings and that of the 1881 edition was very conservative. The volume was bound in light yellow cloth and the front cover carried in a frame Whitman's signature in gilded letters. The backstrip naturally bore the title and the author's name and was decorated with some very simply designed blades of grass and a hand on which a butterfly was perched, a motif which had already appeared on the binding of the 1860 edition. Facing page 29, where "Song of Myself" began, was, as in most of the previous editions, a portrait of Whitman, but it was that of the 1855 volume.

There was nothing new in all this. But the table of contents showed a certain number of changes. All the poems without exception were now classified and individualized. There were no more undifferentiated sections casually entitled "Leaves of Grass" as in 1871 and 1876. Each section now had its own subtitle. This was the most highly organized edition thus far, and its arrangement of the poems was definitive; Whitman made no further changes afterwards. Curiously, the "Songs of Insurrection" had disappeared. The poems which belonged to it had been scattered among several other sections, as if Whitman had wanted to attenuate the revolutionary aspect of the book. It seems that artistic considerations had now become more important than political concerns. Most often he had gathered his poems around an image under a symbolic title such as "Sea-Drift," "Birds of Passage," "From Noon to Starry Night," [92] rather than under an explicit formula. Generally speaking, throughout the book he had been solicitous of the typographical presentation, and in particular he had completely revised the punctuation, omitting many superfluous commas and replacing dashes with commas, which gave his book a much more conventional aspect and a less personal appearance.[93]

His main concern had been with the organization; he had introduced only twenty new poems, all very short, an insignificant addition in view of the fact that he had had five years to write them and that he had made several journeys which ought to have stimulated his creative activity.[94] But, as we have had occasion to remark, he had derived only four poems from his trip to the West [95] and from his Canadian journey only a few notes. His inspiration, threatened with exhaustion since 1873, was almost completely gone. The impetuous torrent of 1855 was now reduced to a trickle. It was also symptomatic that several of these new poems had a purely literary inspiration. This is particularly true of "Roaming in Thought," subtitled "After Reading Hegel"; [96] of "The Dalliance of the Eagles," which was a paraphrase of a description by John Burroughs; [97] and of "To the Man-of-War Bird," which had been inspired by a passage from Michelet.[98] Also it seems that in order to enlarge the book he had raked up some old material. "My Picture Gallery," as Emory Holloway has shown, is a fragment of a long poem written when he was preparing the first edition of *Leaves of Grass*.[99] And, unless "Patrolling Barnegat" was a recollection of a recent excursion, it may well have been an unused sketch dating from the period of "Out of the Cradle Endlessly Rocking." [100] It has the same stormy air, the same savage and melancholy music, and in the line-endings the same repetitions of present participles. As in 1876 he included several unimpressive occasional poems, such as "What Best I See in Thee" celebrating General Grant's return from his world's tour,[101] and "The Sobbing of the Bells" written to order a few days after the death of President Garfield.[102] In addition, several other poems seem to have been composed merely in order to introduce the book or one of its sections; for instance, "Thou Reader" [103] and "As Consequent." [104]

Thus the new poems which he felt compelled to write and in which an authentic inspiration can be sensed are extremely rare. It is remarkable, however, that in spite of his illness and infirmity there is no complaint, no cry of rebellion. On the contrary, "Hast Never Come to Thee an Hour" [105] and "A Clear Midnight" [106] convey serenity and detachment. His faith remained intact. He had emerged victorious from his trials and he now awaited further events with confidence. He had formerly praised "the grandeur and exquisiteness of old age," [107] and it might be feared that after his paralytic stroke fate would give him the lie, but with patience and energy he had overcome his misfortune. Therefore old age did not disappoint him, and he did not have to renounce what he had said before his experience of it. In "Youth, Day, Old Age and Night," he solemnly reaffirmed his belief in the equality of old age and youth:

> Youth, large, lusty, loving — youth full of grace, force, fascination,
> Do you know that Old Age may come after you with equal grace, force, fascination? [108]

— a relative equality and illusory strength when we think of the poverty of his inspiration after 1871. He now only mentioned for the record the themes he had formerly chanted with so much vigor and of which "A Riddle Song" [109] is merely a rather cold inventory. Even the memory of his mother could not put warmth into "As at Thy Portals also Death," [110] which hardly echoes the great sadness her loss had caused him in 1873. And, when he undertook to sing a hymn to the sun, "Thou Orb Aloft Full Dazzling," [111] there was no trace of the fervor which once animated him in "Song of Myself." His sensuality was not altogether dead, but it was moribund. It had outlived itself.

It is not surprising therefore that he tried to tone down certain boldnesses of expression, the urgency of which he no longer felt so strongly as in his youth. Even before the controversy over the Boston edition, he had on his own initiative expurgated a certain number of poems where sexual images were not absolutely necessary. Thus, in "Year of Meteors" he suppressed some homosexual lines addressed to the Prince of Wales [112] and in "Pensive on Her Dead Gazing" an allusion to the beautiful bodies of young men.[113] He modified "Native Moments" [114] in "Children of Adam" in a similar way, and made other suppressions of that kind here and there.[115] This quiet labor of self-censorship had begun in 1867, but it had never before been carried so far. He made no mention of it, however, and was careful to let alone the more compromising poems, the absence or weakening of which would have been remarked. For he was especially anxious that these changes should not be noticed. This is clearly indicated in his letters to Osgood at the time when he was thinking of making concessions to Stevens. He insisted on the greatest secrecy: ". . . the change to be just silently made — the book, etc. at casual view all its pages to look just the same — only those minutely looking detecting the difference. . ." He specified also that "all lines and passages marked in pencil [must] come out and their places [must] be exactly filled with other matter — so that the pages will superficially present the same appearance as now." And he further requested that the copy containing his corrections be returned to him, probably so that there would be no evidence of his action.[116] An inverted form of hypocrisy, one might say — not at all. He was merely being proud and stubborn and wanted at any cost to avoid the appearance of abandoning the position which he had taken in opposition to Emerson in 1860.[117] His voluntary corrections show that he no longer insisted on his verbal audacities, but he refused to disavow his past self, thus preserving at the same time the unity of his life and the integrity of his work, his "identity," as he would have said.

In 1882, he had a volume published at Philadelphia by Rees Welsh and Company entitled *Specimen Days and Collect*, intended as a companion piece to *Leaves of Grass*,[118] the format and binding of the two books being exactly the same. He had already had the same idea in 1876 with *Two Rivulets*. But *Specimen Days* contained only prose. It included "Democratic

Vistas," "Memoranda during the War," the various prefaces of *Leaves of Grass*, a certain number of articles previously printed in periodicals, the text of his commemorative lecture on the death of Lincoln, and even, as an appendix, several juvenilia never before collected in book form. The only original material was the part of *Specimen Days* that recounted very briefly his childhood and youth, and his Civil War diary, some hundred and fifty pages in all.[119] Since 1876 he had written more in prose than in verse — a bad sign for a poet, but even in prose his output had not been abundant. This second volume definitely confirms the impression of impoverishment [120] and relative sterility given by the first.

In 1882, Whitman was sixty-three years old, and he had not yet won recognition. Thanks to Osgood and even more to the scandal occasioned by the Boston edition, *Leaves of Grass* had enjoyed a certain success, but a number of critics greeted his work with the same old sarcasms.[121] "He is a wicked Tupper; he is an obscene Ossian; he is a poetical Zola; he is — Walt Whitman," declared the New York *Examiner*.[122] He was charged with not having purified his work,[123] with having remained himself after having raised with *Drum-Taps* a momentary hope that he had reformed. This was the point made by a reviewer in the New York *Independent*:

> Whitman changed with the war. He ceased to chant the phallus; *Drum-Taps* and the like came on. His rhythms drew nearer to poetry, to the common movement of blank verse and to rhyme; but in preparing the new edition of his poems, he has preserved the old leaves and strown them all through the book.[124] Shame on the publisher who is sending them with his imprint to unsuspecting American homes.[125]

Still the same reproach of obscenity and formlessness. But some of the critics strongly defended him and completely denied these two main accusations. A reviewer in the New York *Sun* even justified his catalogues,[126] and the Reverend

Mr. Morrow, pastor of the Tabernacle Methodist Episcopal Church in Philadelphia, approved the sexual frankness of his poems.[127] The New York *Sun* review concluded that "the belief is growing in cultivated minds that in Walt Whitman we have one of the most remarkable and original individualities in literature." [128]

Even the detractors, such as the critic in the *Dial*, were obliged to recognize that Whitman had written some worthwhile poems, "Ethiopia Saluting the Colors," "O Captain! My Captain!" and "When Lilacs Last in the Dooryard Bloom'd," [129] the taste of the average reader generally running to these poems because of their patriotic and sentimental appeal and also because of their more conventional form. But the great mass of the public remained indifferent. Whitman was appreciated only by the connoisseurs. This paradox had struck the reviewer in the *Critic*: "One great anomaly of Whitman's case has been that, while he is an aggressive champion of democracy and of the working-man, in the broad sense of the term working-man, his admirers have been almost exclusively of a class the farthest possibly removed from that which labors for daily bread by manual work. . ." [130] But it could hardly have been otherwise. As a writer signing himself "Deuceace" in the St. Louis *Daily Globe Democrat* very justly remarked: "The mass of people seldom read verse (unless it be exceptionally bad, and contributed to a cheap weekly). . ." [131]

There was probably another reason, purely practical, but equally important, for Whitman's lack of popularity — namely, the lack of publicity. A New York bookseller complained about it in an interview with a reporter for the *Tribune*:

There is some call for the book from dealers to fill orders, but I do not think the sales now are large. I guess the Philadelphia firm are trying to push it in the hope of making money out of it. The book never was well advertised, and of course that makes a difference. A book that is advertised well, is sure to sell.[132]

To console himself for the apathy of the masses and the hostility of his detractors, Whitman had the fanatic zeal of his admirers, the Whitmaniacs, as they were now beginning to be called.[133] We have seen how vigorously they supported him when the 1881 edition was attacked. In calmer times they published dithyrambic articles or even poems about Whitman.[134] They considered him, if not as a god, at least as a very great prophet. He was for them the equal of Christ, the founder of a new religion, and they were proud of being the first disciples. It was in this spirit that R. M. Bucke wrote the book on Whitman which he published in 1883,[135] and in which he included as an appendix the complete text of *The Good Gray Poet.*[136] But all this hagiographic literature could have only a very limited influence, and Whitman's more sober and judicious admirers — such as Edward Dowden,[137] Robert Louis Stevenson,[138] James Thomson,[139] and even John Burroughs [140] — who did not share this blind devotion, certainly gained more readers for *Leaves of Grass* than the noisy chorus of the enthusiasts.[141]

If Whitman's position was not precisely that which his worshipers claimed for him, neither was it that to which his detractors tried to relegate him.[142] A growing number of readers were beginning to be aware of this, as the *Critic* noted:

. . . in spite of all the things that regard for the decencies of drawing-rooms and families may wish away, he certainly *represents* as no other writer in the world, the struggling, blundering, sound-hearted, somewhat coarse, but still magnificent vanguard of Western civilization that is encamped in the United States of America. Wide [*sic*] readers are beginning to guess his proportions.[143]

Whitman realized this and looked to the future with confidence. He was sure that a more refined and spiritual civilization would eventually replace the gross commercialism of his time. He had already said so and he repeated it to his Santa Fe admirers in 1883:

The seething materialistic and business vortices of the United States, in their present devouring relations, controlling and be-littling everything else, are, in my opinion, but a vast and indis-pensable stage in the new world's development and are certainly to be followed by something entirely different, at least by immense modifications. Character, literature, a society worthy the name, are yet to be established through a nationality of noblest spiritual, heroic and democratic attributes. . .[144]

Thus, in spite of failures, difficulties, and disappointments, his faith in himself, in democracy, and in his country won through; he was now able to face old age with serenity.

CHAPTER X

THE DECLINE (1883-1890)

THOUGH he thought for a time of leaving Camden,[1] Whitman finally decided to remain; but, in order to keep his independence, he bought in March 1884, with the money which the Philadelphia edition had brought him, a small two-story wooden house at 328 Mickle Street.[2] This was the first time that he had owned a house, a home of his own. Previously, to use his own words,[3] he had "possessed a home only in the sense that a ship possesses one." But he no longer had the courage to pursue his nomadic life, going from boarding-house to boardinghouse. The ship had been drawn up on shore, and was never again to take to sea.[4]

Mickle Street was undoubtedly democratic, but extremely ugly. There was the noise of the trains which passed on the nearby track and frequently the air brought the odor of a neighboring fertilizer factory, but Whitman was indifferent to these matters. He had never lost his Bohemian habits and the most picturesque disorder reigned in his house. He camped rather than really lived there. The furniture consisted mainly of trunks and wooden boxes, as if he were always ready to depart. The floor was littered with old newspapers, books, and piles of letters, but Whitman knew where to find what he wanted and felt perfectly happy in these almost sordid surroundings.[5] He sat with Olympian serenity in the midst of all this confusion, and his numerous visitors were struck by his beauty and nobility.[6]

He had hired as a housekeeper an elderly widow, Mary Davis, a mediocre but very devoted housewife who freed him from all material care. This arrangement gave him more independence than he had at his brother's house and more privacy, without however reducing him to complete solitude. As a matter of fact, he was visited by more and more admirers, who sometimes came from faraway places, and he welcomed them all, except the bores, with the greatest simplicity and kindness. There were actors such as Henry Irving [7] and Bram Stoker; English writers such as Edmund Gosse,[8] Ernest Rhys,[9] H. R. Haweis,[10] Edward Carpenter,[11] Sir Edwin Arnold,[12] and Oscar Wilde; [13] and more humble pilgrims such as Dr. J. Johnston,[14] Emily Faithfull,[15] and C. Sadakichi-Hartmann; [16] or even obscure students and utopians of all kinds who expected from him the consecration of their hopes.[17] Sometimes he had to pose for painters such as Thomas Eakins, Herbert Gilchrist, and J. W. Alexander, or sculptors such as Sidney Morse, who worked for weeks on a bust of him.[18] He avoided no one (on the contrary), and he offered himself with the same complacence to the demands of the photographers.[19] He had always liked to have his portrait made.

In addition to these passing visitors, Whitman also welcomed several faithful friends from Camden and Philadelphia, especially reporters such as Talcott Williams, Harrison Morris, and Thomas Donaldson,[20] and above all Horace Traubel, a clerk who every day after work came to gossip with him and keep him company. The enthusiasm of this young and rather naïve radical amused Whitman. He was not a friend or even a disciple, but a worshiper. He scrupulously recorded the slightest utterances of his idol. A minute and inexhaustible Boswell, he has left in the four fat volumes of his *With Walt Whitman in Camden* an artless account of the last years of Whitman,[21] in

which the innumerable details tend to hide the man, but which
constitute a valuable collection of the literary and political
opinions of the aging poet. Traubel's brother-in-law, Thomas
B. Harned, a lawyer in Philadelphia, was another member of
the cult. Moreover, Whitman was entertained by several of
the best families of the City of Brotherly Love; he frequently
visited in particular the home of R. Pearsall Smith, a very
strict and austere Quaker, whose daughters were great admirers
of his works.[22] And on February 22, 1887, the Contemporary
Club in Philadelphia gave a large reception in his honor.[23]
The disgraceful author of *Leaves of Grass* was now considered,
at least by some people, as an eminently respectable person.

However, in spite of all his friends and all these tokens of
esteem, his material situation remained precarious. The magazines still refused to publish his poems. In 1887 he was complaining again: "I sent a little poem to Harpers — (Alden) —
but it came back refused — this is the fourth refusal within a
few months, & I shall try no more." [24]

He had better luck the following year, for the New York
Herald published some of the poems which were later to
appear under the title of *November Boughs*.[25] But, most of
the time, his only income was from the sale of his books, which
did not bring him a living. In the last half of 1885, his royalties
amounted to the ridiculous sum of twenty dollars.[26] Informed
of his destitution by Mrs. Gilchrist, Rossetti tried to come to
his rescue. He thought at first of asking President Cleveland
to intervene,[27] but realizing the inappropriateness of such a
move, he launched a subscription in England which raised
more than five hundred dollars.[28] This unexpected windfall
permitted Whitman to wait for better times. His American
friends were also active. During the same year (1885), with
funds raised by a subscription limited to ten dollars per person,
they offered him a horse and buggy, by means of which, in

spite of his infirmity, he was able to ride about Camden. In 1886, in spite of his protests, Sylvester Baxter undertook to get him a pension in recognition of his war services.[29] A bill was introduced in the House of Representatives, but it did not pass.[30] Then a new subscription was launched, this time for the purpose of buying him a small country house so that he could get away from his sordid surroundings in Camden. The Staffords were ready to offer him a piece of land at Timber Creek. But, when he received the money, he preferred to stay where he was.[31] At his age he did not want to change, and he was probably afraid that he would have fewer visitors in the country. He preferred the warmth of human contacts to the beauty of nature.

His friends had found another very tactful way of helping him. He liked every year on the fifteenth of April to deliver his lecture on the death of Lincoln. Every year, therefore, this was an occasion for his admirers to help him. In 1887 he spoke at New York in the Madison Square Theater to an audience of over three hundred people. Mark Twain was present, and Andrew Carnegie sent a check for $350. This lecture brought him $600.[32]

These contributions enabled Whitman, in spite of his meager income as an author, to enjoy a peaceful old age free from financial worry.[33] He had at last attained complete serenity. He realized that his work was relatively unsuccessful, but he was resigned to it. He offered his *Leaves of Grass* confidently to the coming generations. It was his "carte de visite" to posterity.[34] He also looked back with satisfaction into the past "o'er Travel'd Roads." [35] In the poems of these years he evoked the memory of his parents, "precious ever-lingering memories, (of you my mother dear — you father — you, brothers, sisters, friends)." [36] He thought nostalgically of his native island:

Sea-beauty! stretch'd and basking! [37]

And he sang the sweetness of memories:

> How sweet the silent backward tracings!
> The wandering as in dreams — the meditation of old
> times resumed — their loves, joys, persons, voy-
> ages.[38]

He was proud of having emerged victorious from the long battles of life, like a soldier covered with scars.[39] But he did not live solely in the past and future. The present still held many pleasures for him. He was always keenly sensitive to the joy of spring, to "the simple shows, the delicate miracles of the earth," [40] namely, birds and flowers. In one poem he even celebrated the appearance of the first dandelion.[41]

But this noble serenity and these moments of quiet happiness were temporary victories over the sufferings and apathy of old age. For, over the years, the burden of his half-paralyzed body was becoming heavier.[42] A sunstroke in 1885 had aggravated his illness,[43] and in June 1888 a new paralytic stroke almost killed him. Luckily, Dr. Bucke was nearby at the time, and by means of a vigorous treatment he succeeded in bringing him through.[44] But this marked the end of his outings. He had to sell the horse and buggy and buy a wheel chair instead. He was now almost completely powerless and could move about only with the help of an attendant. His friends came to his aid and furnished the services of a male nurse so that, after a fashion, he was still able to come and go.[45] But his health was precarious. He had to fight continually against all kinds of infirmities and against the torpor of his weakened body:

> As I sit writing here, sick and grown old,
> Not my least burden is that dulness of the years,
> querilities,
> Ungracious glooms, aches, lethargy, constipation, whim-
> pering *ennui*,
> May filter in my daily songs.[46]

Therefore he welcomed all the more the moments of respite which his illness left him:

> After a week of physical anguish,
> Unrest and pain, and feverish heat,
> Toward the ending day a calm and lull comes on,
> Three hours of peace and soothing rest of brain.[47]

He was still capable sometimes of a short buggy ride around Camden.[48] "The burning fires down in [his] sluggish blood [were] not yet extinct." He still had an "undiminish'd faith" and "groups of loving friends." [49] But his creative power was almost gone, as he knew very well himself; he complained of a "strange inertia falling pall-like round" him,[50] and he confided to Traubel that "his grip [was] gone — irretrievably lost: I seem to have lost the power of consecutive thought, work — mental volition. . . Said he had tried to go over the Hicks manuscript, but didn't get far along: ten minutes of it did me up." [51]

In spite of all this he did not give up. With admirable tenacity he forced himself to write, to scribble a few lines whenever he felt a little better and more clear in his mind. He resisted step by step the numbness which threatened to overcome him. He wanted to imitate the snow bird which in the Arctic wastes sang with a blithe throat in spite of the surrounding desolation.[52] And once more he gained the victory. In 1888, after a seven years' silence, a new volume appeared at Philadelphia, published by David McKay: *November Boughs*.[53] Like the *Two Rivulets* of 1876, it was a mixture of prose and verse. It included a long preface, "A Backward Glance o'er Travel'd Roads," [54] some sixty very short poems (none longer than one page) collected under the title of "Sands at Seventy," and some reprints of articles already published in magazines or in English editions of his works. In the same year he also published his *Complete Poems and Prose*, a thick volume of 900 pages,[55] and during the following year (1889), for his seventieth birthday, he brought out the ninth edition of *Leaves of Grass*.[56] The text was basically the same as that of the 1881 edition, but "A Backward Glance" served as a preface and "Sands at Seventy" was added as an appendix. From this time on, all the new poems were annexed to *Leaves of Grass* instead of being truly incorporated. He no longer had the strength to rearrange his book or to modify the structure so slowly and so patiently built up. "Sands at Seventy" contained only one important poem, "With Husky-Haughty Lips, O Sea," [57] composed on the seashore in 1884. Its tone and imagery recall "Sea-Drift" (1860). In it, Whitman sang the future of the world which appeared to him as an endless battle, with the soul at the center of things perpetually trying to realize itself and in spite of all its efforts never succeeding — a battle similar to the one going on within himself. Thus he felt complete sympathy with the ocean ceaselessly tossed by winds and tempests:

> Ever the soul dissatisfied, curious, unconvinced at last;
> Struggling to-day the same — battling the same.[58]

In spite of the lethargy of his body, the battle still continued, and as usual, his soul overcame his doubts and once more he concluded:

> Life, life an endless march, an endless army, (no halt,
>   but it is duly over,)
> The world, the race, the soul — in space and time the
>   universes,
> All bound as is befitting each — all surely going some-
>   where.[59]

There was no longer any need to repress desires disapproved by social morality; his "turbulent passions" had been calmed.[60] It was no longer love that disturbed him, but the approach of death.[61] Was he afraid? Certainly he preferred to wait a little longer, not to leave his friends and the world too quickly,[62] but he no longer had to struggle so violently to achieve serenity. He resigned himself more willingly to the inevitable:

The soft voluptuous opiate shades,
The sun just gone, the eager light dispell'd — (I too
will soon be gone, dispell'd,)
A haze — nirwana — rest and night — oblivion.[63]

He looked forward to the "halcyon days" to come.[64] He now faced the political problems which had always troubled him so much with the same optimism and the same tranquillity. The current condition of the United States did not entirely please him, but again he consoled himself with the thought that all efforts thus far had been applied to the material foundations and that the spiritual superstructure would come later. Such was the answer of "the United States to Old World critics." [65]

There is evidence therefore in "Sands at Seventy" of a still rich and varied interior life, but one that naturally lacks the power and intensity of the earlier poems. Whitman was well aware himself of the weakness and infrequency of his inspiration [66] and compared the frail poems of *November Boughs* to the sparse and lingering leaves of a tree at the approach of winter.[67] He valued them all the more, however, as they were "confirming all the rest" and were "the faithfulest, hardiest — last." [68] He was right. The remarkable thing is that this tired, paralyzed, old man renounced no part of the message of his youth [69] and, in spite of illness and suffering, continued to celebrate the joy of living. By dint of will power and tenacity — in spite of his reputation for letting himself drift lazily along — he had arrived precisely where he wanted to be. Though an invalid, he had become just such a majestic, Olympian old man, loved and respected by all, as he had described in 1855 in *Leaves of Grass*.[70] His life to the very end ran parallel to his work.

This is certainly not to say that he did not change over the years. In particular, the arrogant pride which he had displayed at the beginning had given way to an unexpected modesty and humility. After setting out in 1855 to conquer the world and imagining himself the author of the greatest masterpiece of all times, he recognized now that "not only the divine works that to-day stand ahead in the world's reading, but dozens more, transcend (some of them immeasurably transcend) all I have done, or could do." [71]

Leaves of Grass, he now maintained, had never been for him any more than an experiment, and it would take another hundred years to assess it properly. Therefore he disapproved of what he regarded as the excessive enthusiasm of O'Connor and Bucke.[72] He was now capable of a judicious detachment with regard both to himself and to others. Having outgrown his dogmatic intransigence, he had become broad-minded and tolerant. He conceded that he was not the only great poet and that "The Poetic area is very spacious — has room for all — has so many mansions!" [73] He was now philosopher enough not to be absolutely certain of anything or of any conclusion.[74] He was no longer even sure of himself; for the first time, we find him speaking humorously of his own work. He no longer presented himself as an infallible prophet and a savior of mankind, but occasionally made fun of his old man's garrulity.[75] We do not find much of this kind of mild humor in Whitman's earlier work.

His attitude toward war had also changed. He was still thinking of it: the Civil War occupied considerable space in the prose of *November Boughs* [76] and supplied the imagery of "Thanks in Old Age." [77] As in 1865, he preached the reconciliation of North and South,[78] but with the passage of years, he had forgotten the horrors of battle and now sang of the heroism and grandeur of war as he had done at first in 1860–61:

The perfume strong, the smoke, the deafening noise;
Away with your life of peace! — your joys of peace!
Give me my old wild battle-life again! [79]

What did the public think of this new Whitman? Apparently
the noble dignity of the old man had disarmed at least some of
his enemies. Only the die-hards — like the Boston *Traveller*
— [80] continued to attack him. In general, the critics were
favorable. The *Saturday Review* of London made almost complete amends for the slashing review of *Leaves of Grass* it had
published in 1855.[81] This fact alone shows how far Whitman
had come since the first edition of his book. His admirers,
realizing that his strength was declining, were lavish with
tokens of affection.[82] His birthdays became apotheoses. In
1889, to celebrate his seventieth anniversary, they gave a big
dinner in his honor at Morgan's Hall in Philadelphia, and the
newspapers of Camden and Philadelphia unanimously chanted
his praises.[83] In 1890, they did better still. Colonel Ingersoll,
the eloquent champion of free-thought, attended Whitman's
seventy-first birthday celebration and delivered a long speech
glorifying *Leaves of Grass* and, after the banquet, with reporters in attendance, disputed with Whitman about the immortality of the soul. The orator denied it, but, in spite of his
arguments, the poet refused to give up his belief in it.[84] On
October 21 of the same year, Ingersoll made another appearance. This time he delivered a lecture in Horticultural Hall in
Philadelphia [85] on Liberty in Literature;[86] it was of course a
eulogy of *Leaves of Grass,* and the poet was present on the
stage in his wheel chair. On that occasion he must have remembered that forty years earlier he had dreamed of becoming
a great orator himself. But he felt too tired to do more than
say a few words of thanks and it was the last time he was able
to appear in public.

He became more and more of a popular figure and the newspapers often mentioned him and his picturesque den in Mickle

Street. He even had a cigar named after him,[87] which in the land of publicity was a great distinction. But he still had very few readers. At the beginning of 1889, he had sold only 700 copies of *November Boughs*.[88] Nevertheless he would continue to write until the end.

CHAPTER XI

LAST MONTHS AND DEATH (1891–1892)

On June 4, 1890, three days after his seventy-first birthday, a newspaper announced that Whitman's death was imminent.[1] The report was exaggerated, but certainly his strength was declining. He no longer went out of doors and only rarely left his room. In the summer, when the heat was stifling, he was forced to wait at his window for the evening breeze.[2] He was permanently condemned to immobility and only death could free him or put an end to this passive and patient existence.[3] Nevertheless he still had moments of happiness, for example, when the sun warmed him into life. He then felt as sportive as a wave, and he would have liked to play like a child or a young kitten: that "perfect physique" which he had sung formerly still survived in the depths of his being.[4] His seventy-second birthday was also a great occasion. Unlike the preceding ceremonies, it was celebrated privately. Some thirty of his friends gathered in the ground-floor sitting room of his house. He was so weak that he could not come down by himself and had to be carried. But the presence of his friends and the champagne which they gave him stimulated and braced him so much that he presided over the feast with spirit and gossiped indefatigably [5] for three hours.

But this was his last flurry. He soon grew worse, and Traubel called in one of the best physicians in Philadelphia, Dr. Daniel

Longaker, who has left a circumstantial account of the poet's last months.[6]

Longaker at first did not discover any particularly disturbing symptoms. Whitman mainly complained of the sleepiness which almost constantly oppressed him and which he attributed to constipation. He also suffered from an enlarged prostate and was often obliged to use a sound in order to urinate.[7] He was a model patient, very docile and courageous, who analyzed with serene lucidity the progress of the disease in his worn-out body. He noted with the greatest care for the benefit of his doctor what food and how many pills he took each day, the state of his bowels, and any pain or discomfort that he felt.[8] He seemed rather surprised that his system refused to function normally or to obey his will. He thought he saw a spiritual reason for this. He had deflected his vital powers from their proper object for too long a time; all his vitality had been absorbed by his creative work; his stomach and bowels left to themselves had gradually become inactive.[9] Open air and a little exercise would doubtlessly have done him good, but he was now too weak to apply this remedy which had succeeded so well after his first paralytic attack. If he tried to go out, he felt dizzy; he had to stay shut up in his room, his den, as he called it.[10]

However, in spite of his great weariness, he did not give up. He was still able to forget his physical sufferings and be interested in other things than his illness. He discussed the personalities and the questions of the day with his visitors and his doctors.[11] At no time, even when his condition became more serious, did he behave as a testy or peevish invalid. He declared one day to Dr. Longaker that "he thought it a grand thing to grow old gracefully," [12] and so far as he was concerned, he had managed to do so. He kept his serenity to the very end and succeeded in embodying the ideal of Olympian old age that he had always admired. This was the result of a conscious and thorough effort to keep his life in harmony with his work in order not to betray the message of *Leaves of Grass*. The following passage indicates his feelings:

> On, on the same, ye jocund twain!
> My life and recitative, containing birth, youth, mid-
> age years,
> Fitful as motley-tongues of flame, inseparably twined
> and merged in one — combining all. . .

His purpose was to preserve both the unity of his life and the unity of his work:

> My verses, written first for forenoon life, and for the
> summer's, autumn's spread,
> I pass to snow-white hairs the same, and give to pulses
> winter-cool'd the same. . .[13]

He refused to give up the struggle:

> . . . Think not we give out yet,
> Forth from these snowy hairs we keep up yet the lilt.[14]

He wanted to sing "our joys of strife and derring-do to the last." [15] In spite of the illness and paralysis of his body, he therefore continued to write and to create. In 1891 he even brought out a new collection of poetry and prose, *Good-Bye My Fancy*,[16] which he had prepared during the preceding year [17] and which later became a second annex to *Leaves of Grass*.

But this thin volume, which was bound exactly like *November Boughs*, contained only thirty-one poems, all very short,[18] in which Whitman hardly did more than take up again, with less energy, some of the themes he had treated earlier.[19] He realized this very clearly and wondered whether he should publish them or not:

Had I not better withhold (in this old age and paralysis of me) such little tags and fringe-dots (maybe specks, stains,) as follows a long dusty journey, and witness it afterward? I have probably not been enough afraid of careless touches, from the first — and am not now — nor of parrot-like repetitions — nor platitudes and the commonplace. . . Besides, is not the verse-field, as originally plann'd by my theory, now sufficiently illustrated — and full time for me to silently retire? — (indeed amid no loud call or market for my sort of poetic utterance).

In answer, or rather defiance, to that kind of well-put interrogation, here comes this little cluster, and conclusion of my preceding clusters. Though not at all clear that, as here collated, it is worth printing (certainly I have nothing fresh to write) — I while away the hours of my 72nd year — hours of forced confinement in my den — by putting in shape this small old age collation.[20]

In spite of the lack of inspiration — or at least of any new inspiration — and the indifference of the public,[21] Whitman still had to keep on writing. He had no illusion about the value of his current work, but he could not persuade himself to stop. His work had become the condition of his life. He may also have seen in this activity a way of preparing for death, which was becoming more and more threatening and which he was now almost looking in the face.[22] The thought of his approaching end haunts most of the poems of *Good-Bye My Fancy*, the very title of which is a farewell to life.[23] Yet, as soon as this collection was finished, he went on to write new poems, taking advantage of the respite that death still left him. These were gathered into a posthumous annex to *Leaves of Grass*, but Whitman himself gave them their title, "Old Age Echoes," [24] which suggests that to the very end he had only one concern: the enrichment and the organization of his book. The tenth edition of *Leaves of Grass*, called the death-bed edition, the printing of which he had supervised himself in spite of his weakness, appeared almost at the time of his death.[25]

He was not only composing poems, but was still writing tirelessly to his friends, such as Bucke and especially J. W. Wallace and J. Johnston, his two faithful admirers in Lancashire. Besides informing them about the state of his health, he told them of articles being published about him, of his literary projects, of the beauty of autumn, the future of democracy, and so on.[26] His eyesight was failing, his brain more and more palpably refusing even slight tasks or revisions,[27] yet he tried to maintain contact with the mass of his readers by means of new poems and with his favorite disciples by means of letters which he awkwardly scribbled on his bed.

Nevertheless disease finally conquered this extraordinary spiritual energy. On December 17, 1891, he had a chill which quickly developed into pneumonia.[28] On the twenty-first Bucke hastened to his bedside. He was thought to be dying, but he did not do so yet. Two weeks later, to the great surprise of the doctors,[29] his worst symptoms had disappeared and his breathing and circulation had almost returned to normal. But he was not by any means cured. He was still very weak and had to stay in bed. The smallest effort exhausted him; the least conversation tired him. Still, almost every day, he had enough strength to glance through the newspapers and read his mail. He was even able to write a few more letters.[30] But he fully realized that he was condemned.[31] He was not afraid of death; he awaited it calmly and serenely. Had he not recently apostrophized it in these terms:

> Thee, holiest minister of Heaven — thee, envoy,
>   usherer, guide at last of all,
> Rich, florid, loosener of the stricture-knot call'd life,
> Sweet, peaceful, welcome Death.[32]

Thus, when the time came, the man adopted the resignation of the poet. He not only accepted death, but he also bore his suffering without complaint. His body, however, had become so thin that he could no longer rest comfortably in any position. (As a last resort, his friends were obliged to put him in a water-bed.)[33] The disease progressed in proportion as his strength declined. He was soon suffering discomfort in his abdomen as well as in his chest, and at the very end he even felt severe pains in one ankle.[34] In addition, a cruel hiccup shook his body.[35] But he never had a complaint or a word of impatience for those who took care of him.[36]

Finally, in March, his long martyrdom came to an end. He died on the twenty-sixth a little before seven in the evening. He remained conscious and lucid to the last.[37]

The next day, the doctors who had cared for him and two professors of the University of Pennsylvania conducted an autopsy of his body. They made some startling discoveries. Whitman's brain during these last months had atrophied and showed symptoms of arteriosclerosis. His lungs had been ravaged by tuberculosis and only about an eighth of the right one was usable for breathing. The intestines and liver had also been attacked by tuberculosis, and tubercular abscesses, invisible from the outside, had formed under the sternum and the fifth rib and in the left foot (which explained the pains in his ankle). One of his suprarenal glands contained a cyst and his kidneys were in very bad condition. The prostate was enlarged and the bladder contained an enormous stone.[38] As Dr. Longaker concluded: "Another would have died much earlier with one-half of the pathological changes which existed in his body." [39] Only his indomitable will had enabled him to live so long in spite of all these maladies. The poet of perfect health had fought off illness and had finally been overcome by a combination of diseases the least of which would have been enough to kill another man.

He was buried on March 30 in Harleigh Cemetery, in Camden, where he had had a simple but imposing granite mausoleum built at great expense.[40] There was no religious service, but his friends had conceived a new kind of ceremony suitable for the founder of a new religion which transcended all others. At the entrance of the cemetery, before a large crowd, Francis Heward Williams read the invocation to death from "When Lilacs Last in the Dooryard Bloom'd" and quotations from Confucius, Buddha, Jesus Christ, the Koran, Isaiah, the Book of Revelation, the Zend-Avesta, and Plato. Then, Thomas B. Harned, Daniel Brinton, Dr. Bucke, and Colonel Ingersoll spoke in turn to praise the memory of the great prophet who had died.[41]

Whitman was dead, but the work in which he had embodied himself continued to live its own independent life. And we shall study it in another volume.

NOTES

ABBREVIATIONS USED IN THE NOTES

AL: *American Literature.*

AM: *Atlantic Monthly.*

CP: *The Complete Prose of Walt Whitman*, edited by Malcolm Cowley, New York: Pellegrini and Cudahy, 1948.

CW: *The Complete Writings of Walt Whitman*, 10 vols., New York: Putnam's Sons, 1902.

FC: *Faint Clews and Indirections*, edited by Clarence Gohdes and Rollo G. Silver, Duke University Press, 1949.

G of the F: *The Gathering of the Forces*, edited by Cleveland Rogers and John Black, 2 vols., New York: Putnam's Sons, 1920.

Imprints: *Leaves of Grass Imprints*, 1860.

Inc. Ed.: *Leaves of Grass*, Inclusive Edition, edited by Emory Holloway, New York: Doubleday, Doran, 1927.

In Re: *In Re Walt Whitman*, Philadelphia: David McKay, 1893.

LG: *Leaves of Grass.*

NB: *November Boughs*, 1888.

N & F: *Notes and Fragments*, edited by R. M. Bucke, London, Ontario, 1899.

N & Q: *Notes and Queries.*

NEQ: *New England Quarterly.*

RAA: *Revue Anglo-Américaine.*

SD: *Specimen Days.*

Sequel: *Sequel to Drum-Taps*, 1865.

SPL: Walt Whitman, *Complete Verse, Selected Prose and Letters*, edited by Emory Holloway, London: The Nonesuch Press, 1938.

Uncoll. PP: *The Uncollected Poetry and Prose of Walt Whitman*, collected and edited by Emory Holloway, 2 vols., 1921.

With WW in C: Horace Traubel, *With Walt Whitman in Camden*, 4 vols.

WWW: *Walt Whitman's Workshop*, edited by C. J. Furness, Harvard University Press, 1928.

NOTES

INTRODUCTION

1. *Figaro Littéraire*, September 9, 1944; reprinted in *Journal des Années Noires*, p. 51.
2. Emory Holloway and Ralph Adimari, *New York Dissected* (New York: R. R. Wilson, 1936), pp. 1–2, or "Whitman and Physique," *CW*, V, 274.
3. It should be said in fairness that the appendix of the Inclusive Edition of Leaves of Grass edited by Emory Holloway (New York: Doubleday, Page, 1927) contains a considerable number of variants collected by Oscar L. Triggs. But, unfortunately, the inventory is incomplete, and it is practically impossible to reconstruct the history of a given poem on the basis of this material.
4. "My book and I — what a period we have presumed to span! those thirty years from 1850 to '80 — and America in them!" "A Backward Glance o'er Travel'd Roads," *Inc. Ed.*, p. 525.
5. *Inc. Ed.*, p. ix, *LG 1892*, p. 2.
6. "An Executor's Diary Note," *Inc. Ed.*, p. 539.
7. Boston *Globe*, August 24, 1881, quoted by Oscar L. Triggs in *Conservator*, VIII (August 1897), 87b, and in "The Growth of Leaves of Grass," *CW*, VII, 119.
8. Interview of Whitman by J. B. S. in New York *World*, May 21, 1876, under the title of "Walt Whitman: The Athletic Bard Paralyzed and in a Rocking-Chair."
9. Letter to Sarah Tyndale dated Brooklyn, June 20, 1857, *SPL*, p. 885.
10. *WWW*, p. 135.
11. *Ibid.*
12. See n. 8 above.
13. Preface to 1876 edition, *Inc. Ed.*, pp. 513–514n.
14. Preface to 1872 edition, *Inc. Ed.*, p. 510.
15. *N & F*, p. 55.
16. *WWW*, pp. 9–10.
17. *CW*, X, 101.
18. "Or from That Sea of Time," ll. 8–9, *Inc. Ed.*, p. 486.
19. Preface to 1876 edition, *Inc. Ed.*, p. 518n.
20. *Ibid.*, p. 517n.

21. "A Backward Glance o'er Travel'd Roads," *Inc. Ed.*, p. 531.
22. "A Thought on Shakspere," *NB* (1888), p. 56, *SPL*, p. 824.
23. "Ah Poverties, Wincings, and Sulky Retreats," *Inc. Ed.*, p. 398.
24. *Inc. Ed.*, p. 457.
25. "A Backward Glance o'er Travel'd Roads," *Inc. Ed.*, p. 522. In *SD* he affirms his preference for artists who have lived wildly, who have suffered disasters, but have persevered and always recovered their balance: "And yet there is another shape of personality dearer far to the artist-sense (which likes the play of strongest lights and shades), where the perfect character, the good, the heroic, although never attain'd, is never lost sight of, but through failures, sorrows, temporary downfalls, is return'd to again and again, and while often violated, is passionately adhered to as long as mind, muscles, voice, obey the power we call volition." *SD*, pp. 156–157, *CP*, p. 156.
26. "So Long!" ll. 53–54, *Inc. Ed.*, p. 418.
27. "Song of Myself," §1, l. 1, *Inc. Ed.*, p. 24.
28. "A Backward Glance o'er Travel'd Roads," *Inc. Ed.*, p. 535.
29. Reprinted in "Leaves-Droppings," *LG 1856*, p. 361.
30. *Inc. Ed.*, p. 444.
31. W. B. Yeats, *A Vision* (privately printed by T. Werner Laurie Ltd., 1925), p. 46, or *ibid.* (New York: Macmillan, 1938), pp. 113–114.
32. "Walt Whitman, an American, one of the roughs, a kosmos. . ." *LG 1855*, p. 29, "Song of Myself," §24, l. 1, *Inc. Ed.*, p. 565.
33. Esther Shephard, *Walt Whitman's Pose* (New York: Harcourt, Brace, 1938).
34. Preface to 1856 edition, *Inc. Ed.*, p. 501.
35. J. P. Sartre, *Introduction à Baudelaire — Ecrits Intimes* (Monaco: Editions du Point du Jour).
36. Frédéric Lefèvre, *Entretiens avec Paul Valéry* (Paris: Le Livre, 1926), p. 107.
37. ". . . the vagaries of my life, the many tearing passions of me. . ." "My 71st Year," *Inc. Ed.*, p. 445.
38. He very early felt this soothing influence of artistic creation. He wrote in June 1848: "You may be tired of such outpourings of spleen, but my experience tells me that I shall feel better after writing them. . ." "The Shadow and the Light of a Young Man's Soul," *Union Magazine of Literature and Art*, 11, 280–281. See also *Uncoll. PP*, I, 231.

I. YOUTH — THE UNSUCCESSFUL QUEST

1. *SD*, p. 9, *CP*, pp. 4–5.
2. *Uncoll. PP*, II, 5, 224–227, 300.

3. See "An Incident on Long Island Forty Years Ago," *Uncoll. PP*, I, 149–151.

4. "My old daddy used to say, it's some comfort to a man if he must be an ass anyhow to be his own kind of an ass!" *With WW in C*, II, 41.

5. *SD*, pp. 14–15, *CP*, p. 10.

6. "There Was a Child Went Forth," ll. 24–25, *Inc. Ed.*, p. 307.

7. John Burroughs, *Notes on Walt Whitman as Poet and Person*, quoted in *SD*, p. 12, *CP*, pp. 8–10.

8. *SD*, pp. 12–14, *CP*, pp. 8–10.

9. *Ibid.*

10. "There Was a Child Went Forth," ll. 5–18, *Inc. Ed.*, p. 306.

11. "Out of the Cradle Endlessly Rocking," l. 136, *Inc. Ed.*, p. 214.

12. *Uncoll. PP*, II, 86.

13. *Inc. Ed.*, p. 7.

14. *SD*, p. 16, *CP*, p. 11.

15. See *SD*, pp. 15, 290, *CP*, pp. 10, 297, and above all *With WW in C*, I, 96–97.

16. Many American writers started as printers: Bayard Taylor, W. D. Howells, Mark Twain, Bret Harte, J. C. Harris, Artemus Ward, Edward Eggleston, Ambrose Bierce, Stedman, Gilder, without forgetting Benjamin Franklin.

17. Van Wyck Brooks, *The Times of Melville and Whitman* (New York: E. P. Dutton, 1947), p. 126.

18. See Theodore A. Zunder, "William B. Marsh — The First Editor of the Brooklyn Daily Eagle," *American Book Collector*, IV (August 1933) 93–95. Marsh was in turn a type-setter and an editor before becoming chief editor of the Brooklyn *Eagle*.

19. *SD*, p. 15, *CP*, p. 11.

20. *Uncoll. PP*, II, 86. The date given in *SD*, p. 16, is wrong (*CP*, p. 11).

21. *Uncoll. PP*, II, 126–127.

22. *SD*, p. 16, *CP*, p. 11: "Fond of the theatre, also, in New York, went whenever I could — sometimes witnessing fine performances." See also *SD*, pp. 19–20, or *CP*, pp. 14–15.

23. *Uncoll. PP*, II, 254–255.

24. *Ibid.*, I, 229–234.

25. *Ibid.*, II, 86–87.

26. *Ibid.*, I, 48–51, 164–166; II, 319–320.

27. *CP*, pp. 336–340.

28. See "Education — Schools," etc., *Uncoll. PP*, I, 144–146, an article originally published in the Brooklyn *Eagle*, November 23, 1846.

29. "We consider it a great thing in education that the learner be

taught to rely upon himself. The best teachers do not profess to *form* the mind, but to *direct* it in such a manner and put such tools in its power — that it builds up itself." *Ibid.*, p. 146.

See "Song of Myself," §46, ll. 10–11, 24, *Inc. Ed.*, pp. 70–71:
> "Not I, not any one else can travel that road for you,
> You must travel it for yourself . . .
> I answer that I cannot answer, you must find it out for yourself."

30. Whitman had devoted one of his "Sun-Down Papers" to a eulogy of loafing; see *Uncoll. PP*, I, 44–46, an article reprinted from the *Long Island Democrat*, November 28, 1840.

31. *Uncoll. PP*, vol. I, pp. xxxiii–xxxiv, n. 1.

32. *Ibid.*, p. 37 (*Long Island Democrat*, September 29, 1840).

33. "Was at Jamaica and through Queens Co. electioneering in fall of 1840." MS notebook quoted in *Uncoll. PP*, II, 87.

34. See "Report of Walter Whitman's Speech in the Park, in New York City, July 29, 1841," *Uncoll. PP*, I, 51.

35. "This latter I consider one of my best experiences and deepest lessons in human nature behind the scenes and in the masses." *SD*, p. 16, *CP*, p. 11.

36. *Uncoll. PP*, I, 32–51.

37. *Ibid.*, pp. 1–16.

38. See Bliss Perry, *Walt Whitman* (1906), pp. 17–18.

39. Katherine Molinoff, *An Unpublished Whitman Manuscript: The Record Book of the Smithtown Debating Society, 1837–1838* (New York, 1941).

40. Katherine Molinoff, *Some Notes on Whitman's Family* (Brooklyn, privately printed by the author, 1941). See also the review of Frances Winwar's *Walt Whitman and His Times* by Clifton J. Furness in *AL*, XIII (January 1942), 423–432. Furness insists on the more sordid aspects of the Whitman family and quotes unpublished letters by Mrs. Whitman.

See also: "The time of my boyhood was a very restless and unhappy one: I did not know what to do." Grace Gilchrist, "Chats with Walt Whitman," *Temple Bar Magazine*, CXIII, no. 447 (February 1898), 200–212.

41. See *Uncoll. PP*, II, 87: "Went to New York in May 1841 and wrote for *Democratic Review*, worked at printing business in *New World* office. . ."

42. *Ibid.*, pp. 87–88.

43. See *The Gathering of the Forces*, ed. by Cleveland Rodgers and John Black (1920) II, 6.

44. Quoted by Bliss Perry, *Walt Whitman* (1906), pp. 22–23.

45. See Canby, *Walt Whitman* (1945), plate IV.

46. *SD*, pp. 18-19, *CP*, pp. 13-14.

47. *Inc. Ed.*, pp. 386-389.

48. John Burroughs, *Notes on Walt Whitman as Poet and Person*, quoted by Bliss Perry, *Walt Whitman*, p. 39. It has been proved that Whitman wrote himself the first chapters of Burroughs' book; see F. P. Hier, "End of a Literary Mystery," *American Mercury*, I (April 1924), 471-478. One therefore cannot trust the biographical indications which it contains. This passage in particular is as suspicious as Whitman's reply to Symonds which we shall discuss later.

49. For this period see *Uncoll. PP* and *G of the F*.

50. Canby, *Walt Whitman*, pp. 52-56.

51. "Song of Myself," §52, l. 3, *Inc. Ed.*, p. 75.

52. *Uncoll. PP*, I, 123 (Brooklyn *Eagle*, November 5, 1846).

53. "Song of Myself," §32, l. 6, *Inc. Ed.*, p. 50.

54. "A City Fire," Brooklyn *Eagle*, February 24, 1847, *Uncoll. PP*, I, 154-156.

55. "Song of Myself," §33, ll. 139-147, *Inc. Ed.*, pp. 56-57.

56. See n. 54.

57. "Philosophy of Ferries," Brooklyn *Eagle*, August 13, 1847, *Uncoll. PP*, I, 168.

58. "Crossing Brooklyn Ferry," *Inc. Ed.*, pp. 134-139.

59. Quoted by Bliss Perry, *Walt Whitman*, p. 276, n. 1.

60. W. A. Chandos, for instance, in an article entitled, "The Local Press," Brooklyn *Standard*, October 22, 1864, quoted by Holloway in *Uncoll. PP*, vol. I, p. xliii, n. 4.

61. See Emory Holloway's introduction to *I Sit and Look Out*, pp. 3-8.

62. See *G of the F*, vol. I, pp. xxvi-xxxiii.

63. *Ibid.* p. xxxiii.

64. See Whitman's own account of the event in the first number of the Camden N.J., *Courier*, quoted by Bliss Perry, *Walt Whitman*, pp. 41-42.

65. "Excerpts from a Traveller's Note-Book," *Crescent*, March 5, 6, 10, 1848, *Uncoll. PP*, I, 181-186.

66. *Ibid.*, pp. 185-186.

67. *Ibid.*, p. 187.

68. *Ibid.*, p. 185.

69. See "The West," Brooklyn *Eagle*, December 26, 1846, *Uncoll. PP*, I, 151-152.

70. See R. M. Bucke, *N & F*, pp. 41-42.

71. "From the Desk of a Schoolmaster," *Long Island Democrat*, Sept. 29, 1840, *Uncoll. PP*, I, 37.

72. *Crescent*, March 16, 1848, *Uncoll. PP*, I, 202-205.

73. *With WW in C*, II, 283.

74. "The Old Cathedral," *Crescent*, April 22, 1848, *Uncoll. PP*, I, 221–222.
75. For instance: corps de réserve (*ibid.*, p. 200); marchande des (*sic*) fleurs, em (*sic*) bon point, brune, brunette, blonde (p. 203); jolie grisette, tout à fait, nonchalance (p. 204); distingué, coiffeurs (p. 208); ecaille (*sic*) (p. 211); sans culottes (p. 212); sans froid, chaqu'un a son goût, chaqu'un a son gré (*sic*) (p. 215); bijouterie (p. 216).
76. "O Magnet-South," *Inc. Ed.*, pp. 393–394.
77. Henry Bryan Binns, *A Life of Walt Whitman* (London: Methuen, 1905), p. 51.
78. *Uncoll. PP*, vol. I, pp. xlvii–xlviii.
79. *With WW in C*, II, 316, 328, 425, 510–511; III, 80, 119–120, 140, 253, 364.
80. See above, n. 77.
81. Léon Bazalgette, *Walt Whitman, l'homme et son oeuvre* (Paris: Mercure de France, 1908), II, 80–103.
82. *Uncoll. PP*, vol. I, pp. xlii–lii. See also Emory Holloway, "Walt Whitman's Love Affairs," *Dial*, LXIX (November 1920), 473–483.
83. Emory Holloway, *Whitman, an Interpretation in Narrative* (New York: Knopf, 1926), pp. 65–71.
84. *Uncoll. PP*, II, 63–76; for the date of this notebook see p. 63, n. 1.
85. *Uncoll. PP*, II, 77–78.
86. *Ibid.*, p. 78.
87. See his letter to his mother March 28, 1848, quoted by Holloway in *Uncoll. PP*, vol. I, p. xlvi, n. 2.
88. See Canby, *Walt Whitman*, p. 78.
89. Jean Catel, *Walt Whitman* (Paris, 1929), pp. 239–241.
90. "New Orleans in 1848," *NB*, p. 102, *CP*, p. 453.
91. *Uncoll. PP*, II, 77. On Jeff's home-sickness, see n. 3.
92. *Uncoll. PP*, II, 78–79. He went sight-seeing like a tourist: "We went under the Falls, saw the whirlpool, and all the other things, including the suspension bridge" (p. 79).
93. *Uncoll. PP*, vol. I, p. liii, n. 2.
94. Catel, *Walt Whitman*, pp. 293–301.
95. "Song for Certain Congressmen," reprinted in *CP*, pp. 334–335, under the title of "Dough-Face Song."
96. *SPL*, pp. 503–504 and n., p. 1087. Whitman also reprinted this poem in *SD*, pp. 372–373 (*CP*, pp. 389–390), but for some reason or other antedated it.
97. *Uncoll. PP*, I, 27–30.
98. See Brooklyn *Freeman*, September 9, 1848. The *Catalogue of the Trent Collection* contains a facsimile of this particular number.

99. *Uncoll. PP*, vol. I, p. n. 3.

100. See chap. xvii, entitled "Slavery."

101. *SD*, pp. 258–263, *CP*, pp. 264–268.

102. These pages are not dated in *SD*. Most of them were probably written after the Civil War, but some passages — notably the one to which we allude in the next sentence — were composed much earlier. The string of abuse which Whitman fires at the delegates sent to Democratic conventions is already to be found in *The Eighteenth Presidency* which he thought of publishing in 1856 (see Clifton J. Furness, *WWW*, pp. 99–100). Furness felt that some parts of this tract had been written several years before (*ibid.*, p. 227, n. 84). All this accounts for the exceptional virulence and vigor of such passages in *SD*.

103. *SD*, p. 259, *CP*, p. 265.

104. *Selected Poems* (Oxford University Press, 1913), pp. 186–187.

105. On Emerson's attitude during all this period, see Marjory M. Moody, "The Evolution of Emerson as an Abolitionist," *AL*, XVII (March 1945), 1–21. See also his *Journal*, VIII, 185–186.

106. See Thoreau, "Slavery in Massachusetts," in *Works* (Riverside ed., 1894), Vol. X.

107. "The House of Friends," New York *Tribune*, June 14, 1850, *Uncoll. PP*, I, 26, or "Wounded in the House of Friends," *SD*, p. 373, *CP*, pp. 390–391.

108. *Ibid.*

109. "The shriek of a drowned world, the appeal of women . . . Would touch them never in the heart, But only in the pocket." ("The House of Friends," *Uncoll. PP*, I, 27.)

110. "Liberty, let others despair of thee, But I will never despair of thee. . ." "Resurgemus," *Uncoll. PP*, I, 30. The very title of this poem expresses hope.

111. *Uncoll. PP*, I, 234–235.

112. "A Plea for Water," Brooklyn *Advertizer*, May 18–June 6, 1850, *Uncoll. PP*, I, 254–255.

113. See his article in the Brooklyn *Eagle*, reprinted in *G of the F*, II, 52–55.

114. *LG 1855*, p. 47, "Song of Myself," §42, ll. 22–24, *Inc. Ed.*, p. 65. After the Civil War, "wars" replaced "churches" in this list.

115. "Memorial in Behalf of a Freer Municipal Government, and against Sunday Restrictions," Brooklyn *Evening Star*, October 20, 1854, *Uncoll. PP*, I, pp. 259–264. He had already developed some of these ideas, but with less vigor, in the *Eagle* in 1846–47 (*G of the F*, II, 55–72). He took them up again in *LG*; see "To the States" (*Inc.*

Ed., p. 8) and "Poem of Remembrances for a Girl or a Boy of These States" (*ibid.*, pp. 467–468).

116. Brooklyn *Daily Advertizer*, April 3, 1851, *Uncoll. PP*, I, 241–247. He realized himself the importance of this text, for he reprinted a fragment of it in *SD*, p. 372 (*CP*, pp. 388–389).

117. *Uncoll. PP*, I, 241.

118. "Read well the death of Socrates, and of greater than Socrates." *Ibid.*, p. 246.

119. "The beautiful artist principle sanctifies that community which is pervaded by it. A halo surrounds forever that nation." *Ibid.*, p. 244.

120. "'51, '53, occupied in house-building in Brooklyn." *SD*, p. 20, *CP*, p. 15. See also *FC*, p. 49.

In "A Whitman Collector Destroys a Whitman Myth," *Papers of the Bibliographical Society of America*, LII (1958), 73–92, Charles E. Feinberg refutes the assumptions made by the editor of *FC* and very convincingly proves that Whitman was not only a carpenter, but also occasionally a contractor and a businessman. This, however, does not invalidate the testimony of George Whitman and others who saw him work — or play — at carpentering; see below n. 122.

121. O'Connor, "The Carpenter — A Story," *Putnam's Magazine*, I (January 1868), 55–90. In this tale Whitman is identified with Christ, who also worked as a carpenter before he began preaching.

122. *In Re* (Philadelphia: David McKay, 1893), p. 35.

123. Bazalgette, *Walt Whitman*, I, 112.

124. *Uncoll. PP*, I, 83–86.

125. See *The Half-Breed and Other Stories*, ed. by Thomas Ollive Mabbott (Columbia University Press, 1927).

II. THE 1855 EDITION — BIRTH OF A POET

1. Whitman probably borrowed the idea of this binding from a literary friend, Mrs. Sarah Payson Willis Parton, whose *Fern Leaves from Fanny's Portfolio* was first published in 1853 and was reprinted in 1854. This *Fern Leaves* was a duodecimo volume bound in brown or red cloth according to the edition, whereas *Leaves of Grass* was a quarto; but the cover was decorated, front and back, with a tangle of branches and roots, especially on the backstrip, where the letters of the title also had roots and were caught in the roots of a plant which branched out widely over them. Of course, the content of the book was entirely different, consisting of moralizing stories, but Whitman may have been inspired by the title. The resemblance did not escape Mrs. Parton, for she entitled the enthusiastic review of *Leaves of Grass* which she contributed to the New York *Ledger*, May 10, 1856:

"Fresh Fern Leaves: Leaves of Grass." But the borrowing — if it was one — amounted to little more than the word "leaves," which was then fashionable. Clifton J. Furness has found the word in the titles of four books, which appeared between 1852 and 1855. See his introduction to the facsimile edition of the 1855 *Leaves of Grass* (Columbia University Press, 1939).

2. Whitman even helped to set type for the book. According to his own testimony: "I had some friends in the printing business there — the Romes — three or four young fellows, brothers. They had consented to produce the book. I set up some of it myself: some call it my handiwork: it was not strictly that — there were about one hundred pages: out of them I set up ten or so — that was all." *With WW in C*, II, 471.

3. This relative anonymity elicited the following comments from the reviewer in *Putnam's Monthly* (September 1855): "As seems very proper in a book of transcendental poetry, the author withholds his name from the title-page, and presents his portrait, neatly engraved on steel, instead. This, no doubt, is upon the principle that the name is merely accidental: while the portrait affords an idea of the essential being from whom these utterances proceed. We must add, however, that this significant reticence does not prevail throughout the volume, for we learn on page 29, that our poet is 'Walt Whitman, an American, one of the roughs, a kosmos' " (*Leaves-Droppings*, pp. 368–369).

This article had been written by Charles Eliot Norton in 1855; see *A Leaf of Grass from Shady Hill*, with a review of Walt Whitman's *Leaves of Grass*, ed. Kenneth B. Murdock (Harvard University Press, 1928).

4. This portrait was a steel engraving by Samuel Hollyer, after a daguerreotype taken at Brooklyn in July 1854 by Gabriel Harrison; see Introduction to the facsimile edition of the 1855 *Leaves of Grass* by Thomas Bird Mosher, p. 10.

5. "Song of Myself," §2, l. 9, *Inc. Ed.*, p. 40.

6. *Uncoll. PP*, II, 63–76.

7. H. B. Binns, *A Life of Walt Whitman* (London: Methuen, 1905), pp. 51–52.

8. Léon Bazalgette, *Walt Whitman, l'homme et son oeuvre* (Paris: Mercure de France, 1908), I, 81–103.

9. Basil de Selincourt, *Walt Whitman, a Critical Study* (London: Martin Secker, 1914), pp. 18–24.

10. Emory Holloway, *Whitman, an Interpretation in Narrative* (New York: Knopf, 1926), pp. 64–71.

11. *Uncoll. PP*, II, 62–76.

12. In his first book, *Walt Whitman* (Philadelphia: David McKay, 1883), Bucke drew a fairly conventional portrait of the poet. It was

only after Whitman's death that he brought forward the mystical hypothesis in an essay entitled "Walt Whitman and the Cosmic Sense," which appeared in *In Re Walt Whitman* (Philadelphia: David McKay, 1893), pp. 329–347. He developed his theory in *Cosmic Consciousness: A Study in the Evolution of the Human Mind* (Philadelphia: Innes and Sons, 1901).

13. *In Re*, p. 341.

14. *Ibid.*, pp. 341–342.

15. *LG, 1855*, p. 32, *Inc. Ed.*, p. 27, "Song of Myself," §5, ll. 6–14.

16. "Prayer of Columbus," *Inc. Ed.*, pp. 352–354.

17. *Inc. Ed.*, pp. 440–441.

18. *Ibid.*, p. 449.

19. Edward Hungerford, "Walt Whitman and His Chart of Bumps," *AL*, II (January 1931), 350–384. Mark Van Doren accepted his conclusions in "Walt Whitman Stranger," *American Mercury*, XXXV (July 1935), 277–285.

20. L. N. Fowler and his brother O. S. Fowler had a phrenological office in New York (with branches in Boston and Philadelphia), which was also a bookshop and a publishing center for books on phrenology. They themselves had written a whole series of books not only on phrenology, but also on sexual education and eugenics; they were therefore in full sympathy with Whitman on at least these two points.

21. As early as November 16, 1846, he reviewed enthusiastically in the Brooklyn *Eagle* J. G. Spurzheim's *Phrenology or the Doctrine of the Mental Phenomena*. In his papers were found many clippings from the *American Phrenological Journal*; see CW, X, 75, 86, 89, 94, or *N & F*, pp. 205 (376), 207 (419) & (424), 210 (424). All these clippings are now in the Trent Collection of the Duke University Library (*Catalogue of the Trent Collection*, pp. 66–67).

22. *With WW in C*, II, 385.

23. *Leaves-Droppings*, p. 362.

24. *Ibid.*, p. 362. See also *In Re*, p. 25n.

25. See above, Chapter I, pp. 22–23.

26. Haniel Long, *Walt Whitman and the Springs of Courage* (Santa Fe: Writers' Editions, 1938).

27. In the 1855 Preface, among the qualities which he attributes to the great poet, are to be found precisely some of those which Fowler had detected in him: "Extreme caution or prudence, the soundest organic health, large hope and comparison . . . large alimentiveness and destructiveness and causality." *Inc. Ed.*, p. 501.

28. Quoted by Hungerford, p. 366.

29. Long, pp. 16f.

30. *Leaves-Droppings*, pp. 346–358.

31. Burroughs, pp. 16–17.

32. *SD*, p. 321. This essay had first been published in the *Literary World*, May 22, 1880.

33. *SPL*, pp. 1045–1046.

34. Bazalgette, for instance, who wrote: "L'originalité de son livre est la plus absolue peut-être qui ait été jamais manifestée en littérature." *Walt Whitman, l'homme et son oeuvre*, I, 195. See also O'Connor's introduction to R. M. Bucke's *Walt Whitman*, 1883.

35. See what he replied to Traubel when the latter reproached him with calling Emerson "Master" after having declared in "Poem of You Whoever You Are" (later "To You," *Inc. Ed.*, p. 198, l. 17), "I only am he who places over you no master, owner, better, God, beyond what waits intrinsically in yourself": "They were salad days. I had many undeveloped angles at that time. I don't imagine I was guiltless; someone had to speak for me; no one would; I spoke for myself." Horace Traubel, "Walt Whitman on Himself," *American Mercury*, III (October 1924), 186–192.

36. J. T. Trowbridge, *My Own Story with Recollections of Noted Persons* (Boston: Houghton Mifflin, 1903), pp. 360–401. See also "Reminiscences of Walt Whitman," *Atlantic Monthly*, LXXXIX (February 1902), 163–175.

37. *My Own Story*, p. 363.

38. *G of the F*, II, 270–271.

39. *Catalogue of the Trent Collection*, p. 76.

40. See Catel, *Walt Whitman*, pp. 335–336.

41. *Good-Bye My Fancy* (1891), p. 58, *CP*, p. 529.

42. *Pictures, an Unpublished Poem of Walt Whitman*, with an introduction by Emory Holloway (New York: June House, 1927), p. 25.

43. See above, n. 32.

44. F. M. Smith, "Whitman's Poet-Prophet and Carlyle's Hero," *PMLA*, LV (1940), 1146–1164, and "Whitman's Debt to Carlyle's Sartor Resartus," *MLQ*, III (March 1942), 51–65.

45. See *G of the F*, II, 290–293, and *Uncoll. PP*, I, 129–130.

46. See *Heroes and Hero-Worship*, Everyman's Library ed., p. 313, and also p. 281.

47. See *Heroes and Hero-Worship*, Lecture II, "The Hero as Prophet. Mahomet: Islam," and Lecture IV, "The Hero as Priest. Luther: Reformation; Knox: Puritanism."

48. Speaking of the birth of the myth of Odin, Carlyle wrote: "Fancy your own generous heart's love of some greatest man expanding till it *transcended* all bounds, till it filled and overflowed the whole field of your thought! Or what if this man Odin — since a great deep

soul, with the *afflatus* and mysterious *tide of vision* and impulse rush-
ing on him he knows not whence, is ever an enigma, a kind of terror
and wonder to himself — should have felt that perhaps he was divine;
that he was some effluence of the 'Vuotan', Supreme Power and
Divinity, of whom to his *rapt vision* all Nature was the awful Flame-
image." *Ibid.*, pp. 261–262 (italics supplied to indicate all the words
that Whitman took up in "Song of Myself," "By Blue Ontario's Shore,"
and in his notebooks).

49. *Ibid.*, pp. 316–323.

50. "Novalis beautifully remarks of him, that those great Dramas
of his are Products of Nature too, deep as Nature herself. I find a
great truth in this saying. Shakespeare's Art is not Artifice. It grows up
from the deeps of Nature, through this noble sincere soul, who is a
voice of Nature." *Ibid.*, pp. 339–340.

51. "Islam, like any great Faith, and insight into the essence of
man, is a perfect equaliser of men. . ." *Ibid.*, p. 307. Cf. "He is the
equalizer of his age and land" in the Preface to *LG 1855, Inc. Ed.*,
p. 291.

52. *Heroes and Hero-Worship*, p. 394.

53. Lecture V.

54. "To which of these Three Religions do you specially adhere?
inquires Meister of his Teacher. To all three! answers the other: To
all the Three; for they by their union first constitute *the True Religion.*"
Ibid., p. 277.

55. "To his eyes it is forever clear that this world wholly is
miraculous." *Ibid.*, p. 303.

56. Smith points out in particular that the adjective "electric,"
which Carlyle applies to Blumine's charm, is one of Whitman's
favorites.

57. "Whitman's Debt to Sartor Resartus," *MLQ*, III, 65.

58. Esther Shephard, *Walt Whitman's Pose* (New York: Harcourt,
Brace, 1936). For a constructive criticism of her thesis, see Henri
Roddier, "Pierre Leroux, George Sand et Walt Whitman, ou l'éveil
d'un poète," *Revue de Littérature Comparée*, XXXI (January–March
1957), 5–33.

59. Shephard, p. 140.

60. *Ibid.*, p. 280.

61. *Ibid.*, p. 312.

62. *Ibid.*, p. 315.

63. *Ibid.*, p. 283.

64. *Ibid.*, p. 282.

65. *Ibid.*, p. 284.

66. *Ibid.*, p. 313.

67. *Ibid.*, p. 304, and also p. 315.

68. *Inc. Ed.*, pp. 313–316, or Preface to the 1855 edition, pp. 501–502.

69. Shephard, p. 320.

70. *Ibid.*, p. 154.

71. *Inc. Ed.*, p. 501.

72. *Uncoll.* PP, I, 135.

73. See Shephard, pp. 201–210, 420–428.

74. *Inc. Ed.*, pp. 27–28, §5.

75. Shephard, pp. 312–313.

76. Esther Shephard herself (p. 189) is obliged to admit: "Whitman, it may be like many of the rest of us, could not remember where his many seething ideas had originally come from." It is regrettable that she should not have shown the same moderation in the rest of her book.

77. There were times when Whitman judged rather severely George Sand's heroes, as when he wrote to W. S. Kennedy: "J N J [a planter who had called on him and claimed to be a great admirer of *Leaves of Grass*] is certainly crazy — a cross between Zdenko [in *Consuelo*] & something more intellectual and infernal." FC, p. 113.

78. See in particular: "Le moi que Whitman célèbre à chaque page des *Brins d'Herbe* est la projection de l'inconscient." Catel, *Walt Whitman*, p. 400.

79. Allen, pp. 61–62.

80. See above, p. 54.

81. *Uncoll.* PP, II, 63–90.

82. In the *Inc. Ed.* the punctuation of the preface has been simplified and the number of points of suspension cut down to three in all cases.

83. *Inc. Ed.*, pp. 286–299.

84. They have been taken up again only in a short passage in the poem later entitled "Song of Myself" *LG 1855*, p. 29, *Inc. Ed.*, p. 44, in "Suddenly Out of Its Stale and Drowsy Lair" *LG 1855*, pp. 87–88, *Inc. Ed.*, pp. 227–228, under the title of "Europe," in "Clear the Way There Jonathan!" (*LG 1855*, pp. 89–90, *Inc. Ed.*, pp. 225–227, under the title of "A Boston Ballad"), and finally in "Who Learns My Lesson Complete" (*LG 1855*, pp. 92–93, *Inc. Ed.*, pp. 329–330).

85. See above, Chapter I, pp. 40–41.

86. Translators have not always paid attention to this peculiarity. André Gide called *Leaves of Grass* "Brins d'Herbe," as if it had been "Blades of Grass." Only Bazalgette rendered the title correctly.

87. "Spontaneous Me" (1856), *Inc. Ed.*, p. 90, ll. 44–45. The same idea occurs in "Scented Herbage of My Breast" (1860, *Inc. Ed.*, pp. 95–97), and "You Lingering Sparse Leaves of Me" (1887, *Inc. Ed.*, p. 439). The pun is particularly unmistakable in such titles as

"Here the Frailest Leaves of Me" (1860, *Inc. Ed.*, p. 109), "A Leaf of Faces" (thus called in 1860, later entitled "Faces," *Inc. Ed.*, pp. 386–389), "A Leaf for Hand in Hand" (1860, *Inc. Ed.*, p. 110), and "Proto-Leaf" (which was, in 1860, the title of "Starting from Paumanok").

88. See above, p. 280, n. 1.

89. "So Long!" *Inc. Ed.*, p. 418, ll. 53–54.

90. Whitman purposely used the word "leaf" in its botanical sense. See what he said to Traubel; "I am well satisfied with titles — with Leaves of Grass, for instance, though some of my friends themselves rather kicked against it at the start — particularly the literary hair-splitters, who rejected it as a species of folly. 'Leaves of Grass', they said: there are no *leaves* of grass; there are spears. But *Spears* of Grass would not have been the same to me. Etymologically *leaves* is correct — scientific men use it so. I stuck to leaves, leaves, leaves, until it was able to take care of itself. Now it has got well started on its voyage — it will never be displaced." *With WW in C*, I, 186.

91. Whitman may have found the germ of this image in *Heroes and Hero-Worship*: "To us also, through every star, through every blade of grass, is not a God made visible, if we will open our minds and eyes?" (Everyman's Library ed., p. 247). It is known that he had read this book, and had reviewed it briefly in the Brooklyn *Eagle* (October 17, 1846); see *Uncoll. PP*, I, 129.

92. *LG 1855*, p. 24, *Inc. Ed.*, p. 38, §17, l. 5.

93. *LG 1855*, p. 16, *Inc. Ed.*, p. 28, §6, ll. 9–11.

94. *LG 1855*, pp. 16–17, *Inc. Ed.*, pp. 28–29, §6, ll. 13–15, 28.

95. In the introduction to the facsimile edition of the 1855 *Leaves of Grass* (Columbia University Press, 1939), C. J. Furness suggests that Whitman may have used "grass" as printer's slang meaning "a person who does casual work around the shop" or "the work such a person does." But this seems unlikely since he never mentioned the possibility when he discussed the meaning and purpose of his title with Traubel. See also Charles M. Adams, "Whitman's Use of 'Grass,'" *American N & Q*, VI (February 1947), 167–168.

96. "I celebrate myself," *LG 1855*, p. 13, "Song of Myself," *Inc. Ed.*, p. 24, §1, l. 1.

97. *LG 1855*, p. 29, *Inc. Ed.*, "Song of Myself," pp. 43–44, §24, ll. 1–4.

98. *LG 1855*, p. 44, "Song of Myself," *Inc. Ed.*, p. 62, §39, l. 1.

99. *LG 1855*, p. 44, "Song of Myself," *Inc. Ed.*, p. 62, §39, ll. 6–7.

100. *LG 1855*, p. 86, "Song of the Answerer," *Inc. Ed.*, p. 141, §1, ll. 28–29.

101. *LG 1855*, p. 39, "Song of Myself," *Inc. Ed.*, p. 56, §33, ll. 124–135.

102. *LG 1855*, p. 45, "Song of Myself," *Inc. Ed.*, p. 63, §40, ll. 17–18.

103. *LG 1855*, p. 51, "Song of Myself," *Inc. Ed.*, p. 70, §46, ll. 2–3, 6.

104. *LG 1855*, p. 18, *Inc. Ed.*, p. 31, §9.

105. *LG 1855*, p. 18, *Inc. Ed.*, p. 31, §10, ll. 16–18.

106. *LG 1855*, p. 20, *Inc. Ed.*, p. 33, §13, ll. 13–14.

107. *LG 1855*, p. 21, *Inc. Ed.*, p. 34, §14, ll. 11–13.

108. *LG 1855*, pp. 90–91, *Inc. Ed.*, pp. 90–91.

109. *LG 1855*, p. 15, "Song of Myself," *Inc. Ed.*, p. 27, §4, l. 9.

110. "Song of Myself," *Inc. Ed.*, p. 27, §2, l. 16.

111. *Inc. Ed.*, p. 616, in a variant of "Song of the Broad-Axe," dating back to 1856.

112. *LG 1855*, p. 15, "Song of Myself," *Inc. Ed.*, p. 27, §4, l. 15.

113. *LG 1855*, p. 48, *Inc. Ed.*, p. 67, §43, ll. 17–19.

114. *LG 1855*, p. 48, *Inc. Ed.*, p. 67, §43, ll. 22–23.

115. *LG 1855*, p. 39, *Inc. Ed.*, p. 56, §33, l. 136.

116. *LG 1855*, p. 43, *Inc. Ed.*, p. 61, §37, l.9.

117. See for instance *LG 1855*, pp. 32–33, *Inc. Ed.*, pp. 48–49, §28, of "Song of Myself," and *LG 1855*, p. 78, *Inc. Ed.*, "I Sing the Body Electric," p. 80, §2, ll. 5–9, 20.

118. *LG 1855*, p. 15, "Song of Myself," *Inc. Ed.*, p. 27, §4, ll. 10–14.

119. *Uncoll. PP*, II, 88–89.

120. One may even wonder if the following line is not a confession: "If you remember your foolish and outlaw'd deeds, do you think I cannot remember my own foolish and outlaw'd deeds?" *Inc. Ed.*, "A Song for Occupations," p. 179, §1, l. 17.

121. See above, n. 120.

122. See above, Chapter I, pp. 23, 38–39.

123. ". . . talking like a man unaware that there was ever such a production as a book, or such a being as a writer." Review of *Leaves of Grass* published in the *United States Review* and written by Whitman himself. See *Leaves of Grass Imprints* (1860), p. 8.

124. Here is another contradiction: he claimed that the writing of his book had been sheer joy (*N & F*, p. 63, item 37); later he had to admit that the process had been very painful and that he had been torn by doubts. See *ibid.*, p. 62, a passage which he took up in "My Book and I" and in "A Backward Glance."

125. See above, Chapter I, p. 45.

126. See "A Backward Glance," *Inc. Ed.*, pp. 523–524. In one of his early notebooks (1848–49) he was already writing: "True noble expanded American Character is raised on a far more lasting and universal basis than that of any of the characters of the 'gentlemen' of aristocratic life, or of novels, or under the European or Asian forms

of society or government. . . It is to accept nothing except what is equally free and eligible to anybody else. It is to be poor rather than rich." *Uncoll. PP*, II, 63. See the same idea in *LG 1855*, p. 29, "Song of Myself," *Inc. Ed.*, p. 44, §24, l. 11.

127. *Uncoll. PP*, II, 66.

128. *Imprints*, p. 56.

129. *Leaves-Droppings*, pp. 383–384.

130. *Ibid.*, p. 375. Whitman had actually written: "I talk wildly . . . I have lost my wits." *LG 1855*, p. 33, "Song of Myself," *Inc. Ed.*, p. 49, §28, l. 20. He was referring to a state of mystical exaltation, not to a permanent condition.

131. *Ibid.* The passage which the reviewer refers to corresponds to §5 of "I Sing the Body Electric" (*Inc. Ed.*, p. 49).

132. *Leaves-Droppings*, p. 379.

133. *Imprints*, p. 18. The reviewer was William J. Stillman.

134. *Ibid.*, p. 17.

135. *Leaves-Droppings*, pp. 381–383. See also *New York Dissected*, pp. 167–170.

136. *Imprints*, pp. 23–24.

137. *Leaves-Droppings*, pp. 368–369. For some unknown reason, W. S. Kennedy, in *Fight of a Book for the World*, pp. 12–13, classed this review among the hostile articles. But for Whitman's fanatical disciples, anything which was not unqualified praise was an attack. Norton, who was only twenty-eight years old, was already a member of the Harvard faculty. This article shows a remarkable breadth of mind on the part of the future historian and translator of Dante. It is interesting to note that Whitman, who often complained of the narrowness of academic criticism, was thus greeted by a professor at the beginning of his career — without however being aware of it, since the review was anonymous.

138. *Imprints*, pp. 3–4.

139. *Leaves-Droppings*, pp. 366–367.

140. *New York Dissected*, pp. 162–163.

141. *Ibid.*, pp. 166–167.

142. "We give a cordial welcome to *Leaves of Grass*, which we look upon as the most considerable poem that has yet appeared in our country." *Imprints*, p. 51.

143. "No one . . . can read this singular prose-poem without being struck by the writer's wonderful power of description and of word-painting . . ." Quoted by Canby, *Walt Whitman*, p. 124.

144. See *Imprints*, pp. 52–54.

145. *Leaves-Droppings*, p. 374.

146. Brooklyn *Times*, September 29, 1855, *Leaves-Droppings*, pp. 360–363, and *In Re*, pp. 23–26; *American Phrenological Journal*,

October 1855, under the title of "An English and an American Poet" (Whitman compares himself to Tennyson, to the disadvantage of the latter, naturally), *Leaves-Droppings*, pp. 369–375, and *In Re*, pp. 27–32; *United States Review*, September 1855, *In Re*, pp. 13–21.

147. The New York *Daily Times* in particular; see *Imprints*, p. 21. It is remarkable that Whitman should have reprinted this article. He was apparently indifferent to such attacks, probably because he did not feel in the least guilty.

148. "Leigh Hunt criticised his own poems. Spenser criticised himself." *CW*, VI, 119.

149. "Whitman has remarked to us that in a period of misunderstanding and abuse their publication seemed imperative." The editors of *In Re*, p. 13.

150. He once declared to Traubel: "I expected hell: I got it." *With WW in C*, II, 472.

151. "A Visit to Walt Whitman," Brooklyn *Eagle*, July 11, 1886.

152. *With WW in C*, II, 472.

153. See F. O. Matthiessen, *American Renaissance* (Oxford University Press, 1941), p. x.

154. Ralph Adimari, "Leaves of Grass, First Edition," *American Book Collector*, V (May-June 1934), 150–152. See also John T. Winterich, "Romantic Stories of Books — I. Leaves of Grass," *Publishers' Weekly*, CXII (November 1927), 1869–1873.

155. See Carolyn Wells and Alfred F. Goldsmith, *A Concise Bibliography of the Works of Walt Whitman* (Boston: Houghton Mifflin, 1922), pp. 3–5.

156. See Joseph Jay Rubin, "Carlyle on Contemporary Style," *MLN*, LVII (May 1942), 362–363.

157. *LG 1856*, p. 346.

158. *Leaves-Droppings*, p. 345.

159. For instance, in "The American Scholar" (1837), and in his essay on "The Poet" (1844).

160. He thus wrote toward the end of the Preface to the 1855 edition: "The soul of the largest and wealthiest and proudest nation may well go half-way to meet that of its poets. The signs are effectual. There is no fear of mistake . . . The proof of a poet is that his country absorbs him as affectionately as he has absorbed it." *Inc. Ed.*, p. 507.

III. THE 1856 EDITION

1. See *Imprints*, p. 2.

2. Fowler and Wells probably preferred not to have it known that they had published *Leaves of Grass*, since some critics had accused the book of obscenity. They may have been afraid of its effect on the

sale of other books bearing their imprint. But we have definite proof that they were in fact the publishers of the second edition in Whitman's letter of July 22, 1857, to an unknown correspondent, in which he complains of their ill-will — probably because of their prudence and their fear of scandal. See *SPL*, p. 885.

3. It gives a list of their agencies in the United States and abroad.

4. See above, Chapter II, p. 79.

5. Whitman was violently criticized on this count by the *Christian Examiner*; see *Imprints*, p. 7.

6. Especially in the poems now entitled "Song of Myself" and "The Sleepers."

7. This poem had already been published in 1855, but it then celebrated the human body in rather general terms; it was only in 1856 that Whitman added the very frank and bold passage which constitutes §9 of the final version (*Inc. Ed.*, pp. 85–86).

8. *Inc. Ed.*, pp. 88–90.

9. *LG 1856*, p. 356.

10. It was about this time that Whitman wrote the following note, found among his papers after his death: "Make the *Works* — Do not go into criticism or arguments at all. Make full-blooded, rich, flush, natural works. Insert natural things, indestructibles, idioms, characteristics, rivers, states, persons, etc. Be full of *strong sensual germs*" (underlined by Whitman); *CW*, VI, 7, or *N & F*, p. 57 (16). The editor, R. M. Bucke, thought that this fragment dated back to 1856.

11. See *LG 1855*, pp. 51–52, "Song of Myself," *Inc. Ed.*, pp. 70–71, §46. The theme was not new even in 1855; it was already to be found in an 1847–48 notebook (*Uncoll. PP*, II, 66–67); but the image was still very close to the banal comparison of life with a road.

12. *LG 1856*, pp. 223–239, *Inc. Ed.*, pp. 124–133.

13. *LG 1856*, pp. 124–133, *Inc. Ed.*, pp. 223–239.

14. For instance, pp. 21–24 and 35–40 in *LG 1855*, *Inc. Ed.*, "Song of Myself," pp. 34–37, §15, and pp. 51–57, §33.

15. *Leaves-Droppings*, pp. 345–346. Whitman had published this letter on October 10, 1855, in the New York *Tribune*, at the request of the editor, Charles A. Dana, who was a friend of his. He then pasted clippings from this into some of the review copies of the first edition. He also had it reprinted, and he included it as an appendix to the 1855 volume, specifying, however, that this was "Copy for the convenience of private reading only." For the publication of this letter had been violently criticized. He had in fact been guilty of discourtesy. The letter was strictly personal, and ought not to have been published without the consent of its author, who would probably have expressed himself somewhat differently if he had been writing for publication (see Bliss Perry, *Walt Whitman*, 1906, pp. 114–115).

However, Emerson, although he was sometimes taken to task for having so rashly approved such a daring book (in particular in the New York *Criterion*; see *Imprints*, pp. 55–56), never reproached Whitman for his use of the letter, and did not even speak of it when Whitman called on him a year later. Therefore, Whitman probably felt justified in publishing it as an appendix to his second edition. Moreover, he apparently found convincing arguments to justify this move. Thoreau, after his first meeting with Whitman, wrote to his friend Harrison Blake: "In his apologizing account of the matter, he made the printing of Emerson's letter seem a little thing — and to some extent throws the burden of it — if there is any, on the writer." Curiously, this sentence does not appear in the edition of Thoreau's *Letters* edited by Emerson (Thoreau, *Letters to Various Correspondents* [Boston, 1865], p. 142); it is given in Viola C. White, "Thoreau's Opinion of Whitman," *NEQ*, VIII (June 1935) 262–264.

The reviewer for the New York *Times*, otherwise favorable to Whitman, attacked him sharply for using Emerson's letter in his 1856 edition, because, he said, its praise was intended for the twelve original poems only; see *Imprints*, p. 26.

16. *LG 1856*, p. 346.

17. These poems were: "Poem of Many in One" (later "By Blue Ontario's Shore"), "Poem of the Last Explanation of Prudence" (later "Song of Prudence"), "Liberty Poem for Asia" (later "To a Foil'd Revolutionaire"), and "Poem of the Singers of the Words of Poems" (later the second part of "Song of the Answerer"). See Willie T. Weathers, "Whitman's Poetic Translations of His 1855 Preface," *AL*, XIX (March 1947), 21–40.

18. Later called "By Blue Ontario's Shore."

19. *LG 1860*, pp. 108–125.

20. A verse of the 1860 version shows the strange interconnection of the two themes: "The Many in One — what is it finally except myself?" *LG 1860*, p. 125, *Inc. Ed.*, p. 665.

21. "Whitman, the Poet," *New Republic*, October 20, 1947, p. 27.

22. See above, p. 290, n. 14.

23. *LG 1856*, p. 316, *Inc. Ed.*, p. 469.

24. *LG 1855*, pp. 89–90, *Inc. Ed.*, p. 225.

25. "Let us all, without missing one, be exposed in public, naked, monthly. . ." *LG 1856*, p. 319, *Inc. Ed.*, "Respondez," p. 471, l. 39.

26. "Let there be no God!" *LG 1856*, p. 319, *Inc. Ed.*, "Respondez," p. 471, l. 42.

27. *LG 1856*, p. 319, *Inc. Ed.*, "Respondez," p. 471, ll. 41–43.

28. *LG 1856*, pp. 318, 320, *Inc. Ed.*, "Respondez," p. 471, l. 28, and 472, l. 53.

29. *LG 1856*, pp. 321, 317, *Inc. Ed.*, p. 472, ll. 65–66, and p. 470, l. 22.

30. *LG 1856*, p. 317, *Inc. Ed.*, p. 470, ll. 13–14, 23, 26.

31. *LG 1856*, p. 321, *Inc. Ed.*, p. 472, ll. 59–62, 64.

32. *LG 1856*, pp. 317–320, *Inc. Ed.*, p. 470, l. 21, p. 471, l. 27, and p. 472, l. 50.

33. *LG 1856*, pp. 319, 321, *Inc. Ed.*, p. 471, l. 39, and p. 472, l. 63.

34. *LG 1856*, p. 255, *Inc. Ed.*, "Excelsior," p. 397, l. 4.

35. *LG 1856*, "Sun-Down Poem," pp. 216–217, *Inc. Ed.*, "Crossing Brooklyn Ferry," pp. 136–137, §6, ll. 1–12. It is to be noted that in 1860 he canceled the phrase "a solitary committer." He probably thought that it was too disquieting, and he now preferred to be considered merely as a "solitary singer."

36. *Imprints*, p. 27.

37. *Ibid.*, pp. 6–7.

38. *Ibid.*, p. 27.

39. See *I Sit and Look Out*, pp. 186–187.

40. This volume was entitled *Abbie Nott and Other Knots* (Philadelphia: Lippincott, 1856), and was the work of a mysterious "Katinka" whose identity was never established. The quoted lines came from "Song of Myself" (*Inc. Ed.*, p. 40, §20, ll. 22–24). They were taken from the 1855 edition since *Abbie Nott* appeared before the 1856 volume.

This curious book presents a problem. Some scholars have wondered whether it might have been by Whitman himself. (See John T. Winterich, "Good Secondhand Condition," *Publishers' Weekly*, March 1928, pp. 1309–1310, and Carolyn Wells, "On Collecting Whitman," *Colophon*, vol. I, no. 4, 1940.) But the problem seems insoluble. The copyright was granted under the name of Katinka (Eastern District of Pennsylvania, April 5, 1856, no. 148), and the publishers cannot give any further information, part of their record having been destroyed by a fire in 1898. One theory is that the author was Mrs. Catherine Brooks Yale (1818–1900), the wife of Linus Yale, inventor of the Yale lock. She was a writer in her spare time, publishing among other things *Nim and Cum and the Wonderland Stories* (Chicago, 1895), but there is no real evidence for this hypothesis and no close parallel between the known works of Mrs. Yale and Katinka. On the other hand, the resemblances between Katinka and Whitman are rather striking. The stories recall those which Whitman had written earlier and the sketches closely resemble descriptions in some of his articles. The same Quaker influences appear. There is frequent mention of "the inner natural light." Like Whitman, Katinka was much concerned with the problem of evil. Like him she advocated feminism (pp. 108, 216, etc.) and believed in the value of hydrotherapy (p. 96); she also describes a trip down the Mississippi (pp. 131–133), and in a chapter devoted to childhood memories she portrays an ideal mother who might have been Whitman's own (pp. 290–293). She even speaks of a poem in regular verse as a "rhythmical jingle" (p. 112). Finally, Cunningham, with whom Abbie Nott falls in love, shows a remarkable resemblance to Whitman, at least to Whitman as he would have liked to be: "He followed this interior conviction, laid aside his books and commenced his uncertain travels, following only the attraction of magnetism. Wherever he went, he scattered his rich intellectual wealth in the form of lectures and conversations." It is also remarkable that one of the terms most often used by Katinka is "magnetism" or "magnetic," which is also one of Whitman's favorites. All these are disquieting coincidences, but without further evidence, they remain inconclusive.

41. "Poem of Many in One," *LG 1856*, p. 196, *Inc. Ed.*, "By Blue Ontario's Shore," p. 296, §14, l. 16.

42. "Poem of the Sayers of the Words of the Earth," *LG 1856*, p. 331, *Inc. Ed.*, "A Song of the Rolling Earth," pp. 190–191, §4, ll. 6, 8–12.

43. See above, Chapter III, no. 2.

44. Among his papers is an article on "Egotism" clipped from *Graham's Magazine* (XXVII [March 1845] 97–103; see *Catalogue of the Trent Collection*, p. 69), in which he had underlined in pencil the following passage on Wordsworth: "His poems originally were unpopular, the principles of taste on which they are written were misrepresented and ridiculed, their faults were magnified and their merits underrated with a dishonesty almost unprecedented in the history of criticism." And further on: "A more humble spirit would have been crushed by the opposition he received and ceased to write with the condemnation of the *Lyrical Ballads*." At the bottom of this page, he wrote in ink: "See above and Beware!" which shows that he was thinking of himself. Several other passages are also underlined, including this one, two pages further on: "A great author, hated, reviled, persecuted, starved, in his own age, is almost sure of deification in the next."

It is impossible to know exactly when he read and annotated this article, but it may have been long after the date of publication, when he was beginning to work on *Leaves of Grass*, or even after he had published one or more editions.

The case of Wordsworth seems to have interested him very much, for the Berg Collection of the New York Public Library has another article on Wordsworth from an unidentified periodical, a review of Christopher Wordsworth's *Memoirs of William Wordsworth*, and of a Boston edition of Wordsworth's poems dated 1851. Whitman here also underlined several passages which he must have found encouraging; these in particular: ". . . we are always ready to ask help of him whose vision is clearer than our own. We welcome therefore the true seer [see 1855 preface, *Inc. Ed.*, p. 492]. He is eyes for the world; he is the true keeper of keepers. . . An age of imitation never recognizes the inspired teacher who is true to his own nature. . . Happy the age in which a strong devout soul converses with the Spirit of the Universe in the hearing of men!"

Thus Wordsworth must have exerted a certain influence on Whitman, not so much through his work, which the American poet hardly knew and did not like (in the margin of the same article, next to the sentence, "Wordsworth is not equal in imagination to the greatest poets," he wrote in pencil this indignant exclamation: "Well, I should say not!"), as by his example and personality, in so far as Whitman was able to understand it through the medium of magazine articles. (See Roger Asselineau, "Whitman et Wordsworth. Etude d'une influence indirecte," *Revue de Littérature Comparée*, XXIX [October-December 1955], 505–512). With Whitman we must recognize in addition to the direct literary influences on his work other influences, more diffuse, but also derived from literature, which affected the development of his personality.

IV. NEW UNCERTAINTIES

1. *The Journals of Bronson Alcott*, ed. Odell Shepard (Boston: Little, Brown, 1938), pp. 289–290, entry for November 10, 1856.

2. See above, Chapter I, n. 40.

3. His friendship for the Broadway omnibus drivers soon became legendary. It began during his early years in New York but after *Leaves of Grass* had given him a certain notoriety the newspapers took it up. For example, the New York *Tribune* remarked in 1859: "The *Boston Courier* thinks it very likely that the poet Walt Whitman, as is reported, now drives a Broadway omnibus and says:

'Whitman's extraordinary abilities have always been fettered by an unconquerable laziness. The last time we saw him his dress was wonderful beyond description; high heavy boots, tight trousers, an unprecedented rough jacket, and a tapering tower of a hat. It was said last winter that he was getting up a series of lectures, but it seems that his natural indolence has conquered his poetic inspiration.' " New York *Tribune*, 1859, quoted in *Imprints*, p. 64.

A few days later the New York *Constellation* replied: "An omnibus driver or not? — A leading journal in this city has recently been duped by a communication or a statement manufactured in its own office into saying that Walt Whitman, the writer of *Leaves of Grass*, one of the most remarkable and original contributors to our literature for many years, was driving an omnibus. Now whether he has ever done so or not, we neither know nor care; but certain are we that he is not, at present, doing so, as we have repeatedly seen and conversed with him in the course of the present month. And we regard the attempt to stain the supposititious act with a ludicrous celebrity, as having been made in the worst of tastes." Quoted in *Imprints*, p. 64.

The somewhat extravagant tone of this reply would seem to indicate that the correction came from Whitman himself, and it is possible that the communication which had led the New York *Tribune* into its error was also his work. It is fairly probable that this series of articles constituted a small advertising campaign which he had engineered to attract public attention. This would have been entirely consistent with his usual practice.

4. See above, Chapter I.

5. At one time he was so short of money that he had to borrow two hundred dollars from his friend James Parton, the husband of Fanny Fern, and it seems that he had great difficulty in repaying it two months later, partly in cash, partly in kind. Parton may even have had to institute proceedings. At any rate, the two friends quarreled after this incident. Whitman was later accused by his enemies of never having paid this debt, and he thought it necessary to justify himself to posterity by explaining the whole affair to Horace Traubel (see *With WW in C*, III, 235–239).

Some of the details of this rather confused story can be found in *New York Dissected*, pp. 152–153, n, 20, p. 239; *I Sit and Look Out*, p. 211, n. 6; O. S. Coad, "Whitman vs. Parton," *Rutgers University Library Journal*, December 1940, pp. 1–8.

Coad, who was able to consult the letters of Kennedy, Harned, Traubel, and Ethel Parton (a niece of Parton's) now in the Rutgers University Library, believes that Whitman completed the payment of his debt in June 1857. Bliss Perry, however, apparently on hearsay evidence, at one time accused Whitman of having dissipated the fortune which a young man of letters, Parton, had imprudently lent him (see his *Walt Whitman*, pp. 123–124). Traubel protested violently against this unwarranted accusation ("Questions for Bliss Perry," *Conservator*, November 1906, pp. 137–138) and Bliss Perry was obliged to make a partial retraction in the appendix of the second edition. Whitman's version of the affair is very clearly given in a letter to O'Connor dated September 28, 1869 (see *SPL*, pp. 986–987).

6. In this respect he merely followed the example of Emerson, Thackeray, Dickens, Philips, and Curtis. The American public was always eager to listen to lectures. On the importance of the oratorical

tradition in the United States, see F. O. Matthiessen, *American Renaissance*, pp. 18–23.

7. *LG 1856*, p. 346.

8. *N & F*, p. 57, or *CW*, VI, 7–8. This manuscript note is dated April 24, 1857.

9. See above, Chapter I.

10. See above, Chapter I.

11. *In Re*, p. 19.

12. *In Re*, p. 35.

13. Part of this material was published by C. J. Furness in his *WWW*, pp. 33–68. See also T. B. Harned, "Walt Whitman and Oratory," *CW*, VIII, 244 ff. *New York Dissected* contains an article by Whitman (pp. 179–181) in which, after criticizing the lecturers he had heard in Brooklyn in the course of the year, he tried to define what the ideal lecturer should be. In 1851 he had himself lectured before the Brooklyn Art Union (see Brooklyn *Daily Advertizer*, April 3, 1851, *Uncoll. PP*, I, 241–247, and Bliss Perry, *Walt Whitman*, pp. 49–55).

14. See *WWW*, pp. 39–60.

15. *WWW*, pp. 66–67.

16. *WWW*, pp. 197–198, n. 31. The MS, now in the Trent Collection (see *Catalogue of the Trent Collection*, p. 58), bears the date of 1858.

As Furness remarks, the two media of expression were so closely associated in his mind that the notes which he collected were used indiscriminately for his projected lectures or for his poems. On one of the scraps of paper which he used for his rough drafts he first wrote the title "Poem-Religious" and then added: "or in lecture on Religion." Sometimes the process was reversed; materials intended for a lecture were later incorporated into a poem, as in the case of these two lines of "Starting from Paumanok" (*Inc. Ed.*, p. 16, §7, ll. 18–19):

"Nor character nor life worth the name without religion,
    Nor land, nor man, nor woman, without religion."

Whitman had first written over these two lines "Lecture"; nevertheless he used them in the poem without any alteration.

17. *WWW*, p. 198, n. 31.

18. Often, moreover, in his notes, side by side with the word "lecture," he used the word "lesson." For him it was less a matter of lectures in the ordinary sense than of lay sermons. He wanted to preach above all. See *WWW*, p. 32.

19. Maurice Bucke discerned the same evolution; see *N & F*, p. vi.

20. *WWW*, p. 197, n. 31. His reason for wanting so much to

publish the text of his lectures was not merely his desire to make money; he believed profoundly in the superiority of writing over speech. In an article from the *Edinburgh Review* (Am. Ed., LXXXIX [April 1949] 149–168, see *Catalogue of the Trent Collection*, p. 80), entitled "The Vanity and Glory of Literature," he underlined the following passage: "Great as has been the influence of Socrates, he owes it almost entirely to the books he refused to write, and it might have been greater still, had he condescended to write some of his own." The article bears the date 1856 in Whitman's hand. Therefore he must have read it precisely at the time with which we are concerned. Though it may seem curious, it is possible that he may have been thinking of becoming an orator mainly for reasons of health. He had clipped and carefully preserved an article from the *American Phrenological Journal*, which contains the following statement: "This constant excitability of men of letters not unfrequently leads to inflammation, and sometimes to a softening of the brain. Dean Swift and Daniel Webster, both of whom possessed great intellects and thought profoundly, died of this affection. . . Yet, notwithstanding these evils incident to a literary life, its average duration is of a respectable length and frequently extends to great age. This was particularly the case among ancient philosophers, who alternated their time between abstruse studies in the closet and conversations and speeches in the midst of their fellow-citizens in the open air and public buildings in which they were wont to assemble. Plato died at 81, Xenocrates at 82, Thales at 89 and Democritus at 100" (*Catalogue of the Trent Collection*, pp. 66–67).

These newspaper clippings and magazine articles which Whitman so carefully annotated and underlined have not yet received the attention they deserve. A very large number have survived to give precise evidence regarding Whitman's habitual concerns and his opinions about certain literary and philosophical problems. This source of information is particularly important because Whitman read a great many periodicals and very few books, especially after 1848.

21. There are many allusions to this profession in the 1860 edition. Whitman mentions the power of the orator over crowds several times, as for example in "Poem of Joys," p. 268, §39. But in the edition of 1871 this passage has disappeared. Elsewhere ("Leaves of Grass," no. 16, pp. 189–190, later entitled "Mediums," *Inc. Ed.*, p. 399), he regards orators as mediums, as spokesmen for God. He speaks also of his intention to travel throughout the United States giving lectures or speeches ("Leaves of Grass," no. 17, pp. 190–191, later entitled "On Journeys through the States," *Inc. Ed.*, p. 8), a dream which he never gave up; in the definitive edition, the poem which expresses it is placed in the "Inscriptions," with which the

book begins, as if to give it more weight. But his finest hymn to the glory of orators was "Leaves of Grass," no. 12, pp. 183–185, later entitled "Vocalism" (*Inc. Ed.*, pp. 321–322, and variant readings, pp. 674–675).

22. *I Sit and Look Out*, p. 17.

23. He had previously resumed his journalistic activities in 1856 by contributing from time to time to *Life Illustrated*, a Fowler and Wells publication. He had in particular written a series of articles under the title of "New York Dissected," which have been collected by Emory Holloway and Ralph Adimari in *New York Dissected* (New York: R. R. Wilson, 1938). A chronological list of these articles may be found in *Catalogue of the Trent Collection*, pp. 101–102.

24. See Canby, *Walt Whitman*, Plates VI, VII, VIII. See also the description by Frederick Huene, a young German poet who came to America after the Revolution of 1848 and worked as a typographer on the Brooklyn *Times* in *I Sit and Look Out*, p. 12.

25. See *I Sit and Look Out*, p. 17. But he was only an occasional contributor.

26. The paper, however, had campaigned for Frémont, the Republican candidate in 1856, but this, as we shall see, could only please Whitman.

27. *I Sit and Look Out*, pp. 59–60.

28. *Ibid.*, pp. 47–49.

29. *Ibid.*, pp. 54–55.

30. "A Dialogue," *Democratic Review*, XVII (November 1845), 360–364, *Uncoll. PP*, I, 97–103; "Hurrah for Hanging," Brooklyn *Eagle*, March 23, 1846, *Uncoll. PP*, I, 108–110.

31. "Capital Punishment," Brooklyn *Times*, May 22, 1858, *Uncoll. PP*, II, 15–16; "The Death-Penalty," January 13, 1858, *I Sit and Look Out*, pp. 46–47.

32. "The Radicals in Council," June 29, 1858, *I Sit and Look Out*, pp. 45–46.

33. "The Temperance Movement," March 10, 1858, *ibid.*, p. 49.

34. "A Delicate Subject," June 20, 1859, *ibid.*, pp. 119–120.

35. "Reformers," *ibid.*, pp. 44–45.

36. "Our Pecuniary Difficulties," October 5, 1857, *ibid.*, pp. 169–170.

37. "We progress!" November 7, 1857, *ibid.*, p. 43.

38. See his contributions to the Brooklyn *Eagle* collected in *G of the F*, I, 240–266.

39. "The Spanish American Republics," September 10, 1858, *ibid.*, pp. 162–163.

40. Jean Catel first published it in pamphlet form: *The Eighteenth*

Presidency (Montpellier: Causse, Graille et Castelnau, 1928). C. J. Furness published a slightly different version in *WWW*, pp. 87–113. The best edition is that of Edward F. Grier, *The Eighteenth Presidency* (University of Kansas Press, 1956).

41. *WWW*, p. 92.
42. *WWW*, p. 93.
43. *WWW*, p. 95.
44. *WWW*, pp. 99–100.
45. *WWW*, p. 100.
46. *WWW*, p. 109.
47. *WWW*, p. 110.
48. *WWW*, pp. 112–113.
49. *WWW*, pp. 111–112.
50. *Inc. Ed.*, p. 236. This poem was written in 1857, probably shortly after the election of Buchanan. Whitman himself wrote this date in the copy of the 1860 edition that he used to prepare the next edition. This so-called "blue-copy" is now in the Lion Collection in the New York Public Library.
51. *Inc. Ed.*, p. 236.
52. *N & F*, p. 57 (14).
53. *SPL*, p. 885. See also Rollo G. Silver, "Seven Letters of Walt Whitman," *AL*, *VII* (March 1935), 78.
54. Yet there is one between an article published on September 30, 1857, "The Cure" (*I Sit and Look Out*, pp. 42–43), and several poems of the 1860 edition: "You Felons on Trial in Courts" (*Inc. Ed.*, p. 323), "To a Pupil" (*Inc. Ed.*, p. 327), and "Of the Visage of Things" (*Inc. Ed.*, p. 480).
55. Whitman himself wrote this article, which he probably intended to publish in a friendly periodical. The MS is now in the Yale University Library. See Canby, *Walt Whitman*, pp. 135–136.
56. Thanks to Clapp's friendship, Whitman published in the *Saturday Press* first "A Child's Reminiscence" (later "Out of the Cradle. . .") on December 24, 1859, and on January 7, 1860, an anonymous article entitled "All about a Mocking-Bird," which was a reply to an attack of the Cincinnati *Commercial* of December 28, 1859 (reprinted in *Imprints*, pp. 57–59). In this article he triumphantly announced the approaching publication of the third edition of *Leaves of Grass*. On May 19, 1860, the *Press* published a very favorable review of his book — which he had written himself. See T. O. Mabbott and Rollo G. Silver, "*A Child's Reminiscence by Walt Whitman*" (University of Washington Bookstore, 1930).
57. On Whitman and the New York Bohemia, see Van Wyck Brooks, *The Times of Melville and Whitman* (New York: Dutton,

1947), pp. 192–216; W. S. Kennedy, "Notes on the Pfaffians," *Conservator*, March 1897; Charles I. Glicksberg, "Walt Whitman and Bayard Taylor," *N & Q, CLXXIII* (July 3, 1937), 5–7.

58. W. D. Howells, *Literary Friends and Acquaintances*, 1900, p. 74.

59. *Uncoll. PP*, II, 93.

60. *With WW in C*, I, 417.

61. *Uncoll. PP*, II, 91. This notebook dates back to 1859. This fragment has been used partly in "That Shadow My Likeness," *Inc. Ed.*, p. 112. (*LG 1860*, "Calamus" no. 40, p. 376). The same idea is to be found in "Song of Myself," *Inc. Ed.*, p. 27, §4, ll, 10–14.

62. See introduction to *I Sit and Look Out*, pp. 13–17.

63. *I Sit and Look Out*, pp. 119–120.

64. *Ibid.*, pp. 120–122.

65. *Uncoll. PP*, II, 91, n. 1.

66. *Ibid.*; Holloway, *Whitman*, p. 164, and *I Sit and Look Out*, p. 16.

67. Canby, *Walt Whitman*, p. 130.

68. *SD*, p. 20, *CP*, pp. 15–16. There is nothing on the years between 1857 and 1860.

69. *Uncoll. PP*, II, 91.

70. He may have been for some time ready to defy public opinion; see his article in the Brooklyn *Times* on February 4, 1858 (*I Sit and Look Out*, p. 172).

71. The poem which best expresses this obsession is "To You" (*LG 1860*, p. 403, *Inc. Ed.*, p. 479) which was also suppressed in 1867. Other characteristic poems are: "A Glimpse" (*LG 1860*, "Calamus" no. 29, p. 371, *Inc. Ed.*, p. 109), "Among the Multitude" (*LG 1860*, "Calamus" no. 41, p. 376, *Inc. Ed.*, p. 112). In the "Poem of Joys" (*LG 1860*, p. 261, §§13–14, *Inc. Ed.*, "A Song of Joys," p. 610, in the variant readings) there is a discreet allusion to his secret desires: "O the young man as I pass! O I am sick after the friendship of him who, I fear, is indifferent to me. . . The memory of one only look — the boy lingering and waiting." This revealing passage was suppressed in 1881.

72. The date 1858–59 which we suggest is based on no document; it is however extremely probable, for if we may believe "Long I Thought that Knowledge. . ." (*Inc. Ed.*, pp. 477–478), the sentimental crisis was posterior to the political crisis. The latter, as we have seen, occurred in 1856–57. Fredson Bowers, after a careful study of Whitman's MSS, has reached exactly the same conclusion; see *Whitman's Manuscripts — Leaves of Grass 1860* (University of Chicago Press, 1955), pp. xli–l, and Fredson Bowers, *Textual and Literary Criticism* (Cambridge University Press, 1959), pp. 35–65.

73. *LG 1860*, "Calamus" no. 8, pp. 354–355, *Inc. Ed.*, "Long I Thought that Knowledge," pp. 477–478, ll. 5–12.

74. *LG 1860*, "Calamus" no. 26, p. 369, *Inc. Ed.*, p. 108.

75. *LG 1860*, "Calamus" no. 9, pp. 355–356, *Inc. Ed.*, pp. 478–479.

76. *LG 1860*, pp. 269–277, *Inc. Ed.*, p. 210 ("Out of the Cradle Endlessly Rocking").

77. *LG 1860*, p. 276 (30), *Inc. Ed.*, p. 637, variant reading of l. 150.

78. G. W. Allen, *Walt Whitman Handbook*, pp. 143–144.

79. *Inc. Ed.*, p. 212, l. 74, p. 213, ll. 111–112, 115.

80. *Inc. Ed.*, p. 638, variant reading of ll. 158ff. The passage was canceled in 1881. It was quite out of place since it expressed the despair of Whitman in 1858–59 rather than the feelings of the child.

81. *LG 1860*, pp. 195–199, *Inc. Ed.*, pp. 216–218.

82. *LG 1860*, pp. 410–411, *Inc. Ed.*, p. 377, under the title of "Thought," ll. 9–10. See also "Yet, yet, Ye Downcast Hours," *Inc. Ed.*, p. 372, l. 4 (*LG 1860*, p. 422).

83. *LG 1860*, "Calamus" no. 17, pp. 362–363, *Inc. Ed.*, p. 372. In his various editions of *Leaves of Grass*, Emory Holloway erroneously gives 1871 as the first publication date of this poem. See my article, "A propos de Walt Whitman," *Langues Modernes*, 42ème Année, no. 4, p. 65 (August–October, 1948).

84. *LG 1860*, p. 425, *Inc. Ed.*, p. 373 ("As if a Phantom Caress'd Me").

85. *LG 1860*, "So Long!" p. 464 (15), and 456 (23), *Inc. Ed.*, p. 417, l. 33, pp. 418–419, ll. 64–71, and variant readings, p. 704.

86. *LG 1860*, p. 423, *Inc. Ed.*, p. 482.

87. *LG 1855*, p. 55, *Inc. Ed.*, p. 75, "Song of Myself," §50, l. 10.

88. "A Word out of the Sea," *LG 1860*, p. 276 (31), *Inc. Ed.*, p. 638, "Out of the Cradle Endlessly Rocking," variant reading of ll. 158f.

89. *Walt Whitman*, trans. Evie Allison Allen, with an introduction by Gay W. Allen (New York: Columbia University Press, 1951), pp. 160–179.

90. *Ibid.*, p. 143. Schyberg believes that his period of dissipation ended on April 16, 1861, on which day Whitman recorded the following resolution in one of his notebooks: "Thursday, April 16, 1861, I have this hour, this day resolved to inaugurate a sweet, clean-blooded body by ignoring all drinks but water and pure milk — and all fat meats, late suppers — a great body — a purged, cleansed, spiritualized invigorated body."

However, Schyberg's thesis is greatly weakened by the fact that these dietary rules do not imply that Whitman had previously led a life of debauchery. There are several other similar resolutions in his notebooks, some of which are even more disquieting than this one, notably that which he took on July 15, 1868 or 1869 (*Uncoll. PP,* II, 95).

91. See C. J. Furness, "Walt Whitman Looks at Boston," *NEQ,* July 1928, pp. 353, 370. See also *SD,* p. 183, W. S. Kennedy, *The Fight of a Book for the World,* p. 15, and J. T. Trowbridge, "Reminiscences of Walt Whitman," *Atlantic Monthly,* LXXXIX (February 1902), 163–175.

92. See above, n. 85.

v. the 1860 edition

1. As this passage in *Fourteen Thousand Miles Afoot* (New York, 1859) shows: "Nothing can more clearly demonstrate the innate vulgarity of our American people, their radical immodesty, their internal licentiousness, their unchastity of heart, their foulness of feeling, than the tabooing of Walt Whitman's *Leaves of Grass.* It is quite impossible to find a publisher for the new edition which has long since been ready for the press." (Quoted in *Imprints,* pp. 51–52.)

2. See Chapter IV, n. 56.

3. According to Kennedy, it was Col. Richard J. Hinton who gave Thayer and Eldridge the idea of publishing *Leaves of Grass (The Fight of a Book for the World,* p. 242).

4. See C. J. Furness, "Walt Whitman Looks at Boston," *NEQ,* I, (July 1928), 353–370.

5. See *NB,* pp. 47–49, *CP,* pp. 399–401.

6. Frank Sanborn himself recalled the incident in a letter to the Springfield *Republican* (April 19, 1876). See Furness, "Walt Whitman Looks at Boston," *NEQ,* I (July 1928), and Holloway, *Whitman,* pp. 164–165.

7. *Atlantic Monthly,* April 1860.

8. "Reminiscences of Walt Whitman," *ibid.,* LXXXIX, 163–175, later reprinted in *My Own Story* (Boston: Houghton Mifflin, 1903), pp. 360–401.

9. After the failure of Thayer and Eldridge in 1861, the plates were bought by an unscrupulous publisher, Richard Worthington, who later printed thousands of fake copies of the third edition (10,000 according to Kennedy). The copies of this spurious edition can easily be distinguished from the genuine ones by their coarser binding and the absence on p. 2 of the indication: "Electrotyped at the Boston Stereotype Foundry," the mention of which would have enabled Whitman to take legal action against Worthington. See *With WW in C,* I, 195–196, 250–251, 255–256; W. S. Kennedy, *The Fight of a*

Book for the World, p. 243, and Carolyn Wells and Alfred F. Goldsmith, *A Concise Bibliography of the Works of Walt Whitman* (Boston: Houghton Mifflin, 1922), p. 107.

10. The name of the author, however, is given on the backstrip, but, unlike the title, is not gilded.

11. This butterfly reappeared in *SD*, which contains between pages 122 and 123 a fine photograph showing Whitman with a butterfly on his forefinger. Esther Shephard (*Walt Whitman's Pose*, pp. 250–251 and plate 16, p. 212) has proved that this protograph was a fake. She has found among Whitman's papers a cardboard butterfly which he probably tied to his finger with a piece of wire on that occasion. But this does not detract from the symbolic value of the picture.

12. See above, Chapter IV, n. 53.

13. The 45 poems of "Calamus" were new and so were 12 or 15 of the poems which made up "Enfans d'Adam" — 57 in all. It is probable that the poems entitled "Chants Democratic" were composed earlier, in 1856–57 when Whitman went through his political crisis — and so were most of the longer poems (for the date of "Proto-Leaf," see below, n. 38).

14. *LG 1860*, p. 13, "Proto-Leaf," §34, *Inc. Ed.*, p. 17, "Starting from Paumanok," §10, ll. 3–5. He also announced "Calamus":

    "And sexual organs and acts! do you concentrate in me —
        For I am determined to tell you with courageous clear
        voice, to prove you illustrious."

LG 1860, p. 10, "Proto-Leaf," §21, *Inc. Ed.*, p. 18, "Starting from Paumanok," §12, l. 11.

15. From an article published anonymously by Whitman in the New York *Saturday Press* (January 7, 1860), reprinted in Mabbott and Silver, *A Child's Reminiscence by Walt Whitman* (University of Washington Press, 1930).

16. From a letter dated July 20, 1857; see *SPL*, p. 885.

17. *LG 1860*, p. 239, *Inc. Ed.*, p. 475, "So Far and So Far and On Toward the End."

18. *LG 1860*, pp. 451–456, *Inc. Ed.*, pp. 416–419.

19. He wanted his book to look like a Bible. All the longer poems are divided into numbered paragraphs so that it is possible to give chapter and verse, so to speak, for any quotation.

20. *LG 1860*, p. 29, *Inc. Ed.*, p. 44, "Song of Myself," §24, ll. 20–22.

21. *LG 1855*, pp. 77–82, *Inc. Ed.*, pp. 79–86, "I Sing the Body Electric."

22. "Poem of Women," *LG 1856*, pp. 100–102, *Inc. Ed.*, p. 327–328, "Unfolded out of the Folds"; "Poem of Procreation," *LG 1856*, pp. 240–243, *Inc. Ed.*, pp. 86–88, "A Woman Waits for Me"; "Bunch

Poem," *LG 1856*, pp. 309–312, *Inc. Ed.*, pp. 88–90, "Spontaneous Me."

23. He said so himself in *LG 1860*, p. 11, "Proto-Leaf," §22, *Inc. Ed.*, p. 15, "Starting from Paumanok," §6, ll. 21–23.

24. In a letter to Harrison Blake, *Thoreau's Familiar Letters* (Boston: Houghton Mifflin, 1894), p. 345.

25. He already aimed at this kind of symmetry in the fifth poem of *LG 1855*, *Inc. Ed.*, pp. 79–86, "I Sing the Body Electric."

26. *N & F*, p. 169 (63).

27. See above, Chapter IV, pp. 107–113.

28. *LG 1855*, p. 79, *Inc. Ed.*, p. 81, "I Sing the Body Electric," §4, l. 165.

29. *LG 1856*, pp. 240–243, *Inc. Ed.*, pp. 86–88, "A Woman Waits for Me."

30. *LG 1856*, p. 312, *Inc. Ed.*, p. 90, "Spontaneous Me," l. 42.

31. This was in 1856 the beginning of the first line of "Poem of Procreation."

32. Is it not symptomatic that all the poems that make up "Calamus" were published in 1860, while several of the more important poems in "Enfans d'Adam" date from the first two editions? It proves that he became aware of the abnormal character of his instincts only in 1859–60.

33. *SD*, p. 191, *CP*, p. 189.

34. *LG 1867*, p. 7, *Inc. Ed.*, p. 12, "Starting from Paumanok," §1, ll. 3–4. As early as 1860 he declared:

> "See in my poems, old and new cities, solid, vast, inland, with paved streets, with iron and stone edifices, and ceaseless vehicles and commerce."

LG 1860, p. 21, "Proto-Leaf," §63, *Inc. Ed.*, p. 22, "Starting from Paumanok," §18, l. 6.

35. "Calamus" no. 10, *LG 1860*, p. 356, *Inc. Ed.*, p. 593, among the variant readings of "Recorders Ages Hence."

36. "Calamus" no. 8, *LG 1860*, p. 354, *Inc. Ed.*, "Long I Thought that Knowledge," p. 478, l. 4.

37. *LG 1860*, p. 105.

38. "Proto-Leaf," *LG 1860*, p. 5 (1), *Inc. Ed.*, p. 557. This poem, the exuberance and optimism of which are so close to those of the first edition, may have been written as early as 1856, since Whitman declared:

> "In the Year 80 of the States. . .
> I, now thirty-six years old. . ."

LG 1860, p. 8 (11), *Inc. Ed.*, pp. 548–549, variant reading of §3. The year of Independence, 1776, plus 80, equals 1856.

39. *Ibid.*

40. "Leaves of Grass" no. 20, *LG 1860*, p. 239, *Inc. Ed.*, p. 475.

41. *LG 1860*, pp. 451–456, *Inc. Ed.*, pp. 416–419.

42. "Apostroph," *LG 1860*, pp. 105–106, *Inc. Ed.*, pp. 473–475. This poem was suppressed in 1867, probably because it expressed unwarranted fears and also because it was extremely awkward with all its "O" 's. Besides, in 1860 it served mainly as a prologue to "Chants Democratic" and in 1867 these poems were dispersed.

43. "Proto-Leaf," *LG 1860*, p. 10 (20), *Inc. Ed.*, "Starting from Paumanok," p. 14, §6, ll. 7–9.

44. From a notebook dated 1860–61 now in the Library of Congress.

45. See above, Chapter IV.

46. *LG 1860*, p. 286, *Inc. Ed.*, p. 398, ("Thought," ll. 1–4, 8–10).

47. *LG 1860*, pp. 179–180 ("Chants Democratic" no. 9), *Inc. Ed.*, p. 408 ("Thoughts," §1, ll. 1–2, 5–8).

48. *LG 1860*, pp. 182–183 ("Chants Democratic" no. 11), *Inc. Ed.*, p. 409 ("Thoughts," §2, ll. 1, 9, 11, 15).

49. See the title page: "Year 85 of the States (1860–1861)."

50. *LG 1860*, p. 179 ("Chants Democratic" no. 9), *Inc. Ed.*, p. 408 ("Thoughts," §1, l. 3).

51. See above Chapter III.

52. *LG 1860* ("Leaves of Grass" no. 13), *Inc. Ed.*, p. 323 ("You Felons on Trial in Courts"), and variant readings, pp. 675–676.

53. *LG 1860*, pp. 237–238 ("Leaves of Grass" no. 18), *Inc. Ed.*, pp. 395–396 ("All is Truth," ll. 6–8, 16–17).

54. *LG 1860*, p. 236 ("Leaves of Grass" no. 17), *Inc. Ed.*, p. 232 ("I Sit and Look Out," ll. 1, 9–10).

55. *Ibid.*, l. 2.

56. *LG 1860*, pp. 361–362 ("Calamus" no. 16), *Inc. Ed.*, p. 479 ("Who Is Now Reading This," ll. 1–2, 5–7).

57. See for instance "Calamus" no. 36, *LG 1860*, p. 374, *Inc. Ed.*, p. 110.

58. *LG 1860*, p. 343 ("Calamus" no. 2), *Inc. Ed.*, p. 96 ("Scented Herbage of my Breast," ll. 10–11, 14).

59. "As the Time Draws Nigh," *Inc. Ed.*, p. 405 and 697, which gives the text of the original poem entitled "To My Soul" in 1860.

60. *LG 1860*, pp. 5–22, *Inc. Ed.*, "Starting from Paumanok," pp. 12–23.

61. *LG 1860*, pp. 259–268, *Inc. Ed.*, "A Song of Joys," pp. 149–155.

62. "Leaves of Grass" no. 10, *LG 1860*, pp. 224–226, *Inc. Ed.*, "Myself and Mine," pp. 201–202, ll. 2–4, 30–33, and variant readings p. 633.

63. ". . . full of life now. . ." "Calamus" no. 45, *LG 1860*, p. 378, *Inc. Ed.*, p. 113, l. 1. "I, forty years old. . ." he added; so the poem was written in 1859.

64. *Walt Whitman Handbook*, pp. 143–144, where Schyberg's views are summed up. See Frederik Schyberg, *Walt Whitman* (Copenhagen: Gyldendalske Boghandel, 1933), or the translation by Evie Allison Allen (Columbia University Press, 1951).

65. *LG 1860*, p. 196, "Leaves of Grass" no. 1, §4, *Inc. Ed.*, "As I Ebb'd with the Ocean of Life," p. 216, §2, ll. 5–6.

66. *LG 1860*, p. 342 ("Calamus" no. 2), *Inc. Ed.*, pp. 95–96 ("Scented Herbage of My Breast," ll. 3–5).

67. *LG 1860*, p. 359 ("Calamus" no. 13), *Inc. Ed.*, p. 593 among the variant readings of "Roots and Leaves Themselves Alone."

68. "Whitman: the Poet," *New Republic*, October 20, 1947, p. 27.

69. *LG 1855*, p. 55, *Inc. Ed.*, p. 74, "Song of Myself," §50, l. 4.

70. *LG 1860*, p. 277, §33, *Inc. Ed.*, p. 215, "Out of the Cradle Endlessly Rocking," ll. 165–173.

71. *LG 1860*, p. 268, §41, *Inc. Ed.*, p. 155, "A Song of Joys," ll. 157–161, and p. 612.

72. *LG 1860*, p. 14 (39), *Inc. Ed.*, p. 18, "Starting from Paumanok," §11, l. 4.

73. For example in "Calamus" no. 10 (*LG 1860*, pp. 356–357, *Inc. Ed.*, p. 102, "Recorders Ages Hence"), "Calamus" no. 11 (*LG 1860*, pp. 357–358, *Inc. Ed.*, pp. 102–103, "When I Heard at the Close of the Day"), "Calamus" no. 19 (*LG 1860*, p. 364, *Inc. Ed.*, p. 105, "Behold This Swarthy Face"), "Calamus" no. 29 (*LG 1860*, p. 371, *Inc. Ed.*, p. 109, "A Glimpse"), and "Calamus" no. 20 (*LG 1860*, pp. 364–365, *Inc. Ed.*, p. 106, "I Saw in Louisiana a Live-Oak Growing").

74. See "Calamus" no. 2, *LG 1860*, p. 343, *Inc. Ed.*, p. 96, "Scented Herbage of My Breast," l. 21.

75. *LG 1860*, p. 353 ("Calamus" no. 7), *Inc. Ed.*, p. 101, "Of the Terrible Doubt of Appearances," ll. 14–16.

76. See in particular "Calamus" no. 20, l. 9, *LG 1860*, p. 365, *Inc. Ed.*, p. 106, "I Saw in Louisiana a Live-Oak Growing."

77. "Calamus" no. 39, *LG 1860*, p. 375–376, *Inc. Ed.*, p. 111, "Sometimes with One I Love."

78. See "Proto-Leaf," §22, *LG 1860*, pp. 10–11, *Inc. Ed.*, p. 15, "Starting from Paumanok," ll. 18–26; "Calamus" no. 5, *LG 1860*, pp. 349–351, *Inc. Ed.*, pp. 200–201, "For You O Democracy," and pp. 266–267, "Over the Carnage Rose Prophetic a Voice," and p. 476, "States"; "Calamus" no. 23, *LG 1860*, p. 367, *Inc. Ed.*, p. 107, "This Moment Yearning and Doubtful"; "Calamus" no. 35, *LG 1860*, p. 374, *Inc. Ed.*, p. 111, "To the East and to the West"; "Calamus" no.

37, *LG 1860*, p. 375, *Inc. Ed.*, p. 110, "A Leaf for Hand in Hand"; "Calamus" no. 33, *LG 1860*, p. 373, *Inc. Ed.*, p. 109, "No Labor-Saving Machine"; "Calamus" no. 34, *LG 1860*, p. 373, *Inc. Ed.*, p. 110, "I Dream'd in a Dream."

79. "Calamus" no. 45, *LG 1860*, p. 450, *Inc. Ed.*, p. 113, "Full of Life Now." Gay W. Allen in *The Solitary Singer* (New York: Macmillan, 1955, or Grove Press, 1959), p. 257, points out that the MS version of this poem gives Whitman's age as thirty-eight. But the fact that the poet later changed it to forty shows that he thought his statement was still valid two years later.

80. "To My Soul," *LG 1860*, p. 450, *Inc. Ed.*, p. 405, "As the Times Draws Nigh," l. 8.

81. "Quicksand Years that Whirl Me I Know not Whither," *Drum-Taps*, p. 30, *Inc. Ed.*, p. 374. Though this poem was published only in 1865, it is obvious that it applies to the prewar years and was probably composed toward the end of 1860 or in 1861.

82. "Leaves of Grass" no. 18, *LG 1860*, p. 191, *Inc. Ed.*, p. 9, "Me Imperturbe."

83. "Leaves of Grass" no. 20, *LG 1860*, p. 239, *Inc. Ed.*, p. 475, "So Far and So Far and On Toward the End."

84. *LG 1856*, pp. 211–212, *Inc. Ed.*, pp. 134–139, "Crossing Brooklyn Ferry."

85. For example in "Chants Democratic" no. 14, pp. 186–187, *Inc. Ed.*, p. 11, "Poets to Come," and variant readings, pp. 546–547.

86. See end of "Chants Democratic" no. 11, p. 183, *Inc. Ed.*, p. 409, "Thoughts," §2 ll. 15–18, and: "The market needs to-day to be supplied — the great West especially — with copious thousands of copies" (anonymous article entitled "All about a Mocking-Bird," published in New York *Saturday Press* on January 7, 1860; reprinted in Mabbott and Silver, *A Child's Reminiscence by Walt Whitman*).

87. *LG 1860*, pp. 391–403.

88. "To Him That Was Crucified," p. 397, *Inc. Ed.*, pp. 322–323.

89. *LG 1860*, p. 398, *Inc. Ed.*, p. 376.

90. *LG 1860*, p. 399, *Inc. Ed.*, p. 324.

91. See *Uncoll. PP*, II, 66, 69, 71–72.

92. "Proto-Leaf," §25, *LG 1860*, p. 11, *Inc. Ed.*, p. 16, "Starting from Paumanok," §7, ll. 8–10.

93. *Uncoll. PP*, II, 91–92.

94. According to Trowbridge, Whitman occasionally played the Redeemer's part in everyday life. This is how he described his first encounter with the poet in 1860 at Boston: "We found a large, gray-haired and gray-bearded, plainly dressed man, reading proof-sheets at a desk in a dingy little office, with a lank, unwholesome looking lad at his elbow, listlessly watching him. . . . After he had gone out,

Whitman explained: 'He is a friendless boy I found at my boarding-place — I am trying to cheer him up and strengthen him with my magnetism.' " "Reminiscences of Walt Whitman," *Atlantic Monthly,* LXXXIX (February 1902), 164.

95. Many parodies, in particular, were written. Mabbott and Silver give a list of ten in *A Child's Reminiscence by Walt Whitman.* Whitman reprinted one in his *Imprints,* pp. 61–62. See also Mabbott and Silver, "William Winter's Serious Parody of Walt Whitman," *AL,* V (March 1933), 63–66, and Charles I. Glicksberg, "Walt Whitman Parodies Provoked by the 3rd Edition of *Leaves of Grass,*" *American N & Q,* VII (March 1948), 163–168. The richest collection of these parodies is Henry S. Saunders, *Parodies on Walt Whitman,* preface by Christopher Morley (New York: American Library Service, 1923). Some are to be found in *The Antic Muse,* ed. Robert P. Falk (New York: Grove Press, 1955), pp. 115–126.

96. *Southern Field and Fireside,* June 9, 1860.

97. Reprinted in *Imprints,* p. 58.

98. For instance in the Brooklyn *Times* of July 5, 1860: "In the studied taste and expensiveness of this edition, the publishers have proclaimed the high value they have set upon Mr. Whitman's effusions, whatever divisions of opinions may exist in the rest of the world about them. Years ago we knew him as New York editor and for several years later he has been a miscellaneous contributor to the Press; and during all this time his writings were like other men's, no more strikingly marked with individuality of style. . . . We make no doubt that the singularity of the Leaves is a matter of principle with their author, the embodiment of a piece of profound sagacity."

The Brooklyn *Standard* of November 24, 1860, was still more enthusiastic: "We are not disposed to review or criticize these Leaves because we like them in toto and that's enough. We have read them lovingly and reverently like a true Brooklynite."

99. In the New York *Saturday Press* in particular; see Mabbott and Silver, *A Child's Reminiscence by Walt Whitman.* A list of reviews of the 1860 edition is to be found in W. S. Kennedy, *The Fight of a Book for the World,* pp. 14–15.

100. Reprinted in Charles I. Glicksberg, "A Friend of Walt Whitman," *American Book-Collector,* VI (March 1935), 91–94.

101. Quoted by Kennedy, *The Fight of a Book for the World,* p. 14.

102. "Walt Whitman and *Drum-Taps,*" *Galaxy,* II, 606–615.

103. The best proof of this is probably the fact that Thayer and Eldridge planned to publish another collection of poems by Whitman under the title of "Banner at Daybreak." This book was announced as being "in preparation" in O'Connor's *Harrington,* in 1860, p. 560, and also in two issues of the *Liberator,* an antislavery paper, on

November 2 and 9, 1860: "A new volume of poems by Walt Whitman — a handsome brochure of 150 pages — 1 volume 16mo." It is therefore probable, as the title suggests, that this volume had a strong abolitionist bias. See Goodale, "Some of Walt Whitman's Borrowings," *AL*, X (May 1938), 205.

There is no way of establishing the contents of this abortive volume. But "Song of the Banner at Daybreak" would probably have had a prominent place in it, as it did at the beginning of *"Drum-Taps"* and also in the definitive edition of *Leaves of Grass*. It was probably this poem which gave the volume its title. It is not about the Civil War, but about the irreconcilable ideological conflict which divided the North and the South. It is likely also that Whitman would have included all of the poems not specifically about the Civil War which later appeared in *Drum-Taps*. They were probably written at this time, with the exception of "The Centenarian's Story," which was probably composed at the same time as the series of historical articles on Brooklyn that Whitman contributed to the Brooklyn *Weekly Standard* in 1861 (*Uncoll. PP*, II, 222–321). The table of contents might therefore have included the following titles:

"Rise O Days from Your Fathomless Deeps," *Drum-Taps*, p. 35, *Inc. Ed.*, p. 247; "Pioneers! O Pioneers!," *Drum-Taps*, p. 25, *Inc. Ed.*, p. 194; "Year of Meteors," *Drum-Taps*, p. 51, *Inc. Ed.*, p. 202; "Quicksand Years that Whirl Me I Know not Whither," *Drum-Taps*, p. 30, *Inc. Ed.*, p. 374; "When I Heard the Learned Astronomer," *Drum-Taps*, p. 34, *Inc. Ed.*, p. 230; "A Child's Amaze," *Drum-Taps*, p. 37, *Inc. Ed.*, p. 233; "Mother and Babe," *Drum-Taps*, p. 41, *Inc. Ed.*, p. 234; "Did You Ask Dulcet Rhymes from Me," *Drum-Taps*, p. 50, *Inc. Ed.*, p. 272 ("To a Certain Civilian"); "The Torch," *Drum-Taps*, p. 52, *Inc. Ed.*, p. 331; "Years of the Unperform'd," *Drum-Taps*, p. 53, *Inc. Ed.*, p. 405 ("Years of the Modern"); "The Ship," *Drum-Taps*, p. 60, *Inc. Ed.*, p. 9 ("The Ship Starting"); "A Broadway Pageant," *Drum-Taps*, p. 61, *Inc. Ed.*, p. 206; "Flag of Stars, Thick-Sprinkled Bunting," *Drum-Taps*, p. 65, *Inc. Ed.*, p. 402 ("Thick-Sprinkled Bunting"); "Old Ireland," *Drum-Taps*, p. 66, *Inc. Ed.*, p. 307; "Look Down Fair Moon," *Drum-Taps*, p. 66, *Inc. Ed.*, p. 270; "Out of the Rolling Ocean the Crowd," *Drum-Taps*, p. 67, *Inc. Ed.*, p. 91; "Others May Praise What They Like," *Drum-Taps*, p. 68, *Inc. Ed.*, p. 329; "Solid, Ironical, Rolling Orb," *Drum-Taps*, p. 68, *Inc. Ed.*, p. 483; "Shut not Your Doors to Me Proud Libraries," *Drum-Taps*, p. 8, *Inc. Ed.*, p. 11; "Beginning My Studies," *Drum-Taps*, p. 18, *Inc. Ed.*, p. 7.

Two of these poems, if we agree that they were composed in 1860, strongly confirm the hypothesis of Whitman's moral regeneration in 1859–60; for "Out of the Rolling Ocean the Crowd" is a remarkably

appropriate answer to the cry of despair of "Out of the Cradle Endlessly Rocking," and "Solid, Ironical, Rolling Orb" expresses a complete and unreserved reconciliation with the world.

104. It was only in 1881 that James R. Osgood and Company
offered to publish *Leaves of Grass.*

VI. THE WOUND DRESSER

1. "Leaves of Grass" no. 20, *LG 1860*, p. 239, *Inc. Ed.*, "So Far
and So Far and On Toward the End," p. 475, ll. 9–12.

2. "Messenger Leaves," *LG 1860*, p. 399, *Inc. Ed.*, p. 232.

3. *SD*, p. 21, *CP*, p. 16.

4. Quoted by Emory Holloway, *Whitman*, p. 185.

5. "Give Me the Splendid Silent Sun," *Drum-Taps*, pp. 48–49, §3,
Inc. Ed., pp. 264–265.

6. Quoted by Jean Catel, "Whitman et la Guerre Civile," *Revue
Anglo-Américaine*, II (June 1934), 437.

7. *Uncoll. PP*, II, 222–321.

8. *Ibid.*, pp. 1–5.

9. *SD*, pp. 22–25, *CP*, pp. 18–20.

10. *Uncoll. PP*, II, 306–321.

11. In "First O Songs for a Prelude," *Drum-Taps*, p. 5 (under the
title of "Drum-Taps"), *Inc. Ed.*, pp. 237–239; "Eighteen Sixty-One,"
Drum-Taps, p. 17, *Inc. Ed.*, pp. 239–240; "Beat! Beat! Drums!"
Drum-Taps, p. 38, *Inc. Ed.*, p. 240.

12. "(I am more and more surprised at the very great proportion
of youngsters from fifteen to twenty-one in the army). . ." *SD*, p.
28, *CP*, p. 22. See DeWolfe Miller's refutation of Higginson's charges
in his introduction to his facsimile of *Drum-Taps* (Gainesville, Florida:
Scholars' Facsimiles and Reprints, 1959), p. xv.

13. *Drum-Taps*, p. 18, *Inc. Ed.*, pp. 240–241, ll. 1–2, 9–11.

14. Preface to 1855 edition, *Inc. Ed.*, p. 491; see "Poem of Many
in One," *LG 1856*, p. 189, "By Blue Ontario's Shore," *Inc. Ed.*,
p. 292, §10, l. 9. Whitman liked this idea so much that he took it up
again in 1860; see "Calamus" no. 31 (2), *LG 1860*, p. 372, "What
place is besieged?" *Inc. Ed.*, p. 10.

15. See his letter to his mother dated July 15, 1863: "I have had
it much on my mind what could be done if it should so happen that
Jeff should be drafted of course he could not go without its being the
downfall almost of our whole family. . ." *SPL*, p. 912.

16. See Emory Holloway, "Some New Whitman Letters," *American
Mercury*, XVI (February 1929), 187.

17. *SPL*, p. 940.

18. *SPL*, p. 888.

19. SD, p. 26, CP, p. 21.

20. Ibid.

21. SD, pp. 26-27, CP, pp. 21-22.

22. Uncoll. PP, II, 21.

23. SD, pp. 27-28, CP, pp. 22-23. In SD Whitman says he came back from Falmouth in January 1863, but this is an error. In 1882 he did not remember the exact date. In fact he was back in Washington as early as December 29, 1862. He wrote a letter to his mother from there on that day; see SPL, p. 888.

24. SD pp. 26-27, CP, pp. 21-22.

25. This is the title which he gave in 1898 to a collection of letters sent by Whitman from Washington during the war. Whitman himself had used the phrase as a title for one of his poems, called "The Dresser" in 1867 (Drum-Taps, p. 31), and later, in 1881, "The Wound-Dresser," Inc. Ed., p. 261.

26. Dr. D. B. St. John Roosa, a house surgeon of the old New York Hospital, wrote in 1896 an interesting account of Whitman's visits there which was printed in the Philadelphia Evening Telegraph, June 30, 1896, under the title "Recollections of Whitman." The article had also been published by the New York Mail and Express with the following subtitle: "Dr. D. B. St. John Roosa writes of the poet's visits to the New York Hospital — Fond of stage drivers — The young physician never took his poetry seriously and thought him a crank — His sympathetic nature." See Bliss Perry, Walt Whitman, p. 131.

27. Quoted by Canby, Walt Whitman, pp. 217-218.

28. "I am the only one that doles out this last [i.e., tobacco] and the men have grown to look to me." Letter to W. S. Davis, October 1, 1863, SPL, p. 919.

29. See SD, pp. 27-28, CP, p. 23: "Then went thoroughly through ward 6, observ'd every case in the ward, without, I think, missing one." See also letter to Mrs. Margaret S. Curtis, October 4, 1863, SPL, p. 922.

30. Some of these notebooks are now in the Library of Congress; A Catalog Based upon the Collections of the Library of Congress, 1955, p. 19. See also SD, pp. 57-58, CP, pp. 32-34, 54.

31. See the second volume of this study (in preparation), or Roger Asselineau, L'Evolution de Walt Whitman, Part II, Chapter V.

32. Many of the letters sent to Whitman after the war by young soldiers he had cared for are now in the Berg Collection. Whitman must have kept them religiously. One of these young men, E. D. Fox, wrote to him: ". . . you know I used to call you Father or 'Pa' and I still think of you as such for I am sure no Father could have cared for their [sic] own child better than you did me. . ." Another, Joe Harris,

began his letter, "Dear Uncle Walt. . ." See also *Catalogue of the Trent Collection,* p. 60.

33. *SD,* p. 29, *CP,* p. 24.

34. "Hospitals Visits," July 1863, quoted by Canby, *Walt Whitman,* p. 218.

35. "October 1st (1863) — Among other things in my visits to hospitals I commence reading pieces." Notebook in the Library of Congress.

36. See above, p. 138.

37. *LG 1855,* p. 45, *Inc. Ed.,* "Song of Myself," p. 63, §40, ll. 21–23, and §41, l. 1.

38. "The doctors tell me I supply the patients with a medicine which all their drugs and bottles and powders are helpless to yield." *SPL,* p. 920.

39. Letter to his mother, June 30, 1863, *SPL,* pp. 908–909.

40. Letter to his mother, September 8, 1863, *CW,* IV, 195.

41. Letter to his mother, April 15, 1863, quoted by Canby, *Walt Whitman,* p. 220.

42. *CW,* IV, 158.

43. Letter to his mother, June 30, 1863, *SPL,* p. 908.

44. Letter to Mrs. Abby Price, October 11, 1863, *SPL,* p. 926.

45. One of the notebooks in the Library of Congress, dated 1863, contains the fellowing entry:

"Nov. 5: am home these days.

Dec. 2nd: Returned to Washington."

46. "Nelly . . . I got home about 8 in evening — was up bright and early to the polls next morning . . . I shall probably stay five or six days longer . . . I have been several times to the Opera and the French Theatre . . ." Letter to Mrs. O'Connor, November 15, 1863, now in the Berg Collection.

47. Letter to Elijah Fox, November 21, 1863, *SPL,* p. 935.

48. One night, however, it was thought that the Confederates were going to attack, but nothing happened; see letter to Trowbridge, February 8, 1864, quoted by Bliss Perry, *Walt Whitman,* p. 145.

49. Letter to his mother, February 12, 1864, *SPL,* p. 937.

50. "I am well as usual; indeed first rate every way." Letter to his mother, April 10, 1864, *SPL,* p. 941.

51. Letter to his mother, June 3, 1864, *ibid.,* pp. 943–944.

52. Letter to his mother, June 7, 1864, *ibid.,* p. 945.

53. The first letter in which he mentioned his ill-health was dated March 31, 1863: "I have felt well of my deafness and cold in my head for four days or so, but it is back again bad as ever this morning." *SPL,* p. 900. See also letter to his mother, June 9, 1863, *ibid.,* p. 905;

letter to Lewis Kirk Brown, August 1, 1863, *ibid.*, p. 914, and letter to his mother, June 14 and 17, 1864, *ibid.*, pp. 947–948.

54. Letter to O'Connor, January 6, 1865, SPL, pp. 949–950.

55. Two letters help us to reconstruct his stay in Brooklyn at this time:

"The political meetings in New York and Brooklyn are immense. I go to them as to shows, fireworks, cannons, clusters of gaslights, countless torches, banners, and mottos [*sic*], 15, 20, 50, 100 people. Per contra I occasionally go riding into the country, in quiet lanes, or a sail on the water, and many times to the seashore at Coney Island." Letter to Charles Eldridge, October 8, 1864, Berg Collection.

"There is a hospital here, containing a couple of hundred soldiers, it is only a quarter of a mile from our house, and I go there a good deal — am going this afternoon to spend the afternoon and evening.

"Strange as it may seem days after days elapse without their having any visitors — so you see I am still in business — some of the cases are very interesting." Letter to O'Connor, September 11, 1864, Berg Collection.

56. SD, p. 76, CP, pp. 72–73; NB, pp. 116–117, CP, pp. 467–468; and letter to his mother, January 1, 1867, in *Letters Written by Walt Whitman to His Mother*, with an introductory note by Rollo G. Silver (New York: Alfred Goldsmith, 1936), p. 21. His visits to the hospitals lasted at least until April 16, 1867. This is the date of the last letter to his mother in which they are mentioned. See *ibid.*, p. 43.

57. See SD, p. 57, CP, pp. 53–54. At the end of the war he claimed that he had distributed thousands of dollars in the hospitals. See also SPL, pp. 893, 919–920, 921–923, 953.

58. Letter to Mrs. Abby H. Price, SPL, p. 927. He tried at first to find a job in a government service, but without success. He told his office-hunter's disappointments to Jefferson Whitman in a letter dated February 13, 1863, SPL, pp. 893–894. In August he still had found nothing; see letter to Lewis Kirk Brown, August 1, SPL, p. 914, and his letter to Nat and Fred Gray, May 19, 1863, SPL, p. 898. In the meantime, however, he must have found his part-time job with Major Hapgood, for he finished writing the letter last mentioned in the office of the latter: "Friday Morning 20th — I finish my letter in the office of Major Hapgood, a paymaster, and a friend of mine." He had apparently already worked as a copyist, for in *Lain's Brooklyn Directory* for 1860 one could read: "Walt Whitman, copyist"; see *Uncoll. PP*, II, 23, n. 2.

59. To the Brooklyn *Daily Union* in particular (see *Uncoll. PP*, II, 26–29) and to the New York *Times* (*ibid.*, pp. 29–36). He also sent some articles to the Brooklyn *Eagle*, but they edited them and

then refused to publish them any longer; see his letter of May 26, 1863, *CW*, IV, 161. Raymond of the New York *Times* sent him $50 for one of his articles; see *With WW in C*, III, 77.

60. Letter to his mother, May 5, 1863, *SPL*, p. 902.

61. Letter to his mother, June 9, 1863, *SPL*, p. 907. See also letters to the same, July 15, 1863, *SPL*, p. 912, and March 2, 1864, *The Wound Dresser*, 1898, p. 153.

62. His correspondence contains no allusions to this project, but several documents now in the Yale University Library show that he thought of it very seriously. He had already found a title:

MEMORANDA
OF A YEAR
(1863)
by Walt Whitman.

And here is the rough draft of the letter he sent to Redpath (October 21, 1863) to tell him of his project:

"At all events the year 1863 is the most important in the history of America. And this book with its framework jotted down on the battlefield in the shelter tent or by the wayside amid the rumble of passing artillery train or the march of cavalry . . . I should think two or three thousand sell out to be certainly depended on, here in hospitals in Washington, Army Depts and etc. My idea is a book of handy size and form 16mo or smallish 12mo first rate paper (this is indispensable) ordinary binding strongly stitched. It should be got out immediately I think — an edition elegantly bound might be pushed off for books for presents etc. for the holidays, if advertised for that purpose — it would be very appropriate. I think it is a book that would please women. I should expect it to be popular with the trade.

"Of course I propose the affair to you publisherially — as something to invest in, to make out (for both of us). I take it it would be a very handsome speculation only it is to be done while the thing is warm, namely *at once*. I have been and am in the midst of these things. I feel myself full of them and I know, and would readily absorb and understand my memo — wherefore let us make and publish this book and out with it so as to have it for sale by middle or 20th of November."

Unfortunately these War Memoranda were to come out only in 1876 in *Two Rivulets*.

63. See above, n. 58.

64. See "Where I Lived, and What I Lived For" in *Walden*.

65. Letter to his mother, June 9, 1863, *SPL*, p. 906.

66. J. T. Trowbridge, "Reminiscences of Walt Whitman," *Atlantic Monthly*, LXXXIX (February 1902), 164–168.

67. He lived at first with the O'Connors, 394 L Street, then, in

October 1863 he moved to an attic, 456 Sixth Street (see letter dated October 20, 1863, *CW*, IV, 210–220); it is there that Trowbridge visited him. Finally, in May 1864, he moved to 502 Pennsylvania Avenue (see letters dated May 23, 1864, *CW*, IV, 267, and June 7, 1864, *SPL*, p. 947).

68. He had not renounced beer however; see letter to Hugo Fritsch, August 7, 1863, *SPL*, pp. 916–917.

69. See his letter to his mother, June 14, 1863: "My boarding place, 502 Pennsylvania av., is a miserable place, very bad air . . . " *SPL*, p. 947.

70. See above, Chapter IV, p. 313, n. 58.

71. He saved money even on his clothes and wore shirts made by his mother and old suits: "How welcome the shirts were — I was putting off, and putting off, to get some new ones . . . and the coats too, worn as they are, they come in very handy . . ." Letter to his mother, May 19, 1863, *SPL*, p. 903.

72. See "First O Songs for a Prelude," *Drum-Taps*, pp. 5–7, *Inc. Ed.*, pp. 237–239.

73. *Drum-Taps*, p. 45, *Inc. Ed.*, p. 263, "Long, Too Long America."

74. *Drum-Taps*, p. 7 (8), *Inc. Ed.*, p. 239, "First O Songs for a Prelude," ll. 54–57.

75. See this MS note in the Library of Congress: "Battles and death condense a nationality."

76. "Eighteen Sixty-One," *Drum-Taps*, p. 17, *Inc. Ed.*, pp. 239–240. The last line, however, contains the word "sad."

In 1846–47, during the Mexican War, he had similarly extolled war in the Brooklyn *Eagle* (see *G of the F*, I, 242). Whatever may have been the circumstances at the beginning, the American cause was, in his opinion, just; because the United States represented democracy, whereas the Mexican government was nothing but a ridiculous and odious parody of it (Brooklyn *Eagle*, June 6, 1846, *G of the F*, I, 244). Thus it seemed to him quite proper for the United States simply to annex if not all Mexico, at least all of the territory down to the peninsulas of Yucatan and California, not for imperialistic reasons, but in order to bring the benefit of democracy to oppressed and badly governed people (Brooklyn *Eagle,* June 6, 1846, *G of the F*, I, 242). These naïve views have also been expressed by two historians: Justin H. Smith, in *War with Mexico*, and more recently by Alfred Hoyt Bill, in *Rehearsal for Conflict: The War with Mexico*, 1947.

Whitman nevertheless condemned war: "But war is a dreadful evil, in any event and under any circumstances . . ." (*G of the F*, I, 248). But he soon qualified this condemnation: "War is a horrible evil: so is anarchy but as the latter is less horrible than despotism so is war far less in its evils than quieter, but deeper dangers" (*ibid.*, p. 256).

He reacted in the same way in 1861. Though by nature opposed to violence, he willingly resigned himself to its use to assure the victory of democracy and to preserve his country from the "quieter but deeper dangers" which had threatened it since 1850. No doubt, the Mexican War having been fought far to the west, occasioned a much less complex and human reaction than Whitman had to the Civil War. The editor of the Brooklyn *Eagle* theorized about remote events, the author *Drum-Taps* responded as a man to his own experience among the suffering wounded soldiers.

77. "Did you ask dulcet rhymes from me?" *Drum-Taps*, p. 50, *Inc. Ed.*, p. 272, under the title "To a Certain Civilian."

78. "Drum-Taps," *Drum-Taps*, p. 7 (5), *Inc. Ed.*, "First O Songs for a Prelude," pp. 238–239, ll. 47, 49.

79. "The Veteran's Vision," *Drum-Taps*, p. 56, *Inc. Ed.*, p. 268, "The Artilleryman's Vision."

He took up the same theme much later in "The Dying Veteran" (1888), although this may have been a rejected poem dating from the time of the Civil War. But even if it was written in his old age, it need not surprise us, because, even after having experienced all the horrors of war, he still remained very responsive to its heroic aspect. In "Some War Memoranda" published in *NB*, he mentions several acts of extraordinary bravery (pp. 80–112, *CP*, pp. 432, 462–463).

He never rejected the poems written during the time when he believed that war was heroic and which he printed in *Drum-Taps* side by side with those expressing his sadness and disillusion. He clung to these contradictions imposed by the complexity of life. Always primarily preoccupied with the future, he never tried to erase the past. After 1855, his evolution was accomplished without revolution.

Jean Catel in "Walt Whitman et la Guerre Civile" (*RAA*, XI [June 1934], 434–439) accuses Whitman of having disseminated false propaganda at the beginning of 1862 in reassuring articles on the military hospitals, which he published in the New York *Leader*; but Whitman was sincere in writing them; they were composed at the same time as the patriotic and warlike poems of *Drum-Taps*. The fact that he used the pseudonym of Velsor Brush and that he never mentioned these articles to anyone does not prove that he was ashamed of them. He generally preferred to have his journalistic work remain anonymous, for he had no illusions concerning its value.

Curiously, although Whitman formed a much more accurate idea of war after December 1862, and described it much more realistically, he never in his poems or in his memoirs talked about fear. This omission is the more surprising as he was much concerned with the question of deserters. Evidently the "wound-dresser" never completely supplanted the belligerent poet of 1861. At any rate, *Drum-Taps*, in spite of the profound pity which inspires many poems, still presents to some extent an idealized picture of war.

80. "Poem of Joys," *LG 1860*, pp. 263–264 (23), *Inc. Ed.*, pp. 151–152, "A Song of Joys," ll. 65–72.

81. See "Beat! Beat! Drums!" *Drum-Taps*, p. 38, *Inc. Ed.*, p. 240. This poem was first published in *Harper's Weekly* on September 28, 1861, and on the same day in the New York *Leader* (SPL, p. 1071). This proves that it was written at the very beginning of the war. From the same period we have "Old Ireland," which seems out of place in *Drum-Taps*, but Whitman probably wrote it to stimulate the patriotic ardor of the Irish in New York and to encourage them to engage in the defense of their new country. The poem first appeared in the New York *Leader*, November 2, 1861 (see SPL, pp. 1074–1075).

82. "I would like to see *every man* in the land — I would like to see the people embodied en masse . . . for that will be something like our nation getting itself up in shape." Letter dated March 1863; see E. Holloway, "Some New Whitman Letters," *American Mercury*, XVI (February 1929), 187.

83. See above Chapter V, n. 103.

84. "Song of the Banner at Daybreak," *Drum-Taps*, p. 16 (18), *Inc. Ed.*, p. 246, l. 139.

85. "Song of the Banner at Daybreak," *Drum-Taps*, p. 12 (12), *Inc. Ed.*, p. 243, l. 63.

86. ". . . O Libertad! arm'd Libertad!" in "Shut not Your Doors to Me Proud Libraries," *Drum-Taps*, p. 8, *Inc. Ed.*, p. 546, among the variant readings.

87. "Rise O Days from Your Fathomless Deeps," *Drum-Taps*, p. 35, *Inc. Ed.*, pp. 247–248, esp. §§2 and 3.

88. "Song of the Banner at Daybreak," *Drum-Taps*, p. 12 (12), *Inc. Ed.*, p. 244, l. 75.

89. *Drum-Taps*, p. 26 (9), *Inc. Ed.*, p. 195, ll. 33–36.

90. *Drum-Taps*, p. 25 (2), *Inc. Ed.*, p. 194, l. 7.

91. The period of enthusiasm lasted from April 13, 1861, when Fort Sumter was bombarded, until July 20–21, 1862, the date of the first battle of Bull Run, which clearly showed that the war would be longer and harder than anyone had thought and that the Union could not be sure of winning. But it may have lasted until December 1862, since the passage in *SD* in which Whitman describes the arrival of the retreating army in Washington is not an eye-witness report. He probably did not realize the full horror of war until he

had seen it close up on the Rappahannock. His point of view changed along with that of the Northern public. In this respect he was the spokesman of his time. He summarized the history of the Civil War on a scrap of paper, preserved in the Library of Congress, in this way: "the electric uprising of the North in vast paroxysm of contempt and astonishment and rage — the first Bull Run the utter cast-down shock and dismay — the call for troops — the chaos of divided counsel and then followed the war in full-blood — the war with all its hope — holocaust of death four years of fratricidal war."

92. "The Wound-Dresser," *Inc. Ed.*, p. 261, ll. 4–6. These three lines were added in 1881; they admirably sum up his evolution during the war. He became conscious of it afterwards.

93. Ellen M. Calder (ex-Mrs. O'Connor), "Personal Recollections of Walt Whitman," *Atlantic Monthly*, XCIX (June 1907), 833.

94. Letter to his mother, September 8, 1863, CW, IV, 193.

95. See "Vigil Strange I Kept on the Field One Night," *Drum-Taps*, p. 42, *Inc. Ed.*, pp. 257–258, and "A Sight in Camp in the Daybreak Gray and Dim," *Drum-Taps*, p. 46, *Inc. Ed.*, p. 259, esp. the last three lines.

96. See "A March in the Ranks Hard-Prest and the Road Unknown," *Drum-Taps*, p. 44, *Inc. Ed.*, pp. 258–259.

97. See "In Clouds Descending in Midnight Sleep," *Sequel to Drum-Taps*, p. 20, *Inc. Ed.*, p. 402, under the title "Old War-Dreams."

98. See "Come up from the Fields Father," *Drum-Taps*, p. 39, *Inc. Ed.*, pp. 255–257. He may have used a real incident; see SPL, pp. 1071–1072.

99. "One of the drifts [of his *Memoranda of a Year*] is to push forward the very big and needed truth that our national military system needs entirely shifting and revolutionizing and made to tally with democracy — the people — The officers should almost invariably rise from the ranks. The entire capacity keenness and courage of our army are in the ranks. There is an absolute want of democratic spirit exclusively . . ." From the rough draft of a letter to Redpath dated October 21, 1863 (Yale University Library). See also SD, pp. 24–25, CP, pp. 19–20.

100. SD, pp. 24–25, CP, pp. 19–20.

101. *Drum-Taps*, p. 54, *Inc. Ed.*, pp. 260–261.

102. Letter to his mother, September 8, 1863, CW, IV, 193.

103. Letter to his mother, April 10, 1864, SPL, p. 940.

104. Letter to Tom Sawyer, April 21, 1863 (Berg Collection).

105. Letter to his mother, July 15, 1863, SPL, pp. 911–912.

106. Letter dated August 18, 1863, CW, IV, 183.

107. *Drum-Taps*, pp. 42, 46, *Inc. Ed.*, pp. 257, 259.

108. "Pensive on her dead gazing, I heard the mother of all," *Drum-Taps*, p. 71, *Inc. Ed.*, p. 412.

109. See "Over the Carnage Rose Prophetic a Voice," *Drum-Taps*, p. 49, *Inc. Ed.*, p. 266. He incorporated in this poem almost word for word, a fragment from "Calamus" no. 5 (*LG 1860*, p. 349, *Inc. Ed.*, pp. 476–477, under the title of "States").

110. He made significant additions to some of the 1860 poems. Thus, in 1871, he added to "Thoughts" (*Inc. Ed.*, pp. 408–409) the clause printed below in italics (l. 14):
"And how all people, sights, combinations, the democratic masses too, serve — and how every fact, *and war itself; with all its horrors, serves* . . . "

111. Military parades even aroused his warlike enthusiasm: "I tell you, mother, it made everything ring — made my heart leap . . . I tell you it had the look of *real war* — noble-looking fellows; a man looks so proud on a good horse and armed . . . Alas! how many of these healthy handsome rollicking young men will lie cold before the apples ripen in the orchard." (Letter to his mother, June 30, 1863, *SPL*, pp. 910–911.) He would not have added the note of pity in 1862, though.) A more sober description of the same parade is given in *SD*, pp. 39–40, *CP*, p. 35.

112. See "Lo, Victress on the Peaks," *Sequel to Drum-Taps*, p. 23, *Inc. Ed.*, p. 273, ll. 7–9; "Camps of Green," *Drum-Taps*, p. 57, *Inc. Ed.*, pp. 413–414; and "Hymn of Dead Soldiers," *Drum-Taps*, pp. 59–60, *Inc. Ed.*, "Ashes of Soldiers," pp. 406–408.

113. See "Turn O Libertad," *Drum-Taps*, p. 70, *Inc. Ed.*, pp. 274–275, ll. 10–12.

114. "Years of the Unperform'd," *Drum-Taps*, pp. 53–54, "Years of the Modern," *Inc. Ed.*, pp. 405–406, ll. 1–3, 7, 25, 29–30.

115. *SD*, p. 32, *CP*, p. 28. See also *NB*, p. 81, *CP*, p. 433.

116. *SD*, p. 80, *CP*, p. 76.

117. *SD*, p. 78, *CP*, p. 74, and also *SD*, p. 48, *CP*, pp. 43–44. He took up the subject again in *Democratic Vistas* (*CP*, pp. 219–221). See also a letter to his mother, September 15, 1863, *The Wound-Dresser*, 1949, p. 116.

118. The Civil War had the same happy influence on Melville.

119. "Reconciliation," *Sequel*, p. 23, *Inc. Ed.*, p. 271. See also the last two lines of "To the Leaven'd Soil They Trod," *Sequel*, p. 24, *Inc. Ed.*, p. 275.

120. See his letter to his mother, April 10, 1864, *SPL*, p. 940. Almost the same passage occurs in *NB*, p. 111, *CP*, p. 462. See also this sentence from a letter to Lewis Kirk Brown, August 15, 1863

(now in the Library of Congress): "I agree with you that a rebel in the Southern army is much more respectable than a Northern copperhead."

121. *SD*, p. 78, *CP*, pp. 74–75.

122. "A Secesh Brave," *SD*, p. 33, *CP*, p. 28.

123. "The Dresser," *Drum-Taps*, p. 31, "The Wound-Dresser," *Inc. Ed.*, p. 261, l. 8.

124. "Camps of Green," *Drum-Taps*, p. 57, *Inc. Ed.*, pp. 413–414, ll. 20–21.

125. Article published in *Army Square Hospital*, May 20, 1865, and reprinted by E. Holloway in *Colophon*, Part I, 1930, under the title of "Whitman on War's Finale."

126. *Sequel*, pp. 15–17, *Inc. Ed.*, pp. 370–372.

127. F. DeWolfe Miller has established the exact date in the introduction of his facsimile edition of *Drum-Taps* (Gainesville, Florida: Scholars' Facsimiles and Reprints, 1959), p. l.

128. Whitman did not follow a chronological order in this volume, except for the first few poems, which are undoubtedly the earliest. For the remainder, he was guided by purely aesthetic and sometimes even typographical criteria. In order to obtain an attractive typographical arrangement on the page and at the same time to include the largest amount of material in the smallest number of pages — for the sake of economy perhaps — he added here and there some very short poems, such as "Cavalry Crossing a Ford" (p. 8), "By the Bivouac's Fitful Flame" (p. 16), "Beginning My Studies" (p. 18 — this is an extreme case; its theme makes it irrelevant here, and Whitman later placed it in "Inscriptions"), "A Child's Amaze" (p. 37), "Mother and Babe" (p. 41), etc. Sometimes he placed poems together because they had similar titles. Three poems, the titles of which begin with "Year" or "Years," are thus grouped together toward the end of the volume, although "Year of Meteors" would be better placed at the beginning and "Year that Trembled and Reel'd beneath Me" serves as a sort of tail-piece to "Years of the Unperform'd," which should be the last of the three since it phophesies the future.

129. Letter to his mother, March 31, 1863, *SPL*, p. 900.

130. Letter to his mother, April 10, 1864, *SPL*, p. 941.

131. Trowbridge, "Reminiscences of Walt Whitman," *Atlantic Monthly*, LXXXIX (February 1902), 171.

132. Letter to O'Connor, January 6, 1865, *SPL*, pp. 949–950.

133. *Ibid.*

134. The great metaphysical themes were almost completely absent from it. They reappeared only in "When Lilacs Last . . ." and "Chanting the Square Deific," which both belong to *Sequel*.

135. Letter to O'Connor, January 6, 1865, *SPL*, pp. 949–950.

136. Other things being equal, there is the same difference between *Leaves of Grass* and *Drum-Taps* as between nonrepresentational and traditional painting.

137. Letter to O'Connor, January 6, 1865, SPL, pp. 949–950.

138. *Ibid.*

139. This collection of poems was never published separately. See Wells and Goldsmith, *A Concise Bibliography of the Works of Walt Whitman*, p. 11.

140. *SD*, pp. 43–44, *CP*, pp. 38–39.

141. *Drum-Taps*, p. 69, *Inc. Ed.*, pp. 284–285.

142. *Sequel*, pp. 3–12, *Inc. Ed.*, pp. 276–283.

143. By Swinburne, in particular, in "Under the Microscope" (1872); by Bliss Perry (*Walt Whitman*, 1906, p. 157); and by Canby (*Walt Whitman*, p. 240). A dissenting voice is that of Malcolm Cowley (see *The Complete Poetry of Walt Whitman*, 1948, pp. 34–36). The beauty of the poem has, on the contrary, been extolled by Richard P. Adams in "Whitman's 'Lilacs' and the Tradition of Pastoral Elegy," *PMLA*, LXXII (June 1957), 479–487.

144. "I Heard You, Solemn-sweet Pipes of the Organ," *Sequel*, p. 17, *Inc. Ed.*, pp. 93–94; "Not my enemies . . . ," *Sequel*, p. 17, *Inc. Ed.*, p. 484; "O Me! O Life!" *Sequel*, p. 18, *Inc. Ed.*, p. 231; "Ah poverties . . . ," *Sequel*, p. 18, *Inc. Ed.*, p. 398.

145. In fact, we know that "I Heard You Solemn-Sweet Pipes of the Organ" was first published in the New York *Leader* (October 12, 1861) under the title of "Little Bells Last Night" (*SPL*, pp. 1066–1067). The other poems may very well date from the same time. They are perfectly consistent with what we know of the spiritual crisis that Whitman underwent shortly before publishing the third edition of *Leaves of Grass*. "I Heard You . . ." is a poem of love and regret. "O Me! O Life!" and "Ah Poverties . . ." are both very melancholy and express the grief of a broken heart, but they end on a note of resignation and courageous acceptance. "This Day, O Soul" corresponds to a recovery and a reconciliation with the world. The whole conclusion of the 1859–60 crisis is therefore summarized in these few poems, if our hypothesis is correct. "Not My Enemies . . ." seems to have a more general meaning, having to do with the homosexual tendencies that continued to trouble Whitman secretly throughout the war, in spite of the apparent propriety of his behavior.

146. *Sequel*, p. 13, *Inc. Ed.*, p. 284.

147. *Sequel*, pp. 15–17, *Inc. Ed.*, pp. 370–372.

148. See above, n. 62.

149. Kennedy in *The Fight of a Book for the World*, pp. 16–18, gives a list of reviews of *Drum-Taps*.

150. *Ibid.*, p. 16.

151. *Ibid.*
152. *Galaxy*, II (December 1866), 612–613.
153. *Round Table*, November 1865, pp. 147–148.
154. This review has been reprinted in *Views and Reviews*, 1908, pp. 101–110.
155. See above, n. 145.
156. For instance, "Drum-Taps" (later "First O Songs for a Prelude"), "Song of the Banner at Daybreak," "1861," "Pioneers! O Pioneers!" "Rise O Days from Your Fathomless Deeps," "Beat! Beat! Drums!" "City of Ships," "Long, Too Long, O Land," and "Give Me the Splendid Silent Sun."
157. *Drum-Taps*, pp. 19–24, 68, *Inc. Ed.*, pp. 250–254, 267.
158. See "Cavalry Crossing a Ford" (*Drum-Taps*, p. 8, *Inc. Ed.*, p. 254); "Bivouac on a Mountain-side" (*Drum-Taps*, p. 68, *Inc. Ed.*, p. 267); and "The Most Inspiriting of All War's Shows" (*SD*, pp. 39–40, *CP*, p. 35). See also "The Veteran's Vision" (*Inc. Ed.*, pp. 268–269), and the beginning of "Hymn of Dead Soldiers" (*Drum-Taps*, p. 59, *Inc. Ed.*, pp. 406–407, under the title "Ashes of Soldiers").
159. *SPL*, pp. 949–950.
160. See above, p. 157.
161. *The Poems of Wilfred Owen* (London: Chatto and Windus, 1933), p. 40.
162. There was no contemporary collection of poems or even of memoirs in which any attempt was made to give a realistic account of the fighting. This was not done until much later. General John Beatty's *Memoirs of a Volunteer* appeared only in 1879 (see critical edition by Harvey S. Ford, with an introduction by Lloyd Lewis, New York, 1946) and Ambrose Bierce's *Tales of Soldiers and Civilians* in 1891. The bitter and disillusioned letters of Oliver Wendell Holmes, Jr., the son of the Autocrat of the Breakfast Table, whose reaction to the horrors of infantry combat resembled those of Siegfried Sassoon during World War I, were not published until 1946.
163. As the title indicates, most of the poems describe battles or celebrate generals. Melville, as a poet, was not interested in ordinary soldiers.
164. Letter to O'Connor, January 6, 1865, *SPL*, pp. 949–950.
165. O. L. Triggs, "The Growth of Leaves of Grass," *Conservator*, VIII (August 1897), 84–88.
166. *NB*, p. 13, *Inc. Ed.*, p. 531.
167. *Ibid.*
168. See "So Long!" *LG 1860*.
169. See above, Chapter V, p. 130.
170. He was not unaware of the existence of evil and did not try to conceal it. See for example his description (*SD*, pp. 55–57, *CP*,

pp. 52–53) of the atrocities committed by a band of Southern raiders. See also the passage on Southern prison camps (*SD*, pp. 54–55, *CP*, pp. 50–51). He was also aware of the sadism of the punishments inflicted on some of the Union soldiers: there are jottings on the subject in some of his notebooks now in the Library of Congress. Even in the hospitals, as he knew, the soldiers were sometimes robbed and the corpses rifled. There were times when he almost lost faith in humanity; see letter to his mother, March 29, 1864, *SPL*, p. 939. But his despair did not last; the heroism of the wounded soldiers made up for all these failings. See also his letter to his mother, March 8, 1863, quoted by Rollo G. Silver in "Thirty-One Letters of Walt Whitman," *AL*, VIII (January 1937), 417–418.

171. See above, p. 93.

172. See above, Chapter IV, p. 104.

173. This struck W. D. Howells; see above, Chapter IV, p. 105.

174. See above, Chapter V, p. 132.

175. Many were published in *The Wound Dresser*, A Series of Letters Written from the Hospitals in Washington by Walt Whitman, ed. by R. M. Bucke (Boston: Maynard, 1898), reprinted with an introduction by Oscar Cargill (New York: The Bodley Press, 1949).

176. See above, p. 144.

177. "Whoever You Are Holding Me Now in Hand," *Inc. Ed.*, p. 98, l. 20.

178. Letter to Mrs. Abby H. Price, October 11, 1863, *SPL*, p. 927, or letter to Hugo Fritsch, August 7, 1863, *SPL*, p. 916. Also letter to W. S. Davis, October 1, 1863, *SPL*, p. 918, and letter to Nat and Fred Gray, March 19, 1863, *SPL*, p. 896. Strangely enough he never mentioned this to his mother, and there are hardly any allusions to it in *SD*.

179. "Pioneers! O Pioneers!" *Drum-Taps*, p. 27 (10), *Inc. Ed.*, p. 195, l. 38.

180. "The Dresser," *Drum-Taps*, p. 33, *Inc. Ed.*, "The Wound-Dresser," p. 263, §4, l. 7.

181. "First O Songs for a Prelude," *Drum-Taps*, p. 6, *Inc. Ed.*, p. 238, ll. 32–33.

182. "Pensive on Her Dead Gazing, I Heard the Mother of All," *Drum-Taps*, p. 71, *Inc. Ed.*, p. 701, among the variant readings.

183. For instance, this is what he wrote from Brooklyn on November 21, 1863, to Elijah Fox, a young wounded soldier: "Dearest son: it would be more pleasure if we could be together just in quiet, in some plain way of living, with some good employment and reasonable income, where I could have you often with me, than all the dissipations and amusements of this great city." *SPL*, p. 935.

184. "Vigil Strange I Kept on the Field One Night," *Drum-Taps*,

pp. 42–43, *Inc. Ed.*, pp. 257–258, ll. 3–4, 23. He may have been thinking of an episode described in *SD*, p. 37, *CP*, p. 32.

185. Letter to Benton Wilson, April 15, 1870, *SPL*, p. 988.

186. *Drum-Taps*, p. 67, *Inc. Ed.*, p. 91. Such an encounter is recorded in one of Whitman's notebooks; see *Uncoll. PP*, II, 93.

187. See above, nn. 178 and 183.

188. "Calamus" no. 5, *LG 1860*, pp. 349–351, *Inc. Ed.*, "States," pp. 476–477.

189. "As I Lay with My Head in Your Lap Camerado," *Sequel*, p. 19, *Inc. Ed.*, p. 272, ll. 10–11.

190. *LG 1860*, p. 277 (33), *Inc. Ed.*, p. 215, l. 168.

191. *LG 1860*, p. 275 (28), *Inc. Ed.*, p. 214, l. 133.

192. *LG 1860*, p. 276 (31), *Inc. Ed.*, p. 638 in the variant readings of l. 158.

193. "When Lilacs Last. . ." *Sequel*, pp. 9–10 (28 and 31), *Inc. Ed.*, p. 281, §14, ll. 28, 40–43.

194. See, for instance, *NB*, pp. 111, 113, *CP*, pp. 462, 464. Hence his conclusion: "Then I should say, too, about death in war, that our feelings and imaginations make a thousand times too much of the whole matter. Of the many I have seen die, or known of, the past year, I have not seen or known one who met death with terror. In most cases I should say it was a welcome relief and release." *NB*, p. 112, *CP*, p. 463.

195. "Death's Valley," *Inc. Ed.*, p. 462, ll. 5–6. This poem was published in 1892 only.

196. Letter to Nat and Fred Gray, March 19, 1863, *SPL*, p. 897.

197. "When Lilacs Last. . . ," *Sequel*, p. 11, §18 (39), *Inc. Ed.*, p. 283, §15, ll. 18–20.

198. See above, n. 170.

199. See above, n. 145.

200. *Sequel*, p. 6, §8 (12), *Inc. Ed.*, p. 278, §8, l. 6.

201. *Sequel*, p. 6, §4 (7), *Inc. Ed.*, p. 277, §4, ll. 7–8.

202. *Drum-Taps*, p. 69, *Inc. Ed.*, p. 399, ll. 1, 5–8.

VII. HAPPY BUREAUCRAT AND TORMENTED POET

1. Ellen M. Calder, "Personal Recollections of Walt Whitman," *Atlantic Monthly*, XCIX (June 1907), 825.

2. See "Walt says he had a prospect of getting a good berth in Washington." Letter from George Whitman to his mother, January 22, 1863, *Faint Clews and Indirections*, ed. Clarence Gohdes and Rollo G. Silver (Duke University Press, 1949), p. 155. See also above, Chapter VI, n. 58.

3. See Dixon Wecter, "Walt Whitman as Civil Servant," *PMLA*, LVIII (January 1943), 1094-1109.

4. Letter to O'Connor, January 6, 1865, *SPL*, p. 949.

5. It was a copy of the third edition. He mentioned it in a letter to his mother, March 31, 1863 (*SPL*, p. 900). This copy is now in the Lion Collection, New York Public Library.

6. See Bliss Perry, *Walt Whitman*, p. 165.

7. For a detailed study of Whitman's career as a civil servant, see Wecter, "Walt Whitman as a Civil Servant," *PMLA*, LVIII 1094-1109.

8. *The Good Gray Poet: A Vindication* (New York: Bunce and Huntington, 1866 — but the text itself is dated September 2, 1865), reprinted in R. M. Bucke, *Walt Whitman* (Philadelphia: MacKay, 1883), pp. 99-130. See also *In Re*, pp. 149-157, which gives under the title of "The Good Gray Poet: Supplemental," a long letter dated January 22, 1866, which O'Connor had sent to the Boston *Transcript*, but which this paper did not print. It vigorously sums up the main ideas of his pamphlet.

9. See Bliss Perry, *Walt Whitman*, p. 176.

10. In January, according to Kennedy, *The Fight of a Book for the World*, p. 18.

11. In particular, in the *Round Table*, January 20, in which Stoddard wrote that it was "one of the most extraordinary things we ever encountered." For the reception of *The Good Gray Poet*, see Kennedy, *The Fight of a Book for the World*, p. 19.

12. Whitman was even amused at times by O'Connor's zeal: "He grows stronger and fiercer in his championship of Leaves of Grass — no one can ever say a word against it in his presence without a storm," he wrote to his mother on December 4, 1866, *Letters Written by Walt Whitman to His Mother*, 1866-1872, with an introductory note by Rollo G. Silver (New York: Alfred Goldsmith, 1936), p. 17.

13. "I have an agreeable situation here — labor moderate and plenty of leisure." Letter to his mother, August 1, 1866, "Letters of Walt Whitman to His Mother and an Old Friend," *Putnam's Monthly*, V (November 1908), 167.

14. See above, n. 1.

15. Letter to Jefferson Whitman, January 30, 1865, *SPL*, p. 952.

16. Letters to his mother, January 22 and March 12, 1867, *Letters Written by Walt Whitman to His Mother*, pp. 26, 38.

17. All his letters are dated: "Attorney General's Office. . ." and in one of them he wrote: "Mother I am writing at my table, by the big window I have mentioned several times in former letters — it is very pleasant indeed — the river looks so fine and the banks and hills in the distance — I can sit sometimes and look out for a long time —

It is mighty lucky for me I fell in with such a good situation." *Letters Written by Walt Whitman to His Mother*, 1936, p. 37. See also the letters dated March 26, 1867, and February 2, 1869, *ibid.*, pp. 39–41, 67.

He kept repeating that he had very little to do: "We have not much to do in the office" (August 13, 1868, *ibid.*, p. 58). "I am sitting at my desk writing this — there is not much to do to-day in the office" (February 2, 1869, *ibid.*, p. 67). He sometimes jested about it: ". . . since I began this letter, I have been sent for by the Cashier to receive my pay for the arduous and invaluable services I have already rendered to the government" (letter to Jefferson Whitman, January 30, 1865, *SPL*, p. 952; he was referring here to his first month's salary). In the Indian Bureau he worked as a mere copyist, but in the General Attorney's office he was sometimes assigned more complex tasks (see letter dated August 1, 1866 in "Letters of Walt Whitman to His Mother and an Old Friend," *Putnam's Monthly* V [November 1908]). So in December 1871 he could write to his mother: "The new Attorney Gen'l, Mr. Williams, has assigned me there [the office of the Solicitor of the Treasury] but several important bits of work have had to be done just now and to-day and yesterday I have had to do them — (as the old ladies say, I guess they'll miss me a good deal more than they 'spected)" (*SPL*, p. 999).

18. Letter to O'Connor, April 17, 1865, *SPL*, p. 954.

19. In August-September 1866 he prepared in Brooklyn the publication of the fourth edition of *Leaves of Grass* (see letter to O'Connor, August 26, 1866, Berg Collection). Same thing in 1870 when he prepared the fifth edition (see letter to Peter Doyle, September 6, 1870, *SPL*, p. 993). In 1872 he beat all his previous records. He was in Brooklyn from the middle of February to the beginning of April, and again from June to the middle of July. See Wecter, "Walt Whitman as a Civil Servant," *PMLA*, LVIII, 1094–1109.

20. Letter to his mother, November 16, 1866, *SPL*, p. 960.

21. "I have lots of money — in fact untold wealth." Letter to Mrs. Price, September 14, 1866, *Putnam's Monthly*, V (November 1908), 168. "I can send you whatever money you need, dear mother, any time." *Letters Written by Walt Whitman to His Mother*, p. 45.

22. Letters to his mother, February 12, 1867, *ibid.*, p. 31.

23. Letters to his mother, March 5 and 12, 1867, *ibid.*, pp. 35–38. Later, however, he was less enthusiastic (letter dated August 24, 1868, *ibid.*, p. 60).

24. This letter, now in the Berg Collection, was written by Whitman himself, but it was meant to be sent and signed by O'Connor. It was probably composed at the end of 1866 when there was already some question of publishing an English edition of *Leaves of Grass*.

Whitman must have intended to send in this roundabout way information that W. M. Rossetti could use in his preface. This letter may have been sent. There is a passage in Rossetti's preface which seems to echo it: "His ordinary appearance is masculine and cheerful: he never shows depression of spirits, and is sufficiently undemonstrative, and even somewhat silent in company." *Poems By Walt Whitman,* 1868, p. 14.

25. *Inc. Ed.,* p. 488.

26. It might be objected that he purposely toned down his portrait to reassure potential English readers; but it is a fact that his vitality had decreased and that he had become a stay-at-home.

27. See letter to his mother, June 29, 1866, *Letters Written by Walt Whitman to His Mother,* pp. 8–9, and *ibid.,* p. 13, or *SPL,* p. 961.

28. Letter to Peter Doyle, August 21, 1869, *SPL,* p. 984, and letter to the same, September 3, 1869, *Calamus,* 1897, p. 56.

29. See letter to his mother, June 29, 1866, *Letters Written by Walt Whitman to his Mother,* pp. 8–9.

30. Letter to Peter Doyle, September 6, 1870, *SPL,* p. 993.

31. Letter to Peter Doyle, June 27, 1872, *Calamus,* p. 96, and letter to the same, July 12, *ibid.,* p. 98.

32. Letter to George Whitman, October 23, 1872, Rollo G. Silver, "Thirty-One Letters of Walt Whitman," *AL,* VIII (January 1937), 421.

33. Later Whitman mixed up dates. Thus in *SD* (p. 81, *CP,* p. 78) he wrote that his stroke occurred in February. But the date of January 23 is given by Bucke in his *Walt Whitman* and also in the letter that Whitman scribbled in pencil the next day for his mother (this letter is now in the Yale Library).

34. See R. M. Bucke, *Walt Whitman* (Philadelphia; MacKay, 1883), pp. 45–46.

35. *In Re,* p. 115.

36. *Inc. Ed.,* p. 538. See also letter to Peter Doyle, September 3, 1869, *Calamus,* p. 56: "The doctor says it is all from that hospital malaria, hospital poison absorbed in the system years ago."

37. Burroughs protested against this allegation in the New York *Evening Post,* March 28, 1892 (reprinted in the *Nation,* April 7). See Clara Barrus, *Whitman and Burroughs: Comrades* (Boston: Houghton Mifflin, 1931), p. 297.

38. Eduard Bertz, *Der Yankee-Heiland* (Dresden: Carl Reissner, 1906), p. 30.

39. On Whitman's family, see Katherine Molinoff, *Some Notes on Whitman's Family* (privately printed, Brooklyn, 1941), and Josiah C. Trent, "Walt Whitman — A Case History," *Surgery, Gynecology and Obstetrics,* LXXXVII (July 1948), 113–121.

40. *Ibid.*

41. Whitman seems to have had several premonitory strokes. See Mrs. Whitman's letter to Mrs. Price quoted in "Letters of Walt Whitman to His Mother and an Old Friend," *Putnam's Monthly*, V (November 1908), 169. "He had a very slight attack soon after the war, but it seemed to pass over."

42. Letter dated May 16, 1866, and quoted in Florence Hardiman Miller, "Some Unpublished Letters of Walt Whitman's Written to a Soldier Boy," *Overland Monthly*, XLIII (January 1904), 62.

43. *Ibid.*

44. See above, Chapter II, p. 66.

45. At least after 1867, and anyway he could visit them only on Sundays now.

46. See letter to his mother, May 4, 1868, *SPL*, p. 976. He told his mother he was happy (letter from Mrs. Whitman to Walt Whitman, August 19, 1868, *FC*, p. 198). But a little later he had to confess: "You say you think I like Washington so much — Well I am satisfied here, but not particularly attached to the place — only I think it is better for me as things are, & better all round — if it could only be so that I could come home for a little while, & frequently, I should want nothing more — but one mustn't expect to have everything to suit perfectly" (Letter to his mother, August 24, 1868, *Letters Written by Walt Whitman to His Mother*, p. 61.) He felt happy and safe only at home with his mother, and that is why he went back to Brooklyn as often as possible. After his stroke, he took refuge with his brother George in Camden, and he hoped to proceed from there to Brooklyn (see his letter to his mother quoted in *FC*, p. 78).

47. "Leaves of Grass" no. 2, *LG 1867*, pp. 249–250, *Inc. Ed.*, "Tears," p. 218.

48. See O'Connor's testimony quoted by R. M. Bucke in his introduction to *Calamus*, p. 18, and Burroughs's, *ibid.*, p. 16.

49. *Uncoll. PP*, Vol. I, p. lviii, n. 15.

50. Frances Winwar, *American Giant: Walt Whitman and His Times* (New York: Harper, 1941).

51. See his review of Frances Winwar's book, *AL*, XIII (January 1942), 423–432. Furness, in particular, proves that Whitman could have known the Beaches only in New York before the Civil War.

52. *Whitman: An Interpretation in Narrative* (New York: Knopf, 1926).

53. *Uncoll. PP*, II, 95–96.

54. See above, the beginning of Chapter VI.

55. See, for instance, "Song of Myself," §28, *Inc. Ed.*, pp. 48–49, and ". . . the furious storm through me careering. . ." in "From Pent-up Aching Rivers," *Inc. Ed.*, p. 78, l. 31. Also: "The torment,

the irritable tide that will not be at rest. . ." in "Spontaneous Me," *Inc. Ed.*, p. 89, l. 29.

56. "Leaves of Grass" no. 3, *LG 1867*, p. 250, *Inc. Ed.*, pp. 219–220, ll. 3–8, 10–11.

57. I have examined this MS in the Library of Congress. It is written in pencil and "him" and "his" are still very clearly legible under "her."

58. *Uncoll. PP*, II, 95. As to the two mysterious numbers 16 and 164, Edward Hungerford thinks that they are the numbers attributed by Fowler to "Hope" and "Adhesiveness"; see "Walt Whitman and His Chart of Bumps," *AL*, II (January 1931), 350–384.

59. See "To You," *LG 1860*, p. 403, *Inc. Ed.*, p. 479.

60. *LG 1860*, "Enfans d'Adam" no. 6, p. 309 (6), *Inc. Ed.*, "One Hour to Madness and Joy," p. 90, l. 19.

61. *Sequel*, p. 18, *Inc. Ed.*, p. 398.

62. *Uncoll. PP*, II, 95.

63. *Sequel*, "Not My Enemies Ever Invade Me," p. 17, *Inc. Ed.*, p. 484, l. 4.

64. See above Chapter VI, n. 145.

65. *Uncoll. PP*, II, 94.

66. *Ibid.*, p. 97.

67. See *Calamus*, p. 23.

68. Letter to Peter Doyle, July 30, 1870, *Calamus*, p. 61.

69. *Passage to India*, p. 15, *Inc. Ed.*, p. 351, §9, ll. 19–20, 22, 25–26, 29–31. The idea of this passage to India was already in germ in "Enfans d'Adam" no. 10, *LG 1860*, p. 312, *Inc. Ed.*, p. 94, "Facing West from California."

70. *Passage to India*, p. 84, §6, *Inc. Ed.*, p. 221, ll. 25, 30–32.

71. "Warble for Lilac Time," *Passage to India*, p. 97, *Inc. Ed.*, p. 318, ll. 16–20. The same aspirations are expressed in "The Last Invocation," *Passage to India*, p. 69, *Inc. Ed.*, p. 378; "Now Finale to the Shore," *Passage to India*, p. 117, *Inc. Ed.*, p. 416; "Joy, Shipmate, Joy!" *Passage to India*, p. 120, *Inc. Ed.*, p. 415.

72. *Passage to India*, p. 50–51, §15, *Inc. Ed.*, p. 154, ll. 126–133.

73. "Poems bridging the way from Life to Death. . ." in "Proud Music of the Storm," *Passage to India*, p. 24, §15 (32), *Inc. Ed.*, p. 342, §6, l. 21.

74. "Leaves of Grass" no. 3, *LG 1867*, p. 250, *Inc. Ed.*, p. 219, "Aboard at a Ship's Helm."

75. *Passage to India*, p. 120, *Inc. Ed.*, p. 415.

76. *Passage to India*, p. 117, *Inc. Ed.*, p. 416.

77. "The Untold Want," *Passage to India*, p. 118, *Inc. Ed.*, p. 415.

78. "Shut Not Your Doors. . ." *Passage to India*, p. 118, *Inc. Ed.*, p. 415.

79. See above, p. 182.

80. *As a Strong Bird on Pinions Free*, p. xi, *Inc. Ed.*, pp. 484–485.

81. *Leaves of Grass*, New York, 1867, 338 pp. + *Drum-Taps*, New York, 1865, 72 pp. + *Sequel to Drum-Taps*, Washington, 1865–66, 24 pp. + *Songs before Parting*, no place or date, 36 pp.

82. Wells and Goldsmith, *A Concise Bibliography of the Works of Walt Whitman*, p. 114.

83. Gay W. Allen in his *Walt Whitman Handbook* lists one too many: "Not the Pilot" was already included in the edition of 1860, p. 425.

84. *LG 1867*, p. 5, *Inc. Ed.*, p. 434, "Small the Theme of My Chant."

85. *LG 1867*, p. 214, *Inc. Ed.*, p. 233.

86. *LG 1867*, pp. 249–250, *Inc. Ed.*, p. 218.

87. *LG 1867*, p. 250, *Inc. Ed.*, pp. 219–220.

88. *LG 1867*, p. 268, *Inc. Ed.*, p. 7.

89. *LG 1867*, p. 284, *Inc. Ed.*, pp. 308–309.

90. *LG 1867*, p. 284.

91. *LG 1867*, "Starting from Paumanok," p. (7), §1, *Inc. Ed.*, p. 12, §1, l. 5.

92. In "By Blue Ontario's Shore" for instance; see *Inc. Ed.*, p. 659, variant reading of §6, ll. 40–41, and p. 661, variant reading of §12, l. 10.

93. "Chants Democratic" no. 1, *LG 1860*, pp. 108–125, "As I Sat Alone by Blue Ontario's Shore", *LG 1867*, pp. 4–21, *Inc. Ed.*, pp. 286–299.

94. The importance of the poet was further reduced in 1871. See, for instance, the 1867 version of §1 (*Inc. Ed.*, pp. 656–657) and that of 1871 (*Inc. Ed.*, p. 286), esp. ll. 4–6.

95. He thus added §§1, 7, 11, 19, and 20. Besides, he added between parentheses at the end of pre-existing paragraphs groups of verses devoted to democracy, which he personified and called "Mother"; this image is one of the leit-motifs of the poem.

96. *Songs before Parting*, §22 (70), *Inc. Ed.*, p. 666, variant readings of ll. 9–13 of §20.

97. See *Inc. Ed.*, p. 658, an 1856 reading of l. 9 of §6. The word "defections" disappeared in 1867.

98. *LG 1856*, "Poem of Many in One," p. 196, *Inc. Ed.*, p. 662, variant reading of l. 4 of §14, and *Songs before Parting*, 1867, "As I Sat Alone by Blue Ontario's Shore," p. 16, §14 (45), *Inc. Ed.*, p. 295, §14, l. 4.

99. *Songs before Parting*, "As I Sat Alone by Blue Ontario's Shore," *Inc. Ed.*, p. 286, §2, ll. 10–11. These two lines were added in 1867.

100. *Songs before Parting*, "As I Sat Alone by Blue Ontario's

Shore", p. 5, §4 (11–12), *Inc. Ed.*, p. 657, variant reading of ll. 7f of §3.

101. *LG 1860*, pp. 354–355, 355–356, 361–362, *Inc. Ed.*, pp. 477–478, 479.

102. "Calamus" and "Children of Adam," however, were expurgated too. See, for instance, *Inc. Ed.*, p. 585, variant readings of ll. 3 and 4 of §11 of "I Sing the Body Electric," and p. 588, variant readings of "A Woman Waits for Me," etc.

103. "Walt Whitman," *LG 1860*, p. 51 (118), *Inc. Ed.*, p. 562, variant reading of §21.

104. "Walt Whitman," *LG 1860*, p. 86 (276), *Inc. Ed.*, p. 576, variant reading of §41.

105. See, for instance, the variant readings of l. 19 of "There Was a Child Went Forth. . ." *Inc. Ed.*, p. 668. See also the variant readings of l. 12 of §10 of "Starting from Paumanok," *Inc. Ed.*, p. 550.

106. At the same time he dropped a number of lines in which he had claimed to be not the Messiah but a John the Baptist preparing the way; see Gay W. Allen, *Walt Whitman Handbook*, p. 186. J. T. Trowbridge was the first critic to draw attention to this discreet process of expurgation; see "Reminiscences of Walt Whitman," *Atlantic Monthly*, LXXXIX, 174.

107. In this selection the emphasis was laid on Whitman, the poet of democracy. The two sections entitled "Chants Democratic" and "Drum-Taps" took up nearly one half of the book. The others were entitled: "Walt Whitman," "Leaves of Grass," "Songs of Parting" (and not "Songs before Parting," for Rossetti already knew of some of the changes which were to take effect in the next edition).

108. They are: "Whoever you are holding me now in hand" (which Rossetti entitled "Fit Audience"), "These I singing in spring" (entitled "Singing in Spring"), "Not heaving from my ribb'd breast only" (entitled "Pulse of my life"), "For you O Democracy" (entitled "Love of Comrades").

109. See Whitman's letter to M. D. Conway, July 24, 1867, *SPL*, p. 963. Rossetti used the text of the 1867 edition. Whitman sent him a copy of it with manuscript revisions. In *WWW*, Furness gives the text (pp. 150–154) and tells the story (pp. 141–149) of an introduction, probably written by Whitman himself but signed by O'Connor, which Whitman wanted Rossetti to use. This introduction came too late and could not be printed. It was better in any case for the English public to have a qualified presentation by Rossetti than an extravagant eulogy by O'Connor.

110. Letter to Conway, November 1, 1867, *SPL*, p. 964.

111. Letter to W. M. Rossetti, December 3, 1867, *SPL*, pp. 966–967.

112. *Ibid.*, p. 967.

113. See his prefatory notice, pp. 20–23.

114. See *With WW in C*, II, 447–448. Traubel quotes several letters from F. S. Ellis.

115. *With WW in C*, II, 420.

116. *Galaxy*, December 1867, pp. 919–933.

117. *Ibid.*, May 1868, pp. 540–547.

118. *Democratic Vistas* (Washington, 1871).

119. "In Cabin'd Ships at Sea," *LG 1871*, p. 9, §2, *Inc. Ed.*, p. 2, l. 15.

120. See *CP*, pp. 214–215.

121. *LG 1871*, "Respondez," pp. 333–334, *Inc. Ed.*, p. 470, ll. 17–20.

122. The date of the copyright is 1870. The book was probably printed during Whitman's stay at Brooklyn from July 25 to October 1, 1870. See letter to Peter Doyle, September 6, 1870: "I am at the printing-office several hours every day. . ." *Calamus*, p. 72, or *SPL*, p. 993.

123. The copyright notice reads: "Entered according to Act of Congress in the year 1870. . ." The book may even have been ready as early as the beginning of 1869, if we are to believe an article in the Washington *Commercial*, May 9, 1869, which was probably inspired by Whitman if not written by him. See Emory Holloway, "Whitman as His Own Press-Agent," *American Mercury*, XVIII (December 1929), 482–488.

124. Whereas the pages on the right bear the title "Passage to India," those on the left bear the title "Leaves of Grass."

125. *After All Not to Create Only*, Boston: Roberts Bros., 1871, vii + 24 pp.

126. The 1872 edition was merely a reprinting: "I have attended to the bringing out the new edition of my book, but as the plates were all ready before, it is not much of a job." Whitman to Peter Doyle, March 4, 1872, *Calamus*, p. 89.

127. *LG 1867*, p. 273, §5 (14), *Inc. Ed.*, p. 610, last line of the passage following l. 31 in 1860.

128. *LG 1867*, p. 258, *Inc. Ed.*, p. 479. This poem dated back to 1860 (*LG 1860*, p. 403).

129. The 1865 *Drum-Taps* were now split into three groups: "Drum-Taps," "Marches Now the War is Over," and "Bathed in War's Perfume," separated by groups of poems entitled "Leaves of Grass." There was a fourth group of former "Drum-Taps" in *Passage to India* under the title of "Ashes of Soldiers."

130. *LG 1871*, pp. 337–338, *Inc. Ed.*, p. 274.

131. "Proud Music of the Storm," *Passage to India*, p. 17, §1, *Inc. Ed.*, p. 337, §1, ll. 10–11.

132. Same poem, *Passage to India*, p. 18, §3 (5), *Inc. Ed.*, p. 338, §2, ll. 13–15.

133. *After All Not to Create Only*, p. 17, §8, *Inc. Ed.*, p. 170, §7, ll. 1–3 ("Song of the Exposition"). See also "The Mystic Trumpeter," *Inc. Ed.*, p. 391, §6, ll. 1–4, in which he depicts war as one of the evils which afflict mankind.

134. See "Virginia — The West," *As a Strong Bird on Pinions Free*, p. 15, *Inc. Ed.*, pp. 248–249. See also the end of *After All Not to Create Only*, pp. 23–24, §§ 13–14, *Inc. Ed.*, "Song of the Exposition," pp. 173–174, §9. In the Preface to the edition of 1872 he expressed the hope that the wounds caused by the war would soon be healed; see *Inc. Ed.*, p. 511.

135. *LG 1871*, p. 11–12, *Inc. Ed.*, pp. 3–4. See also *Inc. Ed.*, p. 409, §1, 1.14, and variant readings, p. 699. In the same year he added to "Song of the Banner at Daybreak," the following line (*Inc. Ed.*, p. 647):

"The war is over — yet never over. . . out of it, we are born to real life and identity."

136. "As I Ponder'd in Silence," *LG 1871*, p. 8, §2, *Inc. Ed.*, p. 2, ll. 13, 15–16.

137. *LG 1871*, p. 309.

138. See above, Chapter VI, pp. 160, 174.

139. *LG 1867*, p. (5), *Inc. Ed.*, p. 1. The 1867 poem subsists in the definitive edition (*Inc. Ed.*, p. 434); Whitman included it in his "Sands at Seventy."

140. *LG 1867*, p. (5), "Inscription."

141. *Inc. Ed.*, pp. 511–512.

142. *LG 1871*, pp. 363–369.

143. *LG 1871*, p. 363, *Inc. Ed.*, p. 10.

144. Mark Twain and C. D. Warner, *The Gilded Age: A Tale of Today*, 1873.

145. *WWW*, p. 229, n. 95.

146. The title page bears the following indication: "Recited by Walt Whitman on invitation of Managers American Institute, on Opening their 40th Annual Exhibition, New York, noon, September 8, 1871."

147. The germ of this poem was already contained in "Enfans d'Adam" no. 10, in *LG 1860*. This poem was later entitled "Facing West from California's Shores."

148. *Passage to India*, pp. 108–111, *Inc. Ed.*, "Outlines for a Tomb," pp. 319–320.

149. *Passage to India*, pp. 94–96, *Inc. Ed.*, pp. 316–318.

150. *Passage to India*, pp. 87–93, *Inc. Ed.*, pp. 301–306, "The Return of the Heroes."

151. There were eleven new poems in all in 1871: "One's Self I

Sing," "As I Ponder'd in Silence," "In Cabin'd Ships at Sea," "To Thee Old Cause," "For Him I Sing," "Still though the One I Sing," "The Base of all Metaphysics," "Ethiopia Saluting the Colors," "Delicate Cluster," "Adieu to a Soldier," plus "After All Not to Create Only," though it was published separately.

Passage to India also contained some new poems: "Gliding o'er All," "Passage to India," "Proud Music of the Storm," "To a Certain Civilian," "This Dust Was Once a Man," "Whispers of Heavenly Death," "Darest Thou Now O Soul," "A Noiseless Patient Spider," "The Last Invocation," "As I Watch'd the Ploughman Ploughing," "Pensive and Faltering," "On the Beach at Night," "A Carol of Harvest for 1867" (later "The Return of the Heroes"), "The Singer in the Prison," "Warble for Lilac Time," "Sparkles from the Wheel," "Brother of All with Generous Hand" (later "Outlines for a Tomb"), "Gods," "Lessons," "Now Finale to the Shore," "Thought" (later "As They Draw to a Close"), "The Untold Want," "Portals," "These Carols," "Joy, Shipmate Joy."

152. *As a Strong Bird on Pinions Free and Other Poems* (Washington, D.C., 1872), XIII + 16 pp. This booklet contained the following poems: "One Song, America, before I Go," "Souvenirs of Democracy" (later "My Legacy"), "As a Strong Bird. . ." (later "Thou Mother with Thy Equal Brood"), "The Mystic Trumpeter," "O Star of France," "Virginia — The West," "By Broad Potomac's Shore."

153. For the circumstances of this invitation, which seems to have originated in a practical joke that the students of Dartmouth wanted to play on the faculty, see Bliss Perry, *Walt Whitman*, pp. 203–210. But in a letter to Peter Doyle June 27, 1872 (*SPL*, pp. 1007–1008), Whitman declared: "All went off very well." And in the Burlington *Free Press and Times* there appeared on July 1, 1872, a flattering account of the poet's performance — which may have been written by Whitman himself.

154. He himself announced on p. 5 of *As a Strong Bird. . .* : "The Mystic Trumpeter, and O Star of France, and indeed all Walt Whitman's other pieces since 1871–72, follow."

155. *As a Strong Bird. . .* pp. 13–14, *Inc. Ed.*, pp. 331–332. He hated Napoleon III, but loved the French, see his letter to Peter Doyle, September 6, 1870, *SPL*, p. 993.

156. *Inc. Ed.*, pp. 507–508.

157. See above, p. 182.

158. Letter to Peter Doyle, September 6, 1870, *SPL*, pp. 993–994.

159. *Inc. Ed.*, p. 508.

160. *Inc. Ed.*, pp. 484–485.

161. *LG 1871*, pp. 8–9, *Inc. Ed.*, pp. 2–3, ll. 1–2, 4–6, 10, 12, 15, 17, 19.

162. Letter to O'Connor, September 27, 1867 (Berg Collection).
163. See above, p. 199.
164. Later entitled "The Return of the Heroes," *Inc. Ed.*, pp. 301–306.
165. See Portia Baker, "Walt Whitman's Relations with Some New York Magazines," *AL*, VII (November 1935), 274–301.
166. A review signed "C." in the *Round Table*, January 19, 1867.
167. *Nation*, January 2, 1868, p. 8.
168. On Whitman's reception in Great Britain, see Harold Blodgett, *Walt Whitman in England* (Cornell University Press, 1934).
169. "Walt Whitman's Poems," London *Chronicle*, July 6, 1867. Robert Buchanan a little later published a very warm article in his turn in the *Broadway Magazine*, November 1867. He reprinted it the following year in *David Gray and Other Essays*.
170. Letter to J. C. Hotten, April 24, 1868, *SPL*, p. 974.
171. Letter to M. D. Conway, February 17, 1868, *SPL*, pp. 969–970.
172. See above, n. 169.
173. Swinburne had already compared Whitman to Blake in his essay on the latter in 1867. In 1871, in his *Songs before Sunrise*, he greeted him as the prophet of Liberty in a poem entitled "To Walt Whitman in America." But in 1872, in *Under the Microscope*, he began to qualify his praises, and in 1887 he attacked Whitman violently in the *Fortnightly Review*. See G. W. Allen, *Walt Whitman Handbook*, pp. 477–478.
174. In *The Poetry of the Period* (London: R. Bentley, 1870).
175. This article has been reprinted in *In Re*, pp. 41–55. The quotation is borrowed from p. 48.
176. Thus Robert Buchanan's article in the *Broadway Magazine*, November 1867, was immediately reprinted in the New York *Citizen*, November 2, and in the Washington *Sunday Morning Chronicle*, November 10. In the same way, Rossetti's article in the London *Chronicle*, July 6, 1867, was reprinted in the New York *Citizen* as early as August 10.
177. Ferdinand Freiligrath's three articles on Whitman (*Wochenausgabe der Augsburger Allgemeine Zeitung*, May 10 *et seq.*, 1868) were later reprinted in his complete works, *Gesammelte Dichtungen* (Stuttgart, 1877), IV, 75 ff.
178. *Revue Britannique*, May 1868.
179. *Revue des Deux Mondes*, XLII (June 1, 1872), 556–577.
180. *Renaissance Littéraire et Artistique*, III, no. 7 (June 8), no. 11 (July 6), and no. 12 (July 13, 1872).
181. "Walt Whitman det amerikanske Demokratis Digter," *For Ide og Virkelighed*, I, 152–216.

182. Thus a translation of Freiligrath's articles was published in the Boston *Commonwealth* as early as July 4 and in the July issue of the *New Eclectic*. Mme Bentzon's article, though less favorable, was published in the New York *Spectator and Weekly Commercial Adviser* of July 19, 1872, under the title of "A French Opinion of Walt Whitman." The same journal had published in April a translation of Rudolf Schmidt's article. Whitman was so proud of this Danish tribute that he gave a summary of it among the advertisements printed at the end of *As a Strong Bird on Pinions Free*. The full article was later printed in *In Re*, pp. 231–248.

183. Such was the conclusion drawn by R. J. H. (R. J. Hinton) in "The Poet Walt Whitman — His Fame and Fortunes in Europe and America," Rochester *Evening Express*, March 17, 1868. This article was reprinted in the *Kansas Magazine* in December 1872. Whitman alluded to it in a letter to his mother (April 28, 1868, *SPL*, p. 975).

Most English critics insisted on the essentially American quality of his personality and art: "Walt Whitman is by far the most original product of his time, the sum and expression of the great democracy of the West . . ." (Review of Rossetti's edition, *Academia*, March 21, 1868, p. 278) "He is the first characteristic writer that the United States have produced . . . Whitman's very faults are national. The brag and bluster, and self-assertion of the man are American only . . ." (*Chambers's Journal*, July 4, 1868). But most of his compatriots refused to recognize themselves in the mythical American character whom English critics discovered in *Leaves of Grass*. The *New Eclectic* was even indignant: "That he is an American, in one sense, we must admit. He is something no other country could have produced. He is American as certain forms of rowdyism and vulgarity, excrescences on American institutions, are American. But that he is American in the sense of being representative of American taste, intellect, or cultivation, we should be very sorry indeed to believe." *New Eclectic*, July 1868.

184. *As a Strong Bird . . .* , p. xiii, *Inc. Ed.*, p. 412, which, however does not give the original version of the poem.

185. "Most readers will be surprised at the tone of unqualified, panegyric which runs through this little volume." An anonymous review, New York *Tribune*, July 20, 1867.

186. See F. P. Hier, "End of a Literary Mystery," *American Mercury*, I (April 1924), 471–478.

187. "The Carpenter," *Putnam's Magazine*, I (January 1868). This tale was later reprinted in *Three Tales* (Boston: Houghton Mifflin, 1892), pp. 211–320.

188. Letter to Peter Doyle, July 16, 1871, *SPL*, p. 996.

189. "The Poetry of Democracy: Walt Whitman," *Westminster Review*, XCVI (July 1871), 33–68. See Harold Blodgett, "Whitman and Dowden," *AL*, I (May 1929), 171–182.

190. Letter to O'Connor, July 14, 1871, *SPL*, p. 995.

191. John C. Dent, "America and Her Literature," *Temple Bar*, Vol. XXXVII, no. 147, p. 401.

VIII. THE HEROIC INVALID (1873–1876)

1. "I call myself a half-paralytic these days, and reverently bless the Lord it is not worse . . ." *SD*, p. 82, *CP*, p. 78.

2. See Josiah C. Trent, "Walt Whitman — A Case History," *Surgery, Gynecology and Obstetrics*, LXXXVII (July 1948), 3; see also letter to his mother, May 11, 1873, in *Wake* 7, pp. 14–15.

3. Letter to Peter Doyle, August 28, 1873, *Calamus*, p. 109.

4. Preface to *Two Rivulets*, p. 7n, *Inc. Ed.*, p. 514n.

5. Martha was Jeff's wife; she died of tuberculosis at St. Louis, where the couple had settled after the war.

6. See Dixon Wecter, "Walt Whitman as Civil Servant," *PMLA*, LXVIII (January 1943), pp. 1094–1109.

7. *In Re*, p. 114.

8. Letter to Peter Doyle, July 7, 1873, *Calamus*, pp. 102–103.

9. July 24, 1873, *ibid.*, p. 104.

10. September 5, 1873, *ibid.*, p. 112.

11. "I am going to try to get down to the ferry boat, and cross to Philadelphia — so you see I am not altogether disabled — but it is awful tough work." August 28, 1873, *ibid.*, p. 110. See also letter to Mrs. Abby H. Price and Helen Price, January 1874, *SPL*, p. 1017.

12. ". . . but I have so many times got a little better, only to fall back again as bad as ever, or worse . . ." (September 12, 1873, *Calamus*, p. 112). ". . . the worse of my case is these *fall backs* — But I have been out a little to-day. My walking does not improve any at all. (Then to make things more *cheerful*, there are many deaths here about from paralysis)" (October 16, 1873, *ibid.*, p. 112).

13. October 13, 1873, *ibid.*, p. 119.

14. "I keep a bully good heart, take it altogether . . ." (January 19, 1874, *ibid.*, p. 140). See also letter of April 16, 1874, *ibid.*, p. 152. After April 1874 he had other worries. Owing to lack of exercise, he suffered from dyspepsia (letters to Peter Doyle, May 22 and April 30, 1874, and December 3, 1875, *Calamus*, pp. 153, 160, 163).

15. See letters to Peter Doyle, September 26, 1873, March 26, 1874, and 1875, *Calamus*, pp. 116–117, 150, 159.

16. Letter to Peter Doyle, October 3, 1873, *SPL*, p. 1014.

17. Letter to Peter Doyle, January 30, 1874, *Calamus*, p. 141.
18. *Two Rivulets*, pp. 25–26, *Inc. Ed.*, pp. 392–393.
19. See above, n. 6.
20. "I don't fret about being discharged — I wonder it didn't come before." July 10, 1874, *Calamus*, p. 155.
21. *SD*, p. 93, *CP*, p. 89.
22. First published in *Harper's Monthly Magazine*, XLVIII (March 1874), 524–525, and then in *Two Rivulets*, pp. 21–23.
23. *Two Rivulets*, p. 21, *Inc. Ed.*, p. 682. Whitman himself realized the autobiographical value of the poem: ". . . as I see it now I shouldn't wonder if I have unconsciously put a sort of autobiographical dash in it." Letter to Mrs. O'Connor, February 3, 1874, Berg Collection.
24. *Inc. Ed.*, p. 352, ll. 1, 4, 6, 15–19.
25. *Ibid.*, pp. 352–353, ll. 27–30.
26. *Ibid.*, p. 353, ll. 51–55.
27. *Ibid.*, l. 46.
28. "Song of the Redwood Tree," *Inc. Ed.*, p. 175, §1, ll. 6–7.
29. *Ibid.*, p. 176, §1, ll. 39–40.
30. *Ibid.*, p. 177, §1, l. 62.
31. Preface to *Two Rivulets*, p. 7n, *Inc. Ed.*, p. 514n.
32. Whitman seems, at this time, to have been little interested in the social problem, which, however, had reached an acute stage in 1873–1876. In his letters to Peter Doyle (January 16, 1874, *Calamus*, p. 139; February 6, 1874, *ibid.*, p. 142 or *SPL*, p. 1019) he sometimes alluded to the sufferings of the unemployed, but never mentioned the matter in print. In 1871 (see Newton Arvin, *Whitman*, p. 138) he thought of prefixing a violent protest against "the more and more insidious grip of capitalism" to his "Songs of Insurrection" (*WWW*, p. 229, n. 95), but he eventually gave up the idea.
33. *Inc. Ed.*, p. 460, ll. 1–4.
34. *Ibid.*, p. 461, ll. 11–12, 17–18.
35. Letter to Mrs. O'Connor, March 22, 1874, Berg Collection.
36. From an article published in a series entitled " 'Tis But Ten Years Since," which appeared in the *Graphic* from January 27 to March 7, 1874. Whitman reprinted it partially in his *Memoranda during the War*. The passages which he left out are to be found in Thomas Mabbott and Rollo G. Silver, " 'Tis But Ten Years Since," *AL*, XV (March 1943), 51–62. The passage quoted above occurs on p. 52.
37. "Song of the Redwood Tree," *Two Rivulets*, p. 15, *Inc. Ed.*, p. 178, §3, ll. 8–11.
38. Preface to *Two Rivulets*, p. 14, *Inc. Ed.*, p. 521.
39. "Wandering at Morn," *Two Rivulets*, p. 28, *Inc. Ed.*, p. 334

40. "Prayer of Columbus," *Two Rivulets*, p. 23, *Inc. Ed.*, p. 354, ll. 64–66.

41. See letter to Peter Doyle, December 3, 1875, *Calamus*, p. 163.

42. See letter to Einstein, November 26, 1875, *SPL*, p. 1023, and *SD*, pp. 157–158 (*CP*, p. 157).

43. Letter to Mrs. Gilchrist, *SPL*, p. 1024.

44. Letter to Einstein, November 26, 1875, *SPL*, p. 1023.

45. *Two Rivulets* (Camden, N.J., 1876, 384 pp.) contained:

1. "Two Rivulets," 32 pp., which included fourteen new poems: "Two Rivulets," "Or from That Sea of Time," "Eidólons," "Spain, 1873–74," "Prayer of Columbus," "Out from behind This Mask," "To a Locomotive in Winter," "The Ox Tamer," "Wandering at Morn," "An Old Man's Thought of School," "With All Thy Gifts," "From My Last Years," "In Former Songs," "After the Sea-Ship."

2. "Democratic Vistas," 84 pp.

3. "Centennial Songs," 18 pp., which included "Song of the Exposition" (first published in 1871 as "After All Not to Create Only"), "Song of the Redwood Tree," "Song of the Universal," "Song for All Seas, All Ships," the last three being new poems.

4. "As a Strong Bird on Pinions Free," X+16 pp. (first published in 1872).

5. "Memoranda during the War," 68 pp.

6. "Passage to India," 120 pp.

As usual, the title page did not give the author's name. Some parts of the volume were printed in New York and others in Camden on different kinds of paper.

The 1876 edition of *Leaves of Grass* was an exact reproduction of the 1871–72 volume, but in some copies, notably those sent to English purchasers, some of whom paid three or four times the price of the book, and to whom Whitman wanted to give something extra, a few new poems were inserted. These additional poems had originally been printed on a single sheet intended to be cut in such a way as to permit the various poems to be glued to the page indicated in a supplementary table of contents. One of these sheets is preserved in the Carolyn Wells Houghton Collection of the Library of Congress and contains the following poems:

"The Beauty of the Ship," *Inc. Ed.*, p. 485.

"As in a Swoon," which was never printed again and is not included in *Inc. Ed.*:

> "As in a swoon, one instant,
> Another sun, ineffable, full-dazzles me
> And all the orbs I knew — and brighter, unknown orbs;
> One instant of the future land, Heaven's land."

"When the Full-grown Poet Came," *Inc. Ed.*, pp. 451–452. This poem was not included in the 1881 edition of *Leaves of Grass*; it reappeared only in *Good-Bye My Fancy* in 1891.

"After an Interval," *Inc. Ed.*, p. 485.

These poems were to be glued respectively on pages 207, 247, 359, and 369, to fill the blanks left at the bottom of each of these pages. As we have had occasion to notice with the 1860 edition, Whitman hated to leave blank spaces.

Thus, *Two Rivulets* contained seventeen new poems and *Leaves of Grass* four. Since the 1871–72 edition, Whitman had written twenty-one new poems, as well as "To the Man-of-War Bird," which appeared in the *Athenaeum* on April 1, 1876.

46. ". . . the present melange," Preface to 1876 edition, *Inc. Ed.*, p. 512.

47. See letter to Edmund C. Stedman, June 17, 1875, *SPL*, p. 1021, and Preface to *Two Rivulets*, p. 6, *Inc. Ed.*, p. 513. See also "Two Rivulets," *Inc. Ed.*, pp. 485–486.

48. Preface to *Two Rivulets*, p. 5n, *Inc. Ed.*, p. 513n.

49. Preface to *Two Rivulets*, p. 6n, *Inc. Ed.*, p. 513n; see also "In Former Songs," *Two Rivulets*, p. 31, *Inc. Ed.*, p. 487.

50. Preface to *Two Rivulets*, p. 5n, *Inc. Ed.*, p. 513n.

51. *Two Rivulets*, pp. 17–20, *Inc. Ed.*, pp. 4–7.

52. "The Ox Tamer," *Two Rivulets*, pp. 27–28, *Inc. Ed.*, pp. 332–333.

53. *Centennial Songs*, p. 16, *Inc. Ed.*, p. 192, §2, ll. 7–10.

54. Preface to *Two Rivulets*, p. 7, *Inc. Ed.*, pp. 514–515.

55. Preface to *Two Rivulets*, p. 7, *Inc. Ed.*, p. 514n.

56. *Two Rivulets*, p. 24, *Inc. Ed.*, p. 321, ll. 4–5, 7. Line 7 is a Biblical reminiscence; see Revelation 9:2. Mrs. O'Connor recounts the following incident which may have inspired the poem: "It was about this time [during Whitman's stay in Washington] that one evening . . . he was accosted by a policeman and ordered to remove that 'false face', his name for a mask. Walt quietly assured him that the only face he wore was his very own, but added, 'Do we not all wear false faces?'" Ellen M. Calder, "Personal Recollections of Walt Whitman," *Atlantic Monthly*, XCIX (June 1907), 831.

57. Preface to *Two Rivulets*, p. 11n, *Inc. Ed.*, p. 518n.

58. *Ibid.*

59. *Ibid.*, p. 520.

60. *Ibid.*, p. 517.

61. "After an Interval," *LG 1876*, p. 369, *Inc. Ed.*, p. 485, ll. 5–6.

62. *Inc. Ed.*, p. 400. This poem was inspired by the proclamation of the Republic in Spain under the presidency of Emilio Castelar.

63. *Two Rivulets*, p. 29, *Inc. Ed.*, pp. 333–334.

64. *Two Rivulets*, "Centennial Songs," pp. 15–17, *Inc. Ed.*, pp. 192–194.

65. See letter to Mrs. O'Connor, June 10, 1874, Berg Collection.
66. Letter to Robert Buchanan, May 16, 1876, *SPL*, pp. 1027–1028.
67. *The Hour*, March 1876.
68. New York *Independent*, June 29, 1876.
69. This article was entitled "Walt Whitman — True Reminiscences of His Writings." A few months earlier, the same paper had published an article in which, almost in the same terms, Whitman complained of being boycotted (January 26, 1876); see *WWW*, pp. 245–248, n. 220.
70. See above, nn. 22 and 28.
71. In 1873, the New York *Graphic* had published "Nay,Tell Me Not To-day the Publish'd Shame" (March 5); "The Singing Thrush" (March 15 — later "Wandering at Morn"); "Spain 1873–'74" (March 23); " 'Tis But Ten Years Since" (January 27–March 7); "An Old Man's Thought of School" (November 3); "A Christmas Garland," (Christmas number), which was composed of "In the Wake Following" (later "After the Sea-Ship") and "The Ox-Tamer."
The Camden *New Republic* had published "Song of the Universal" on June 20, 1874.
72. London *Athenaeum*, March 11, 1876.
73. He referred to American poets as "rooks" and "caws" and called Whitman "a sick eagle." Two days earlier, the same paper had published an article by its special correspondent in the United States on Whitman's difficult situation: ". . . while the stories of his extreme poverty and suffering which recently obtained circulation, are, I am glad to say, untrue, he has fallen into obscurity, if not into positive neglect, and apparently into a mood of sorrow." It was probably this report which, coming after the article in the *Athenaeum*, provoked Buchanan's letter. The public quickly responded to his appeal. On March 14 and 15, he thanked the generous donors who had immediately sent contributions, but on March 16 the *Daily News*, probably somewhat worried, tried in an editorial to calm the American public, maintaining that after all it was free to ignore a poet whom, from the start, it had refused to recognize. According to Traubel, Whitman granted the justice of this view; see *With WW in C*, I, 343–344.
74. New York *Tribune*, March 31, a note by E. C. Stedman on O'Connor's part in the Harlan affair; April 12, a new attack by Taylor charging Whitman with obscenity; April 13, an article by Burroughs; April 22, an article by O'Connor, "Walt Whitman; Is He Persecuted?"; July 10, an occasional poem by Whitman, "A Death-Sonnet for Custer" (later "From Far Dakota's Cañons"; on the origin of this poem, see *SD*, pp. 187–188, *CP*, pp. 184–185); July 13, "Robert Buchanan and Walt Whitman in Court," on the action for libel

brought by Buchanan against P. A. Taylor, the owner of the *Examiner,* who had published Swinburne's attack against Whitman.

75. New York *Herald,* April 2, 1876.

76. See W. S. Kennedy, *The Fight of a Book for the World,* p. 27. On the English subscription, see Clarence Gohdes, "The 1876 English Subscription for Whitman," *MLN,* L (April 1935), 257–258.

77. See letters to Buchanan, May 16 and September 4, 1876, *SPL,* pp. 1026–1028, and to W. M. Rossetti, March 17, *ibid.,* pp. 1024–1025. He was justly proud of the dignity of his attitude throughout this affair and quoted the last-mentioned letter in *SD,* pp. 316–317 (*CP,* pp. 324–325); see also *With WW in C,* I, 344–347.

78. See Bliss Perry, *Walt Whitman,* pp. 217–218.

79. See Robert Dudley Adams, "Walt Whitman, the American Poet," Sydney *Evening News,* May 20, 1876.

80. *With WW in C,* I, 343.

81. Quoted by Bliss Perry, *Walt Whitman,* p. 217.

82. Letter to Peter Doyle, December 13, 1876, *Calamus,* p. 165.

IX. NEW VICTORIES (1876–1882)

1. See *The Letters of Anne Gilchrist and Walt Whitman,* ed. with an introduction by T. B. Harned (New York: Doubleday, Doran, 1918).

2. See above, Chapter VII, p. 209.

3. Letter to Anne Gilchrist, August 17, 1873, *SPL,* p. 1013.

4. See E. Holloway, *Whitman,* pp. 290–293.

5. Letter to Anne Gilchrist, March 17, 1876, *SPL,* p. 1023.

6. Letter to John R. Johnston, June 20, 1877, *SPL,* pp. 1029–1030.

7. "A Visit to Walt Whitman in 1877," *Progressive Review,* I, no. 5 (February 1897), 413.

8. *SD,* pp. 82–123, *CP,* pp. 78–121.

9. *SD,* pp. 82–84, *CP,* pp. 78–80.

10. See "Bumble-Bees," "Summer Perfume — Quail — Notes — The Hermit-Thrush," "The Sky — Days and Nights — Happiness," "Colors — A Contrast," *ibid.*

11. See "Birds Migrating at Midnight," "Autumn Side-Bits," *ibid.*

12. "I sit here amid all these fair sights and vital influences . . ." *SD,* p. 92, *CP,* p. 86.

13. *SD,* p. 82, *CP,* p. 78.

14. "The Lesson of a Tree," *SD,* p. 89, *CP,* p. 86.

15. *Inc. Ed.,* p. 461, l. 6, echoes the title of a chapter in *SD,* "The Sky — Days and Nights — Happiness," which confirms the fact that the poem was in all likelihood composed at Timber Creek.

16. *SD*, pp. 104–105, *CP*, pp. 101–102.

17. *SD*, pp. 103–104, *CP*, pp. 99–101. On his health at the end of his second summer at Timber Creek, see letter to Peter Doyle, June 20, 1877, *Calamus*, p. 167, and letter to Tennyson, August 9, 1878, *SPL*, p. 1032. On his stays at Timber Creek, see Sculley Bradley, "Walt Whitman on Timber Creek," *AL*, V (November 1933), 235–246.

18. See Camden *Daily Post*, March 29, 1877: "Walt Whitman — He visits New York after 5 years' absence — High Tone Society now takes him to its bosom — Yet he rides again atop of the Broadway Omnibuses and fraternizes with drivers and boatmen — He has a new book under way — He is better in health."

19. See Baltimore *American*, March 17, 1877: "Our New York Letter: . . . Walt Whitman on the Woman Question . . . he talked in an easy delightful way regarding the new social and political aspects which life had taken since his banishment from its activities and seemed to feel very much as if he had gone to sleep ten years ago in New Jersey . . . Mr. Whitman recited with his old fire some lines from Henry Murger, the French Bohemian poet, called the 'Midnight Visitor.' They were very sad." The text of this poem will be found in Traubel, "Walt Whitman and Murger," *Poet Lore*, VI (October 1894), 484–491. It was an adaptation of "Ballade du désespéré," in *Les Nuits d'Hiver*.

20. *SD*, pp. 113–114, *CP*, pp. 110–111.

21. *SD*, pp. 114–115, *CP*, pp. 111–112.

22. *SD*, p. 117, *CP*, 114.

23. *SD*, p. 117, *CP*, 115.

24. See "A Poet's Recreation," New York *Tribune*, July 4, 1878, and "Gathering the Corn," *ibid.*, October 24.

25. See *Walt Whitman's Diary in Canada*, p. 55.

26. Letter to George Whitman, June 15–17, 1878, *SPL*, pp. 1030–1031.

27. *SD*, p. 306, *CP*, p. 315.

28. *SD*, pp. 129–133, *CP*, pp. 127–131.

29. He was the guest of the Old Settlers of Kansas Committee.

30. *SD*, p. 142, *CP*, pp. 140–141. On his western journey, see R. R. Hubach, "Walt Whitman and the West," a digest of a doctoral dissertation, Indiana University, 1943.

31. *SD*, pp. 141–142, *CP*, pp. 139–140.

32. *SD*, pp. 147–148, *CP*, p. 146.

33. *SD*, p. 145, *CP*, p. 144.

34. *SD*, p. 143, *CP*, p. 142.

35. *Inc. Ed.*, p. 334–335.

36. *Inc. Ed.*, p. 403.

37. *Inc. Ed.*, p. 336. He may also have composed at this time the poem entitled "Mirages," to which he prefixed the following note: "Noted verbatim after a supper talk outdoors in Nevada with two old miners." But he published it only in 1891 in *Good-Bye My Fancy*.

38. *SD*, p. 155, *CP*, pp. 154–155. On his stay in St. Louis, see also letter to Peter Doyle, November 5, 1879, *Calamus*, pp. 170–172, and R. R. Hubach, "Walt Whitman visits St. Louis," *Missouri Historical Review*, XXXVII (July 1943), 386–394. See also "Plate Glass Notes," *NB*, pp. 78–79, *CP*, pp. 430–431.

39. R. R. Hubach, "Three Uncollected St. Louis Interviews of Walt Whitman," *AL*, XIV (May 1942), 141–147.

40. *SD*, p. 159, *CP*, p. 158–159.

41. *SD*, pp. 160–161, *CP*, p. 160. ". . . a remembrance always afterwards."

42. Letter to Peter Doyle, July 24, 1880, *Calamus*, p. 172.

43. See above, n. 25.

44. *SD*, pp. 161–165, *CP*, pp. 160–166.

45. "To Walt Whitman," *Galaxy*, January 1877, p. 29.

46. See *Calamus*, p. 10.

47. *SD*, p. 180, *CP*, pp. 179–180.

48. St. Louis *Post Dispatch*, October 17, 1879; see above, n. 39.

49. Trent Collection, Duke University.

50. *Walt Whitman's Diary in Canada*, pp. 58–59.

51. Letter from J. G. Holland to R. W. Gilbert, September 19, 1880, quoted in Johnson, *Remembered Yesterdays* (Boston, 1923), pp. 337–338.

52. See Portia Baker, "Walt Whitman's Relations with Some New York Magazines," *AL*, VII (November 1935), 274–301.

53. E. C. Stedman, "Walt Whitman," *Scribner's*, XXI (November 1880), 47–64. This article was reprinted by Stedman in his *Poets of America* (Boston and New York: Houghton, Mifflin, 1885), pp. 349–395.

54. *SD*, p. 179, *CP*, p. 178.

55. *SD*, p. 180, *CP*, pp. 179–180.

56. *SD*, pp. 181–182, *CP*, pp. 180–181.

57. For instance, in the Boston *Herald*, April 18, 1881: "Walt Whitman — His second visit to the New England Metropolis — A cordial welcome in literary circles — Sketch of his life and poetic characteristics." See also, Boston *Evening Traveller*, April 16, 1881: "Walt Whitman on the death of Lincoln."

58. *SD*, pp. 182–183, *CP*, p. 182.

59. *SD*, pp. 185–186, *CP*, pp. 182–183. See also New York *Tribune*, August 4, 1881, "Letter from Walt Whitman — Week at

West Hills," and Mrs. Mary Wager-Fisher, "Walt Whitman," *Long Islander*, August 5, 1881.

60. *SD*, pp. 9–10, *CP*, pp. 5–6.

61. *SD*, pp. 186–187, *CP*, pp. 183–184.

62. *With WW in C*, I, 60.

63. Boston *Herald*, April 18, 1881.

64. Thomas B. Harned, "Walt Whitman and His Second Boston Publishers," *CW*, V, 275–300.

65. *Ibid.*, 276.

66. "I was in Boston from August 19 to October." MS note in Trent Collection, Duke University; see *Catalogue*, p. 49, no. 34.

67. Letter to Burroughs, September 24, 1881, *SPL*, p. 1039.

68. *SD*, pp. 189–190, *CP*, pp. 186–187.

69. See letter quoted by Harned, *CW*, V, 288.

70. *Ibid.*, 289–290.

71. *Ibid.*, 290.

72. Bucke gives the list in his *Walt Whitman*, p. 149.

73. Letter to Osgood quoted by Harned, *CW*, V, 294. The poems which Whitman intended to censor were: "I Sing the Body Electric" (§§5 and 8), "A Woman Waits for Me," and "Spontaneous Me."

74. *CW*, V, 294.

75. *Ibid.*, p. 295.

76. *Ibid.*, p. 296.

77. *Ibid.*

78. Letter to O'Connor, May 25, 1882, Berg Collection.

79. The only difference was that the title page bore the indication: "Camden, Author's Edition."

80. "They are now on their fourth Philadelphia edition of *Leaves of Grass*." Postcard to O'Connor, September 17, 1882, Berg Collection. See also letter to Burroughs, *SPL*, p. 1042.

81. See Springfield *Republican*, September 24, 1882: "It is to be regretted that Whitman had not the patience to wait for some firm of consequence to take up the task Osgood so feebly laid down. The Philadelphia firm advertise in this fashion in the Philadelphia *Press*: '*Leaves of Grass* by Walt Whitman, is not an agricultural book in the haymakers' parlance; but it is a daisy, and don't you forget it.' "

82. This edition is identical with the Osgood, Author's, and Rees Welsh editions.

83. A few periodicals approved the suppression of *Leaves of Grass*: *The Literary World* (June 3, 1882), the New York *Tribune*, and the Boston *Advertiser* (May 24), the latter in an article entitled "Dirt in Ink." But there were many protests: in the Boston *Globe* (May 31), a letter from Dr. Bucke in the Springfield *Republican* (May 23), the

Camden *Post* (May 22), the *Critic* (June 3), the Boston *Commonwealth* (September 23), an article entitled "Old Obscenity Comstock" in the Washington *Capital* (July 23), *Man*, "a liberal journal of progress and reform," September 1 ("The liberties of this country ar [*sic*] not worth a brass copper when its citizens hav [*sic*] to beg or hire distinguished lawyers and politicians to intercede with the Heads of Departments to get rights that have been unlawfully and arbitrarily refused . . ."), and *Dr. Foote's Health Monthly* (July and August 1882).

84. He sent three letters: on May 25, June 18, and August 27. See *With WW in C*, I, 52–54.

85. See New York *Tribune*, July 15: "Whitman's *Leaves of Grass* — Movement in Philadelphia to suppress the work — Opinion of a prominent clergyman" and Philadelphia *Press*, same date: "Walt Whitman's Work — The Society for the Prevention of Vice to stop the sale — A clergyman defends the poet — He thinks that the Association will make a mistake — Rev. James Morrow, a prominent Methodist, invited to write a review of the poems for the author's edition."

86. See *This Word*, III, no. 13 (April 1, 1882): "We need some of the Gospel of Walt Whitman, who grandly and heroically dares to say: 'Divine am I, inside and out' . . ." In no. 24 (June 17), under the title of "Keep off the Grass," Chainey printed the full text of "To a Common Prostitute"; and in no. 26 (July 1), Chainey told the story of the difficulties raised by Tobey, the Boston postmaster, and published a letter of thanks which Whitman had sent him: "My dear friend, I to-day mail you a copy of *Leaves of Grass* as a little gift and testimonial of thanks. Please send me a word if it is safely received. I sent you a little package of printed sheets last week by mail." It was a rather cold and noncommittal letter. O'Connor, on the other hand, had sent an impassioned missive.

87. See *Liberty*, July 22, 1882.

88. Letter to O'Connor, April 14, 1883, Berg Collection; see also letter to the same, November 12, 1882, *SPL*, pp. 1042–1043.

89. *Ibid.*

90. *Critic*, I (November 5, 1881), 303; reprinted in *Essays from the Critic* (Boston: Osgood, 1882), pp. 175–185.

91. Letter to Osgood, May 27, 1881, *CW*, V, 278.

92. "Birds of Passage" was not an original title. Whitman may have borrowed it from Longfellow.

93. Here is an example:
1876:
　　"ONE'S-SELF I sing — a simple, separate Person;
　　Yet utter the word Democratic, the word En-masse.

Of Physiology from top to toe I sing;
Not physiognomy alone, nor brain alone, is worthy for the
    muse — I say the Form complete is worthier far;
The Female equally with the Male I Sing."
1881:
    "ONE'S-SELF I sing, a simple, separate person,
    Yet utter the word Democratic, the word En-Masse.
    Of physiology from top to toe I sing,
    Not physiognomy alone nor brain alone is worthy for the
        Muse, I say the Form complete is worthier far,
    The Female equally with the male I sing."

94. Here is the list of the twenty new poems: "Thou Reader," "Youth, Day, Old Age and Night," "To the Man-of-War Bird," "Patroling Barnegat," "The Dalliance of the Eagles," Roaming in Thought," "Hast Never Come to Thee an Hour," "As Consequent," "Italian Music in Dakota," "My Picture-Gallery," "The Prairie States," "Paumanok Picture," "Thou Orb Aloft Full-Dazzling," "A Riddle Song," "From Far Dakota's Cañons," "What Best I See in Thee," "Spirit That Form'd This Scene," "A Clear Midnight," "As at Thy Portals also Death," "The Sobbing of the Bells."

However, "Youth, Day, Old Age and Night" was not really new; it was a fragment from "Great Are the Myths" and thus dated from 1855.

95. "Italian Music in Dakota," "The Prairie States," "From Far Dakota's Cañons," and "The Spirit That Form'd This Scene." One might add to these "A Paumanok Picture," which Whitman probably wrote during his trip to Long Island with Dr. Bucke in 1881.

96. *LG 1881*, p. 216, *Inc. Ed.*, p. 233.

97. *LG 1881*, p. 216, *Inc. Ed.*, pp. 232–233. See Clara Barrus, *Whitman and Burroughs: Comrades*, p. xxiv.

98. *LG 1881*, pp. 204–205, *Inc. Ed.*, p. 219. See Adeline Knapp, "Walt Whitman and Jules Michelet; Identical Passages," *Critic*, XLIV, 467–468, and Gay W. Allen, "Walt Whitman and Jules Michelet," *Etudes Anglaises*, I (May 1937), 230–237.

99. *LG 1881*, p. 310, *Inc. Ed.*, p. 335. See *Pictures*, an unpublished poem by Walt Whitman, with an introduction and notes by E. Holloway (New York: June House, 1927), pp. 9–10.

100. *LG 1881*, pp. 208–209, *Inc. Ed.*, p. 223. See "Out of the Cradle Endlessly Rocking," §1, ll. 130–143 (*Inc. Ed.*, p. 214).

101. *LG 1881*, p. 368, *Inc. Ed.*, p. 403.

102. *LG 1881*, p. 378, *Inc. Ed.*, p. 414. According to Joaquin Miller ("An Anecdote on Whitman," *Poet Lore*, X [1898], 618), Whitman had at first declined to write a poem on Garfield in spite of an offer of $100 from a Boston editor. Yet Whitman did write one

eventually, and it was published in the Boston *Globe*, September 27, 1881. He must have finally yielded to temptation. Moreover, he knew Garfield personally (see *With WW in C*, I, 324), and there is among his papers in the Library of Congress a note describing the President's death and the emotion of the American people: "All this while . . . the silent half-light through which everything else is seen, is the condition of President Garfield lying low on his bed there at the White House with death lurking stealthily nigh and sometimes almost showing his grisly visage while as gallant a struggle as was ever made against him is day and night dauntlessly kept up by the surgeons and doctors to say nothing of the splendid endurance of the patient himself.

"Besides the personal and technically political points of this whole affair, I often think of it in its bearings upon the American people, the whole fifty millions of them — giving them a common centre, essentially human, eligible to all, where they can all and each agree and where the warmest and best emotions of the heart are identified with abstract patriotism, union, nationality and made one."

When writing "The Sobbing of the Bells," Whitman probably remembered the last line of Poe's poem entitled "The Bells": "To the sobbing of the bells . . ." He was aware of it himself and for this reason was reluctant to include this piece in *Leaves of Grass*; see *With WW in C*, III, 129.

103. *LG 1881*, p. 18, *Inc. Ed.*, p. 11.

104. *LG 1881*, pp. 277–278, *Inc. Ed.*, pp. 300–301. Lines 13–33 of this poem originally belonged to "Two Rivulets" and so date back to 1876. Lines 13–15 were part of "Two Rivulets" proper (*Inc. Ed.*, p. 486); ll. 22–23 were §1 of "Or from That Sea of Time," and ll. 13–21 were §2 of the same poem, which thus should not have been placed among the "Rejected Poems" in the *Inc. Ed.*

105. *LG 1881*, p. 218, *Inc. Ed.*, p. 235.

106. *LG 1881*, p. 369, *Inc. Ed.*, p. 404.

107. "Chants Democratic" no. 8, *LG 1860*, p. 177 (4), "Song at Sunrise," *Inc. Ed.*, p. 410, l. 20.

108. "Youth, Day, Old Age and Night," *LG 1881*, p. 180, *Inc. Ed.*, p. 191. This is all that Whitman kept in 1881 of the long poem entitled in 1867 "Great Are the Myths," which dated back to 1855.

109. *LG 1881*, pp. 362–363, *Inc. Ed.*, pp. 396–397.

110. *LG 1881*, p. 376, *Inc. Ed.*, p. 412.

111. *LG, 1881*, p. 352, *Inc. Ed.*, pp. 385–386.

112. This poem was written in 1860 but included in *LG* only in 1867. The canceled passage is quoted in *Inc. Ed.*, p. 634 (after l. 13).

113. See *Inc. Ed.*, p. 701, for variant reading of l. 11.

114. He thus canceled l. 7: "I take for my love some prostitute." *Inc. Ed.*, p. 590.

115. Thus, in "The Sleepers," he canceled all the description of an erotic dream (*Inc. Ed.*, p. 683, after §1); in "To Think of Time," a line in §6 (*Inc. Ed.*, p. 686, before l. 3); and in "A Song of Joys," a whole passage that he had already toned down in 1867 (*Inc. Ed.*, p. 610, after l. 31).

116. Letter to Osgood, March 7, 1882, *CW*, V, 291–294.

117. The reviewer in the New York *Tribune*, November 19, 1881, was quite aware of Whitman's dilemma: "Of late years we believe that Mr. Whitman has not chosen to be so shocking as he was when he had his notoriety to make, and many of his admirers, the rational ones — hoped that the *Leaves of Grass* would be weeded before he set them out again. But this has not been done; and indeed Mr. Whitman could hardly do it without falsifying the first principle of his philosophy, which is a belief in his own perfection, and the second principle, which is a belief in the preciousness of filth . . ."

118. Whitman was already planning this book in 1879; see letter to Mrs. Gilchrist, *SPL*, p. 1033. He had thought of other titles before choosing the present one: "Nota Benes — Note-Posts of a Life in the New World in the nineteenth century — Dawns noons and (starry) nights of a half-paralytic — Only some days and nights of a half-paralytic — Resumes, notes and recallés [*sic*] of a half-paralytic — Odds and omnes — Far and near at 64 — Omnes" (a MS note in the Library of Congress). In March 1882, in a letter to Osgood, he spoke of "Specimen Days and Thoughts" (*CW*, V, 292–293).

119. For the memories of his childhood and youth, see *SD,* pp. 7–21 (*CP*, pp. 3–16), and for his diary from 1865 to 1882, *SD*, pp. 81–200 (*CP*, pp. 77–206).

120. The more so since this prose volume merely skimmed the surface of the subject, as Whitman himself knew very well: "Do you know what *ducks and drakes* are? Well S.D. is a rapid skimming over the pond-surface of my life, thoughts, *expressions* that way — the real are altogether untouched, but the flat pebbles making a few dips as it flies and flits along — enough at least to give some living touches and contact points — I was quite willing to make an immense negative book." Letter to O'Connor, November 12, 1882, *SPL*, p. 1043.

121. As the reviewer in *Papers for the Times* (no. 22, April 1886, p. 181), noted, most critics did not even take the trouble to read his book: "These opponents may be divided into two classes: persons who honestly object to Whitman's plainness of speech, because they regard it as unnecessary and unfitting . . . These persons we can respect; their opinion is honest and intelligible. The other class we cannot respect. It consists for the most part of hack writers to the press who think it no portion of their duty to know anything of the works they

are paid to review." And he gave the following example: "For instance here is a Saturday Reviewer boldly denouncing Whitman, who does not even know the name of Whitman's book — Blades of Grass he calls it."

122. New York *Examiner*, January 19, 1882.

123. No critic seems to have been aware of the discreet work of expurgation carried out by Whitman since 1867. E. P. M. thus wrote in the New York *Sun*, November 19, 1881: "Of this side of the matter it is enough to say that if the new edition is a triumph for the poet, it has been achieved without any concession on his part. He has modified nothing. He has canceled no objectionable line or offensive phrase. He has confessed no sin against good taste or decency."

124. See above, n. 123.

125. "Walt Whitman's Leaves of Grass Redivivus," New York *Independent*, December 29, 1881. There were other attacks in *The Dial*, January 1882; the New York *Tribune*, November 19, 1881; the New York *Evangelist*, January 26, 1882; the *Literary World*, June 3, 1882; and the Detroit *Free Press*, January 7, 1882.

126. New York *Sun*, November 19, 1881.

127. His answer to the Philadelphia officers of the Society for the Suppression of Vice was quoted in the New York *Tribune*, July 15, 1882: "Walt Whitman is robust and virile but not obscene . . . The book, were its publication unobstructed, would speedily find its own level and its circulation would be limited to that level . . ."Other vindications of *Leaves of Grass* appeared in an article by B. W. Ball entitled "Two American Poets" in *The Index*, January 12, 1882; *The Scottish Review*, Vol. II, no. 4, pp. 281–300; *The Pioneer Press*, December 12, 1881; the Philadelphia *Times*, December 3, 1881; *The Mace*, March 21, 1882; an article by G. E. M. entitled "Whitman, Poet and Seer," New York *Times*, January 22, 1882; the Springfield *Republican*, September 24, 1882; the Boston *Herald*, May 24, 1882; an article by G. C. Macaulay in the *Nineteenth Century*, December 1881, pp. 903–918. See also in the *Iconoclast* (Indianapolis, Indiana), November 11, 1882, an article by Elmira, "the Quaker Infidel": "Suggestions and Advice to Mothers," in which the author advised mothers to make their children read *Leaves of Grass* because Whitman sang the body with admirable purity.

128. A review by E. P. M. in the New York *Sun*, November 19, 1881.

129. "In view of his savage contempt for anything musical in poetry, it will be a fine stroke of the irony of fate if he should be destined to be remembered only by the few pieces which are marked by the 'piano-tune' quality that he derides — the true and tender

lyric of My Captain and the fine poem on Ethiopia Saluting the Colors. These pieces with the magnificent threnody on Lincoln — When Lilacs Last in the Dooryard Bloomed — and a few others in which there is an approach to metrical form . . . are likely to be preserved in memory . . ." *The Dial*, January 1882, p. 219.

130. *Critic*, November 5, 1881, pp. 177–178. The reviewer in the London *Nineteenth Century* offered the following explanation: "The mass of his countrymen were not and are not strong enough to accept him. They have too little confidence in their own literary originality to appreciate duly one from among themselves who breaks through all the conventional usages of literature . . . It is necessary perhaps that this writer . . . should be first accepted in the Old World before he can be recognized by the New, which at present can see nothing in literature but by reflected light." G. C. Macaulay, "Walt Whitman," *Nineteenth Century*, XII, December 1882.

131. Deuceace, "Walt Whitman, Rhapsodist and Loafer," St. Louis *Daily Globe Democrat*, July 2, 1882.

132. New York *Tribune*, August 6, 1882.

133. O'Connor claimed the paternity of the word in a letter to Dr. Bucke (February 23, 1883), now in the Harris Collection of Brown University Library: "I wrote once, gaily, to the fellows in New York, that I was a Hugolater and a Whitmaniac. Soon after I saw in some of the ring papers sneers at us Whitmaniacs! . . . They are indebted to us for even their epithets of abuse . . ."

134. For instance: Joaquin Miller, "To Walt Whitman," *Galaxy*, January 1877; Robert Buchanan, "To Walt Whitman" (a sonnet), *Progress*, April 3, 1880; Linn B. Porter, "Walt Whitman," Boston *Transcript*, April 18, 1881; Walter R. Thomas, "A Sonnet to Walt Whitman," Boston *Index*, December 20, 1883, etc.

135. Richard Maurice Bucke, *Walt Whitman* (Philadelphia: David McKay, 1883).

136. O'Connor made a few alterations in the original text at Whitman's own request: ". . . I have been looking through the GGP as Dr. B sent it in his copy and it comes to my soul over the dozen years more eloquent and beautiful than ever — seems to me . . . it deserves to stand just as it is — two passages in the last page only might be left out — and I should so suggest. Seems to me all that is wanted is a brief prefatory dated present time, distinctly confirming your faith etc. That is without diminution (it couldn't have 'increase') . . ." Letter to O'Connor, February 19, 1883, Berg Collection.

137. Dowden's *Studies in Literature*, 1789–1877 (London: C. Kegan Paul, 1878), contained a chapter entitled "The Poetry of Democracy: Walt Whitman," pp. 468–523.

138. Stevenson's *Familiar Studies of Men and Books* (London,

1882), contains a chapter on Whitman, pp. 104–136, on which W. S. Kennedy passed the following comment: "R. L. Stevenson discussed Whitman . . . in a tone of frigid admiration, mingled with semi-sneering flippant detraction" (*The Fight of a Book for the World,* p. 32). Whitman, on the contrary, was perfectly satisfied with it: "Yes, he was complimentary to the Leaves; not outrightly so — saying yes with reservations: but being a man in whom I dare not waits upon I would he does not state his conviction unequivocally . . . His wife assured me that he felt far more strongly on the subject than he wrote." *With WW in C,* I, 145–146.

139. Thomson, "Walt Whitman," *Cope's Tobacco Plant,* II (May, June 1880), 471–473, 483–485. These two essays were reprinted with an introduction by Bertram Dobell in James Thomson, *Walt Whitman, the Man and the Poet* (London 1910).

140. Burroughs, *Birds and Poets* (Boston: Houghton Mifflin, 1877), pp. 185–235. This is how Whitman judged Burroughs' attitude toward him: "John is a milder type — not the fighting sort — rather more contemplative: John goes a little more for usual, accepted things, respectable things, than we do . . . though God knows he is not enough respectable to get out of our company." *With WW in C,* I, 334.

141. About this time, however, he was violently attacked by Sidney Lanier, who took him to task for his inverted dandyism and concluded: "The truth is, that if closely examined, Whitman, instead of being a true democrat, is simply the most incorrigible of aristocrats, masquing in a peasant's costume; and his poetry, instead of being the natural outcome of a fresh young democracy, is a product which would be impossible except in a highly civilized society." *The English Novel and the Principle of Its Development* (New York: Scribner's Sons, 1883). Yet Lanier had written a very friendly letter to Whitman in 1878 with an order for a copy of *Leaves of Grass* (see *With WW in C,* I, 208). It is true that at that time he made some reservations concerning the form of Whitman's poetry. This passage from enthusiasm to disillusionment was not unusual among Whitman's admirers. He accepted it serenely (*ibid.,* 209). We might note, however, that Mrs. Lanier protested against the omission by W. D. Browne, the editor of her husband's papers, of a whole passage favorable to Whitman. In 1897 she published a complete edition of this posthumous work.

142. In 1884 the *Critic* conducted a poll of its readers in order to establish a list of forty authors who deserved to be members of an imaginary American Academy. Whitman was placed twentieth on the list. To be sure, the *Critic* had always been favorable to him. See Portia Baker, "Walt Whitman's Relations with Some New York Magazines," *AL,* VII (November 1935), 274–301.

143. *Critic*, November 5, 1881, pp. 177–178.
144. Philadelphia *Press*, August 5, 1883.

X. THE DECLINE (1883–1890)

1. "I shall break up from here in the spring and leave Camden —
I don't know where . . ." Letter to Harry Stafford, January 2, 1884,
Berg Collection.
2. See Bliss Perry, *Walt Whitman*, p. 245.
3. George Selwyn, "Walt Whitman in Camden," *Critic*, February
28, 1885, reprinted in *Uncoll. PP*, II, 58.
4. See "The Dismantled Ship," *NB*, p. 37, *Inc. Ed.*, p. 440. On
the origin of this poem, see *With WW in C*, I, 390. An earlier version
is included in "Walt Whitman; Unpublished Notes," *Wake* 7, p. 9.
5. *Uncoll. PP*, II, 60.
6. See, for instance, Stuart Merrill, *Walt Whitman* (Toronto:
Henry S. Saunders, 1922), pp. 6–8, a reprint of an article in *Masque,*
Series II, no. 9–10, pp. 303–307. Edmund Gosse, who visited Whitman in 1885, had the same impression; see E. Gosse, "A Note on Walt
Whitman," Littell's *Living Age*, May 26, 1894, p. 498.
7. See "Mr. Irving's Second Tour of America," *The Theatre,*
April 1885.
8. See above, n. 6; also "The Poet and His Guests," Camden *Post,*
January 8, 1885, and "A Poet's Symposium: Edmund Gosse brings
Walt Whitman kind words from Tennyson," *ibid.*, January 7, 1885.
9. See *With WW in C*, I, 161–163. Rhys had published a rather
timid selection of *Leaves of Grass* in England: *Poems by Walt Whitman* (London: Canterbury Poet Series, 1886); see also E. Rhys, "The
portraits of Walt Whitman," *Scottish Art Review*, June 1889.
10. H. R. Haweis, "A Visit to Walt Whitman," *Pall Mall Budget,*
no. 930, January 14, 1886, reprinted in the *Critic*, February 27,
1886.
11. Edward Carpenter, *Days with Walt Whitman and Some Notes
on His Life and Works* (London, 1906). He visited Whitman twice,
in 1877 and in 1884.
12. "Arnold and Whitman," Philadelphia *Press*, September 15,
1889; "Arnold and Whitman; The Light of Asia Visits the American
Poet — Kind Greetings sent by Browning and Rossetti to the Good
Gray Poet," Philadelphia *Times*, September 15, 1889. See also Edwin
Arnold, *Seas and Lands* (London, 1892), pp. 78–84.
13. Wilde's visit dated back to 1882; see "The Aesthetic Singer
Visits the Good Gray Poet: He asks the advice of the latter and is
told to go ahead in his missions to shatter the ancient idols," Phila-

delphia *Press*, January 19, 1882. See also Helen Gray Cone, "Narcissus in Camden," *Century*, November 1882.

14. J. Johnston, *Notes of a Visit to Walt Whitman* (privately printed, Boston, 1890), and J. Johnston and J. W. Wallace, *Visits to Walt Whitman in 1890–91 by two Lancashire Friends* (London, 1917; New York, 1918).

15. Emily Faithfull, *Three Visits to America* (New York: Fowler and Wells, 1884), pp. 94–96.

16. C. Sadakichi-Hartmann, "Notes of a Conversation with the Good Gray Poet by a German Poet and Traveller," New York *Herald*, April 14, 1888. See also his *Conversations with Walt Whitman*, (New York: E. P. Coby, 1895). Whitman protested against the unreliability of these interviews in a letter to Kennedy, August 4, 1890; see *FC*, p. 139.

17. See, for instance, "The Good Poet's Guest — A Southern Admirer Visits Walt Whitman — John Newton Johnson travels from his cotton plantation to call on Nature's bard . . ." New York *Tribune*, June 5, 1887. On this picturesque character, see Sidney Morse, "My Summer with Walt Whitman," *In Re*, pp. 376–377.

". . . have some nice visitors — sometimes foreigners — two or three American girls now and then — great comfort to me" (postcard to O'Connor, January 26, 1885, Berg Collection). Whitman enjoyed such visits very much; see *With WW in C*, I, 71.

18. Sidney Morse, "My Summer with Walt Whitman, 1887," *In Re*, pp. 376–391.

19. Whitman was also frequently interviewed by journalists; see, for instance, Richard Hinton in New York *World*, April 14, 1889, or J. L. G. "A Visit to Walt Whitman's Shanty," *Critic*, November 28, 1891.

20. Thomas B. Donaldson, *Walt Whitman, the Man* (New York: Harper, 1896).

21. *With Walt Whitman in Camden*, in 3 volumes of over 500 pages each, appeared from 1906 to 1914. A fourth volume edited by Sculley Bradley was published in 1953 by the University of Pennsylvania Press (reprinted in 1959); a fifth one is in the press. These four volumes cover only about a year of the poet's life.

In 1890 Traubel founded a monthly review with philosophical pretensions, *The Conservator*, and after Whitman's death, he devoted it to the worship of his hero and made it the organ of the fanatical Whitmaniacs. It continued to appear until 1919, but during the last years of its existence articles on Whitman became less and less frequent, and Traubel spoke increasingly as a prophet of socialism rather than the high priest of the Whitman cult.

22. See above, n. 15.

23. See Bliss Perry, *Walt Whitman*, p. 251. Several members of the Club resigned in protest; see L. D. Morse, "Dr. Daniel Brinton on Walt Whitman," *Conservator*, November 1899, p. 134.

24. Letter to Kennedy, September 14, 1887, *FC*, p. 115. However, the Springfield *Republican* had accepted "The Dying Veteran" for $25, and the *Critic* sent him $10 for "Twilight" (see postcard to Kennedy, July 9, 1887, *FC*, p. 113); and on August 18, 1886, Whitman wrote to O'Connor: ". . . have been writing somewhat busily for me in the last three or four weeks — articles, generally ordered one — *Century* — *North American Review* and *Lippincott's* — a little bit about Shakespeare in last *Critic*" (Berg Collection). See also postcard to *Century Magazine* in *SPL*, p. 1045. He also received $25 for an article of reminiscences in the New Orleans *Picayune*, January 25, 1887, for the centenary of this paper.

In February 1886 he delivered his Lincoln lecture at Elkton, Maryland; see Rollo G. Silver, "Walt Whitman's Lecture in Elkton," *N & Q*, March 14, 1936, pp. 190–191.

25. "My writing for the *Herald* continues on — they have lately written to me to continue — they have paid me so far dol. 165, wh' I call first rate, 25 for Whittier bit, also enclosed." Letter to O'Connor, April 18, 1888, Berg Collection.

26. "My last half-annual return of royalties for both my books just rec'd — dol. 20.71 cts." Letter to O'Connor, January 22, 1886, Berg Collection. See also: "I get a miserable return of royalties from McKay my Philadelphia publisher — not dol. 50 for both books Leaves of Grass and Specimen Days for the past year." Letter to Burroughs, December 21, 1885, Berg Collection.

27. See letters of W. M. Rossetti to Mrs. Gilchrist, June 15, July 5, August 28, 1885, and letters of the same to Herbert Gilchrist, December 23, 1885 and May 9, 1886.

28. "The English 'offering' (through Rossetti and Herbert Gilchrist) will am't over 500 dollars — the principal part of which has already been sent to me — and on which I am really living this winter." Letter to O'Connor, January 22, 1886, Berg Collection. The first subscription took place in 1885, but there was a second one in December 1886, launched by the *Pall Mall Gazette*; see Whitman's letter to the editor of this magazine, *SPL*, pp. 1048–1049.

29. See Whitman's letter to S. Baxter, December 8, 1886, Berg Collection: "I thank you deeply and Mr. Lovering also — but do not consent to being an applicant for a pension as spoken of — I do not deserve it. Send word to Mr. Lovering or show him this . . ."

30. See postcard to Kennedy, January 26, 1887, *FC*, p. 106.

31. Sylvester Baxter, "Walt Whitman in Boston," *New England Magazine*, August 1892, pp. 720–721.

32. Letter to Eldridge, April 21, 1887, quoted by Bliss Perry, *Walt Whitman*, pp. 252–253. In 1886 his Lincoln lecture had been delivered at Philadelphia (*ibid.*, p. 251) and the last one was also delivered in Philadelphia at the Contemporary Club, in 1890.

33. He still sometimes complained of his poverty, though: see "To the Pending Year," which was published in the *Critic*, (January 5, 1889, under the title of "To the Year 1889" (*Inc. Ed.*, p. 447).

34. *Inc. Ed.*, p. 522.

35. See title of the preface to *NB*.

36. *NB*, p. 19, *Inc. Ed.*, p. 435, l. 3.

37. "Paumanok," *NB*, p. 19, *Inc. Ed.*, p. 420, l. 1.

38. "Memories," *NB*, p. 21, *Inc. Ed.*, p. 423. See also "By That Long Scan of Waves," *NB*, pp. 24–25, *Inc. Ed.*, pp. 426–427.

39. See "True Conquerors," *NB*, p. 31, *Inc. Ed.*, p. 434. See also: "Result of seven or eight stages and struggles extending through nearly thirty years . . ." "A Backward Glance . . . ," *Inc. Ed.*, p. 522.

40. "Soon Shall the Winter's Foil Be Here," *NB*, p. 33, *Inc. Ed.*, p. 436, l. 6.

41. "The First Dandelion," *NB*, p. 21, *Inc. Ed.*, p. 423.

42. See the photograph of him at seventy in *Uncoll. PP*, II; the dissymmetry of the face caused by paralysis became more and more marked as he grew older.

43. See postcard to Kennedy, August 5, 1885, *FC*, p. 100. He had had a sunstroke in 1858; see letter to Lewis Kirk Brown, August 1, 1863, *SPL*, p. 914.

44. See letter to O'Connor, June 14, 1888, Berg Collection: ". . . Have been pretty ill, indeed might say pretty serious, two days likely a close call — but Dr. Bucke was here and took hold me [*sic*] without gloves . . ."

45. See E. Holloway, *Whitman*, pp. 311–312. His first nurse was a medical student, Eddie Wilkins; he was succeeded by Frank Warren Fritzinger, a young sailor and Mrs. Davis' adopted son. Whitman was very fond of him: "Frank Warren Fritzinger, my friend and gillie," he called him in a letter to J. W. Wallace, September 22, 1890, *SPL*, p. 1053. See Elizabeth L. Keller, *Walt Whitman in Mickle Street*, 1921.

46. *NB*, p. 20, *Inc. Ed.*, p. 422.

47. "An Evening Lull," *NB*, p. 37, *Inc. Ed.*, p. 441. See *With WW in C*, I, 354.

48. "Drove down yesterday three or four miles to Gloucester, on the Delaware below here, to a fine old public house close to the river, where I had four hours and a good dinner of planked shad and champagne . . . enjoyed all and was driven back to Camden at sundown — so you see I get out and have fun yet — but it is a

dwindling business." Letter to O'Connor, April 25, 1888, Berg Collection.

49. "A Carol Closing Sixty-Nine," *NB*, p. 20, *Inc. Ed.*, p. 421, ll. 8–9.

50. *Ibid.*, l. 7.

51. *With WW in C*, I, 354.

52. "Of that blithe throat of thine," *NB*, p. 28, *Inc. Ed.*, p. 430.

53. *November Boughs*, Philadelphia: David McKay, 1888, 140 pp.

54. See *Walt Whitman's Backward Glances*, ed. Sculley Bradley and John A. Stevenson (University of Pennsylvania Press, 1947).

55. *Complete Poems and Prose of Walt Whitman, 1855–1888*, Philadelphia: published by the author, 1888, 900 pp.

56. *Leaves of Grass* with *Sands at Seventy* and *A Backward Glance O'er Travel'd Roads*, Philadelphia, 1889, 422 pp.

57. *NB*, p. 26, *Inc. Ed.*, p. 428. This poem was written during a stay at Ocean Grove with Burroughs in 1884; see *Walt Whitman's Diary in Canada* (Boston: Small, Maynard, 1904), p. 63, n. 1, and *With WW in C*, I, 406.

58. "Life," *NB*, p. 30, *Inc. Ed.*, p. 433, ll. 5–6.

59. "Going Somewhere," *NB*, p. 31, *Inc. Ed.*, p. 433, ll. 6–8.

60. "Halcyon Days," *NB*, p. 22, *Inc. Ed.*, p. 424, l. 3. The change struck Sidney Morse, who had done his bust and saw him again eleven years later in 1887; see *In Re*, p. 372.

61. "Queries to my Seventieth Year," *NB*, p. 21, *Inc. Ed.*, p. 422.

62. "After the Supper and Talk," *NB*, p. 38, *Inc. Ed.*, p. 142, esp. l. 11.

63. "Twilight," *NB*, p. 35, *Inc. Ed.*, p. 439. According to Traubel, some of Whitman's admirers protested against this poem, especially on account of the last word which they considered inconsistent with the rest of his work. See *With WW in C*, I, 140–141. The poem is not really inconsistent with the rest of *Leaves of Grass*; it merely expresses a mood and is not a philosophical pronouncement.

64. "Halcyon Days," see above, n. 60.

65. *NB*, p. 32, *Inc. Ed.*, p. 434. See also "Not Meagre, Latent Boughs Alone," *Inc. Ed.*, p. 439.

66. As in the 1876 and 1881 editions there is a high percentage of occasional poems, which shows the weakening of his inspiration: "Abraham Lincoln," "Election Day, November 1884," "Death of General Grant," "Red Jacket," "Washington's Monument," "The Dead Tenor," "Orange Buds by Mail from Florida," "The Dead Emperor." He also used old poems. Thus, "Small the Theme of My Chant," which had been included in *Leaves of Grass* in 1867, now reappeared after an eclipse.

67. "You Lingering Sparse Leaves of Me," *NB*, p. 36, *Inc. Ed.*, p. 349

68. *Ibid.*, ll. 5–6.

69. On the contrary, he congratulated himself on having made no concessions: "I had my choice when I commenc'd. I bid neither for soft eulogies, big money returns, nor the approbation of existing schools and conventions . . . unstopp'd and unwarp'd by any influence outside the soul within me, I have had my say entirely my own way, and put it unerringly on record . . ." *Inc. Ed.*, p. 523.

70. For instance, in "Song of Myself," *LG 1855*, p. 51, *Inc. Ed.*, p. 69, §45, l. 11; and in "Debris," *LG 1860*, p. 423, *Inc. Ed.*, p. 482, ll. 9–11.

71. *Inc. Ed.*, p. 527.

72. *Ibid.*, p. 523.

73. *Ibid.*, p. 530.

74. *Ibid.*, p. 523.

75. "Continuing the subject, my friends have more than once suggested — or may be garrulity of advancing age is possessing me." *Ibid.*, p. 529. Also: ". . . garrulous to the very last . . ." in "After the Supper and Talk," *NB*, p. 38, *Inc. Ed.*, p. 422, last line.

76. "Some War Memoranda," "Abraham Lincoln," and "Last of the War Cases."

77. *NB*, p. 32, *Inc. Ed.*, p. 435, particularly ll. 11–14.

78. "While Not the Past Forgetting," *NB*, p. 33, *Inc. Ed.*, pp. 436–437.

79. "The Dying Veteran," *NB*, p. 34, *Inc. Ed.*, p. 437, ll. 16–18.

80. "If there are readers who find intellectual greatness and spiritual uplifting in Walt Whitman, we can only say that for those who enjoy this kind of 'poetry', it is poetry that they will enjoy . . ." Boston *Traveller*, January 17, 1889.

81. "That work . . . was reviewed in the earliest days of the *Saturday Review* by a very eminent hand. We shall not say that it was unjustly reviewed, nor do we think so. From certain points of view Walt Whitman deliberately laid himself open to what he has abundantly received, the process known technically as 'slating' . . . Now it seems to us that Walt Whitman's unfavorable critics hitherto have failed to distinguish between the faults which false premisses to start from and misconceived aim tend to have produced in him on the one side, and the faculties, and even to a certain extent the accomplishments as a poet, which in spite of all these evil influences he has displayed on the other . . . let us none the less confess that this strayed reveller, this dubiously well-bred truant in poetry, is a poet still, and one of the remarkably few poets that his own country

has produced." Review of *NB* in *Saturday Review* (London), March 2, 1889, pp. 260–261.

82. Thus an admirer sent him orange-buds by mail from Florida; see the poem on this subject, *NB*, p. 35, *Inc. Ed.*, pp. 438–439.

83. The Camden *Post* in particular published an article entitled "Camden Honors Him — Poet Whitman's 70th Birthday" (June 1, 1889) and announced on May 10: "A Camden Compliment — On Walt Whitman's 70th Birthday — An Imposing Celebration — Morgan's Hall has been secured for dinner which will be attended by prominent literary characters." The speeches delivered on that occasion were published by Horace Traubel under the title *Camden's Compliment to Walt Whitman*.

84. See Philadelphia *Press*, June 1, 1890: "The old poet talks across table on immortality with the agnostic — A dinner of intimate friends in honor of the Camden sage's seventy-second [*sic*] birthday."

85. If we are to believe the local newspapers, the organizers of this ceremony encountered difficulties: "Refused to Col. Ingersoll — Walt Whitman's testimonial benefit cannot be held in the Academy — Horticultural Hall chosen — Directors will not allow the famous atheist to lecture on 'art and morality' — What President Baker says." Philadelphia *Press*, October 5, 1890.

86. *In Re*, pp. 253–283.

87. "In fact, his personality had such advertising value that an enterprising manufacturer in 1889 named a cigar after him." C. Gohdes, "Walt Whitman and the Newspapers of His Day," *Library Notes, a Bulletin Issued for the Friends of the Duke University Library*, I, no. 2, (October 1936), 3–4.

88. ". . . of *November Boughs* over 700 have been sold." Postcard to O'Connor, February 16, 1889, Berg Collection.

XI. LAST MONTHS AND DEATH (1891–1892)

1. "Walt Whitman's End — It seems to be approaching rapidly now." London, Ontario, *Free Press*, June 4, 1890.

2. "To the Sunset Breeze," *Good-Bye My Fancy*, p. 12, *Inc. Ed.*, p. 449.

3. ". . . nothing left but behave myself quiet, and while away the days yet assign'd . . ." Preface Note to 2nd Annex, *Inc. Ed.*, p. 538.

4. *Ibid.*, p. 548.

5. *In Re*, pp. 297–327.

6. *Ibid.*, pp. 393–411. See also letter to J. Johnston, June 1, 1891, *SPL*, p. 1057.

7. *In Re*, pp. 394–395.

8. *Ibid.*, p. 395.

9. *Ibid.*, p. 396.

10. *Ibid.*, p. 397.

11. *Ibid.*, p. 398.

12. *Ibid.*

13. *Good-Bye My Fancy*, p. 8, *Inc. Ed.*, p. 444, ll. 1–3, 10–11. See also "L of G's Purport," *ibid.*, p. 456, ll. 6–9.

14. "Sounds of Winter," *Good-Bye My Fancy*, p. 13, *Inc. Ed.*, p. 451, ll. 6–7.

15. "Old Age's Ship and Crafty Death's," *Good-Bye My Fancy*, p. 10, *Inc. Ed.*, p. 446, l. 4.

16. Some of these poems had already appeared in magazines in 1890 and some of them even as early as 1889. Thus, "My 71st Year" was first published in the *Century Magazine* in November 1891; "Old Age's Ship and Crafty Death's" in the same magazine in February 1890; "To the Pending Year" in the *Critic*, January 5, 1889, under the title "To the Year 1889"; "Bravo, Paris Exposition!" in *Harper's Weekly*, September 28, 1889; "Interpolation Sounds" in the New York *Herald*, August 12, 1888 (see *With WW in C*, II, 125); "To the Sunset Breeze" in *Lippincott's Magazine*, December 1890; "Old Chants" in *Truth*, March 19, 1891; "A Twilight Song" in *Century Magazine*, May 1890; "Osceola" in *Munson's Illustrated World*, April 1890; "A Voice from Death" in the New York *World*, June 7, 1889; "The Commonplace" in *Munson's Illustrated World*, March 1891; and "The Unexpressed" in *Lippincott's Magazine*, March 1891. As for "Sail Out for Good, Eidólon Yacht," it had appeared in *Lippincott's* as early as March 1881.

17. ". . . I shall put in order a last little six or eight page annex (the second) of my L of G and that will probably be the finish . . ." Letter to Kennedy, June 18, 1890, *Rains Catalogue*, p. 79.

18. Among them, as in *November Boughs*, there were several occasional poems: "My 71st Year," "To the Pending Year," "Bravo Paris Exposition!" "Interpolation Sounds," "A Christmas Greeting" (to Brazil), "Osceola," and "A Voice from Death." To this list might be added "For Queen Victoria's Birthday," which was published in the *Critic*, May 24, 1890, but was never incorporated in *Leaves of Grass*. At this time of his life, Whitman often spoke as the poet laureate of the United States.

19. Thus "When the Full Grown Poet Came" took up an idea already expressed in "Passage to India" in 1876.

20. *Good-Bye My Fancy*, p. 5, *Inc. Ed.*, p. 537. See also letter to J. Johnston, March 30, 1891, *SPL*, p. 1055.

21. As usual, he put all his hope in the judgment of posterity; see "Long, Long Hence," *Inc. Ed.*, p. 447.

22. See "L of G's Purport," *Inc. Ed.*, p. 456, ll. 11–12.

23. See in particular: "Sail Out for Good, Eidólon Yacht!" "Lingering Last Drops," "Good-Bye My Fancy," "Old Age's Ship and Crafty Death's," "Osceola," "A Voice from Death," and "L of G's Purport."

24. See "An Executor's Diary Note," *Inc. Ed.*, p. 539.

25. *Leaves of Grass*, Philadelphia: David McKay, 1892, 438 pp. It was a very plain edition; the volume was bound in green cloth, and the backstrip bore the following indication: "Leaves of Grass, Complete, 1892" and a facsimile of Whitman's signature. It included, besides *Leaves of Grass* proper (i.e., the text of the 1881–82 edition), "Sands at Seventy," "Good-Bye My Fancy," and "A Backward Glance o'er Travel'd Roads."

26. The last one that he sent to J. Johnston was dated February 6, 1892; see *SPL*, pp. 1058–1059.

27. Preface to 2nd Annex, *Inc. Ed.*, p. 537.

28. See Daniel Longaker, "The Last Sickness and the Death of Walt Whitman," *In Re*, pp. 398–399.

29. *Ibid.*, p. 402.

30. The last letter that he wrote was dated March 17, 1892, and was addressed to his sister, Hannah Heyde; see *In Re*, p. 432.

31. "He did not, as is usual with consumptives, entertain any hopes of recovery . . ." *Ibid.*, p. 404.

32. "Death's Valley," *Inc. Ed.*, p. 463, ll. 18–20.

33. "Walt just put in his water-bed . . ." J. W. Wallace (quoting a letter from Traubel), "Last Days of Walt Whitman," *In Re*, p. 433.

34. "March 18 . . . the severe pain in W.'s left ankle increases." *Ibid.*, p. 433.

35. *Ibid.*, p. 403.

36. *Ibid.*, p. 410.

37. See *In Re*, pp. 434–435 and R. M. Bucke, "Memories of Walt Whitman," *Walt Whitman Fellowship Papers*, May 1897, pp. 35–42. On the exact time of his death, see "Virbius," "Walt Whitman's Death," *N & Q*, CLXVII (August 18, 1934), 116.

38. See the notes of the post-mortem examination in *In Re*, pp. 406–409, and Josiah C. Trent, "Walt Whitman — A Case History," *Surgery, Gynecology and Obstetrics*, LXXXVII (July 1948), 113–121.

39. *In Re*, p. 409.

40. This grave became a topic of controversy. Whitman's enemies accused him of feigning poverty in order to save up enormous sums which were swallowed up in his mausoleum. He was in particular accused of stinginess and ingratitude toward Mrs. Davis, notably by

Elizabeth Leavitt Keller (his nurse during his last illness) in *Walt Whitman in Mickle Street* (New York: Mitchell Kennerley, 1921). These accusations were taken up by Frances Winwar in *American Giant: Walt Whitman and His Times*, but C. J. Furness in his review of this book in *AL*, XIII (January 1942), 423–432, justified Whitman by quoting passages from Thomas B. Harned's diary. It seems that Whitman did not spend more than $1,500 on his tomb and let himself be drawn too far by unscrupulous contractors. For a vindication of Whitman's generosity, see Helena Born, "Whitman's Altruism," *Conservator*, September 1895, pp. 105–107.

41. *In Re*, pp. 437–452.

GENERAL INDEX

INDEX OF POEMS AND PROSE–WRITINGS

THE EVOLUTION OF
WALT WHITMAN

THE CREATION OF
A BOOK

FOREWORD

THIS volume corresponds to the second part of my book
on *L'Evolution de Walt Whitman.* As the subtitle indicates,
its subject is "the creation of a book," namely, *Leaves of Grass,*
whereas the first volume was devoted to the "creation" of
Whitman's personality. After a study of the events of Whitman's life with the help of his works whenever possible, the
time has now come to study his works with the help of what
we know of his life whenever necessary. The wisdom of an
approach which separates the man from his work has been
questioned by some reviewers, because, they claim, it separates
the man from his work in the very act of demonstrating their
inseparability. This is true, of course, but what else can one
do? The purely biographical approach enables the critic to
analyze the work only sporadically and, conversely, a critical
study requires constant reference to the poet's life. So the
two methods are complementary and must be applied jointly,
but in turn, for the sake of clarity, rather than simultaneously.
And this strategy is all the more legitimate as it does not necessarily imply an absolute separation of the two points of view.
The biographical part of *The Evolution of Walt Whitman,*
for instance, was already to a large extent critical while the
critical part constantly involves biographical data; it even
includes a whole biographical chapter devoted to Whitman's
sex life in which all the facts that bear on this peculiar aspect
of his personality are brought together and studied with much

more thoroughness than would have been possible in the biographical part, where the chronological arrangement would have scattered them. As it is, their concentration throws a strong light on some of the more mysterious poems. Thus, in spite of appearances, the splitting of this study into two volumes respects the fundamental unity of Whitman's life and work; — his "jocund twain," as he called them, "continue on the same." They seem to be parallel, but they are actually one.

Much to my regret, Professor Richard P. Adams, who helped me translate the first volume, was no longer in France when I prepared the translation of this one. But I had the luck to have the assistance of Mr. Burton L. Cooper, then American "lecteur" at the University of Lyons. I wish to express my thanks to him as well as to Mrs. Robert Marr of the Editorial Department of Harvard University Press, who has prepared my typescript for the printer with the same admirable thoroughness that Mrs. James E. Duffy showed for the first volume.

May 1962   R. A.

CONTENTS

CONTENTS

PART ONE

THE MAIN THEMES OF LEAVES OF GRASS

CHAPTER I

MYSTICISM AND THE POETRY OF THE BODY

Who goes there! hankering, gross, mystical, nude?
("Song of Myself," §20, line 1.)

WHOEVER reads *Leaves of Grass* in the text of the 1855 edition cannot avoid being struck by the importance which Whitman gives to the body. He continually takes pleasure in evoking naked men and women and in singing their beauty, their vigor, and the violence of their desires.

The word "body" recurs as often in his poems as the word "soul," and it is clear that it had the same poetic value for him, that "body" is encircled by the same halo of mystery and of infinity. The two words have the same resonance in his poetry, the same richness of suggestion. Moreover he proclaims in many instances the equality of the body and the soul and calls himself as much the poet of one as of the other.[1] He vindicates the body and brings it up to the level of the soul. He even makes it divine:

> The man's body is sacred and the woman's body is
>   sacred . . .[2]
> A divine nimbus exhales from it from head to foot . . .[3]

There are new notes here. No poet before him had had such audacity or had ever taken his flight from so low a base. Never had the word "body" been pronounced with so much respect and with so much voluptuousness at the same time.

As early as 1855–56 Whitman deliberately made it one of the major themes of his poetry:

> Walking freely out from the old traditions . . . American poets and literats . . . recognize with joy the sturdy living forms of the men and women of These States, the divinity of sex . . .[4]

"I believe in the flesh and the appetites,"[5] he announces proudly, and he introduces himself to the reader as "turbulent, fleshy, sensual,"[6] "materialism first and last imbuing."[7]

However, he is not merely sensual. For him the body is not simply an end in itself, but a means. It does not represent the goal, but a starting-point. He very quickly leaves it behind and, transcending material appearances, reaches a spiritual reality, the soul, of which the body is the outward manifestation. In other words, his sensuality, instead of remaining exclusively carnal, opens out and is sublimated. The spirit, in order to be manifest, cannot do without matter and, of course, all mysticism depends on and is accompanied by emotions of the flesh. But what is original with Whitman, at least in 1855–56, is that, contrary to Wordsworth, Shelley, or Emerson, for instance, he always has the sharp consciousness of the purely sensual source of his mystical intuitions. Instead of proceeding at once to a spiritualization, like the English romantics or the American transcendentalists, he never forgets that his body is the theater and the point of origin for his mystical states.[8] He never attempts to hide their physical concomitants. The descriptions which he gives of them are entirely candid. He had no illusions whatever about the nature of religious fervor. "Even in religious fervor, he said, there is a touch of animal heat."[9] No wonder that he later reproached Elias Hicks for what he called his sentimentality, in other words for the naïveté of his spiritualism. As for himself, he was, he added, "mainly sensitive to the wonderfulness and perhaps spirituality of things *in their physical and concrete expressions.*"[10] Much as he wished to hold an equal balance between the body and the soul, at this period he leaned toward the body.[11]

He went even further. No social taboo stopped him. He does not disguise the fact that the source of his mysticism is not only a diffuse sensuality, but emotions or joys of a purely sexual nature.[12] In short, he transposes the center of sensibility. It is no longer the heart, but the genitals. On this point he prefigures Freud. So, when he sings of the body, he reserves a prime place for the sexual organs:

> If I worship one thing more than another it shall be the
>   spread of my own body, or any part of it,
> Translucent mould of me it shall be you!
> Shaded ledges and rests it shall be you!
> Firm masculine colter it shall be you! . . .
> You my rich blood! your milky stream pale strippings of
>   my life! [13]

Thus he rejects all conventional modesty, for by the simple fact that they exist, are not the sexual organs the equals of the other organs?

> Welcome is every organ and attribute of me, and of any
>   man hearty and clean,
> Not an inch nor a particle of an inch is vile, and none
>   shall be less familiar than the rest.[14]

As early as 1856, he unblushingly names them among the other parts of the body: ". . . man balls, man root' [15] and celebrates them in a lyric tone:

> This poem drooping shy and unseen that I always
>   carry, and that all men carry,
> (Know once for all, avow'd on purpose, wherever are
>   men like me, are our lusty, lurking masculine
>   poems,)
> Love-thoughts, love-juice, love-odor, love-yielding, love-
>   climbers, and the climbing-sap,

> Arms and hands of love, lips of love, phallic thumb of
> love, breasts of love, bellies press'd and glued to-
> gether with love . . .[16]

One often has the impression of dealing with a sexuality
overshadowed with mysticism rather than with a mysticism
overshadowed with sensuality. Mystical joy and sexual climax
are confused. The rush of irresistible force which suddenly
and inexplicably overcomes him at the moment of the sexual
act is as upsetting to him as a revelation:

> Is this then a touch? quivering me to a new identity,
> Flames and ether making a rush for my veins . . .[17]

Therefore he makes the sexual organ the center of the world:

> Sex contains all, bodies, souls,
> Meanings, proofs, purities, delicacies, results, promul-
> gations . . .[18]

The result is a curious pansexualism based on a sexual
mysticism which, from 1855 on, makes him consider the coitus
as a mode of knowledge.[19] The poet, according to Whitman,
ought to inscribe himself in the world by plunging his seminal
"muscle" [20] into it, and "the sobbing liquid" [21] which rushes
from his body in the transport of the sexual act seems to him
to be the very essence of life. He feels himself indisputably
united with his fellow-men by the desires of his flesh, "the
shuddering longing ache of contact" [22] which he sometimes
calls either "adhesiveness," from a term that the phrenologists
had put into currency, or "efflux": [23]

> The efflux of the soul comes from within through em-
> bower'd gates, provoking questions,
> These yearnings why are they? these thoughts in the
> darkness why are they?
> Why are there men and women that while they are
> nigh me the sunlight expands my blood?
> Why when they leave do my pennants of joy sink flat
> and lank?

Why are there trees I never walk under but large and
   melodious thoughts descend upon me? . . .
What is it I interchange so suddenly with strangers? [24]

In short, in desiring bodies, he communicates mystically with
souls:

Do you know what it is as you pass to be loved by
   strangers?
Do you know the talk of those turning eye-balls? [25]

What is more subtle than this which ties me to the
   woman or man that looks in my face?
Which fuses me into you now, and pours my meaning
   into you? [26]

It seems that with the years he became more and more
clearly conscious of the sexual origin of his mysticism or, at
least, expressed himself on that subject with more and more
boldness. Thus in the 1860 edition of *Leaves of Grass* he
devoted two entire groups of new poems to carnal love, "Enfans
d'Adam" (*sic*) and "Calamus," in which he intoned with a
strong voice the song of the phallus, the song of procreation,[27]
and celebrated with enthusiasm and fervor, without the least
inhibition, what he called "the mystic deliria, the madness
amorous, the utter abandonment," [28] the "brief hour of madness and joy" [29] which procured him both supreme happiness
and the knowledge of essential reality. For, if he sometimes
happened to doubt the reality of the physical world and the
immortality of the soul, if his reason revealed itself as incapable of solving the riddle of creation, the trance which accompanied the sexual act or the simple presence at his side of
someone he loved gave him the reassuring certitude that all
that he perceived really existed and everything was in order:

Of the terrible doubt of appearances,
Of the uncertainty after all, that we may be deluded,
That may-be reliance and hope are but speculations
   after all,

That may-be identity beyond the grave is a beautiful
    fable only . . .
When he whom I love travels with me or sits a long
    while holding me by the hand,
When the subtle air, the impalpable, the sense that
    words and reason hold not, surround us and pervade
    us,
Then I am charged with untold and untellable wisdom,
    I am silent, I require nothing further.[30]

Thus he proclaimed in 1860 with more clarity than ever
the absolute value, in his eyes, of the illuminations which
accompanied his sexual transports, the content of which was
inexpressible in rational language. It is undeniable that for him
sexual climax was the source — and condition — of suprara-
tional communication, of mystical revelations.

It seems, moreover, that Whitman knew at least once
(William James [31] and R. M. Bucke [32] are both in agreement
on this point) a genuine mystical ecstasy. He recalled it in 1855
in the first poem of his collection:

I mind how once we lay such a transparent summer
    morning,
How you settled your head athwart my hips and gently
    turn'd over upon me,
And parted my shirt from my bosom-bone, and plunged
    your tongue to my bare-stript heart,
And reach'd till you felt my beard, and reach'd till you
    felt my feet.
Swiftly arose and spread around me the peace and
    knowledge that pass all the arguments of the earth,
And I know that the hand of God is the promise of my
    own,
And I know that the spirit of God is the brother of my
    own,
And that all the men ever born are also my brothers,
    and the women my sisters and lovers,
And that a kelson of the creation is love . . .[33]

So this was both a rapture and an illumination, and we recognize in it the four qualities which, according to William James, characterize mystical states: ineffability, the revelation of a truth ("noetic quality"), transiency, and passivity [34] — ineffability, because he is incapable of defining what was communicated to him; the revelation of a truth, since he now has the unshakable certainty of the presence of God in the world; transiency, because the illumination lasted only as long as a stroke of lightning; finally, passivity, since he was there lying in the grass, motionless, thinking of nothing, and he had the sudden impression of being dominated, overcome by exterior forces. He does not however minimize the importance of the part played by his body on this occasion and, in spite of the importance of the spiritual element in this particular case, he represents this mystical state as a form of sexual intercourse. Thus, even then, he remains essentially the poet of the body.

This ecstasy, which took place, according to Bucke, in June 1853,[35] was probably a real consecration for Whitman. Like Wordsworth in similar circumstances [36] he must have felt himself chosen and dedicated by a force which transcended him and from that moment he undertook to communicate in his poems the content of the extraordinary revelation he had had. But he no doubt never experienced another trance of the same violence.[37] His mysticism became chronic and more subdued; he lived after that in a state of almost permanent religious emotion, but of greatly reduced intensity, which permitted him to perceive mysterious spiritual presences beyond the inert appearances of material objects:

> Melange mine own, the unseen and the seen,
> Mysterious ocean where the streams empty,
> Prophetic spirit of materials shifting and flickering around me,
> Wondrous interplay between the seen and the unseen,

> Living beings, identities, now doubtless near us, in the
>   air, that we know not of,
> Extasy everywhere touching and thrilling me,
> Contact daily and hourly that will not release me . . .[38]

Space is always for him the "sphere of unnumber'd spirits"
and water is undoubtedly alive:

> How the trees rise and stand up, with strong trunks,
>   with branches and leaves!
> (Surely there is something more in each of the trees,
>   some living soul.) [39]

This intuitive perception of living presences in inanimate
objects persisted in him for a long time. Did he not as late as
1876, after his stroke of paralysis, try to make the young
force of the shrubs of Timber Creek pass into his weakened
body? [40] And, in *Specimen Days,* he interpreted mystically
the curious instinct which in the solitude of the woods or
the mountains makes us constantly turn our heads to assure
ourselves that we are not being followed. It is, he says, because
we feel an invisible presence.[41] However, with the years —
if it ever entirely disappeared, it was doubtless very late —
this faculty of mystical perception little by little decreased.
It is symptomatic in this respect that Whitman in 1876 suppressed in "Starting from Paumanok" the most striking line:

> Extasy everywhere touching and thrilling me . . .

In spite of their supreme importance, sexual sensations are
not, however, the only physical concomitants of his mystical
states. His sensuality participates in all the activity of his
senses, even his sense of smell, as this passage, found on the
very first page of the 1855 edition of *Leaves of Grass,* indicates:

> Houses and rooms are full of perfume, the shelves are
>   crowded with perfumes,
> I breathe the fragrance myself and know it and like it,

> The distillation would intoxicate me also, but I shall
>   not let it.[42]

It is the same with his sight and his sense of taste, as is shown
by this cry of joy which escapes him before the beauty of dawn:

> To behold the day-break!
> The little light fades the immense and diaphanous
>   shadows,
> The air tastes good to my palate.[43]

But it is the sense of touch which is for him the source of
the most intense and the most voluptuous sensations — so
intense and so voluptuous as a matter of fact that they are
almost painful to him: " . . . the shuddering longing ache of
contact . . ." [44] All the other senses are supplanted by that
one,[45] and it is his entire body and not only his hands which
receives tactile impressions. The mere contact of his foot with
the earth upsets him and swells him with force.[46] When he
walks in the woods, it seems to him that the branches caress
him and the wind rubs against him lovingly.[47] He defines
himself as "the caresser of life" [48] and sometimes experiences
an irresistible desire to expose his naked body to the air:

> I will go to the bank by the wood and become undis-
>   guised and naked,
> I am mad for it to be in contact with me.[49]

He later described this mystical nudism in *Specimen Days*:

> Perhaps the inner never lost rapport we hold with earth, light,
> air, trees, etc., is not to be realized through eyes and mind only,
> but through the whole corporeal body, which I will not have
> blinded or bandaged any more than the eyes.[50]

Hence also his love of water. He likes to walk barefoot on
the solitary dunes of Long Island [51] or to bathe naked in a
swimming-pool or in the sea — the sea which, it seems to him,
extends its curved fingers toward him as if it, too, wished to

caress his body.[52] He gives himself up with the same joy to the "generous sun." [53]

> A show of the summer softness. . . . a contact of
>   something unseen. . . . an amour of the light and
>   air;
> I am jealous and overwhelmed with friendliness,
> And will go gallivant with the light and the air myself,
> And have an unseen something to be in contact with
>   them also.[54]

Curiously enough, the night produces the same effect upon him; he seeks contact with it as if it were a naked body:

> Press close bare-bosom'd night — press close magnetic
>   nourishing night!
> . . . mad naked summer night.
>
> Smile O voluptuous cool-breath'd earth! [55]

Thus all his sensations are profoundly sensual. The external world overwhelms him with amorous caresses which create a violent erotic exaltation in him:

> Mine is no callous shell,
> I have instant conductors all over me whether I pass
>   or stop,
> They seize every object and lead it harmlessly through
>   me.
>
> I merely stir, press, feel with my fingers, and am
>   happy,
> To touch my person to some one else's is about as much
>   as I can stand.[56]

Living and feeling are such joys that he celebrates his senses as though they were miracles:

> Seeing, hearing, feeling, are miracles . . .[57]

And he attaches the highest value to the least of his kinesthetic sensations:

Alone far in the wilds and mountains I hunt,
Wandering amazed at my own lightness and glee.[58]

Each moment and whatever happens thrills me with
joy,
I cannot tell how my ankles bend, nor whence the
cause of my faintest wish . . .
That I walk up my stoop, I pause to consider if it really
be . . .[59]

Coenesthetic sensations, which generally pass unnoticed
by the majority of men, are also for him an inexhaustible
source of joy and wonder:

My respiration and inspiration, the beating of my heart,
the passing of blood and air through my lungs . . .[60]

he exclaims. And it was doubtless in order to experience them
more intensely that he sought, in his youth, the stimulation
of walking, as he confides to us in *Specimen Days*.[61]

Thus there is in him a hyperesthesia of all the senses,
particularly that of touch, which explains the chronic nature
of his mysticism and which is perhaps connected with the
repression of his sexual instincts. He appears constantly to feel
the need of rubbing himself, in his imagination, against things
and against people, probably because he could not satisfy his
desires otherwise.[62] But so frantic is his joy and so intense
is his happiness that one continually has the impression of a
vigor that nothing can check and of an insolent health — a
"reckless health," as he himself calls it.[63]

Such was the mystical and carnal temperament of Whitman
from 1855 to 1860 during the first years of his career as a
poet, but, little by little, as he grew older, his sensations lost
their sensuality and his desires and joys their violence — a
decline which was probably accelerated by the overwhelming
fatigue caused on the one hand by his visits to military hospitals during the Civil War and by his stroke of paralysis on
the other hand. As early as 1860 he no longer dared to boast

of his "reckless health"; he now called it less bombastically his "perfect health." [64] But the difference between the impetuous, almost frantic Whitman of 1855 and the settled poet who is revealed to us in *Specimen Days* is still more considerable. The former cannot sit still, he must rush out, take to the open road, wander the world from one pole to the other. The latter, twenty years later, seated on a camp-stool in the woods observes patiently the spectacle which the birds and insects present to him and makes lists of plants. He describes minutely in prose instead of glorifying in verse. In his poems — for he still writes poems, but so few after the proliferation of 1855–56 — nature scarcely has a place any more. It seems that he now looks forward to departing from the earth which formerly gave him so much joy and to setting off in order to lose himself on the high seas.[65] The supremacy has passed from his half-paralyzed body to his soul. Doesn't he, in 1878, entitle one of the chapters of his memoirs "Hours for the Soul"? [66] And it is no longer through voluptuousness or a desire to caress things that, in 1875–76, during his stays at Timber Creek, he offers his naked body to the sun and to the air. It is rather for reasons of hygiene and because he wants to recover his health.

The contrast is more striking still if one compares the poet of 1855 with the old man of Camden. And no comparison is easier, for he happens to have rewritten in "Old Age Echoes" under the title "To be at all" [67] a passage which already figured in the first edition of *Leaves of Grass*.[68] What a difference! The subject is the same, the ideas have not changed, he uses practically the same words, but the triumphant tone of former times has disappeared. Try as he will to affirm:

> One [one of the "conductors" which cover his body]
>   no more than a point lets in and out of me such bliss
>   and magnitude,
> I think I could lift the girder of the house away if it
>   lay between me and whatever I wanted.[69]

he does not convince us. We no longer feel passing through his verse the thrill of sensuality which authenticated the earlier version:

> I merely stir, press with my fingers and am happy,
> To touch my person to some one else's is about as much
>   as I can stand.[70]

He now proceeds by calm affirmations which are certainly more explicit and clearer than his vehement and passionate declarations of 1855, but they remain flat and without force. He explains and comments where formerly he sounded his "barbaric yawp." [71] He remembers his emotions, but he no longer feels them, or at least no longer feels them with the same intensity. The mystical fervor subsists, but the sensuality is calmed, cleansed, purified, and, as a result, the dash and the *élan* of his youth have disappeared.[72]

However, though the violence decreased little by little with age, his senses remained active almost till the end and were only very slowly dulled by the passage of time. In short, his sensibility survived his sensuality by many years. Thus, in 1880, he still perceived very distinctly, while walking through the woods at the end of winter, a light resinous odor mixed with the snow — something to which very few of us would be sensitive — and he added:

> For there is a scent to everything, even the snow, if you can only detect it — no two places, any two hours, anywhere, exactly alike. How different the odor of noon from midnight, or winter from summer, or a windy spell from a still one.[73]

In 1872, at the age of fifty-three, he still attached the same importance to coenesthetic sensations as he did at the time when he discovered life and its joys, and he exclaimed in a transport of delight in "The Mystic Trumpeter":

> Enough to merely be! enough to breathe! [74]

Though the wind after a few years ceased to caress his body

amorously, it nonetheless remained for him a dear presence
with which he was always avidly seeking contact. In 1865
he recommended to a reporter who had come to interview
him that he wear his shirts with the collar open so that the
wind might touch his body,[75] and in 1890, when illness had
definitively nailed him to his armchair, he awaited impatiently
all through the summer the arrival of the evening breeze which,
even though it addressed itself more to his imagination and
to his soul than to his senses, seemed deliciously cool and
refreshing to his poor wasted body.[76] In the same way he remained faithful for a long time to his almost pagan cult of
the sun as is proved by the fervent invocation which he addressed to it in 1881, "Thou Orb Aloft Full-Dazzling":

> Hear me illustrious!
> Thy lover me, for always I have loved thee . . .[77]

Generally speaking, he paid the greatest attention to impressions of a physiological nature. Thus, during his stay
in Denver in the course of his trip to the Far West, he carefully noted the stimulating effect that the lighter mountain
air produced on his body, that "aerial ozone" as he called it,
and he praised the "delicious rare atmosphere" and "the cli-
matic magnetism of this curiously attractive region." [78]

It seems however that, as he grew older, Whitman had a
tendency to accord a greater value to auditory sensations than
to others — probably because, being less easy to locate in space,
they appeared to him more spiritual, more detached from
matter and closer to the soul. Thus, in "Proud Music of the
Storm" he gives to hearing a privileged place in the hierarchy
of the senses:

> Such led to thee O soul,
> All senses, shows and objects, lead to thee,
> But now it seems to me sounds lead o'er all the rest.[79]

It must be noted besides that about the same time he

composed another poem in honor of music, "The Singer in Prison." [80] This undeniable tendency to spiritualism can also be detected in his attitude toward night. In 1865 it has already ceased to be the passionate lover that he depicted ten years earlier;[81] he now treats it more coldly, it is only "the cool transparent night," "the transparent shadowy night," [82] and in 1878 he regards it with so much serenity and equanimity that he can write:

> I am convinced there are hours of Nature, especially of the atmosphere, mornings and evenings, address'd to the soul. Night transcends, for that purpose, what the proudest day can do.[83]
> Ah, where would be any food for spirituality without night and the stars? [84]

The sky also becomes "a vast voiceless simulacrum — yet may-be the most real reality and formulator of everything." [85] As to the sea, which he saw only at rare intervals after 1862, it lost with the years the strange attraction it had had for him in his youth; in *Specimen Days* he only recalls the obsessive rhythm of its waves breaking on the shore, which had become, if we are to believe him, the very rhythm of his own internal life.[86]

Thus his senses were gradually stilled. At the end of this slow evolution he still uses them to perceive and — sometimes even with a remarkable keenness — they continue to inform him about the external world, but they are no longer a source of troubled emotions and of violent transports. Nature no longer has the heat and the reality of a desirable body; he sees in it only a spiritual presence:

> For thou art spiritual, Godly, most of all known to my
> sense . . .[87]

Thus, in proportion as he grew older and his body wore out, Whitman's mysticism shed its more sensual elements, but, in spite of this progressive spiritualization due to the de-

cline of his physical vigor and the failing of his senses, a powerful animality persisted in him right up to the end, and, as
the preceding quotation demonstrates, he never forgot what he
owed to his body.[88] Hence the unity of his book. Whatever the
date of composition of his poems, one always has the impression of hearing the same voice. Besides, even in his old age,
he never repudiated the sensuality of his youth. On the contrary, he protested against the narrow puritanism of Whittier;
to the asceticism of the Quaker poet he preferred the pagan
conception of life of the ancient Greeks.[89] And this explains
why he never consented to a radical expurgation of *Leaves
of Grass.* He refused it not through foolish obstinacy nor
out of conceit, but because until his death he preserved an
unshakable faith in the dignity of the body and the validity of
the sexual instinct.

But up to here our study of Whitman's mystical states has
been limited exclusively to a description of their organic
concomitants. Their repercussions on the emotional level
still have to be examined. It is certainly an artificial method
to distinguish between these two inseparable aspects of the
the same reality, but this effort of abstraction is necessary for
the clarity of the analysis.

All mystical emotion is accompanied by an intense and
unutterable joy and Whitman is no exception to the rule. In
his first poems he can scarcely contain himself, he is transported, he utters shouts of joy:

> Each moment and whatever happens thrills me with
> joy . . .[90]

> The efflux of the soul is happiness, here is happiness,
> I think it pervades the open air, waiting at all times,
> Now it flows unto us, we are rightly charged.[91]

> O the joy of my spirit — it is uncaged — it darts like
> lightning.[92]

It is this joy which gives to his first *Leaves of Grass* their irresistible dynamism and which explains why each of his perceptions in those years was a form of wonder before the splendor of the world.

In 1872 he still sings of the joy of life with apparently the same vigor:

> Joy! joy! in freedom, worship, love! joy in the ecstasy
> of life!
> Enough to merely be! enough to breathe!
> Joy! joy! all over joy! [93]

But this time the context is not the same. In the interval he has been crushed by the war, disappointed and revolted by the scandals of the Reconstruction. He has just written the bitter pages of *Democratic Vistas,* and he is seeking to regain control of himself. So, in this poem, he invokes a "mystical Trumpeter" whose prophetic music he seems to hear and whom he begs to "sing to [his] soul, [and to] renew its languishing faith and hope." [94] He sings of a joy which he hopes to find again some day, but does not experience any longer. He did find it again, however, in spite of his paralysis, since in 1877 he noted in his journal:

> I have had this autumn some wondrously contented hours —
> may I not say perfectly happy ones? [95]

But this is no longer the intense joy that ran through him before, but only a pale reflection of it. He adds significantly:

> What is happiness anyhow? Is this one of its hours, or the
> like of it? — so impalpable — a mere breath, an evanescent
> tinge? [96]

And he is so unsure of holding on to it that a little further on he no longer even dares to call himself completely happy: ". . . why am I so (almost) happy here. . ." [97] His mystic joy of life thus knew the same inexorable decline as his sensuality.

But this was to be expected since the joy was nothing else but the projection of his sensuality upon the emotional level. *Leaves of Grass,* in so far as it is a poem of the body, necessarily reflects the decline of the body of its author and his final decrepitude.

However, it is grossly oversimplifying to represent the mystical life of Whitman by a uniformly descending curve corresponding to the gradual decline of his vital energy. Indeed, he experienced in turn, — as we have shown in re-tracing his life, — periods of exaltation and periods of de-pression, the violence of which went on diminishing as he was growing older. Most mystics have known this alternation and have passed like him from certitude to doubt and from torturing spiritual drought to the drunkenness of ecstasy. Allusions to similar crises can be found in *Leaves of Grass:*

> Down-hearted doubters dull and excluded . . .
> I know every one of you, I know the sea of torment,
>   doubt, despair and unbelief.[98]

But such moments of doubt and despair hold only an insignificant place in his work, because it is, above all, a song of victory which celebrates, after each crisis, his renewed faith and joy. It is fitting, however, in order to appreciate the true value and scope of his poems, not to forget the struggles which preceded them.

CHAPTER II

THE IMPLICIT METAPHYSICS

ALL poetry, in order to be valid, must be the expression of a *Weltanschauung*, and Whitman's verse offers no exception. It continually implies a confused and complex metaphysic upon which, at first, it seems impossible to impose an order. Doesn't he himself boast of his own contradictions?

> Do I contradict myself?
> Very well then I contradict myself,
> (I am large, I contain multitudes.) [1]

Malcolm Cowley has picturesquely described the chaos of Whitman's thought. Speaking of the philosophic notions that Whitman borrowed right and left with remarkable eclecticism, he says:

. . . he contained them, not as the sky contains stars, by fixed laws, and not as a tree has roots; but rather as a river in flood contains driftwood or an attic contains the family relics.

He never went over the relics, discarding those of no value and arranging the others systematically. He was indolent, as he often said, and opposed on principle to any form of intellectual discipline. His work is full of separate statements and hints and intuitions, some of great value and all making it richer as poetry . . . but they are dangerous as philosophical guides because they point in all directions. Nationalism and internationalism, socialism, fascism (including its racial doctrines) and private enterprise, naturalism and idealism; the love of life and the blind hunger for death . . .[2]

Such is certainly the impression that Whitman's works in effect produce, but the contradictions are explained and the logic of his position becomes evident if one considers, instead of the present totality of *Leaves of Grass*, the temporal succession of the ideas which Whitman in turn tried to express. We will therefore attempt in this study to rediscover the underlying logic of his thought by following its chronological development. It is the only method which will allow us to extricate from his work a relatively coherent metaphysic.

But can one speak of a metaphysic of Walt Whitman, and did he really think of expressing one in *Leaves of Grass*? It is probable that, at the beginning, the philosophical content of his poems escaped him and he evolved a metaphysic without being aware of it, just as Monsieur Jourdain expressed himself in prose without realizing it. Little by little, however, he became conscious of the intellectual content of his poetry and in 1872 he declared:

When I commenced, years ago, elaborating the plan of my poems . . . one deep purpose underlay the others, and has underlain it and its execution ever since — and that has been the Religious purpose.[3]

And "religious" is, in his mind, synonymous with "philosophical," as is shown by these two notes discovered among his papers and probably written about the same time:

Philosophy of Leaves of Grass.

Walt Whitman's philosophy — or perhaps metaphysics, to give it a more definite name — as evinced in his poems, and running through them, and sometimes quite palpable in his verses, but far oftener latent, and like the unseen roots or sap of trees — is not the least of his peculiarities . . .[4]

What name? Religious Canticles. These perhaps ought to be the *brain,* the *living spirit* (elusive, indescribable, indefinite) of all L of G.[5]

Moreover, had he not declared as early as 1860:

I too, following many and follow'd by many, inaugurate a religion . . .[6]

All these statements justify our enterprise.

INSTINCTIVE MATERIALISM AND
MATERIALISTIC SPIRITUALISM

That poetry of the body, so special to Whitman, which, as we have shown, impregnates all of *Leaves of Grass*, necessarily results in a materialistic affirmation on the intellectual plane. His body is the source of such great joys for him that he makes it the center of the world and the supreme reality. What matters in his eyes is not at all the soul, as in traditional religions, but the body:

> Was somebody asking to see the soul?
> See, your own shape and countenance, persons, substances, beasts, the trees, the running rivers, the rocks and sands . . .
> Behold, the body includes and is the meaning, the main concern, and includes and is the soul . . .[7]

> And if the body were not the soul, what is the soul?[8]

> O I say these are not the parts and poems of the body only, but of the soul,
> O I say now these are the soul,
> If these are not the soul, what is the soul?[9]

He was already taking a similar position in the manuscript notebooks which preceded the 1855 edition:

> I am the poet of reality
> I say the earth is not an echo
> Nor man an apparition;
> But that all the things are real,
> The witness and albic dawn of things equally real

I have split the earth and the hard coal and rocks and
   the solid bed of the sea
And went down to reconnoitre there a long time,
And bring back a report,
And I understand that those are positive and dense
   everyone
And that what they seem to the child they are . . .[10]

In sum, he proclaims here in a lyric key the existence and
reality of matter and naïvely refutes subjective idealism in the
name of common sense. In 1855 he even goes so far as to
write

A word of reality, materialism first and last imbue-
   ing . . .[11]

And, in 1860, evoking the men and women of the future,
he announces:

They shall fully enjoy materialism and the sight of
   products . . .[12]

But these are not, properly speaking, professions of materialistic faith. The word "materialism" has no precise philosophical sense for him, it is only a more sonorous synonym
for "matter." True, under the influence of the violent sensations to which he was subject — and especially the tactile
sensations which were particularly intense with him, and
which more than all the others were always accompanied by
an impression of irrecusable reality — he was very sensitive
to the material aspect of the world. But nothing in the
Christian education he had received at school,[13] in the Quaker
principles his parents had inculcated upon him, or in the
books he had read [14] prepared him to accept the materialistic
conception of the world which, however, his senses revealed
to him as an indisputable fact, a "donnée immédiate." Poets
before him had celebrated the soul, the spirit, but not the
body. Moreover, the ecstasies and mystical emotions into which

his sensations had soon blossomed out had put him in contact with an order of suprasensible reality which he could not but interpret in terms of spiritualism.[15] He thus found himself under the necessity of admitting the existence of a spiritual principle along with matter, and was consequently torn between two equally plausible solutions, each of which corresponded to one aspect of his temperament and of his experience which he could not repudiate. The rough drafts of the 1855 edition of *Leaves of Grass* show the extent of his confusion. One sees there how the traditional spiritualism obsessed and disturbed him:

You have been told that mind is greater than matter. I cannot understand the mystery, but I am always conscious of myself as two — as my soul and I . . .[16]

In other words, he is always conscious of having both a soul and a body. He does not want the body to be forgotten, or, what amounts to the same thing, he does not want the soul to be given more importance than the body:

When I see where the east is greater than the west, — where the sound man's part of the child is greater than the sound woman's part — or where a father is more needful than a mother to produce me — then I guess I shall see how spirit is greater than matter . . . My life [i.e., the spiritual principle which impels me] is a miracle and my body which lives is a miracle; but . . . I know that I cannot separate them, and call one superior and the other inferior, any more than I can say my sight is greater than my eyes.[17]

He was so bewildered, however, and the influence of the spiritualist tradition was so strong with him that it seems that for a time, during the years 1850–1855, he did lean toward idealism, for, taking up again the image of the eyes and sight, he recorded in another notebook:

Is not the faculty of sight better than the [an illegible word, perhaps "substance"] of the eye? — Is not the human voice more than the rings of the windpipe? [18]

Nevertheless, in another passage of the same period, where he compares the soul and the body, he insists on the contrary on the indispensable character of the latter:

> The effusion or corporation of the soul is always under the beautiful laws of physiology — I guess the soul itself can never be anything but great and pure and immortal; but it makes itself visible only through matter . . .[19]

The only way to put an end to these hesitations and to mitigate this irritating antinomy was boldly to affirm the absolute equality of the body and the soul, and this is what Whitman did as early as 1855:

> I believe in you my soul, the other I am must not abase
>   itself to you,
> And you must not be abased to the other.[20]

> I am the poet of the Body and I am the poet of the
>   Soul . . .[21]

The passage from his instinctive materialism to this compromise between materialism and spiritualism was facilitated by the very peculiar character of his initial intuitions. From the beginning indeed matter was less for him an objective reality than a "donnée," a body of data, supplied by his consciousness. His position might be defined by that formula of André Gide which parodies Descartes's *cogito*: "I feel therefore I am." [22] Did not Whitman declare in 1856:

> I too had receiv'd identity by my body,
> That I was I knew was of my body, and what I should
>   be I knew I should be of my body.[23]

> We realize the soul only by you, you faithful solids
>   and fluids,
> Through you color, form, location, sublimity, ideality,

Through you every proof, comparison, and all the
suggestions and determinations of ourselves.[24]

Thus one might almost say that his materialism was a
subjective materialism or a materialistic idealism. At any rate,
the paradoxical character of the formula shows how unstable
the "mélange," as he called it,[25] was. Yet he still tried in 1860
to hold on to his position:

I believe materialism is true and spiritualism is true,
I reject no part.[26]

But in that same year — or at least in the same edition, for
certain poems in the 1860 edition were composed from 1856
to 1857 and the others only in 1859–60 — a short poem,
which disappeared from the book later, indicated a complete
reversal of his position:

I have said many times that materials and the Soul are
great, and that all depends on physique;
Now I reverse what I said, and affirm that all depends
on the aesthetic or intellectual . . .
And I affirm now that the mind governs — and that all
depends on the mind.[27]

And so he exclaimed in his "Song at Sunset":

Surely there is something more in each of the trees, some
loving soul.

. . .

O spirituality of things! [28]

And he fervently intoned the praises of the soul:

Here the heir-ship and heiress-ship of the world, here
the flame of materials,
Here spirituality the translatress, the openly-avow'd,
The ever-tending, the finalè of visible forms,
The satisfier, after due long-waiting now advancing,
Yes here comes my mistress the soul.[29]

He now even went so far as to doubt matter and the testimony of his senses:

> May-be the things I perceive, the animals, plants, men,
>   hills, shining and flowing waters,
> The skies of day and night, colors, densities, forms,
>   may-be these are (as doubtless they are) only appari-
>   tions, and the real something has yet to be known
>   . . .[30]

And in "Scented Herbage of My Breast" he considered matter as only a "mask" which hid the "real reality" from him.[31]

So he now calls in question the very existence and the reality of what, a short time before, had appeared to him as an irrefutable certainty. How did such a reversal occur? We know that in the years which preceded the 1860 edition of *Leaves of Grass* he passed through a profound moral crisis — of a sexual origin. His body was tormented by troubled desires and he sought everywhere at that period an object of love, and he believed that he had found one — this explains the composed tone of the rest of the poem which we have quoted above — but he finally lost it. It was probably at the time of the disorder of all his senses which preceded his great passion that this sudden disaffection for matter took place. Did not matter betray him in refusing to satisfy the aspirations of his flesh? At any rate, whatever the origin of this change in point of view may have been, henceforth in his poems the emphasis was placed no more on matter, but on the spirit. And so it was that in 1867 in "The City Dead-House" the body of a prostitute appears to him not only as the "tenement of a soul," but as "itself a soul," [32] and, as early as the following year, he dreamed of composing poems exclusively dedicated to the soul,

> . . . to a new rhythmus fitted for [it],
> Poems bridging the way from Life to Death, vaguely
>   wafted in night air, uncaught, unwritten . . .[33]

"Passage to India" is probably one of these poems. For the

word "body," so frequent in his verse until then, no longer figures here and seems to have disappeared from his vocabulary. On the contrary, it is the word "soul" which constantly recurs, charged with fervor and always preceded with incantatory O's. The soul, if we are to believe him, has become his "actual Me." [34] In short, he is already prepared to follow the "Mystic Trumpeter" whose call he was soon to hear (in 1872).[35]

Thus, more and more, he detached himself from and lost interest in his body which undoubtedly became calmer with age and ceased to be for him alternately a source of intense joys and intolerable torments. The stroke of paralysis which left him infirm and diminished must have reinforced that tendency toward spiritualism which reached its full flowering in 1876 in "Eidólons."

By this curious word of Greek origin, which is the doublet of "idol," he means images, the ethereal essences of things. In the poem in which he celebrates them it seems that the physical world disintegrates and dissolves before our eyes. Matter disappears. Objects are only "the ostent evanescent." [36] Time and space are filled by myriads of "eidólons." The universe itself is only an immense "eidólon" and the essential Me, "the real I myself," which is no longer the body, but the immaterial body hidden inside the body, is only "an image, an eidólon." [37]

Consequently it seems that at the end of his evolution he reaches a subjective idealism almost as absolute as that of Berkeley. But, at the very moment when we believe him finally settled and in possession of a well-defined monistic philosophy, he slips away and escapes us again. For in the course of the same year that he composed — or at least published — "Eidólons," he wrote in the preface to the sixth edition of *Leaves of Grass*:

It was originally my intention, after chanting in LEAVES OF GRASS the songs of the Body and Existence, to then compose a further, equally needed Volume, based on those convictions of perpetuity and conservation which, enveloping all precedents, make the unseen Soul govern absolutely at last.[38]

(This confirms the change of orientation which we have already observed in his book from 1860 on. In fact, he had begun to write poems for this second volume at least as early as 1868, with "Proud Music of the Storm" and "Passage to India.")

But the full construction of such a work (even if I lay the foundation, or give impetus to it) is beyond my powers, and must remain for some bard in the future. The physical and the sensuous, in themselves or in their immediate continuations, retain holds upon me which I think are never entirely releas'd; and those holds I have not only not denied, but hardly wish'd to weaken.[39]

His materialism then is not dead at all. It is he himself who tells us so. Should we believe him? It is true that after 1860 he did not write a single poem which exalts matter and really sings the joys of the flesh, and, when in 1891 he undertook to celebrate the visible world, he lapsed back into the subjective idealism of "Eidólons":

> Grand is the seen . . .
> But grander far the unseen soul of me, comprehending,
>   endowing all those . . .
> (What were all those, indeed, without thee, unseen
>   soul? of what amount without thee?) [40]
>
> (Sometimes how strange and clear to the soul,
> That all these solid things are indeed but apparitions,
>   concepts, non-realities.) [41]

Nevertheless the fact remains that until the end he affirmed the rights and the importance of the body and never repudiated his primitive materialism.[42] In order to steer a middle course and not to go to extremes, he always took great care to correct the "extravagance" of the idealist position by setting it — at least in his prose works — against its contrary.[43] In his old age he even went so far as to declare himself delighted with a portrait which Eakins had made of him, although some of his disciples found it much too sensual and almost Rabelaisian and preferred Herbert Gilchrist's idealized portrait.[44]

Thus one may conclude that, on the whole, Whitman passed from a materialism colored with spirituality to a spiritualism tinged with materialism [45] without ever permitting this dualism to resolve itself into monism.[46] The proportions of the combination changed with time, but the components always remained the same. The variations which occurred were caused, as we have indicated, by the failing of his vitality and the progressive dulling of his sensuality. But to these, purely intellectual factors must be added. In particular, his initial materialism was very probably encouraged by the theories of the phrenologists. Phrenology indeed emphasized the dependence of the soul upon the body — even though Fowler repudiated the charge of materialism by replying that his theories implied a parallelism between matter and spirit and not an identity of the two elements, and that consequently they were compatible with the immortality of the soul.[47] At all events, it is certain that Whitman, at least about 1850–1855, considered science in general as a prestigious confirmation of materialism.[48]

But later, at a date which it is difficult to determine,[49] before 1860 according to some, between 1860 and 1870 according to others, he made the belated discovery of the German idealists whom Carlyle and the transcendentalists had brought into fashion long before.[50] It is infinitely probable that he never read any of their works and that he had only a second-hand knowledge of their ideas drawn from encyclopedias [51] and such works of popularization as Gostwick's *German Litera-*

ture [52] and Hedge's *Prose Writers of Germany*. At any rate he immediately adopted their conclusions without troubling himself about the reasonings which had led to them. Their aridity repelled him.[53] As early as 1871 he mentioned Kant, Fichte, Schelling, and Hegel alongside of Plato and Christ, and saw in them "The Base of All Metaphysics." [54] During the same period he even thought of devoting a whole lecture to them and he prepared very detailed notes which have come down to us.[55] He exalted their subjectivity which seemed to him their most original contribution:

. . . Kant's tremendous and unquestionable point, namely that what we realize as truth in the objective and other Natural worlds is not the absolute but only the relative truth from our existing point of view . . .[56]

But he was especially excited by Hegel's spiritualism in which he saw the most profound explanation that had yet been given of the mystery of creation:

Penetrating beneath the shows and materials of the objective world we find, according to Hegel . . . , that in respect to human cognition of them, all and several are pervaded by *the only absolute substance* which is SPIRIT . . . As a face in a mirror we see the world of materials, nature with all its objects, processes, shows, reflecting the human spirit and by such reflection formulating, identifying, developing and proving it. Body and mind are one; an inexplicable paradox, yet no truth truer. The human soul stands in the centre, and all the universes minister to it, and serve it and revolve round it. They are one side of the whole and it is the other side.[57]

Whitman, dazzled by this brilliant synthesis, was sometimes tempted to express himself, too, in terms of spiritualistic monism in spite of his natural tendency toward dualism. Torn between the teaching of the German idealists and his own intuitions, he constantly wavered between the two extremes and these oscillations contributed to blur the outlines of his philosophy and to make his metaphysical thought elusive and full of contradictions. But that mattered little to him; his ambition was not to bring to his reader *a* ready-made philosophy, but simply *some* philosophy.[58]

THE NOTION OF IDENTITY — ME AND NOT-ME

This same problem of the soul and the body also tormented Whitman under another form. In his childhood, if one is to believe what he says of it in "There Was a Child Went Forth," [59] so intense were his perceptions that he literally identified himself with the objects he perceived:

> . . . the first object he look'd upon, that object he
> became,
> And that object became part of him for the day or a
> certain part of the day,
> Or for many years or stretching cycles of years.[60]

He thus lived in a strange continuum where all things were inextricably mingled with himself. There was no clear line of demarcation between him and the others. The universe was in dissolution and he himself was dissolved in that mixture. This confusion was not lacking in charm.

But soon a question took form in his mind: What am I if I am all? Where does the Me stop and the Not-Me begin? It was perhaps in order to answer these questions that he undertook to write *Leaves of Grass*, for he again and again brought up the problem in the poem which he later called "Song of Myself," but he might just as well have entitled it "Looking for Myself":

> What is a man anyhow? what am I? what are you? [61]

> To be in any form, what is that? [62]

But, in 1855, he no longer lived in the same confusion as before. He was now conscious of being endowed with a distinct existence, of being placed at the center of the world — however fluid this world may have seemed to him:

> I know I am solid and sound,
> To me the converging objects of the universe perpetually flow . . .[63]

He no longer dissolves in objects, he bumps into them and they make him conscious of his own existence:

> You objects that call from diffusion my meanings and give them shape! [64]

It then seems to him that an easy way of distinguishing the Me from the Not-Me is to call Me that body which keeps bumping into things. It is the body, he tells us, which gives us the sense of our identity:

> I too had receiv'd identity by my body . . .[65]

— a provisional solution. Very soon he reaches the soul. The body is only an intermediary. It is the means whereby the soul receives its "identity":

> O the joy of my soul . . . receiving identity through materials . . .
> My soul vibrated back from them . . .[66]

His sexual ecstasies reveal to him, too, to what extent he can be dependent upon the physical world:

> Is this then a touch? quivering me to a new identity . . .[67]

From then on it is clear to him that the Me is the soul and the Not-Me all the rest:

> People I meet, the effect upon me of my early life or the ward and city I live in, or the nation,
> The latest dates, discoveries, inventions, societies, authors old and new,

My dinner, dress, associates, looks, compliments,
   dues
. . .

These come to me days and nights and go from me
   again,
But they are not the Me myself.

Apart from the pulling and hauling stands what I
   am . . .[68]

This soul, this Me which is at the center of the world and
of each being differentiates itself more and more as we live
and confers upon us an irreducible individuality and an eternal
existence. For, once the Me has been formed, nothing henceforward can destroy it. Through it we escape death and the
flux of things. It will survive the body:

It is not to diffuse you that you were born of your
   mother and father, it is to identify you . . .
You are henceforth secure, whatever comes or goes.[69]

Thus the composition of *Leaves of Grass* has rapidly permitted Whitman to put the confused world of his perceptions
in order and clearly to distinguish between the Me and the
Not-Me. However, the problem never ceased to preoccupy
him and, in 1882, he went back to it again in *Specimen Days*:

The most profound theme that can occupy the mind of man —
the problem on whose solution science, art, the bases and pursuits
of nations, and everything else, including intelligent human
happiness . . . depends for competent outset and argument, is
doubtless involved in the query: What is the fusing explanation
and tie — what the relation between the (radical, democratic)
Me, the human identity of understanding, emotions, spirit, &c.,
on the one side, of and with the (conservative) Not Me, the
whole of the material objective universe and laws, with what is
behind them in time and space, on the other side? [70]

Thus he reduced the problem to the matter-spirit dualism,

and, as the rest of the passage shows, entrusted Hegel with the care of finding a solution.

He had himself posed the problem under still another form by trying to understand the meaning of the dualism God-man, and, as we are going to see, under the influence of his mysticism he had arrived at a solution which seemed acceptable to him and by which he always abided.

PANTHEISM — FROM GOD TO THE "SQUARE DEIFIC"

On that memorable summer morning when Whitman had his ecstasy, it was revealed to him that the spirit of God was the eldest brother of his own.[71] But what did he then mean by "God"? Was it the God of the Christians? It does not seem so, for it is not God the Father. In 1855 he calls him his "eldest brother," which still implies a certain hierarchy, but, as early as the following year, he boldly proclaims Him his brother, and from now on they are equal:

> I only am he who places over you no master, owner,
>   better, God, beyond what waits intrinsically in your-
>   self.[72]

He thus broke almost from the start with the traditional Christian concept of a transcendent God,[73] distinct from His creation and superior to His creatures; he preferred an immanent God, mingled with the world, incarnated in each creature. He suggested this in symbolic language as early as 1855:

> I hear and behold God in every object . . .
> I see something of God each hour of the twenty-four,
>   and each moment then,
> In the faces of men and women I see God, and in my
>   own face in the glass,
> I find letters from God dropt in the street, and every
>   one is sign'd by God's name . . .[74]

In 1856 he was still more direct and explicit:

> A vast similitude interlocks all . . .
> All souls, all living bodies though they be ever so dif-
> ferent, or in different worlds,
> All gaseous, watery, vegetable, mineral processes, the
> fishes, the brutes . . .
> All identities that have existed or may exist on this
> globe, or any globe . . .
> This vast similitude spans them, and always has
> spann'd,
> And shall forever span them and compactly hold and
> enclose them.[75]

Very soon therefore Whitman's mysticism resulted on the metaphysical plane in a pantheistic conception of the divinity. He prized it so highly that in 1856 he entitled the poem from which we have drawn the preceding quotation "Clef Poem," meaning by that that the poem, according to him, gave the key to the mystery of the universe. But it was only gradually, however, that his thought became clear. The 1867 edition is particularly important in this respect, for it contains an essential poem: "Chanting the Square Deific." [76]

As early as 1855 he set himself as the successor of the ancient founders of religions:

> Outbidding at the start the old cautious hucksters,
> Taking myself the exact dimensions of Jehovah,
> Lithographing Kronos, Zeus his son, and Hercules
> his grandson,
> Buying drafts of Osiris, Isis, Belus, Brahma, Bud-
> dha . . .[77]

He promised himself to surpass them all:

> Accepting the rough deific sketches to fill out better
> in myself . . .[78]

He later kept his word with his "square deific." In the poem bearing this title he offered his reader a well-defined dogma, a precise credo. His new religion was meant to be a synthesis of all the religions of the past. His God, "the square entirely divine," has for its first side the cruel and always wrathful Jehovah of the Old Testament and also the Kronos of the ancient Greeks, that is to say, Time, which, contrary to space, is the sphere of our impotence and sanctions the inflexible determinism which rules the physical world. The second side counterbalances the first; it represents Christ, Hermes, Hercules, the pity of the Divinity for creatures, and charity, which softens the rigor of the laws. The third side is more unexpected; it is Satan, but a Satan whose traits are a little hazy; he is both the incarnation of the principle of evil (the "comrade of criminals") and the Satan of Milton,[79] the Satan of the romantics, "brother of slaves," always in revolt against tyrants and as such a factor of progress. The fourth side is an original creation, Whitman gives it a name of his own, "Santa Spirita," [80] but, at this point, his thought becomes confused, for his "Santa Spirita" is both the fourth side of the square and the sum of the three others, since it includes God, the Savior, and Satan. This contradiction was in keeping with Whitman's desire to conciliate the traditional religions and his own, which he would probably have found difficulty in defining, but which was undeniably a form of pantheism. This is unmistakable. We find here again the pantheism which was already latent in *Leaves of Grass* in 1855. This "Santa Spirita" is universal life:

> Ethereal, pervading all . . .
> Essence of forms, life of the real identities, perma-
>   nent, positive, (namely the unseen,)
> Life of the great round world, the sun and stars, and
>   of man . . . the general soul . . .

He thus tried in 1865 [81] to give a precise intellectual meaning to the mystical revelation which he had had a few years before and to rationalize his intuitions, but the theology which he so carefully elaborated was still full of uncertainties. He wished to open the mystical triangle of the trinity and to add a fourth side to it, but this only resulted in confusion. Besides, his pantheism itself was still very far from having the rigor of a philosophical system. Swept away by his infatuation for spiritualism, he made his supreme divinity, as the name "Santa Spirita" indicates, a pure spirit, contrary to Spinoza, who, being a systematic thinker, never forgets the material part of the universe.

And so we find again on the theological level Whitman's constant vacillations between spiritualism and materialism. A few years later, probably impelled by that care for compensation and balance which we have already noticed in him, he tried to repair his omission and fill up the lacuna which his "Santa Spirita" so unfortunately presented. For, summing up the themes of his poems at the end of *Passage to India* in 1872, he added this:

> Through Space and Time fused in a chant, and the
>   flowing, eternal identity,
> To Nature, encompassing these, encompassing God —
>   to the joyous, electric All, . .
> The entrance of Man I sing.[82]

It is clear that by God he means here only the soul of the world and that it is not by it alone that he is attracted, but by what he calls "Nature," which encompasses at one time the physical world and God, spirit and matter. That is why he exclaims in another poem in the same collection:

> Thought of the Infinite — the *All*!
> Be thou my God.[83]   [italics ours]

A few years later, however, in *Two Rivulets*, when he spoke of God, he used more conventional expressions, as if he returned to the more orthodox conception of a transcendent divinity. He evoked "the Eternal Ocean," "the mystic Ocean" toward which all things flow, but which apparently does not include them yet.[84] And, before the Rocky Mountains, he thought of the "Spirit that form'd this scene" [85] as if it were the God of Genesis. But these were probably mere lapses into more banal language due to age, for he once more used images which implied a pantheistic philosophy:

> You unseen force, centripetal, centrifugal, through
>   space's spread . . .
> What central heart — and you the pulse — vivifies
>   all?
> . . . what fluid, vast identity,
> Holding the universe with all its parts as one — as sail-
>   ing in a ship? [86]

> Thou laws invisible that permeate them and all,
> Thou that in all, and over all, and through and under
>   all, incessant!
> Thou! thou! the vital, universal, giant force resistless,
>   sleepless, calm . . .[87]

> Allah is all, all, all — is immanent in every life and
>   object . . .[88]

This pantheism was, of course, a conception of his mind and not a raw product of his mystical perceptions. So it is suitable that we should ask ourselves what influences shaped them. As always with Whitman these influences were extremely diffuse. His most considerable debt was probably to Emerson. His notion of a "general soul" singularly recalls the Emersonian oversoul, but he may also have been influenced by the English romantics and notably by Wordsworth, of whom he had at least read the ode "On Intimations of Immortality," [89] and by Coleridge, whose *Biographia Literaria* he had known for a long time.[90] Finally, later, the German idealists confirmed all these borrowed ideas. He noted in one of his notebooks apropos of Schelling:

His palace of idealistic pantheism was never completed, is more or less deficient and fragmentary, yet is one of the most beautiful and majestic structures ever achieved by the intellect or imagination of man . . .[91]

As for Hegel, as we shall see, he played a decisive part in the formation of the square deific.[92]

In any event, whatever the book sources for his pantheistic system may have been, Whitman, to the end of his life, remained faithful to his first intuitions and never sought, like Wordsworth for instance, to return to orthodoxy. He never thought of repudiating the natural religion which he had at first intended to found. Yet, a more subtle but no less redoubtable danger than conformity for some time hung over his work. The rationalization to which he submitted his intuitions in "Chanting the Square Deific" might very well have killed his inspiration and dried up his poetry, but we have seen to what extent even then his theology, which he wanted to be clear and logical, in fact remained confused and uncertain. He never succeeded in imposing on his thought the rigidity of a dogma or a system, and he thus escaped the sclerosis of intellectualism. In short, it was his lack of "esprit géométrique," of intellectual rigor, which saved him. Besides, as he grew older, all dogmatism became more and more distasteful to him and, four years after composing "Chanting the Square Deific," he wrote in "Passage to India":

> Ah more than any priest O soul we too believe in God,
> But with the mystery of God we dare not dally.[93]

This distrust of reason and instinctive sense of mystery prevented him both from accepting unreservedly the conclusions of science and from accepting the credo of any established church.

ANTI-INTELLECTUALISM AND THE SCIENTIFIC SPIRIT

The *Leaves of Grass* of 1855 are essentially a long cry of wonder before the beauty of the world and of astonishment before the mystery of life:

A child said *What is the grass?* fetching it to me with
full hands,
How could I answer the child? I do not know any more
than he.[94]

On almost every page one finds similar acknowledgments
of impotence.[95] It is the normal reaction of a mystic who
vividly feels the vanity of all attempts at rational explanation.
This attitude was natural in him, but it was probably reinforced by his reading — by Carlyle, in particular.[96] He may
even have been influenced by the Keatsian theory of "negative
capability" which a magazine article had revealed to him.[97]
At any rate, during his whole life, he evinced the same distrust of reason. In 1860 he represented the poet as "unap-
proachable to analysis," [98] and in 1867 he maintained that
no one can know himself, still less the world.[99] And, in his
old age, he constantly reverted to that idea that the mystery
of creation will always escape us:

Ever the grappled mystery of all earth's ages old and
new . . .
Ever the soul dissatisfied, curious, unconvinced at
last . . .[100]

He almost concluded: "Happy are the poor in spirit." [101]
He did not go quite so far, however, for he added in 1860:

I say nourish a great intellect, a great brain;
If I have said anything to the contrary, I hereby retract
it.[102]

In 1855–56 he had affected ignorance and posed as an
autodidact who owes nothing to anyone. He now realized his
mistake and the naïveté of such a claim. Henceforth he recognized the necessity of culture and he no longer tried to hide
the fact that he had always read.[103] Nevertheless up to the
end of his life he insisted that one must go beyond books:

The open air I sing . . .
(Take here the mainest lesson — less from books —
less from the schools,) . . .[104]

These general considerations help to understand better Whitman's attitude toward science. Given his profoundly religious spirit, one might expect that he would reject science or at least regard it with suspicion; on the contrary, at the beginning at least, he enthusiastically adopted all its conclusions and that at a time when the churches were cool toward it, when poets ignored it, and Emerson declared that it was "apt to cloud the sight." [105] He devoured books on astronomy like Denison Olmsted's *Letters on Astronomy*, Elijah Burritt's *Geography of the Heavens*, O. M. Mitchell's *Course of Six Lectures on Astronomy*, and C. S. Rafinesque's *Celestial Wonders and Philosophy*,[106] and books on physics, on chemistry, and so on; [107] he carefully cut out all the popular science articles that fell into his hands, and, in 1855, he exclaimed:

Hurrah for positive science! long live exact demonstration! [108]

For science did not disturb him. True, it destroys the belief in miracles and the supernatural, but that did not matter very much, since for the poet it is the real itself which is the supernatural, since the smallest blade of grass and all that exists is a miracle. Besides, does not science complete our senses and enlarge our universe by revealing to us the infinitely small and the infinitely large and by opening up to us the infinity of space and time? Moreover, by showing that man was the product of a cosmic and millenary evolution, does it not confirm the divine character which the traditional religions have already attributed to him? [109] Far from rendering the world banal and prosaic, it makes it appear more wonderful than ever. Science thus became a springboard for the imagination of the poet who sought to reach the soul and the secret life of things beyond inert material appearances:

Gentlemen, to you the first honors always!
Your facts are useful, and yet they are not my dwelling,
I but enter by them to an area of my dwelling.[110]

Such was his point of view all his life: science is only a stage at which we must not stop. He returned to this point in his preface to the 1872 edition. Under the influence of Hegel [111] he then presented science as the antithesis of religion [112] and he announced the synthesis to come, "the New Theology," "the supreme and final Science," "the Science of God." [113] He developed the same idea in 1876 in "Song of the Universal" [114] and in "Eidólons":

Beyond thy lectures, learn'd professor,
Beyond thy telescope or spectroscope observer keen,
    beyond all mathematics,
Beyond the doctor's surgery, anatomy, beyond the
    chemist's with his chemistry,
The entity of entities, eidólons.[115]

Whitman also affirmed in the preface to the *Leaves of Grass* of that year the necessity of adopting the conclusions of science and, at the same time, of transcending them by soaring to what he called "the worlds of Religiousness." [116]

Thus, from the beginning of his poetic career, Whitman sought boldly to integrate science and poetry, as Lucretius had done before,[117] and to make one complement the other instead of unprofitably setting them at loggerheads. But he never let himself be bound by scientific materialism. He admired the discoveries of science, but he knew very well that the explanations it proposed were only provisional theories without any absolute value. He rejected that dogmatism to which all narrow rationalism tends and, on the contrary, appreciated the spirit of free inquiry which enables science to progress without cease.[118] Far from regarding it as an enemy, he considered it as religion's best ally. Was it not going to

destroy all the medieval superstitions which hid the true face
of the Divinity? It seemed to him that science was destined to
cause the disappearance of all religions and so to assure the
triumph of true Religion.[119] He hoped that with its support
Poetry, Literature, would supplant the established churches
and would eventually become the religion of the future and
of democracy.

WHITMAN'S ATTITUDE TOWARD THE CHURCHES

As was natural for a child of Quakers, and, what is more, of
Quakers belonging to a dissident sect, in his youth Whitman
felt only contempt for all established churches. As early as
1840, in his "Sun-Down Papers," he ridiculed the diversity
of religions, every one of which sees truth through the colored
lenses of its own dogmas: "Many of the glasses were of so
gross a texture that the temple was completely hid from
view." [120]

This criticism distinctly recalls the attacks of the French
eighteenth-century "philosophes." Whitman had not read
their works, but, from childhood, he had been familiar with
The Ruins by Volney,[121] according to whom all religions
amount to the same thing and are nothing more than instru-
ments of domination in the hands of priests and kings. It is
probable that it was from Volney, too, that Whitman borrowed
the idea of the relativity of religions and of their gradual
evolution, expressed repeatedly in *Leaves of Grass*.[122] Walter
Whitman senior, besides, seems to have been a man of a
very independent spirit, in revolt against Christianity and in
sympathy with the free-thinkers of his time. He much admired
Thomas Paine and, in all likelihood, made his son at a very
early age read *The Age of Reason* as well as Frances Wright's
Free Inquirer, to which he subscribed. Afterwards, when
young Walt became a journalist in New York, he attended the

lectures she gave in Tammany Hall and read over and over again her little Socratic dialogue entitled *A Few Days in Athens,* which in his old age he remembered as *Ten Days in Athens.*[123] It has even been possible to compile a fairly long list of all the borrowings he made from that book.[124] Though he later qualified their theses, he never repudiated his first masters. In 1877 he even publicly took the defense of Paine.[125] And later he followed with interest the efforts of a new generation of rationalists. In the last years of his life he was a great admirer of Robert Ingersoll whose vigor and dynamism he liked, though he did not approve of all his ideas,[126] and of Thomas Huxley, the biologist. He even declared to all and sundry that those two "without any others could unhorse the Christian giant." [127]

These rationalistic notions, however, were qualified by idealistic influences. Had not Carlyle declared — and Emerson been in agreement with him on this point — that:

> Literature is but a branch of Religion and always participates in its character: however, in our time, it is the only branch that still shows any greenness; and, as some think, must one day become the main stem.[128]

Those grievances of philosophers condemning the religions of their time on the grounds of historic relativism and of evolution were further reinforced by a personal element. Like many mystics in direct communication with the Divinity, Whitman refused to acknowledge the authority of the churches, which, according to him, were each and all paralyzed by the routine of their liturgy, and he wanted, in his turn, to found a purer and more vital religion based on his personal illuminations. Wishing to be a prophet, he could not but be anti-clerical.

All this helps to explain the violence of his attacks on priests in the first two editions of *Leaves of Grass:*

There will soon be no more priests. Their work is done. They may wait awhile . . . perhaps a generation or two . . . dropping off by degrees. A superior breed shall take their place. A new order shall arise and they shall be the priests of man, and every man shall be his own priest.[129]

Priests are only "cautious hucksters," [130] clinging to their "formules," "bat-eyed and materialistic." [131] In his open letter to Emerson in 1856 he was even harsher:

> The churches are one vast lie; the people do not believe them, and they do not believe themselves; the priests are continually telling what they know well enough is not so, and keeping back what they know is so. The spectacle is a pitiful one.[132]

Thus, pushing protestant revolt against ritual to extremes, Whitman refused to worship and pray according to consecrated formulas [133] and intended, if not to repudiate altogether, at least to transcend, all established religions.[134]

In 1860 we find the same criticism almost in the same terms. He thinks with contempt "Of the mumbling and screaming priest, (soon, soon deserted,) . . ." [135] And in his newspaper articles he is no less severe than in his poems. Calling up childhood memories in the *Brooklyn Standard* in 1862, he pitilessly ridiculed the Methodist revivals he had had occasion to attend in the past.[136]

Once he was in Washington, however, his attitude changed. Caught in the turmoil of the Civil War, he realized his powerlessness and renounced his role as prophet and founder of a new religion. It was enough for him now to be a "man of letters" in the sense which Carlyle gives to the word. Besides, he had the opportunity to see Catholic priests and nuns devoting themselves at the bedsides of the wounded,[137] and the dying finding a spiritual comfort which he had never suspected in those religions which he believed dried out and dead.[138] From then on, he was more indulgent and less aggressive. When he still happens to attack priests, the tone of his criticism is less violent.[139] In 1879 he went so far as to include "ecclesiasticism" among the assets of the United States,[140] and, the following year, during his stay in Ontario at the home of Dr. Bucke, he attended an Episcopalian service and described it sympathetically in *Specimen Days*.[141]

Moreover, his more and more marked leaning toward spiritualism between 1860 and 1876 [142] brought him closer to Christianity and, in particular, made him conscious of a certain kinship between his philosophy and the Quaker doctrine. In the rough draft of a preface for *Two Rivulets* he even wrote: "With these comes forward more prominently in *Two Rivulets* than in the preceding volume, the moral law, the 'inner light' of the Quakers . . ." [143]

The same year, he quoted George Fox in one of his poems [144] and defined poetic inspiration in terms of which a Quaker would not have disapproved.[145]

Nevertheless, in spite of his increasingly comprehensive attitude, he remained inflexible, until the end, on the doctrinal plane and, in 1888, he still affirmed in his essay on Elias Hicks that the churches in the United States were devoid of sense and no longer interested anyone,[146] repeating, in short, but without acrimony or personal animosity, what he had with so much violence proclaimed in 1855.

That fear of the routine of rites and the dryness of dogmas which saved his poetry from sclerosis gave him a sharp sense of the constant becoming of the world which we must now examine.

FROM THE SENSE OF THE BECOMING OF THE WORLD
TO EVOLUTIONISM

The immanent God whom Whitman places at the center of the world and whom he calls now "Nature," now "Santa Spirita," is not a static spirit, an immobile presence, but a perpetual becoming, "the joyous electric all." [147] His first illuminations had revealed to him the existence of living presences beyond inert material appearances.[148] When he wrote his first *Leaves of Grass,* he felt himself surrounded by mysterious forces circulating through water and rocks, through inanimate objects as well as through animals or men. The entire universe appeared to him essentially as a vital impulse, an irresistible current without beginning or end ceaselessly impelling the enormous mass of creation toward the future:

> All goes onward and outward, nothing collapses . . .[149]

> There is that in me — I do not know what it is — but
>   I know it is in me . . .
>   . . . it is eternal life — it is Happiness.[150]

> Urge and urge and urge,
> Always the procreant urge of the world.
> Out of dimness opposite equals advance, always sub-
>   stance and increase, always sex . . .[151]

He knew very well, as we have noted, that he owed his mystical intuitions to his sexual transports and so, as our last quotation shows, he often represents the vital impulse of the world as a universal sexual desire. This pansexualism even sometimes gives birth to phallic images of cosmic dimensions:

> Something I cannot see puts upward libidinous prongs,
> Seas of bright juice suffuse heaven.[152]

Fairly quickly, however, his senses calmed down and this sexual obsession ceased. One no longer finds such audacious metaphors in the poems which he wrote during and after the war. But, until the end of his life, he retained that dynamic conception of the world as a constant becoming:

> Ever the mutable,
> Ever materials, changing, crumbling,
>   re-cohering . . .[153]

. . . creation's incessant unrest, exfoliation . . . Indeed,
what is Nature but change, in all its visible, and still more its
invisible processes? [154]

> Unseen buds, infinite, hidden well . . .
> Urging slowly, surely forward, forming endless,
> And waiting ever more, forever behind.[155]

His vitalism was so intimately fused with his sensibility
that it circulates like a living current through all his poetical
works, even through his last poems. (The last quotation is
borrowed from a poem published in 1891.) Of course, it
loses its force little by little, but its nature never changes and
it remains itself right up to the end.

Whitman perceives this life force not only in the immensity
of space, but also in the infinity of time:

> I am an acme of things accomplish'd, and I an encloser
>   of things to be . . .
> Immense have been the preparations for me,
> Faithful and friendly the arms that have help'd me.
> Cycles ferried my cradle, rowing and rowing like cheer-
>   ful boatmen . . .
> Before I was born out of my mother generations guided
>   me,
> My embryo has never been torpid, nothing could over-
>   lay it.
> For it the nebula cohered to an orb,
> The long slow strata piled to rest it on,
> Vast vegetables gave it sustenance,
> Monstrous sauroids transported it in their mouths and
>   deposited it with care.[156]

In short, as early as 1855 and even before,[157] Whitman had had
the prescience of evolutionism, not by a sort of genial intuition,
but because the idea had already been in the air for a long
time.[158] As early as 1856 Emerson had begun to speak of

evolution [159] (after Leibniz, Kant, Goethe, and many others), and, above all, the newspapers and the reviews had warmly discussed the theories of Lamarck,[160] Sir Charles Lyell,[161] and Robert Chambers.[162] Thus Whitman invented nothing, he simply adopted the astronomical [163] and geological hypotheses of the time which happened to confirm and complete his personal vitalism.

We do not know what his reactions were when the first American edition of *The Origin of Species* appeared in 1860, but it is quite probable that, not being hindered by any religious prejudices, he immediately accepted Darwin's theories, which were so close to his own. In 1876, in *Two Rivulets,* he devoted one of his prose notes to Darwinism.[164] He thus became gradually conscious of his intuitive evolutionism and his progress on this point followed that of his time. It is symptomatic that he never used the word "evolution" before 1871.[165] He was never, though, a blind follower of Darwin.[166] In *Two Rivulets,* reasoning according to the methods of Hegelian dialectics, he declared that the confrontation of the traditional explanation with the Darwinian hypothesis would eventually give birth to a third theory which, synthesizing the other two, would be much closer to the truth than any other. Even though he himself never went beyond the Darwinian stage, he was thus, later, won over to the side of Hegel,[167] probably because Hegel revealed to him a discontinuous form of evolution much more in keeping, as we are going to see, with his own experience.

Up to here, we have examined only the positive aspects of his philosophy, the profound convictions born of his mysticism. But his thought was not always so serene. He had to struggle to save his faith and two difficulties especially, again and again, tormented him: the existence of evil and the mystery of death. It thus remains for us to study the crises they provoked and the solutions he found for them.

THE PROBLEM OF EVIL

The exuberant Whitman, brimming over with health, who in 1855 boldly set off for the conquest of the world and sounded his barbaric yawp over the roofs of the earth, was impelled by such a joy of life that it seemed to him that everything was perfect and that this was the best of all possible worlds:

> The soul is always beautiful,
> The universe is duly in order, everything is in its place,
> What has arrived is in its place and what waits shall be
>   in its place . . .[168]

> Pleasantly and well-suited I walk,
> Whither I walk I cannot define, but I know it is good,
> The whole universe indicates that it is good,
> The past and present indicate that it is good.[169]

> I inhale great draughts of space . . .
> All seems beautiful to me . . .[170]

So fervent is his joy and so passionate his optimism that he accepts everything, even evil. Evil itself becomes perfect in his eyes:

> How perfect the earth is, and the minutest thing upon
>   it!
> What is called good is perfect, and what is called bad
>   is just as perfect . . .[171]

> Great is wickedness — I find I sometimes admire it
>   just as much as I admire goodness . . .[172]

Does that mean that he is devoid of the "Vision of Evil," as W. B. Yeats reproached him with being? [173] Not at all; his optimism is lucid. The existence of evil does not escape him and he does not seek to deny it. He even probes in imagination all the sufferings and all the turpitudes of the world:

> Agonies are one of my changes of garments . . .[174]

> The pleasures of heaven are with me and the pains of
>   hell are with me . . .[175]

He lets his eyes roam on all the exploited, all the sick and all
the criminals of the world.[176]

For, far from trying to dodge the problem of evil, for a long
time he kept pondering it with anguish. What more tragic
problem can there be for a mystical pantheist? It has been
revealed to him that God is everywhere, he knows that God
is all, but, at the same time, he sees evil everywhere around
him. Is it possible that God should be evil, that evil should
partake of God? These torturing questions obsessed Whitman.
His ecstasies enabled him to commune with the great current
of joy which flows through the world, but he did not forget
that there are millions of suffering beings on the earth and
was himself sometimes horribly tormented by troubled desires
which society reproved and which he had to hold in check:

> It is not upon you alone the dark patches fall . . .
> Nor is it you alone who know what it is to be evil,
> I am he who knew what it was to be evil,
> I too knitted the old knot of contrariety . . .
> Had . . . lust, hot wishes I dared not speak . . .[177]

The rough drafts which preceded the first edition of *Leaves
of Grass* reflect his efforts to find, before proceeding, a solution to that agonizing problem, and the text of 1855 shows
that he had already gathered the elements of an answer. Evil,
he concluded, is only a temporary accident; it is not an absolute
reality:

> What has arrived is in its place and what waits shall be
>   in its place,
> The twisted skull waits, the watery or rotten blood
>   waits,
> The child of the glutton or venerealee waits long, and
>   the child of the drunkard waits long, and the
>   drunkard himself waits long . . .[178]

> In each house is the ovum, it comes forth after a thou-
>   sand of years.
> Spots or cracks at the windows do not disturb me . . .
> I read the promise and patiently wait.[179]

In short, he leaned toward a spiritualistic solution of the
problem: the soul is always good and beautiful, but the flesh
is sometimes rotten; in other words, matter is the obstacle
which provisionally prevents the soul from blossoming out.
This doctrine was even more clearly set out in his rough
notes:

> In the silence and darkness
> Among murderers and cannibals and traders in slaves
> Stepped my spirit with light feet, and pried among
>   their heads and made fissures to look through
> And there saw folded foetuses of twins, like the bodies
>   in the womb,
> Mute with bent necks waiting to be born, —
> And one was Sympathy and one was truth.[180]

According to him, there are no wicked, but only sick, people
(he prefigures the psychoanalysts in this respect):

> Wickedness is most likely the absence of freedom and
>   health in the soul.[181]

Evil being a mere accident and not an essence, he thus quite
naturally reaches the conclusion, in a poem belonging to the
1860 edition, that it does not really exist:

> I make the poem of evil, I commemorate that part also,
> I am myself just as much evil as good, and my nation
>   is — and I say there is in fact no evil . . .[182]

So he hesitates between the pure and simple negation of
evil [183] and an optimistic manicheism which, while recognizing
the existence of evil beside that of good, announces and
proclaims the final victory of the latter over the former. Evolu-

tion for him becomes synonymous with progress; in short, he adopts the serene optimism of the transcendentalists; [184] he believes in it with all his soul:

> Wisdom is of the soul, is not susceptible of proof, is
> its own proof . . .
> Is the certainty of the reality and immortality of things,
> and the excellence of things;
> Something there is in the float of the sight of things
> that provokes it out of the soul.[185]

However, he has to fight to protect this spontaneous optimism against the assaults of life which again and again disappoint him and ceaselessly recall to him the existence of evil. In 1856 the ugliness of the world even wrung from him the cry of despair of "Respondez," [186] but he must have recovered his faith, his "wisdom," [187] or his "satisfaction," [188] as he called it, almost immediately, for the other poems of the book sing the joy of life and his unalterable confidence in the future. But in 1858–1860 there was a new crisis. His instincts were tearing and torturing him, tension between the North and South was mounting, he despaired of himself and of others:

> I sit and look out upon all the sorrows of the world,
> and upon all oppression and shame,
> I hear secret convulsive sobs from young men at
> anguish with themselves [like himself], remorseful
> after deeds done . . .
> I mark the ranklings of jealousy and unrequited love
> attempted to be hid . . .
> I observe the slights and degradations cast by arrogant
> persons upon laborers, the poor, and upon negroes,
> and the like . . .[189]

Life has no more sense for him. We are, he concludes, only flotsam and jetsam cast up haphazardly on the shore.[190] But he soon breaks away from this sterile despair. He very quickly rediscovers the consoling notion of an "eternal progress" [191]

which was already in germ in "Faces" [192] and which in 1856
he called "amelioration." [193] True, he thought, life is a continual struggle, a succession of painful convulsions,[194] but the
present is only the germ of the future,[195] and why doubt the
future when the past shows a constant progress? The future
will justify the present and retrospectively give it its true
sense:

> . . . all I see and know I believe to have its main pur-
> port in what will yet be supplied.[196]
>
> Where has fail'd a perfect return indifferent of lies or
> the truth?
> . . . nothing fails its perfect return . . . and what
> are called lies are perfect returns . . .
> . . . there is no flaw or vacuum in the amount of
> the truth — but . . . all is truth without excep-
> tion;
> And henceforth I will go celebrate any thing I see or
> am,
> And sing and laugh and deny nothing.[197]

His sense of the becoming of the world and of evolution thus
saved him. He could once more conclude:

> . . . I do not see one imperfection in the universe,
> And I do not see one cause or result lamentable at last
> in the universe.[198]

Thereafter came the Civil War with its train of sufferings
and horrors. Was evil going to prevail over good? He trembled
for the North after the defeat of Bull Run. For, at the beginning, it seemed to him that the cause of the North was that
of good, but, soon after his first contact with the realities of
combat, he understood that the problem was far more complex
and that the North did not have the monopoly of heroism or
suffering. Moreover, the spectacle of the martyrdom endured
by the wounded became gradually so intolerable to him that he

revolted and called for the end of the slaughter. He then realized that it was War itself that was Evil, and not just the South. But how could one stop it? One must resign oneself to the inevitable. So he submitted to it, but its horror crushed him.[199] The brutality of military discipline, the atrocious greed of the grave-diggers and hospital thieves revealed to him all the sadism and all the blackness that the human soul can harbor.[200] Fortunately the magnificent courage of the wounded and the dying who bore their sufferings stoically, without a word of bitterness, reconciled him with his own kind and saved him from despair:

> Democracy, while weapons were everywhere aim'd at
>   your breast,
> I saw you serenely give birth to immortal children, saw
>   in dreams your dilating form,
> Saw your spreading mantle covering the world.[201]

This terrible trial ended in 1865. The South was defeated, the attempt at secession definitively thwarted. The cause of democracy had won and there was once more legitimate ground for hope. Peace opened up infinite prospects of progress, even more beautiful than before the war since slavery was abolished and there remained nothing to divide the nation. The storm had cleared the sky and it seemed to Whitman that this happy result amply justified its occurrence. And so he came to wonder if that war which had torn him [202] and his country was not indispensable, if, in a general way, evil was not indispensable to progress. Hegel, whom he had just discovered,[203] at this juncture supplied him with a solution to the problem:

The varieties, contradictions and paradoxes of the world and of life, and even good and evil, so baffling to the superficial observer, and so often leading to despair, sullenness or infidelity, become a series of infinite radiations and waves of the one sea-like universe of divine action and progress, never stopping, never hasting. "The heavens and the earth" to use the summing up of Joseph Gostick whose brief I endorse: "The heavens and the earth and all things within their compass — all the events of history — the facts of the present and the development of the future (such is the doctrine of Hegel) all form a complication, a succession of steps in the one eternal process of creative thought." . . . A curious, triplicate process seems the resultant action; first the Positive, then the Negative, then the product of the mediation between them; from which product the process is repeated and so goes on without end.[204]

Interpreting the Civil War in the light of Hegelian dialectic, Whitman could then write:

> I know not what these plots and wars and deferments
> are for,
> I know not fruition's success, but I know that through
> war and crime your work goes on, and must yet go
> on.[205]

It was at this moment, too, that he conceived of his "square deific," his God in four persons who is the synthesis of Good and Evil.[206]

Thus he found in Hegel the explanation of the discontinuity and the convulsions of the becoming. Up to then he had had to deny evil in the present or in the future; now he could boldly affirm its necessity and accept its existence without despair. No wonder that in his gratitude he saluted Hegel as "Humanity's chiefest teacher and the choicest loved physician of [his] mind and soul" who had helped him to resolve "the dark problem of evil, forming half of the infinite scheme." [207]

Under the pressure of external events, he knew other periods of distress and of doubt, but he always re-affirmed his faith in the necessarily happy outcome of the crises of the becoming. This is what he did for instance in 1871 in spite of his disgust for all the scandals of the Reconstruction. Under the influence of the Civil War, which was still so close, he compared life to a perpetual war of varying fortunes.[208] But, he proclaimed, something "more immortal even than the stars" will eventually triumph over evil, just as the stars themselves always triumph over the storm clouds which for a time hide them from view.[209] And, just as the thrush transforms into ecstatic songs the repulsive worms it eats, so will the Union sooner or later emerge from its difficulties.[210] These analogous reasonings inspired by Hegel enabled him to recover his optimism whenever it was obscured.

In 1873, when he was struck by paralysis, true to his philosophy, he refused to acknowledge defeat. He struggled valiantly against evil and eventually triumphed over it, too. He did not lose his way "along the mighty labyrinth" of the world because he knew "the guiding thread so fine" which enables its owner to find the exit. He knew that:

> In this broad earth of ours,
> Amid the measureless grossness and the slag,
> Enclosed and safe within its central heart,
> Nestles the seed perfection.[211]

He did not despair because he knew the slowness of the process of evolution by means of thesis and antithesis:

> In spiral routes by long detours,
> (As a much-tacking ship upon the sea,)
> For it [the soul] the partial to the permanent flowing,
> For it the real to the ideal tends.[212]

He thus takes up again here, with more clarity than before, combining it with his Hegelianism,[213] the spiritualistic solution which he had already outlined in 1855 in the poem later entitled "Faces":

> Forth from their masks, no matter what,
> From the huge festering trunk, from craft and guile
> and tears,
> Health to emerge and joy, joy universal.[214]

Hegel's meliorism now crowns his initial evolutionism:

> For it the mystic evolution,
> Not the right only justified, what we call evil also justi-
> fied.[215]

"What we call evil," since evil is a mere element of the becoming, represents a transitory phase which will disappear in the final synthesis. Whitman made his thought more explicit a few years later in "Roaming in Thought," which bears a symptomatic subtitle: "After Reading Hegel."

> Only the good is universal.[216]
> Roaming in thought over the Universe, I saw the little
>   that is Good steadily hastening towards immortality,
> And the vast all that is call'd Evil I saw hastening to
>   merge itself and become lost and dead.[217]

In other words, evil is only a part of the whole and, in order to resolve the problem posed by its existence, one must never forget the "ensemble" which includes and assimilates it.

Until his death, Whitman thus had the conviction that he would eventually be "going somewhere" [218] where everything would be perfect, but until his death, too, he retained his sense of evil.[219] When in 1891 (or one or two years earlier) he heard a preacher celebrate the perfection of the universe, he could not refrain, once he had returned home, from drawing up a list of all the horrors of creation under the ironic title of "The Rounded Catalogue Divine Complete." [220] He defined his own final position as an "optimism with a touch of pessimism," [221] probably wishing to indicate thereby that his optimism was neither blind nor naïve.

Whitman's struggle with the problem of evil thus ended with a victory. He passed, after all kinds of vicissitudes, from the joyous optimism of a mystic to a more subdued and more rational optimism based on Hegelianism and evolutionism. He was perfectly conscious of the influences which had brought him to such a position. Describing the poets of the future, who of course bore a striking resemblance to himself, he said in *Democratic Vistas*:

. . . I say there must, for future and democratic purposes, appear poets, (dare I to say so?) of higher class even than any of those [the great poets of the past] — poets not only possess'd of the religious fire and abandon of Isaiah . . . but consistent with the Hegelian formulas, and consistent with modern science.[222]

It also follows from this study that the need which Whitman had to affirm, in order to survive, the essential reality of good beyond too often repugnant or repulsive material appearances, was one of the factors which led him to lean more and more toward a spiritualistic conception of the world.

THE OBSESSION WITH DEATH

All his life, Whitman was haunted by the thought of death even more than by the problem of evil. It was not for him a matter of purely speculative interest, but a permanent threat hanging over his existence as a perceiving subject set in the center of the universe and tied to the physical world by every fiber of his body. So the theme of death recurs again and again in his works. As early as 1838, at the age of nineteen, he devoted to it one of his first poetic attempts, a short poem in traditional form entitled "Our Future Lot" which appeared in the *Long Islander* and the *Long Island Democrat*. The sentiments and the phraseology were both Christian:

Thy form, re-purified, shall rise,
In robes of beauty drest.

The flickering taper's glow shall change
To bright and starlike majesty,
Radiant with pure and piercing light
From the Eternal's eye! [223]

Almost all the poems he published then are similarly on the subject of death: "My Departure," [224] "The Love that is hereafter," [225] where he represents faith in a better world as the only comfort here below, "We shall rest at last," [226] and "The End of All." [227]

But these are exercises in rhetoric rather than personal effusions; neither the thought nor the expression are original. More striking is "Time to Come" which appeared in 1842 in the *New York Aurora* of which he was then editor. It is a revised version of "Our Future Lot," but the tone has changed. He no longer celebrates in conventional terms the happy fate of an elect soul; he now expresses his anguish before the unfathomable mystery of death:

> O, Death! a black and pierceless pall
> Hangs round thee, and the future state;
> No eye may see, no mind may grasp
> That mystery of Fate.[228]

And toward 1850 he wrote again in one of his notebooks:

O Mystery of Death, I pant for the time when I shall solve you! [229]

In 1855, in the first edition of *Leaves of Grass*, there remained no trace of this anxiety. He felt so full of life and strength that it seemed impossible to him that he should ever cease to be:

> I know I am deathless . . .
> I laugh at what you call dissolution,
> And I know the amplitude of time.[230]
> No array of terms can say how much I am at peace
>   about God and about death.[231]
> And as to you Death, and you bitter hug of mortality,
>   it is idle to try to alarm me.[232]
> Has any one supposed it lucky to be born?
> I hasten to inform him or her it is just as lucky to die,
>   and I know it.[233]

Why indeed should we fear death since we will not really die? Our infinite past and our present guarantee our survival.[234] His optimism is total: "What will be will be well, for what is is well." [235] He denies death as he denies evil. He dissolves it in immortality: "I swear I think there is nothing but immortality!" [236] He even exults:

Is it wonderful that I should be immortal? as every one
    is immortal;
I know it is wonderful . . .[237]

This joyous acceptance of death, where one can feel the indifference of a young man, full of health, who cannot realize that he will die one day, is, of course, found again in the 1856 version of *Leaves of Grass,* when he evokes for example "the delicious near-by freedom of death" which gives to old people their nobility and serenity.[238] So passionate is his love of life that he can think without disgust of all the corpses whose rotten flesh has become mixed with the water in which he bathes and the fruit which he eats. The "compost" of death is necessary to life.[239] And the thought of the dissolution of bodies does not frighten him since he knows that he is limitless and that the universe is infinite.[240]

Moreover, one must die in order to live; does not he himself die a little every hour? But the past does not matter much to him, he hurls himself with enthusiasm and joy toward the future:

To pass on, (O living! always living!) and leave the
    corpses behind.[241]

Is it not paradoxical however that such a sensual poet should resign himself so easily to the loss of his body, however remote that prospect may appear to him? No wonder that from time to time he is struck with the regret of having one day to leave this terrestrial existence, so rich in sensations, so fertile in joys:

To think of all these wonders of city and country, and
others taking great interest in them, and we taking
no interest in them.[242]

It seems to me that every thing in the light and air
ought to be happy,
Whoever is not in his coffin and the dark grave let him
know he has enough.[243]

I am not uneasy but I shall have good housing to myself, [after death]
But this is my first — how can I like the rest any
better? [244]

In 1860, on the contrary (or rather in the poems written
between 1857 and 1860), the tone changes completely. In
the interval he has been disappointed by life, he has been
hurt and wounded. He who a short while before was walking
along the open road with confidence and joy now has the
impression of traveling through an unknown and hostile
world:

O baffled, balk'd, bent to the very earth,
Oppress'd with myself that I have dared to open my
mouth,
Aware now that amid all that blab whose echoes recoil
upon me I have not once had the least idea who or
what I am . . .[245]

And so he now aspires to break completely with his past and
to drift away:

O something pernicious and dread!
Something far away from a puny and pious life! . . .
Something escaped from the anchorage and driving
free.[246]

He has but one desire: to escape, to get away. He would like
to leave his body behind and all the hateful world of matter,
to say "so long!" to his friends and to die.[247]

But where did this sudden disgust come from? The origin of it must have been some disturbance of a sexual nature. He himself suggests this explanation when taking leave of his reader:

> Enough O deed impromptu and secret,
> Enough O gliding present — enough O summ'd-up past.[248]

"Enfans d'Adam" and "Calamus" confirm the interpretation. In these poems we see him full of anguish, unsettled, tormented by an exasperated sensuality. He aspires to lose himself, to sink either into the ecstasy of love or into death, it does not matter which:

> O something unprov'd! something in a trance!
> To escape utterly! from others' anchors and holds!
> To drive free! to love free! to dash reckless and dangerous!
> To court destruction with taunts, with invitations!
> To ascend, to leap to the heavens of the love indicated to me!
> To rise thither with my inebriate soul!
> To be lost if it must be so! [249]

> . . . what indeed is finally beautiful except death and love? . . .
> Death or life I am then indifferent, my soul declines to prefer,
> (I am not sure but the high soul of lovers welcomes death most) . . .[250]

Life, he now claims, was until then choking him, but death is going to liberate him, to relieve him of his body, finally to put him in contact with the essential, eternal reality which material appearances were hiding from him.[251] Thus, at the end of his sensual raving, he paradoxically repudiates his senses. The daily miracle of life which shortly before enchanted him has now lost all its charm. Simply to be is no longer sufficient for him; he would like to live beyond the physical world in a constant state of intoxication, in a perpetual trance.

There may have been several reasons for this change. First of all, it is possible that Whitman, perhaps after a belated revelation of carnal love, should have led a rather dissolute life at that period. Some of his poems at least suggest it:

> Give me now libidinous joys only . . .
> I am for those who believe in loose delights, I share
>   the midnight orgies of young men . . .[252]

If these statements are not purely Platonic, however, he was evidently trying to annihilate himself in the violent joys of the flesh by giving himself up completely to the "shuddering longing ache of contact" which had long obsessed him.[253] But his need for love may have been frustrated even then and, feeling incapable of satisfying it here below, he may have put off its fulfillment until later in the hope that death would procure for him that annihilation in voluptuousness after which he sighed in vain.

Finally, perhaps he wished to die because the death or the betrayal of him whom he loved passionately had broken his heart.[254] In the absence of reliable biographical information, one is reduced to suppositions. But one thing is certain; between 1857 and 1860, Whitman went through a tormented period in the course of which sentimental disappointments and sexual obsessions constantly threatened to destroy his moral equilibrium. He even experienced moments of despair and unbearable doubt when the immortality of the soul appeared to him as a myth,[255] and the future frightened him:

> As the time draws nigh glooming a cloud
> A dread beyond of I know not what darkens me.[256]

But, in a general way, he still had confidence in "the exquisite transition of death"[257] and thought wistfully of its "superb vistas."[258] He even sometimes dreamed of its "beautiful

touch," of its "soothing and benumbing" caresses,[259] and pronounced its name with an almost sensual voluptuousness.[260]

This morbid state of mind, however, did not last, Even
before publishing the third edition of *Leaves of Grass* he had
surmounted that crisis and recovered his zest for life. Moreover, the Civil War soon diverted his attention from himself
and put forward other problems.

His visits to the hospitals from 1863 to 1865 affected him
profoundly. For three years the spectacle of death was daily
before him. Day after day young men, a short while before
full of life and energy, died before his eyes, often in the midst
of horrible sufferings, but always with an unshakable courage.
They welcomed death, if not with joy, at least with serenity,
since it put an end to their martyrdom. And Whitman — a
little like Montaigne — kept wondering at the ease with which
all these uncultivated young men accepted death without ever
having been prepared for it. Living in the midst of the dying
gradually hardened him and it soon seemed to him that death
was not quite so redoubtable as he had imagined. (In fact, a
few years before he had prayed for it, but the very fact that
he had already forgotten that earlier state of mind is the best
proof of his recovery.) He eventually saw in it a benevolent
force and a liberator:

> Lingering and extreme suffering from wounds or sickness seem
> to me far worse than death in battle. I can honestly say the latter
> has no terrors for me, as far as I myself am concerned . . . Of
> the many I have seen die . . . I have not seen or known one
> who met death with terror. In most cases I should say it was a
> welcome relief and release.[261]
>
> This then, what frightened us all so long. Why, it is put to
> flight with ignominy — a mere stuffed scarecrow of the fields.
> Oh death, where is thy sting? Oh grave, where is thy victory? [262]

And so, at the end of the war, on the occasion of Lincoln's
death, he sang of "sane and sacred death," [263] "lovely and

soothing," "cool-enfolding," "strong deliveress." [264] Thus it appeared to him more and more as a refuge and a comfort. For, if he intones such a hymn of joy at the thought of death, it is because life is sad. Through the entire poem there resounds contrapuntally a note of poignant melancholy which does not derive from Lincoln's death, but from an older deeper sadness. Does not he avow to us that he suffered from insomnia at that period? [265] He does not tell us the cause of that dull pain, but it is clear that life was once more disappointing him. He saw around him too many skeptics, too many greedy and unscrupulous shysters. The ordinary activities of men seemed to him nothing but a vain and sterile agitation.[266] And that is probably the reason why, when revising "On the Beach at Night Alone," he canceled the whole passage where, in 1856, he voiced his reluctance to die and his desire to remain as long as possible here below.[267]

In 1871, he expressed the same profound dissatisfaction, the same eagerness to escape to a world which would at last fill the emptiness of his heart:

> The untold want by life and land ne'er granted,
> Now voyager sail thou forth to seek and find.[268]

Consequently, as he grew older, a growing weariness detached him from life and made him envisage death with more and more serenity:

> O Death (for Life has served its turn,)
> . . .
> Be thou my God,[269]

he exclaimed in 1870.

> . . . O soul, thou actual Me,
> . . .
> Thou . . . smilest content at Death . . .[270]

In 1869 he again, as in 1860, went so far as to wish to die immediately:

Passage, immediate passage! the blood burns in my
veins!
Away O soul! hoist instantly the anchor! [271]

But his despair, mainly caused this time by the collapse of
his political dreams, did not last and he soon resigned himself
to living and to waiting patiently for death.

Also, with time, his conception of death became increasingly spiritualistic. He grew tired of matter and of his body; he
wanted his soul to be free at last and to dissolve in time and
space:

To break the stagnant tie — thee, thee to free, O
soul . . .[272]

It was not I that sinn'd the sin,
The ruthless body dragg'd me in;
Though long I strove courageously,
The body was too much for me.
Dear prison'd soul bear up space,
For soon or late the certain grace;
To set thee free and bear thee home,
The heavenly pardoner death shall come.[273]

He further explained his thought in the 1876 preface. His
intention, he said, was henceforward to sing

those convictions of perpetuity and conservation which, enveloping all precedents, make the unseen soul govern absolutely at last
. . . [and to show] the resistless gravitation of Spiritual Law,
and with cheerful face estimating Death, not at all as the cessation, but as somehow what I feel it must be, the entrance upon by
far the greatest part of existence, and something that Life is as
much for, as it is for itself.[274]

In 1881, he went even so far as to replace in his "Song of
Joys" the exclamation:

O Death! the voyage of Death,

which he probably considered too flat, by this dithyrambic line:

> For not life's joys alone I sing, repeating — the joy of
> death! [275]

In spite of this enthusiasm, he still on many occasions experienced moments of doubt and fear, "downcast hours,"
when he wondered with anguish if the soul really survived
the body and if it was not matter alone which was eternal.[276]
Sometimes, too, though ready to die and already taking leave
of his friends, he thought with pangs of regret of all that he
was going to leave and felt "loth to depart." [277]

But such falterings did not last. Good Hegelian that he was,
Whitman knew how to resign himself to the necessity of death,
the antithesis to life,[278] and, in 1891, he once more declared
himself ready to weigh anchor and set off far from the shore
on the deep waters of death:

> I will not call it our concluding voyage,
> But outset and sure entrance to the truest, best, ma-
> turest . . .[279]

Thus, during his whole life, Whitman was strangely fascinated by death. Does it mean that he was afraid of it, as
some have maintained, and that he sang of it in a strong voice
to reassure himself, like a child who whistles while going
through a wood alone? It seems rather that, in spite of his
love of life, death exercised a curious and almost morbid
attraction upon him and that he was more and more drawn
to it. In 1855–1856 he celebrated it as the equal of life of
which it was the natural extension, just as sleep is the natural
extension of waking; then from 1857 to 1860 came the years
of sexual torment when death and voluptuousness were confused; the war calmed him and from then on he considered
death as a deliverance; he spiritualized it; it was no longer
synonymous with sexual ecstasy, but, on the contrary, promised
a calm, ethereal, and serene life.

He himself offered, in "A Persian Lesson," an explanation

of the attraction which death exercised over him and, he claimed, over all men as well. He saw in it a manifestation of what some psychoanalysts nowadays call the "death-wish," a desire for annihilation.

> . . . the urge and spur of every life;
> The something never still'd — never entirely gone,
>   the invisible need of every seed.
> It is the central urge in every atom . . .
> To return to its divine source and origin, however distant . . .[280]

Perhaps, too, in his case, it was the nostalgia for that purely physiological happiness which the embryo feels in the womb of its mother. Certain passages suggest this subconscious regret and give some appearance of verisimilitude to psychoanalytical explanation. When, for example, addressing himself to night, which is always associated in his mind with death, he declares:

> I will duly pass the day O mother, and duly return to you.[281]

And, again, in his elegy on the death of Lincoln, he calls the ocean, death, his "dark mother," and says:

> And the soul turning to thee O vast and well-veil'd death,
> And the body gratefully nestling close to thee.[282]

Death undeniably attracts him, but how does he conceive of the after-life? It seems that all his life he hesitated between the mystical concept of a dissolution in the Great All and the belief in personal survival. Sometimes he distinguishes them, sometimes he confuses and reconciles them.

In 1855–1856, he evokes with serene indifference the decomposition of corpses — his own as well as others — the elements of which are immediately put back into service to form new beings.[283] On this point he unreservedly adopts the conclusions of positive science. For him, as for chemists, "nothing is lost, nothing is created, everything is transformed." But he did not stop there. As he himself declared in one of the anonymous reviews he wrote for the first edition of *Leaves of Grass*: "He is a true spiritualist. He recognizes no annihilation, or death, or loss of identity." [284]

According to him, our body and our terrestrial life have conferred a certain individuality ("identity") upon our soul and death is incapable of destroying it.[285] In 1860, he developed this idea: our body is not really ourself and we can leave it behind after our death as a residue; our essential being is not at all changed. Our "real body," that is to say, our soul, which is modeled after our body, survives intact after the chemical decomposition of our "excrementitious body," [286]

> Myself discharging my excrementitious body to be
>   burn'd, or render'd to powder, or buried,
> My real body doubtless left to me for other spheres,
> My voided body nothing more to me, returning to the
>   purifications, further offices, eternal uses of the
>   earth.[287]

This is the period when he celebrates the body, when death appears to him hardly believable and, in any case, hardly different from life, and living, according to him, consists in earning ". . . for the body and the mind whatever adheres and goes forward and is not dropt by death . . ." [288]

But, after the war, he asked only to be dissolved and lost. Dying became for him synonymous with the mystical fusion of the individual soul in the soul of the universe:

> Then we burst forth, we float,
> In Time and Space O soul, prepared for them,
> Equal, equipt at last, (O joy! O fruit of all!) them to
>   fulfil O soul.[289]

"All, all, toward the mystic Ocean tending," he exclaimed

in 1876.[290] But he nonetheless continued to believe in the persistence of individuality after death, for that same year he wrote in a projected preface for *Two Rivulets*: "The Body and the Soul are one, and in the latter, the former is immortal," [291] which recalls his notions of "real body" and of "identity." Moreover, in 1881, on the occasion of Carlyle's death, he solemnly reaffirmed his faith:

And now that he has gone hence, can it be that Thomas Carlyle, soon to chemically dissolve in ashes and by winds, remains an identity? . . . I have no doubt of it.[292]

To his mind, these are not two contradictory conceptions, but rather two complementary aspects of the same reality. As early as 1860 he wrote:

Melange mine own, the unseen and the seen,
Mysterious ocean where the streams empty . . .
Living beings, identities now doubtless near us in the
air that we know not of . . .[293]

In 1865, he defined his "Santa Spirita" as the "essence of forms, life of the real identities." [294] Thus, for him, souls were at the same time distinct entities and parts of the whole, endowed with an indestructible individuality and run through by the great current of universal life which animates all that is, as he explained in *Democratic Vistas*:

. . . the pulsations in all matter, all spirit, throbbing forever — the eternal beats, eternal systole and diastole of life in things . . .[295]

And so the essence of each being is both "unfix'd yet fix'd," [296] static and dynamic, but, in any event, eternal.

Up to his old age Whitman retained this duality in his point of view. In 1888, a few pages apart in the same book, he proclaimed the immortality of "identities," [297] and then defined death as "A haze — nirwana — rest and night — oblivion." [298]

By that he meant dissolution, fusion, loss in the soul of the world.

All his life, consequently, Whitman retained his faith in the existence of that great cosmic life force of which he had had the revelation during the mystical ecstasies of his youth. Though his own vitality waned with age, he never ceased to believe in the inextinguishable and eternal vitality of the universe, and he saw there a guarantee of his own survival. The arguments of Ingersoll, the most eloquent of the agnostics of his time, never shook his conviction.[299] But he never lapsed into dogmatism, for he had no illusions about the purely subjective character of his belief. He knew very well that life and death are insoluble problems which each generation vainly attempts to solve. He realized that he had succeeded no more than his predecessors in piercing the mystery.[300]

Yet, in his youth, he had been more presumptuous and had tried to define with some precision what he meant by the survival of the soul. Indeed one finds a trace in his first poems of a curious doctrine which recalls the metempsychosis of Pythagoras[301] and certain eastern religions.[302] Several poems of 1855–1856 very clearly imply a belief in the transfer and reincarnation of souls.[303]

> And as to you Life I reckon you are the leavings of
>   many deaths,
> (No doubt I have died myself ten thousand times be-
>   fore.)
> I hear you whispering there O stars of heaven,
> O suns — O grass of graves — O perpetual transfers
>   and promotions . . .[304]

In 1871, at the moment of taking leave of his reader, he added in "So Long!"

> I receive now again of my many translations, from my
>   avataras ascending, while others doubtless await
>   me . . .
> Remember my words, I may again return . . .[305]

(He even used the Sanscrit form of the word "avatar.")[306]

His evolutionism, besides, reinforced and confirmed this belief. He imagined himself in turn a mineral, a plant, a bird, a quadruped, and finally a man.[307] He saw himself watching his herd on the Asiatic steppes, exploring Kamtschatka in a sledge, then temporarily settled in the Ganges valley and adoring the divinities of ancient India, and so on and on.[308]

This doctrine, at least at the outset, implied the idea of moral retribution:

> Not one word or deed . . .
> But has results beyond death as really as before death.[309]

> Are your body, days, manners, superb? after death you
> shall be superb . . .[310]

Thus the Christian notion of sin and punishment persisted, but in a very diffuse manner. Moreover, probably under the influence of transcendentalist optimism and in particular of Emerson's essay on "Compensation," [311] he refused to admit the idea of eternal damnation. On the contrary, for him, sooner or later all will be saved, for all the transfers undergone by living beings are "promotions." Each one rises gradually in the hierarchy of the universe.[312] There is never any mention in his poems of setbacks or regressions. Sinners are only "laggards" who will one day catch up with their betters:

> In each house is the ovum, it comes forth after a thou-
> sand years.[313]

These moral preoccupations, however, appear almost exclusively in his first poems. Very soon apparently Whitman ceased to be interested in that aspect of the matter. Yet he retained his belief in reincarnation much longer. In 1871, he still sang of the "many deaths" of each being [314] and, in 1876, in "Eidólons," he described life as a series of cycles:

> Ever the dim beginning,

Ever the growth, the rounding of the circle,
Ever the summit and the merge at last, (to surely start
again,) . . .[315]

But, in his last writings, even though his faith in the immortality of the soul remained unchanged, he no longer seemed
to believe in the possibility of a return. The yacht of his soul
was bearing off from the shores of this earth and would never
return to it, he thought.[316]

What caused this change? Probably the slow decline of his
strength. Gradually his senses lost their hold on him, his body
more and more appeared to him as a burden. Death would
rid him of it. So why should he wish to be reincarnated? To
experience the torments of the flesh again? He preferred to
survive in an immaterial form. We find here again his leaning
toward spiritualism, which was reinforced, as we have seen,
by his distrust of all categorical positions before the insoluble
mystery of death. "May be," "who knows?" he murmurs at the
moment of bidding goodbye for ever to his fancy.[317]

So Whitman's position with regard to the different problems
posed by existence and the nature of God and of the soul,
by evil and death, always followed approximately the same
evolution. In 1855–1856, in the full flush of youth and under
the influence of his mystic illuminations, he proceeded by
passionate affirmations and proclaimed with fervor his faith
in God and his belief in the immortality of the soul and the
excellence of life. Then came all sorts of physical and moral
trials, moments of doubt and of despair. But he triumphed
over these crises one after the other and in his old age attained
a perfect serenity which permitted him, until his death, to
sing, with more purity, but less force, the same themes as in
his youth. Moreover the gradual quieting of his desires and of
the torments of his flesh made him lean more and more toward
a spiritualistic conception of the world and of human destiny.
In spite of this evolution, however, he remained all his life

astonishingly faithful to himself and never repudiated the image of himself which he presented to his reader in his first book. But, helped by his reading, he became more and more clearly conscious of the particularities of his position,[318] without ever letting this progressive intellectualization dry him up; it only made him better understand the infinite complexity of the problems. So he approached them at the end of his life with a sincere humility and no longer with the assurance and presumption of his youth. In this respect the following remarks which he once made to Traubel in 1888 very plainly show both the persistence of his faith and the complete absence of dogmatism which characterize his last years:

Of all things, I imagine I am most lacking in what is called definiteness, in so far as that applies to special theories of life and death. As I grow older I am more firmly than ever fixed in my belief that all things tend to good, that no bad is forever bad, that the universe has its own ends to subserve and will subserve them well. Beyond that, when it comes to launching out into mathematics — tying philosophy to the multiplication table — I am lost — lost utterly. Let them all whack away — I am satisfied: if they can explain, let them explain: if they can explain, they can do more than I can do. I am not Anarchist, not Methodist, not anything you can name. Yet I see why all the ists and isms and haters and dogmatists exist — can see why they must exist and why I must include them all.[319]

CHAPTER III

THE ETHICS

AT first sight this title is surprising. Can one, indeed, speak of an ethical philosophy in the case of a pantheist who deifies life in its totality, evil included, who attributes to evil the same value as to good and believes it necessary to the becoming of the world?

> Great is wickedness [he even dared to write in 1855],
>   I find I often admire it just as much as I admire
>   goodness;
> Do you call that a paradox? It certainly is a paradox.[1]

> What blurt is this about virtue and about vice?
> Evil propels me and reform of evil propels me, I stand
>   indifferent.[2]

In one of the notebooks which he used between 1850 and 1855 he went even so far as to deny the validity of the notion of sin:

> I am the poet of sin
> For I do not believe in sin.[3]

In *Leaves of Grass* he refuses to make the slightest distinction between sinners and the just. They have the same value in his eyes:

> This is the meat equally set, this the meat for natural
>   hunger,

It is for the wicked just the same as the righteous, I
    make appointments with all,
I will not have a single person slighted or left away,
The kept woman, sponger, thief, are hereby in-
    vited . . .
There shall be no difference between them and the
    rest.[4]

For him all men are strictly equal since they are all equally
repositories of the same principle of life. The mere fact of
existence implies perfection:

I do not call one greater and one smaller,
That which fills its period and place is equal to any.[5]

And so he neither condemns nor damns anyone:

The little plentiful manikins skipping around in collars
    and tail'd coats . . .
I acknowledge the duplicates of myself, the weakest
    and shallowest is deathless with me . . .[6]

Why should he look away from the prostitute? The sun
does not refuse her its light.[7] Moreover, there is no fundamental difference between sinning in action and sinning in
thought, and we have all sinned in thought. All men are
equally guilty.[8] Evil is inextricably mixed with good and forms
with it a Gordian knot which no one can untie.[9] Under these
conditions, all judgments of value are impossible and all attempts at moralizing absurd as he himself recognizes in the
1855 preface:

The greatest poet does not moralize or make applica-
    tions of morals.[10]

This mystical amoralism is accompanied by a violent reaction against puritan ethics. He admits no sexual taboo [11] and
proclaims the sacred character of the reproductive organs of
men and women. Prefiguring modern psychoanalysts he even

shows the evils of repression and denounces asceticism.[12] Who tries to be an angel, becomes a beast, Pascal said. For his part, Whitman would gladly choose to be a beast; he often envies the happy and healthy life of animals who are fettered by no morality.[13] According to him, one must follow one's instincts instead of repressing them. As a result of his love of life, he becomes, like the romantics, the apologist of a passion which permits us to participate more intensely in the becoming of the world. He despises "neuters and geldings" and favors "men and women fully equipt." [14]

That enthusiasm and the boldness of those principles singularly differ from the views he put forth during the same period (1857–1859) in his editorials for the *Brooklyn Times*.[15] One can scarcely believe that the fiery revolutionary poet of *Leaves of Grass* from 1855 to 1860 was the same person as this prudent journalist. True, the newspaper for which he was working was his livelihood and he had to take into account the prejudices of his readers, but, nonetheless, at first sight, the man that he claimed to be in his poems bears only a remote resemblance to what he was in real life. This antinomy, however, is more apparent than real and the difference becomes less important when one discovers, under the aggressive amoralism of his first poems, the elements of a morality which is still to some extent traditional.

Indeed one must not forget that he celebrates good as well as evil and that his amoralism never turns into immoralism. On the contrary, he has a very sharp sense of certain values, of justice, for instance, which he regards as an unalterable absolute:

> Great is Justice!
> Justice is not settled by legislators and laws — it is in
>   the Soul . . .
> It is immutable — it does not depend on majori-
>   ties . . .[16]

Thus he still believes in the dictates of conscience and also in what he calls Truth, that is, as it appears, the belief in God and in immortality.[17] For he understands and forgives everything except a lack of faith:

> The wonder is always and always how there can be a mean man or an infidel.[18]

And not only does he think some religious faith necessary, but he still retains in the inmost recesses of his heart the notion of sin from which, in his moments of mystical exaltation, he may seem to be free. "The difference between sin and goodness is no delusion," he peremptorily affirmed in 1855.[19] Besides, in spite of his sensuality and apparent epicureanism, he sometimes advocates rules of conduct which are in fact quite close to stoicism:

> O while I live to be the ruler of life, not a slave,
> To meet life as a powerful conqueror . . .
> To these proud laws of the air, the water, and the
> ground, proving my interior impregnable,
> And nothing exterior shall ever take command of me.[20]

These internal contradictions came from the fact that he was torn between his instincts and the Christian morality which had been inculcated upon him, between his instinctive materialism and his spiritualistic aspirations. It is symptomatic that in 1876, when his spiritualism triumphed,[21] he insisted upon the moral significance of his poetic work:

> Since I have been ill (1873–74–75,) mostly without serious pain, and with plenty of time and frequent inclination to judge my poems . . . I have felt temporary depression more than once; for fear that in LEAVES OF GRASS the *moral* parts were not sufficiently pronounc'd. But in my clearest and calmest moods I have realized that as those LEAVES, all and several, surely prepare the way for, and necessitate Morals, and are adjusted to them, just the same as Nature does and is, they are what, consistently

with my plan, they must and probably should be . . . (In a certain sense, while the Moral is the purport and last intelligence of all Nature, there is absolutely nothing of the moral in the works, or laws, or shows of Nature. Those only lead inevitably to it — begin and necessitate it.) [22]

Thus, of course, he does not claim to have written a moralizing and preaching poetry like Whittier; he is convinced, however, that his works express a very high morality which may not be what is usually meant by that word, but which is in harmony with the deeper meaning of the world.

We have already brought out certain principles of this implicit morality, but they recalled traditional morality and presented no original characteristics. That to which Whitman makes allusion in the passage above is rather the notion of "prudence," on which, indeed, his entire moral philosophy is based. This "prudence" which he also calls sometimes "caution," sometimes "wisdom" — which is the Latin meaning of "prudence" — appeared as early as 1855 in the preface to *Leaves of Grass*; [23] in the following edition he devoted an entire poem to it, the "Song of Prudence." [24] In spite of this fine enthusiasm, neither the word nor the idea are quite his own. He borrowed them from Emerson. [25] But he has so well assimilated his borrowing that almost no one has noticed it. What does he mean by this strange notion? For him, "prudence" is the sense of the infinity of time and space where our actions have repercussions, the never-sleeping consciousness of the supreme importance of their distant consequences beyond their immediate effects, and the result is not prudence in the usual sense of that word, but disinterested self-sacrifice and love. For, at the moment of acting, one must not be preoccupied with the practical results, the "direct" consequences of our action, with the pleasure or the ephemeral advantage which we may derive from it, but with its "indirect" consequences, as much for others here below as for ourselves after our death. According to him, the least of our acts lastingly, even eternally, modifies our soul (this is the equivalent of the notion of mortal sin) and the fate of our "identity," of our individual soul, is for ever changed by it (which is the equivalent of the Christian notion of responsibility and punishment). The most trivial of our deeds has infinite extensions, which he calls "spiritual results," [26] and which resemble Emerson's "compensations." [27] After death, there will be neither forgiveness nor expiation.[28] Everyone will have to expiate his sins; the injustices of this world will be rectified while sacrifices and heroic deeds will be rewarded.[29] And so he reaches the conclusion that:

> Charity and personal force are the only investments worth any thing.[30]

That is the reason why he has celebrated in the epic mode in his first *Leaves of Grass* the indomitable courage of the revolutionaries of 1848,[31] of John Paul Jones, the commander of the *Bonhomme Richard*,[32] the rescuers of the *San Francisco*,[33] and the prisoners massacred near Goliad in Texas.[34]

This problem of the compensation of earthly injustices preoccupied him a great deal in the years 1855–1856 and he devoted several poems to it.[35] Was not it one of the aspects of that problem of evil which he so much wanted to solve? But his "prudence," which was essentially an awareness of what he called "ensemble," and his pantheistic optimism prevented him from believing in eternal damnation. Here he broke with Christianity. Though punishment seemed to him necessary, he could not resign himself to the loss of a single soul and to the irremediable separation of the wicked from the good,[36] all men being equal and, like him, of divine origin.[37] Sinners and degenerates would gradually rise in the hierarchy of living beings and would sooner or later become themselves at last and catch up with the just. He had a presentiment of this in

1855 while contemplating the "faces" of those who passed him by in the street,[38] and he proclaimed it in 1876: "Health, peace, salvation universal." [39] In short, on this point, he is closer to the Buddhists than to the Christians.

But how could he condemn anyone when he was persuaded that "wickedness is most likely the absence of freedom and health in the soul?" [40] For him, the body and the soul are interdependent, but, contrary to Mary Baker Eddy, he believed more, at least at that period, in the influence of the body upon the soul than in that of the soul upon the body. Thus, if the body is ill, the soul will be unhealthy, and, consequently, the drunkard,[41] the glutton, the unchaste person are no more responsible for their condition than a congenital idiot. His materialism, in other words, leads him to deny free will in such cases; but for himself or for those whose bodies are healthy and vigorous, such servitude is out of the question. "Healthy, free, the world before [them], the long brown path before [them]" leads them "wherever [they] choose." [42]

True, they are subject to gravity and to all the laws which govern the physical as well as the moral world (to his eyes there is no fundamental difference between the two),[43] but they are nonetheless free to play their parts well or ill, "the role that is great or small according as one makes it." [44] This is a paradox which Christianity also admits and of which he became increasingly conscious. Thus is 1871 he wrote:

> With time and space I him dilate and fuse the immortal laws,
> To make himself by them the law unto himself.[45]

As he grew older, he more and more insisted on that idea of the freedom of the soul which lives in harmony with the world, for age liberated him from his passions, and his struggle with paralysis revealed to him the extent of the power of the soul. So he devoted to free will an entire prose note in *Two Rivulets* in 1876: [46]

While we are from birth to death the subjects of irresistible law, enclosing every movement and minute, we yet escape, by a paradox, into true free will. Strange as it may seem, we only attain to freedom by a knowledge of, and implicit obedience to, Law. Great — unspeakably great — is the Will! the free Soul of man! . . . The shallow, as intimated, consider liberty a release from all law, from every constraint. The wise see in it, on the contrary, the potent Law of Laws, namely the fusion and combination of the conscious will, or partial individual law, with those universal, eternal, unconscious ones, which run through all Time, pervade history, prove immortality, give moral purpose to the entire objective world, and the last dignity to human life.[47]

And that is why he celebrated in the same year in "Eidólons," "the separate countless free identities." [48]

Such is his ideal. But how is one to carry it out? One solution would be to abandon everything and set out, poor but merry, on the open road, in search of beauty, happiness, love, and infinity; [49] but Whitman never took to that open road which he pointed out with a flourish to his disciples. The other solution — and this is the one he adopted — consists in remaining in the city, in accepting life in the community, but relentlessly questioning everything and seeking beyond the routine of institutions and beliefs the living spirit of which they are or have been the emanation.[50] And, therefore, Whitman in 1855, in spite of his outward conformity,[51] was led by his mystical morality to condemn the materialism, the greed, the "mania of owning things" [52] of his fellow-beings who walked through life with dimes on their eyes [53] and wasted their lives earning a livelihood, as Juvenal had already pointed out.[54] For, in 1855, he regarded work as a harmful and dangerous activity which diverted man from the true end of life. In this respect, animals, it seemed to him, are superior to us: "they do not sweat," they are not "industrious." [55] On this point he disapproved of Carlyle's Gospel of Work, of his "laborare est orare," which so well sums up the puritan ideal of life. But, with the years, Whitman's opinion about work changed. He fairly soon understood the importance and necessity of it in a new country and he stopped condemning it. Such is probably the reason why, in 1881, he no longer said of animals "not one is . . . industrious," but "not one is . . . unhappy." [56]

Besides these recommendations of an essentially negative character, Whitman's morality does not contain any precise precept. The supreme duty is to believe and to behave like a free man. That done, you have only to abandon yourself to the becoming of the world. For, if you conform to the great law of the universe, you will find yourself obeying all the little secondary laws which, to men of little faith, impose duties, but which for you will become sources of living impulses:

> I give nothing as duties,
> What others give as duties I give as living impulses,
> (Shall I give the heart's action as a duty?) [57]

For the man who lives in harmony with the immense current of force which runs through the world, a moral comportment is as natural and instinctive as the functioning of the organs of the body. Here is the morality of a mystic. It abolishes the notion of duty and springs quite naturally from the vitalism and optimism of his metaphysics.

For Whitman, whoever conforms with these principles will find happiness. For he believed in the possibility of happiness here below and he proclaimed it in the preface to his first edition of *Leaves of Grass.*[58] This was not, however, the same sort of happiness as that which the French "philosophes" and, after them, the authors of the American Constitution recognized as the birthright of all men. For him it was not synonymous with the free and peaceful enjoyment of the goods which you accumulate by work and industry, but with the feeling of plenitude which you experience when you let yourself be carried away into the infinity of space by the whirling earth, when you hurl yourself with hope and confidence into a future still more marvelous than the present.

Did he forget the infirmities and illnesses which follow in the wake of old age? One might indeed believe that a conception of life so resolutely optimistic reflects the presumption of a young man, full of strength and incapable of imagining that one day he will be old and weak. But not at all. There is no lack of foresight there, only the consequence of a principle. As early as 1855 Whitman considered life not as a slow and inexorable decline, but, on the contrary, as a constant and uninterrupted ascent toward death which itself would only be the beginning of a freer and more satisfying existence. He did not admit the Christian dogma of the fall of man. According to him, the fate of every being is a steadily ascending curve from the first drop of protoplasm to our incarnation in the body of a man.[59] Our earthly life being only a section of that curve, our old age occupies a privileged position on it by comparison with our youth. And so he sang of "old age superbly rising" [60] and "the welcome, ineffable grace of dying days." [61] In 1860, he delighted in evoking beautiful and noble old men:

> One sweeps by, old, with black eyes, and profuse white hair,
> He has the simple magnificence of health and strength,
> His face strikes as with flashes of lightning whoever it turns toward.[62]

He went so far as to imagine himself old:

> O the old manhood of me, my noblest joy of all!
> My children and grand-children, my white hair and beard,

My largeness, calmness, majesty, out of the long stretch
of my life.[63]

It was at this time that he cut out of the newspapers all
the articles that dealt with cases of exceptional longevity,
which proves that he was vividly interested in the problem
and that he aspired to reach a good old age himself.[64] But it
is to be noted that all the old men he evokes have remained
strong and vigorous, in perfect health. Under these conditions,
one realizes what a disaster his stroke of paralysis must have
been for him. He was left an invalid at only fifty-four years
of age. This was the collapse of all his dreams. But, as we have
seen, he refused to acknowledge defeat, fought tenaciously
and valiantly with the disease and eventually triumphed over
it. After a few years nothing more than a light infirmity remained and in 1881 he could take up again, at the age of
sixty-two, the imprudent declaration which he had made
in 1855:

Youth, large, lusty, loving — Youth, full of grace,
force, fascination!
Do you know that Old Age may come after you, with
equal grace, force, fascination? [65]

His own life had proved it and continued to prove it. Until
the end, in spite of the redoubled assaults of disease, he endeavored to remain true to himself, to bear all his trials without recrimination, to compensate for the decline of his forces
by the dignity of his bearing. To a large extent he succeeded;
his photographs show it and his friends have borne witness
to it. His face, in aging, attained an Olympian serenity.
Shortly before his death, he confided to Dr. Longaker, who
was taking care of him, that it was a very fine thing to grow
old gracefully.[66] This simple detail shows to what extent he
was anxious to remain faithful to his own moral notion of
progress.

Such an undertaking, however, demanded vigilance and constant efforts. But this poet, who is too often imagined as a mere indolent dreamer, had, deep in his heart, a tenacious and indomitable will which enabled him to maintain his life until the end in the direction he had chosen. He was not just that swimmer whom he sometimes evokes, who lets himself be rocked by the waves; he was also the pilot who guides his ship among the rapids with admirable sureness and who knows where he is going.[67] So it is not surprising that he took for his master Epictetus, whose *Enchiridion* he read off and on all his life. He discovered it in his youth in a second-hand bookshop in New York and in 1888 he confided to Traubel:

Epictetus is the one of all my cronies who has lasted to this day without cutting a diminished figure in my perspective. He belongs with the best — is a universe in himself. He sets me free in a flood of light . . .[68]

Toward this period he had one of the maxims of the *Enchiridion* printed on his stationery.[69] It is thus quite probable that his reading of Epictetus reinforced his indomitable pride.

Pride, did we say? This was indeed one aspect of his secret will and toughness. He often used the word himself, as in these two lines from "The Mystic Trumpeter" which so well sum up his life of struggle:

Yet 'mid the ruins Pride colossal stands unshaken to
    the last,
Endurance, resolution to the last.[70]

This pride, which probably was natural to him, was also partly the result of his pantheistic attitude. All pantheism leads to pride, since, in this system, God being immanent in man, man becomes an emanation of God. In the first *Leaves of Grass,* man is constantly deified and exalted:

It is also not consistent with the reality of the soul to admit that there is anything in the known universe more divine than men and women.[71]

> Divine am I inside and out, and I make holy what-
>   ever I touch or am touch'd from . . .[72]
> And nothing, not God, is greater to one than one's self
>   is . . .[73]

This pride was not special to Whitman; it was current in the nineteenth century, an epoch when man was breaking free from traditional churches and discovering, with science, his unlimited power over matter,[74] but, with Whitman, this feeling was frequently sobered down by the humility which the thought of the infinity of the universe and its awesome mystery imposed upon him, at least in his moments of depression.[75] In 1888, however, he still affirmed in his preface to *November Boughs*:

Defiant of ostensible literary and other conventions, I avowedly chant "the great pride of man in himself," and permit it to be more or less a *motif* of nearly all my verse. I think this pride indispensable to an American. I think it not inconsistent with obedience, humility, deference, and self-questioning.[76]

So, on the moral as on the metaphysical plane, Whitman's thought, for all his hesitations and gropings, remains on the whole remarkably consistent. However, though in 1876 and again in *November Boughs* (in the notes on Elias Hicks) [77] he insisted on the supreme importance of moral philosophy and on the moral content of his works, nearly all the poems which we have quoted in this chapter date from the years 1855–1860. Apparently, in spite of his declarations of principle, he ceased to be interested in the matter after 1860 and, indeed, as we will see in studying his ideas on democracy he had, after the war, preoccupations of another kind.

CHAPTER IV

THE FUNDAMENTAL AESTHETICS

W HITMAN'S aesthetics derives quite naturally from his mysticism. For, in poetry, he saw above all the expression of the supreme truths which had been revealed to him. So, though he took pleasure in reading Homer, Shakespeare, and Walter Scott's narrative poems, he conceived no other poetry but lyric poetry. As to the novels whose aim is mere entertainment, he had nothing but contempt for them.[1] To his mind, the purpose of any literature worthy of the name is not to entertain but to bring the reader's soul into contact with the soul of the world. He never diverged from that opinion. In the preface to the 1855 edition of *Leaves of Grass* Whitman expresses the same views as he does in the *Democratic Vistas* of 1871 and the essay on "Poetry To-day in America" which he published ten years later and reprinted in 1892 in his *Complete Works*.[2] The poet is he who "sees the farthest" and "has the most faith." [3] The great man of letters (in the Carlylean sense of the word) is known by "his limitless faith in God, his reverence and by the absence in him of doubt . . ." [4] He deciphers Nature —

. . . the only complete, actual poem, existing calmly in the divine scheme, containing all, content, careless of the criticisms of a day or these endless and wordy chatterers.

He is conscious of the existence of

. . . the soul, the permanent identity, the thought, the something . . . that fully satisfies . . . That something is the All, and the idea of the All, with the accompanying idea of eternity, and of itself, the soul, buoyant, indestructible, sailing space forever, visiting every region, as a ship the sea.

He feels life circulating through all things,

. . . the pulsations in all matter, all spirit, throbbing forever — the eternal beats, eternal systole and diastole of life in things . . .

And he thus knows that neither the soul nor matter ever die.[5]

In other words, for Whitman, the poet is essentially a seer[6] and a prophet in the broad meaning of the word, such as he defined it himself in *Specimen Days*:

The word prophecy is much misused; it seems narrow'd to prediction merely. That is not the main sense of the Hebrew word translated "prophet"; it means one whose mind bubbles up and pours forth as a fountain, from inner, divine spontaneities revealing God. Prediction is a very minor part of prophecy. The great matter is to reveal and outpour the God-like suggestions pressing for birth in the soul. This is briefly the doctrine of the Friends or Quakers.[7]

On this point, he was near not only to the doctrine of the Quakers, but also to the romantic [8] — and transcendentalist [9] — conception of the visionary poet. The poet whom he called up in his preface to the 1855 edition, and whom he intended to become, is in relation to mankind what sight is in relation to man: he sees eternity latent in men and women [10] and his glance pierces the future; "he places himself where the future becomes present." [11] Like the old Testament prophets, he leads his fellow-countrymen in wartime and shakes their inertia in peacetime.[12]

Whitman's ambition in 1855 was still higher; his rival and model was Christ. Indeed, in the first version of *Leaves of Grass*, he introduces himself as the successor and even as a

reincarnation of the Messiah.[13] He too brings a message of
solace to the poor and to all social outcasts,[14] and, like Christ,
he leads his disciples along the open roads of the world [15] and
stops from time to time to preach to the crowd that follows
him:

> A call in the midst of the crowd,
> My own voice, orotund sweeping and final.
> Come my children,
> Come my boys and girls . . .[16]

He leans over the slave at work in the cotton-fields or the
servant who has just cleaned the privies, and puts on his cheek
the kiss of peace.[17] He visits the sick as they pant on their
beds, and, outbidding all "the old cautious hucksters" of the
religions which preceded him,[18] he brings to all the good news
that death and evil are mere illusions and that all shall be
saved. What is more, he works miracles and restores the dying
to health:

> To any one dying, thither I speed and twist the knob
>   of the door,
> Turn the bed-clothes toward the foot of the bed,
> Let the physician and the priest go home.
> I seize the descending man and raise him with resist-
>   less will . . .
> I have embraced you, and henceforth possess you to
>   myself,
> And when you rise in the morning you will find that
>   what I tell you is so.[19]

It was probably at that time that he proposed to write a new
Bible to be finished in 1859 which was to include 365 parts,
in order that the faithful might have one text to read and
meditate upon every day of the year.[20] He even thought for a
time of writing a new burial service.[21]

This exaltation, however, was to subside fairly soon and
such lyrical exaggerations are no longer to be found in later

editions. Though he still treated Christ as an equal in 1860 in "To Him that was Crucified," [22] most of the time from then on he gave up posing as the savior of mankind and the founder of a new religion. He was now merely one prophet among many others, the John the Baptist who announces the coming of poets greater than himself:

> I announce greater offspring, orators, days and then
> depart.[23]

In 1872, wishing to reaffirm ostentatiously his faith in the future of democracy, he prophesied again (in the narrow meaning of the word), but he did so with modesty and without claiming any supernatural powers:

> Now trumpeter for thy close . . .
> Rouse up my slow belief, give me some vision of the
> future,
> Give me for once its prophecy and joy.[24]

He now introduced himself as a mere precursor of the "resplendent coming literati," "sacerdotal bards," and "kosmic savans" who would adorn the democracy of the future.[25] This moderation surprises after the bombast and pretentiousness of his first poems. It can probably be accounted for by the decline of his forces, and it is likely that it was imposed upon him by the hard lessons of life and the relative failure of his work. This belated modesty did not prevent his first disciples, R. M. Bucke and Horace Traubel, for instance, from considering *Leaves of Grass* as the Bible of democracy and the Holy Book of a new civilization.[26] Whitman himself, though more and more reserved with regard to his personal role, nevertheless kept to the end of his life his belief in the quasi-sacred character of the poet as the successor of the prophets and priests in modern society.

> There will soon be no more priests. Their work is done . . .
> A superior breed shall take their place,[27]

he affirmed in 1855, and, in 1871, he repeated in *Democratic
Vistas*: "The priest departs, the divine literatus comes," [28]
taking up again on his own responsibility the theory Carlyle
had set forth in *Heroes and Hero-Worship*. In his opinion,
literature was the supreme art, and was destined to supplant
and supersede religion. This borrowed idea, which became
one of the main themes of *Democratic Vistas*,[29] is the principle
that guided all his life and inspired all his work.[30]

Besides, as befits a mystic, Whitman was deeply convinced
of the divine character of his inspiration. When he wrote, it
seemed to him that he was "divinely possessed, blind to all
subordinate affairs and given up entirely to the surgings and
utterances of the mighty tempestuous demon" that was in
him.[31] At such times, he can only "scream electric" and deliver
"curious envelop'd messages"; he has no will left; he is no
longer conscious and he acts passively, "[his] commission
obeying, to question it never daring." [32] In short, he is merely
a medium.[33]

The poets [he wrote in the margin of an article on poetry]
are the divine mediums — through them come spirits and materials to all the people, men and women.[34]

His songs, he asserted, spring from "irresistible impulses" [35]
"as total and irresistible as those which make the sea flow, or
the globe revolve." [36] As he grew older, of course, his inspiration gradually lost its strength and became short-winded, his
poems became shorter and shorter; in 1876, after his illness,
he even used the past tense to speak of his work, as if it were
completed,[37] and in his "Prayer of Columbus," he utters a cry
of doubt: "Is it the prophet's thought I speak, or am I
raving?" [38]

This doubt, however, was short-lived and soon overcome,
for in his preface of that year he congratulated himself precisely on having never repudiated, when winter came, the

songs which his soul had dictated to him during the summer
months.[39] And he never really doubted the authenticity of his
inspiration. In 1881, in "Spirit that form'd this Scene," he
even affirmed that the force which created the world and the
one which created his poems were akin.[40] Besides, up to the
time of his death, he lent an attentive ear to the increasingly
tenuous voice of his inspiration and piously collected its most
trivial utterances.

The inspired poet is thus one of the elect of God, but, as for
Whitman there exist close connections between the spirit and
the body, between spiritual purity and physical beauty,[41] the
poet is not only a person endowed with a superior spirituality;
he is also a man of an impeccable "physiology," who has received from nature "the soundest organic health" and a
vigorous well-fed body assimilating food completely.[42] Consequently, it is incumbent upon him to keep this choice organism
in a state of grace and to observe certain rules of physical
and moral hygiene.

In this respect, Whitman's aesthetics is inseparable from
his ethics and, his spiritualism being inextricably mixed up
with his materialism, his prescriptions concern the body as
well as the soul. He attempted very early to formulate a certain
number of rules of conduct meant to secure health and
longevity.[43] Numerous are the newspaper articles he devoted
to this subject in the *Brooklyn Eagle* and in the *Brooklyn
Times*. He believed neither in medicine nor in drugs; he put
all his hopes in hygiene and sport. Under the influence of
the Fowler brothers, he recommended to his readers that they
look after the cleanliness of their bodies and bathe frequently.
You gain a fine complexion by it, he declared, and a feeling
of great physical well-being.

A lightness and elasticity — a dissolving away of all heaviness
and dullness of spirits — a buoyancy become a habit of mind and
body in the bather.[44]

His enthusiasm shows that he was speaking from experience. And, for the same reason, he advised his contemporaries to go in for athletics.[45] Did not he at that time swim every day after his day's work? [46] Furthermore, according to Peter Doyle,[47] he never smoked and he drank very little. Though he had not always been so abstemious,[48] it is probable that, on the whole, he was quite temperate and that he was sincere when he wrote *Franklin Evans* — what he said about it later was only for fear of being laughed at.[49]

According to him, the strict observance of all these precepts enabled one to preserve good health and, in his opinion, health was of supreme importance.

The Egyptian priests (the Greeks also) regarded the preservation of health as a point of the first importance and indispensably necessary to the practice of piety and the service of the Gods.[50]

For, without health, there is no "magnetism," that is to say, no spiritual power, no inspiration, no effulgence, and, consequently, no poet.[51]

This physical hygiene, however, does not suffice; the poet must also conform his life to very strict moral rules. For poetry is a priestly function which demands complete self-denial. Whoever wants to serve it, must give up the pursuit of wealth and take a vow of poverty.

> You shall not heap what is call'd riches,
> You shall scatter with lavish hands all that you earn or
> achieve . . .[52]

He so advised his disciples in 1856, and he himself put into practice this ethic of absolute disinterestedness. He could have made a fortune as a contractor; he preferred to follow his vocation instead. As a journalist, he always refused to sacrifice his convictions to his career. During the Civil War, instead of trying to make money, he devoted himself to the service of the wounded and was later content with a modest clerkship in a government department. As a poet, lastly, he could rightly claim in 1876 that he had "never composed with an eye on the book-market, nor for fame, nor for any pecuniary profit," [53] for, right to the end, in spite of attacks and entreaties, he maintained in his book, almost without making any changes, the audacities of language and thought which hampered its sale and diffusion. He never had any needs beyond those which he defined in 1855:

> . . . a little sum laid aside for burial money and . . . a few clapboards around and shingle overhead on a lot of American soil owned, and the easy dollars that supply the year's plain clothing and meals.[54]

He always lived very frugally in almost miserable houses. His tomb was his only luxury. But this contempt for riches and this self-imposed poverty were, to his mind, the indispensable condition of the greatness of his poetry.

> Words follow character, nativity, independence, individuality . . .[55]

he thought. So he had to some extent to sacrifice his life to his work. He accepted this form of asceticism without any regret.[56]

The same austerity and sense of greatness are found again on the plane of pure aesthetics. For he despised that imaginative faculty which Wordsworth and Coleridge called "fancy" [57] and had nothing but contempt for ingenious images, far-fetched comparisons, and super-added ornaments — as well as for all exclusively narrative poetry.

> The theory and practice of poets [he wrote in 1856] have hitherto been to select certain ideas or events or personages, then describe them in the best manner they could, always with as much ornament as the case allowed. Such are not the theory and practice of the new poet.[58]

"He possesses the superiority of genuineness over fiction and romance," [59] he stated in a poem of the same year. So, according to him, the poet must celebrate the present and not the past, the real and not the imaginary. He insisted on this idea to the very end and reverted to it in 1888:

For grounds for *Leaves of Grass*, as a poem, I abandon'd the conventional themes, which do not appear in it: none of the stock ornamentation, or choice plots of love and war, or high, exceptional personages of Old World song: nothing, as I may say, for beauty's sake — no legend, myth, or romance, nor euphemism . . .[60]

Nothing is truer, except that, as he grew older, his repugnance to "fancy" decreased and he had recourse to its good services in some of his poems, in particular in 1860 in "Out of the Cradle Endlessly Rocking," in which he personified the mocking-bird and made him speak exactly as a poet of the old school would have done. He proceeded in the same manner in 1876 in "Song of the Redwood Tree" and in 1888 in "The Voice of the Rain," which recalls "The Cloud" of Shelley. Besides, in numerous poems, he personified America, which he sometimes even called "Columbia," for beauty's sake probably.[61] He went even further. In 1871, in his "Song of the Exposition," he called upon the Muse, whom he invited to leave Greece to come and live in the United States.[62]

These, however, are only minor departures from the rules he had laid down for himself. On the whole, he remained faithful to the aesthetics which he had defined at the beginning of his career, and the prime mover of his poetry is less that "fancy" which he condemned than a faculty which he thought was new and called "the Kosmic Spirit" [63] — it was nothing else than Wordsworth's and Coleridge's "imagination." Here is how he defined it himself:

I will not make poems with reference to parts,
But I will make poems, songs, thoughts, with reference to ensemble,

And I will not sing with reference to a day, but with
    reference to all days . . .[64]
All must have reference to the ensemble of the world,
There shall be no subject but it shall be treated with
    reference to the ensemble of the world and the com-
    pact truth of the world.[65]

In other words, he wants the least object in his poems to
imply and call up the rest of the world and suggest the infinity
of space and time, as in the following passage:

O the gleesome saunter over fields and hillsides!
The leaves and flowers of the commonest weeds . . .[66]

The lines recall Wordsworth's:

To me the meanest flower that blows can give
Thoughts that do often lie too deep for tears.[67]

He seems to have become more and more clearly conscious
of the cosmic quality of his poems, for the two fragments
that we have quoted above, in which he so plainly defined his
intentions, both date from 1860, but, as early as 1855, he
already mentioned among the qualities of the poet a "perfect
sense of the oneness of nature" [68] and declared that "anything
is but a part." [69]

Even in his first poems there occur striking examples of this
desire for spatial and temporal ubiquity. Again and again in
"Song of Myself" his imagination soars beyond the data of
his senses and reveals to him the infinity of space and time;
he then draws up ecstatic inventories of all the sights of the
world; [70] and he did the same thing in 1856 in such poems
as "Salut au Monde" and "Song of the Broad-Axe." In 1860,
he exclaimed:

O to realize space!
The plenteousness of all, that there are no bounds,
To emerge and be of the sky, of the sun and moon
    and flying clouds, as one with them.[71]

Then, "great thoughts of space and eternity fill" him and he thinks of all the globes of the past and the future, of the immensity of the universe.[72] Yet, as he grew older, the dimensions both of his subjects and of his poems shrank. He needed no less than the whole earth at the beginning of his career; in his old age, he was satisfied with a flower, a bird, a street, a printer's case — and a few lines.[73] And yet, these humble vignettes still imply and suggest the rest of the world in the manner of the Japanese hokkus of the best period. "The first dandelion" reminds us of the everlastingness of life, the canary in its cage celebrates the "joie de vivre" in its own way; all mankind walks up and down Broadway and the "font of type" contains in latent form all the passions of men. His imagination has lost its former vigor, but his glance has remained as piercing as ever and his sight still carries to the utmost confines of the universe:

> Distances balk'd . . .
> I feel the sky, the prairies vast — I feel the mighty
>   northern lakes,
> I feel the ocean and the forest — somehow I feel the
>   globe itself swift-swimming in space . . .[74]

he exclaimed as late as 1890.

This cosmic sense was probably natural to him, but he seems to have cultivated it systematically — for the following note has been found among his papers:

First of all prepare for study by the following self-teaching exercises. Abstract yourself from this book; realize where you are at present located, the point you stand that is now to you the centre of all. Look up overhead, think of space stretching out, think of all the unnumbered orbs wheeling safely there, invisible to us by day, some visible by night . . . Spend some minutes faithfully in this exercise. Then again realize yourself upon the earth, at the particular point you now occupy. Which way stretches the north, and what countries, seas, etc.? Which way the south? Which way the east? Which way the west? Seize these firmly in your mind, pass freely over immense distances. Turn your face a moment thither. Fix the direction and the idea of the distances of separate sections of your own country, also of England, the Mediterranean Sea, Cape Horn, the North Pole, and such like distinct places.[75]

These are true spiritual exercises which he practiced in order to reach a state of grace; they show to what extent he strove never to forget the existence around him of the infinite space of the universe. When, in his poems, he draws up long inventories of things, towns, rivers — "catalogues," as they are usually called — his aim is probably the same. He simply tries to make us realize the immensity of the world; he does so to warm up his imagination, and ours.[76]

Science, in this respect, was a great help to him — and this is one of the reasons why he greeted it as the helpmate of poetry:

Without being a Scientist, I have thoroughly adopted the conclusions of the great Savans and Experimentalists of our time, and of the last hundred years, and they have interiorly tinged the chyle of all my verse, for purposes beyond. Following the Modern Spirit, the real Poems of the Present, ever solidifying and expanding into the Future, must vocalize the vastness and splendor and reality with which Science has invested Man and the Universe (all that is called Creation,) and must henceforth launch Humanity into new orbits, consonant with that vastness, splendor and reality, (unknown to the old poems) . . .[77]

Astronomy in particular opened endless vistas to his mind:

All the vastness of Astronomy — and space — systems of suns [here a blank in the manuscript] carried in their computations to the farthest that figures are able or that the broadest? mathematical faculty can hold . . .[78]

On the other hand, geology and astronomy combined gave him a sense of the immensity of time — a sense which few

writers have possessed to the same degree.[79] He felt suspended
between two infinites: the dark past of the geological eras
whose duration is measured in millions of years and the endless and glorious future which mankind was entering with
confidence, sure as it was of the ultimate triumph of democracy and science.[80]

"[I am] a novice beginning yet experient of myriads of
seasons," [81] he proclaimed in 1855. In 1891, in two of his last
poems, he called up the long line of epics and sacred books
which, since the remotest times, had prepared the coming of
Leaves of Grass and, in the same way, he imagined the centuries and centuries that would elapse before his book at last
should triumph.[82] So, to his death, he was conscious of the
infinity of time as well as of the infinity of space. His cosmic
sense inspired him right to the end of his life.

In this poetic universe of his in which everything is an
inseparable part of the Whole, all that exists is a wonderful
miracle which one never tires of contemplating:

> The bull and the bug never worshipp'd half enough,
> Dung and dirt more admirable than was dream'd . . .[83]

For nothing is contemptible; his "imagination" confers on the
most trivial object a greatness which escapes those who forget
the cosmic context of which it is a part:

> . . . the majesty and beauty of the world are latent
> in any iota of the world . . .[84]

And this is another justification of the "catalogues." They
may tire the reader, but they never tired their author, who
inserted whole pages of them in his poems — at least until
1860, after which date they disappeared. A disappearance to
which little attention has been paid so far, but which probably
corresponds to the decline of his faculty of wonder. From this
date on, he could write a poem only after a shock — until

then his subject was the world, the "ensemble," and he descended from the whole to the parts. From now on, he could re-ascend from the parts to the whole only when a part had particularly struck him. His cosmic sense was unchanged, his vision of the world was the same, but his sensibility, like any human sensibility, had gradually been worn out by habit. Such wear and tear is inevitable and, in his case, was connected with the decrease of his mystic joys and the decline of his vitality. The difference is obvious if one compares, for instance, "Miracles," which was composed in 1856, to "The Commonplace," which dates from 1891. The subject is fundamentally the same; his purpose, in both cases, is to celebrate the wonderful beauty of everyday things. But, while in the first poem the most commonplace words vibrate with joy and suggest intense sensations, the second, in spite of a lyrical start, soon founders in trivial generalities and never succeeds in moving us.

At any rate, this comparison shows that his conception of beauty never varied, even if he perceived it more rarely and less strongly, as he grew older. Beauty for him was not the exclusive attribute of things endowed with harmonious proportions. True, he was sensitive to plastic beauty, and in "Song of Myself" has described with a sculptor's enthusiasm the perfect body of a negro teamster at work,[85] but, generally speaking, he conceives beauty not as an aesthetic value, but as a mystic property. He even condemns what he calls "the beauty disease" and he adopted as his own Baudelaire's protest against art for art's sake and aestheticism.[86] Beauty is for him inherent in all that exists.[87]

> Each precise object or condition or combination or process exhibits a beauty . . . the multiplication table its — old age its — the carpenter's trade its — the grand-opera its . . . the hugehulled cleanshaped New-York clipper at sea under steam or full sail gleams with unmatched beauty . . . [88]

The whole being beautiful and the parts interdependent and inseparable from the whole, every thing cannot but be beautiful. The great merit of his art is precisely to rehabilitate the humblest scenes by surrounding them with a halo of infinity. Thus he does not forget, and does not allow us to forget, that the knife-grinder "sharpening a great knife" at his wheel in the street is nothing but "an unminded point set in a vast surrounding." [89] Hence the greatness and vastness of his *Leaves of Grass,* and its superiority, according to him, over all the poems which preceded it.[90]

Besides imagination, there is another faculty which in Whitman's eyes is indispensable to the poet; it is sympathy. He introduces himself as "he attesting sympathy" [91] and, according to him, ". . . whoever walks a furlong without sympathy walks to his own funeral drest in his shroud . . ." [92] He means by this that the poet must always feel mysteriously connected to the "locations and times," "forms, colors, densities, odors," [93] which are the concrete manifestations of universal life. In relation to nature, sympathy is the mystic perception of the spiritual reality which lies hidden behind material appearances, or, what amounts to the same thing, the consciousness of the projection of the subject's soul on the objects which are perceived. Very early, before 1855 probably, Whitman had read in a review the following sentence:

The mountains, rivers, forests, and all the elements that gird them round, would be only blank conditions of matter, if the mind did not fling its own divinity around them.

Whitman was so much struck by this that he wrote in the margin: "This I think is one of the most indicative sentences I ever read." [94] And, in 1891, he expressed exactly the same idea in a short poem:

Grand is the seen . . .
But grander far the unseen soul of me, comprehend-
ing, endowing all those . . .

(What were all those, indeed, without thee, unseen
    soul? of what amount without thee?) [95]

This sympathy also implies, especially toward mankind, a
total acceptance of all that is, since all things have an equal
right to exist:

. . . nothing in its place is bad . . .
He [the poet] judges not as the judge judges, but as
    the sun falling round a helpless thing . . . [96]

In this respect, Whitman's main objection to Wordsworth
was that he lacked that universal sympathy toward all men,[97]
which made Whitman for his part "appoint an appointment"
with a prostitute in a poem which he never disowned in spite
of all attacks.[98] In 1888, he again emphatically affirmed the
existence of what he called "continuities," [99] by which he meant
the mystic solidarity of all things and the deep underlying
unity of all that is beyond the diversity of appearances. Thus,
his sympathy, like his imagination, remained alive right to
the end.

Yet, in spite of his universal tolerance, he could not help
harboring personal preferences and occasionally showing his
disapproval. He could even be quite violent at times, as when
he wrote "The Eighteenth Presidency" and his "Boston Ballad."
But he never published the former and thought of suppressing
the latter; he preserved it in his book only at the urgent en-
treaty of his friend Trowbridge.[100] As to his "Poem of the
Propositions of Nakedness' [101] whose tone is so bitterly ironical,
he removed it from *Leaves of Grass* after 1876 and at the
same time canceled the satirical allusions which occurred at
the beginning of his "Song of the Exposition." [102] It must be
added that he periodically made a resolution to abstain from
sarcasm. Thus, on November 25, 1868, he noted on a slip
of paper: "No more attempts at smart sayings or scornful
criticisms, or harsh comments, on persons, or actions, or private

and public affairs." Again on July 15, 1870, he wrote: "Never attempt puns or plays upon words, or utter sarcastic comments." [103] He kept his word on the whole, since there are hardly any left in *Leaves of Grass* now.[104] He thus succeeded in preserving the purely lyric quality of his inspiration.

So, to all intents and purposes, Whitman's aesthetics is the logical outcome of his mystic intuitions and the faithful reflection of his pantheistic metaphysics. He became more and more clearly conscious of its implications and put its principles into practice until his death — but his body gradually betrayed him and the last edition of *Leaves of Grass* has neither the glamor nor the power of the first ones. The same "cosmic spirit" pervades all his work, but, as years went by, his exaltation declined progressively and his wondering gaze became accustomed to the glory of the world.

CHAPTER V

SEX LIFE

"The Love that dare not speak its name." [1]

Recorders ages hence,
Come, I will take you down underneath this im-
    passive exterior, I will tell you what to say of
    me . . .
Whose happiest days were far away through fields,
    in woods, on hills, he and another wandering
    hand in hand, they twain apart from other
    men . . .[2]

U P to here we have studied but a single source of Whitman's poetic inspiration, namely, his mysticism. We have
examined its influence in turn on his metaphysics, his ethics,
and his aesthetics; we have seen from what profound regions
of his subconscious this mysticism sprang and how closely
connected it was, at least at the outset, with his sensuality.
We must now retrace our steps and try to determine the
nature of the sexual emotions which sometimes accompany
his mystical trances and sometimes develop independently.
Side by side with songs of religious inspiration, his book indeed
contains some poems of carnal love almost all grouped together in "Calamus" and "Children of Adam." In the middle
of his mystical Leaves of Grass there rise here and there high
tufts of calamus or sweet-flag with long pointed leaves, yellow-

ish green spikes (or spadices), and huge snaky rhizomes, mysterious and troubling phallic symbols.³ What meaning may we
ascribe to them? Their presence poses a problem but it is
essential to solve it, as Whitman himself repeatedly insists on
the capital importance of calamus for the understanding of
his work:

> O I do not know whether many passing by will dis-
> cover you (delicate tall leaves of the sweet-flag) or
> inhale your faint odor, but I believe a few will;
> O slender leaves! O blossoms of my blood! I permit you
> to tell in your own way of the heart that is under
> you . . .⁴

> I am not what you supposed, but far different.
> . . .
> But these leaves conning you con at peril,
> For these leaves and me you will not understand,
> They will elude you at first and still more afterward,
> I will certainly elude you . . .
> Already you see I have escaped from you . . .
> For all is useless without that which you may guess
> at many times and not hit, that which I hinted at;
> Therefore release me and depart on your way.⁵

> Here the frailest leaves of me and yet my strongest
> lasting,
> Here I shade and hide my thoughts, I myself do not
> expose them,
> And yet they expose me more than all my other poems.⁶

Thus he constantly piques our curiosity and yet obstinately
refuses to satisfy it. He glides just to the brink of confession,
but suddenly regains his self-control and keeps to himself the
great secret to which he has nevertheless drawn our attention.
One feels that he would like to tell us all, but that, for some
reason or other, he cannot — a disconcerting and unexpected
attitude on the part of a poet who is at first sight so open and

exuberant. Why does he not go to the end of his confidence? Such a reserve seems suspect. Did he have some failing to hide? There is a mystery to elucidate and, as the facts are lacking, the commentators have thrown themselves whole-heartedly into it and proposed the most diverse explanations.

The most generally accepted hypothesis today is that Whitman was, at least virtually, a homosexual. J. A. Symonds was the first to suggest it in Whitman's own lifetime. He had studied Greek friendship [7] and the Italian Renaissance and such an anomaly was neither surprising nor shocking to him. He thought, when he read "Calamus," that he had discovered Whitman's secret and, a long time later, in 1890, he wrote to him to ask if he had guessed correctly. But Whitman, probably in a panic at the idea that what he had taken such great care to hide was going to be made public, protested vehemently in his reply against such a "terrible" interpretation which, he said, had never occurred to him and which he disavowed completely. Moreover, in order to prove beyond doubt that he was perfectly normal, he added that in the course of his restless and jolly youth he had begotten six illegitimate — and apparently adulterine — children, of whom two were dead. He was even a grandfather, he claimed, for one of his grandsons lived in the South and wrote to him occasionally.[8] The reply was clever and the argument might have seemed ir-refutable, but, though it satisfied his disciples, it failed to convince Symonds who, not without reason, kept to his position.[9] For this denial can easily be explained by the fear of scandal [10] and did not rectify the ambiguous character of the poems which Whitman had written thirty years before. His thesis was even in flagrant contradiction with the many almost transparent allusions contained in "Calamus." And as for his illegitimate children, it seems that this was pure invention on his part, and that he wished to set the curious on a false trail. The most exhaustive research has never uncovered the trace of a single one.[11] Besides, even if their existence were proved, the homosexual theory would still be valid, for it sometimes happens that homosexuals do have children as the result of some normal sexual intercourse. But this eventuality seems a priori fairly improbable in Whitman's case. We know from his brother George, from Peter Doyle, and from others that he was not interested in women.[12] When, during the war, a comrade of his offered to put a young French nurse in his arms, he excused himself on the ground that he had just had an affair with a French girl in Washington with deplorable results to his health, which, in all likelihood, was nothing but a white lie.[13] Later, when Mrs. Gilchrist courted him, he similarly resorted to all kinds of evasions.[14] Finally, one of his letters shows us the insurmountable repulsion which he felt when some friends took him along to a house of ill-repute in New York.[15] All these facts seem to confirm what the poems suggest about Whitman's homosexuality.

The first critic who dared frankly to discuss the problem posed by "Calamus" was the German, Eduard Bertz, who as early as 1905 boldly affirmed that Whitman was, to use his own terminology, an "Urning," that is to say, an invert.[16] And he argued from this, as did Mark Van Doren later, that *Leaves of Grass* could not be regarded as universally valid poetry.[17] On the contrary, the Englishman, Edward Carpenter, for whom mankind in its evolution was eventually to create an "intermediate sex," [18] saluted Whitman as a precursor and exalted his homosexuality.[19] In France the problem was passionately discussed for ten months in the pages of the *Mercure de France* as a result of a letter from Apollinaire, who claimed that the poet's funeral had been the occasion of scandalous manifestations on the part of fellow-homosexuals.[20] Stuart-Merrill and Bazalgette protested and claimed that Whitman was perfectly normal, while Bertz and Harrison Reeves sided with Apollinaire. In Great Britain, doctors and psychologists

soon joined in. Havelock Ellis [21] and W. C. Rivers [22] studied
Whitman's case scientifically and dispassionately. But a long
time elapsed before American critics attained such detachment.[23] Emory Holloway, after digging out a document of
cardinal importance — the original text of "Once I Pass'd
through a Populous City" in which the beloved was a man and
not a woman as in the published version — [24] refused to accept
the necessary consequences in his biography and, juggling the
problem away, maintained without any valid reason that Whitman's sexuality was perfectly normal.[25] It was only gradually
under the influence of English critics and of Jean Catel's book,
that American commentators came to admit the anomaly of
the poet, which is now accepted by authors as diverse as Newton
Arvin,[26] H. S. Canby,[27] Gay Wilson Allen,[28] and Malcolm
Cowley.[29]

We must in our turn study this fundamental problem and
analyze Whitman's sexual poetry, considering it, according
to our usual method, not as a body of static data, but as a constantly changing continuum whose evolution must be carefully observed.

Whitman's exceptional interest in the physiology of love
appeared very early. In 1847, he had already published several
articles in the *Brooklyn Eagle* to advocate a greater frankness
of expression in matters of sexual life.[30] And in 1855, in his
first *Leaves of Grass,* he himself set an example by devoting
an entire poem to the body in which the evocation of the sexual
organs and functions was hardly veiled at all by the use of
partly symbolic language.[31] The opening poem celebrated them
in passing without naming them directly [32] and his poem on
work began, curiously enough, with this invocation:

> Come closer to me;
> Push close my lovers and take the best I possess,
> Yield closer and closer and give me the best you pos-
>   sess.[33]

One feels that he is obsessed with and hungry for the joys of love like those two women whom he describes to us, one of whom caresses nude bathers in imagination [34] while the other, in her frenzy, rubs against darkness as if it were some incubus.[35] No one knows what his sexual life had been up to then. Malcolm Cowley supposes that he had a revelation of love between 1850 and 1855 and that that explains the sudden change in the tone of his poetry and the sudden birth of *Leaves of Grass*.[36] He sees in the passage where Whitman celebrates the ecstasy which consecrated him the memory of that first experience.[37] But nothing in the text permits us to suppose this. On the contrary, all the details show that it was a mystical state, perhaps of an auto-erotic nature at the start. The 1855 version moreover, suggests an unsatisfied sexual instinct which seeks its object everywhere and does not find it. The exuberance it exhibits is only a compensation for the repression from which he suffers and which his dreams reveal to us. Does not he imagine in the course of one of them that he is naked outdoors and does not know where to hide? [38] He even confesses in scarcely veiled terms that he is subject to involuntary ejaculations at night.[39] All these are so many signs of a retarded adolescence and of a surprising immaturity for a man of thirty-six. Does he not avow it himself in this line:

> [I] am curious to know where my feet stand — and
> what is this flooding me, childhood or manhood —
> and the hunger that crosses the bridge between.[40]

The 1856 edition reveals the same torments, the same tortures and the same erotic dreams.[41] So strong is his obsession that the simple sight of a bee alighting on a flower makes him think of copulation.[42] But, if he still represses his desires, "lust, hot wishes [he] dared not speak," [43] for the first time he lets us have a glimpse of the direction which they take:

> [I] was call'd by my nighest name by clear loud
> voices of young men as they saw me approaching
> or passing,
> Felt their arms on my neck as I stood, or the negli-
> gent leaning of their flesh against me as I sat,
> Saw many I loved in the street or ferry-boat or public
> assembly, yet never told them a word . . .[44]

These, however, are only sparse allusions. In 1860, on the
contrary, he gave free course to his passion and it broke forth
with the violence of an explosion. From the crater which had
just formed, two streams of burning lava shot out and no
less than two new groups of poems were necessary to collect
the overflow. "Enfans d'Adam" and "Calamus"; the former was
ostensibly devoted to the love of man for woman whereas the
latter, with its more mysterious title, sang the love of comrades.
But we know that Whitman composed "Enfans d'Adam" after
"Calamus" as a companion to it, as it were, and in order to
reassure those of his readers who might have been upset by
the strangeness of "Calamus." [45] The same preoccupation with
camouflage made Whitman add "or woman" whenever he used
the word "man." As to "Enfans d'Adam," in spite of the artificial character of the fiat which gave birth to the group, all
the poems which make it up are not as cold as some critics have
claimed. Some of them, in fact, date from the first two editions
and express the same feelings as the poems of "Calamus."
Besides, many of the others very probably are mere transpositions. But, naturally, the most revealing passages occur in
"Calamus."

When he composed those poems, Whitman certainly yielded
to an irresistible need to confess in order to free himself, but
he also had to take into account the taboos of the society in
which he lived. Hence his use of a number of terms with a
hidden meaning, like "calamus" for instance. To the uninitiated
reader the word may seem perfectly innocent, and that is

exactly what Whitman sought. When Conway asked him its meaning, Whitman explained that it was a kind of "very large and aromatic grass . . . often called sweet-flag [which] grows all over the Northern and Middle States." "The recherché or ethereal sense" which he gave it in his book, he answered, came from the fact that it presented "the biggest and hardiest kind of spears of grass, and [a] fresh, aromatic, pungent bouquet." [46] In fact, this calamus had for him the value of a phallic image and had evidently haunted his mind for some time, since it is already to be found in a line of the first edition:

> Root of wash'd sweet-flag! timorous pond-snipe! nest
> of guarded duplicate eggs! [47]

In 1860, this same root became unequivocally the symbol of manly love and a secret token for the initiates:

> And this, O this shall henceforth be the token of com-
> rades, this calamus-root shall,
> Interchange it youths with each other! let none ren-
> der it back.[48]

As for the word "adhesiveness" which recurs so often in his verse, he does not use it in the sense of "the faculty of making friends" as do the phrenologists from whom he borrowed it; he confers a secret meaning upon it which he revealed much later incidentally in the course of an interview. It is, he said, "a personal attachment between men that is stronger than ordinary friendship." [49] Sometimes, too, he has recourse to purposely ambiguous words like "comrade,[50] which can be taken both in a democratic sense and in a more intimate meaning. And so he creates an esoteric vocabulary which permits him to communicate his message to a small number of initiates who take the hint,[51] but keep silent in order not to betray him.

In the very first poem of "Calamus" he dashes forward along "paths untrodden" and repudiates all the moral principles which have guided his life so far. He has just found out, he explains,

> That the soul of the man [he] speak[s] for rejoices in comrades . . .[52]

Contrary to what Malcolm Cowley thinks, he seems to have become aware of his anomaly very late. For a long time this abnormal instinct had been brewing in him,[53] but he probably did not dare to give it free rein and perhaps did not even understand all its implications [54] — until in 1858 or 1859 he met a "comrade" who felt the same desires as he did and whom he loved passionately. This was a brief and tumultuous idyll which we have tried to retrace.[55] It is probable that he then at last realized that his feelings were not as monstrous as he thought and could be shared.[56] In all likelihood it was at that moment that he solemnly decided not to be ashamed of them any more [57] and henceforth to celebrate "manly attachment," "athletic love," and "the need of comrades." [58] He even notes the date of this vital resolution: "September 1859," [59] which shows what importance he attached to it.

The poems which compose "Calamus" were thus so many "light, blushing drops" which trickled from him, from that self which he finally had the courage to be.[60] The essential theme of these confessions is the obsession of desire, the sighs which his tormented and unsatisfied body heaves at night, his efforts at self-control, the promises which he makes and cannot keep, the images which haunt his dreams and obsess him during the day, that constant erotic excitation which little by little has become the very "pulse" of his life.[61] His long walks in Manhattan are only an incessant quest for love. He is always looking for a glance which responds to his own.[62] The eyes, the faces, the bodies of the strangers who pass by give him an inexplicable pleasure. He does not exchange a single word with them, but their image afterwards pursues him.[63] Sometimes it seems to him that he has met the perfect comrade, the "lover and perfect equal" for whose encounter he has been craving,[64] but most often he is content to dream of all the "other men in other lands" who would become attached to him if they knew him.[65] His sensuality, thus constantly exasperated by his imagination, in the end becomes a source of distress; he is "he that aches with amorous love." [66]

Thus the dominant impression which these confessions give is that all these secret desires belonged to a world of dreams rather than to reality. He acknowledged it himself:

> Ethereal, the last athletic reality, my consolation,
> I ascend, I float in the regions of your love O man,
> O sharer of my roving life.[67]

He also speaks of "many a hungry wish told to the skies only." [68] Under these conditions one may wonder whether his passion was ever anything but Platonic, whether, in order to write "these songs," he was not satisfied with mere "unreturned love." [69] Yet, if he was he

> Who often walk'd lonesome walks thinking of his dear
> friends, his lovers,

he was also, at least so he claimed, he

> Whose happiest days were far away through fields, in
> woods, on hills, he and another wandering hand
> in hand, they twain apart from other men . . .[70]

He also evoked furtive meetings:

> . . . on a high hill, first watching lest any person for
> miles around approach unawares,
> Or possibly with you sailing at sea, or on the beach
> of the sea or some quiet island,
> Here to put your lips upon mine I permit you . . .[71]

And what is to be thought of this poem, which, though it is part of "Enfans d'Adam," has not even been transposed:

> I am for those who believe in loose delights, I share
>   the midnight orgies of young men . . .
> . . . I pick out some low person for my dearest friend,
> He shall be lawless, rude, illiterate, he shall be one con-
>   demned by others for deeds done,
> I will play a part no longer, why should I exile myself
>   from my companions?
> O you shunn'd persons, I at least do not shun you,
> I come forthwith in your midst, I will be your
>   poet . . .[72]

Did these orgies and encounters really take place, or did
he merely dream them for want of something better, because
he could not live them? No one can tell. The biographical data
are insufficient on this point. Some, like Bertz and Donaldson,[73] think that his homosexuality remained Platonic,[74] an
interpretation toward which we lean and which the following
admission seems to confirm:

> The untold want by life and land ne'er granted,
> Now voyager sail thou forth to seek and find.[75]

Others, like Symonds and Malcolm Cowley, consider on
the contrary that he was an active homosexual. We know
indeed that he liked to associate with New York bus drivers,
that he was popular among the ferry-boat crews and noted in
his notebooks the descriptions and sometimes the addresses of
the young men whom he met. On the other hand it would
certainly have been easy for him to satisfy his abnormal instincts, for, according to certain testimonies,[76] homosexuality
was then current in the United States. But all these facts only
constitute presumptions,[77] not proofs, and it is probable that
we will never know the truth. However, whether his anomaly
was real or virtual does not matter very much; the result is
the same for us. Whether his poems were the result of a compensatory activity or the transposition of certain hidden
episodes in his life, one fact at any rate is certain: his *Leaves*

of Grass plunge their roots into a murky and unhealthy part of himself and, in this respect, they are "Fleurs du Mal." Whitman felt this so strongly that for a time he thought of a similar title, if not for the whole book, at least for "Calamus." He jotted down the following names: "Flames of Confession," "Drops of My Blood" (which is close to "Trickle Drops"), "Drops of Evil," "Flames of Evil," "Verses of Evil." [78] But they were also flowers of good, "fleurs du bien," as Vigny called Baudelaire's *Fleurs du Mal,*[79] for they had indeed helped him to escape the torment and despair that his anomaly caused him. His art saved him, by purifying his passions:

> I loved a certain person ardently and my love was not
>   return'd,
> Yet out of that I have written these songs.[80]

> I will therefore let flame from me the burning fires
>   that were threatening to consume me,
> I will lift what has too long kept down those smoulder-
>   ing fires,
> I will give them complete abandonment,
> I will write the evangel-poem of comrades and of love.[81]

And that is why he recognized himself in the solitary thrush:

> Song of the bleeding throat,
> Death's outlet song of life, (for well dear brother I
>   know,
> If thou wast not granted to sing, thou wouldst surely
>   die.) [82]

And he was probably thinking of the transmutation into poetry of the impure elements which were in him when, a long time later, he wrote:

> Not the right only justified, what we call evil also justi-
>   fied.
> Forth from their masks, no matter what,

> From the huge festering trunk, from craft and guile
>   and tears,
> Health to emerge and joy, joy universal.[83]

In all likelihood he was only generalizing his own experience
there and attributing to the world as a whole his own struggles
and his final recovery.

Thus his art really had that power of catharsis which Aristotle attributed to tragedy. In "Calamus" and in many places
in *Leaves of Grass* we witness the metamorphosis of the torments of his flesh and the morbid obsessions of his imagination
into hymns and songs. He is transformed into a priest of some
phallic worship,[84] he celebrates the "mystic deliria" of sexual
ecstasies,[85] and this exhibitionism frees him. The "contact
daily and hourly that will not release" him [86] dissolves itself
into the current of universal desire which, as irresistible as
gravity, pushes all the particles of matter toward each other.[87]
He ceases to think exclusively of himself, he becomes integrated
in the world and then,

> O nor down-balls nor perfumes, nor the high rain-
>   emitting clouds, are borne through the open air,
> Any more than my soul is borne through the open air,
> Wafted in all directions . . .[88]

He regains his balance within his unbalance; the metaphysical doubts which assailed him are now dissipated, he feels
surrounded, penetrated by an unutterable certitude, "the sense
that words and reason hold not," and "untold and untellable
wisdom." [89] At the end of these strange metamorphoses, the
troubled emotions of his abnormal sensuality are thus sublimated into rapturous mystical intuitions.

This sublimation does not take only a metaphysical form,
it has a social aspect too, for the beloved beings whose presence
at his side reassure him as to the reality of the world and the
immortality of the soul are also his comrades on the plane of
democracy. Fraternity and comradeship are not cold and life-

less abstractions for him. He feels them in his flesh, as can be seen in that poem where he kisses the lips of a dear New York comrade from whom he is going to part.[90] And he recommended the multiplication of such robust, virile friendships in all the United States:

> Come I will make the continent indissoluble,
> I will make the most splendid race the sun ever shone
>   upon,
> I will make divine magnetic lands,
> With the love of comrades . . .
> I will make inseparable cities with their arms about
>   each other's necks,
> By the love of comrades . . .[91]

As early as 1860, therefore, he succeeded in reconciling his homosexual instinct with his political ideal, which was one way of justifying his anomaly in his own eyes and in the eyes of the others. Under the favor of this confusion, he was able, in the years which followed, to express his abnormal predilections without fear of shocking.

The equilibrium which "Calamus" permitted him to attain was, however, very precarious. His personal notebooks show that he continued to be interested in the young men whom he met, and, even though he took a solemn vow of abstinence and chastity when the Civil War broke out,[92] the desires which obsessed him would not be calmed so easily. Even in the military hospitals in Washington, at a time when he apparently had succeeded in controlling himself and giving his homosexuality the noble form of an untiring devotion for the wounded, his impure sensuality still had violent convulsions. He attached himself passionately to some of the young soldiers,[93] and was torn by passions of the same order as those which had tortured him in 1858–1859. Here, for example, is what he wrote in April 1863 to a certain Tom Sawyer after the latter had gone back to his regiment:

Dear comrade, you must not forget me, for I never shall you. My love you have in life or death forever. I don't know how you feel about it, but it is the wish of my heart to have your friendship and also that if you should come safe out of this war, we should come together again in some place where we could make our living and be true comrades and never be separated while life lasts — and take Lew Brown too,[94] and never separate from him.[95]

Less than a week later he wrote to him again to reproach him for his silence and for not having picked up at his house the shirt, the pair of drawers, and the socks which he had prepared for him:

I should have often thought now Tom may be wearing around his body something from *me* . . . Not a day now passes nor a night but I think of you . . .[96]

Whitman's presentiments proved correct. Tom Sawyer replied nicely but rather coldly to the first letter and left the second unanswered. At the end of May, Whitman wrote again:

My dearest comrade, I cannot though I attempt it put in a letter the feelings of my heart. I suppose my letters sound strange and unusual to you as it is, but as I am only expressing the truth in them, I do not trouble myself on that account. As I intimated before, I do not expect you to return for me the same degree of love I have for you.[97]

This correspondence continued until November, but Tom Sawyer's lack of enthusiasm gradually cooled Whitman's ardor and the conclusion of his last letter is melancholy and resigned:

Well [dear brother — deleted] comrade, I must close. I do not know why you do not write to me. Do you wish to shake me off? That I cannot believe for I have the same love for you that I exprest in my letters last spring and I am confident you have the same for me . . . Good-by, dear comrade, & God bless you, if fortune should keep you from me here, in this world, it must not hereafter.[98]

So, even during the war, Whitman experienced new relapses, but, as these letters show, if his homosexual tendencies remained unchanged and his abnormal desires were still as obsessive as ever, his passions had no longer the intensity and the violence of former times and no longer wrung from him the same cries of anguish and despair. Very quickly he resigned himself to not being understood, to not being loved as much as he himself loved. He did not demand much. He would have been satisfied even with a "ménage à trois," since a closer intimacy was apparently impossible. He would be happy with the mere presence near him of the one — or of those — whom he loved. The most convinced believer in Whitman's active homosexuality will not find in all this correspondence any definite proof in support of his theory.[99] The feelings which these letters express are not normal, but they remain Platonic. There is even a passage where we witness their idealization, as it were. Whitman is thinking of all the young soldiers who, like Tom Sawyer, were part of the Army of the Potomac, and he writes:

O how much I think about them though I suppose that does no good. Tom, you tell the boys of your company there is an old pirate up in Washington, with the white wool growing all down his neck — an old comrade who thinks about you & them every day, for all he don't know them, and will probably never see them, but thinks about them as comrades and younger brothers of his, just the same.[100]

He thus transferred to all young men without exception that love which some of them had rejected, and his abnormal passion, now diluted, lost all its noxiousness.

Shortly after the war, in 1866, Whitman accidentally met a young Irishman of nineteen or twenty years of age, Peter Doyle, who was at that time a streetcar conductor in Washington.[101] They were immediately attracted to each other and began a long friendship which was ended only by Whitman's death. It was a strange comradeship, since a priori everything should have separated the two men: age, position, and even education, for Peter Doyle was illiterate. Yet, during all the time that Whitman spent in Washington they were inseparable. He often waited for his young friend to leave work and they took long walks in the moonlight or bought a watermelon and ate it unceremoniously in the street seated on a doorstep.[102] On Sundays they spent the day together, strolling along the banks of the Potomac.[103] Sometimes Whitman gave him flowers,[104] or, when he was on vacation in New York, invited him to come and spend a few days with him so that their separation would not be so long.[105] When he fell ill in 1873, Peter Doyle came to see him every day, ran his errands and cared for him devotedly.[106] After Whitman settled in Camden, they met only at rare intervals, but they wrote to each other very often.[107] The sick poet did not forget his young protégé and sent him money whenever the young man found himself out of work.[108] Besides, Whitman mentioned him in his will,[109] and when in 1880 he visited Dr. Bucke in Canada, Peter Doyle joined him there and accompanied him on the return trip.[110] It was probably a very pure and almost paternal friendship, or rather a Socratic friendship of the sort which existed between Socrates and Alcibiades, for it was ennobling. Whitman tried to bring his young friend up to himself, he taught him arithmetic, geography, and spelling,[111] gave him lessons in stoicism, and exhorted him to bear the trials of life valiantly.[112]

However, in the meantime, as we know,[113] he was still tortured by abnormal desires — perhaps for Peter Doyle himself. Did he not offer in 1869, making a pretext of a skin disease which then disfigured the young man, to move in with him in a little apartment in a quiet place? [114] But once more he succeeded in controlling himself and probably nothing happened. In 1871, carrying still further the idealization which he had started in 1860, he wrote in *Democratic Vistas*:

Intense and loving comradeship, the personal and passionate attachment of man to man — which, hard to define, underlies the lessons and ideals of the profound saviours of every land and age, and which seems to promise, when thoroughly develop'd, cultivated and recognized in manners and literature, the most substantial hope and safety of the future of these States, will then be fully express'd.[115]

Love of comrades thus blossoms out into love of mankind and becomes synonymous with universal brotherhood. He took up the idea again the same year in the poem symptomatically entitled "The Base of All Metaphysics" [116] and developed it with still more force in the preface to the Centenary Edition, at a time when, feeling weakened by his paralysis, he laid stress on the soul:

I also sent out LEAVES OF GRASS to arouse and set flowing in men's and women's hearts, young and old, (my present and future readers,) endless streams of living, pulsating love and friendship, directly from them to myself, now and ever. To this terrible, irrepressible yearning, (surely more or less down underneath in most human souls,) — this never-satisfied appetite for sympathy, and this boundless offering of sympathy — this universal democratic comradeship — this old, eternal, yet ever-new interchange of adhesiveness, so fitly emblematic of America . . .

He even went so far as to claim that "the special meaning of the *Calamus* cluster of LEAVES OF GRASS . . . mainly resides in its Political significance." [117]

However his soul was not yet in complete control and his trials were not ended. When he was restored to health after his stroke of paralysis, new temptations assailed him. In 1876, he made the acquaintance of a young man who worked as a printer in the shop of the *New Republican* at Philadelphia.

His name was Harry Stafford and his parents had a small farm at Timber Creek north of Camden.[118] This time again Whitman seems to have been in the grip of a violent passion. H. B. Binns, during his visit to the United States in 1904 to prepare his book on Whitman, copied from a notebook which Traubel had in his possession but had not even opened the following notes which could refer only to Harry Stafford:

> November 25–28, 1876. At White Horse [Timber Creek]. Memorable talk with H.S. settles the matter for life.
> December 19. Evening sitting in room [probably in Camden] had serious inward revelation and conviction about H.'s course in the matter. Saw clearly what it really meant. Very profound meditation on all — more happy and satisfied at last about it — singularly so.
> April 29, 1877. Scene with H. in front room.
> July 20, 1877. Scene in the room at White Horse. Good bye.[119]

These notes, probably intentionally obscure, suggest a difficult, even a stormy friendship which each of the participants perhaps understood in a different way. One might suppose that once the ambiguity on which their first association rested was dissipated, young Stafford refused to let himself be led away. In any case, Whitman's attachment for him was singularly profound, as is evidenced by these extracts from some letters which he sent to him:

> Dear son, how I wish you could come in now, even if but for an hour and take off your coat and sit down on my lap . . . I shall be down *Friday,* in the 6 o'clock train — I want to see the creek again — and I want to see you darling son, and I can't wait any longer . . . I wish I was with you this minute down by the creek or off in the woods somewhere [last sentence underlined in the original].[120]

Such an obsession pertains to passion rather than friendship. Whitman, however, succeeded in regaining his self-control and the letters which he wrote afterwards show mainly his anxiety to enrich the mind of his young friend. We witness the same sublimation as in the case of Peter Doyle. He encourages him to write,[121] points out to him the beauties of true religion as he conceived it,[122] and so on. Harry Stafford got married a few years later, but, to the end, Whitman kept his friendship for him. He even left him his gold watch, which he had at first intended for Peter Doyle.

In spite of the place which this attachment seems to have occupied in his life, no echo of it is found in his poetic works. The reason for this silence is probably that all the passions which he experienced after 1860 had the same character and approximately the same history and that he had already said everything he had to say on the subject in 1860 in "Calamus" and "Enfans d'Adam." But the persistence of his sensuality explains why he refused with such obstinacy to cut out of his book the poems or the passages which too glaringly referred to this aspect of his life. They still expressed his secret desires; he was still living them. This is the reason why in 1881 he glorified the "sexual passion" and the beauty of nude bodies in *Specimen Days*.[123] And, in 1888, he insisted with unchanged vigor on the primordial importance of sexuality in life in general and in his work in particular.[124] True, with age, his senses calmed down and his lack of balance mitigated, but he kept alive for a long time the memory of his "many tearing passions." [125] Hence the heat of his reactions, even in his old age, whenever carnal desires were mentioned, and the nostalgic tone of this poem which recalls the struggles and torments of his middle-age:

From Montauk Point
I stand as on some mighty eagle's beak,
Eastward the sea absorbing, viewing, (nothing but the
    sea and sky,)
The tossing waves, the foam, the ships in the distance,

The wild unrest, the snowy, curling caps — that in-
   bound urge and urge of waves,
Seeking the shores forever.[126]

He, too, had always experienced an incessant urge and his whole life had been a restless and — perhaps — ever-disappointed quest, the passionate eagerness and secret despair of which he had tried to express in *Leaves of Grass* from 1860 on.

"THESE STATES" —
EGOCENTRISM AND PATRIOTISM

IF the first *Leaves of Grass* sing principally the "Song of Myself," the preface to the 1855 edition is, on the contrary, in many places a hymn to the United States, which, Whitman tells us, "themselves are essentially the greatest poem." [1] Above all, he admires their immensity which makes them a subject worthy of his cosmic imagination. That vast continent and that multitudinous nation give him a sense of the infinity of space:

> Here is not merely a nation, but a teeming Nation of nations,
> Here the doings of men correspond with the broad-cast doings of the day and night . . .[2]

And not only does America offer unlimited boundaries, but her future, which is predetermined by no past, is rich with infinite promise.[3] So ardent is his patriotism that he goes so far as to proclaim: "Great is the greatest Nation — the nation of clusters of equal nations . . ." [4] She is so great and so noble, why wouldn't she one day dominate the world? He dreams of universal hegemony for her:

> Great is the English brood — what brood has so vast a destiny as the English?

It is the mother of the brood that must rule the earth
with the new rule;
The new rule shall rule as the Soul rules, and as the
love, justice, equality in the Soul rule.[5]

This enthusiasm, which he shared with a number of his fellow-citizens,[6] went back to his youth. He had already had occasion, at the time of the Mexican War, to express it in his editorials for the *Brooklyn Eagle*. He had then declared himself in favor of the annexation of new territories. In his eyes the cause of humanity was identical with that of his country. If the United States expanded, it would be a gain for human happiness and for liberty. Mexico, with her weak and corrupt government, could offer only a parody of democracy and was unworthy of the great mission, devolving upon the new world, to populate America with a noble race. This mission, he had already affirmed, only the United States was capable of fulfilling.[7] And so he expected one day to see it annex Alaska and Canada.[8] Of course, he would have been very surprised if he had been accused of imperialism. It was not for him a matter of conquering territories, but of liberating men and bringing them happiness.[9] It was less a question of patriotism than of democratic proselytism. He saw liberty diffused all over the world, thanks to the United States:

Shapes of a hundred Free States, begetting another
hundred north and south . . .[10]

So, in 1856, he quite naturally included Montreal and Havana in a list of American cities;[11] and his poems of 1860 reflect the same expansionist zeal. He dreams of the time when the same current of life will circulate from Mexico and Cuba to New York, when the Canadian will sacrifice himself for the Kansan and vice versa.[12] He even sings of the supremacy of the United States over the Pacific Islands, of "the new empire grander than any before" of which America will be the "mistress," but which she will refresh and rejuvenate.[13]

His convictions on this point never changed. In 1871, he affirmed with the greatest confidence in *Democratic Vistas*: "Long ere the second centennial arrives, there will be some forty to fifty great States, among them Canada and Cuba." [14] In 1873, in a letter to Peter Doyle, he declared himself in favor of military intervention in Cuba,[15] and, in 1879, during his trip to the West, he thought of proclaiming, in a speech which he did not have an opportunity of delivering; ". . . the day is not yet, but it will come, including Canada entire . . ." [16] The following year, while visiting Canada and the Great Lakes region, he noted:

It seems to me a certainty of time, sooner or later, that Canada shall form two or three grand States, equal and independent, with the rest of the American Union. The St. Lawrence and lakes are not a frontier line, but a grand interior or mid-channel.[17]

At any rate, this pan-Americanism, perhaps tainted with chauvinism at the beginning, was gradually purified. It seems in particular that, after the war, Whitman systematically eliminated from his poems all the lines where nationalism was too arrogant. It is certainly not by accident that in 1867 he suppressed this verse, which until then concluded "I Hear America Singing":

Come! some of you! still be flooding The States with hundreds and thousands of mouth-songs, fit for The States only.[18]

He must eventually have thought this restriction too arrogant and offensive to those who, all over the world, were fighting for the liberation of man. And it was probably for the same reason that, in the same year, he canceled this line in "So Long!"

When there is no city on earth to lead my city, the city of young men, the Mannahatta city — But when the Mannahatta leads all the cities of the earth . . .[19]

Moreover, in "Years of the Modern" he evokes the universal democracy of the future for which "not America only, not only Liberty's nation, but other nations" are preparing.[20] The star-spangled banner ceases to represent the United States exclusively, it becomes the "flag of man." [21] Under the influence of his repeated political disillusionments, he lost his absolute faith in his country and, in 1871, in "Passage to India," instead of setting up America as an example, he subordinated its destiny to a cosmic design. The United States was no longer the supreme outcome of the evolution of the world, but merely a link in the chain, a transition stage through which humanity on the march will have to go, a temporary goal which will be attained and then inevitably transcended in conformity with Hegelian dialectic.[22] As for the proud poet of America whom the 1885 preface evoked, he now yields his place to "the poet worthy that name, the true son of God." [23]

Thus Whitman gradually rose from a rather narrow Americanism to a very broad internationalism which sang the universal brotherhood of men rather than the particular merits of the American nation.[24] In 1876, for instance, he composed a "Song for All Seas, All Ships" [25] in memory of all the heroes and all the captains who lost their lives at sea, regardless of their nationality, and, in 1881, to broaden the scope of his book, he detached from "Drum-Taps" a number of specifically American poems like "Thick-Sprinkled Bunting" "Pioneers! O Pioneers!" [26] and conferred a universal meaning upon them by placing them in a new context. His point of view ceased to be exclusively national. In 1871 he addressed a moving poem to France after her defeat by Prussia; [27] he sent the fraternal salute of the United States to the young republic of Brazil.[28] He announced that the day would come when poets would compose "international poems" [29] and was rejoiced to hear that someone should think of translating *Leaves of Grass* into Russian.[30] The little journalist from Brooklyn, excited over local politics, thus became by degrees the poet laureate of international democracy who imagined, at the end of his life,

> That in the Divine Ship, the World, breasting Time
> and Space,
> All Peoples of the globe together sail, sail the same
> voyage, are bound to the same destination.[31]

This internationalism, based on a belief in the universality of reason which Whitman had borrowed from the "philosophes" of the eighteenth century via the Constitution of the United States,[32] does not, however, lead to cosmopolitanism, for like all his contemporaries he had a very vivid sense of the reality of nationalities in general and of the American nationality in particular.[33] He preached the brotherhood of races and of peoples, but at the same time he felt profoundly American. He himself was perfectly aware of this contradiction:

> You know [he once said to Traubel] there is a sense in which I want to be cosmopolitan: then again a sense in which I make much of patriotism — of our native stock, the American stock, ancestry, the United States . . . That is the same old question — adjusting the individual to the mass . . .[34]

The nation, thus, might be to the world what the individual is to the nation. In 1856 he had already made patriotism a principle of his aesthetics in his "Letter to Ralph Waldo Emerson." The poet, he declared, must not be ashamed of his "native-born perceptions," but must on the contrary "recognize with joy the sturdy living forms of the men and women of These States."[35] And we have seen to what extent he was attached to Long Island and Brooklyn his little fatherland; he even minutely recorded its history in his "Brooklyniana."[36] But he was capable of transcending this parochialism. As early as 1855 he mystically identified himself in *Leaves of Grass* with the most diverse landscapes and inhabitants of the United States in order to give an image as complete and varied as possible of his country. Some readers were taken in and believed that he had really traveled everywhere.[37] In fact, outside of New York and Long Island he then knew only New Orleans, the valleys of the Ohio and the Mississippi, the Great Lakes, and Niagara Falls. It was only after the major part of his works had been written that he visited the Far West and Canada; and he never saw the Pacific. He realized himself the inadequacy of his preparation for the role of poet of America which he wanted to assume,[38] but he got over it by telling himself that the wisest men are often those who stay at home, as the example of Kant shows.[39] The argument is specious. What will do for a transcendental philosopher will not necessarily do for a poet. In his case, however, imagination made up for lack of experience and, when reading him, one never has the impression of dealing with a stay-at-home poet. He "absorbed" the South so well during his rapid visit to New Orleans that he almost believed in the end that he was a Southerner by birth; [40] he acquired the feel of the West by crossing it and he read descriptions of the rest of the country in books — and magazines. His cult of America was thus the fruit of a systematic generalization of his scanty experience, the result of a bold imaginative extrapolation. He loved all the states without exception,[41] even during the Civil War, because they were all equally part of the land of democracy. In the last analysis his patriotism was not a form of parochialism (after 1862 he fairly easily detached himself from Brooklyn and New York), but a sort of political nationalism. What he loved was not any given place, but a certain human climate made up of liberty, equality, and fraternity, which he knew was common to all the states. That is why he was as happy at Camden in spite of the ugliness of his surroundings as in the middle of the rural scenery of Long Island.

These ideological preoccupations also explain why, very early, even before he knew it, he celebrated the West with particular fervor. It seemed to him, as it did to many of his contemporaries,[42] that it was the land of triumphant democracy and perfect equality, a prefiguration of the United States to come and the only true America. As early as 1846, he regarded its inhabitants as the hope of the United States, because, he said, they "begin at the roots of things — at first principles — and scorn the doctrines founded on mere precedent and imitation," [43] and the following year he wrote in another article in the *Brooklyn Eagle*:

It is to us a cheering and grand idea, that the agricultural and *domestic* West must eventually outtopple in means, extent and political power, all the rest of this Republic — and carry sway in what it listeth. The boundless democratic free West! [44]

His first contact with the West, in 1848, when he crossed it quickly on his way to New Orleans did not disappoint him; it only confirmed his high opinion of it. He found the Westerners more virile than the Easterners and he praised their sense of reality and their spirit of independence: ". . . in the [Eastern] cities, frippery and artificial fashions are too much the ruling powers." [45]

But, curiously enough, in the first two editions of *Leaves of Grass*, which were, it is true, of a more personal than political inspiration, he did not even touch on this theme. It was only in 1860 that he began to treat it poetically and to evoke

. . . what Indiana, Kentucky, Arkansas, and the rest,
   are to be . . .
[the] mighty inland cities yet unsurvey'd and unsuspected,
. . . the modern developments . . . inalienable
   homesteads
. . . a free and original life . . .[46]

He sang the immensity of the prairie and the spiritual results which come of it: "the most copious and close companionship of men," those men "that go their own gait, erect, stepping with freedom and command, leading, not following . . ."⁴⁷

He even solemnly promised California and "the great pastoral Plains" that he would soon leave the East and visit them "to teach robust American love." ⁴⁸ It was probably at that time that he thought of preparing a special edition of *Leaves of Grass* for the West containing poems on Wisconsin, Missouri, Texas, Lake Superior — and on the rifle.⁴⁹

The Civil War, during which he had frequent opportunities for meeting young soldiers from the West ⁵⁰ and for appreciating their moral health and their stamina, reinforced his faith in the average man and in democracy. It was then that he composed the most fervent of his poems in honor of the West: "Pioneers! O Pioneers!" ⁵¹ In his enthusiasm he even went so far as to dedicate "To a Western Boy" a poem he had addressed to young Americans in general in the preceding edition.⁵² In 1876, in *Two Rivulets,* he similarly offered his "last thoughts" to the West because he believed that they would germinate better there than anywhere else,⁵³ and that soon "the Muse of the Prairies and of the Peaks of Colorado" would sing of the body and the soul, science, and universal brotherhood in a new language which would be neither prose nor verse.⁵⁴ In short, he transferred to the West the hope of that democratic literary revolution which he had called for and announced in 1855, but which the too traditional East had declined to make. He felt encouraged by the birth on the Pacific Coast of a young independent literature and he immediately greeted Joaquin Miller as the precursor of American poets to come.⁵⁵

In 1879, his "first real visit to the West" finally took place,⁵⁶ and he could only admire and exclaim. The immensity of the plains, the savagery of the mountains, the tonic quality of the air, the dynamism and the generosity of the inhabitants, everything filled him with wonder.⁵⁷ His dreams had come true, it seemed to him, and the reality was worthy of the ideal which he had sung. He returned home very proud of the enormous work which had been done to clear these vast territories and make them habitable; he was full of hope for the future. From then on he never took up the subject again — except to relate his trip in *Specimen Days*. It was as if he had stored enough optimism for the rest of his life. He never again doubted the grandeur of the destiny which awaited his country and democracy. In particular, he showed a touching attachment for General Grant in whom he saw above all a child of the prairies, a representative of the uncrowned kings of the West.[58]

This myth of a realizable democracy, already partially realized in the Great Plains of the Middle West and on the Pacific Coast, was what enabled Whitman to escape the despair which "Respondez," [59] "The Eighteenth Presidency," and certain passages in *Democratic Vistas* had betrayed at various moments of his life. But he had another refuge, which was not spatial, but temporal: he had an unshakable faith in the future. Is that to say that he despised the past? Not at all. On this point, his disciples went much too far. O'Connor, for example, who, speaking of *Leaves of Grass*, wrote during Whitman's lifetime: "It is, in the first place, a work purely and entirely American, autochthonic, sprung from our own soil; no savor of Europe nor of the past, nor of any other literature in it . . ." [60]

Whitman let him talk, as he often did. If he owed nothing to the past, the originality and the force of his genius were all the greater, but his own point of view was much more complex.

One may consider that since the middle of the eighteenth century America had been torn by a new Quarrel between the Ancients and the Moderns. Should one remain attached to Europe and transplant on the new continent the ways of life of the old world or, on the contrary, break all ties and boldly

set out on different routes toward a better future? Such was
the question which it became more and more imperative to
answer. The War for Independence in appearance settled the
matter once for all. The Moderns carried the day and Great
Britain had to recognize the right of the United States to
follow its own destiny. But, in fact, the young Republic continued to depend on the mother country and on Europe for
many years, in particular in all that concerned the arts. It
was only at the beginning of the nineteenth century that the
revolt broke out anew among American writers. It was then
that Emerson — after several others [61] — launched his appeal
to the "American Scholar," [62] which was like a second Declaration of Independence — intellectual independence this time.
Eighteen years later, in the preface to *Leaves of Grass*, Whitman took up fundamentally the same idea when he called for
a specifically American poetry in keeping with the new world
which democracy had built up on the new continent. He thus
sided with the Moderns, with infinitely more spirit than
Emerson. As he, himself, said, he uttered the "word of the
modern, the word En-Masse." [63] Yet, for all his enthusiasm,
he no more than Emerson thought of denying the importance
of the past and of Europe. From the very first words of the
manifesto he warned the reader:

America does not repel the past or what it has produced
under its forms or amid other politics or the idea of castes or the
old religions . . . accepts the lesson with calmness . . . is not
so impatient as has been supposed that the slough still sticks to
opinions and manners and literature while the life which served
its requirements has passed into the new life of the new
forms . . .[64]

During all his life Whitman thus held a difficult position;
he was both a bold innovator looking forward to a glorious
future and a cautious conservative respectful of the past. His
first writings show him already torn between his pride in

belonging to a new country and a very vivid sense of his
indebtedness to the old world. So, in 1846, he wrote in the
Brooklyn Eagle:

Removed on the one hand from the servile copyists who believe that under the portals of the past, and to the moping phantoms there, we must look for masters and for examples, and to
pay our highest worship — and, on the other hand, from the
officious thruster forward of the claims in every ridiculous connection, of *writing that is merely American because it is not
written abroad* — there is a true public opinion forming here
that will ere long do equal and exact justice to all, in this
matter.[65]

The moderation of these views is unexpected. The passage
almost sounds like an anticipatory condemnation of *Leaves
of Grass*. But, one year later, returning to the same problem,
he emphatically affirmed, and without any restriction this
time, the superiority of the Moderns:

It may seem a tall piece of coolness and presumption, for an
humble personage like ourself to put *his* opinions of governments
on the same page with those of the wise men of the ancient days;
but, as a common engineer, now, could tell Archimedes things
to make the latter stare, so the march of improvement has
brought to light truths in politics which the wisest sages of Greece
and Rome never discovered. And it is, at the same time, painful
to yet see the servile regard paid by the more enlightened present
to the darker past.[66]

The contradiction which seems to exist between his moderate attitude in 1846 and the extreme position which he took
in 1847, is, however, only apparent. If he evinced a certain
humility in the first case, it was because he knew very well
that, as regards art and literature, his country still had much
to learn. In the second case, on the contrary, intoxicated by
the success of science and the triumph of democracy in the
new world, he felt only contempt for a past now superseded.

This distinction accounts for the alternations of arrogance and relative modesty through which he constantly went.

To this opposition another must be added. As we have many times had the occasion to notice, Whitman had a keen sense of the becoming and of the constant evolution of the world. As a result, he felt instinctively the dependence in which the present found itself at every moment in connection with the past. But, on the other hand, his belief in progress made him turn his back on the past and set out toward the future with a blind faith in its superiority.

These contradictory influences and these internal tensions explain why, according to the circumstances, he sometimes insisted on the importance of the past, sometimes, on the contrary, called for a resolute break with it and a bold march forward without a backward glance.

At the moment when he began his great adventure with *Leaves of Grass,* he confided to one of his notebooks his dream of an entirely new American literature which he believed himself destined to found:

> We suppose it will excite the mirth of many of our readers to be told that a man has arisen, who has deliberately and insultingly ignored all the other, the cultivated classes as they are called, and set himself to work to write "America's first distinctive Poem" . . . he either is not aware of the existence of the polite social models, and the imported literary laws, or else he don't value them two cents for his purposes.[67]

> I say we have here, now, a greater age to celebrate, greater ideas to embody, than anything ever in Greece or Rome — or in the names of Jupiters, Jehovahs, Apollos and their myths . . . Because, what is America for? — To commemorate the old myths and the gods? — To repeat the Mediterranean here? — No; — (Nä-o-o) but to destroy all those from the purposes of the earth, and to erect a new earth in their place.[68]

But, curiously enough, in 1856, the same man, in his

"Letter to Ralph Waldo Emerson," celebrated the richness of the English language and literature, "all the rich repertoire of traditions, poems, histories, metaphysics, plays, classics, translations" without which future American literature could not be born.[69] And, in 1858, in an article in the *Brooklyn Times,* he went so far as to make fun of all the fanatical reformers, the "amiable lunatics," by whom "everything new was declared to be right, and everything old was pronounced to be wrong." [70]

The same waverings were in evidence in 1860. Meditating on "Antecedents," he declared:

> I respect Assyria, China, Teutonia, and the Hebrews,
> I adopt each theory, myth, god, and demi-god . . .[71]

Then, without being aware of the inconsistency, he recovered his splendid self-assurance and proclaimed:

> I was looking a long while for Intentions,
> For a clew to the history of the past for myself, and
>   for these chants — and now I have found it.
> It is not in those paged fables in the libraries, (them I
>   neither accept nor reject,) . . .
> It is in the present — it is this earth to-day . . .[72]

The Civil War seems to have exacerbated Whitman's nationalism. The fervor with which he celebrated the Union made him unjust to other nations. He had fits of xenophobia. Thus he inserted in "By Blue Ontario's Shore" these lines full of hatred which he suppressed in later editions:

> America isolated I sing;
> I say that works made here in the spirit of other lands,
>   are so much poison in These States.
> How dare these insects assume to write poems for
>   America?
> For our armies and the offspring following the
>   armies? [73]

When the war was over, the intoxication of victory and of regained peace made him renew his declaration of independence with regard to the past:

> Turn O Libertad . . .
> Turn from lands retrospective recording proofs of the past,
> From the singers that sing the trailing glories of the past,
> From the chants of the feudal world, the triumphs of kings, slavery, caste,
> . . . give up that backward world . . .[74]

But this presumptuous attitude did not last. Presently, sickened by the turpitudes of the Reconstruction and probably disappointed again in his love affairs, he took refuge in spiritualism. And that is why, in spite of his enthusiasm for the material progress which had culminated in the building of the Suez Canal, the laying of underwater cables, and the construction of the first transcontinental railroad, he affirmed above all, in "Passage to India," his respect for the past:

> The Past! the Past! the Past!
> The Past — the dark unfathom'd retrospect!
> . . .
> The past — the infinite greatness of the past!
> For what is the present after all but a growth out of the past? . . .
> . . . the present, utterly form'd, impell'd by the past.[75]

Far from turning from the past as in 1867, he now thought with nostalgia of the ancient religions of Asia with which it seemed to him he had mystically come into contact again. It was a sort of looping of the loop: western man rediscovered eastern mysticism and recognized its value after the failure of science to replace the old religions.[76] He then realized more clearly than ever that America is only an extension of the past and that she can neither condemn nor reject it:

> Sail, sail thy best, ship of Democracy,
> Of value is thy freight, 'tis not the Present only,
> The Past is also stored in thee . . .
> Venerable priestly Asia sails this day with thee,
> And royal feudal Europe sails with thee.[77]

America can no more be separated from the old world than a son can be separated from his father.[78]

This was the time when, under the influence of Hegel, he conceived of progress as a synthesis of opposites. So it is not surprising to see him announce in *Democratic Vistas* the transcending and even the destruction of the past by the fusion of present democracy with the spirit of the great men of the past.[79] Moreover, one has the impression that the older he gets the more disappointed he becomes with the present and the more he admires what made the grandeur of the past. Does not he recommend us in "Poetry To-day in America"

. . . to saturate ourselves with, and continue to give imitations, yet awhile, of the aesthetic models, supplies, of that past of those lands we spring from . . .

Ah [he exclaims] never may America forget her thanks and reverence for samples, treasures such as these — that other life-blood, inspiration, sunshine, hourly in use to-day, all days, fore-ever, through her broad demesne! [80]

Thus he insisted more and more on all that America owed to the old world; in the end he even recognized the importance of his own debt:

If I had not stood before those poems with uncover'd head, fully aware of their colossal grandeur and beauty of form and spirit, I could not have written "Leaves of Grass" . . .[81]

We are far here, in 1888, from the poet of 1855 who introduced himself to his reader as a thoroughly uncultivated man of the people, "a rough," as he said.

True, he retained until the end his faith in the future and in democracy, but, in the last years of his life, finding himself still alone on the open road to which he had taken in 1855, he sometimes experienced a certain sadness and one understands the disillusioned conclusion with which he closed his essay on "American National Literature" in 1891: "To all which we conclude, and repeat the terrible query: American National Literature — is there distinctively any such thing, or can there ever be?" [82]

He had dreamed of founding such a literature and he had failed; he realized it now. However, neither that failure nor all the disappointments which had been inflicted upon him as much by the governments as by the governed succeeded in destroying his cult of the United States, of that precious Union [83] for which he had trembled during the Civil War and which was the only present incarnation of his political ideal. It had not been granted to him to enter into the Promised Land, but he was sure that mankind would some day enter into it and that it would be found in America — where he had prophesied.

CHAPTER VII

DEMOCRACY —
"MYSELF" AND MAN "EN-MASSE"

ONE might be tempted, as Newton Arvin was in particular,[1] to exaggerate the influence of the Civil War on Whitman's evolution and to see there a break in his life. True, it would be interesting to contrast the mystical individualist of the years 1855 to 1860 with the fervent democrat of the post-bellum period, whose conversion to altruism would be explained by the spectacle of the sufferings endured by the soldiers. Unfortunately reality is much more complex and does not lend itself readily to such arbitrary oversimplifications. In fact, Whitman's faith in democracy is present in his work from the beginning:

> I speak the pass-word primeval [he exclaimed in 1855]
>   I give the sign of democracy . . .[2]

And, on the other hand, his individualism persisted right to the end. The two elements coexisted continually in him and were combined in different ways according to circumstances. The proportions of the mixture varied, but the mixture itself never really changed. It always consisted of the same inseparable components. The war did not modify it. It constituted a terrible moral trial for Whitman, but it did not destroy his individualism or make him discover a democratic ideal which

146 THE EVOLUTION OF WALT WHITMAN

he had had for a long time. It merely confirmed his faith in it.[3]

This faith in democracy plunged its roots into the most profound part of his being. Had he not inherited it from his Dutch ancestors so fond of liberty? [4] Was it not the natural extension of the Quaker principles of his mother? "I wear my hat as I please indoors or out," [5] he confides to us, for, if he has not retained the Quaker use of "thee" and "thou," he does not concede to any man the right to consider himself his superior. His father, for his part, was an ardent democrat of the old school who hated priests and kings and swore by the founders of the republic. The names which he gave to three of his sons declare clearly enough who were his favorite heroes: George Washington, Thomas Jefferson, and Andrew Jackson.

Whitman never denied his plebeian origins. On the contrary he was proud of them: "I advance from the people in their own spirit . . ." [6] He even had a Tolstoyan concern to have nothing more than others:

> [I] claim nothing to myself which I have not carefully
> claim'd for others on the same terms . . .[7]

And he felt all his life attracted by humble people of unpolished natures whom no education had deformed or dried up:

> The young mechanic is closest to me, he knows me
> well,
> . . .
> The farm-boy ploughing in the field feels good at the
> sound of my voice . . .[8]
> [I have] gone freely with powerful uneducated per-
> sons . . .[9]

All those who knew him admired the naturalness with which he talked with common people and noted how popular and loved he was wherever he went.

It is not surprising therefore that from his first poems, even before the birth of *Leaves of Grass*, Whitman took the defense of the oppressed against tyrants. In 1850, in "Blood-Money," he lashed the slave-owners who, in his eyes, were as guilty as Judas since they sold "the like of God," [10] and the same year he entoned a song of vengeance against the kings of Europe who had suppressed the revolution of 1848 in a blood-bath and thought that they had stifled liberty forever.[11] He believed so much in this last poem that he kept it in *Leaves of Grass* until the end.[12] In 1855, in the poem which he later rightly entitled "Song of Myself," he solemnly affirmed his solidarity with all the victims of intolerance and oppression: the witch who is burned alive, the slave chased by the hounds, and so on.[13] He "beat the gong of revolt, and stop[ped] with fugitives and them that plot and conspire." [14] He has always "hated tyrants," he claims.[15]

This profound faith in democracy, moreover, was as much in harmony with his personal religious credo as with that of his Quaker ancestors. Had not his mysticism revealed to him the divine character of all beings? If he, Walt Whitman, was a god placed at the center of the universe, the same applied to the others who were all in the same way sentient subjects. A democratic society is a sum of subjects all equally centers of the world:

> Underneath all to me myself, to you yourself, (the same
>   monotonous old song.) [16]

He constantly reverted to this idea of the divinity of the individual. In *Democratic Vistas,* for instance, he wrote:

> . . . it remains to bring forward and modify everything else with the idea of that Something a man *is,* (last precious consolation of the drudging poor,) standing apart from all else, divine in his own right, and a woman in hers, sole and untouchable by any canons of authority, or any rule derived from precedent, state-safety, the acts of legislatures . . .[17]

It was fundamentally a Christian notion, as he himself pointed out a few pages later.[18]

His political thought was also influenced by another principle of his metaphysics. At least from 1860 on, he recognized the existence of evil and the necessity of its presence in creation. On the human level he could thus reject no one. The most degraded being contained the same potentialities as the most noble one and was entitled to the same fundamental rights as the others. Besides, how could he have condemned anyone when he felt himself as guilty as the most criminal. The secret inadaptation which resulted from his sexual anomaly obliged him, unless he excluded himself from the human community, to admit into his democracy all men and all women irrespective of their merits or condition. Finally, his political credo was not only an intellectual conception or a combination of abstract ideas, it was also the expression of an elemental instinct, his love of city crowds, which was as lively as his love for the sea or for nature. From his youth he had been a "lover of populous pavements." [19] He loved to spend whole afternoons strolling along Broadway, looking for faces which attracted him, for eyes which furtively answered the caress of his glance:

> Sauntering the pavement thus, or crossing the ceaseless ferry, faces and faces and faces,
> I see them and complain not, and am content with all . . .[20]

So he confides to us in 1856, but in 1860 he makes a more revelatory confession:

> O the streets of cities!
> The flitting faces — the expressions, eyes, feet, costumes! O I cannot tell how welcome they are to me;
> O of men — of women toward me as I pass — The memory of only one look — the boy lingering and waiting.[21]

Thus it is clear that, if he sought out crowds, it was because they gave him all sorts of troubled pleasures. It was one way for him to satisfy his homosexual desires without running any risk, by merely dreaming of adventures which he knew would never come true. One understands now why he felt human solidarity so intensely. For him, it was not simply a moral notion, but the effect of an irresistible magnetism.

The two democratic principles which Whitman proclaimed with the greatest enthusiasm as early as 1855 were Liberty and Equality: "Great is Liberty! great is equality!" [22] Individual liberty seemed to him the indispensable condition of democracy. It answers an immemorial need of the human soul.[23] In all times, heroes and poets have called out for it for the men whom despots had reduced to slavery. History, according to Whitman, is the endless recital of the ever-renewed struggles of tyranny and liberty.[24] It sometimes may seem that the tyrants win, but their temporary victory means nothing, for liberty is imperishable. The "good old cause," [25] as he calls it after Milton, progresses ceaselessly and irresistibly and at last one day will triumph for ever.[26]

This conviction was shared by all his contemporaries. Was it not in particular the central theme of Victor Hugo's *Légende des Siècles*? But, in his love of liberty, Whitman went much further than most of the liberals of his time. For fear that it might wither, he was ready to accept its going as far as license and disorder. As early as 1847, he protested in an editorial in the *Brooklyn Eagle* against the timid souls who were afraid of the turbulence of the democratic spirit.[27] For his part, he regarded it as the best safeguard of liberty and in 1856 he sang of "the audacity and sublime turbulence of the States." [28] A great city, according to him, is a place

> Where the men and women think lightly of the
> laws . . .

Where the populace rise at once against the never-ending audacity of elected persons.[29]

He returned to the subject in his open letter to Emerson:

Always America will be agitated and turbulent. This day it is
taking shape, not to be less so, but to be more so, stormily,
capriciously, on native principles, with such vast proportions of
parts . . . As for me, I love screaming, wrestling, boiling hot
days . . .[30]

This preference for living disorder rather than for dead
order ought not to surprise us. Was not he the poet of the flux
of the world? Had he not sung with a juvenile enthusiasm in
1855 (in spite of his thirty-six years of age) of the intense and
unconstrained life, of dynamism and exuberance? No wonder
that he exclaimed:

Piety and conformism to them that like,
Peace, obesity, allegiance, to them that like,
I am he who tauntingly compels men, women, nations,
Crying, Leap from your seats and contend for your
    lives! [31]

On the political level, he could only praise "the American
contempt for statutes and ceremonies, the boundless impatience
of restraint." [32]

In 1860, going still further, he proclaimed the right to revolt
and recommended permanent disobedience:

. . . I hold up agitation and conflict . . .[33]

Resist much, obey little . . .[34]

In so doing he remained in that protestant tradition of non-
conformity which Thoreau in 1849 had carried to its extreme
limit by preaching "Civil Disobedience," [35] and, at the same
time, ranged himself with those eighteenth-century liberals
for whom any government, any authority is a necessary evil.
The danger of such a doctrine is that by depreciating and

undermining institutions, it may eventually lead to anarchy. Whitman foresaw this objection and answered it in advance in "I Hear It Was Charged against Me":

> I hear it was charged against me that I sought to destroy institutions,
> But really I am neither for nor against institutions,
> (What indeed have I in common with them? or what with the destruction of them?) [36]

The letter of the law mattered little to him. In his eyes, the only thing that really counted was the spirit of democracy. Brotherhood seemed to him to be a sufficient tie between men.

Nevertheless his intransigent individualism sometimes took the form of an insolent defiance of society and of a destructive anarchism, as when he proclaimed:

> . . . I confront peace, security, and all the settled laws, to unsettle them,
> I am more resolute because all have denied me than I could ever have been had all accepted me . . .[37]

These lines were written between 1860 and 1865 (as early as 1859–1860 perhaps, for the phraseology is exactly like that of "Calamus") in a moment of revolt. It is clear that we deal here with a maladjusted person who has a grudge against the society which has rejected him and thwarted his plans. He sets himself up against it. The context reveals that this was the reaction of a disappointed homosexual whose way to happiness had been barred by the laws then in force.

However, the extravagances and the revolts of the poet must not make us forget the man, who knew how to control himself. The rhapsodist sang his ideal and his secret sufferings, but, in the meantime, the journalist wrote sensible and moderate editorials. Much as he wanted to present himself in his poems as "une force qui va," a force on the go [38] — and which even does not know very well where it is going — he was much more reasonable and lucid in real life. Thus, in 1857, he raised a protest against the anarchy then reigning in the Western Territories (though the West was the incarnation of his democratic ideal) and supported Dickens who had very severely criticized all these disorders.[39] Besides, as he grew older, having learned by experience and become less enthusiastic, he gradually understood the dangers of liberty. The views which he expressed on that subject in *Democratic Vistas* are much more moderate than his proclamations in *Leaves of Grass*:

> The eager and often inconsiderate appeals of reformers and revolutionists are indispensable, to counterbalance the inertness and fossilism making so large a part of human institutions. The latter will always take care of themselves — the danger being that they rapidly tend to ossify us. The former is to be treated with indulgence, and even with respect.[40]

So his own appeals must not be taken literally, they have only a provocative value. He believed in a sort of division of labor: the duty of governments is to govern, to give orders, and the duty of poets and intellectuals is to resist and occasionally rebel and disobey. Both functions are equally indispensable in a harmonious society.

But, in 1876, he apparently leaned more toward order than toward liberty. He subordinated freedom to law on the moral as well as on the political plane:

> It is not only true that most people entirely misunderstand Freedom, but I sometimes think I have not yet met one person who rightly understands it. The whole Universe is absolute law. Freedom only opens entire activity and license *under the law*. To the degraded or undevelopt — and even to too many others — the thought of freedom is a thought of escaping from law — which, of course, is impossible. More precious than all worldly riches is Freedom . . . and better than all, a general freedom of One's-Self from the tyrannic domination of vices, habits, appe-

tites, under which every man of us, (often the greatest brawler for freedom,) is enslaved.[41]

So, with age — this evolution is frequent — Whitman became more and more of a conservative.[42] Without renouncing the ideal of his youth, he tended to put the emphasis on law and order rather than on liberty at all costs. That is why, in 1885, in a tribute to George Washington, he referred to "Freedom, pois'd by toleration, sway'd by Law." [43]

The second democratic principle in which Whitman believed was equality. As early as 1855, he insisted with as much vigor on the fundamental equality of all men as on their right to liberty. Holding himself up as a point of comparison, he declared:

> In all people I see myself, none more and not one a
> barley-corn less . . .[44]

Consequently, he felt himself to be the equal of the President and on a level with the sailors whom he met and who for their part took him for one of their own.[45] How could he have made discriminations? Had he not affirmed that "what is commonest, cheapest, nearest, easiest is Me?" [46]

According to him, the mere fact of living conferred a divine character even upon the most despicable being. Was not the body of each man the supreme outcome of the evolution of the universe for thousands of years? [47] He knew, besides — did not his own case prove it? — that social origin and education were of little importance and that the most humble being contained infinite potentialities of grandeur: "Always waiting untold in the souls of the armies of common people is stuff better than anything that can possibly appear in the leadership of the same." [48] So, in 1860, he quite naturally arrived at the notion of "average man" and of "divine average" which from then on was everywhere present in *Leaves of Grass*.[49] He underlined its importance in one of his last poems:

> I chant . . . the common bulk, the general average
> horde, (the best no sooner than the worst) . . .[50]

Yet, in the course of the first years of his poetical career, the pride of the prophet of a new religion clashed in him with the humility of the mystic, brother in God of all creatures. So, even though he proclaimed the equality of all men and extolled the average man with genuine fervor, he could not help celebrating great men almost in the same breath:

> A great city is that which has the greatest men and
> women,
> If it be a few ragged huts it is still the greatest city in
> the whole world.[51]

> All waits or goes by default till a strong being appears;
> A strong being is the proof of the race and of the ability
> of the universe,
> When he or she appears materials are overaw'd,
> The dispute on the soul stops,
> The old customs and phrases are confronted, turn'd
> back, or laid away.[52]

> Produce great Persons, the rest follows.[53]

The contradiction, however, is not so absolute as might at first appear. The great men of whom Whitman thought were neither the Übermenschen of Nietzsche nor the heroes of Carlyle (he reproached the latter with his inhumanity and his scorn for average man): [54]

> Let others praise eminent men and hold up peace . . .
> I praise no eminent man, I rebuke to his face the one
> that was thought most worthy.[55]

> . . . there is to me something profoundly affecting in
> large masses of men following the lead of those who
> do not believe in men.[56]

The great men whom he admires do not behave in an overbearing manner toward average humanity and do not use violence. They are not statesmen and temporal chiefs, but, like himself, thinkers and prophets — poets, in short, such as he has been calling for since 1855, who inspire and lead the masses, or heroes who sacrifice their lives for them,[57] or great engineers who work for their well-being. To the hero-worship which Carlyle had recommended, Whitman in 1871 opposed a "worship new," that of "captains, voyagers, explorers, engineers, architects and machinists." [58]

His own hopes of greatness had been rather quickly disappointed. After the first edition of *Leaves of Grass,* he had dreamed of becoming the poet-orator of the United States, the supreme arbiter of the destiny of his country,[59] but this dream never materialized and his failure made him more modest. In the meantime, the Civil War revealed to him the heroism and the spirit of sacrifice of the average American and confirmed his faith in man "en-masse." [60] Far from exalting the leaders, he then preferred to celebrate the gallantry of the unknown soldiers who fell in combat,[61] and to take up the defense of the men in the ranks against the officers who abused their privileges.[62] When he happened to sing of Lincoln (without ever naming him in his poems), he showed him, above all, not as a great leader of men, but as a "representative man" in the Emersonian meaning of the word, as a magnificent example of the virtues of the average man whom power does not corrupt. Later, he attached himself to Johnson, Grant, and Garfield for exactly the same reasons.[63] When the war was ended, he proclaimed with still more enthusiasm, if possible, than in 1860, the grandeur of the average man:

> Never was average man, his soul, more energetic, more
> like a God . . .[64]

A few years later, in *Democratic Vistas,* he stated once for all that a real democracy is not a government of the best men, of born "heroes," of the natural leaders of the race, but a government whose aim is to teach all the citizens how to govern themselves by granting equal political rights to all.[65]

In this very lucid little treatise, he courageously recognized a certain number of difficulties which he had not been able to mention in his poems, in particular, that

. . . general humanity . . . has always, in every department, been full of perverse maleficence, and is so yet. In downcast hours the soul thinks it always will be . . . I myself see clearly enough the crude, defective streaks in all the strata of the common people; the specimens and vast collections of the ignorant, the credulous, the unfit and uncouth, the incapable, and the very low and poor.[66]

If he accords equality to all, it is, therefore, not through naïveté or blindness, but because he sees there an indispensable condition for the development of mankind. The pessimism which he usually repressed, but which appears for instance in his "Notes Left Over," where he wrote that "Man is about the same, in the main, whether with despotism, or whether with freedom," [67] explains why, as he grew older, he came more and more to insist upon the importance of great personalities. The disgust which the scandals of the Reconstruction caused him and the adulation with which his disciples surrounded him perhaps contributed to this change. At any rate, one fact is certain: toward 1888, his attitude was no longer the same. Whereas in an interview given to a St. Louis journalist in 1879 he had been ecstatic over the vitality of the masses and had declared, "We will not have great individuals or great leaders, but a great average bulk, unprecedently great," [68] he was now upset at the idea that a misunderstood democratic egalitarianism might produce unrelievedly standardized personalities. What he wanted was a leveling not downward, but upward,[69] and his new program called for "the building up of the masses by building up grand individuals." [70] It was then that to the great scandal of his friends he lamented in a very brief poem the death of William I, "a faithful shepherd, patriot." [71]

But [he confided to Traubel] too many of the fellows forget that I include emperors, lords, kingdoms, as well as presidents, workmen, republics . . . I do not see why a democrat may not say such a thing and remain a democrat.[72]

True, but he undoubtedly saw himself more lucidly when he added:

I look in all men for the heroic quality I find in Caesar, Carlyle, Emerson . . . If that is aristocracy then I am an aristocrat.[73]

So, at the end of his life, without ever renouncing his faith in the average man, he leaned very strongly toward the Carlylean concept of great men as an indispensable leaven for the progress of the masses. He must have drawn a certain comfort from that idea. Was it not an exaltation of his own role?

Besides liberty and equality, which safeguard the rights of the individual, a democracy cannot be conceived without brotherhood, which binds the citizens together and assures the unity of the group. It is a curious thing that Whitman hardly ever uses such words as fraternity, brotherhood, brothers. Perhaps he regarded them as devalued because of the excessive and often insincere usage made of them by the churches. At any rate, he always preferred to express his very keen sense of human brotherhood in terms of comradeship. As early as 1855 he used several times the word "comrade," [74] which suggests ties of friendship between workers, or the word "companion," which has the same connotations,[75] but these two words were then fairly colorless and suggested nothing more than "workingmen and workingwomen," a phrase of which he was also very fond. On the contrary, in 1860, the word "comrade" invaded the whole book and expressed an emotion which it did not imply until then. This sudden flowering coincided with the appearance of the Calamus motif and, besides, it was in "Calamus" that the word recurred most often. It is clear when one reads a poem like "Behold this Swarthy Face" [76] that his sense of comradeship was only one form of his homosexual tendencies. But apparently in the irresistible attraction which urged him toward some and which he felt in others he saw a tie capable of uniting all men indissolubly. And so he recommended this "new friendship" and prophesied that

> Affection will solve every one of the problems of free-
> dom,
> Those who love each other shall be invincible . . .
> The most dauntless and rude shall touch face to face
> lightly,
> The dependence of Liberty shall be lovers,
> The continuance of Equality shall be comrades.[77]

Little by little, however, his ardor calmed down and the almost physiological concomitants of his sense of comradeship disappeared. The poem which we have just quoted was even dropped from *Leaves of Grass* as early as 1867. But, in *Democratic Vistas* and in the preface to the 1876 edition, Whitman reaffirmed his faith in the value and necessity of comradeship, giving it, it is true, a more noble and normal form.[78] He even carried the idealization so far as to speak of God as "the great Camerado" or "the Comrade perfect." [79] Thus one observes a gradual spiritualization and a constant enlargement of the notion of what a comrade should be, that ideal comrade whom Whitman doubtlessly sought in vain all his life, for whose presence he craved so passionately in order to escape his solitude.

In addition to liberty, equality, and fraternity, which belong to democracy at all times, Whitman preached a new democratic dogma, particular to his century, namely feminism.[80] In doing so, he renewed a certain Quaker tradition, for the Quakers had for long been in favor of this. There even appeared in 1856 a book entitled *Abbie Nott and Other Knots,* signed with the impenetrable pseudonym of "Katinka," which had a Quaker and a feminist inspiration at the same time and the epigraph of which was borrowed from *Leaves of Grass.*[81] On the other hand, Margaret Fuller, for whom Whitman always had a very great admiration, had been the founder of a feminist movement in the United States; [82] it must not be forgotten either that Whitman was a fervent and faithful reader of the works of George Sand and Frances Wright. As early as 1846 he wrote in the *Brooklyn Eagle* a eulogy of feminine refinement and purity and protested against gallantry which, to his mind, was only skin-deep and rarely came from a profound respect for women — for all women whatever their social rank.[83] His first poetic notes show him anxious to become "the poet of women as well as men":

> The woman is not less than the man
> But she is never the same . . .[84]

Consequently, in 1855, he proclaimed in the preface to *Leaves of Grass* "the perfect equality of the female with the male" [85] and sang:

> I am the poet of the woman the same as the man,
> And I say it is as great to be a woman as to be a
> man . . .[86]

The following line reveals to us the deep reason for his attitude:

> And I say there is nothing greater than the mother of
> men.

Thus his feminism was a form of mother-worship. Above all, he sees the mother in woman, the mother who, in the folds of her body, contains in a latent state all the generations to come and the whole future of mankind.[87] So his feminism implies duties as well as rights. True, as early as 1856 he recognized the same political rights for women as for men:

> Where women walk in public processions in the streets
>   the same as the men,
> Where they enter the public assembly and take places
>   the same as the men . . .
> There the great city stands.[88]

He also admitted that they might practice the same professions as men,[89] but he wanted them to remain feminine and by that he meant maternal, a "sane athletic maternity" being to his mind "their crowning attribute." [90] The future of the United States and of democracy depends upon them, let them not forget it! [91] They must not seek to be "ladies," but on the contrary endeavor to remain women.[92] In his editorials in the *Brooklyn Eagle* [93] and later in *Democratic Vistas* [94] he condemned the artificial and unhealthy fashions which deformed the bodies and ruined the health of women.[95] Nothing was so disappointing to him as, in 1879, to see these fashions spread to the cities of the West,[96] where he had expected to find the robust wives of the pioneers proud of leading a simple and natural life.[97] What irritated him in these fashions was their "abnormal libidousness," [98] an unexpected reproach on the part of the poet of sexual desire, but which can be explained by his homosexuality. The "child of Adam" in practice did not want any mistresses, but only mothers. And so he condemned free love with vigor.[99] And, as regards education, since what mattered above all was to form healthy women capable of bearing children, he was in favor of as simple a system of instruction as possible.[100] Was not his own mother almost illiterate and yet the best of mothers?

So this feminist, even though after the death of his mother he deified woman, "womanhood divine, mistress and source of all, whence life and love and aught that comes from life and love," [101] ended paradoxically by opposing the emancipation of woman as it was understood by the fighters for feminism in his time. He was well aware of it. Did not he write in one of his notebooks: "We have, too, the radical equality of the sexes (not at all from the 'woman's rights' point of view however) . . ." [102] Hence his veneration for Queen Victoria in whom, in 1846, he admired "a gentle-hearted woman" whose "benignant and kindly influence" reconciled him with monarchy.[103] In 1890 he even went so far as to compose a few lines on the occasion of her birthday.[104] In short, she came much closer to the ideal of this strange feminist than most of the American women whom he saw about him.

Whitman's democratic inspiration occupied an increasingly important place in his work. In 1855, one scarcely finds it at all except in the preface, in the eighth and the ninth poems (later entitled respectively "Europe" and "A Boston Ballad," [105]) and here and there in the last poem (later excluded from *Leaves of Grass*).[106] In 1856, the "Poem of Many in One" replaced the preface,[107] and the second poem of the first edition received a title which gave it a more democratic meaning: "Poem of the Daily Work of the Workmen and Workwomen of These States." [108] Besides this, a new poem, "Liberty Poem for Asia, Africa, Europe, America, Australia, Cuba and the Archipelagoes of the Sea" [109] and the Letter to Emerson [110] enriched the democratic message of *Leaves of Grass*, but the main subject of the book nonetheless remained "Myself." The third edition, in 1860, gave still more importance to the theme of democracy by gathering together in two special sections entitled "Chants Democratic" and "Messenger Leaves" most of the poems bearing upon it.[111] After the war, on the very first page of his new *Leaves of Grass*, in a brief introductory poem, Whitman warned the reader of the dualism of his inspiration: "One's-Self" and "the word of the modern, the word EN-MASSE," [112] From then on the two themes were placed on the same footing — theoretically at least, for, in fact, up to the end, "One's-Self" continued to dominate the book.

In his youth, Whitman had always been excited by political questions. The newspapers for which he wrote had always been party papers and he had even been active for a time in the ranks of the Democrats.[113] When he became a poet, he did not retire into an ivory tower. On the contrary, he continued to take an interest in the affairs of the city: "Whatever interests the rest interests me, politics, churches, newspapers, schools . . ." [114] Thus it is not surprising that during the presidential campaign of Fillmore and Buchanan he thought of diffusing through the entire country a violent tract on "The Eighteenth Presidency" [115] which only came to light a long time after his death. But one can perceive echoes of it in his open letter to Emerson.[116] We must not forget either that he assumed his journalistic activities and was chief-editor of the *Brooklyn Times* from 1857 to 1859. During the Civil War, though he did not take an active part in politics, he was nevertheless a fervent unionist and a faithful follower of Lincoln. When the hostilities were over, of course, he celebrated the victory of the Union, but he immediately thought of the dangers which still menaced democracy. This is shown in particular by the additions which he made to his "Poem of Many in One." [117] With a great deal of foresight he understood that the fight was not over and that in spite of the defeat of the Rebels the cause of democracy had not definitively triumphed:

> Democracy, the destin'd conqueror, yet treacherous
>   lip-smiles everywhere,
> And death and infidelity at every step.[118]

His fears were soon realized. The corruption of politicians and the greed of businessmen during the period of the Reconstruction shocked and revolted him.[119] All around him, there was nothing but

. . . incredible flippancy, and blind fury of parties, infidelity, entire lack of first-class captains and leaders, added to the plentiful meanness and vulgarity of the ostensible masses . . .[120]

Sometimes he felt almost tempted to side with Carlyle.[121] But as usual, he refused to give way to discouragement and it was then that, in order to regain valid reasons for still believing in his ideal in spite of all set-backs, he wrote two essays: "Democracy" and "Personalism," which he published in *Galaxy* in 1867 and 1868 and later collected in one volume under the title of *Democratic Vistas*.[122]

In this book, he tries above all to reconcile and unite the two themes he had interwoven in *Leaves of Grass*: the "I" and the masses. He tries to resolve the problem of the harmonious integration of the individual in society.

We shall, it is true, quickly and continually find the origin-idea of the singleness of man, individualism, asserting itself, and cropping forth, even from the opposite ideas. But the mass, or lump character, for imperative reasons, is to be ever carefully weigh'd, borne in mind, and provided for . . . The two are contradictory, but our task is to reconcile them.[123]

The solution seemed to him to reside in something which he called by a name which he was probably the first to use in this acceptation, "personalism." [124] He never defines the word but it is clear that what he means by it is not at all individualism in an ordinary sense but a transcendent form of it, for "personalism" posits the participation of the individual in a cosmic reality. The individual is simultaneously a distinct "identity" and a part of the whole. On the political plane, the consequence of this metaphysical concept is that each man or woman is at the same time a human personality separate from all others and a citizen, that is, an inseparable member of a certain society.[125] Whitman's ideal is a "healthy average personalism" [126] which, according to him, democracy alone is capable of achieving. For, in time, democracy will permit the merging of individualism and "patriotism" (by which he meant the solidarity of the individual with the totality of his country); it contains the promise of the reconciliation, or rather synthesis, of these two opposites.[127] (We find here again the influence of Hegelian dialectic.)

A number of principles which Whitman had affirmed for a long time are grouped around this central doctrine and thus acquire a new significance. Notable among these is his instinctive individualism even though he now seeks to transcend it. From 1855 to 1860, he had proclaimed his "egotism" with vigor:

> I will effuse egotism and show it underlying all, and
>   I will be the bard of personality.[128]

Each individual is an end in himself or herself; only individuals really matter. He repeats these fundamental truths again and again:

> Underneath all, individuals,
> I swear nothing is good to me now that ignores individuals,
> The American compact is altogether with individuals,
> The only government is that which makes minute of individuals,
> The whole theory of the universe is directed unerringly to one single individual — namely to You.[129]

Consequently, he went on, the governors are only the delegates of the governed; they are in power to serve the people, not the other way round: "The President is there in the White House for you; it is not you who are here for him . . ." [130]

One recognizes here some of the ideas Rousseau had developed in the *Social Contract* and it was there in fact that Whitman found them. He had carefully copied whole pages of a translation of that book and annotated them for his own use. His comments show that, though he was taken with the idea of a contract between the governors and the governed (he even uses the word "compact" in this meaning in one of the poems which we have quoted), he laid greater emphasis on individualism than Rousseau did.[131] On that point his opinion had not changed in 1871. For him the ideal still remained the free development of the personality of each member of the community and he deplored the standardization imposed by modern society with its increasingly complex and artificial institutions.[132]

So, in his eyes, the task of a government is not to repress and constrain but, on the contrary, to protect and liberate from constraints so that the individual can expand and develop fully.[133] It is not at all politics which ought to govern the life of each citizen, but morality:

. . . man properly train'd in sanest, highest freedom, may and must become a law, and series of laws, unto himself, surrounding and preparing for, not only his own personal control, but all his relations to other individuals, and to the State . . .[134]

So Whitman ultimately returned to and vindicated the Jeffersonian concept which he had developed in his editorials in the *Brooklyn Eagle*: "The best government is that which governs least." [135]

Such are the constant and fundamental principles of Whitman's political thought, but reality was very different from that ideal and in all his writings one again and again encounters muffled echoes of his disappointments and of his apprehensions.[136] "Great are the plunges, throes, triumphs, downfalls of democracy," he exclaimed in 1835 [137] in a passage which he suppressed ten years later in the joy of recovered peace. In 1860, he threatened those who were responsible for the failures of democratic institutions:

And I will make a song for the ears of the President,
full of weapons with menacing points,
And behind the weapons countless dissatisfied faces
. . .[138]

Democratic Vistas shows it: he was not ignorant of political corruption, he knew about dishonest electoral practices, he was aware of the insincerity and lack of faith of politicians.[139] Later he even went so far as to recognize that all the animadversions made by Carlyle on democracy had solid foundations.[140]

However, none of the contradictions which reality inflicted upon him succeeded in impairing his faith. In his eyes the present evils were always mere accidents and not at all failings inherent in the essence of democracy. The present might be disappointing, but the ideal would eventually triumph.[141] If he remained optimistic in spite of his lucidity, it was because he put all his hope in the future, in 1855 as well as in 1871. Like all his contemporaries, he believed in progress, without, however, ignoring the fact that human nature changes very little [142] and that a ceaseless struggle would be necessary to assure the victory of democracy.[143] He thus applied to politics his Hegelian conception of the becoming.

His other reason for hope was his absolute confidence in the average American. He expressed it very early. In his editorials in the *Brooklyn Eagle*, in the preface to the first edition of *Leaves of Grass*,[144] he sang the praises of the little people, their fundamental honesty, the warmth of their friendship, their passionate love of liberty, their generosity, their vigor. On this point he admitted neither the condescending attitude of Carlyle nor the contemptuous indifference of Thoreau. Moreover, as we have seen, the Civil War confirmed his judgment in a striking manner. It seemed to him that it gave definite proof of the grandeur of the average man by bringing out the sense of responsibility which impelled soldiers to volunteer, their endurance, their heroism in the midst of danger and the stoicism which, in the hospitals, made them bear atrocious sufferings without complaint.[145] The turpitudes of the regime were thus not their fault; a minority of avid profiteers, insatiable industrialists, and greedy politicians were alone responsible.[146]

Such was Whitman's democratic credo. It never varied in its essence. In his newspaper articles, in his poems, in his essays, in spite of crises and reverses, Whitman always remained faithful to it. If his political thought remained so coherent and so constant, it was because, as we have pointed out, it corresponded to certain profound needs of his temperament.

There was, however, one problem in the face of which Whitman's thought always remained very hesitant, and that was the social problem, or "the poverty question," as he sometimes called it.[147] He was preoccupied very early with the existence of this scandalous anomaly in a democratic society and he devoted numerous articles to it in the *Brooklyn Eagle* in 1846 and 1847. He protested in particular against the paltry wages paid to women in the garment industry, which gave them only the choice of two evils, utter destitution or prostitution.[148] He protested against the slavery to which servants were reduced (since any personal life was practically denied them) and he was also against the abusive exploitation of young clerks who were often obliged to remain in the shops from five in the morning to nine-thirty at night.[149] In the same way he took violent exception to the rich industrialists who ruthlessly cut down the wages of unskilled workers under the pretext that the supply of labor was greater than the demand.[150] One finds an echo of these courageous protests in the first poem of the 1855 edition of *Leaves of Grass*:

> Many sweating, ploughing, thrashing, and then the chaff for payment receiving,

> A few idly owning, and they the wheat continually
> claiming.[151]

But this is only one rapid allusion and the question of
capitalistic exploitation is nowhere else mentioned in his poetic
work. Moreover, if he condemns it here in passing, it is less
for political than for moral reasons. Capitalism is denounced
less as a form of social oppression than as one aspect of that
"mania of owning things" of which he disapproved thoroughly.
The economic crisis of 1857 and its attendant ills once
more attracted his attention to this painful problem. He stigmatized in the *Brooklyn Times* the indifference of the rich
who, in their watering-places, forgot the distress of the unemployed, and he attacked the stupidity of the female welfare
workers who campaigned against alcoholism instead of taking
the defense of the poor garment workers against the insatiable
greed of their employers.[152] The absurdity of capitalism in a
period of crisis revolted him:

> The granaries of the land are filled with the harvests of the
> year, and, strange to tell, the philanthropic are everywhere medi-
> tating by what means famine shall be kept from our doors.[153]

But, for his part, he saw no remedy for the situation. It
seemed impossible to him for psychological reasons to suppress
individual profit, the basis of a capitalistic economy. He regarded as utopian the nationalizations which some had recommended.[154] Thus he felt completely powerless. Besides, he was
a poet and not a man of action. He could only look out and
record the sufferings which it was not in his power to prevent
or alleviate. He expressed this purely passive attitude in a poem
of 1860:

> I sit and look out upon all the sorrows of the world, and
>   upon all oppresssion and shame . . .
> See, hear, and am silent.[155]

After the war, "the labor question," as he then called it,

continued to preoccupy him. In *Democratic Vistas* he mentioned ". . . that problem, the labor question, beginning to open like a yawning gulf, rapidly widening every year . . ." [156] In a note which he seems to have thought of using as an introduction to his "Songs of Insurrection" in 1871, he indicated among other dangers "the more and more insidious grip of capital." [157] On the other hand, the same year, he published a dithyrambic poem in honor of George Peabody, certainly a great philanthropist but nonetheless a great capitalist, who, after all, had merely given back to the poor with one hand what he had taken from them with the other.[158] That this fact escaped Whitman shows that he had never reflected much on the question and that his reactions were, above all, sentimental.

Before long his kind heart had other reasons for sadness. In 1873 a financial panic occurred and was followed by a new economic crisis. Hundreds of thousands of Americans found themselves ruined or jobless and were obliged to beg and sleep on the streets. Whitman's letters to Peter Doyle are full of allusions to all the distressing scenes he had the occasion of witnessing at the time.[159] In the years which followed, the situation only got worse; the workers tried to organize and strikes multiplied. In 1877 serious trouble broke out in Pittsburgh and in Baltimore (not very far, in short, from Camden where Whitman was then living). Railroad employees incensed by repeated wage cuts set round-houses and workshops on fire. Martial law had to be proclaimed and the federal troops and the militia called out to restore order. Whitman followed these events with passion. There has been found among his papers a series of five long articles which he cut out of an English journal, the *Sunderland Times*.[160] And it was then that he wrote his essay on "The Tramp and Strike Questions," [161] where once more, and with bitterness, he complained of the existence of a gulf between the rich and the

poor. What difference was there, he asked, between the Old
and the New World? If the situation became worse, the social
question would slowly but surely eat away the entire structure
of American democracy "like a cancer of lungs or stomach,"
and "then our republican experiment, notwithstanding all its
surface-successes, [would be] at heart an unhealthy failure"
and a revolution as terrible as the French Revolution of 1789
would finally break out one day.[162]

However, even in that critical period, he envisaged the
problem less from a social than from a moral angle. His point
of view remained the same as in 1855: the profound cause
of all these evils was none other than the sordid materialism of
the nation.[163] In his old age, even at the time of the violent
strikes of 1886, as the conversations which he had with Traubel show, his scapegoat was still money, the thirst for money.[164]

F. O. Matthiessen believed that he discerned an evolution
in Whitman's political thought and that the poet "veered
inevitably, though by no very coherent course, from individualism towards socialism." [165] Newton Arvin thought the
same.[166] But each of them, in fact, imposed his own convictions upon Whitman, for this evolution is nowhere apparent.
On the contrary, Whitman was conscious of the social problem
all his life and reverted to it again and again from his articles
in the *Brooklyn Eagle* until his death — which, of course,
does not mean that he did not at times cease to think of it.
Indeed, he seems to have been preoccupied with it mainly
under the pressure of external events, when some particularly
shocking facts were brought to his notice. On the other hand,
the intermittent interest which he had for that question does
not at all imply that he leaned toward socialism. He scarcely
knew anything about that doctrine and what he did know did
not satisfy him at all.

It is surprising, at first sight, that this poet with so curious
and so open a mind, usually anxious to keep himself well in-

formed on scientific discoveries and new ideas, never tried to
learn about the theories of Karl Marx. One might almost believe that the social problem did not torment him as much as
certain critics have thought. His work does not contain a single
allusion to *Das Kapital*.[167] But if the ideas of Marx were hardly
known in America at the time, it was not the same with those
of Henry George. *Progress and Poverty* had appeared in 1878
and soon excited universal interest. Yet, ten years later, Whitman had still not read it and asked Traubel to sum it up for
him. The remarks which he made on that occasion are characteristic of the superb contempt which he felt for social thinkers:

> Horace [he said to Traubel one day] what is this Henry George
> thing — this single tax fandangle: tell me about it: tell me all
> you know: I hear so much said for it, against it, that I feel as if
> I should know what all the fireworks are about. [Traubel] talked
> for the next half hour about *Progress and Poverty*. [Whitman]
> asked a lot of questions . . . finally he said: That'll do: now
> I begin to know what the hullaballoo means. It's a plausible
> scheme, too, it seems to me, at first blush. I have no doubt the
> statisticians could come along and disprove it — but what can't
> they disprove? . . . It is my impression of him, however, that
> he too is the victim of a special twist, bias . . .[168]

This judgment is characteristic of his attitude toward socialism in general. Being the poet of the cosmos, the poet of the
whole of mankind, he could not accept the limitations of a
doctrine which reduced all problems to those of the working
class. And so he bitterly criticized the fanaticism of labor
unionists:

> They would set on their fellow-workingmen who didn't belong
> to their "union" like tigers or other beasts of prey. It was their
> "union" against the world.[169]

He wanted to deal with men, not with workers. The
workers, he thought, must not cut themselves off from the rest

of the human community. He considered himself the champion of humanity rather than the champion of one class.

On the other hand, though he sometimes admitted that a social revolution might break out some day and become as necessary and inevitable as were, in their times, the American Revolution and the Revolution of 1789, he never called for it; he hoped on the contrary that it could be averted. He had no confidence whatever in these great upheavals. To a brutal revolution he preferred a slow evolution. And he was confident that things would mend and that all would end well:

. . . once open the eyes of men to the *fact* of the intimate connection between *poor pay* for women, and *crime among women*, and the greatest difficulty is overcome. The remedy will somehow or other follow — for benevolence when aroused among the body of the people, tends to the reform of whatever abuse it is directed against . . .[170]

So he wrote in 1847, and, in his old age, he confided to Sidney Morse, while sitting for his bust, that

He was not sure but things were working well enough as they were, evolving in their natural course far better results than any theory of socialism could promise.[171]

Thus the ideal solution for him was a liberal capitalism of the sort which Carnegie had advocated in *Triumphant Democracy*.[172] Far from wishing for the abolition of private property and the communal sharing of all goods which seemed to him impossible anyway, he put all his hope in a world of small property owners,[173] for the simple reason that

. . . the laws are always advantageous to the possessors, and injurious to non-possessors — from which it follows that the social state can only be beneficial to men when all possess some, but none too much, property.[174]

Such a Jeffersonian conception is certainly better adapted to an agricultural than to an industrial society, and that is the reason why, in spite of his enthusiasm for the astounding achievements of modern industry, Whitman sometimes dreamed with nostalgia of the agricultural civilization of former times.[175] However, for all these anachronistic preoccupations, unexpected from the poet of the future, the moderate solution he recommended was not altogether absurd. To some extent events have vindicated him. American society has not quite evolved in the way he predicted, but capitalism nevertheless has known how to adapt and amend itself so as to avoid that excessive concentration of wealth which Marx believed inevitable and to procure indispensable material comfort for a ceaselessly increasing number of people.

On the other hand, one must not forget that Whitman, who placed liberty above all, even above material achievements,[176] could never have accepted the socialist concept of a minute regulation of all economic activities. On this particular point he had very fixed ideas which never varied: he was a free-trader. He championed that doctrine in the *Brooklyn Eagle* [177] and in 1855, rather unexpectedly, he exclaimed "Great is . . . free-trade . . . !" in *Leaves of Grass*,[178] and his conversations with Traubel show that in his old age he still believed in it with unabated fervor. Absolute free trade appeared to him as a panacea capable, in particular, of putting an end to war and he rejoiced that Henry George was also in favor of it.

One other reason for his indifference to socialism, and a no less potent one, was his idealism. He regarded the life of the spirit as infinitely more important than the problem of the redistribution of wealth. In all his poetical works, and with increasing insistence after 1860, there recurs like a leitmotiv the affirmation that what really matters in a republic is neither material abundance, nor institutions; nor even knowledge, but the virtue of the citizens and the saving grace of an ideal among a few orators and poets.[179] Religion, he constantly claims, is more valuable than wealth, and he gives to "religion" a very broad sense:

> But behold! such [that is, "ostensible realities," the
> world of material appearances] swiftly subside,
> burnt up for religion's sake . . .
> I say that the real and permanent grandeur of these
> States must be their religion,
> Otherwise there is no real and permanent grandeur
> . . .[180]

He is still more explicit in *Democratic Vistas*:

It may be claim'd, (and I admit the weight of the claim,) that
common and general worldly prosperity, and a populace well-to-
do, and with all life's material comforts, is the main thing, and is
enough. It may be argued that our republic is, in performance,
really enacting to-day the grandest arts, poems, &c., by beating up
the wilderness into fertile farms, and in her railroads, ships,
machinery, &c . . . I too hail those achievements with pride and
joy: then answer that the soul of man will not with such only —
nay, not with such at all — be finally satisfied; but needs what,
(standing on these and on all things, as the feet stand on the
ground,) is address'd to the loftiest, to itself alone.[181]

Such is the real problem for him. He is afraid lest the United
States sink into materialism, lest what ought to be only a stage
in its evolution become a permanent condition. And so he puts
all his hopes in the formation of an elite of completely disinterested poet-apostles who will inject their spiritualism into the
masses,[182] but he does not close his eyes to the fact that the
process is extremely slow.[183] At any rate, it is clear that the
most important element in the democratic society of which
he dreams will not be the holders of temporal power, but the
writers, the representatives of spiritual power. In the last
analysis, it does not matter much to him whether the democratic regime is or is not the best means of assuring an equitable
distribution of consumers' goods; what counts in his eyes is
that it would permit the free development of individuals and
the full growth in all men of the moral and religious sense
which feudal and ecclesiastical institutions usually had stifled

and stunted in the past. In short, democracy is for him, above all, a means of working out one's salvation on earth; his supreme aim is to allow the development in all of

. . . a towering selfhood, not physically perfect only — not satisfied with the mere mind's and learning's stores, but religious, possessing the idea of the infinite . . . realizing, above the rest, that known humanity, in deepest sense, is fair adhesion to itself, for purposes beyond — and that, finally, the personality of mortal life is most important with reference to the immortal, the unknown, the spiritual, the only permanent real, which as the ocean waits for and receives the rivers, waits for us each and all.[184]

His point of view is thus not that of a socialist, but that of a transcendentalist. Had not Emerson already declared that ". . . the highest end of government is the culture of men . . ."?[185] Whitman was conscious of that filiation and quoted him several times.[186] Like his master, he yearned after a spiritual democracy and boldly prophesied its advent.[187]

So, ultimately, Whitman's democratic doctrine is, despite appearances, the credo of a solitary man. He admits it himself:

I should say, indeed, that only in the perfect uncontamination and solitariness of individuality may the spirituality of religion positively come forth at all . . . Bibles may convey, and priests expound, but it is exclusively for the noiseless operation of one's isolated Self, to enter the pure ether of veneration, reach the divine levels, and commune with the unutterable.[188]

Democratic Vistas and all his poetic works are the credo of a solitary man, but of a solitary man who is looking for the way out of his metaphysical solitude — which perhaps was nothing but the isolation of a maladjusted person — in order to integrate himself in the human community, because, according to him:

The master sees greatness and health in being part of the mass; nothing will do as well as common ground. Would you

have in yourself the divine, vast, general law? Then merge yourself in it.[189]

And this explains why he undertook to write *Leaves of Grass*
and the reason for the book's growth. He composed it in order
to commune and communicate with the mass of men. Hence
the importance and frequency of the passages in which in 1855
and 1856 he evoked the soul of crowds. Much as his self is
the center of most of his poems, he is never really alone. He
feels encouraged and supported by the impalpable presence
of the whole of mankind. He has "the certainty of others, the
life, love, sight, hearing of others." [190]

His cosmic sense was thus complemented by a unanimistic
sense — long before unanimism existed; and indeed the unanimists have recognized him as a precursor.[191] If he takes the
Brooklyn ferry, he is conscious of the existence about him of
the innumerable troop of all the men who have taken it before
him or will take it in the future.[192] He imagines "the progress
of the souls of men and women along the grand roads of the
universe" [193] and he enjoys being carried along by this uninterrupted tide. Hence his attachment to New York where he
has everyday on Broadway the spectacle of humanity "en-
masse," where he can "merge with the crowd and gaze with
them." [194] He knows that under ordinary circumstances very
few men feel this unanimism with the same intensity that he
does, but, let some catastrophe occur, he says, and then

. . . mark how eagerly [the newspaper accounts] are seized
upon, and devoured by millions who are entirely destitute of
selfish and personal interest in the matter, and who are only
moved by that mysterious sympathy which is the universal bond
underlying all mankind . . . despite the sneers of the cynics
and the doubters . . . it will be seen that in every man's better
nature beats something responsive to the "still sad music of humanity" . . .[195]

This is precisely what happened during the Civil War and

Whitman's unanimism was then reinforced. He sang of the patriotic enthusiasm which electrified the first volunteers, "the torrents of men" which poured over Manhattan,[196] and he rejoiced to hear the tramping of millions of feet.[197] He absorbed the "electric spirit" of those "dreadful hours." [198] But he also hoped that one day there would be a communion of all nations and there would be only one heart for the whole world.[199] Humanity, he thought, would eventually become as unanimous as the United States.[200] And during all his life he kept that belief in the existence of a collective soul. In 1881, in his essay on "Poetry To-day in America," he explained that each nation has a soul which is not merely the sum of the individual souls of which it is composed, but, on the contrary, transcends all those willful and selfish egos.[201] That same year, he felt the unanimous soul of the United States shiver at the assassination of President Garfield,[202] and in 1888 he celebrated again with nostalgia the "hurrying human tides" of Broadway.[203]

His unanimism, in short, was the meeting-point of his mysticism and his democratic faith, and, like his mysticism, it gradually lost its force. One might even wonder if in his old age his enthusiasm for democracy did not to some extent cool down. Did he not write in 1883 in the preface to *November Boughs*:

. . . I consider "Leaves of Grass" and its theory experimental — as, in the deepest sense, I consider our American republic itself to be, with its theory. (I think I have at least enough philosophy not to be too absolutely certain of anything, or any results.) [204]

But his moderation and Olympian detachment must not deceive us. This belated relativism is not really skepticism. Whitman only wished thus to indicate his indifference to doctrines and to the letter of dogmas. His ideal in fact remained the same and his faith was unchanged. Indeed, a few pages further he affirms:

. . . the New World needs the poems of realities and science and of the democratic average and basic quality, which shall be greater . . . The new influences, upon the whole, are surely preparing the way for grander individualities than ever . . . One main genesis-motive of the "Leaves" was my conviction (just as strong to-day as ever) that the crowning growth of the United States is to be spiritual and heroic.[205]

However, it is clear that, in the political as well as in the metaphysical domain, as his life approached its end, Whitman increasingly emphasized the spirit and insisted more and more on the liberty and grandeur of the individual who is eventually to face death alone rather than on the needs and the aspirations of the anonymous masses.

CHAPTER VIII

DEMOCRACY AND RACIALISM — SLAVERY

U NTIL 1862, American democracy presented a singular anomaly: while the Constitution promised "the blessings of liberty" to the inhabitants of the Union and to their posterity, the colored population of the South was reduced to slavery. This scandal tormented many consciences, but the problem was much more complex than was realized by the European readers of Dickens' *American Notes* or of *Uncle Tom's Cabin*, and it took Emerson for instance, a long time, despite all his idealism, to espouse the cause of abolitionism.[1] So one may wonder whether Whitman knew the same hesitations and was held back by the same scruples.

Traubel asked him one day if he had been an abolitionist in his youth. "Certainly," Whitman replied — "From the first?" — "Yes, from the first: and not only anti-slavery: more than anti-slavery: a friend, indeed, all around of the progressist fellows: that's where, why, how, I finally cut off from the Democratic party." [2] But, in so saying, either he was lying in order not to bring discredit upon himself and disappoint a young admirer whose radical opinions he knew, or his memory betrayed him, for, in fact, his attitude with regard to the Negro question had been more hesitant and uncertain than he suggested.

During his childhood, he had seen Negro slaves in Long Island; he mentions the fact in *Specimen Days* without indignation.[3] It is true that in the North the masters worked in the fields side by side with their slaves and in general treated them well. Perhaps that is why he maintained in *Franklin Evans* that the Negroes would be much worse off if they were free. They were housed, fed, and clothed, and their masters were full of solicitude for them since they represented a part of their capital. Indeed their condition was preferable to that of the proletarians in Europe. Theirs was a "merely nominal oppression." Consequently, our young author concluded, the philanthropists of the Old World should not interfere with the systems of the New.[4] And he reasoned in the same way in an editorial which he wrote that same year for the *New York Aurora,* "Black and White Slaves." [5]

It was only in 1846 that he began to protest against slavery.[6] One of the first articles which he published in the *Brooklyn Eagle* was a violent attack against the slave trade. He described the horrors of a passage on board a slave ship and demanded that condign punishment should be meted out, not to the crews, but to the brokers who organized that infamous trade.[7] He was not an abolitionist for all that. A few months later, he attacked "the mad fanaticism or ranting of the ultra 'Abolitionists,' " whose zeal, he claimed, had done "more harm than good to the very cause [they] professed to aid." [8] He regarded them as dangerous agitators and monomaniacs ready to destroy everything in order to liberate the slaves. Their haste seemed excessive to him and their convictions much too simplistic. On the contrary, he fully approved the principles set forth in the State Address of Massachusetts:

Speaking of a well-developed and healthy Democracy, it says, — "It may regard slavery anywhere and everywhere, as a great evil, a direct, practical denial of the essential truths of Democracy. It may deplore the misfortune, the misconduct, or the inconsistency of every sister State where slavery exists. It may . . . lament that Congress has no power to purchase the freedom of every slave, and proclaim a universal emancipation. But it will not the less remember, that the power of Congress is limited within narrow and well-defined boundaries," etc.

"But while we deprecate . . . the perversion of a benevolent association into a fierce political party, we discountenance and despise that morbid and sickly fear of disunion, which sometimes robs our private citizens and public officers of their manhood, so far that they dare not whisper an honest word or attempt a proper act, concerning slavery, lest the slave-holding States take offence. This base surrender of opinion, this cowardly apprehension of Southern discontent, is as offensive to the Southern Democrat as it ought to be to all; and let us recollect, as a fact pregnant with meaning, that it was a Virginia Democrat, in the National Congress, who first stigmatized temporizing Northern politicians by the expressive epithet of 'dough-faces' " . . .⁹

So, at that date, Whitman disapproved of the principle of slavery and felt that one must not be afraid to say so, but he considered abolitionism as an illegitimate attempt to intervene in the affairs of the South and he feared that the consequences would be disastrous for the Union. He preferred therefore to retain the *status quo* and wait patiently for a change of heart in the South. In this respect, he thought, like Jefferson and the anti-Federalists at the end of the eighteenth century, that the federal power must bow to the "sovereignty and independence of the States."

This policy of non-intervention was not at all, however, a policy of capitulation, for Whitman was violently opposed to all new concessions, notably regarding the extension of slavery in the new territories of the West. This was a delicate problem which had already cropped up at the time of the Louisiana Purchase. It had been resolved in 1820 by the Missouri Compromise, but it reappeared in an acute form after the Mexican War. It was then that Whitman led a violent campaign against extension in the *Brooklyn Eagle,* invoking the authority of

Washington and Jefferson, both of whom had condemned slavery.[10] He pointed out in particular that the Southern states had taken only an insignificant part in the operations.[11] He also very cleverly tried to divide the Southerners by opposing to the rich planters who owned slaves the small farmers who worked with their own hands.[12] And here we discover the basic reason for his hostility to slavery: it not only degraded the Negroes (that seems to have mattered very little to him), but also the white workers whose standard of living it reduced to a scandalously low level.[13] He could not bear that idea and vituperated the slave-owners. Let these men be content with the advantages conceded to them in violation of the Constitution [14] and let them beware: the free men of the North might get tired of their "insolent demands":

Already the roar of the waters is heard; and if a few short-sighted ones seek to withstand it, the surge, terrible in its fury, will sweep them too in the ruin.[15]

Thus he went as far as threats and coldly envisaged the necessity of a war to oblige the South to give in.

One other reason for his anger was that he was beginning to be afraid for the sake of that Union which he placed above all. If the Southerners, by their obstinacy, put it in danger, it might be the end of liberty in America and perhaps in the whole world:

Quite all the happiness that we enjoy, which springs from the political institutions of our country — much of our ability to confer happiness on the thousands from abroad that annually claim homes here — all the respect paid our names in foreign climes, the regard to our citizens' rights, and the opening of avenues to commercial profit — depend likewise on the same Union. Further than this: the perpetuity of the sacred fire of freedom, which now burns upon a thousand hidden, but carefully tended, altars in the Old World, waits the fate of our American Union. O, sad would be the hour when that Union should be dissolved! Then might the good genius of humanity weep tears of blood, bitterer than any ever before shed for the downfall of her high hopes! [16]

As one sees, there is no mention of Negroes in all that. The only thing that matters in Whitman's eyes is the cause of liberty, his own and that of the white workers, his brothers. But on this point he was intransigent. In 1847 the only acceptable solution seemed to him to be the Wilmot Proviso which would forbid slavery in the new territories. He praised it to his readers [17] and, when Isaac Van Anden, the owner of the *Eagle,* sought to impose a different political line on him, he preferred to resign and lose his position rather than go back on his free-soil convictions.[18]

Yet, two or three months later, he was on the staff of the *New Orleans Crescent,* in which he could daily read advertisements offering slaves for sale. But this was not the result of a sudden revulsion; to his mind, he remained perfectly consistent. Did he not hate the dough-faces of the North more than the planters of the South? At the bottom of his heart he even had a secret indulgence for the latter. He condemned them insofar as they were slave-owners, but he could not help admiring them as men. Being a great reader of Walter Scott, he had been conquered by their nobleness and their chivalric spirit even before he went to the South.[19] And then perhaps he had no choice. He had just lost his job and accepted the first interesting offer which was made to him. Besides, his stay in New Orleans was of only a short duration. In September 1848 he was back in Brooklyn as editor of the *Freeman,* a free-soil newspaper.

Unfortunately, the dough-faces whom he hated so much were not long in triumphing over the free-soilers within the Democratic party, and, one year later, Whitman was obliged to hand in his resignation. Moreover, under the leadership of Henry Clay and Daniel Webster, the Whigs took over Congress and, to appease the South, accepted the Compromise of 1850 which in Whitman's eyes amounted to a capitulation. Under the new law about fugitive slaves, the federal authorities henceforth had to return escaped slaves to their masters and, as regards new territories, they would decide themselves, at the time of their admission into the Union, whether they would or would not be slave-states. There was thus a risk that slavery would extend further and the stain spread even to the Northern states, which could no longer offer legal refuge to fugitive slaves. These concessions roused indignation in the North. Whittier, Emerson, and Thoreau were all three equally revolted.[20] As for Whitman, he gave free course to his pain and and his rage in four poems which he published at once in the New York newspapers: "Song for Certain Congressmen," "Blood-Money," "The House of Friends," and "Resurgemus." [21] There he attacked above all the cowardice and the corruption of the professional politicians who for sordid reasons of personal interest had just betrayed the ideal of the nation. He reserved all his rage for the infamous "dough-faces" and forgave the slave-owners:

> Virginia, mother of greatness,
> Blush not for being also the mother of slaves.
> You might have borne deeper slaves —
> Doughfaces, Crawlers, Lice of Humanity . . .[22]

It was probably at that time that he frequented the anti-slavery meetings.[23] He imagined himself ascending the platform, "silent, rapid, stern, almost fierce," and delivering "an oration of liberty — up-braiding, full of invective — with enthusiasm." [24] As so often with him, this was only a stray impulse and a dream; in fact, he took no action; and yet he went so far as to prepare notes for such a speech. They have been found among his papers. He proclaimed in them his intention to help any fugitive, whether he be "an Irish fugitive or an Italian or

German or Carolina fugitive," "whether he be black or white,"
even if he is "coarse fanatical, and a nigger," for "while he has
committed no crime further than seeking his liberty and defending it, as the Lord God liveth, I would help him and be
proud of it, and protect him if I could." [25] Thus, once more,
he broadened the problem. In his eyes it is not so much a
question of the emancipation of the Negroes as of the liberty
of all men. And so he puts forward a new argument: slavery
degrades not only the slave, but also his master, and not only
his master, but all the citizens of the community where he lives:

What real Americans can be made out of slaves? What real
Americans can be made out of the masters of slaves? . . .
Some simple person or worse, asks how this degrades us. —
We are not in personal danger of degradation. — Why, what
can be a greater meanness and degradation than for a proud and
free community to have forced upon it from an outside power,
officers who go at their pleasure and say to a man, come, this
soil is no protection to you? [26]

Such was the position of the journalist and it helps us to
understand that of the poet. For we find in the first version
of *Leaves of Grass* the very same revolt against the Fugitive
Slave Law as in his articles of the *Brooklyn Eagle*.[27] "Resurgemus" is even included in the book; only its typographical
aspect has changed,[28] and, on the other hand, the ninth poem,
later entitled "A Boston Ballad," [29] fiercely attacks the federal
authorities of that city who had arrested a fugitive slave and
returned him to his master. Here and there Whitman also
evokes painful or frightening scenes which show all the horror
of slavery: a fugitive slave caught up by his pursuers and
killed on the spot,[30] the sale of a Negro by auction,[31] and, in
the following edition, slaves chained together by twos and
threes,[32] and a Negro woman beaten with a whip.[33] Despite
the impassive tone and the objectivity of these descriptions,
one feels him deeply moved and indignant. Moreover, he puts

"the family kiss" on the right cheek of a "cotton-field drudge" [34] and imagines himself receiving a fugitive slave in his home and making ready to shoot at those who might come to claim him.[35] Are not the blacks "divine-soul'd," "nobly-form'd, superbly destin'd, on equal terms with [us]"? [36] So slavery appeared to him as one of the cruelest manifestations of evil on earth:

> Damn him [Lucifer]! how he does defile me,
> How he informs against my brother and sister, and
>   takes pay for their blood,
> How he laughs when I look down the bend after the
>   steam boat that carries away my woman.[37]

Yet, despite the indignation which he felt, he could not help praising "the noble Southern heart." [38] For he wanted to stand above the struggle and be at the same time "the poet of slaves and of the masters of slaves." [39] His aim was to penetrate to "the essence of the real things" and thus understand both

> . . . slavery and the tremulous spreading of hands to protect it, and the stern opposition to it which shall never cease till it ceases or the speaking of tongues and the moving of lips cease.[40]

The articles which he wrote for the *Brooklyn Eagle* a few years later reflect his perplexity. Then he even went so far as to admit that slavery had its good points; but what, more than all the rest, prevented him from taking sides was that "there are just as great reforms needed in the Northern States. Perhaps, there are greater reforms needed here, than in the Southern States." [41]

Thus he discovered, like Emerson, a supplementary reason to be indifferent to abolition: the social problem,[42] which seemed to him infinitely more serious and more urgent than that of slavery. And so, in 1860, he painted an idyllic picture of the life of the slave in the South:

> There are the negroes at work in good health . . .

> In Virginia, the planter's son returning after a long
> absence, joyfully welcom'd and kiss'd by the aged
> mulatto nurse . . .[43]

This does not prevent him from strongly condemning in
another poem of the same edition the possession of a man by
a man,[44] or, above all, from affirming once more:

> . . . where liberty draws not the blood out of slavery,
> there slavery draws the blood out of liberty . . .[45]

And he added:

> Once more I proclaim the whole of America for each
> individual, without exception.[46]

Moreover, his hatred for the Fugitive Slave Law was un-
diminished, as his attitude during the Sanborn affair shows.
He happened to be in Boston in 1860 at the time when the
Supreme Court of Massachusetts was trying an abolitionist
named Frank Sanborn, who had been arrested by the federal
authorities for helping negro slaves to escape. His acquittal
was in no doubt, but his friends invaded the courtroom to
prevent, by force if necessary, the bailiffs from arresting him
a second time. Whitman had joined them to give them a hand,
should the occasion arise.[47] John Brown's condemnation to
death by a Virginia court certainly moved him much less [48]
(even though he celebrated the old man's heroism in "Year
of Meteors").[49] He could only disapprove of the recourse to
violence of that fanatic abolitionist, whatever respect he felt
for his courage and thirst for martyrdom.

During the whole Civil War, as must be expected after such
premises, Whitman's sole preoccupation was the Union.[50] On
this point he shared Lincoln's views and he was grateful to the
President for not having yielded to the pressure of the abolitionists, those "fire-eaters." [51] He was angry with the "slave-
ocrats" of the South,[52] not because they owned slaves, but

because they had tried to break the sacrosanct Union. He damned them in 1860; he called them murderers in 1867.[53] But is it not strange that he did not devote a single poem to the Emancipation Proclamation? [54] The only allusion to the liberation of the slaves that can be found in *Leaves of Grass* is a short poem, "Ethiopia Saluting the Colors," [55] which he added to his *Drum-Taps* only in 1871, as if he had belatedly realized that this was a rather serious omission.

Such a lack of enthusiasm is surprising on the part of a poet who placed liberty and equality above all, and one may wonder if the reasons which he gave for his indifference are sufficient. It seems not. In fact, he was obeying a motive which he never mentioned anywhere and which he perhaps did not dare to avow to himself: he instinctively felt a kind of aversion for Negroes. In a sketch which he never published he described a group of slaves in these terms:

And here are my slave-gangs, South, at work upon the roads, the women indifferently with the men — see, how clumsy, hideous, black, panting, grinning, sly, besotted, sensual, shameless.[56]

He goes so far as to reproach them with the color of their skins and he can scarcely hide his disgust. Eldridge, his publisher in 1860, who knew him well in Washington during the war, has reported that:

Of the Negro as a race he had a poor opinion. He said that there was in the constitution of the negro's mind an irredeemable trifling or volatile element, and that he would never amount to much in the scale of civilization. I never knew him to have a friend among the negroes while he was in Washington, and he never seemed to care for them . . . In defence of the negro's capabilities I once cited to him Wendell Phillips' eloquent portrait of Toussaint L'Ouverture, the pure black Haytian warrior and statesman . . . He thought it a fancy picture much overdrawn, and added humorously, paraphrasing Betsy Prig in "Martin Chuzzlewit", "I don't believe there was no such nigger." [57]

Indeed Whitman believed Negroes quite incapable of governing themselves.

We hear a monstrous deal about the horrors of negro slavery
[he had written in the *Brooklyn Times*], cannot some one who
has visited the court of his Majesty Foustin I, give us an idea of
the results of negro freedom there, and also in the West Indies?⁵⁸

In short, he felt, like Carlyle, that God had created the
blacks to act as servants to the whites. So he took good care
not to raise the slightest protest in *Democratic Vistas* against
the anti-abolitionist passages in *Shooting Niagara*.⁵⁹ In *Leaves
of Grass* he even went so far as to hide the fact that the heroic
fireman who dies, crushed by a wall while fighting a fire was
originally a Negro, as the first version of the passage shows.⁶⁰
Sometimes, however, he made an effort to conquer his prejudice. In the hospitals, during the war, he treated the wounded
Negroes whom he encountered with kindness, he tells us, and
always gave them something. But he does not dwell on it and
there is hardly any mention of it in his notebooks.⁶¹ They did
not interest him. Many times, on the contrary, he scarcely
concealed the repugnance or contempt which he felt for that
race — in his letters to his mother in particular.

We had the strangest procession here last Tuesday night [he
wrote to her in 1866], about 3000 darkeys, old & young, men &
women — I saw them all — they turned out in honor of *their*
victory in electing the Mayor, Mr. Bowen — the men were all
armed with clubs or pistols — besides the procession in the
street, there was a string went along the side walk in single file
with bludgeons and sticks, yelling and gesticulating like madmen
— it was quite comical, yet very disgusting & alarming in some
respects — They were very insolent, & altogether it was a strange
sight — they looked like so many wild brutes let loose.⁶²

In the war reminiscences which he published, however, he
rendered homage to the good conduct and gallantry of the

colored troops, but, even then, remarks of this sort sometimes escape him:

> Certes, we cannot find fault with the appearance of this crowd — negroes though they be . . .
> Occasionally, but not often, there are some thoroughly African physiognomies, very black in color, large, protruding lips, low forehead, etc. But I have to say that I do not see one utterly revolting face.[63]

A little later, attending a military parade, he found it quite curious to see Lincoln "standing with his hat off" to a regiment of black troops "just the same as the rest" as they passed by.[64] Finally, in 1872, in the course of a visit to his sister's home in Vermont, he rejoiced at not seeing a single Negro.[65] One has the impression that their vast numbers in Washington where they had flocked after the war almost frightened him. Of course, he nowhere dares to express his fear of a black peril for America, but one feels that he cannot help thinking of it.[66]

Thus Whitman's position with regard to the Negro problem never changed. In his old age, he told Traubel things which he might as well have told forty years before:

> The negro was not the chief thing: the chief thing was to stick together. The South was technically right and humanly wrong . . . Phillips — all of them — all of them — thought slavery the one crying sin . . . I never could quite lose the sense of other evils in this evil — I saw other evils that cried to me in perhaps even a louder voice: the labor evil . . . to speak of only one . . .[67]

Thus, contrary to Emerson who had at first shown the same indifference as he, but who was not long in becoming an ardent abolitionist,[68] Whitman always held the same views and even broke with his faithful friend, William O'Connor, sooner than declare the abolitionists to be in the right. Much as he approved of Rousseau's declarations on the fundamental equality of all men beyond racial differences,[69] he nevertheless continued to behave and to react like a Long Island peasant whose grand-parents had owned slaves.[70] As often with him, his attitude was determined by instinctive and deeply rooted preferences rather than by reasoning and logic. His obstinacy and his complete imperviousness to the arguments of the abolitionists can thus be accounted for.

CHAPTER IX

INDUSTRIAL CIVILIZATION

IN 1889, Mark Twain sent to Whitman the following message on the occasion of the poet's seventieth birthday:

You have lived just the seventy years which are the greatest in the world's history and richest in benefit and advancement to its peoples. These seventy years have done much more to widen the interval between man and the other animals than was accomplished by any five centuries which preceded them.

What great births you have witnessed! The steam press, the steamship, the steel ship, the railroad, the perfected cotton gin, the telegraph, the telephone, the phonograph, the photograph, photogravure, the electrotype, the gaslight, the electric light, the sewing-machine and the amazing infinitely varied and innumerable products of coal tar, those latest and strangest marvels of a marvelous age . . .[1]

That reminder was quite appropriate. Had not the nineteenth century seen the United States pass from an agricultural to an industrial era with extraordinary rapidity? And no poet was more alive to that prodigious growth than Walt Whitman. In 1871, he rapturously proclaimed in *Democratic Vistas*:

When the present century closes, our population will be sixty or seventy millions. The Pacific will be ours, and the Atlantic mainly ours. There will be daily electric communications with every part of the globe. What an age! What a land![2]

Most of the poets of his time, however, did not share his enthusiasm.[3] The intrusion of factories and railroads in landscapes which had up till then been undisturbed and pastoral had been deplored or even cursed by the romantics. The attitude of Vigny turning away from "servile cities" ("les cités serviles") and observing with mistrust "the railroads which cut across the hills" ("le fer des chemins qui traverse les monts") had been general. Like him poets thought that

> Sur le taureau qui fume, souffle et beugle,
> L'homme a monté trop tôt . . .[4]

And, like him, they had carefully avoided the use in verse of the impure words which served to designate the new inventions. Most often the romantics did not even have his boldness and deliberately ignored the existence of industry. The Past and Nature alone seemed to them worthy of being sung in verse. There appeared to be an incompatibility between industry and poetry.[5]

The American transcendentalists had been bolder. Thoreau, unsociable and old fashioned as he was, was not insensible to the beauty of the locomotives which rode through the woods not far from his retreat at Walden Pond.[6] As for Emerson, he very clearly saw the problem which industrial civilization created for poets and readers of poetry:

> Readers of poetry see the factory-village and the railway, and fancy that the poetry of the landscape is broken up by these; for these works of art are not yet consecrated in their reading; but the poet sees them fall within the great Order not less than the beehive or the spider's geometrical web.[7]

He was thus in favor of the integration of industry into poetry.

But, whereas Emerson had only very timidly put into practice himself the principles he had formulated,[8] Whitman undertook intrepidly, as early as 1855 in the first edition of

Leaves of Grass, to incorporate in his poems the most prosaic industries and to mention machines or tools which no one had dared to name in verse before him.[9] Thus it is that in his poem on occupations he lists:

> The etui of surgical instruments, and the etui of oculist's or aurist's instruments, or dentist's instruments;
> Glassblowing, grinding of wheat and corn . . . casting, and what is cast . . . tinroofing, shingledressing,
> Shipcarpentering, flagging of sidewalks by flaggers . . . dockbuilding, fishcuring, ferrying;
> The pump, the piledriver, the great derrick . . . the coalkiln and brickkiln,
> Ironworks or whiteleadworkers . . . the sugarhouse . . . steamsaws, and the great mills and factories;
> . . .
> The cylinder press . . . the handpress . . . the frisket and tympan . . . the compositor's stick and rule,
> The implements for daguerreotyping . . . the tools of the rigger or grappler or sailmaker or blockmaker,
> Goods of guttapercha or papiermache. . . . colors and brushes . . . glaziers' implements . . .[10]

He does not shrink from the most technical terms, he even goes so far as to enumerate the different parts of the steam-engine [11] and the different tools of the shoemaker.[12] "The steam-whistle, the solide roll of the train of approaching cars," [13] the crash of the triphammers, and the press whirling its cylinders,[14] seem to him as worthy of interest as the virgin forests of Florida or the wildest mountains. For the poet, according to him, contains "the essences of the real things . . . the wharf-hem'd cities and superior marine" [of the United States] as well as "the unsurveyed interior . . . the factories and mercantile life and laborsaving machinery" as well as "the Southern plantation life." [15]

> Great are marriage, commerce, newspapers, books, free-
> trade, railroads, steamers, international mails and
> telegraphs and exchanges . . .[16]

he already exclaimed in 1855, and, in 1856, returning to the
same idea in his open letter to Emerson, he listed some of the
subjects available for American poets:

> . . . the different trades, mechanics . . . money, electric tele-
> graphs, free-trade, iron and the iron mines . . . those splendid
> resistless black poems, the steam-ships of the seaboard states, and
> those other resistless splendid poems, the locomotives, followed
> through the interior states by trains of rail-road cars.[17]

So great was his enthusiasm that, to the already long list
of occupations and tools which he had compiled the preceding
year in the second poem of his book, he now added a certain
number of new inventions which he had omitted to note,
like "the permutating lock that can be turned and locked as
many different ways as there are minutes in a year . . . electro-
plating, stereotyping," and so on. He even added a few more
parts to his steam-engine and took the occasion to describe in
detail the melting and refining of iron and the manufacturing
of "strong clean-shaped T rail for rail-roads." [18] On the other
hand, his "Broad Axe Poem" retraced the epic of the exploration and conquest of the American continent and called up
with fervor:

> Shapes of factories, arsenals, foundries, markets,
> Shapes of the two-threaded tracks of railroads,
> Shapes of the sleepers of bridges, vast frameworks,
> girders, arches . . .
> Shapes of turbulent manly cities . . .[19]

Thus it is not surprising that he proudly declared in his letter
to Emerson:

> Of the twenty-four modern mammoth two-double, three-double,
> and four-double cylinder presses now in the world, printing by
> steam, twenty-one of them are in the United States.[20]

As the country became increasingly industrialized, he thus gave industry more and more importance in his poems. In 1860, he thought of writing poems on the different occupations:

> O I will make the new bardic list of trades and tools!
> . . .
> O for native songs! carpenter's, boatman's, ploughman's
>   songs! shoemaker's songs! [21]

He summed them up in the long poem which later became "I Hear America Singing." [22] And, to begin with, he intoned this hymn:

> O to work in mines, or forging iron,
> Foundry casting, the foundry itself, the rude high roof,
>   the ample and shadow'd space,
> The furnace, the hot liquid pour'd out and running.[23]

He also invited his readers to look at the steamers "steaming through [his] poems," "immigrants continually coming and landing," "ceaseless vehicles, and commerce" in "cities, solid, vast . . . with paved streets, with iron and stone edifices," "the many-cylinder'd steam printing press," "the electric telegraph stretching across the continent," "the strong and quick locomotive as it departs, panting, blowing the steam-whistle" "the numberless factories," and the "mechanics busy at their benches." [24]

Nor did he forget to sing the arrival of the "Great Eastern" in the port of New York, "well-shaped and stately," "600 feet long," the proud symbol of the wealth and power of this New World whose population and production figures were ceaselessly increasing.[25] To modernize his text and keep up with improvements, he went even so far as to change "sail'd" into "steam'd." [26] With his sense of the becoming of the world he could not but approve of the dynamism of American economy. So he called out for

. . . the choicest edifices to destroy them;
Room! room! for new far-planning draughtsmen and
  engineers!
Clear that rubbish from the building-spots and the
  paths! [27]

He thus already had the typically American taste for change
and renovation, for destroying in order to rebuild. He was
carried away by the national desire for ceaselessly going ahead.

The organizers of the annual exhibition of the American
Institute were therefore well inspired when, in 1871, they
invited him to read a poem at the opening ceremony. No one
was better qualified than he to celebrate in verse the achievements of American industry. For that occasion he composed
his "Song of the Exposition" which is a hymn to the glory of
technology. In the first lines he invites the Muse to leave the
Old World in order to come and settle in the "great cathedral"
of "sacred industry." [28] For the monuments and artistic treasures of Europe belong to a dead past. With its incessantly
renewed creations, with its intense life, industry alone ought
henceforth to matter in the eyes of poets. Thus he leads his
poor Muse, somewhat frightened at first by the thud of the
machines and the sharp sound of the steam-whistles, among
the drain-pipes, the gasometers and artificial fertilizers, and
enthrones her in the middle of kitchen utensils,[29] more useful
and closer to the realities of life than Greek or Roman temples
or "Rhenish castle-keeps." [30] Then he takes her about the
stands and does not spare her any detail. She must watch the
harvesting and weaving of cotton, the coining of money and
the printing of a newspaper on a marvelous Hoe press.[31] He
speaks highly to her of the latest successes of technology from
the transatlantic cables to the Suez Canal by way of the Mont-
Cenis tunnel.[32] Finally he exalts the infinite resources of the
United States, the inventive mind of its inhabitants and their
innumerable patents.[33]

In 1876, the same enthusiasm makes him discover the beauty of a locomotive in winter, with its black cylindrical body, its decorations of golden copper and silver-colored steel, its rhythmic breathing, its "long, pale, floating vapor pennants," "tinged with delicate purple," and the "dense and murky clouds out-belching from [its] smoke-stack." [34] But usually it is not aesthetic pleasures that he asks of machines. What he admires in industry and what attracts him toward it is its prodigious vitality, its power, and the magnitude of its achievements. To the end of his life, he was in ecstasy before the miracles of modern technology. Thus, during his trip to the Far West, he was amazed by the ingenuity of Pullman sleeping cars [35] and in 1888 he devoted a poem to the orange blossoms which had been sent to him by mail from Florida.[36] The idea of protesting against the overrunning of the country by industrial progress never occurred to him. On the contrary, during his stay at Burroughs' farm, in 1878, he noted with pleasure that in the night "the rolling music of the RR. trains" could be heard across the Hudson.[37] And he rejoiced to find factories and telegraph poles even in the Rocky Mountains.[38]

What were the reasons which led this poet of the solitary beaches of Paumanok and of the vast, free spaces thus to give his unqualified approval to modern industry which destroyed solitude and spoiled nature? There is no lack of reasons and there is no contradiction between his love of nature and his enthusiasm for industry. Is he not first of all the poet of the body as well as of the soul? It is natural therefore that he should be sensitive to the material aspect of civilization. And then, especially in the second half of the nineteenth century when it made such prodigious progress in this new country, industry was not merely a quest after material rewards, it also implied a desire to dominate matter; it is a passionate outburst of vitality and energy, a manifestation of man's "élan vital" and as such it seduced the mystic in Whitman for whom the world was essentially a constant becoming. It merged quite naturally in his conception of the universe as a force which goes continually forward, as perpetual evolution. Far from interfering with the schemes of nature, it is going in the same direction, for it is

. . . strong, real, rank and practical, like Nature — doing just the thing that is needed without timid regard to nicety — with an opulence of power . . .[39]

He thus eventually reasserted in his own way Carlyle's "work is worship," "laborare est orare":

Ah little recks the laborer,
How near his work is holding him to God,
The loving laborer through space and time.[40]

On the political plane, there was the same pre-established harmony between industry and his democratic ideal. For he saw in industry the promise and guarantee of infinite progress for mankind. Thanks to the steamboats, to the telegraph, to the press, to the innumerable factories which were appearing everywhere, thanks even — this was indeed the height of optimism — to more and more perfect engines of war, soon, all over the earth, men would be united and free, universal democracy would triumph.[41] There would then prevail everywhere

Practical, peaceful life, the people's life, the People themselves,
Lifted, illumin'd, bathed in peace — elate, secure in peace.[42]

The industrial power of modern nations also flattered his sense of the grandeur of man. In 1848, after visiting the engine-room of the Brooklyn ferry, he noted:

It makes one think that man — he who can invent such powers as this — is not such an insignificant creature after all. All the immense power of this able-to-kill-and-destroy structure is controlled by a couple of men, who stop it or set it going as easily as a child rolls his hoop.[43]

For all these reasons Whitman was very early excited over factories and machines. Being careful to keep up with his time [44] and to accept the scientific conception of the world, it was natural that he should also be interested in the practical applications of science. All his life, with an untiring curiosity — which was perhaps, if we are to believe Freud, a sublimation of his abnormal sexual instincts [45] — he visited factories, questioned workers,[46] cut out of the newspapers all the accounts of new inventions. As early as 1848, he wrote a dithyrambic article in the *Brooklyn Eagle* on the power of steam-engines in boats.[47] In 1856, the line on metallurgy which he added to his "Song for Occupations" was the fruit of a visit which he made to a factory in the Adirondacks.[48] Before composing his poem on the axe, he methodically collected information on the "process of making, tempering and finishing" an axe. "Inquire fully," he noted in one of his rough draughts. "What wood is the kelson generally?" he even asked himself.[49] In 1857 he wrote an article for the *Brooklyn Times* on the porcelain factories of Greenpoint,[50] and he noted on a newspaper clipping:

> The list of one week's issue of patents from the National Patent Office at Washington illustrates America and the American character about as much as anything I know. Remember the Crystal Palace and the American Institute Fairs.[51]

No invention seemed beneath his notice. He was keenly interested in sewing-machines, and wrote to friends in 1857: "What a revolution this little piece of furniture is producing — Isn't it quite an *encouragement* . . ." [52] He was probably thinking of the poor dressmakers whose fate he had so often pitied and whose burden was going to be lightened. Twenty years later he cut out of a Philadelphia newspaper the account of an exhibition of sewing and knitting machines.[53] The importance of a new product like gutta-percha did not escape him either; he at once told the readers of his newspaper about it,[54] and mentioned it in one of the poems of the first edition of *Leaves of Grass*.[55] In 1879, during his trip to the West, he did not fail to visit an important glass-works near Saint Louis and one night admired from a distance the blaze produced by a zinc-smelting establishment.[56]

For him industry was also an inexhaustible treasury of new words with which he loved to enrich his poems in order to give them a force and a character which no other poem had had before.

Factories, mills, and all the processes of hundreds of different manufacturers grow thousands of words [he noted in 1856]. This is the age of the metal Iron. *Iron, with all that it does, or that belongs to iron, or flanges from it,* results in words: from the mines they have been drawn, as the ore has been drawn . . . They are ponderous, strong, definite, not indebted to the antique — they are iron words, wrought and cast . . . I love these iron words of 1856.[57]

This was the reason he compiled those long lists of technical words with which he cluttered up some of his poems.

The metaphysical, political, journalistic, and artistic motives which made him take an interest in industry did not blind him to its dangers, however. Already in 1855, placing himself on a purely mystical plane, he condemned in the opening poem the commercial activities of which he approved in the preface.[58] Businessmen, engrossed in their deals, too often forget the feast of life, it seemed to him. What is the point of making so much money? [59] In any form of work there is both much more and much less than is generally believed. Much more, for the ultimate end of work, which is the liberation of man, is noble; much less, for what is the value of the money which it brings? [60] What matters, he affirmed in 1856, is not

> a teeming manufacturing state . . . or the best built
>   steamships . . .
> Or hotels of granite and iron . . . or any chef-
>   d'oeuvres of engineering . . .[61]

but the quality of the men who make up that nation and the liberty which they enjoy. He insisted more and more on the fact that work and industry are only means and not ends in themselves — especially after the war. He thus declared in *Democratic Vistas*:

> I too hail those achievements with pride and joy: then answer that the soul of man will not with such only — nay, not with such at all — be finally satisfied; but needs what, (standing on these and on all things, as the feet stand on the ground,) is ad-dress'd to the loftiest, to itself alone.[62]

Instead of going into ecstasies, as in 1856, over the number and power of the rotatory presses owned in the United States, he now complained that they were never used to print anything great and enduring.[63] For his part, if he had to, he would sacrifice all the merchant ships in the world to save the great masterpieces of antiquity.[64] He knew that such views were exceptional and he emphatically condemned the materialism (which he called "realism") of his contemporaries.

> To the cry, now victorious — the cry of sense, science, flesh, incomes, farms, merchandise, logic, intellect, demonstrations, solid perpetuities, buildings of brick and iron, or even the facts of the shows of trees, earth, rocks, &c., fear not, my brethren, my sisters, to sound out with equally determin'd voice, that conviction brooding within the recesses of every envision'd soul — il-lusions! apparitions! figments all! [65]

The soul alone is important. Hence the conclusion which he gives to his "Song of the Exposition," even though it is a hymn to industry:

> While we rehearse our measureless wealth, it is for
>   thee, dear Mother, [that is, Democracy]
> We own it all and several to-day indissoluble in thee;
> Think not our chant, our show, merely for products
>   gross or lucre — it is for thee, the soul in thee, elec-
>   tric, spiritual! [66]

He repeated this nobly idealistic profession of faith less
ostentatiously, but with no less fervor in 1888 in a short five-
line poem, "The United States to Old World Critics." [67]

His increasingly marked leaning toward a spiritualistic con-
conception of the world thus appears even here. And that is
why, in spite of his fundamental adhesion to industrial civilization, he now and then had weak moments during which, tired
of "cities, and artificial life, and all their sights and scenes," [68]
he regretted "the smell of sun-fried hay, where the nimble
pitchers handle the pitch-fork," "new wheat," and "fresh-
husk'd maize." [69] Much as he expected industry to secure the
final liberation of man, he could not help being frightened by
the materialism of industrial society and dreaming, like Jefferson a century earlier, of an agricultural republic of pure
morals:

> There is a subtle something in the common earth, crops, cattle,
> air, trees, &c., and in having to do at first hand with them, that
> forms the only purifying and perennial element for individuals
> and for society. I must confess I want to see the agricultural oc-
> cupation of America at first hand permanently broaden'd. Its gains
> are the only ones on which God seems to smile. What others —
> what business, profit, wealth, without a taint? What fortune else
> — what dollar — does not stand for; and come from, more or
> less imposition, lying, unnaturalness? [70]

Thus the journalist, the "lover of populous pavements," had
not killed in him the little Long Island peasant.

PART TWO

THE PROGRESS OF HIS ART

CHAPTER X

STYLE — FROM MYSTICISM TO ART

EMERSON one day confided to a friend that *Leaves of Grass* reminded him at one time of the *Bhagavad-Gita* and the *New York Herald*.[1] Its style is indeed most incongruous. Lyrical flights are to be found side by side with prosaic banalities, mystical effusions with the most familiar expressions from the spoken language. Sometimes Whitman transcribes an everyday scene with extreme simplicity and the greatest transparence:

> The little one sleeps in its cradle,
> I lift the gauze and look a long time, and silently brush
>   away flies with my hand.[2]

Sometimes he heaps up abstract words interminably with an enthusiasm which the reader does not always share:

> Great is Liberty! great is Equality! . . .
> Great is Youth — equally great is Old Age . . .
> Great is Wealth — great is Poverty — great is Expres-
>   sion — great is Silence . . .[3]

Even more, the same verse sometimes brings these two clashing elements together:

> I concentrate toward them that are nigh, I wait on the
>   door-slab.[4]

Too often one passes without transition from the loose, woolly, pretentious language of the journalist who pads his text with big words to the rapid and precise evocation of a concrete detail. It even happens that his best passages are spoiled by the brusque intrusion of a learned word in a very simple context:

> The field-sprouts of Fourth-month and Fifth-month be-
> came part of him.
> Winter-grain sprouts and those of the light-yellow corn
> and the *esculent roots* of the garden . . .[5] [italics
> ours]

The same jarring note is sometimes produced by the unex-pected use of a slang term:

> The spotted hawk swoops by and accuses me, he com-
> plains of my *gab* and my loitering.[6] [italics ours]

Thus, most often, the different stylistic elements, instead of being used separately and kept free from all admixture, enter into complex combinations. The concrete passages, in partic-ular, are not always the realistic and perfectly objective little pictures of the sort which we have quoted above. Habitually, the mind of the poet diffuses its own divinity over the void of the external world; [7] grass is not that inert substance which a child carries to him in his fist, but "the flag of [his] disposition, out of hopeful green stuff woven." [8] His sensibility and, all the more, his sensuality, often modify the image of things which he gives to us:

> Smile O voluptuous cool-breath'd earth!
> Earth of slumbering and liquid trees . . .
> Earth of the vitreous pour of the full moon just tinged
> with blue . . .[9]

Matter then is dissolved; trees become liquid and contours fluid (these two adjectives "liquid" and "fluid" recur frequently in his verse). One is witness to a mysterious transmutation of the real in which his imagination also intervenes.[10] For Whitman is not content with what he has before his eyes; he wants to evoke, to imply, as it were, all the rest of the world, the infinity of space, and the "amplitude of time."[11] He soon abandons the stallion whose beauty and dash so much impressed him:

> I but use you a moment and then I resign you stallion —
>   and do not need your paces, and outgallop them,
> And myself as I stand or sit pass faster than you.[12]

Hence cosmic visions of this sort:

> My ties and ballasts leave me, I travel — I sail — my
>   elbows rest in sea-gaps,
> I skirt sierras, my palms cover continents . . .
> I fly those flights of a fluid and swallowing soul,
> My course runs below the soundings of plummets
>   . . .[13]

He is transformed into a comet and travels round the universe with the speed of light:

> I depart as air, I shake my white locks at the runaway
>   sun,
> I effuse my flesh in eddies, drift it in lacy jags.[14]

This dissolution of himself and this fluidity of the world permit the boldest and most unexpected images:

> My foothold is tenon'd and mortis'd in granite . . .[15]

> . . . a leaf of grass is no less than the journey-work of
>   the stars . . .
> . . . [I] am stucco'd with quadrupeds and birds all
>   over[16]

> . . . the sobbing liquid of life . . .[17]

The complexity and the discords of his style are not due solely to his lack of education and to his habits as a journalist, they derive also from the duality of his point of view on the world. Sometimes he places himself on the plane of the senses and describes the visible in simple and direct terms. Sometimes, as a mystic, he transcends physical appearances and tries to suggest the invisible. As he himself says:

> I help myself to material and immaterial . . .[18]

Thus is explained the co-existence in his work of descriptive passages and of somewhat obscure lines where he tried to express the inexpressible and translate those mysterious hiero-glyphics which in his eyes all material objects were.[19] The problem of the inexpressible haunted him.

> There is something that comes to one now and per-
> petually,
> It is not what is printed, preach'd, discussed, it eludes
> discussion and print . . .
> It is for you whoever you are, it is no farther from you
> than your hearing and sight are from you,
> It is hinted by nearest, commonest, readiest, it is ever
> provoked by them . . .[20]

> I do not know it — it is without name — it is a word
> unsaid,
> It is not in any dictionary, utterance, symbol . . .[21]

How can one resolve this insoluble problem? A frontal attack is impossible. One can only approach it indirectly. And that is precisely what Whitman does. As early as 1855 he understood that in order to evoke "transcendent" reality he had to be "in-direct and not direct or descriptive or epic" [22] (what Paul Claudel calls "la divine loi de l'expression détournée"):

> I swear [he said the following year] I see what is
> better than to tell the best,
> It is always to leave the best untold.[23]

And, in 1860, defining the "laws for creation," he formulated this precept:

There shall be no subject too pronounced — all works
shall illustrate the divine law of indirections.[24]

So, instead of saying, he must suggest [25] — not by means of
the music of his verse, as the symbolists tried to do later, for
it never for a moment occurred to him — but by means of
images since "the unseen is proved by the seen." [26] This may
lead to a certain obscurity, but a poem must be a beginning
rather than an end and it belongs to the reader to take up the
poet's suggestions and to finish it.[27] In short, Whitman defined
here beforehand the fundamental principles of symbolism;
and he was still more explicit in *Specimen Days*: "The play of
imagination with the sensuous objects of Nature for symbols,
and Faith . . . make up the curious chess-game of a poem
. . ." [28] These ideas were not altogether new; they had already
broken through in the subjective theories of the romantics and
the transcendentalists,[29] but no one had yet applied them with
as much audacity as Whitman and no poet before him had
dared to express his *joie de vivre* by means of an image as "indirect" as this:

> As God comes a loving bed-fellow and sleeps at my side
>   all night and close on the peep of the day,
> And leaves for me baskets covered with white towels,
>   swelling the house with their plenty.[30]

We have here, it is true, an extreme case where the oneiric
character of the evocation and the gratuitousness of the asso-
ciations almost announce surrealism. Whitman, in general,
was reluctant to go in that direction. Comparing himself to
Blake about 1868–1870 in an essay which he never had
occasion to publish, he wrote:

> Blake's visions grow to be the rule, displace the normal condi-
> tion, fill the field, spurn this visible, objective life, & seat the
> subjective spirit on an absolute throne, wilful & uncontrolled. But
> Whitman, though he occasionally prances off . . . always holds

the mastery over himself, &, even in his most intoxicated lunges or pirouettes, never once loses control, or even equilibrium.[31]

The passing from the objective to the subjective plane is thus deliberate and conscious with him, and conscious, too, is his care never to lose contact with objective reality. One is reminded of Wordsworth's skylark which, unlike Shelley's, never forgets in the midst of her wild flight that she has left her nest on the earth; much as Whitman launched his "yawp" over the rooftops of the world, his feet remained firmly planted on the ground.[32]

The most felicitous passages of *Leaves of Grass* are thus those in which Whitman has succeeded in fusing the diverse elements of his style, those in which he suggests rather than describes and soars rather than trudges through interminable objective catalogues, those, too, in which he takes flight but does not get lost in the clouds. His expression is effective whenever he manages to interweave abstractions and familiar terms as in:

> I believe in those wing'd purposes . . .[33]

Or in:

> Agonies are one of my changes of garments.[34]

These unexpected combinations give a new vigor to his style. But he fails every time he lets one of these elements prevail over the others, notably when he falls into didacticism and preaches in abstract terms his democratic gospel or his personal religion:

> There can be any number of supremes — one does not countervail another any more than one eyesight countervails another, or one life countervails another.
> All is eligible to all . . .[35]

"How plenteous! how spiritual! how résumé!" [36] he went so far as to say in 1860.

Such are the characteristics of Whitman's style in the first two editions of *Leaves of Grass*; but we might have drawn our examples from later editions as well, for until the end his qualities and his faults remained the same. "Grand is the Seen" written at the end of his career is the exact counterpart of "Great are the Myths" published in 1853.[37] Is that to say that he made no progress in the interval? Not at all. The patient labor of revising his work which he undertook from 1856 to 1881 was not in vain and reveals an increasingly finer artistic sense.[38] Matthiessen claims that these corrections are disconcerting and cannot always be justified,[39] but we do not share his opinion on this point. If some of them appear useless, most of them serve a purpose and can be vindicated.

First of all, as we have pointed out,[40] Whitman in growing old understood that it had been maladroit and tasteless to shock his readers by introducing crude details in contexts where one would not expect to find them. So, without really renouncing the poems which had a sexual inspiration, he gradually eliminated from the others such verses as:

> Have you sucked the nipples of the breasts of the
> mother of many children! [41]

and:

> And have an unseen something to be in contact with
> them also.[42]

The first of these lines was suppressed in 1860, that is to say, the very year he added "Calamus" and "Children of Adam" to *Leaves of Grass*.

He very soon also tried to avoid the monotony of certain repetitions and in particular the coordinating conjunctions which he had over-used in the first edition. Numerous are the *and*'s and the *or*'s which disappeared in 1856.[43] Later he got rid of the *O*'s, realizing that that was a little too facile a method for a lyric take-off. As early as 1867 he suppressed "Apostroph," where they swarmed [44] and eliminated many others in 1881, for instance, in "Out of the Cradle Endlessly Rocking," where one critic in 1860 had counted thirty-five O's.[45] It had taken Whitman twenty years to come round to his view. Generally speaking, he attempted to remove all the repetitions which had no expressive value and whose monotony weighted his verse, particularly all the useless *I*'s which came after coordinating conjunctions,[46] as well as the numerous *I swear*'s which in fact added nothing.[47] He also cut out a number of awkward lines such as "A breed whose testimony is behaviour." [48]

> If you would be better than all that has ever been be-
> fore, come listen to me and I will tell you,

in 1867 became:

> If you would be freer than all that has been before
> come listen to me.[49]

He also suppressed a number of colloquial phrases the incongruity of which in certain passages he now perceived. Thus it was that in 1867 he no longer retained "plenty of them" at the end of the following line:

> If you remember your foolish and outlaw'd deeds, do
> you think I cannot remember my own foolish and
> outlaw'd deeds? [50]

"You mean devil" similarly disappeared from "Myself and Mine." [51] The Prince of Wales who had been democratically hailed as "sweet boy" in 1860, became "young prince" in 1881.[52] In "The Centenarian's Story" he avoided the colloquial usage of "good" as an adverb,[53] and in 1871 he eliminated from "Crossing Brooklyn Ferry" "Bully for you!" and "Blab, blush, lie, steal," which were undoubtedly very expressive,

but which he now considered too slangy.[54] In 1881 he redoubled his severity with himself and suppressed not only
these youthful lines from "Song of Myself":

> That life is a suck and a sell, and nothing remains in
> the end but threadbare crape and tears.
> Washes and razors for foofoos — for me freckles and
> a bristling beard.[55]

He suppressed also the playful lines which he had composed
in 1871 to amuse his audience at the American Institute
Exhibition:

> She comes! this famous Female [the Muse] — as was
> indeed to be expected;
> (For who, so ever youthful, 'cute and handsome would
> wish to stay in mansions such as those . . .
> With all the fun that's going — and all the best so-
> ciety?) [56]

But all his corrections did not have such a negative character. He profited from this minute labor of revision to render
his text more expressive and to choose his words with more
care. In particular he rid himself of a number of catch-all
adjectives like "wondrous" or "mystic," [57] either suppressing
them completely, or replacing them by less vague and more
appropriate epithets. Thus, "the mystic midnight" became
"the vacant midnight" [58] and "my insolent poems" was changed
in 1881 into "my arrogant poems," which is certainly more
appropriate.[59] In "To Think of Time," speaking in the name
of the dead, he had at first written:

> To think of all these wonders of city and country and
> . . . we taking small interest in them . . .

but "small" was exaggerated and he replaced it later with "no."
He had in the same way rather imprudently qualified the trot
of the horses of a hearse as "rapid"; after 1860 he contented
himself with "steady." [60]

Sometimes he introduced color adjectives to enhance the descriptive passages. For example, he added the entire line:

> Scarlet and blue and snowy white,

to "Cavalry Crossing a Ford," [61] and appended the complementary indication "yellow-flower'd" to the rather uninteresting mention of a cottonwood in a Southern landscape.[62] Almost everywhere dull and banal expressions gave place to more expressive words. Whereas in 1867 he merely "sang" on the shores of Lake Ontario, in 1881 he "thrill'd." [63] "The English pluck" of John Paul Jones's adversaries later became "the surly English pluck," which is indeed a very apt phrase.[64]

Certain lines were thus completely transformed, like:

> Alone, held by the eternal self of me that threatens to
>   get the better of me, and stifle me,

which was, in 1881, changed to:

> Held by this electric self out of the pride of which I
>   utter poems . . .[65]

The poetic charge of the second version is singularly higher; it is magnetized, as it were, by the introduction of the adjective "electric." "I hear American mouthsongs" was flat and awkward; it became "I hear America singing" in 1867 and the line now really sings.[66]

He also added some images here and there, for example, the line "Thou but the apples, long, long, long, a-growing" to "Thou Mother with Thy Equal Brood," [67] and realizing the evocative power of the historical present he substituted it for the preterite in some stories like that of the seafight between the *Bonhomme Richard* and an English frigate.[68] All these corrections liberated the latent energy of many passages.

But he turned his attention more particularly to titles and first lines and it was there that he obtained the most spectacular results. In 1856 all his titles were of a depressing monotony and an annoying clumsiness: "Poem of Walt Whitman, an American," "Poem of The Daily Work of the Workmen and the Workwomen of These States," "Poem of the Heart of the Son of Manhattan Island," "Poem of the Last Explanation of Prudence," "Poem of the Propositions of Nakedness," and in 1860 they were not much better since most of the poems were simply numbered. In 1867, however, he did his best to find picturesque titles. Thus, "Proto-Leaf," a barbarous expression, was replaced by "Starting from Paumanok" which is concrete and dynamic, and the former "Poem of Walt Whitman, an American" became in 1881, after many metamorphoses, "Song of Myself," a title which admirably sums up its central theme. The "Poem of the Body" which originally began with:

> The bodies of men and women engirth me and I engirth them . . .[69]

started in 1867 with:

> I sing the body electric . . .

which is singularly more promising. It was during that year that he found the title of "One Hour of Madness and Joy,"[70] of "Trickle-Drops,"[71] of "On the Beach at Night Alone."[72] But it was only later and after much searching that he arrived at "As I ebb'd with the ocean of life,"[73] "By Blue Ontario's Shore,"[74] "Aboard at a Ship's Helm,"[75] "Out of the Cradle Endlessly Rocking,"[76] "A Song of the Rolling Earth,"[77] and so on.

He also rounded off certain lines whose ends seemed too abrupt — especially, it appears, while preparing the 1881 edition. Thus,

> You shall sit in the middle well-poised thousands of years,

became:

> You shall sit in the middle well-pois'd thousands and
> thousands of years . . .[78]

In the poem entitled "I was looking a long while" the last line:

> All for the average man of to-day,

which lacked force and vividness, was changed to:

> All for the modern — all for the average man of to-
> day,[79]

which is at once more rhythmical and more vehement. Whitman, moreover, took pains not only with his titles and with the ends of lines but also with the ends of his poems. In particular, he added to "A Farm Picture" a last line which has a most happy effect and enlarges to infinity what was originally a rather banal vignette.[80] And, what was an even more characteristic correction, he introduced into his longer poems, like "Song of Myself," either at the beginning or at the end of the different sections, lines destined to serve, according to the individual instance, as an introduction or a conclusion, in order to prepare the transitions and reinforce the cohesiveness of the whole.[81] In other words, he became increasingly mindful of form.

But at the same time, in proportion as his inspiration lost its force, he tended to be more and more content with very short poems for which no problem of composition existed. He had already used this formula as early as 1856 [82] in *Drum-Taps,* where he had included a number of short descriptive poems like "A Farm Picture," "Cavalry Crossing a Ford," "By the Bivouac's Fitful Flame," "The Torch," "The Ship," and "The Runner," [83] or very brief philosophical poems like "A Child's Amaze." From 1881 on, he wrote only poems of this sort, but, refusing to admit the decline of his inspiration, he claimed that in so doing he was deliberately limiting himself in order to conform to a principle posed by Poe, namely "that (at any rate for our occasions, our day) there can be no such thing as a long poem. The same thought," he added, "had been haunting my mind before, but Poe's argument, though short, work'd the sum and proved it to me." [84] He merely omitted to say that, to Poe's mind, the short poem adapted to the capabilities of the modern reader might reach a length of about a hundred lines, as in the case of "The Raven," [85] and this was rather far from the few lines with which the author of *November Boughs* now contented himself.

Whitman thus attached more and more importance to form as his poetic material became thinner. Whereas in the preface to the 1855 edition of *Leaves of Grass* he affected a sovereign scorn for polish and ornaments,[86] and made everything depend on the power of inspiration, ten years later, he rejoiced that *Drum-Taps* was "certainly more perfect as a work of art, being adjusted in all its proportions, & its passion having the indispensable merit that . . . the true artist can see it is . . . under control." [87] And it is probably during this period that he gave himself this advice:

In future *Leaves of Grass. Be more severe* with the final revision of the poem, nothing will do, not one word or sentence, that is not *perfectly clear* — with positive purpose — harmony with the name, nature, drift of the poem. Also *no ornaments, especially no ornamental adjectives,* unless they have come molten hot, and imperiously prove themselves. *No ornamental similes at all — not one: perfect transparent clearness* sanity and health are wanted — that is the *divine style* — O if it can be attained — [88]

It is obvious that he was then very far from the superb assurance he had shown in 1855 and this text proves that all his later revisions were perfectly conscious. As early as 1860 he had begun to understand his error:

Now I reverse what I said, and affirm that all depends
on the aesthetic or intellectual,
And that criticism is great — and that refinement is
greatest of all . . .[89]

Unfortunately it was too late. He could still revise his early
poems, but he could not recast them, and, in spite of the
progress he achieved, his art remained fundamentally the
same. So, at the end of his life, he himself realized the inferiority of his work from the point of view of form. Casting a
backward glance over the roads he had traveled he readily
acknowledged in 1888 that as far as descriptive talent, dramatic situations, and especially verbal melody and all the
conventional techniques of poetry were concerned, *Leaves of
Grass* was eclipsed by many masterpieces of the past.[90] And
beating his breast three years later he added: "I have probably
not been enough afraid of careless touches, from the first . . .
nor of parrot-like repetitions — nor platitudes and the commonplace." [91]

Thus the mystic who, in 1855, had wished to communicate
the revelation which he had received and announce to the world
a new gospel by slow degrees became an artist more and more
conscious of his imperfections, but, to a large extent, incapable
of remedying them. How could he have done so? In spite
of his growing respect for art, all discipline seemed to him a
useless constraint and any convention a dangerous artifice
which risked raising a barrier between his thought and the
reader. To art he opposed what he called simplicity,[92] that is
to say, strict adherence to nature. As a mystic, he was thus
able to write: "In these *Leaves* everything is literally photo-
graphed. Nothing is poetized, no divergence, not a step, not
an inch, nothing for beauty's sake, no euphemism, no
rhyme." [93] And, in the same year, as an artist, he on the contrary affirmed the necessity of a transposition: "No useless
attempt to repeat the material creation, by daguerreotyping

the exact likeness by mortal mental means." [94] This contradiction gives the measure of his predicament. In fact, of course, he had to transpose, but he was not any less convinced that he had remained completely faithful to nature. When in 1879 he traveled in the Rocky Mountains he thought that he saw in their chaotic mass the symbol of his own poems. "I have found the law of my own poems," he explained at the sight of "this plenitude of material, complete absence of art." [95] To art, for him a synonym for artifice, he thus preferred Nature, "the only complete, actual poem," [96] with its disorder, its immensity, its indescribably secret life.[97]

To this instinctive preference his belief in the unlimited power of inspiration was obscurely related, as well as his faith in the efficacy of the slow germination which precedes the birth of a poem:

The rhyme and uniformity of perfect poems show the free growth of metrical laws and bud from them as unerringly and loosely as lilacs or roses on a bush, and take shapes as compact as the shapes of chestnuts and oranges and melons and pears and shed the perfume impalpable to form.[98]

In other words, thought and inspiration determine expression, so that what counts in the last analysis is thought and not form, which is only its reflection. Whatever its apparent disorder may be, the poem, simply because it grew and matured in the soul of the poet, has the same profound unity and the same beauty as Nature, which was created by God, the supreme poet. The theory was not new. We recognize here the principle of organic unity which Coleridge had borrowed from Schlegel and had discussed many times in his critical writings, in particular in the *Biographia Literaria* where Whitman may have discovered it. This doctrine suited him perfectly since it authorized him to reject every rule of composition and prosody.[99]

If it permits one to break free from rules, the theory of organic unity, however, does not exempt the poet from work. It requires much groping to release what is gestating within him. The impression of ease or "abandon," as he said, which Whitman's work gives, was, in fact, the result of careful planning. His simplicity is labored, and that is why he approved the famous line of Ben Jonson: "A good poet's made as well as born." [100] The first version of *Leaves of Grass*, far from having been written at one sitting, evolved slowly from a considerable number of drafts of the kind which Emory Holloway has published and which represent the work of several years.[101] The short poems of his old age required as much trouble. There exist at the Library of Congress ten different drafts of "Supplement Hours."

An examination of the papers left by Whitman permits a reconstruction of his method. Contrary to poets like Valéry, for whom the starting-point is a rhythm or a musical motif, Whitman seems always to have taken off from a word or an idea expressed in prose. His manuscripts show it. This initial material was later elaborated and expressed rhythmically. That is what happened for instance to this list of words which R. M. Bucke published in *Notes and Fragments*: "Perfect Sanity — Divine Instinct — Breadth of Vision — Healthy Rudeness of Body. Withdrawnness. Gayety. Sun-tan and air-sweetness." Out of this material Whitman later made two lines of the poem which eventually became "Song of the Answerer":

> Divine instinct, breadth of vision, the law of reason,
>   health, rudeness of body, withdrawnness,
> Gayety, sun-tan, air-sweetness, such are some of the
>   words of poems.[102]

The germ of "Night on the Prairies" which has been found in his papers also appears in the form of a brief sketch in prose entitled "Idea of a poem." [103] And on another rough draft one can read this revealing injunction: "Make this more rhythmic." [104] Sometimes the first line provoked a rich germination within him and in that case, as the ideas appeared,

The rough draft of a sentence from Whitman's essay on Burns
(*manuscript fragment in the possession of the author*)

he noted them down on the first scraps of paper he could find: old envelopes, the backs of proof-sheets, all of which gradually accumulated and soon formed a bundle which he pinned together so as not to lose them. (He often proceeded in the same way when he wrote in prose. In the accompanying illustration, we show a facsimile of the rough draft of a sentence from his essay on Burns; one can still see the pin-holes.) Then he would sort his scraps, add, cut out, change the order of the various fragments, re-arrange them endlessly. And, when he felt that the process of germination was complete, he placed his pieces of paper end to end and recopied them, or pasted them on large sheets, as he did for "Eidólons," the definitive manuscript of which may be seen at the Boston Public Library.[105] Thus, his method was essentially agglutinative. His poems were composed like mosaics and, as in mosaics, a number of lines or passages are interchangeable.[106] Whitman himself, in the course of the successive editions, did not hesitate to change the order of certain paragraphs. This method of composition explains the looseness and desultoriness of so many of his poems, but it enabled him to gather all the insights that a poetic idea gave birth to in his mind and to respect the slow organic growth of his work. So he used it all his life. It was his way of reconciling his mysticism with his art, of preserving the spontaneity of his inspiration while imposing upon it a certain form.

This loose method was thus one of the constants of Whitman's art. For him the spirit always took precedence over the letter. He said one day to Horace Traubel: "I have never given any study merely to expression." [107] He was right, but he might well have added: "I have thought increasingly of form."

CHAPTER XI

LANGUAGE —
INNOVATIONS AND TRADITIONS

LANGUAGE always loomed large in Walt Whitman's mind. In a way *Leaves of Grass* was a deliberate and systematic attempt at enriching and renewing the traditional vocabulary of poetry. He said so himself:

> I sometimes think the Leaves is only a language experiment — that it is an attempt to give the spirit, the body, the man, new words, new potentialities of speech — an American, a cosmopolitan (the best of America is the best cosmopolitanism) range of self-expression. The new world, the new times, the new peoples, the new vista, need a tongue according — yes, what is more, will have such a tongue — will not be satisfied until it is evolved.[1]

And indeed an analysis of the language which he used in his poems reveals the same mixture of heterogeneous elements as his style. Archaic words are found side by side with neologisms, abstruse terms next to slang words, and foreign words close to Americanisms. Ezra Pound has strongly reproved him for the heteroclite and disparate character of his art,[2] but, in fact, the violence of the poetic flow usually sweeps away the impurities before the reader has had time to notice them or to be surprised by them.

The presence of archaic terms in Whitman's language is

a priori unexpected. Is he not the poet of "the Modern Man" for whom the past is nothing but a dead body which one keeps in the doorway for a few hours only before sending it off to the cemetery? [3] If he had been consistent, he ought to have mercilessly rejected all old words. And that is precisely the goal which he set for himself: "I had great trouble in leaving out the stock 'poetical' touches, but succeeded at last," he said of the first version of *Leaves of Grass* in *Specimen Days*.[4] He had made it a rule to "take no illustrations whatever from the ancients or classics, nor from the mythology, nor Egypt, Greece or Rome — nor from the royal and aristocratic institutions and forms of Europe, [to] make no mention or allusion to them whatever . . ." [5] In practice, however, despite the rigor of his principles, he more than once let pass some obsolete word or turn borrowed from his predecessors, and the victory which he thought he had won over tradition in 1855 was not as complete as he imagined. Even in the first edition one already comes across archaisms. Thus he uses "betwixt" instead of "between," [6] and in two places "nigh" instead of "near," [7] "anon," [8] "betimes." [9] He had recourse, too, to words which had long fallen into disuse in everyday language like "to drib," [10] "to buss," [11] " to wrig," [12] "eve" for "evening," [13] and "babe" for "baby." [14] On the whole, however, it must be acknowledged that his language is modern and its character changed very little in 1856 and 1860 despite the introduction of several additional archaisms like "climes," [15] "list" (in the meaning of "to please"),[16] "ere," [17] "diminute" [18] in the second edition,[19] and "loins" [20] and "jocund" [21] in the third one. In *Drum-Taps*, on the contrary, archaisms suddenly proliferated, as if Whitman had wished to give his war poems the dignity of ancient epics. In particular he used the second person singular for the first time in *Leaves of Grass*, notably in his elegy on Lincoln.[22] He also resorted to a whole new series of archaisms: "kine," [23] "erewhile," [24] "o'er" instead of "over," [25]

"to harbinge," [26] "a-gone," [27] " 'tis," [28] "cerulean," [29] "lo," with
which he sprinkled several poems,[30] and "darkling." [31] Moreover he added here and there in the poems of the first three
editions some "nigh" 's [32] and some "list" 's (in the meaning
of "to listen") [33] which did not previously appear there. We
thus deal with a perfectly conscious refinement. He deliberately renounced the principles of simplicity and modernity
which had guided him up to then and now no longer hesitated
to fill his poems with borrowed ornaments. In 1871–1872,
moreover, this process gathered speed. In "Passage to India,"
"The Mystic Trumpeter," "Thou Mother with Thy Equal
Brood" (and a little later in "The Prayer of Columbus"), the
second person singular abounds. And what is one to make of
"Darest Thou Now O Soul" [34] which combines the second
person singular with an archaic interrogative form? Henceforth
obsolete and "poetic" words become increasingly frequent: "the
deep," [35] "e'er," [36] "ne'er," [37] "eld," [38] "haply," [39] "isle," [40]
"hark," [41] "to limn," [42] "nay," [43] " 'mid," [44] "obeisant," [45] "me-
thinks," [46] beseems," [47] "emprises," [48] "eterne," [49] "e'en," [50]
"atomies," [51] "bale," [52] "charnel," [53] "i' " for "in," [54] "spake," [55]
"ope," [56] "longeve," [57] "morn," [58] "benison," [59] "unwrit," [60]
"estray," [61] "poesy," [62] "ostent," [63] "brethren," [64] "thereof," [65]
and "whereto." [66] In the "Song of the Redwood Tree" (a specifically American subject though), he even went so far as to
evoke the dryads and the hamadryads of the ancient Greeks.[67]
But that is not all. He also invoked his Muse, humorously in
"Song of the Exposition," but very seriously in "Song of the
Universal" and what is even more unexpected, in the poem
where he celebrated the locomotive.[68] He came finally in one
of his last poems to take for a title "On, on the same ye
jocund twain!" in which the last three words belonged to
traditional poetic diction.[69]

Thus the vocabulary of *Leaves of Grass* became increasingly conventional. After having wished to innovate boldly,

Whitman gradually returned to the tradition. The dignified and high-sounding words which he had at first decided to eliminate from his writings progressively invaded his poems,[70] new ones as well as old. He never discussed this abortive revolution in his critical essays, but apparently, as his inspiration lost its force, he felt more and more the need to fall back on the words which tradition had hallowed and, as it were, charged with poetry in order to enhance the effect of his own verse. Another factor intervened too. As we have seen in the preceding chapter, his taste gradually became more refined; with age his intransigency and his prejudices lost in intensity and virulence. Though he never completely approved of the works of poets who had remained faithful to orthodoxy like Longfellow, Poe, and Tennyson, he at least became more and more open-minded and even on occasion paid homage to them.[71] The past ceased to appear hateful and despicable to him and, as "Passage to India" shows, he finally came to understand the value of tradition. Thus it is not surprising that instead of trying to break with it he was able simply to prolong it and to re-establish contact with the past by borrowing from his predecessors, from Shakespeare, from Walter Scott, from the Bible, words which, in his youth, he had regarded as dead and dried out. He may also have been influenced by the example of Carlyle, for whom he felt increasing admiration and whose language contains numerous archaisms.[72]

A similar evolution appears in his use of Americanisms and neologisms. At the beginning of his career, he enthusiastically announced: "These States are rapidly supplying themselves with new words, called for by new occasions, new facts, new politics, new combinations. — Far plentier additions will be needed, and, of course, will be supplied." [73] For his part he drew copiously upon this picturesque and savory new vocabulary which permitted him to evoke American flora and fauna and all sorts of customs and institutions peculiar to the United

States: "poke-weed," [74] "cotton-wood," "pecan-tree," [75] "qua-haug," [76] "prairie-dog," "chickadee," [77] "katy-did," [78] "camp-meeting," [79] "Kanuck," "Tuckahoe," "Congressman," [80] "quadroon," [81], and so on.[82] He also wanted to incorporate into his poems the most colloquial words of everyday speech. He recognized no difference between the written and the spoken language. "The Real Dictionary," he said, "will give all words that exist in use, the bad words as well as any." [83] Hence his use of words like "cute," [84] "mighty" (as an adverb),[85] and "duds." [86] But, if we class in chronological order, as Rebecca Coy has done,[87] all the Americanisms in *Leaves of Grass*, it becomes apparent that after having abounded in the first two editions, they become rarer in the third and almost completely disappear from the following ones where a dozen at most can be counted. In this respect, too, Whitman's language became more and more conventional. Not that he ever renounced the principles which he had first applied, but because as his thought became more and more abstract he had less and less need for the richly concrete vocabulary which his compatriots had coined. The evolution of his poetic language tended less in the direction of convention than in that of abstraction. (It is to be noted that in the meantime the language of *Specimen Days* remained, on the contrary, quite concrete and picturesque.) This change, which is manifest even in the choice of his archaisms, which are often evocative in the first three editions, and generally dull and colorless in the others, is thus not merely formal; it reflects the evolution of his philosophy and his gradual passage from materialism to spiritualism.

For the same reason all the technical terms associated with industry and commerce which crowd the *Leaves of Grass* of 1855 and 1856 become increasingly rarer in the poems written after the war, even in the "Song of the Exposition" though its subject was the achievements of modern technology. Besides, it seems that Whitman realized in his old age that he had failed in his attempt to create an industrial and democratic poetry. For he wrote in the preface to *November Boughs* in 1888:

Modern science and democracy seem'd to be throwing out their challenge to poetry [at the time when he began to compose *Leaves of Grass*] to put them in its statements in contradistinction to the songs and myths of the past. As I see it now (perhaps too late,) I have unwittingly taken up that challenge and made an attempt at such statements — which I certainly would not assume to do now, knowing more clearly what it means.[88]

He does not elaborate on this subject and his thought remains obscure. Does he mean by that that poetry should systematically avoid treating these two subjects? It is not likely since a few pages later [89] he once more stresses their importance. We should rather conclude then that he regretted at a late date not having been able to better integrate all his scientific, industrial, and political vocabulary in the very texture of his poetry. Too often, indeed, his lists of technical terms constitute a heterogeneous element whose presence in his work seems quite unjustified.

The existence in *Leaves of Grass* of these enumerations and of all the "catalogues," as they are commonly called, poses a problem.[90] We have seen their justification from a metaphysical point of view.[91] They enable Whitman to become conscious of the infinity of space and time and to attain a state of grace, so to speak, but they are also for him a way to indulge in his passion for words. For at the beginning of his poetic career words exerted an irresistible attraction upon him. He celebrated them in the first edition of *Leaves of Grass*:

> Great is Language — it is the mightiest of the sciences,
> It is the fulness, color, form, diversity of the earth,
>   and of men and women, and of all the qualities and
>   processes;
> It is greater than wealth — it is greater than buildings,
>   ships, religions, paintings, music.[92]

Yet, for all that, he does not fall into either verbalism or admiration for purely verbal virtuosity. For him words are not mere sounds or signs on the page of a book. As such, he has only contempt for them:

Words! book-words! what are you? [93]

They interest and excite him only insofar as they are the expression and the condensation of an actual experience ("Erlebnis," as the Germans call it so expressively) either directly, or indirectly in imagination:

Latent, in a great user of words, must actually be all passions, crimes, trades, animals, stars, God, sex, the past, might, space, metals, and the like — because these are the words, and he who is not these, plays with a foreign tongue, turning helplessly to dictionaries and authorities . . .[94]

So each word is for him a fragment hardly detached from cosmic reality yet and still throbbing with life:

The Morning has its words, and the Evening has its words. — How much there is in the word Light! How vast, surrounding, falling, sleepy, noiseless, is the word Night! — It hugs with unfelt yet living arms.[95]

Consequently, it is impossible to replace one word with another, not because each one corresponds to a well-defined intellectual content, but because they all represent concrete realities and separate mystical entities quite distinct from one another:

To me each word out of the — that now compose the English language, has its own meaning, and does not stand for any thing but itself — and there are no two words the same any more than there are two persons the same.[96]

The words of our language are the transcripts of "the substantial words" which are "in the ground and sea," "in the air," and in each of us.[97] They exist first of all in reality and without the presence of this reality the sounds which we articulate are nothing:

> I swear I begin to see little or nothing in audible words,
> All merges toward the presentation of the unspoken meanings of the earth . . .[98]

Each word is the soul of the thing which it reflects and in that way expresses the spirituality of the world:

> All words are spiritual — nothing is more spiritual than words. — Whence are they? along how many thousands and tens of thousands of years have they come? those eluding, fluid, beautiful, fleshless realities, Mother, Father, Water, Earth, Me, This, Soul, Tongue, House, Fire.[99]

There are mysterious correspondences between them and reality. They link us mystically to the world. It is enough to pronounce them to evoke (in the original, magic sense of the word) the object of which they are the symbol and with which we then enter into direct and immediate communication. That is why Whitman calls poets "the Sayers of the Words of the Earth." [100] For his part, he was often content to draw up long lists of them which may appear dry and dull to anyone who forgets what they represent, but which for him were as moving as reality itself.[101] They enabled him to become one with all the things he named in turn and mystically to annex the universe to himself. So they are quite numerous in the first three editions, but after the war, either because he realized their aridity for others, or because they had lost part of their magic power even for himself, he ceased completely to resort to this method of evocation, which shows the decline of his mysticism and his increasingly marked preference for the spiritual side of reality.[102]

Words had not for him only a mystical value; Whitman was also sensitive to their music:

What beauty there is in words! What a lurking curious charm in the sound of some words! [103]

So he collected them with an indefatigable zeal, noting in particular those which struck him for their picturesque quality or their beauty while he was reading. Thus, coming across "scantlings" in an article, he underlined it and wrote in the margin: "a good word" [104] and immediately composed a short poem in which he played with "scant" and "scantlings." [105] He also carefully recorded all the words which he did not know and checked their meanings afterwards in a dictionary. For instance we find notes of this sort in his papers:

"euthanasia, an easy death" — "ad captandum, to attract or captivate." [106]

But books and periodicals were not enough for him. He also conducted all sorts of investigations with sailors and workers in order to enrich his vocabulary.[107] The new words which he discovered immediately gave him the desire to compose a poem incorporating them. He formed, for example, the project of writing a whole poem on insects:

Whole Poem. Poem of Insects.
Get from Mr. Arkhurst the names of all insects — inter-weave a train of thought suitable — also trains of words.[108]

He was also very much interested in etymologies and discovered with delight the forgotten images from which so many abstract words derive.[109] He never ceased being in raptures over the prodigious richness and beauty of the English language, from the preface to the first edition of *Leaves of Grass* [110] to his essay on "Slang in America" in *November Boughs* in 1888.[111] He even seems to have substantially contributed to *Rambles Among Words* which appeared in 1859 under the name of his friend William Swinton alone.[112]

But a language was a living reality for him, something in

constant development which no dictionary could enclose and no list of words exhaust. Hence his interest in slang in which he thought he could catch the language of the future in a nascent state. He fully approved this ceaseless enrichment of the language by the now humorous, now poetic inventions of the popular imagination. Such a process was in keeping with his sense of evolution and his democratic convictions.[113] So he never hesitated to introduce slang words into his poems.[114] He was even the first to use "so long!" in print.[115] New words attracted him irresistibly. Hence all the technical terms with which he crowded some of his catalogues and his frequent use of such adjectives as "magnetic" or "electric." But he was not satisfied with immediately adopting the latest creations; at times he coined new words himself.[116] For instance in 1855 he wrote in the opening poem:

> The blab of the pave, tires of carts, sluff of bootsoles
> and talk of the promenaders . . .[117]

in which "pave" is a personal abbreviation of "pavement" and "sluff" a personal onomatopeia. He sometimes also turns a verb into a noun or conversely, a noun into a verb as the Elizabethans used to do: "the soothe of the waves," [118] "she that had conceived him in her womb and birth'd him." [119] In the first two editions, however, neologisms are still rare (the examples which we have just given almost exhaust the list); [120] they are in general evocative and very felicitously coined because they respect the genius of the language. Such was not the case later. Under the influence of Carlyle, probably, Whitman multiplied them and created horrors, none of which fortunately has survived him: "savantism," [121] "to eclaircise," [122] and "heiress-ship," [123] for instance. After 1865, for the sake of feminism perhaps, he coined a whole series of feminine words in -*ess*: "dispensatress," "all-acceptress," [124] "deliveress," [125] "revoltress," [126] "protectress," [127] "victress," [128] "originatress," [129] "translatress," [130] "tailoress," [131] "oratress." [132] Another of his favorite methods of wordmaking consisted in suppressing suffixes: "apostroph," [133] "philosoph," [134] "literat," [135] (though these last two instances may have been borrowings from the German) "imperturbe" [136] (which corresponds to "imperturbed" or to "imperturbable"), "to promulge." [137] Sometimes, on the contrary, he added a suffix of his own to a standard root as in "deliriate," [138] "oratist," [139] and "venerealee." [140] It was carrying the love of new words a little too far. But, as Mencken has shown, in so doing, he was succumbing to a national rather than to a personal failing.

In 1860 at the same time that he sprinkled his poems with neologisms, Whitman studded them with foreign words, Latin,[141] Spanish,[142] and above all French.[143] We should perhaps see the influence of Carlyle here too, but he may also have wished, in using French words almost always in contexts of democratic inspiration, to indicate his solidarity with the French revolutionists and secretly to link his work to that of George Sand, whom he admired passionately.[144] As for his Spanish words, they were a way of expressing his pan-Americanism.[145] During the Civil War, on the contrary, his preoccupations being exclusively national, he lost the habit of using foreign words,[146] but he returned to that artifice in 1871, at a time when he leaned toward cosmopolitanism — notably in "Proud Music of the Storm," where he introduced a number of Italian words to suggest the music of opera.[147] As he knew none of these languages,[148] he treated them with superb offhandedness, using the word "exposé," for example, as a verb in "I exposé," [149] or creating such philological monsters as "rhythmus," [150] "luminé," [151] "camerado," [152] and "Presidentiad." [153] His friends tried in vain to call his attention to certain errors, but he obstinately stuck to them and perversely refused to admit that he was wrong. William Michael Rossetti in particular once pointed out to him that "Santa Spirita" in "Chanting the Square Deific" was neither Italian nor Latin, but even so Whitman failed to correct his text.[154] Grammatical precision mattered little to him. The sound of these foreign words flattered his ear, which was the only thing that counted.

He also had recourse at times to another source of verbal picturesqueness: words of Indian origin. He seems to have become interested in them between 1856 and 1860. In the notes which Traubel published under the title of *American Primer* and which date back to this period, he wrote:

All aboriginal names sound good. I was asking for something savage and luxuriant, and behold here are the aboriginal names. I see how they are being preserved. They are honest words — they give the true length, breadth, depth. They all fit. Mississippi! — the word winds with chutes — it rolls a stream three thousand miles long. Ohio, Connecticut, Ottawa, Monongahela, all fit . . . California is sown thick with the names of all the little and big saints. Chase them away and substitute aboriginal names. What is the fitness — What the strange charm of aboriginal names? — Monongahela — it rolls with venison richness upon the Palate . . .[155]

And he proposed to change the name of Baltimore and from then on to call the St. Lawrence river Niagara.[156] As early as 1860 he, himself, applied this principle in *Leaves of Grass,* renaming Long Island for instance and reviving its Indian name of Paumanok,[157] calling New York "Mannahatta." [158] In his old age he still celebrated the music of this word:

My city's fit and noble name resumed,
Choice aboriginal name, with marvellous beauty, meaning,
A *rocky founded island — shores where ever gayly dash
the coming, going, hurrying sea waves.*[159]

In the same way he sang the melancholy beauty of "Ynnondio," which means in Iroquois "lament for the aborigines." [160]

Thus the elements of Whitman's vocabulary were numerous

and varied. And this explains the exceptional richness of the language of *Leaves of Grass* which, according to W. H. Trimble, consists of 13,447 words, 6,978 of which (that is to say, about half) are used only once.[161] The period of greatest luxuriance undoubtedly were the years 1855–1856 when everything was an object of wonder for Whitman and he tried to put in his work every creation of God and man. In 1856, his book already contained the whole world; so from then on he was obliged to have recourse to neologisms, archaisms and words of foreign or Indian origin in order to enrich and renew his language. This artificial enrichment, however, did not suffice to make up for the impoverishment of his inspiration and so, for all his efforts at renewal, his vocabulary in fact became increasingly banal and conventional.[162]

Yet, there is one point on which it is possible to discern an improvement: as he grew older, he acquired a finer and finer sense of the propriety of words and of grammatical correctness. In the course of the successive editions of *Leaves of Grass* he corrected a number of improprieties which had at first escaped him. Thus, in 1856, he replaced: "My head evolves on my neck" (where he confused "to evolve" and "to revolve") by "My head slues round on my neck." [163] In 1876, he changed in "Song of the Universal": "In spiral roads by long detours . . ." into: "In spiral routes by long detours . . ." [164] where "routes" is at last the proper word. And, above all, in 1871, he ceased to mistake "semitic" for "seminal," as he had done since 1856.[165] In 1855 he had treated grammar with sovereign contempt:

> The Real Grammar will be that which declares itself a nucleus of the spirit of the laws, with liberty to all to carry out the spirit of the laws, even by violating them, if necessary . . .[166]

In later years, however, he little by little brought himself to eliminate the mistakes which he had made. For example, he corrected as early as 1856 "Was it dreamed whether" into "Was it doubted that . . ." [167] and while he had at first written in 1860 ". . . seeking that is yet unfound," he restored the correct form in the following edition: ". . . seeking what is yet unfound." [168] However, he waited until 1881 to change "you was" into "you were" in "A Song for Occupations." [169] Less serious mistakes did not escape him either. Thus he suppressed "played some," which was a colloquialism,[170] and turned "beside from" into "aside from." [171] He even corrected a construction which he eventually thought too free: ". . . the worst suffering and restless . . ." which in 1860 became: ". . . the worst suffering and most restless . . ." [172]

Leaves of Grass thus slowly gained in correctness what it lost in vigor and raciness. Whitman's poetic language followed through the successive editions of his book a curve parallel to that of his style and similarly reveals an artist becoming steadily more and more conscious, more and more conscientious, but whose material unfortunately keeps dwindling with the years.

CHAPTER XII

PROSODY — ORDER WITHIN DISORDER

I F Whitman attached to form — especially at the beginning of his career — only a secondary importance, his indifference to music was even greater. Long before he had started
writing *Leaves of Grass* he already thought that "whatever
touches the heart is better than what is merely addressed to
the ear." [1] And toward the end of his life he confided to
Traubel:

The first thing necessary is the thought — the rest may follow
if it chooses — may play its part — but must not be too much
sought after. The two things being equal I should prefer to have
the lilt present with the idea, but if I got down my thought and
the rhythm was not there I should not work to secure it . . . I
take a good deal of trouble with words: yes, a good deal: but
what I am after is the content not the music of words. Perhaps
the music happens — it does not harm: I do not go in search of
it. [2]

He even devoted a short poem to the matter:

I have not so much emulated the birds that musically
    sing,
I have abandon'd myself to flights, broad circles.
The hawk, the seagull, have far more possess'd me than
    the canary or mocking-bird,
I have not felt to warble and trill, however sweetly,
I have felt to soar in freedom and in the fulness of
    power, joy, volition. [3]

So, since only the matter and the imagery really mattered to him, as soon as he had something to say he freed himself from all the traditional prosodic constraints which he had respected in his first poetic exercises; he gave up rhyme, broke with rhythmic regularity and, instead of following the standard patterns, used long verses which recall above all the Bible,[4] but also, to some extent, Martin Tupper [5] and Samuel Warren.[6] The first version of *Leaves of Grass*, however, far from indicating a return to primitive techniques, as has too often been claimed, marked an entirely new departure. Such, at least, was Whitman's purpose. His ambition was not to rival the prophets of the Old Testament, but to create a new kind of poetry meant for the eyes of his readers rather than for their ears. He explained that matter very clearly in his old age:

Two centuries back or so much of the poetry passed from lip to lip — was oral: was literally made to be sung: then the lilt, the formal rhythm, may have been necessary. The case is now somewhat changed: now, when the poetic work in literature is more than nineteen-twentieths of it by print, the simple tonal aids are not so necessary, or, if necessary, have considerably shifted their character.[7]

No commentator has, to our knowledge, paid the least attention to this text, which, however, is so essential in explaining the peculiar character of the first version of *Leaves of Grass*. For the exceptional format of the 1855 edition was not at all the result of an accident. Whitman had deliberately planned it so. It allowed his long verses to spread out across the page with a minimum of breaks. The eye could follow them easily. Moreover, everything had been arranged for the pleasure and convenience of the eye, even the punctuation. The rhythmic stops were not indicated by imperceptible commas, but by series of widely spaced points of suspension, even in the prose of the preface. If Whitman's poetry had been meant for the ear, such an artifice would have been unnecessary. For, when one reads a poem aloud, the breaks appear by themselves, whether they were or were not marked by the author.[8] Besides, who would, without getting out of breath, declaim the first *Leaves of Grass*; some of the lines contained over sixty words. Undeniably, Whitman's original ideal was a visual poetry.

It will be objected that the following editions present an entirely different character. It is true, but Whitman regretted that he was not able to preserve the format of the first version. One day, toward the end of his life, one of his admirers brought him a copy of the first edition and Whitman opened it, moved his hand over the broad pages and murmured: "Yes, yes, there was no other way of printing it. The other editions are not accurate." [9] For practical reasons (lower printing costs, for example), he had to adopt for his book a more common format as soon as he decided, in 1856, to publish a commercial stereotyped edition. This new presentation immediately resulted in internal changes. The punctuation of the poems in particular became more banal:

> You shall no longer take things at second or third hand
> . . . . nor look through the eyes of the dead
> . . . . nor feed on the spectres in books . . .[10]

became as early as 1856:

> You shall no longer take things at second or third hand,
> nor look through the eyes of the dead, nor feed on
> the spectres in books . . .[11]

There was another change: the pages of his book being now narrower, he broke up all the verses which were of inordinate length. Thus, he split into four different verses:

> Because you are greasy or pimpled — or that you was once a
> thief, or diseased, or rheumatic, or a prostitute — or are so now
> — or from frivolity or impotence or that you are no scholar, and

never saw your name in print . . . do you give that you are any less immortal? [12]

He sometimes lightened his poems by simply throwing overboard some particularly heavy verses,[13] or by shortening those which could stand amputation without damage. For instance,

> And I will show there is no imperfection in male or female, or in the earth, or in the present — and can be none in the future

was reduced by one third in 1867:

> And I will show there is no imperfection in the present and can be none in the future.[14]

Corrections of this kind were numerous in 1867. It seems that toward this time he wanted to reduce systematically the length of his lines and to indicate the end more clearly by means of semi-colons instead of simple commas.[15] Moreover the lines of the poems composed after 1860 are distinctly shorter than those of the first three editions. Killis Campbell [16] has set up statistics and reached the conclusion that "there are no two poems first published after 1870 with lines that run to as much as twenty-five words, and only one poem published in 1855 or 1856 that retained any considerable number of long lines, — namely 'Our Old Feuillage'. In fact, the longest line in any of the poems first published in the eighties comprises only twenty-one words (and there are only two examples of this), whereas the average long line in the poems written after 1880 runs to about a dozen words." What should we conclude from this, if not that Whitman gradually passed from poetry designed to be read to poetry designed to be recited? Did he not in the meantime try to round off some of his lines whose endings were too flat? [17] And it certainly was not a coincidence if, after 1860, he constantly used the words "Chant," "Song," and "Carol" in the titles of his poems.

On the other hand, Whitman attached more and more importance to rhythm. When speaking of the rhythm of *Leaves of Grass,* it is necessary to distinguish two things: the rhythm of composition which results from the use of parallelisms and repetitions as we find in the Bible and the rhythm of scansion produced by the more or less regular alternation of stressed and unstressed syllables. Both varied through the successive editions.

The poems of the first three versions of *Leaves of Grass* which seem to develop freely without any constraint and to have no formal structure are in fact built on a complex system of parallelisms (or syntactic repetitions) [18] and of verbal repetitions either at the beginning or at the end of verses.[19] Verbal repetitions are obviously the most striking, especially in the 1855 edition, where each verse, in general, occupies only one line; whole paragraphs begin with the same word or same group of words. This is, beyond all question, a technique devised for the eye — at least as much as for the ear — and the equivalent of which we do not find in the Bible.[20] Some commentators,[21] impressed by the fact that there were many notes upon the art of oratory among Whitman's papers,[22] have claimed that he wanted to apply to poetry the rules of rhetoric and eloquence. Nothing is more false. No speech has ever consisted of such enumerations and litanies as are found in *Leaves of Grass.* Besides, oratory and poetry were for Whitman two separate activities which he would have liked to carry on simultaneously, but which he did not confuse, as is shown by this note which he jotted down in 1858:

Henceforth two co-expressions. They expand, amicable from common sources, but each with individual stamps by itself. First POEMS, *Leaves of Grass,* as of INTUITIONS, the Soul, the Body (male or female), descending below laws, social routine, creeds, literature, to celebrate the inherent, the red blood . . . Second, Lectures, or Reasoning, Reminiscences, Comparison, Politics, the Intellectual, the desire for knowledge . . .[23]

Thus, he himself very clearly distinguished the rhapsodic accumulations of his poems from the logical sequences and close concatenations of arguments on which the periodic style of an orator is founded.

He used parallelisms and repetitions even in the poems of his old age, but their character changed gradually. First, the series of lines in which the same words were repeated became less long in proportion as his poems became shorter, but this quantitative difference is trivial. What is important is that these series, instead of extending endlessly, tended to transform themselves into what are sometimes called "envelopes" of parallelism,[24] in which the last line recalls and echoes the first, as in several of the shorter poems of *Drum-Taps* ("An Army Corps on the March," "By the Bivouac's Fitful Flame," and others). The eye is not very sensitive to the symmetry of this pattern, which, besides, is rarely perfect, but the ear, on the contrary, takes pleasure in such echoes.

Whitman's evolution toward a more and more musical poetry will appear still more clearly if we now consider the meter proper. Even in the first edition of *Leaves of Grass,* as Sculley Bradley has shown,[25] it is possible to discover an essential rhythm under the apparent disorder by having recourse to the "hovering accent" on which G. M. Hopkins' "sprung rhythm" is based: [26]

> A child said *What is the grass?* fetching it to me with
>   full hands,
> How could I answer the child? I do not know what it is
>   any more than he.

This is fundamentally a couplet composed of two lines of seven stresses broken by a caesura after the third foot, and the rhythm is on the whole ascending, except in the first foot of the second line, as often happens in lines composed according to the rules of traditional prosody. In short, we have here Paul

Claudel's "iambe fondamental." [27] What counts for Whitman as well as for Claudel is the return at *more or less* regular intervals of stressed syllables separated from each other by a variable number of unstressed syllables (from one to four). Any other meter seemed to Whitman both too monotonous and too narrow:

As to the form of my poetry I have rejected the rhymed and blank verse. I have a particular abhorrence of blank verse, but I cling to rhythm; not the outward, regularly measured, short foot, long foot — short foot, long foot — like the walking of a lame man, that I care nothing for. The waves of the sea do not break on the beach every so many minutes; the wind does not go jerking through the pine-trees, but nevertheless in the roll of the waves and in the soughing of the wind in the trees there is a beautiful rhythm. How monotonous it would become, how tired the ear would get of it, if it were regular! It is the under-melody and rhythm that I have attempted to catch . . .[28]

Such was his aim. Unfortunately, especially in some of the very long lines of the first two editions, this "under-melody and rhythm" do not succeed in coming out and get lost in the endless meandering of the enumerations, as in this line of the 1856 edition:

Iron-works, forge-fire in the mountains, or by the river-
banks, men around feeling the melt with huge crow-
bars — lumps of ore, limestone, coal — the blast-
furnace and the puddling-furnace, the loup-lump
at the bottom of the melt at last — the rolling-mill,
the stumpy bars of pig-iron, the strong clean-shaped
T-rail for railroads.[29]

One has the impression of dealing with loosely rhythmical prose rather than with poetry. Later on, on the contrary, especially after *Drum-Taps,* the rhythm tended to become clearer and more regular in shorter lines. Pure and simple iambs even at times replaced the fundamental iambs of the earlier poems, as in "Joy, Shipmate, Joy!" "Song of the Universal," "To the Man-of-War Bird," and in certain passages of "Prayer of Columbus" and "The Mystic Trumpeter." [30] All these poems date from about 1870, but the tendency persisted and became still more obvious in the edition of 1881 with such poems as "Thou Orb Aloft Full-Dazzling," "A Riddle Song," "Spirit that Form'd This Scene," and later in "With Husky-Haughty Lips, O Sea," "Halcyon Days," "Last of Ebb and Daylight Waning," and in most of the poems which make up "Sands at Seventy," "Good-Bye My Fancy," and "Old Age Echoes." [31]

Moreover, in the later editions, Whitman altered the end of a number of lines so that they might end with an iambic measure. Thus, "The least insect or animal, the senses, eyesight . . ." became in 1871: "The least insect or animal, the senses, eyesight, love.[32] Likewise, the insertion of "yet" in the two following lines gave them a perfectly iambic rhythm:

> I say no man has ever (yet) been half devout enough,
> None has ever (yet) adored or worship'd half enough.[33]

One could quote many more instances.[34] Through the successive editions we thus witness a gradual evolution toward a greater rhythmic regularity, as Karl Shapiro has well observed:

> . . . His prosody in the main may be
> Clocked by the metronome, though curiously
> His later rhythm approached the count of eye
> Scansion . . .[35]

Trowbridge reports that one day in Washington during the Civil War Whitman read to a few friends "Lo, Victress on the Peaks" which he had just composed. O'Connor immediately reproached him with his usual vehemence for saying "poem proud" like any other poet instead of "proud poem" as he would have said ten years earlier. Whitman acquiesced, promised to make the necessary correction, but in fact changed nothing.[36] He had his reasons. This inversion could seem to be a return to obsolete conventions, but it permitted him to obtain in the verse in question a regularly ascending rhythm:

> No poem proud, I chanting bring to thee, nor mastery's
> rapturous verse,[37]

and that was all he wanted. His preoccupation with rhythm had eventually got the better of his contempt for "poetic diction." From then on, he never hesitated to use inversions whenever necessary, as in "On, on the same, ye jocund twain" which contains four:

> I chant my nation's crucial stage (America's, haply
> humanity's) — *the trial great, the victory great*
> . . .
> Here, here from wanderings, strayings, lessons, wars,
> defeats — here at the west *a voice triumphant* . . .
> I pass to snow-white hairs the same, and give to *pulses*
> *winter-cool'd* the same . . .[38]

After the war, he even added inversions to poems dating back from the first editions (which, to tell the truth, were not quite so lacking in them as O'Connor rather naïvely imagined; there were about fifteen in the opening poem in 1855). Thus,

> Walt Whitman, an American, one of the roughs, a
> Kosmos . . .

became in 1867:

> Walt Whitman am I, of mighty Manhattan the son
> . . .[39]

which is certainly more sonorous. And,

> One flitting glimpse, caught through an interstice,

which dated back to 1860, was changed in 1867 to:

> A glimpse through an interstice caught . . .[40]

which is both more rhythmical and more expressive.

With the years, *Leaves of Grass* also gained in melody. If, from the beginning, Whitman had occasionally resorted to alliterations, as in the following line:

> The white wake left by the passage, the quick tremulous whirl of the wheels . . .[41]

he subsequently used them more and more frequently and sought effects of imitative harmony as in the passages quoted below:

> The sibilant near sea with vistas far and foam,
> And tawny streaks and shades and spreading blue
> . . .[42]

> Last of ebb and daylight waning,
> Scented sea-cool landward making, smells of sedge and
> salt incoming . . .[43]

> Some vast heart, like a planet's, chain'd and chafing
> in those breakers,
> By lengthen'd swell, and spasm and panting breath,
> And rhythmic rasping of thy sands and waves,
> And serpent hiss, and savage peals of laughter,
> And undertones of distant lion roar . . .[44]

He played more and more with the music produced by the endings of present participles intentionally placed at the end of a hemistych or a line, as in "Out of the Cradle Endlessly Rocking" in which at one place thirteen consecutive lines each end with a verbal form in -ing,[45] or in "Patroling Barnegat" (1880), all the lines of which, without a single exception, end with a present participle [46] — at the price of inversions, but it did not matter to him; he had now reached a stage where he blithely sacrificed naturalness to music.

He went so far in this direction in *Drum Taps* that in spite of his ostentatious disdain of the "dulcet rhymes" and "piano-tunes" of orthodox poets,[47] he used rhymes himself in two poems: "O Captain! My Captain!" and "Ethiopia Saluting the

Colors." [48] A few years later he again rhymed in the hymn which the singer sings while she visits the prison,[49] but this was a pastiche rather than a personal creation. In 1876, on the contrary, he thought of composing a long rhymed poem entitled "Hands Round" in which he spoke in his own name.[50] But he renounced finishing it, probably realizing that it would jar with the rest of his book. Besides, in that same year, he was writing in one of the notes in *Two Rivulets*:

While admitting that the venerable and heavenly forms of chiming versification have in their time play'd great and fitting parts . . . it is, notwithstanding, certain to me, that the day of such conventional rhyme is ended . . . In my opinion the time has arrived to essentially break down the barriers of form between prose and poetry. I say the latter is henceforth to win and maintain its character regardless of rhyme, and the measurement-rules of iambic, spondee, dactyl, &c., and that even if rhyme and those measurements continue to furnish the medium for inferior writers and themes, (especially for persiflage and the comic, as there seems henceforward to the perfect taste, something inevitably comic in rhyme, merely in itself, and anyhow,) the truest and greatest *Poetry*, (while subtly and necessarily always rhythmic, and distinguishable easily enough,) can never again, in the English language, be express'd in arbitrary and rhyming metre . . .[51]

Though he was at times tempted to resort to rhyme to obtain certain musical effects, he refused for reasons of principle to adorn his poems with this "cheap jewel" ("ce bijou d'un sou"), as Verlaine called it, and remained faithful to the end to the aesthetic of the first edition of *Leaves of Grass*.[52]

But he was not tempted by rhyme only, during the Civil War, he also looked back nostalgically to poems with a set pattern. After years of simmering, the eruption of 1855 had projected out of him streams of molten lava. His first poems give an impression of power, but also of disorder and incoherence (more apparent than real, as Carl Strauch has shown with regard to "Song of Myself").[53] In *Drum-Taps* and their

Sequel, he attempted, on the contrary, to discipline his inspiration and impose a prosodic structure on some of his poems.[54] "Beat! Beat! Drums!" for example, is formed of three stanzas, each containing the same number of lines (of unequal length, though) and each beginning with "Beat! beat! drums! — blow! bugles! blow!" Each stanza ends with a line that varies slightly from one stanza to another while remaining faithful to the same fundamental pattern.[55] The same technique is used in "By the Bivouac's Fitful Flame" [56] and "Thick-Sprinkled Bunting." [57] In each case, the same line opens and closes the poem, thus producing an effect of symmetry and regularity. At other times, on the contrary, one deals with free stanzas; the poem is then divided typographically into stanzas, each one having the same number of approximately equal lines. Such is the case with "Dirge for Two Veterans," [58] "Ethiopia Saluting the Colors," [59] "Pioneers! O Pioneers," [60] and "Old War Dreams." [61] In "O Captain! My Captain!" he went further still. Not only is this poem composed of three identical stanzas which all end up with "Fallen cold and dead," but in addition the lines rhyme two by two.[62] It is the most regular poem in *Leaves of Grass,* but, if we are to believe Thomas B. Harned, Whitman regretted afterwards having written it.[63] In the subsequent editions he had recourse only twice to division into stanzas, for "Gods" (1871) and "Eidólons" (1876), neither of which has as strict a form as "O Captain! My Captain!" The stanzas of "Gods" are of unequal lengths and deserve the name only because their last line makes a refrain. As for those which make up "Eidólons," they are more regular, but still they are not rhymed.[64]

So Whitman never returned to set conventional patterns even in *Drum-Taps.* He aspired for a time to a more regular prosody, but, nevertheless, he refused to copy traditional models servilely, as he had done in his youth. He could not resign himself to casting his poetry in ready-made molds. Any external constraint was repulsive to him. He confusedly sought a mode of composition which assured the cohesion of his poems without destroying their fluidity, and, as the example of his predecessors was of no help to him, it was toward music that he turned. Consciously or not, he adopted the form of the symphony when he wrote in 1865 "When Lilacs Last in the Dooryard Bloom'd." From the first, almost without groping,[65] he reached mastery. This poem, indeed, instead of developing in a straight — or spiral — line like the longer poems of the preceding editions, consists of an intertwining of themes which cross and recross one another with consummate art. Three of them are very distinctly indicated in the first lines: the lilac which blooms in the yard, Venus which appears at the fall of an April night, and the sorrow felt by the poet at the death of Lincoln.[66] To these a fourth theme is added, that of the solitary thrush whose faraway complaint echoes the sadness of the poet. These different motifs are developed individually, taken up again, and then in the last stanza are regrouped in the same way as in the overture. Thus, the reader has an impression of plenitude and completion which no other poem of Whitman gives. He later tried to use this symphonic form again, but never with the same success. "Proud Music of the Storm" (1861), "Passage to India" (1871), "O Star of France" (1871), "The Mystic Trumpeter" (1872), and "Prayer of Columbus" (1874) are also all organized around a central image, sometimes again and again recalled by the repetition of the title as in "The Mystic Trumpeter," [67] but in no other poem do we find that intertwining of themes which gives "When Lilacs Last in the Dooryard Bloom'd" its exceptional beauty. True, "Thou Mother with Thy Equal Brood" does contain two images (democracy is in turn represented as a powerful sea-bird and as a ship), but they do not harmonize at all with each other and the poem must be considered a failure.[68]

Thus, Whitman passed gradually from the monotonous and to some extent disordered effusion of his early solos to a more complex and regular symphonic form of expression and was even tempted for a time to go back to poems divided into stanzas. These experiments, however, did not last and the poems he wrote after 1876 mark a return to the technique of the first edition of *Leaves of Grass* which, actually, he had never completely abandoned. It is nonetheless true that he gave an increasingly significant place to music, and that his poetry became more and more harmonious.[69] In 1860, in an anonymous article, he compared the music of his poems to Italian opera, which the public, accustomed to piano tunes and Negro bands, had at first found cacophonous, and he expressed the hope that his readers would also gradually become accustomed to the new rhythms of *Leaves of Grass*.[70] Everything happened, however, as if, not having the patience to wait, Whitman had himself decided to make some concessions to his rebellious public and provide it with some guidance by using a number of well-tried conventions.

This brief study of Whitman's prosody [71] shows, in short, that although he affected to treat this aspect of his art with scorn and condescension, he attached, in fact, more and more importance to the cadence of his lines, to alliterations, to all that could contribute to enrich the music of his poems. Thus he slowly became a more and more conscious artist, a more and more subtle craftsman, more and more master of himself and of his means of expression.

CONCLUSION

THIS double study of Whitman the man and of Whitman the poet during the forty-odd years during which *Leaves of Grass* germinated and grew reveals that he increasingly understood and used the potentialities present in him from the beginning of his poetic career. Whitman realized it himself in 1888:

. . . I set out with the intention also of indicating or hinting some point-characteristics which I since see (though I did not then, at least not definitely) were bases and object-urgings toward those "Leaves" from the first.[1]

The ideas and the main themes were indeed gradually brought out and clarified. The Protean poet of 1855 who metamorphosed in turn into everything that lived, rejoiced, and suffered,[2] was succeeded as early as 1860 by the less prolix "chanter of pains and joys, uniter of here and hereafter."[3] The sensual and disconnected mystical intuitions of the first edition led ten years later to the geometric theology of "Chanting the Square Deific" which interpreted and systematized his insights without changing their essential nature or warping their meaning. In the course of successive editions, *Leaves of Grass* was subjected to a gradual intellectualization which made the sense and the purpose of the book more accessible by introducing order and logic into the chaos of the original poems.

But this rationalization presented dangers which Whitman

did not completely avoid. For, by insisting more and more on
the intellectual content of his mystic revelations, he ran the
risk of losing contact with the living reality of the physical
world and of insensibly giving the first place to lifeless abstractions. As a matter of fact, we have had occasion to notice the
increasingly abstract character of his poetic language. But one
should not overemphasize this aspect of his evolution, as
Malcolm Cowley, for instance, did.[4] "When Lilacs Last in the
Dooryard Bloom'd" is far from being as conventional as he
would have it, and it must not be forgotten on the other hand
that *Specimen Days,* which was composed between 1876 and
1881, offers the same wealth of concrete details and sensuous
data as the first editions of *Leaves of Grass.* Whatever may be
said, Whitman never completely lost his hold on the real.
Despite his increasing care for order and clarity he never fell
into that other form of dryness which is dogmatism. In a poem
of 1891, near the end of his life, he still evoked the impenetrable mystery of the world, whose secret neither he nor
anyone else has ever been able to pierce:

> In every object, mountain, tree, and star — in every
> birth and life,
> As part of each — evolv'd from each — meaning, be-
> hind the ostent,
> A mystic cipher waits infolded.[5]

While these changes were taking place, Whitman gave in
gradually to the "resistless gravitation of Spiritual Law," [6]
and gave increasing emphasis to the spirit, the soul, in preference to matter, to God rather than the Creation, to death
rather than life, to the future rather than the present. Newton
Arvin, being a materialist himself, has strongly reproached
Whitman for that tendency toward spiritualism which, according to him, involves a diminution of lucidity and a loss
of intellectual vigor.[7] But the problem is not quite so simple,
for Whitman never chose between materialism and spiritual-

ism. His poems of 1855 are already spiritualistic insofar as he interprets his mystic illuminations, and his last writings are still materialistic insofar as they reveal an unchanged attachment to the physical world. He was indeed perfectly aware both of that shift of emphasis and of the permanence of that duality:

> In youth and maturity Poems are charged with sunshine and varied pomp of day; but as the soul more and more takes precedence, (the sensuous still included,) the Dusk becomes the poet's atmosphere. I too have sought, and ever seek, the brilliant sun, and make my songs according. But as I grow old, the half-lights of evening are far more to me.[8]

This victory of the soul was won through the decline of his body. With age and illness, his sensual ardors and, consequently, his mysticism calmed down, and his inspiration became proportionally poorer. The spring gradually dried up. In his old age, the powerful flow of his poetry was reduced to a thin trickle. The last forceful poems that he wrote date from 1871. In 1876 he could add only twenty-one new poems to his book and they were very short at that. There was even one among that number which was not original; its subject was borrowed from Michelet.[9] In 1881, there were only nineteen new poems, and not one of them was longer than one page. Besides, he often evinced, as in "My Picture Gallery," more ingenuity than power. But he nonetheless persisted in writing poetry up to the end and composed two more collections of poems before his death, *November Boughs* and *Good-Bye My Fancy,* in which, unfortunately, he could only repeat weakly what he had formerly proclaimed in a stentorian voice.[10] He was even obliged, in order to fill out his thin volumes, to resort to prose texts and to old material he had originally rejected.[11] He had reached such a stage of decadence that whereas in the years 1855 to 1860 the "leaves of grass" were flourishing and he gathered them profusely,[12] he now had nothing more to offer than a few "lingering sparse leaves." [13]

This loss of force, however, was compensated for by an undeniable progress in form. The disordered impetuosity of the first editions was by degrees disciplined and brought under control. After the Civil War, the chaotic, anarchistic poems were succeeded by well-constructed poems in which the various themes were skilfully intertwined and the reader was guided by repetitions and burdens. The style was more polished, too, and the words chosen with greater care. The successive revisions reveal an increasingly surer taste and a sense of finish which Whitman had lacked completely at the beginning. Negligences of style, improprieties, grammatical errors were thus gradually eliminated. And, at the same time, the rhythm became less loose and more regular. The music, at first neglected, little by little gained in prestige and importance. Imperceptibly, by slow degrees, the inspired mystic of 1855 became more and more involved in problems of form and expression and was eventually metamorphosed into an artist.

Does that mean that Whitman made these concessions in order to reach a larger public? It does not seem so. We have seen the reproaches which were heaped upon him with each new publication of his book. They had practically no influence on him. True, he suppressed here and there, as far as content goes, a few sexual images which were too bold and needlessly gross, but he nonetheless maintained until the end the crudest poems of "Calamus" and "Children of Adam." As to form, he did his best to make his instrument emit more harmonious sounds, but he always refused to go back to regular verse and, until his death, he used the free verse which he had himself created.

The life and career of Whitman thus present a remarkable continuity. During the forty years which he dedicated to *Leaves of Grass,* he made no major change in his philosophy.

The same spirit which had impelled him in 1855 carried him until his death in the same direction — though, it is true, with less and less force. His thought, like his technique, remained fundamentally the same. His life shows a rupture, but it took place between 1850 and 1855, when he abruptly decided to break with his past and devote himself to his great work. "Make the Works," [14] he suddenly resolved one day, a decision which recalls that of Montaigne to withdraw into his "librairie" and turn his back on the world. From then on his evolution continued evenly and his work gives the impression of a gradual maturation and steady enrichment, of a slow and deepening apprehension of certain truths of which he had had an intuition from the beginning. Although it would be a very artificial game, one could almost deduce a posteriori the last poems from the very first. At any rate, it is easy to understand why he never felt the need to divide his poems into several collections. In proportion as they were born, they became integral to the pre-existent ensemble. From this process grew this single book, the work of a whole life.

Despite its unity, *Leaves of Grass* has, of course, neither the rigor nor the cohesion of a philosophical system. It is a bundle of contradictory tendencies, a sum of themes and ideas which are, to some extent, incompatible. Whitman hesitated between matter and spirit, love of life and the attraction of death, liberty, and authority, the individual and the masses.[15] As a matter of fact, he never intended to build up a philosophy. "I will not be a great philosopher," he declared even before beginning his work,[16] and he knew that his book was full of contradictions and paradoxes.[17] As he grew older, he tried to put more order and clarity in his thought, but the original inner tensions subsisted until the end. This did not displease him, however. His work thus encompassed all systems and enabled each reader to remain himself.[18] And, after all, in so doing, he merely followed the example of his master Emerson [19] and illustrated in his own way the principle of "negative capability" formulated by Keats.[20]

This long fidelity of Whitman to himself and to his contradictions is neither stagnation nor immobility. On the contrary, it is the result of a relentless battle. It is not by chance that he loved the adjective "agonistic"; [21] he fully deserves himself the epithet "agonistes," which Milton applied to Samson. He is the poet of optimism and of joy, but all his life he had to struggle with despair — despair which was caused by his contemporaries who were so often unworthy of living in a democracy, despair which was caused by his own condition, too. He had dreamed, as he wrote in one of his notebooks, of becoming "an old man whose life has been magnificently developed," full of "faith in whatever happens" [22] "strong and wise and beautiful at 100 years old" like Merlin,[23] but, at fifty-four, he was struck by a paralytic attack and forced to lead after his sixtieth year a life which became more and more sedentary and dull. He did not give in, however, and all those who knew him in his old age have done homage to his courage:

During these long years of suffering no one has ever heard him utter a word of complaint . . . Every moment of his life tallied with the teachings of his books,[24] [wrote T. B. Harned].

And in 1890 Robert Ingersoll lyrically proclaimed:

He has not been soured by slander or petrified by prejudice; neither calumny nor flattery has made him revengeful or arrogant. Now sitting by the fireside, in the winter of life,
    His jocund heart still beating in his breast,
he is just as brave, and calm and kind as in manhood's proudest days, when roses blossomed in his cheeks.[25]

Indeed, he succeeded in eliminating from his last poems all traces of rancor or physical pain,[26] striving "to keep up yet the lilt" in spite of his "snowy hairs," [27] to sing "with gay heart" and a "blithe throat,"[28] like a "true conqueror" of life.[29]

Under his apparent indolence, this voluptuous loafer had thus a core of strength[30] and a powerful will which no trial could curb, which illness, old age, and failure were equally unable to break.[31] This sensual poet was also a stoic, a disciple of Epictetus, from whose *Enchiridion* he had chosen a quotation which he used as a letter-head in his last years: "a little spark of soul dragging a great lummux [sic] of a corpse-body clumsily to and fro around."[32] This "little spark of soul" effectively animated to the end his great half-paralyzed body and until the last moment inspired his poems.

The most difficult battle, however, was not with illness, but with his wild homosexual desires, which never left him at peace and constantly menaced his balance. All who saw him admired his serenity and his perfect moral health;[33] no one suspected the torments which lacerated him. It was probably his art which saved him by permitting him to express (in the etymological meaning of the word) the turbulent passions which obsessed him. Poetry was for him a means of purification which, if it did not make him normal, at least permitted him to retain his balance in spite of his anomaly. In this sense, as we have tried to show, his *Leaves of Grass* are "fleurs du mal," "flowers of evil." His poetry is not the song of a demigod or a superman, as some of his admirers would have it, but the sad chant of a sick soul seeking passionately to understand and to save itself.[34] He was thinking of himself, perhaps, when he wrote these lines about the actor, Junius Brutus Booth:

He illustrated Plato's rule that to the forming of an artist of the very highest rank a dash of insanity, or what the world calls insanity, is indispensable.[35]

His anomaly, which in all likelihood was what drove him to write *Leaves of Grass,* also explains certain of his limitations, and notably his inability to renew himself as he grew older —

unlike Goethe. He lived too much alone, too much wrapped up in himself. Nothing ever came to change the image of the world which he had made for himself between 1850 and 1855. He spent all his life in the solitude of his inner universe,[36] "solitary, singing in the West." [37] But his isolation weighed upon him (hence his compensatory dreams of democratic brotherhood),[38] and it even drove him to despair sometimes. Hence the cries of suffering which escaped him and which often interrupt his hymn to life. As Federico Garcia Lorca, who knew the same torments, so well understood, he is, despite appearances, the poet of anguish.[39] Whitman, struck by its sadness, even copied this passage from one of Dickens' letters, he probably thought it applied very well to his own case:

Why is it that, as with poor David, a sense comes always crushing on me now, when I fall into low spirits, as of one happiness I have missed in life, and one friend and companion I have never made? [40]

Whitman had thus, at the very core of himself, a sense of defeat and frustration. He had had the ambition to create two masterpieces: a book of immortal poems and a life, the nobility and greatness of which would become legendary. He succeeded in one respect only, but his failure was, perhaps, the condition of that success.

SELECTED BIBLIOGRAPHY

The critical literature about Whitman is already so abundant that its inventory would require a separate volume; so the reader will find here only a selective list of books and articles. If more detailed information is needed, it can be found in the exhaustive checklists that Gay W. Allen has compiled in his *Walt Whitman Handbook* (1946) and his *Walt Whitman as Man, Poet, and Legend* (1961) or in the other bibliographies listed in chronological order below.

A. BIBLIOGRAPHIES

Frey, Ellen Frances, *Catalogue of the Whitman Collection in the Duke University Library, Being a Part of the Trent Collection*, Durham, N.C.: Duke University Library, 1945. 148 pp.

Walt Whitman: The Oscar Lion Collection, New York: New York Public Library, 1953. 78 pp.

Walt Whitman, A Selection of the Manuscripts, Books and Association Items Gathered by Charles E. Feinberg, Detroit: Detroit Public Library, 1955. 128 pp.

Walt Whitman, A Catalog Based Upon the Collections of the Library of Congress, Washington, D.C.: Library of Congress, 1955. 147 pp.

Thorp, Willard, "Whitman," in *Eight American Authors: A Review of Research and Criticism*, edited by Floyd Stovall, New York: The Modern Language Association of America, 1956, pp. 271–318.

White, William, "Whitman: A Current Bibliography," *Walt Whitman Newsletter*, II–IV (1956–1958) and *Walt Whitman Review*, V — (1959 —).

Allen, Gay Wilson, *Walt Whitman as Man, Poet, and Legend*, With a Check-List of Whitman Publications 1945–1960 by Evie Allison Allen, Carbondale: Southern Illinois University Press, 1961. 260 pp. The checklist, pp. 177–244, though not exhaustive, is the most comprehensive one for the period concerned.

B. EDITIONS

The Complete Writings of Walt Whitman, issued under the editorial supervision of his Literary Executors, Richard Maurice Bucke, Thomas B. Harned, and Horace L. Traubel, with additional bibliographical and critical material by Oscar Lovell Triggs, 10 vols., New York and London: Putnam's Sons, 1902.

Leaves of Grass, Inclusive Edition, edited by Emory Holloway, Garden City, Doubleday, Doran, N.Y.: 1925. 728 pp. Contains a list of variorum readings compiled by Oscar L. Triggs.

Complete Poetry and Selected Prose and Letters of Walt Whitman, edited by Emory Holloway, New York: Random House, 1938. 1,116 pp.

Leaves of Grass, facsimile of 1855 edition, with an introduction by Clifton J. Furness, Facsimile Text Society Publication 47, New York: Columbia University Press, 1939. 95 pp.

Leaves of Grass, with an introduction and notes by Emory Holloway, New York: Dutton (Everyman's Library), 1947. 468 pp.

Complete Poetry and Prose of Walt Whitman, with an introduction by Malcolm Cowley, 2 vols., New York: Pellegrini and Cudahy, 1948.

Poetry and Prose of Walt Whitman, edited with a biographical introduction and a basic selection of early and recent commentary by Louis Untermeyer, New York: Simon and Schuster, 1949. 1,224 pp.

The Wound Dresser, edited by Richard M. Bucke, with an introduction by Oscar Cargill, New York: Bodley Press, 1949. 200 pp. A facsimile edition of the 1897 text.

Walt Whitman's Poems, Selections with Critical Aids, edited by Gay Wilson Allen and Charles T. Davis, New York: New York University Press, 1955. 280 pp. Paperback edition, New York: Grove Press (Evergreen Books), 1959.

The Eighteenth Presidency: A Critical Text, edited by Edward F. Grier, Lawrence: University of Kansas Press, 1956. 47 pp.

Poetry and Prose of Walt Whitman, with an introduction and notes by Abe Capek, Berlin: Seven Seas Books, 1958. 552 pp.

Leaves of Grass: The First (1855) Edition, edited with an introduction by Malcolm Cowley, New York: Viking Press, 1959. 145 pp.

Complete Poetry and Selected Prose, edited with an introduction and glossary by James E. Miller, Jr., Boston: Houghton Mifflin (Riverside Editions), 1959. 516 pp.

Walt Whitman's Drum-Taps (1865) and Sequel to Drum-Taps (1865–66), edited with an introduction by F. DeWolfe Miller, Gainesville, Florida: Scholars' Facsimiles and Reprints, 1959. 158 pp.

Leaves of Grass: Facsimile of the 1860 Text, with an introduction by Roy Harvey Pearce, Ithaca, N.Y.: Cornell University Press (Great Seal Books), 1961. 467 pp.

The Collected Writings of Walt Whitman, General Editors, Gay Wilson Allen and Sculley Bradley, New York: New York University Press, 1961 ——. This edition is meant to supersede the 1902 edition of the *Complete Writings*. Two volumes so far have appeared, the first two volumes of *The Correspondence of Walt Whitman*, edited by Edwin Haviland Miller, 1961.

C. UNCOLLECTED WRITINGS

Calamus, a series of letters written during the years 1868–1880, by Walt Whitman to a young friend (Peter Doyle), edited with an introduction by Richard Maurice Bucke, Boston: Laurens Maynard, 1897. 172 pp.

Notes and Fragments, edited by Richard Maurice Bucke, London, Ontario: Privately printed, 1899. 211 pp.

Walt Whitman's Diary in Canada, edited by William Sloane Kennedy, Boston: Small, Maynard, 1904. 73 pp.

An American Primer, edited by Horace Traubel, Boston: Small, Maynard, 1904. 35 pp.

The Gathering of the Forces, editorials and other writings by Whitman as Editor of the Brooklyn *Daily Eagle* in 1846 and 1847, edited by Cleveland Rodgers and John Black, 2 vols., New York and London: Putnam's Sons, 1920.

The Uncollected Poetry and Prose of Walt Whitman, collected and edited by Emory Holloway, 2 vols., Garden City, N.Y.: Doubleday, Doran, 1921.

Pictures, An unpublished poem by Walt Whitman, with an introduction by Emory Holloway, New York: The June House, 1927. 37 pp.

Walt Whitman's Workshop, edited by Clifton J. Furness, Cambridge, Mass.: Harvard University Press, 1928. 278 pp.

I Sit and Look Out, editorials from the *Brooklyn Times*, selected and edited by Emory Holloway and Vernolian Schwarz, New York: Columbia University Press, 1932. 248 pp.

New York Dissected, a sheaf of recently discovered newspaper articles by the author of *Leaves of Grass*, with an introduction and notes by Emory Holloway and Ralph Adimari, New York: Rufus Rockwell Wilson, 1936. 257 pp.

Backward Glances ("A Backward Glance o'er Travel'd Roads" and two contributory essays hitherto uncollected), edited by Sculley Bradley and John A. Stevenson, Philadelphia: University of Pennsylvania Press, 1947. 51 pp.

Faint Clews and Indirections, edited by Clarence Gohdes and Rollo G. Silver, Durham, N.C.: Duke University Press, 1949. 250 pp.

Walt Whitman of the New York Aurora, writings collected by Joseph

Jay Rubin and Charles H. Brown, State College, Pa.: Bald Eagle Press, 1950. 148 pp.

Whitman's Manuscripts: Leaves of Grass (1860), a parallel text edited with notes and introduction by Fredson Bowers, Chicago: University of Chicago Press, 1955. 264 pp.

D. BIOGRAPHIES AND BOOKS OF CRITICISM

Allen, Gay Wilson, *The Solitary Singer: A Critical Biography of Walt Whitman*, New York: Macmillan, 1955. 616 pp. Paperback edition, New York: Grove Press (Evergreen Books), 1959.

—— *Walt Whitman*, New York: Grove Press (Evergreen Profile Books), 1960. 191 pp.

—— (ed.), *Walt Whitman Abroad*, Syracuse: Syracuse University Press, 1955. 281 pp.

—— *Walt Whitman as Man, Poet, and Legend*, Carbondale: Southern Illinois University Press, 1961. 175 pp.

—— *Walt Whitman Handbook*, Chicago: Packard, 1946. 560 pp.

Arvin, Newton, *Whitman*, New York: Macmillan, 1938. 320 pp.

Asselineau, Roger, *L'Evolution de Walt Whitman*, Paris: Didier, 1954. 567 pp.

Beaver, Joseph, *Walt Whitman, Poet of Science*, New York: Columbia University Press (King's Crown Press), 1951. 178 pp.

Blodgett, Harold, *Walt Whitman in England*, Ithaca: Cornell University Press, 1934. 244 pp.

Canby, Henry Seidel, *Walt Whitman, an American*, Boston: Houghton Mifflin, 1943. 381 pp.

Catel, Jean, *Walt Whitman: La Naissance du poète*, Paris: Rieder, 1929. 195 pp.

Chase, Richard, *Walt Whitman*, Minneapolis: University of Minnesota Press, 1961. 48 pp.

—— *Walt Whitman Reconsidered*, New York: Sloane, 1955. 191 pp.

Daiches, David, "Walt Whitman as Innovator," in *The Young Rebel in American Literature*, edited by Carl Bode, London: Heinemann, 1959, pp. 25–48.

—— "Walt Whitman, the Philosopher," in *Walt Whitman: Man, man*, 1959, pp. 25–48.

—— "Walt Whitman, the Philosopher," in *Walt Whitman: Man, Poet, Philosopher — Three Lectures*, Washington, D.C.: Library of Congress, 1955, pp. 35–53.

—— "Walt Whitman's Philosophy," in *Literary Essays*, New York: Philosophical Library, 1957, pp. 62–87.

Dutton, Geoffrey, *Whitman*, Edinburgh and London: Oliver and Boyd, 1961. 120 pp.

Eby, Edwin Harold, *A Concordance of Walt Whitman's "Leaves of Grass" and Selected Prose Writings*, Seattle: University of Washington Press, 1955. 964 pp.

Faner, Robert D., *Walt Whitman and Opera*, Philadelphia: University of Pennsylvania Press, 1951. 249 pp.

Hindus, Milton (ed.), *Leaves of Grass One Hundred Years After,* Stanford: Stanford University Press, 1955. 149 pp.

Holloway, Emory, *Free and Lonesome Heart: The Secret of Walt Whitman*, New York: Vantage Press, 1960. 232 pp.

—— *Whitman; an Interpretation in Narrative*, New York: Knopf, 1926. 345 pp.

Lawrence, D. H., "Whitman," in *Studies in Classic American Literature,* New York: Albert Boni, 1923, pp. 241–264. The original version of this essay has been reprinted in D. H. Lawrence, *The Symbolic Meaning*, London: Centaur Press, 1962, pp. 253–264.

Lewis, R. W. B., *The American Adam: Innocence, Tragedy and Tradition in the Nineteenth Century*, Chicago: University of Chicago Press, 1955. 205 pp. Numerous references to Whitman.

Metzger, Charles R., *Thoreau and Whitman — A Study of Their Esthetics*, Seattle: University of Washington Press, 1961. 113 pp.

Miller, James E., Jr., *A Critical Guide to Leaves of Grass*, Chicago: University of Chicago Press, 1957. 268 pp.

Molinoff, Katherine, *Some Notes on Whitman's Family*, with an introduction by Oscar Cargill, New York: Published by the author, 1941. 43 pp.

—— *Whitman's Teaching at Smithtown, 1837–1838*, New York: Published by the author, 1941. 30 pp.

Pearce, Roy Harvey (ed.), *Whitman — A Collection of Critical Essays*, Englewood Cliffs, N.J.: Prentice Hall, 1962. 183 pp.

Peltola, Niilo, *The Compound Epithet and Its Use in American Poetry: Bradstreet through Whitman*, Helsinki: Suomalainen Tiedakatemia, 1956, pp. 140–160.

Perry, Bliss, *Walt Whitman, His Life and Work*, Boston: Houghton Mifflin, 1906. 318 pp.

Rivers, W. C., *Walt Whitman's Anomaly*, London: George Allen, 1913. 70 pp.

Schyberg, Frederik, *Walt Whitman*, translated from the Danish by Evie Allison Allen, with an introduction by Gay W. Allen, New York: Columbia Press University, 1951. 387 pp.

Traubel, Horace, *With Walt Whitman in Camden*. Vol. I, Boston: Small, Maynard, 1906. 473 pp. Vol. II, New York: D. Appleton, 1908. 570 pp. Vol. III, New York: Mitchell Kennerley, 1914. 590 pp. Vol. IV, edited by Sculley Bradley, Philadelphia: University of Pennsylvania Press, 1953. 528 pp.

E. ARTICLES

Adams, Richard P., "Whitman: A Brief Revaluation," *Tulane Studies in English*, V (1955) 111–149.

—— "Whitman's 'Lilacs' and the Traditional Pastoral Elegy," *PMLA*, LXXII, 479–487 (June 1957).

Allen, Gay Wilson, "Biblical Echoes in Whitman's Works," *American Literature*, VI, 302–315 (November 1934).

—— "On the Trochaic Meter of 'Pioneers! O Pioneers!' " *American Literature*, XX, 449–451 (January 1949).

—— "Walt Whitman: 'Cosmos-Inspired,' " *New World Writing, Eighth Mentor Selection*, New York: New American Library, 1955, pp. 266–280.

—— "Whitman's 'When Lilacs Last in the Dooryard Bloom'd,' " *Explicator*, X. 55 (January 1952).

Amacher, Richard E. "Whitman's 'Passage to India,' " *Explicator*, IX, 2 (December 1950).

Asselineau, Roger, "Etat Présent des Etudes Whitmaniennes," *Etudes Anglaises*, XI, 31–40 (January–March 1958).

—— "Whitman et Wordsworth — étude d'une influence indirecte," *Revue de Littérature Comparée*, XXIX, 505–512 (October–December 1955).

Basler, Roy P. "Out of the Cradle Endlessly Rocking," *Explicator*, V, 59 (June 1947).

Bergman, Herbert, "Ezra Pound and Walt Whitman," *American Literature*, XXVII, 56–61 (March 1955).

—— "Whitman and Tennyson," *Studies in Philology*, LI, 492–504 (July 1954).

Bernbrock, John, "Whitman's Language Study: Work in Progress," *Walt Whitman Review*, VI, 69–72 (December 1960).

Bradley, Sculley, "The Fundamental Metrical Principle in Whitman's Poetry," *American Literature*, X, 437–459 (January 1939).

Bychowski, Gustav, "Walt Whitman — A Study in Sublimation," in *Phychoanalysis and the Social Sciences*, edited by Geza Roheim et al, New York: International Universities Press, 1950, III, 223–261.

Cambon, Glauco, "La Parola come Emanazione — note marginali sullo stile di Whitman," *Studi Americani*, V (1959), 141–160.

Cestre, Charles, "L'Evolution de Walt Whitman," *Langues Modernes*, LI, 158–160 (February 1957).

Chace, F. M., "Notes on Whitman's Mocking-Bird in 'Out of the Cradle Endlessly Rocking,' " *Modern Language Notes*, LXI, 93–94 (February 1946).

Coffman, S. K., Jr., " 'Crossing Brooklyn Ferry,' A Note on the Catalog Technique in Whitman's Poetry," *Modern Philogogy*, LI, 225–249 (May 1954).

——— "Form and Meaning in Whitman's 'Passage to India,'" *PMLA*, LXX, 337–349 (June 1955).

——— "Whitman's 'Song of the Broad-Axe,' Stanza 1, Section 1," *Explicator*, XIII, item 39 (April 1956).

Cooke, Alice Lovelace, "A Note on Whitman's Symbolism in 'Song of Myself,'" *Modern Language Notes*, LXV, 228–232 (April 1950).

Eby, E. H., "Did Whitman Write 'The Good Gray Poet'?" *Modern Language Quarterly*, XI, 445–449 (December 1950).

Eleanor, Sister Mary, "Hedge's 'Prose Writers of Germany' as a Source of Whitman's Knowledge of German Philosophy," *Modern Language Notes*, LXI, 381–388 (June 1946).

Feinberg, Charles E., "A Whitman Collector Destroys a Whitman Myth," *Papers of the Bibliographical Society of America*, LII, 73–92 (2nd quarter 1958).

Finkel, William L., "Sources of Walt Whitman's Manuscript Notes on Physique," *American Literature*, XXII, 308–331 (November 1950).

——— "Walt Whitman Manuscript Notes on Oratory," *American Literature*, XXII, 29–52 (March 1950).

Fletcher, E. G., "Pioneers! O Pioneers!" *American Literature*, XIX, 259–261 (November 1947). (On the scansion of this poem.)

Francis, K. H., "Walt Whitman's French," *Modern Language Review*, LI, 493–506 (October 1956).

Furness, Clifton J., "Walt Whitman's Estimate of Shakespeare," *Harvard Studies and Notes in Philology and Literature*, XIV (1932), 1–33.

Gohdes, Clarence, "A Comment on Section 5 of Whitman's 'Song of Myself,'" *Modern Language Notes*, LXIX, 583–586 (December 1954).

——— "A Note on Whitman's Use of the Bible as Model," *Modern Language Quarterly*, II, 105–106 (March 1941).

——— "Section 50 of Whitman's 'Song of Myself,'" *Modern Language Notes*, LXXV, 654–656 (December 1960).

——— "Whitman and Emerson," *Sewanee Review*, XXXVII, 79–93 (January 1929).

Grier, Edward F., "Walt Whitman, the *Galaxy* and *Democratic Vistas*," *American Literature*, XXIII, 332–350 (November 1951).

Gummere, Richard M., "Walt Whitman and His Reaction to the Classics," *Harvard Studies in Classical Philology*, LX (1951), 263–289.

Harrison, Richard C., "Walt Whitman and Shakespeare," *PMLA*, XLIV, 1201–1238 (December 1929).

Hendrick, George, "Unpublished Notes on Whitman in William Sloane Kennedy's Diary," *American Literature,* XXXIV, pp. 279–285 (May 1962).

—— "Whitman's Copy of the *Bhagavad-Gita,*" *Walt Whitman Review,* V. 12–14 (March 1959).

Hollis, C. Carroll, "Names in 'Leaves of Grass,'" *Names,* V, 129–156 (September 1957).

—— "Whitman and the American Idiom," *Quarterly Journal of Speech,* XLIII, 408–420 (December 1957).

—— "Whitman on 'Periphrastic' Literature," *Fresco,* X, 5–13 (Winter–Spring 1960).

—— "Whitman's Word-Game," *Walt Whitman Newsletter,* IV, 74–76 (March 1958).

Holloway, Emory, "Whitman's Last Words," *American Literature,* XXIV, 367–369 (November 1952).

Hubach, Robert R., "Walt Whitman and Taliessin," *American Literature,* XVIII, 329–331 (January 1947).

—— "Walt Whitman Visits St. Louis," *Missouri Historical Review,* XXXVII, 386–394 (July 1943).

Hungerford, Edward, "Walt Whitman and His Chart of Bumps," *American Literature,* II, 350–384 (January 1931).

Jarrell, Randall, "Walt Whitman: He Had His Nerve," *Kenyon Review,* XIV, 63–79 (Winter 1952).

Johnson, C. W. M., "Whitman's 'Out of the Cradle Endlessly Rocking,'" *Explicator,* V, note 52 (May 1947).

Jones, Joseph, "Whitman's 'When Lilacs Last in the Dooryard Bloom'd,'" *Explicator,* IX, note 42 (April 1951).

Kahn, Sholom J., "The American Background of Whitman's Sense of Evil," *Scripta Hierosolymitana,* II (1955), 82–118.

—— "Whitman's Black Lucifer: Some Possible Sources," *PMLA,* LXXI, 932–944 (December 1956).

Kallsen, T. J., "'Song of Myself': Logical Unity through Analogy," *West Virginia University Bulletin,* IX, 33–40 (June 1953).

Kinnaird, John, "The Paradox of an American Identity," *Partisan Review,* V, 380–405 (Summer 1958).

Lovell, John, Jr., "Appreciating Whitman: 'Passage to India,'" *Modern Language Quarterly,* XXI, 131–141 (June 1960).

Lowell, Amy, "Walt Whitman and the New Poetry," *Yale Review,* XVI, 502–519 (April 1927).

Mabbott, Thomas Ollive, "'Tis But Ten Years Since; with text of what has not been used otherwise by Whitman," *American Literature,* XV, 51–62 (March 1943).

—— "Whitman's 'Song of Myself,'" *Explicator,* V, 43 (April 1947).

McDermott, John Francis, "Whitman and the Partons," *American Literature*, XXIX, 3 1 6–3 1 9 (November 1 9 5 7).

Marks, Alfred H., "Whitman's Triadic Imagery," *American Literature*, XXXIII, 99–1 2 6 (March 1 9 5 1).

Milne, W. Gordon, "William Douglas O'Connor and the Authorship of *The Good Gray Poet*," *American Literature*, XXV, 3 1–4 2 (March 1 9 5 3).

Morgan, Paul, "New Significance to Whitman's 'Song of the Exposition,' " *University of Texas Library Chronicle*, IV, 1 3 7–1 5 0 (Summer 1 9 5 2).

Murry, John Middleton, "Walt Whitman: The Prophet of Democracy," *Pacific Spectator*, IX, 3 2–5 7 (Winter 1 9 5 5).

Paine, Gregory, "The Literary Relations of Whitman and Carlyle," *Studies in Philology*, XXXVI, 5 5 0–5 6 3 (July 1 9 3 9).

Parsons, Olive W., "Whitman, the Non-Hegelian," *PMLA*, LXIII, 1 0 7 7–1 0 9 3 (December 1 9 4 3).

Pound, Louise, "Two Curious Words: Whitman's *Carlacue*," *American Speech*, XXX, 9 5–9 6 (May 1 9 5 5).

——— "Walt Whitman and the French Language," *American Speech*, I, 4 2 1–4 3 0 (May 1 9 2 6).

——— "Walt Whitman's Neologisms," *American Mercury*, IV, 1 9 9–2 0 1 (February 1 9 2 5).

Pulos, C. E., "Whitman and Epictetus: The Stoical Element in Leaves of Grass," *Journal of English and Germanic Philology*, LV, 7 5–8 4 (January 1 9 5 6).

Riese, Teut, "Walt Whitman als politischer Dichter," *Jahrbuch für Amerikastudien*, III (1 9 5 8), 1 3 6–1 5 0.

Roddier, Henri, "Pierre Leroux, George Sand et Walt Whitman, ou l'éveil d'un poète," *Revue de Littérature Comparée*, XXXI, 5–3 3, (January–March 1 9 5 7).

Roundtree, T. J., "Whitman's Indirect Expression and Its Application to 'Song of Myself,' " *PMLA*, LXXIII, 5 4 9–5 5 5 (December 1 9 5 8).

Roy, G. R., "Walt Whitman, George Sand and Certain French Socialists," *Revue de Littérature Comparée*, XXIX, 5 5 0–5 6 1 (October–December 1 9 5 5).

Shephard, Esther, "An Inquiry into Whitman's Method of Turning Prose into Poetry," *Modern Language Quarterly*, XIV, 4 3–5 9 (March 1 9 5 3).

——— "Possible Sources of Whitman's Ideas and Symbols in 'Hermes Mercurius Trismegistus' and Other Works," *Modern Language Quarterly*, XIV, 6 0–8 1 (March 1 9 5 3).

——— "Whitman's Whereabouts in the Winter of 1 8 4 2–1 8 4 3," *American Literature*, XXIX, 2 8 9–2 9 6 (November 1 9 5 7).

Sixbey, G. L., " 'Chanting the Square Deific' — A Study in Whitman's Religion," *American Literature*, IX, 171–195 (May 1937).

Smith, Fred M., "Whitman's Debt to *Sartor Resartus*," *Modern Language Quarterly*, III, 51–65 (March 1942).

—— "Whitman's Poet-Prophet and Carlyle's Hero," *PMLA*, LV, 1146–1164 (December 1940).

Smith, Henry Nash, "Walt Whitman and Manifest Destiny," *Huntington Library Quarterly*, X, 373–389 (August 1947).

Spitzer, Leo, " 'Explication de Texte' Applied to Walt Whitman's 'Out of the Cradle Endlessly Rocking,' " *ELH*, XVI, 229–249 (September 1949).

Stauffer, Ruth, "Whitman's 'Passage to India,' " *Explicator*, IX, 50 (May 1951).

Story, Irving C., "The Structural Pattern of Leaves of Grass," *Pacific University Bulletin*, XXXVIII, 1–12 (January 1942).

Stovall, Floyd, "Main Drifts in Whitman's Poetry," *American Literature*, IV, 3–21 (March 1932).

—— "Notes on Whitman's Reading," *American Literature*, XXVI, 337–362 (November 1954).

—— "Walt Whitman and the American Tradition," *Virginia Quarterly Review*, XXI, 540–557 (Autumn 1955).

—— "Walt Whitman and the Dramatic Stage," *Studies in Philology*, L, 513–539 (July 1953).

—— "Walt Whitman: The Man and the Myth," *South Atlantic Quarterly*, LIV, 538–551 (November 1955).

—— "Whitman, Shakespeare and the Baconians," *Philological Quarterly*, XXI, 27–38 (January 1952).

—— "Whitman, Shakespeare and Democracy," *Journal of English and Germanic Philology*, LI, 457–572 (October 1952).

—— "Whitman's Knowledge of Shakespeare," *Studies in Philology*, XLIX, 643–664 (October 1952).

Sutton, Walter, "The Analysis of Free Verse Form, Illustrated by a Reading of Whitman," *Journal of Aesthetics and Art Criticism*, XVIII, 241–254 (December 1959).

Swayne, Mattie, "Whitman's Catalogue Rhetoric," *University of Texas Studies in English*, XXI, 162–178 (July 1941).

Walcutt, Charles C., "Whitman's 'Out of the Cradle Endlessly Rocking,' " *College English*, X, 277–279 (February 1949).

Ware, Lois, "Poetic Conventions in *Leaves of Grass*," *Studies in Philology*, XXVI, 47–57 (January 1929).

Warfel, Harry R., " 'Out of the Cradle Endlessly Rocking,' " *Tennessee Studies in Literature*, III (1958), 83–88.

—— "Whitman's Structural Principles in 'Spontaneous Me,' " *College English*, XVIII, 190–195 (January 1957).

Wecter, Dixon, "Walt Whitman as Civil Servant," *PMLA*, LXVIII, 1094–1109 (December 1943).

Whicher, Stephen E., "'Pioneers! O Pioneers!'" *American Literature*, XIX, 259–261 (November 1947).

Wiley, Autrey Nell, "Reiterative Devices in *Leaves of Grass*," *American Literature*, I, 161–170 (May 1929).

Wilson, Lawrence, "The 'Body Electric' Meets the Genteel Tradition," *New Mexico Quarterly*, XXVI, 369–386 (Winter 1956–57).

Woodward, Robert H., "Journey Motif in Whitman and Tennyson," *Modern Language Notes*, LXXII, 26–27 (January 1957).

ABBREVIATIONS USED IN THE NOTES

AL: *American Literature.*
AM: *Atlantic Monthly.*
Coll. W: *The Collected Writings of Walt Whitman,* New York University Press, 1961–.
CP: *The Complete Prose of Walt Whitman,* edited by Malcolm Cowley, New York: Pellegrini and Cudahy, 1948.
CW: *The Complete Writings of Walt Whitman,* 10 vols., New York: Putnam's Sons, 1902.
FC: *Faint Clews and Indirections,* edited by Clarence Gohdes and Rollo G. Silver, Duke University Press, 1949.
G of the F: *The Gathering of the Forces,* edited by Cleveland Rogers and John Black, 2 vols., New York: Putnam's Sons, 1920.
Imprints: *Leaves of Grass Imprints,* 1860.
Inc. Ed.: *Leaves of Grass,* Inclusive Edition, edited by Emory Holloway, Garden City, N.Y.: Doubleday, Doran 1925.
In Re: *In Re Walt Whitman,* Philadelphia: David McKay, 1893.
JEGP: *Journal of English and Germanic Philology.*
LG: *Leaves of Grass.*
MLN: *Modern Language Notes.*
MLQ: *Modern Language Quarterly.*
NB: *November Boughs,* 1888.
N & F: *Notes and Fragments,* edited by R. M. Bucke, London, Ontario, 1899.
N & Q: *Notes and Queries.*
NEQ: *New England Quarterly.*
RAA: *Revue Anglo-Américaine.*
SD: *Specimen Days.*
Sequel: *Sequel to Drum-Taps,* 1865.
SPL: *Walt Whitman, Complete Poetry and Selected Prose and Letters,* edited by Emory Holloway, New York: Random House, 1938.
Uncoll. PP: *The Uncollected Poetry and Prose of Walt Whitman,* collected and edited by Emory Holloway, 2 vols., 1921.
With WW in C: Horace Traubel, *With Walt Whitman in Camden,* 4 vols.
WWW: *Walt Whitman's Workshop,* edited by C. J. Furness, Harvard University Press, 1928.

NOTES

PART ONE

THE MAIN THEMES OF LEAVES OF GRASS

I. MYSTICISM AND THE POETRY OF THE BODY

1. *LG 1855,* p. 26, "Song of Myself," *Inc. Ed.,* p. 41, §21, l. 1.

2. *LG 1855,* p. 80, "I Sing the Body Electric," *Inc. Ed.,* p. 83, §6, l. 10.

3. *LG 1855,* p. 79, "I Sing the Body Electric," *Inc. Ed.,* p. 82, §5, l. 2.

4. *LG 1856,* "Leaves-Droppings," p. 354.

5. *LG 1855,* p. 29, "Song of Myself," *Inc. Ed.,* p. 44, §24, l. 26.

6. *LG 1855,* p. 29, "Song of Myself," *Inc. Ed.,* p. 43, §24, l. 2.

7. *LG 1855,* p. 28, "Song of Myself," *Inc. Ed.,* p. 43, §23, l. 8. All these passages probably date back to 1848–1850; cf. *Uncoll. PP,* II, 63–72.

8. It is to be noted that Whitman almost never resorts to the word "to commune" which mystics use so often; he prefers the word "to absorb" with its purely physical connotations:

> Will it absorb into me as I absorb food, air, to appear again in my strength, gait, face?

("Poem of Many in One," *LG 1856,* p. 193, "By Blue Ontario's Shore," *Inc. Ed.,* p. 294, §12, l. 30.) See in the same poem §13, l. 7. Edwin Harold Eby in his *Concordance of Walt Whitman's "Leaves of Grass" and Selected Prose Writings* (Seattle: University of Washington Press, 1949–1955) quotes only one example of "to commune" from the 1855 ed. of *Leaves of Grass* and less than half a dozen instances from the rest of Whitman's works.

9. "Democratic Vistas," *SD,* p. 248, *CP,* p. 251.

10. ". . . Elias at the latent base was *sentimental — religious* like an old Hebrew mystic and though I have something of that kind way in the rear and I guess I am mainly sensitive to the wonderfulness and perhaps spirituality of things *in their physical and concrete expressions* — and have celebrated all that . . ." Letter to O'Connor, April 18, 1888, Berg Collection of the New York Public Library.

11. In 1856 he exclaimed:

All comes by the body, health puts you rapport with the universe.

("Poem of Many in One," *LG 1856*, p. 181, "By Blue Ontario's Shore," *Inc. Ed.*, p. 287, §3, l. 6.)

12. "There Was a Child Went Forth" and "Beginning My Studies" seem to imply on the contrary that his mysticism preceded the awakening of his sexuality, but, as these two poems are in direct contradiction with the rest of his writings, their testimony cannot be trusted. In all likelihood, when he composed them, Whitman projected on his childhood the thoughts and emotions of his adolescence and young manhood, as he did in "Out of the Cradle Endlessly Rocking." Besides, are these two poems really mystical? They merely translate a child's sense of wonder before the world — a reaction which most children have experienced without becoming poets later in life. In any case, even if the two poems in question are the expression of a dim mysticism, it must not be forgotten — as psychoanalysts have proved — that sexual emotions make their appearance long before puberty. So, even then, our thesis is still valid.

13. *LG 1855*, p. 30, "Song of Myself," *Inc. Ed.*, p. 45, §24, ll. 31–34, 36, and variant reading p. 565.

14. *LG 1855*, p. 14, "Song of Myself," *Inc. Ed.*, p. 26, §3, ll. 20–21.

15. "Poem of the Body" (a most characteristic title), *LG 1856*, p. 178, "I Sing the Body Electric," *Inc. Ed.*, p. 85, §9, l. 15.

16. "Bunch Poem," *LG 1856*, pp. 309–310, "Spontaneous Me," *Inc. Ed.*, p. 88, ll. 10–14.

17. *LG 1855*, pp. 32–33, "Song of Myself," *Inc. Ed.*, pp. 48–49, §28. See variant readings pp. 567–568 and *Uncoll. PP*, II, 72, for an earlier draft of this passage.

18. "Poem of Procreation," *LG 1856*, p. 240, "A Woman Waits for Me," *Inc. Ed.*, p. 86, ll. 3–4.

19. "A touch now reads me a library of knowledge in an instant." First draft of "Song of Myself," §28–29, in *Uncoll. PP*, II, 72.

20. ". . . plunge semitic muscle into its merits and demerits . . ." *LG 1855*, p. xi A, "Preface to 1855 Edition," *Inc. Ed.*, p. 505. He took up the same phrase again in 1856 in "By Blue Ontario's Shore," *Inc. Ed.*, p. 289, §6, l. 8. Curiously enough, Whitman uses "semitic" instead of "seminal."

21. *LG 1855*, p. 47, "Song of Myself," *Inc. Ed.*, p. 65, §42, l. 15. See also the variant reading of §28, pp. 567–568.

22. "Poem of the Road," *LG 1856*, p. 231, "Song of the Open Road," *Inc. Ed.*, p. 128, §8, l. 9.

23. "Poem of the Road," p. 229, "Song of the Open Road," *Inc. Ed.*, p. 127, §6, l. 23.

24. "Poem of the Road," *LG 1856*, pp. 229–230, "Song of the Open Road," *Inc. Ed.*, pp. 127–128, §7, ll. 2–4, 8.

25. "Poem of the Road," *LG 1856*, p. 229, "Song of the Open Road," *Inc. Ed.*, p. 127, §6, ll. 24–25.

26. "Sun-Down Poem," *LG 1856*, p. 219, "Crossing Brooklyn Ferry," *Inc. Ed.*, p. 138, §8, ll. 5–6.

27. "Enfans d'Adam," no. 2, *LG 1860*, p. 288, "From Pent-up Aching Rivers," *Inc. Ed.*, p. 77, ll. 4–5.

28. *LG 1860*, p. 289, "From Pent-up Aching Rivers," *Inc. Ed.*, p. 78, l. 26. See also "Enfans d'Adam," no. 6, *LG 1860*, p. 308, "One Hour to Madness and Joy," *Inc. Ed.*, p. 90, l. 4.

29. "Enfans d'Adam," no. 6, *LG 1860*, p. 309, "One Hour to Madness and Joy," *Inc. Ed.*, p. 91, l. 24.

30. "Calamus," no. 7, *LG 1860*, pp. 352–353, "Of the Terrible Doubt of Appearances," *Inc. Ed.*, pp. 100–101, ll. 1–4, 11–13.

31. William James, *The Varieties of Religious Experience* (New York: The Modern Library Edition, 1902), p. 387 (Lectures XVI and XVII).

32. R. M. Bucke, *Cosmic Consciousness* (New York: E. P. Dutton, 1947), pp. 227–228.

33. *LG 1855*, p. 32, "Song of Myself," *Inc. Ed.*, p. 27, §5, ll. 6–14. There is a slight difference between the first and the last versions of this passage.

34. James, *Varieties of Religious Experience*, pp. 371–372.

35. R. M. Bucke, *In Re Walt Whitman* (Philadelphia: David McKay, 1893), "Walt Whitman and the Cosmic Sense," pp. 341–342, and *Cosmic Consciousness*, p. 227.

36. William Wordsworth, *The Prelude* (Version of 1805), Book IV, ll. 340–345.

37. The short poem entitled "Hast never come to thee an hour," *LG 1881*, p. 218, *Inc. Ed.*, p. 235, probably alludes to the 1853 ecstasy.

The strange day-dreams or visions which he attributed to Franklin Evans in 1842 and to which he was probably subject himself (*Uncoll. PP*, II, 200–201), may have been the first manifestations of his mysticism. He describes them as "a strange imaginative mania," "a kind of trance" and though they belong to the field of fancy rather than of imagination, they already suggest a very vivid sense of infinity.

38. "Proto-Leaf," *LG 1860*, p. 13, "Starting from Paumanok," *Inc. Ed.*, p. 17, §10, ll. 6–10, and variant reading p. 550.

39. "Chants Democratic," no. 8, *LG 1860*, pp. 177 (3), 178 (6), "Song at Sunset," *Inc. Ed.*, pp. 410–411, ll. 10, 35–37.

40. See Vol. I, Chapter IX, 232.

41. "One of the Human Kinks," *SD*, p. 98–99, *CP*, p. 95.

42. *LG 1855*, p. 13, "Song of Myself," *Inc. Ed.*, p. 24, §2, ll. 1–3.

43. *LG 1855*, p. 30, "Song of Myself," *Inc. Ed.*, p. 45, §24, ll. 54–56.

44. "Poem of the Road," *LG 1856*, p. 231, "Song of the Open Road," *Inc. Ed.*, p. 128, §8, l. 9.

45. See *LG 1855*, pp. 32–33, "Song of Myself," *Inc. Ed.*, pp. 48–49, §28–29, and an earlier draft of this passage in *Uncoll. PP*, II, 72–73.

46. *LG 1855*, p. 21, "Song of Myself," *Inc. Ed.*, p. 34, §14, l. 9.

47. *LG 1855*, p. 30, "Song of Myself," *Inc. Ed.*, p. 45, §24, l. 45.

48. *LG 1855*, p. 20, "Song of Myself," *Inc. Ed.*, p. 33, §13, l. 8.

49. *LG 1855*, p. 13, "Song of Myself," *Inc. Ed.*, p. 24, §2, ll. 6–7.

50. "A Sun-Bath — Nakedness," *SD*, p. 104, *CP*, p. 101.

51. "Poem of Joys," *LG 1860*, p. 226 (31), "A Song of Joys," *Inc. Ed.*, p. 153, ll. 110–111, and "Proto-Leaf," *LG 1860*, p. 18, "Starting from Paumanok," *Inc. Ed.*, p. 20, §14, l. 26. He later declared to Traubel: "I was a first-rate aquatic loafer." *With WW in C*, II, 21.

52. *LG 1855*, p. 27, "Song of Myself," *Inc. Ed.*, p. 42, §22, ll. 1–6; "Poem of Wonder at the Resurrection of the Wheat," *LG 1856*, pp. 202–204, "This Compost," *Inc. Ed.*, pp. 309–310, §1, ll. 4–5, §2, ll. 17–18. See also "Bunch Poem," *LG 1856*, p. 311, "Spontaneous Me," *Inc. Ed.*, p. 89, l. 35.

In 1857 he wrote several articles in praise of swimming for the *Brooklyn Times* (*I Sit and Look Out*, pp. 100–104). However he was not then expressing his personal sensuality, but merely recommending the practice of swimming for the sake of hygiene. His was the point of view of a journalist concerned with public health. But the subject obsessed him and he returned to it in passing in 1860 in "Enfans d'Adam," no. 2, *LG 1860*, p. 289, "From Pent-up Aching Rivers," *Inc. Ed.*, p. 78, l. 22.

In a review of *Leaves of Grass* which he wrote himself for the *United States Review* he reproached intellectuals with hiding their bodies and avoiding the direct contact of things: ". . . all our intellectual people . . . touch not the earth barefoot, and enter not the sea except in a complete bathing dress . . ." (*Leaves of Grass Imprints*, 1860, p. 8).

53. *LG 1855*, p. 30, "Song of Myself," *Inc. Ed.*, p. 45, §24, l. 42.

54. *LG 1855*, p. 74, "The Sleepers," *Inc. Ed.*, p. 359, §7, l. 1–3, and variant reading p. 684.

55. *LG 1855*, p. 27, "Song of Myself," *Inc. Ed.*, p. 41, §21, ll. 14–16.

56. *LG 1855,* p. 32, "Song of Myself," *Inc. Ed.,* p. 48, §27, ll. 4–7.

57. *LG 1855,* p. 29, "Song of Myself," *Inc. Ed.,* p. 44, §24, l. 27.

58. *LG 1855,* p. 18, "Song of Myself," *Inc. Ed.,* p. 31, §10, l. 1–2.

59. *LG 1855,* p. 30, "Song of Myself," *Inc. Ed.,* p. 45, §24, ll. 49, 50, 52.

60. *LG 1855,* p. 13, "Song of Myself," *Inc. Ed.,* p. 26, §2, l. 10.

61. "Paumanok, and My Life on it as Child and Young Man," *SD,* p. 14, *CP,* pp. 9–10.

In his essay on "L'intuition panthéiste chez les romantiques anglais; essai d'interprétation positive" (*Revue germanique,* juillet-août 1908, reprinted in *L'évolution psychologique et la littérature en Angleterre,* Paris: Felix Alcan, 1920, pp. 22–96), Louis Cazamian has shown the importance of the part played by purely physiological factors and the practice of physical exercises such as walking in the mysticism of the English romantic poets.

62. In "Song of Myself" (§11) he describes a case of repression which probably was a mere transposition of his own.

63. "Broad-Axe Poem," *LG 1856,* p. 158, "Song of the Broad-Axe," *Inc. Ed.,* p. 616 (after section 11).

64. "Proto-Leaf," *LG 1860,* p. 8 (11); in 1881 this passage was transferred from "Starting from Paumanok" to "Song to Myself," §1 (*Inc. Ed.,* p. 24).

As to the passage of "Song of the Broad-Axe" in which he celebrated his "reckless health," he canceled it in 1867; the worries which his health had caused him during the war had probably rendered him more modest and cautious. See *Inc. Ed.,* p. 616.

65. When he wrote "Passage to India" and "Out of the Cradle Endlessly Rocking," for instance.

66. *SD,* p. 118, *CP,* p. 115.

67. *Inc. Ed.,* p. 462.

68. *LG 1855,* p. 32, "Song of Myself," *Inc. Ed.,* p. 48, §27.

69. "To Be At All," *Inc. Ed.,* p. 462, ll. 8–9.

70. "Song of Myself," *Inc. Ed.,* p. 48, §27, ll. 7–8.

71. *LG 1855,* p. 55, "Song of Myself," *Inc. Ed.,* p. 75, §52, l. 3.

72. ". . . of his robust middle age" would be truer to facts since he was between thirty-six and forty-one at the time of the full blossoming of his poetic faculties, but "of his youth" is more suitable after all, since, owing to a curious lag, the youth of the poet coincided with the middle age of the man. So we shall always call "youth" this period in the career of Whitman, as do instinctively all the critics of *Leaves of Grass.*

73. "Loafing in Woods," *SD,* p. 159, *CP,* p. 159.

74. "The Mystic Trumpeter," *As A Strong Bird on Pinions Free,* 1872, p. 12, *Inc. Ed.,* p. 392, §8, l. 16.

See also: "One main object I had from the first was to sing that ecstasy beyond all the pleasures of wealth, love, learning — the simple extasy [sic] of Being . . ." The same idea occurs in the next passage: ". . . merely to breathe and live in that sweet air and clean sunlight was happiness enough for one day . . . there is an ecstatic satisfaction in such lazy philosophy, such passive yielding up of one's self to the pure emotion of Nature, better than the most exciting pleasures." *Uncoll. PP,* II, 314.

75. "In the course of my stay he suggested that I should follow his example and wear a shirt with an open bosom so that the summer breeze could get at me — as he phrased it." Leon Mead, "Memories of Walt Whitman," Lynn (Mass.) *Saturday Union,* June 6, 1885.

76. "To the Sunset Breeze," *Good-Bye My Fancy,* 1891, p. 12, *Inc. Ed.,* p. 499.

77. "Thou Orb Aloft Full-Dazzling," *LG 1881,* p. 352, *Inc. Ed.,* pp. 385–386.

78. "Denver Impressions," *SD,* p. 147, *CP,* p. 146. See also "The St. Lawrence Line," *SD,* p. 154, *CP,* p. 164.

79. "Proud Music of the Storm," *Passage to India,* 1871, p. 23, *Inc. Ed.,* p. 341, §5, ll. 11–13.

80. "The Singer in the Prison," *Passage to India,* 1871, pp. 94–96, *Inc. Ed.,* pp. 316–318.

81. See n. 55.

82. "When Lilacs Last in the Dooryard Bloom'd," *Sequel to Drum-Taps,* 1865–66, pp. 5–6, *Inc. Ed.,* p. 278, §8, ll. 3, 8.

83. "Hours for the Soul," *SD,* p. 118, *CP,* p. 116.

84. "Full-Starr'd Nights," *SD,* p. 101, *CP,* p. 98. See also "Scenes on Ferry and River," "Last Winter's Night," *SD,* p. 125, *CP,* p. 122 (1st para.).

85. "A July Afternoon by the Pond," *SD,* p. 88, *CP,* p. 85.

86. "Sea-Shore Fancies," *SD,* p. 95, *CP,* pp. 91–92.

87. "To the Sunset Breeze," *Good-Bye My Fancy,* 1891, p. 12, *Inc. Ed.,* p. 449, l. 13.

88. See for instance what he declared to a journalist in 1881: ". . . the emotional, the personal, the human, and even the animal are essential parts of a profound poem . . ." *Boston Globe,* August 24, 1881; see Herbert Bergman, "Whitman on His Poetry and Some Poets — Two Uncollected Interviews," *American N & Q,* VIII (February 1950), 164.

89. "Whittier is rather a grand figure — pretty lean and ascetic — no Greek — also not composite and universal enough (don't wish to be, don't try to be) for ideal Americanism. Ideal Americanism

would probably take the Greek spirit for all the globe, all history, all rank . . ." Letter to an unknown correspondent dated Oct. 10, 1889 (Berg Collection). See also his declarations to a Philadelphia journalist in 1880: "The theologians to a man teach humility and that the body is the sinful setting of the immortal soul. I wish men to be proud of their bodies, to look upon the body as a thing of beauty, too holy to be abused by vice and debauchery." *Philadelphia Press,* March 3, 1880; quoted by Henry Bergman, "Whitman on His Poetry," *ibid.,* pp. 163–164.

90. *LG 1855,* p. 50, "Song of Myself," *Inc. Ed.,* p. 45, §24, l. 49.

91. "Poem of the Road," *LG 1856,* p. 230, "Song of the Open Road," *Inc. Ed.,* p. 128, §8, ll. 1–3.

92. "Poem of Joys," *LG 1860,* p. 257 (4), "A Song of Joys," *Inc. Ed.,* p. 149, l. 7. See also *LG 1855,* p. 55, "Song of Myself," *Inc. Ed.,* p. 75, §50, l. 10, and *LG 1855,* p. 59, "A Song for Occupations," *Inc. Ed.,* p. 181, §3, l. 3.

93. "The Mystic Trumpeter," *As a Strong Bird on Pinions Free,* 1872, p. 12, *Inc. Ed.,* p. 392, §8, ll. 15–17.

94. *Ibid.,* l. 3.

95. "The Sky," "Days and Nights — Happiness," *SD,* p. 92, *CP,* p. 89.

96. *Ibid.*

97. "The Oaks and I," *SD,* p. 105, *CP,* p. 102.

98. *LG 1855,* p. 48, "Song of Myself," *Inc. Ed.,* p. 67, §43, ll. 17, 19. See also *LG 1855,* p. 15, "Song of Myself," *Inc. Ed.,* p. 27, §4, l. 15.

II. THE IMPLICIT METAPHYSICS

1. *LG 1855,* p. 55, "Song of Myself," *Inc. Ed.,* p. 75, §51, ll. 6–8. In "Self-Reliance," Emerson said the same thing in almost the same words: "Suppose you should contradict yourself, what then?" Whitman was only following his advice.

2. Malcolm Cowley, *The Complete Poetry of Walt Whitman* (New York: Pellegrini & Cudahy, 1948), p. 26.

3. Preface to 1872 edition, *Inc. Ed.,* p. 510.

4. *CW,* VI, 12, or *N & F,* p. 59 (28).

5. *CW,* VII, 20 (72).

6. "Proto-Leaf," *LG 1860,* p. 11 (25), "Starting from Paumanok," *Inc., Ed.,* p. 16, §7, l. 8.

7. "Proto-Leaf," *LG 1860,* p. 16 (47), p. 17 (51), "Starting from Paumanok," *Inc. Ed.,* p. 19, §13, ll. 1–2, 11.

8. "Poem of the Body," *LG 1856,* p. 167, "I Sing the Body Electric," *Inc. Ed.,* p. 79, §1, l. 8. F. O. Matthiessen who quotes this line in

American Renaissance (Oxford University Press, 1941), p. 52, seems to believe that it was composed in 1860 because "I Sing the Body Electric" is part of "Children of Adam" which was added to *Leaves of Grass* only at that date. The chronological order being thus upset, Whitman's position appears to him full of inconsistencies and contradictions.

9. "Poem of the Body," *LG 1856*, p. 153, "I Sing the Body Electric," *Inc. Ed.*, p. 86, §9, ll. 35–36, and p. 588, variant reading of §9, after l. 36.

10. *Uncoll. PP*, II, 69–70, or *Inc. Ed.*, p. 564.

11. *LG 1855*, p. 28. In 1867 Whitman developed this line in order to make his thought more explicit:

> I accept Reality and dare not question it,
> Materialism first and last imbuing.

("Song of Myself," *Inc. Ed.*, p. 43, §23, ll. 7–8.)

12. "Chants Democratic," no. 16, *LG 1860*, p. 189, "Mediums," *Inc. Ed.*, p. 399, l. 6.

13. One must not underestimate the Christian influences which he underwent in his childhood. There are traces of them in his early writings, in this passage from *Uncoll. PP*, II, 89, for instance, which is anterior to 1855:

> O, Nature! impartial, and perfect in imperfection!
> Every precious gift to man is linked with a curse — and each pollution has some sparkle from heaven.
> The mind, raised upward, then holds communion with angels and its reach overtops heaven; yet then it stays in the meshes of the world too and is stung by a hundred serpents every day.

In order to become himself, Whitman had to cast off the notion of original sin and rid himself of all this Christian mythology. He was capable of writing *Leaves of Grass* only after he had rediscovered the way to the Garden of Eden and could look at the world with the unspoiled freshness of man before the fall. He was quite aware of it himself and that is the reason why in 1860 he proclaimed himself (symbolically) a direct descendant of Adam in "Enfans d'Adam."

14. Notably in Emerson's works where he could read, for instance: "I believe in the existence of the material world as the expression of the spiritual or real." When reading in *Graham's Mazagine* an article on "Imagination and Fact," he was particularly struck by the following sentence, which he underlined: "The mountains, rivers, forests and the elements that gird them round would be only blank conditions of matter if the mind did not fling its own divinity around them." Whitman admiringly wrote in the margin: "This I think is one of the most indicative sentences I ever read." *N & F*, p. 77.

15. As the following passage shows:
> The real life of my senses and flesh transcending my senses
> and flesh,
> My body done with materials, my sight done with my material
> eyes,
> Proved to me this day beyond cavil that it is not my material
> eyes which finally see,
> Nor my material body which finally loves, walks, laughs,
> shouts, embraces, procreates.

("Poem of Joys," *LG 1860*, pp. 265–66 (27), "A Song of Joys," *Inc. Ed.*, p. 153, ll. 100–102.) So, as early as 1855, though he laid stress on the body, he already proclaimed the existence of an immortal soul, even in inanimate things; see for instance *LG 1855*, p. 69, "To Think of Time," *Inc. Ed.*, p. 368, §9, l. 1–2.

16. *Uncoll. PP*, II, 66. This passage of an unpublished note quoted by F. O. Matthiessen in *American Renaissance* (p. 525) shows that he was conscious of the originality of his own position: "Most writers have disclaimed the physical world and they have not overestimated the other, or soul, but underestimated the corporeal."

17. *Uncoll. PP*, II, 66.

18. *Ibid.*, p. 79.

19. *Ibid.*, p. 65.

20. *LG 1855*, p. 15, "Song of Myself," *Inc. Ed.*, p. 27, §5, l. 1–2.

21. *LG 1855*, p. 26, "Song of Myself," *Inc. Ed.*, p. 41, §21, l. 1.

22. *Nouvelles Nourritures* (Paris: Nouvelle Revue Française, 1935), p. 233. Bernardin de Saint Pierre had said before him in his *Etudes de la Nature* (Paris, 1792), III, p. 12: "Je sens, donc j'existe." Whitman reaches almost the same formula in *LG 1855*, p. 32, "Song of Myself," *Inc. Ed.*, p. 48, §28, l. 1, and in "Poem of Joys," *LG 1860*, p. 265 (27), "Song of Joys," *Inc. Ed.*, p. 153, ll. 98–99.

23. "Sun-Down Poem," *LG 1856*, p. 216, "Crossing Brooklyn Ferry," *Inc. Ed.*, p. 136, §5, ll. 10–11.

24. "Sun-Down Poem," *LG 1856*, p. 221, "Crossing Brooklyn Ferry," p. 607, variant reading of §9.

25. "Melange mine own, the unseen and the seen . . ." in "Proto-Leaf," *LG 1860*, p. 13 (35), "Starting from Paumanok," *Inc. Ed.*, p. 17, §10, l. 6.

26. "Chants Democratic," no. 7, *LG 1860*, p. 175 (3), "With Antecedents," *Inc. Ed.*, p. 204, §2, l. 10.

27. "Says," no 7, *LG 1860*, p. 420, *Inc. Ed.*, p. 481.

28. "Chants Democratic," no. 8, *LG 1860*, p. 178 (6–7), "Song at Sunset," *Inc. Ed.*, p. 411, ll. 37, 39.

29. "Proto-Leaf," *LG 1860*, p. 9 (17), "Starting from Paumanok," *Inc. Ed.*, p. 14, §5, ll. 11–15.

30. "Calamus," no. 7, *LG 1860*, pp. 352–53, "Of the Terrible Doubt of Appearances," *Inc. Ed.*, 101, ll. 1–2, 5–6.

31. "Calamus," no. 2, *LG 1860*, p. 344, "Scented Herbage of My Breast," *Inc. Ed.*, p. 97, ll. 33–34.

32. "The City Dead-House," *LG 1867*, p. 284, *Inc. Ed.*, p. 308, l. 12.

33. "Proud Music of the Storm," *Passage to India*, 1872, p. 24 (32), *Inc. Ed.*, p. 342, §6, ll. 20–21.

34. "Passage to India," *Passage to India*, 1872, p. 13 (32), *Inc. Ed.*, p. 350, §8, l. 34.

35. "The Mystic Trumpeter," *As a Strong Bird on Pinions Free*, 1872, pp. 8–12, *Inc. Ed.*, pp. 389–392.

36. "Eidólons," *Two Rivulets*, 1876, p. 17, *Inc. Ed.*, p. 5, l. 21.

37. *Ibid.*, p. 6, ll. 49–52, 57–60, 77–80. He may have borrowed the word "eidólon" from Carlyle or Poe who both used it.

38. Preface to 1876 edition, *Inc. Ed.*, pp. 513–514n.

39. *Ibid.*

40. "Grand is the seen," *Good-Bye My Fancy*, 1891, p. 19, *Inc. Ed.*, p. 457, l. 4, 6.

41. "Apparitions," *Good-Bye My Fancy*, 1891, p. 8, *Inc. Ed.*, p. 445, ll. 2–3. There are many other examples of his spiritualism in his prose works. In 1877 he went so far as to write: ". . . a sunset, filling, dominating the esthetic and *soul senses* [italics ours] . . ." ("An Afternoon Scene," *SD*, p. 99, *CP*, p. 96). As early as 1859–1860 he noted: "Much is said of what is spiritual, and of spirituality, in this, that, or the other — in objects, expressions — For me, I see no object, no expression, no animal, no tree, no art, no book, but I see, from morning to night, and from night to morning, the *spiritual*. Bodies are all spiritual . . ." (*American Primer*, p. 1).

42. He even reasserted his sensuality in 1867 at the very beginning of *Leaves of Grass* in "Inscription":

> Man's physiology complete, from top to toe, I sing. Not physiognomy alone, nor brain alone, is worthy for the muse; — I say the Form complete is worthier far . . .

("One's-Self I Sing," *Inc. Ed.*, p. 1, ll. 3–4). See also in 1881, "Thou Reader" (p. 18), *Inc. Ed.*, p. 11.

43. "What is I believe called Idealism seems to me to suggest, (guarding against extravagance, and ever modified even by its opposite,) the course of inquiry and desert of favor for our New World metaphysics, their foundation of and in literature, giving hue to all." "Democratic Vistas," *SD*, p. 250, *CP*, p. 252. He carried this principle into practice on the very next page: "Thus, and thus only, does a human being, his spirit, ascend above, and justify, objective Nature,

which, probably nothing in itself, is incredibly and divinely service-able, indispensable, real, here."

44. See *With WW in C*, I, *passim*. He once declared for instance: "We need a Millet in portraiture — a man who sees the spirit but does not make a man all flesh — all of him body. Eakins errs just a little, just a little — a little — in the direction of the flesh" (p. 131). In a way he here defined his own poetic ideal.

45. He was quite conscious himself of this evolution and he summed it up very poetically in this note: "In youth and maturity Poems are charged with sunshine and varied pomp of day; but as the soul more and more takes precedence, (the sensuous still included,) the Dusk becomes the poet's atmosphere. I too have sought, and ever seek, the brilliant sun, and make my songs according. But as I grow old, the half-lights of evening are far more to me." "After Trying a Certain Book," *SD*, p. 198, *CP*, pp. 195–96.

46. "My two theses — animal and spiritual — became gradually fused in L. of G. — runs through all the poems and gives color to the whole." *CW*, VII, 15. Curiously enough, this undated note shows by the very ambiguity of its grammar his inability to fuse the two themes.

47. In *Fowler's Practical Phrenology* for instance (New York, 1844), pp. 407–410. On the influence of phrenology on Whitman, see Edward Hungerford, "Walt Whitman and his Chart of Bumps," *AL*, II (January 1931), 350–384.

48. *LG 1855*, p. 28, "Song of Myself," *Inc. Ed.*, p. 43, §23, l. 9, and variant reading p. 564.

49. As early as 1854, according to Mody C. Boatright ("Whitman and Hegel," *University of Texas Bulletin — Studies in English*, no. 9, July 1929, pp. 134–150), because Whitman uses the spelling Gostick instead of Gostwick which was the one used in the first edition of *German Literature* in 1854. But this argument is worthless, since Whitman may have come across this edition long after its publication. Newton Arvin (*Whitman*, New York: Macmillan, 1938, pp. 308–309) much more convincingly maintains that Whitman did not become acquainted with the German idealists before 1862 at the earliest. There appeared in that year an article on Schelling which he used in his notes.

50. On Whitman and the German idealists, see Richard Rieth-müller, "Whitman and the Germans — A Study," *German-American Annals*, IV, nos. 1–3 (January-March 1906), pp. 3–15, 35–49, 78–92. According to him, Whitman underwent the influence of Hegel through the *Journal for Speculative Philosophy* founded in 1876 by W. T. Harris whom Whitman knew personally (see *SD*, p. 191), but the articles which appeared in this journal were much too abstract

and Whitman never read them. He said so himself to Traubel (*With WW in C*, I, 191).

See also W. B. Fulghum, Jr., "Whitman's Debt to Joseph Gostwick," *AL*, XII (January 1941), 491–496.

Sister Mary Eleanor, "Hedge's *Prose Writers of Germany* as a Source of Whitman's Knowledge of German Philosophy," *MLN*, 61 (June 1946), 381–388. This author proves that Whitman also knew Hedge's book which had appeared seven years before that of Gostwick, but she cannot demonstrate that he read it before 1860–1870. This seems unlikely, for Whitman's copy of Hedge's book still exists. It is now kept in the library of Bryn Mawr College and one can read on the fly-leaf this note in Whitman's hand: "Have had this volume over twenty-years and read it off and on many hours, many days and nights. This written Nov. 21 '88 in Mickle Street, Camden. WW." Another note gives a more precise date: "Aug. 29, '62, F. S. Gray (at Raefelle's in 6th Street) requested me to keep this book. He goes in a few days on Gen. Smith's staff, down in the Army in Va." This note has been reprinted in *SPL*, p. 1099 n. of p. 898.

Olive Wrenchel Parsons, "Whitman the Non-Hegelian," *PMLA*, LVIII (December 1943), 1077–1093. Parsons tries to prove that Whitman was not as much of a Hegelian as Boatright thought, but in fact, Boatright had already made all the necessary qualifications.

Robert P. Falk, "Walt Whitman and German Thought," *JEGP*, XL (July 1941), 315–330.

Newton Arvin, *Whitman*, pp. 191–197.

51. In the *Encyclopedia Britannica* and in Dane's *American Encyclopedia*.

52. He acknowledged his debt in the following note now in the Library of Congress: "I am indebted to an abstract of J. Gostick's on German Literature."

53. "Carlyle from American Points of View," *SD*, p. 177, *CP*, p. 176.

54. "The Base of All Metaphysics," *LG 1871*, p. 130, *Inc. Ed.*, p. 101. See also this note dated 1877 in *Specimen Days*: "Doubtless there comes a time — perhaps it has come to me — when one feels through his whole being, and pronouncedly the emotional part, that identity between himself subjectively and Nature objectively which Schelling and Fichte were so fond of pressing" ("The Oaks and I," *SD*, p. 105, *CP*, p. 102). His sensibility thus found itself in its turn modified by his philosophy. There was not simply an influence of the one on the other but an interaction of the two.

55. See *CW*, VI, 166–174. He also dwells at great length on the German idealists in "Carlyle from American Points of View," *SD*, pp. 175–177, *CP*, pp. 174–176.

56. *Ibid.*, p. 185. He drew a similar lesson from Fichte: "Subjectiveness is his principle. Strongly stated nothing exists but the I" (*CW*, VI, 180) and from Schelling: "The chief forte of it . . . is the essential identity of the subjective and objective worlds" (*Ibid.*).

57. *Ibid.*, pp. 171, 172–73. About the same time Whitman read in a review an article entitled "Philosophy, psychology and metaphysics." It is now in the Trent Collection of the Duke University Library. This article appeared in 1871 and Whitman underlined the following passage:

There are, however, reasons compelling man to believe spirit to be the deepest element in the universe; and hence a philosophy has to be sought which ought indeed to amalgamate with the deepest philosophy of the material sciences but ought to underlie it, and be plainly the original of which that is the derivative . . . Metaphysics is the endeavor to demonstrate and bring clearly to light the spiritual unity of the world, not as contradictory of the material unity, but as underlying it, and being the source from which it proceeds.

Whitman must have seen in this article the confirmation of his own tendency toward spiritualism.

58. Brinton had said to Whitman: "You give us no consistent philosophy." Whitman replied: "I guess I don't — I should not desire to do so." I put in: "Plenty of philosophy, but not *a* philosophy." To which Whitman answered: "That's better, that's more the idea." (*With WW in C*, I, 156.)

59. *LG 1855*, p. 90, "There Was a Child Went Forth," *Inc. Ed.*, p. 306, ll. 2–4.

60. *Ibid.*

61. *LG 1855*, p. 25, "Song of Myself," *Inc. Ed.*, p. 39, §20, l. 3.

62. *LG 1855*, p. 32, "Song of Myself," *Inc. Ed.*, p. 48, §27, l. 1.

63. *LG 1855*, p. 26, "Song of Myself," *Inc. Ed.*, p. 40, §20, ll. 15–16.

64. "Poem of the Road," *LG 1856*, p. 224, "Song of the Open Road," *Inc. Ed.*, p. 125, §3, l. 2.

65. "Sun-Down Poem," *LG 1856*, p. 216, "Crossing Brooklyn Ferry," *Inc. Ed.*, p. 136, §5, l. 10.

66. "Poem of Joys," *LG 1860*, p. 265 (27), "A Song of Joys," *Inc. Ed.*, p. 153, ll. 98–99.

67. *LG 1855*, p. 32, "Song of Myself," *Inc. Ed.*, p. 48, §28, l. 1. He had first written:

Only one minute, only two or three sheathed touches,
Yet they gather all of me and my spirit into a knot,
They hold us long enough there to show us what we can be,

And that our flesh, and even a part of our flesh,
seems more than senses and life.

Inc. Ed., p. 567, variant reading of §28.

68. *LG 1855*, p. 15, "Song of Myself," *Inc. Ed.*, pp. 26–27, §4, ll. 2–10.

69. *LG 1855*, p. 68, "To Think of Time," *Inc. Ed.*, p. 366, §7, ll. 1–4. He added two lines in 1881 to make his thought more explicit: *Inc. Ed.*, p. 367, §8 ll. 15–16.

70. "Carlyle from American Points of View," *SD*, p. 175, *CP*, p. 174.

71. *LG 1855*, p. 16, "Song of Myself," *Inc. Ed.*, p. 27, §5, l. 12. See variant reading, p. 556. The equality of God and his creatures is also affirmed *ibid.*, §48, l. 3.

72. "Poem of You, Whoever You Are," *LG 1856*, p. 207, "To You," *Inc. Ed.*, p. 198, l. 17.

73. He used the word in *Passage to India* (*Inc. Ed.*, p. 349, §8 l. 20), but he probably gave it only a laudatory value, for the following lines imply a pantheistic conception. His philosophical terminology was often awkward and unprecise. Besides, the word "transcendent" was so unfamiliar to him that he first spelled it "transcendant."

74. *LG 1855*, p. 54, "Song of Myself," *Inc. Ed.*, p. 73, §48, ll. 13, 16–18.

75. "Clef Poem," *LG 1856*, pp. 250–51, "On the Beach at Night Alone," *Inc. Ed.*, p. 222, ll. 4, 8, 9, 11, 13, 14.

76. "Chanting the Square Deific," *Sequel to Drum-Taps*, 1865–66, pp. 15–17, *Passage to India*, 1872, pp. 60–62, *Inc. Ed.*, pp. 370–372. For information about the sources and meaning of this poem, see George L. Sixbey, "Chanting the Square Deific — A Study in Whitman's Religion," *AL*, IX (May 1937), 171–195.

77. *LG 1855*, p. 45, "Song of Myself," *Inc. Ed.*, pp. 63–64, §41, ll. 6–19. See also "Starting from Paumanok" (1860), *Inc. Ed.*, p. 16, §7, ll. 8–9.

78. *Ibid.*

79. He was indeed thinking of the Satan of Milton and of the romantics as this note found among his papers shows: "Theories of Evil — Festus, Faust, Manfred, Paradise Lost, Book of Job." (*N & F*, p. 126.)
See also: "Poem of the Devil, counteractive of the common idea of Satan." (*Ibid.*, p. 171.) Also: "Lucifer . . . Typhon, made up of all that opposes, hinders, obstructs, revolts." (*Ibid.*, p. 15.)

80. It is a barbarous phrase which does not exist in any language. It seems however that Whitman wanted above all to suggest femininity (see "Thou Mother with Thy Equal Brood"). Mark Van Doren uses this as an argument for Whitman's homosexuality ("Walt Whit-

man Stranger," *American Mercury*, XXXV, July 1935, 277–285. See also John Addington Symonds, *Walt Whitman — A Study* (London: George Routledge, 1893), p. 113. But, according to J. T. Trowbridge (*My Own Story — With Recollections of Noted Persons*, Boston: Houghton Mifflin Co. 1903, pp. 393–394), Whitman simply wanted to translate "Holy Spirit" into Italian and made a mistake: "Whitman . . . in talking of it with me acknowledged the blunder, yet through some perversity he allowed it to pass on into subsequent editions."

On what W. M. Rossetti, who had asked Whitman questions about this strange phrase thought of the matter, see *Letters of W. M. Rossetti*, ed. by Clarence Gohdes and Paull Franklin Baum (Durham, N.C., 1934). p. 61.

81. Though this poem was published only in 1865, Whitman very probably conceived the idea of it long before. There is a note in one of the manuscript notebooks kept in the Library of Congress which shows that as early as 1860–61 he was already looking for the "square deific": "I want a Latin motto which conveys the following sense of the words: Four in one — Quator in Uno or better Quatuor juncta in uno / / au courant Quarto . . ." and, on the next page, "Quatuor — Quatruna — Quadriune — Quatruna."

82. "Shut Not Your Doors to Me . . . ," *Passage to India*, 1871, p. 118, *Inc. Ed.*, p. 546, among the variant readings. Triggs apparently did not notice that this passage was not suppressed in 1881, but merely transferred to "As They Draw to a Close," *Inc. Ed.*, p. 415, ll. 8, 10.

83. "Gods," *Passage to India*, 1871, p. 115 (1), *Inc. Ed.*, p. 643.

84. "Two Rivulets," *Two Rivulets*, 1876, p. 15, *Inc. Ed.*, pp. 485–486, ll. 4, 12. "Eidólons," also published in 1876, implies the same idea.

85. "Spirit that Form'd this Scene," *LG 1881*, p. 368, *Inc. Ed.*, p. 403.

86. "You Tides with Ceaseless Swell," 1885, *Inc. Ed.*, p. 425, ll. 2, 5, 6.

87. "A Voice from Death," *Good-Bye My Fancy*, 1891, p. 16, *Inc. Ed.*, p. 453, ll. 30–32.

88. "A Persian Lesson," *Good-Bye My Fancy*, 1891, p. 17, *Inc. Ed.*, p. 454.

89. *CW*, VI, 14.

90. He had reviewed it in the *Brooklyn Eagle* on Dec. 4, 1847; see *G of the F*, II, 298–299.

91. *CW*, VI, 181.

92. See below, pp. 57–58.

93. "Passage to India," *Passage to India*, 1871, p. 12, §11 (29), *Inc. Ed.*, p. 349, §8, ll. 11–12.

94. *LG 1855*, p. 16, "Song of Myself," *Inc. Ed.*, p. 28, §6; ll. 1–2.
95. See for instance "Song of Myself," *Inc. Ed.*, p. 73, §48, ll. 10–14; p. 27, §4, l. 16; p. 65, §42, ll. 10–16, 33–42; p. 71, §46, l. 24; p. 74, §50, ll. 1, 4–5; "A Song for Occupations," p. 180, §2, ll. 17–25; "Song of the Answerer," p. 140, §1, l. 22; and, among the poems of the 1856 edition, "By Blue Ontario's Shore, p. 295, §14, l. 7; "Song of the Open Road," p. 124, §1, l. 6; p. 127, §6, ll. 15–16.
96. See F. M. Smith, "Whitman's Poet-Prophet and Carlyle's Hero," *PMLA*, LV (December 1940), 1155.
97. In a magazine article on "Modern Poetry and Prose" (*Catalogue of the Trent Collection*, p. 74), Whitman had underlined the following passage:

His [Keats's] mind had itself much of that "negative capability," which he remarked on as a large part of Shakespeare's greatness and which he described as a power "of being in uncertainties, mysteries, doubts, without any irritable reaching after fact and reason" . . . Such is that uncertainty of a large mind which a small mind cannot understand.

98. "Tests," *LG 1860*, p. 416, *Inc. Ed.*, p. 330, l. 1. See also "Shut Not Your Doors to Me Proud Libraries" (1865), l. 6 of the original version, p. 545.
99. "When I Read the Book," *LG 1867*, p. 268, *Inc. Ed.*, p. 7.
100. "Life," *NB*, 1888, p. 30, *Inc. Ed.*, p. 433, ll. 3–6. See also "A Riddle-Song," *LG 1881*, p. 362, *Inc. Ed.*, pp. 396–397; "Shakespeare-Bacon Cipher," *Good-Bye My Fancy*, 1891, p. 10, *Inc. Ed.*, p. 447.
101. See Grace Gilchrist, "Chats with Walt Whitman," *Eclectic Magazine of Foreign Literature*, 1908, p. 454: "Intellect is a *fiend*. It is a curse that our American boys and girls are taught so much." It is also the theme of a passage in his essay on Elias Hicks, *NB*, p. 136, *CP*, pp. 486–487.
102. "Says," *LG 1860*, p. 418 (2), *Inc. Ed.*, p. 480 (2).
103. For instance in "My Canary Bird," *NB*, p. 20, *Inc. Ed.*, p. 422, ll. 1–2.
104. "The Commonplace," *Good-Bye My Fancy*, 1891, p. 17, *Inc. Ed.*, p. 454, l. 5. See also "Passage to India" (1871), *Inc. Ed.*, p. 351, §9, l. 24.
105. *Complete Works*, Centenary Edition (Boston: Houghton Mifflin and Co., 1903–1904), I, 66. See H. H. Clark, "Emerson and Science," *Philological Quarterly*, X (July 1931), 225–260.
106. On Whitman and science, see Joseph Beaver, *Walt Whitman, Poet of Science* (New York: King's Crown Press, 1951), where it is proved that Whitman knew all these books and had a much broader scientific culture than was thought. As "When I Heard the Learn'd

Astronomer" (1865) shows, he even attended lectures on astronomy — probably those given by O. M. Mitchell. Further information on Whitman and the scientific thought of his time will be found in William Gay, *Walt Whitman — His Relation to Science and Philosophy* (Melbourne, 1895), Daniel G. Brinton, "Walt Whitman and Science," *Conservator* (April 1895), pp. 20–21, O. L. Triggs, "Whitman's Relation to Science and Philosophy," *Conservator* (May 1896), a review of William Gay's book. As these studies are all very superficial, one should rather consult: Alice L. Cooke, "Whitman's Indebtedness to the Scientific Thought of His Day," *University of Texas Studies in English*, XIV (July 1934), 89–115, and Clarence Dugdale, "Whitman's Knowledge of Astronomy," *ibid.*, XVI (July 1936), 125–137.

107. According to Beaver, Whitman may also have read Richard Owen's *Key to the Geology of the Globe*, 1857, S. C. Goodrich's *A Glance at the Physical Sciences*, 1844, and all of a series of books which he lists in his bibliography. According to us, Whitman might also have read the works of Edward Livingston Youmans whom he had met several times (*With WW in C*, I, 101): *Handbook of Household Science*, 1857, and others.

108. *LG 1855*, p. 28, "Song of Myself," *Inc. Ed.*, p. 43, §23, l. 9.

109. *LG 1855*, p. vii, Preface to 1855 edition, *Inc. Ed.*, pp. 497–498.

110. *LG 1855*, p. 28, "Song of Myself," *Inc. Ed.*, p. 43, §23, ll. 14–16. See also "Passage to India," *Inc. Ed.*, p. 346, §5, ll. 21–25, and the preface to the 1855 edition, pp. 497, 508, 520, 524–525.

111. See below, pp. 57–61.

112. He very vigorously defined this conflict between science and religion in a note to *Democratic Vistas*, SD, p. 243, CP, p. 262, n. 9.

113. Preface to 1872 edition, *Inc. Ed.*, p. 510.

114. "Song of the Universal," *Two Rivulets*, 1876, "Centennial Songs," pp. 15–16, *Inc. Ed.*, p. 192, §2, ll. 1–10.

115. "Eidólons," *Two Rivulets*, 1876, p. 19, *Inc. Ed.*, p. 6, ll. 61–64.

116. Preface to 1876 edition, *Inc. Ed.*, p. 520. He expressed exactly the same views in his old age:

. . . science is too damned fast for truth sometimes. I often feel like saying to the fellers who are so sure they are sure on all that: hold your horses, hold your horses — don't be too confident that you know the whole story — the kernel, the beginning, the end. Then I have a reaction. After the long period during which the the other view was upheld — the contempt of the body, the horrible, narrow, filthy, poisonous distaste expressed in ascetic religions, for the physical man — I confess that even materialism is a relief, like a new day, like sunlight, like beauty, yes, like truth itself . . . But after all there's more to it than that — more to it than these bodies — than the most superb bodies: more than that: and while I cannot argue the matter out, neither can I surrender my profound conviction. (*With WW in C*, II, 168–169.)

117. Whitman was quite conscious of his kinship with Lucretius — at least at the time when he was writing *Democratic Vistas* in which he praised the Latin poet for the boldness of his attempt, but criticized his negative attitude (*SD*, pp. 253–254, *CP*, p. 255) toward death probably, for he has noted in one of his notebooks (Library of Congress): "The work (De Rerum Natura) is largely aimed at calming the fears of the Romans against suffering after death — it seeks to convince the reader that death is cessation, annihilation, an eternal sleep."

118. *With WW in C*, I, 101:

I like the scientific spirit — the holding off, the being sure, but not too sure, the willingness to surrender ideas when the evidence is against them: this is ultimately fine — it always keeps the way beyond open — always gives life, thought, affection, the whole man, a chance to try after a mistake — after a wrong guess.

119. See preface to 1872 edition, *Inc. Ed.*, pp. 510–511, and "Democratic Vistas," *SD*, p. 249n, *CP*, p. 262, n. 9.

120. "Sun-Down Papers" no. 8, 1840, *Uncoll, PP*, I, 42.

121. "I always associated that book [Frances Wright's *A Few Days in Athens*] with Volney's *Ruins*, on which I may be said to have been raised." *With WW in C*, II, 445.

122. See for instance Chapters XXI (Origin and filiation of religious ideas) and XXIII (The object of all religions identical). Volney's views are taken up again in *LG 1855*, p. 48, "Song of Myself," *Inc. Ed.*, p. 66, §43, ll. 1–15.

123. *With WW in C*, II, 205:

She spoke in the old Tammany Hall there, every Sunday, about all sorts of reform. Her views were very broad — she touched the widest range of themes — spoke informally, colloquially. She published while there the *Free Inquirer*, which my Daddy took and I often read. She has always been to me one of the sweetest of sweet memories: we all loved her . . . Did she write anything, Walt? asked Harned. Oh, yes! one little book I remember well — a little pamphlet, a mere whiffet for size but sparkling with life: *Ten Days in Athens* it was called.

124. See David Goodale, "Some of Walt Whitman's Borrowings," *AL*, X (May 1938), 202–213.

125. See "In Memory of Thomas Paine" (Spoken at Lincoln Hall, Philadelphia, Jan. 28, 1877), *SD*, pp. 96–97, *CP*, pp. 92–94. Whitman knew that Paine belonged to the great school of liberal thought

which developed in Europe in the eighteenth century: "Paine's practical demeanor, and much of his theoretical belief, was a mixture of the French and English schools of a century ago, and the best of both" (p. 93). See also *With WW in C*, II, 135.

126. "Ingersoll is a man whose importance to the time could not be overfigured . . . spiritual importance, importance as a force, as consuming energy . . ." *With WW in C*, I, 82.

"I know quite well why and where I must disagree with him — The Colonel and I are not directly at issue even about God and immortality: I do not say yes where he says no: I say yes where he says nothing." *Ibid.*, 114.

127. ". . . it does seem as if Ingersoll and Huxley without any others could unhorse the whole Christian giant." *Ibid.*, 262.

128. *Heroes and Hero-Worship.*

129. *LG 1855*, p. xi, preface to 1855 edition, *Inc. Ed.*, p. 505. This passage was taken up in 1856 in "By Blue Ontario's Shore," *Inc. Ed.*, p. 295, §13, ll. 14–18. He had formerly written in one of his notebooks: "Not all the traditions can put vitality in churches. They are not alive, they are cold mortar and brick. I can easily build as good, and so can you."

130. *LG 1855*, p. 45, "Song of Myself," *Inc. Ed.*, p. 63, §41, l. 7.

131. "Poem of the Road," *LG 1856*, p. 232, "Song of the Open Road," *Inc. Ed.*, p. 129, §10, l. 7.

132. *LG 1856*, p. 352.

133. *LG 1855*, p. 25, "Song of Myself," *Inc. Ed.*, p. 40, §20, l. 10.

134. *LG 1855*, pp. 60, 64, "A Song for Occupations," *Inc. Ed.*, p. 182, §3, ll. 26–29, and p. 185, §6, ll. 9–16, and "Song of Myself," p. 66, §43, ll. 1–3.

135. "Thoughts," *LG 1860*, p. 286, *Inc. Ed.*, p. 398, l. 5.

136. "Brooklyniana," no. 17 (1862), *Uncoll. PP*, II, 293.

137. "Last of the War Cases," *SD*, pp. 41–42, *CP*, p. 37, and "Summer of 1864," *SD*, p. 52, *CP*, pp. 47–48.

138. "A New York Soldier," *SD*, pp. 41–42, *CP*, p. 37, and "Summer of 1864," *SD*, p. 52, *CP*, pp. 47–48.

139. "Passage to India," *Passage to India*, 1871, p. 12, §11 (29), *Inc. Ed.*, p. 349, §8, ll. 11–12. See also how Peter Doyle described Whitman's religious ideas in those days: ". . . he had pretty vigorous ideas on religion, but he never said anything slighting the church . . . He never went to church — didn't like form, ceremonies — didn't seem to favor preachers at all." *Calamus*, p. 28.

140. "An Interviewer's Item," *SD*, p. 153, *CP*, p. 161.

141. "Sunday with the Insane," *SD*, pp. 161–162, *CP*, p. 161.

142. See pp. 27–30.

143. *CW*, VI, 26–27. From 1860 on, Whitman ceased to designate the days and months by their usual names; he used ordinals instead, thus following an old Quaker custom. But, in so doing, he was not really obeying religious scruples like the Quakers who objected to such words because they were a survival of the old pagan religions. His purpose was different. He wanted to create a specifically American vocabulary and to banish from his works words which smacked too much of Europe:

> I have been informed that there are people who say it is not important about names — one word is as good as another, if the designation be understood. — I say that nothing is more important than names. . . . Great clusters of nomenclature in a land (needed in America) include appropriate names for the months; appropriate names for the Days of the Week (those now used perpetuate Teutonic and Greek divinities) . . . Now the days signify extinct gods and goddesses — the months half unknown rites and emperors — and chronology with the rest is all foreign to America — all exiles and insults here.

American Primer, pp. 31–32. It is for this reason that from 1856 on all the dates mentioned in his poems are based on the year of the Declaration of Independence, 1776, instead of the year of the birth of Jesus Christ. On this point, see J. T. Trowbridge, *My Own Story*, pp. 396–397.

On Whitman and the Quakers, see D. H. Wright, "Whitman — The Inner Light of Quakerism," *Conservator* (April 1906), pp. 24–25; H. W. Hintz, *The Quaker Influence in America* (New York: Fleming H. Revell, 1940), pp. 59–75; Janna Burgess, "Walt Whitman and Elias Hicks," *Friends' Intelligencer*, CI (1944), 54–55, and an unpublished doctoral dissertation by W. B. Fulghum, Jr., "Quaker Influences on Whitman's Religious Thought" (Northwestern University, 1943).

144. "An Old Man's Thought of School," *Two Rivulets*, 1876, p. 29, *Inc. Ed.*, pp. 33–34, ll. 14–15. Later, following Carlyle's lead, he even wrote an essay on George Fox: "George Fox (and Shakspere)," *NB*, 1888, p. 136, *CP*, pp. 488–491.

145. "Prayer of Columbus," *Two Rivulets*, 1876, *Inc. Ed.*, pp. 352–353, ll. 26–30.

146. "Elias Hicks," *NB*, 1888, p. 128, n. 2 (*CP*, p. 487, n. 2), and p. 135 (*CP*, p. 486).

147. "As They Draw to a Close" (1871), *Inc. Ed.*, p. 415, l. 8.

148. "Poem of Walt Whitman, an American," *LG 1856*, p. 98, "Song of Myself," *Inc. Ed.*, p. 75, §50, l. 10.

149. *LG 1855*, p. 17, "Song of Myself," *Inc. Ed.*, p. 29, §6, l. 31.

150. See n. 148.

151. *LG 1855,* p. 14, "Song of Myself," *Inc. Ed.,* p. 25, §3, ll. 7–9 ("always sex" was added in 1856).

152. *LG 1855,* p. 30, "Song of Myself," *Inc. Ed.,* p. 46, §24, ll. 59–60. See also *LG 1855,* p. 79, "I Sing the Body Electric," *Inc. Ed.,* p. 82, §5, ll. 10–12.

153. "Eidólons," *Two Rivulets,* 1876, p. 17, *Inc. Ed.,* p. 4, ll. 13–14.

154. "The Great Unrest of Which We Are Part," *SD,* p. 196, *CP,* p. 194.

155. "Unseen Buds," *Good-Bye My Fancy,* 1891, p. 19, *Inc. Ed.,* p. 457, ll. 1, 7–8.

156. *LG 1855,* p. 50, "Song of Myself," *Inc. Ed.,* pp. 68–69, §44, ll. 15–34. There are many other examples: *LG 1855,* "Song of Myself," *Inc. Ed.,* p. 50, §31, ll. 8–21; p. 51, §32, ll. 11–17; p. 70, §6, ll. 21–28; "I Sing the Body Electric," p. 83, §6, ll. 19–20; "Great Are the Myths," p. 466, §2, ll. 1–3, and "The World Below the Brine" (1860), p. 221.

157. As is shown by this note in a notebook which he used between 1850 and 1855:

Amelioration is the blood that runs through the body of the universe. — I do not lag — I do not hasten — I bide my hour over billions of billions of years. I exist in the void that takes uncounted time and coheres to a nebula, and in further time cohering to an orb, marches gladly round, a beautiful, tangible creature in his place in the procession of God . . . What I shall attain to I can never tell for there is something that underlies me of whom I am a part and instrument.

Uncoll. PP, II, 79–80. See also "Poem of the Sayers of the Earth," *LG 1856,* pp. 323–324, "A Song of the Rolling Earth," *Inc. Ed.,* p. 187, §1, ll. 17–20.

158. See Gay W. Allen, *Walt Whitman Handbook* (Chicago: Packard, 1946), pp. 277–284; Alice Lovelace Cooke, "Whitman's Indebtedness to the Scientific Thought of His Day," *University of Texas Studies in English,* XIV (July 1934), 89–115, and Daniel Brinton, "Walt Whitman and Science," *Conservator* (April 1895), pp. 20–21. According to the latter, Whitman borrowed his historical optimism from J. W. Draper's *History of Civilization.* But Whitman's optimism had, in fact, much deeper roots.

On evolutionism before Darwin, see Henry Fairfield Osborn, *From the Greeks to Darwin,* 1899 (especially Chap. V), and Bentley Glass, Owsei Temkin, and William L. Straus, Jr. (ed.), *Forerunners of Darwin, 1745–1859* (Johns Hopkins Press, 1959).

159. See H. H. Clark, "Emerson and Science," *Philological Quarterly,* X (July 1931), 247.

160. Lamarck, *Système des animaux* (Paris, 1801), *Philosophie zoologique* (Paris, 1809).

161. Sir Charles Lyell, *Principles of Geology* (1832).

162. *Vestiges of Creation,* published anonymously; first American edition in 1845. See Milton Millhauser, "The Literary Impact of 'Vestiges of Creation,' " *MLQ,* XVII (September 1956), 213–226.

163. See A. L. Cooke's article mentioned in n. 158.

164. *Two Rivulets,* 1876, pp. 26–27, reprinted in *SD,* p. 326, *CP,* pp. 335–336. Darwin is also mentioned in "The Great Unrest of which We Are Part," *SD,* p. 196, *CP,* p. 194.

165. Whitman first used the word in "Song of the Exposition" (1871), §3, l. 15. See Eby's *Concordance.*

166. He was too much of an anti-intellectualist for that. Any theory which claimed to explain everything was a priori suspicious to him: "When it comes to explaining absolute beginnings, ends, I doubt evolution clears up the mystery any better than the philosophies that have preceded it. I have felt from the first that my own work must assume the essential truths of evolution or something like them." *With WW in C,* III, 94.

167. He explicitly opposed Hegelianism to Darwinism in *Specimen Days*:

> I am the more assured in recounting Hegel a little freely here, not only for offsetting the Carlylean letter and spirit . . . but to counterpoise, since the late death and apotheosis of Darwin, the tenets of the evolutionists.

"Carlyle from American Points of View," *SD,* p. 177, *CP,* p. 176. He added a note which shows that he was quite conscious of the influence of the geographical factor on the growth of his sense of the becoming of the world:

> In my opinion the above formulas of Hegel are an essential and crowning justification of New World Democracy in the creative realms of time and space. There is that about them which only the vastness, the multiplicity and the vitality of America would seem able to comprehend, to give scope and illustration to, or to be fit for, or even originate. It is strange to me that they were born in Germany, or in the old world at all.

CP, pp. 203–204, n. 16. It thus seemed strange to him that an inhabitant of old Europe could have conceived a philosophy of the becoming which, on the contrary, should have been thought of by an American under the influence of the prodigious growth of his country.

168. *LG 1855,* p. 76, "The Sleepers," *Inc. Ed.,* p. 361, §7, ll. 38–40. See also *LG 1855,* pp. 24, 25, 28, "Song of Myself," *Inc. Ed.,* p. 38, §16, ll. 24–25, p. 39, §19, ll. 1–6, p. 42, §22, ll. 16–19.

169. *LG 1855*, p. 69, "To Think of Time," *Inc. Ed.*, pp. 367–368, §8, ll. 22–25.

170. "Poem of the Road," *LG 1856*, p. 227, "Song of the Open Road," *Inc. Ed.*, p. 126, §5, ll. 6, 10. See also *ibid.*, §4, ll. 11–14, and §6, ll. 1–4.

171. *LG 1855*, p. 69, "To Think of Time," *Inc. Ed.*, p. 368, §8, ll. 26–28, and variant reading p. 687, for in 1856 "sin" was changed to "bad" to emphasize the symmetry and strengthen the contrast.

172. *LG 1855*, p. 95, "Great Are the Myths," *Inc. Ed.*, p. 706.

173. W. B. Yeats, *Autobiographies* (New York: Macmillan, 1927), p. 303. Stephen Spender expresses the same opinion in *Life and the Poet* (London: Secker and Warburg, 1942), pp. 52–53.

174. *LG 1855*, p. 39, "Song of Myself," *Inc. Ed.*, p. 56, §33, l. 136.

175. *LG 1855*, p. 26, "Song of Myself," *Inc. Ed.*, p. 41, §21, l. 2.

176. "Poem of Salutation," *LG 1856*, p. 116, "Salut au Monde," *Inc. Ed.*, p. 120, §10, ll. 14–19.

177. "Sun-Down Poem," *LG 1856*, p. 216–217, "Crossing Brooklyn Ferry," *Inc. Ed.*, pp. 136–137, §6, ll. 1, 5–7, 9. See also "By Blue Ontario's Shore" (1856), *Inc. Ed.*, p. 289, §6, l. 19, where he evokes the ideal bard open both to good and evil.

178. *LG 1855*, p. 76, "The Sleepers," *Inc. Ed.*, p. 361, §7, ll. 40–42.

179. *LG 1855*, pp. 83–85, "Faces," *Inc. Ed.*, p. 388, §4, ll. 13–16. See also §2, l. 1, and §3, ll. 7–12.

180. *Uncoll. PP*, II, 71.

181. *Ibid.*, p. 65.

182. "Proto-Leaf," *LG 1860*, p. 11 (24), "Starting from Paumanok," *Inc. Ed.*, pp. 15–16, §7, ll. 5–7.

183. "Proto-Leaf," *LG 1860*, p. 15 (45), "Starting from Paumanok," *Inc. Ed.*, p. 18, §12, ll. 12–13.

184. See for instance two sentences quoted by F. O. Matthiessen in *American Renaissance*, p. 11: "Purpos'd I know not whither, yet full of faith . . . All bound as if befitting each — all surely going somewhere." In 1887 Whitman used the last phrase as a title for one of his poems: "Going Somewhere." It was a conscious borrowing since he used quotation marks.

185. "Poem of the Road," *LG 1856*, p. 228, "Song of the Open Road," *Inc. Ed.*, p. 127, §6, ll. 8–14.

186. "Poem of the Propositions of Nakedness," *LG 1856*, pp. 316–321, "Respondez," *Inc. Ed.*, pp. 469–472.

187. See n. 185.

188. *LG 1855*, p. 69, "To Think of Time," *Inc. Ed.*, p. 687, variant reading of §9.

189. "Leaves of Grass," no. 17, *LG 1860*, p. 236, "I Sit and Look Out," *Inc. Ed.*, p. 232, ll. 1, 5, 8.

190. "Leaves of Grass," no. 1, *LG 1860*, p. 199, "As I Ebb'd with the Ocean of Life," *Inc. Ed.*, p. 218, §4.

191. "Proto-Leaf," *LG 1860*, p. 6 (2) "Starting from Paumanok," *Inc. Ed.*, p. 12, §2, l. 3.

192. See above, n. 179.

193. "Poem of the Sayers of the Words of the Earth," *LG 1856*, pp. 323–324, "A Song of the Rolling Earth," *Inc. Ed.*, p. 187, §1, ll. 17–20.

194. "Chants Democratic," no. 9, *LG 1860*, pp. 179–180, "Thoughts," *Inc. Ed.*, pp. 408–409, §1.

195. "Leaves of Grass," no. 19, *LG 1860*, p. 238, "Germs," *Inc. Ed.*, p. 230.

196. "Thoughts," no. 2, *LG 1860*, p. 408, *Inc. Ed.*, p. 230, l. 5.

197. "Leaves of Grass," no. 18, *LG 1860*, pp. 237–238, "All is Truth," *Inc. Ed.*, pp. 395–396, ll. 9, 12, 15–17.

198. "Chants Democratic," no. 8, *LG 1860*, pp. 176–179, "Song at Sunset," *Inc. Ed.*, p. 411, ll. 57–58. But this poem is so fervent that it may very well have been written in 1856–1857. For his optimism in 1860, see also "Chants Democratic," no. 7, *LG 1860*, pp. 174–176, "With Antecedents," *Inc. Ed.*, p. 204, §2, ll. 16–19.

199. See Vol. I, pp. 158–159.

200. See the letter to his mother dated March 29, 1864, *SPL*, p. 939.

201. "By Blue Ontario's Shore," *Inc. Ed.*, p. 298, §17, ll. 25–27. These three lines were added in 1867.

202. "As for me, (torn, stormy, amid these vehement days,) . . ." This parenthesis was added in 1867 to "With Antecedents," §2, l. 8, *Inc. Ed.*, p. 204.

203. "Going Somewhere" (published for the first time in *Lippincott's Magazine* in Nov. 1887), *Inc. Ed.*, p. 433.

204. *CW*, VI, 171–173.

205. "By Blue Ontario's Shore," *Inc. Ed.*, p. 298, §18, ll. 15–16. This parenthesis was added in 1867. In 1881, he changed "peace" into "crime," which reinforces the Hegelian character of the statement.

206. Besides this Hegelian idea, there were other much older elements in his square deific, for even before 1855 he had written in *Pictures (An Unpublished Poem by Walt Whitman*. With an introduction and notes by Emory Holloway, New York: The June House, 1927), p. 20: "It is Lucifer's portrait — the denied God's portrait."

207. *CW*, VI, 172.

208. See "As I Ponder'd in Silence," *LG 1871*, p. 8, §2, *Inc. Ed.*,

p. 2; "To Thee Old Cause," *LG 1871*, pp. 11–12, *Inc. Ed.*, p. 4; "Adieu to a Soldier," *LG 1871*, p. 338, *Inc. Ed.*, p. 274.

209. "On the Beach at Night," *Passage to India*, 1872, pp. 83–84, *Inc. Ed.*, pp. 220–221.

210. "Wandering at Morn," *Two Rivulets*, 1876, p. 28 (but published for the first time in the *New York Graphic*, on March 15, 1873, under the title of "The Singing Thrush"), *Inc. Ed.*, p. 334.

211. "Song of the Universal" (read for commencement at Tuft's College, on June 17, 1874), *Two Rivulets*, 1876, Centennial Songs, pp. 15–17, *Inc. Ed.*, pp. 192–194; see in particular §1, ll. 4–9, §3, ll. 4–13, and §4, ll. 13–20. About the same time he identified himself with the man-of-war bird which defies storms: "To the Man-of-War Bird," published for the first time in the London *Athenaeum* in April 1876, *Inc. Ed.*, p. 219.

212. *Ibid.*

213. We do not in the least exaggerate the influence of Hegel on the philosophy of this poem. The best proof of it is that, when Whitman a few years later wanted to define the position of the German philosopher (in his tribute to Carlyle), he took up most of the ideas and even some of the words which he had already used in the "Song of the Universal." See "Carlyle from American Points of View," *SD*, p. 176, *CP*, p. 175.

214. See above, n. 211.

215. *Ibid.*

216. *Ibid.*

217. "Roaming in Thought," *LG 1881*, p. 216, *Inc. Ed.*, p. 233.

218. See above, n. 203.

219. See for instance "With Husky-Haughty Lips, O Sea!," published for the first time in *Harper's Magazine* in March 1884, *Inc. Ed.*, p. 428, l. 10.

220. *Good-Bye My Fancy*, 1891, p. 17, *Inc. Ed.*, p. 455.

221. He made this statement to a visitor in 1883; see "An Impression of Walt Whitman" (an anonymous article), *Atlantic Monthly*, LXIX (June 1892), 853. On Whitman's optimism, see Frederick W. Conner, *Cosmic Optimism* (University of Florida Press, 1949). Chapter VI ("Whitman: High Tide") contains a very precise, but very abstract analysis of Whitman's philosophy. On Whitman's sense of evil, see Sholom J. Kahn, "The American Background of Whitman's Sense of Evil," *Scripta Hierosolymitana*, II (1955), 82–118, and by the same, "Whitman's Black Lucifer," *PMLA*, LXXI (December 1956), 932–944.

222. "Democratic Vistas" (1871), *CP*, p. 255.

223. *Uncoll. PP*, I, 1–2.

224. *Ibid.*, 5–6. He gave another version of this poem a few years

later in a more impersonal form: "The Death of the Nature Lover," *Brother Jonathan*, March 11, 1843, *Uncoll. PP*, I, 7.

225. *Ibid.*, 9–10.

226. *Ibid.*, 10–11.

227. *Ibid.*, 13–15.

228. *Walt Whitman of the New York Aurora*, ed. Joseph Jay Rubin and Charles H. Brown (State College, Pa.: Bald Eagle Press, 1950), p. 134 and p. 147, n. 5.

229. *Uncoll. PP*, II, 89.

230. *LG 1855*, p. 26, "Song of Myself," *Inc. Ed.*, pp. 40–41, §20, ll. 18, 32–33.

231. *LG 1855*, p. 54 "Song of Myself," *Inc. Ed.*, p. 73, §48, l. 12.

232. *LG 1855*, p. 54, "Song of Myself," *Inc. Ed.*, p. 74, §49, l. 1.

233. *LG 1855*, p. 17, "Song of Myself," *Inc. Ed.*, p. 29, §7, ll. 1–2.

234. *LG 1855*, p. 65, "To Think of Time," *Inc. Ed.*, p. 363, §1, ll. 6–7.

235. *LG 1855*, pp. 67–68, "To Think of Time," *Inc. Ed.*, p. 366, §6, l. 1. See also §8, ll. 24–25, p. 368.

236. *Ibid.*, p. 368, §9, l. 3.

237. *LG 1855*, p. 92, "Who Learns My Lesson Complete," *Inc. Ed.*, p. 330, ll. 19–20.

238. "Poem of the Road," *LG 1856*, p. 235, "Song of the Open Road," *Inc. Ed.*, p. 130, §12, l. 17.

239. "Poem of Wonder at the Resurrection of Wheat," *LG 1856*, pp. 202–205, "This Compost," *Inc. Ed.*, pp. 309–310.

240. "Faith Poem," *LG 1856*, p. 265, "Assurances," *Inc. Ed.*, p. 373, l. 4, and variant reading p. 689 (after l. 3).

241. "Calamus," no. 27, *LG 1860*, p. 370, "O Living Always, Always Dying," *Inc. Ed.*, p. 376, l. 6. Though this poem was published only in 1860, it is so full of joy and enthusiasm that it may well have been composed as early as 1856–1857.

242. *LG 1855*, p. 66, "To Think of Time," *Inc. Ed.*, p. 364, §3, l. 2.

243. *LG 1855*, p. 73, "The Sleepers," *Inc. Ed.*, p. 357, §2, ll. 9–10.

244. "Clef Poem," *LG 1856*, pp. 249–250, "On the Beach at Night Alone," *Inc., Ed.*, p. 641 (after l. 3).

245. "Leaves of Grass," no. 1, *LG 1860*, pp. 195–199, "As I Ebb'd with the Ocean of Life," *Inc. Ed.*, pp. 216–217, §2, ll. 7, 8, 15.

246. "Poem of Joys," *LG 1860*, p. 263 (21), "A Song of Joys," *Inc. Ed.*, p. 151, ll. 58–61.

247. "So Long!" *LG 1860*, p. 456, *Inc. Ed.*, pp. 418–419, especially the last two lines.

248. *Ibid.*, ll. 62–63.

249. "Enfans d'Adam," *LG 1860*, pp. 308–309 (6), "One Hour to Madness and Joy," *Inc. Ed.*, pp. 90–91, ll. 16–22. This passage bears a close resemblance to the stanza of "A Song of Joys" which we have quoted above (see n. 246), but the context here is clearer.

250. "Calamus," no. 2, *LG 1860*, p. 343, "Scented Herbage of My Breast," *Inc. Ed.*, p. 96, ll. 11, 14–15.

251. *Ibid.*, l. 21.

252. "Enfans d'Adam," no. 8, *LG 1860*, pp. 310–311, "Native Moments," *Inc. Ed.*, p. 93, ll. 2, 5. See also "Leaves of Grass," no. 13, *LG 1860*, p. 231–232, "You Felons on Trial in Courts," p. 323, especially the last line.

253. "Poem of the Road," *LG 1856*, p. 231, "Song of the Open Road," *Inc. Ed.*, p. 128, §8, l. 9. See also "From Pent-up Aching Rivers," *Inc. Ed.*, pp. 77–79.

254. See "Out of the Cradle Endlessly Rocking" (1860), "Hours Continuing Long Sore and Heavy-Hearted" (1860), and "I Saw in Louisiana a Live-Oak Growing" (1860).

255. "Debris," *LG 1860*, p. 422, "Yet, Yet, Ye Downcast Hours," *Inc. Ed.*, pp. 372–373. He asked himself the same question, but less agonizingly in "Thoughts," no. 5, *LG 1860*, p. 410, "Thought," *Inc. Ed.*, p. 377.

256. "To My Soul," *LG 1860*, p. 449–450, "As the Time Draws Nigh," *Inc. Ed.*, p. 405, ll. 1–2.

257. "Chants Democratic," no. 9 *LG 1860*, p. 180, "Thoughts," *Inc. Ed.*, p. 409 §1, l. 15.

258. "Chants Democratic," no. 8, *LG 1860*, p. 177 (4), "Song at Sunset," *Inc. Ed.*, p. 410, l. 21.

259. "Poem of Joys," *LG 1860*, p. 266 (30), "A Song of Joys," *Inc. Ed.*, p. 154, l. 140.

260. "A Word out of the Sea," *LG 1860*, p. 277 (33), "Out of the Cradle Endlessly Rocking," *Inc. Ed.*, p. 215, ll. 165–173. Line 14 of §12 of "Starting from Paumanok" corresponds more to the careless optimism of the years 1855–56 than to that tragic period when death and sensuality were fused together. Such is the case, too, of "Night on the Prairies," *Inc. Ed.*, pp. 376–377 ("Leaves of Grass," no. 13, *LG 1860*, p. 234).

261. Letter dated August 25, 1863, *CW*, IV, 185–186. See also "Last of the War Cases" (May 23, 1864), *NB*, 1888, p. 112, *CP*, p. 463.

262. Letter to Nat and Fred Gray dated March 19, 1863, *SPL*, p. 897. He here takes up a Biblical phrase.

263. "When Lilacs Last in the Dooryard Bloom'd," *Sequel to Drum Taps*, 1865–66, p. 5, §7 (10), *Inc. Ed.*, p. 278, §7, l. 3.

264. "When Lilacs . . . ," *Sequel to Drum-Taps*, 1865–66, pp. 9–10 §16, *Inc. Ed.*, p. 281–282, §14, ll. 28–55.

265. "When Lilacs . . . ," *Sequel to Drum-Taps*, 1865–66, p. 6, §8, *Inc. Ed.*, p. 278, §8, l. 6.

266. "O Me! O Life!" *Sequel to Drum-Taps*, 1865–66, p. 18, *Inc. Ed.*, p. 231.

267. "On the Beach at Night Alone," *Inc. Ed.*, pp. 641–642. He made another interesting revision in the same edition; he added "the lilacs bloom in the dooryard" to line 13 of §2 of "This Compost" (*Inc. Ed.*, p. 699), which linked up this 1856 poem with his 1865 threnody and with the theme of the acceptance of death.

268. "The Untold Want," *Passage to India*, 1872, p. 118, *Inc. Ed.*, p. 415.

269. "Gods," *Passage to India*, 1872, p. 115, *Inc. Ed.*, p. 229, ll. 8–10.

270. "Passage to India," *Passage to India*, p. 13, §11 (32), *Inc. Ed.*, p. 350, §8, ll. 34, 37. See also the following poems of the same period: "As They Draw to a Close," "Darest Thou Now O Soul," "Whispers of Heavenly Death," and "Pensive and Faltering," and what he confided to Peter Doyle about the same time (*Calamus*, 1897, p. 28).

271. "Passage to India," *Inc. Ed.*, p. 351, §9, ll. 19–20. See also "Joy, Shipmate Joy," *Passage to India*, 1871, p. 120, *Inc. Ed.*, p. 415.

272. "Gods" (1871), *Inc. Ed.*, p. 229, l. 12.

273. "The Singer in the Prison," *Passage to India*, 1871, p. 95, §3, *Inc. Ed.*, p. 317, §2, ll. 18–25.

274. Preface to 1876 edition, *Inc. Ed.*, p. 513n.

275. "A Song of Joys," *Inc. Ed.*, p. 154, l. 139, and variant reading p. 612.

276. "Yet, Yet, Ye Downcast Hours," *Passage to India*, 1871, p. 66, §1, *Inc. Ed.*, p. 372, l. 14. See also the last two lines of "The Last Invocation" (1871), *Inc. Ed.*, p. 378.

277. "After the Supper and Talk," *NB*, 1888, p. 38, *Inc. Ed.*, p. 442.

278. On the occasion, for instance, of the earthquake which devastated Johnstown, Pa., in 1889; see "A Voice from Death" (*Good-Bye My Fancy*, 1891, pp. 15–16, *Inc. Ed.*, p. 452–454). He accepted it more philosophically than Voltaire did the Lisbon earthquake of 1755. But Hegel had taught him ". . . how [to] fuse the material life, the fact of death, chemical dissolution, segregation, with the puzzling thought of Identity's continuance, despite of death . . ." *CW*, VI, 172.

279. "Sail Out for Good, Eidólon Yacht!" *Good-Bye My Fancy*, 1891, p. 7, *Inc. Ed.*, p. 443, ll. 4–5. See also "Death's Valley" (1892), *Inc. Ed.*, p. 463, especially the last two lines.

280. "A Persian Lesson," *Good-Bye My Fancy*, 1891, p. 17, *Inc. Ed.*, p. 454, ll. 11–12, 15.

281. *LG 1855*, p. 77, "The Sleepers," *Inc. Ed.*, p. 362, §8, l. 24; see also last two lines, p. 684.

282. "When Lilacs Last in the Dooryard Bloom'd," *Sequel to Drum-Taps*, 1865–66, p. 10, §16 (33), *Inc. Ed.*, p. 282, §14, ll. 50–51.

283. *LG 1855*, pp. 54–55, "Song of Myself," *Inc. Ed.*, p. 74, §49, ll. 6–8, and p. 76. §52, ll. 9–10.

284. *Imprints*, 1860, p. 12.

285. "To Think of Time," *Inc. Ed.*, p. 367, §8, ll. 15–16, and p. 368, §9, l. 5. The first passage dates back to 1881 and the second to 1855. See also "Sun-Down Poem," *LG 1856*, pp. 216, 218, "Crossing Brooklyn Ferry," *Inc. Ed.*, p. 136, §5, l. 10, and p. 137, §7, ll. 5–6; "Clef Poem" *LG 1856*, p. 249, "On the Beach at Night Alone," *Inc. Ed.*, p. 641, l. 7 of the variant reading (after l. 3); "Proto-Leaf," *LG 1860*, p. 13 (35), "Starting from Paumanok," *Inc. Ed.*, p. 17, §10, l. 9.

286. He may have borrowed this phrase from the Bible; see I Corinthians, XV, 44.

287. "Poem of Joys," *LG 1860*, p. 13 (35), "A Song of Joys," *Inc. Ed.*, p. 154, ll. 141–143. See also "To One Shortly to Die," *LG 1860*, p. 398, *Inc. Ed.*, p. 376, ll. 8–9; "Eidólons" (1876), *Inc. Ed.*, p. 6, ll. 77–80.

288. "Proto-Leaf," *LG 1860*, p. 15 (44), "Starting from Paumanok," *Inc. Ed.*, p. 18, §12, l. 8.

289. "Darest Thou Now O Soul," published for the first time in the *Broadway Magazine* (London) in October 1868, *Inc. Ed.*, p. 369, ll. 13–15. See also "Eidólons," *Two Rivulets*, 1876, p. 17, *Inc. Ed.*, p. 4, ll. 9–12.

290. "Two Rivulets," *Two Rivulets*, 1876, p. 15, *Inc. Ed.*, p. 486, l. 12.

291. *CW*, VI, 26.

292. "Death of Carlyle," *SD*, p. 170, *CP*, p. 170.

293. "Proto-Leaf," *LG 1860*, p. 13 (35), "Starting from Paumanok," *Inc. Ed.*, p. 17, §10, ll. 6–9. Exactly the same idea and the same image occur in "Eidólons" (1855), *Inc. Ed.*, p. 6, ll. 54–55.

294. "Chanting the Square Deific," *Sequel to Drum-Taps*, 1865, p. 17, *Inc. Ed.*, p. 371, §4, l. 7.

295. *SD*, p. 253, *CP*, p. 254.

296. "Eidólons," *Two Rivulets*, 1876, p. 15, *Inc. Ed.*, p. 6, l. 65.

297. "Continuities," *NB*, 1888, p. 30, *Inc. Ed.*, p. 432, ll. 1–2.

298. "Twilight," *Inc. Ed.*, p. 439, l. 3. This line must be given a mystical and positive meaning. In Whitman's lifetime some of his disciples had wrongly interpreted "oblivion" in a negative manner

and protested against such an agnostic statement; see *With WW in C*, I, 141.

299. See Vol. I, p. 261.

300. "Life and Death," *NB*, p. 32, *Inc. Ed.*, p. 435.

301. Among his papers were found "The Golden Verses of Pythagoras" which he had torn out of a book; see *CW*, VII, 84 (334).

302. Eastern thought very early exerted a strong influence on Whitman (see G. W. Allen, *Walt Whitman Handbook*, pp. 457–462). As early as 1840, in an article of the *Long Island Democrat* (October 20), he traveled in imagination from Tibet to Arabia by way of India among lamas, Brahmins, and Moslem pilgrims. He also mentioned Sanscrit and Hindoo sages in *Pictures* (1850–1855). Among his papers were found several magazine articles on Asia which he had carefully preserved and annotated; see *N & F*, p. 204: (332) "Newspaper piece: Persian Poetry"; (338) "Magazine article: 'Indian Epic Poetry,' dated October '48, much scored and annotated." (Concerning the Mahabharata and the Ramayana, Whitman noted: "The style of a great poem must flow on unhasting and unresting." (*CW*, VI, 229.) (Hence perhaps the formlessness of his first *Leaves of Grass*.) (339) "The Hindu Drama — magazine article, much scored and annotated"; p. 206 (395) "newspaper piece: Sanscrit Professorship at Cambridge, April '49, much scored and annotated."

Whitman also possessed *Alger's Poetry of the East*. On the fly-leaf of his copy he wrote:

Given me by WRA the author in Boston it must have been in 1861 or '2. Have often read (dabbled) in the "Introduction to Oriental Poetry", pp. 3 to 92 and over and over again . . . two or three of my jaunts thro' the war I carried this volume in my trunk — read in it — sometimes to hospital groups, to while away the time.

(See H. Traubel, "Notes on the Text of *Leaves of Grass*," *Conservator*, March 1898, pp. 9–11.)

Another of his favorite books was *Flowers Culled from the Gulistan or Rose Garden and from the Boston, or Pleasure Garden of Sadi*. He had written under the title: "Walt Whitman — from Thos. Dixon, Sunderland, England, April '77"; see *Catalogue of Dr. Bucke's Collection* (London: Sotheby, 1935). Later he even bought scholarly books on the East such as William Dwight Whitney, *Oriental and Linguistic Studies; The Veda, The Avesta, The Science of Language* (New York, 1873), and J. Muir, *Religious and Moral Sentiments metrically rendered from Sanscrit* (London & Edinburgh, 1875), both now in the Library of Bryn Mawr College. His respect for Asia was already clearly indicated in 1860 in "Facing West from California's Shores" and "A Broadway Pageant." It became deeper and deeper (perhaps under the influence of Alger's anthology) and Whitman gave it full expression in "Passage to India" in 1871. In 1888, he recalled, in "The Bible as Poetry" (*NB*, pp. 43–45, *CP*, pp. 397–398), the existence of the great religious books of the East and went even so far as to say that after reading such works Western writers appeared to him as "English and French cads, the most shallow, impudent, supercilious brood on earth."

However, all this shows that he read seriously about the East only at a fairly late date. At first he knew it only at second hand through the transcendentalists in general and Emerson in particular (see F. I. Carpenter, *Emerson and Asia,* Cambridge: Harvard University Press, 1930). He had read Emerson's *Essays* and at least his "Brahma." He had clipped the text of this poem from a newspaper; see *CW*, VII, 91 (456). He must also have read articles about the East in the *Dial* from 1840 to 1844.

303. There is in his notes a precise allusion to reincarnation: "That the Egyptian idea of the return of the soul after a certain period of time involved a beautiful . . . nature . . . mystery . . ." *CW*, VI, 151. See also Clifton J. Furness, "Walt Whitman and Reincarnation," *The Forerunner* (Autumn 1942), pp. 9–20.

304. *LG 1855*, p. 54, "Song of Myself," *Inc. Ed.*, p. 74, §49, ll. 9–12. See also p. 29, §6, ll. 25–32; p. 40, §20, ll. 28–33; p. 48, §32, ll. 9–13.

305. "So Long!" *Inc. Ed.*, p. 418, ll. 67, 69, and variant reading p. 704.

306. Under the influence of his scholarly readings probably (see above, n. 302); however, he left "avatars" unchanged in "Salut au Monde," *Inc. Ed.*, p. 118, §6, l. 3.

307. *LG 1855*, p. 34, "Song of Myself," *Inc. Ed.*, p. 50, §31, ll. 8–21.

308. See a manuscript variant of "Salut au Monde," *Inc. Ed.*, p. 601, §6, in which he merely took up again a passage in his "Sun-Down Papers" written in 1840 (*Uncoll. PP*, I, 40).

309. "Poem of the Last Explanation of Prudence," *LG 1856*, p. 258, "Song of Prudence," *Inc. Ed.*, p. 314, ll, 12–14, where he was merely versifying what he had already said in his 1855 preface, *Inc. Ed.*, pp. 502–503.

310. "Poem of Many in One," *LG 1856*, p. 195, "By Blue Ontario's Shore," Inc. Ed., p. 295, §13, l. 16. See also *LG 1855*, p. 69, "To Think of Time," *Inc. Ed.*, p. 367, §8, ll. 10–14.

311. In *Essays*, 1st series.

312. *LG 1855*, pp. 83–84, "Faces," *Inc. Ed.*, 386–387, §2, ll. 1–2, §3, p. 388, §4, ll. 1–2.

313. *Ibid.*, p. 388, §4, l. 13.

314. "Gliding O'er All," *Passage to India*, 1871, titlepage, *Inc. Ed.*, p. 235, l. 5. See also "On the Beach at Night," *Passage to India*, p. 84, *Inc. Ed.*, p. 221, the end.

315. "Eidólons," *Two Rivulets*, 1876, p. 17, *Inc. Ed.*, p. 4, ll. 9–11.

316. "Sail out for good eidólon yacht," *Good-Bye My Fancy*, 1891, p. 7, *Inc. Ed.*, p. 443.

317. "Good-Bye My Fancy," *Good-Bye My Fancy*, 1891, p. 20, *Inc. Ed.*, p. 458, ll. 15–16.

318. To the end of his life he was fond of finding in the writings of others the confirmation of his youthful intuitions. He thus in his old age became interested in the works of Giordano Bruno whose pantheism closely resembled his own. He owned a copy of Daniel G. Brinton (one of his Philadelphia friends) and Thomas Davidson, *Giordano Bruno — Philosopher and Martyr* (Philadelphia, 1890). This book is now in the Library of Bryn Mawr College.

319. *With WW in C, II, 71.*

III. THE ETHICS

1. *LG 1855*, p. 95, "Great Are the Myths," *Inc. Ed.*, p. 706, variant reading of §4.

2. *LG 1855*, p. 27, "Song of Myself," *Inc. Ed.*, p. 42, §22, ll. 16–18.

3. *Uncoll. PP*, II, 71.

4. *LG 1855*, p. 25, "Song of Myself," *Inc. Ed.*, p. 39, §19, ll. 1–6. See also *ibid.*, p. 36, §15, l. 44, p. 38, §16, ll. 17–19; "Proto-Leaf," *LG 1860*, p. 11 (10), "Starting from Paumanok," *Inc. Ed.*, pp. 15–16, §7, ll. 5–7.

5. *LG 1855*, p. 49, "Song of Myself," *Inc. Ed.*, p. 68, §44, ll. 9–10.

6. *LG 1855*, p. 47, "Song of Myself," *Inc. Ed.*, p. 65, §42, ll. 25–27. See also *ibid.*, p. 67, §43, ll. 28–38, and "Proto-Leaf," *LG 1860*, p. 15 (43), "Starting from Paumanok," *Inc. Ed.*, p. 18, §12, l. 6.

7. "To a Common Prostitute," *LG 1860*, p. 399, *Inc. Ed.*, p. 324.

8. *LG 1855*, p. 93, "Great Are the Myths," *Inc. Ed.*, p. 705, variant reading of §1; "Thoughts," no. 1, *LG 1860*, p. 408, "Of the Visage of Things," *Inc. Ed.*, p. 480, and "Leaves of Grass," no. 13, *LG 1860*, pp. 231–232, "You Felons on Trial in Courts," *Inc. Ed.*, p. 323.

9. "Leaves of Grass," no. 18, *LG 1860*, pp. 237–238, "All is Truth," *Inc. Ed.*, pp. 395–396.

10. *Inc. Ed.*, p. 495.

11. *LG 1855*, p. 14, "Song of Myself," *Inc. Ed.*, p. 26, §3, ll. 20–21.

12. *LG 1855*, p. 19, 71–72, "Song of Myself," *Inc. Ed.*, p. 32,

§11, and "The Sleepers," pp. 356–357, §1, ll. 45–58. See also a leading article which he contributed to the *Brooklyn Times* on June 22, 1859: "Can all marry?" (*I Sit and Look Out*, pp. 121–122).

13. *LG 1855*, p. 34, "Song of Myself," *Inc. Ed.*, pp. 50–51, §32, ll. 1–10.

14. *LG 1855*, p. 29, "Song of Myself," *Inc. Ed.*, p. 43, §23, l. 19. See also "Youth, Day, Old Age, and Night," *Inc. Ed.*, p. 191. This poem dates back to 1881, but was in fact a fragment of "Great Are the Myths" which was composed in 1855, but later disappeared from *Leaves of Grass*. O. L. Triggs does not seem to have noticed this transfer.

15. Whereas in 1856 for instance in his "Broad-Axe Poem" (later called "Song of the Broad-Axe") he emphasized the contrast between life and the requirements of middle-class morality (*Inc. Ed.*, §6), in the columns of the *Brooklyn Times* he praised marriage as a necessary institution (*I Sit and Look Out*, pp. 113–114) and denounced abortion as a crime (*ibid.*, pp. 114–115). It is true that, on the other hand, he boldly spoke of the problem of prostitution which he thought should be tolerated and supervised by local authorities (*ibid.* pp. 118–120).

16. *LG 1855*, p. 95, "Great Are the Myths," *Inc. Ed.*, p. 467, §4, ll. 1–4. See also an earlier draft of this passage in *Uncoll. PP*, II, 75, and "Thoughts," no. 4, *LG 1860*, p. 410, "Thought," *Inc. Ed.*, p. 234.

17. *LG 1855*, p. 95, "Great Are the Myths," *Inc. Ed.*, p. 466, §2.

18. *LG 1855*, p. 28, "Song of Myself," *Inc. Ed.*, p. 43, §22, l. 29.

19. *LG 1855*, p. 67, "To Think of Time," *Inc. Ed.*, p. 366, §6, l. 5. See also *ibid.*, p. 365, §5, l. 3.

20. "Poems of Joys," *Passage to India*, 1871, p. 51, §16 (37–38), "A Song of Joys," *Inc. Ed.*, p. 154, ll. 134–138. This passage was added to the poem in 1871, but, as early as 1860, in "Calamus," no. 40 ("That Shadow My Likeness," *Inc. Ed.*, p. 112), Whitman contrasted his essential, impregnable Me with his outward Me frivolously occupied in making a living, chatting and chaffering.

21. See above, pp. 29–30.

22. Preface to 1876 edition, *Inc. Ed.*, p. 517n.

23. Preface to 1855 edition, *Inc. Ed.*, pp. 501–504.

24. "Poem of the Last Explanation of Prudence," *LG 1856*, pp. 257–261, "Song of Prudence," *Inc. Ed.*, pp. 313–316.

25. The word was also used by phrenologists. In 1855 Whitman defined it in phrenological jargon; see *Inc. Ed.*, p. 501.

26. "Poem of Remembrance for a Girl or a Boy of These States," *LG 1856*, p. 227, "To Think of the Soul," *Inc. Ed.*, p. 469, ll. 16–17.

27. *Essays*, 1st series. The resemblances are more verbal than real, for Emerson claims with disarming simplicity that all injustices

are sooner or later redressed here below by a sort of immanent Justice which bears a close resemblance to the Nemesis of the ancient Greeks.

28. "Song of Prudence," *Inc. Ed.*, p. 315, l. 50.

29. *LG 1855*, p. 69, "To Think of Time," *Inc. Ed.*, p. 367, §8, ll. 10–16.

30. "Song of Prudence," *Inc. Ed.*, p. 314, l. 15.

31. "Liberty Poem," *LG 1856*, pp. 268–270, "To a Foil'd European Revolutionaire," *Inc. Ed.*, pp. 310–312.

32. *LG 1855*, pp. 41–42, "Song of Myself," *Inc. Ed.*, pp. 58–60, §35–§36.

33. *LG 1855*, p. 39, "Song of Myself," *Inc. Ed.*, p. 56, §33, ll. 115–124.

34. *LG 1855*, pp. 40–41, "Song of Myself," *Inc. Ed.*, pp. 57–58, §34.

35. Besides "Song of Prudence," see "Assurances" (1856), *Inc. Ed.*, pp. 373–374, and "Song of Myself" (1855), *Inc. Ed.*, pp. 67–68, §43, ll. 29–38. He touched upon the subject again in 1888 in "To Those Who've Fail'd," *Inc. Ed.*, pp. 420–421.

36. "Song of Prudence," *Inc. Ed.*, p. 315, ll. 46–48, and "Poem of You Whoever You Are," *LG 1856*, p. 206–210, "To You," *Inc. Ed.*, pp. 197–199, especially ll. 30–32 and 44–47.

37. "Faces" (1855), *Inc. Ed.*, p. 387, §3, l. 1 and p. 388, §4, l. 11.

38. *LG 1855*, p. 82–85, "Faces," *Inc. Ed.*, pp. 386–389, and "Song of Myself," pp. 67–68, §43, ll. 29–38.

39. "A Song of the Universal" (1876), *Inc. Ed.*, p. 194, §4, l. 20.

40. *Uncoll. PP*, II, 65. See also this passage in "The Wound-Dresser" (April 15, 1863), *CW*, IV, 147: "For the few years to come I should think more of that (good animal health) than anything — that is the foundation of all (righteousness included) . . ."

41. In *Franklin Evans* (1842) he showed how an alcoholic is obliged to go on drinking to prevent his tonus from collapsing; see *Uncoll. PP*, II, 160.

42. "Poem of the Road," *LG 1856*, p. 223, "Song of the Open Road," *Inc. Ed.*, p. 124, §1, ll. 2–3, and p. 126, §5, l. 2.

43. Preface to 1855 edition, *Inc. Ed.*, p. 498.

44. "Sun-Down Poem," *LG 1856*, p. 220, "Crossing Brooklyn Ferry," *Inc. Ed.*, p. 138, §9, l. 11.

45. "For Him I Sing," *LG 1871*, p. 10, *Inc. Ed.*, p. 7, ll. 4–5.

46. "Freedom," *Two Rivulets*, 1876, pp. 31–32, *CP*, pp. 346–347.

47. *Ibid.*, p. 347.

48. "Eidólons," *Two Rivulets*, 1876, p. 19, *Inc. Ed.*, p. 6, l. 55.

49. "Poem of the Road," *LG 1856*, pp. 223–239, "Song of the Open Road," *Inc. Ed.*, pp. 124–133.

50. *LG 1855*, p. 47, "Song of Myself," *Inc. Ed.*, pp. 65–66, §42,

ll. 22–42. See also "Proto-Leaf," *LG 1860*, p. 12, "Starting from Paumanok," *Inc. Ed.*, p. 16, §8.

51. *Ibid.*, ll. 22–24.

52. *LG 1855*, p. 34, "Song of Myself," *Inc. Ed.*, p. 50, §32, l. 6. On November 5, 1846, he had already denounced in an editorial in the *Brooklyn Eagle* what he called "a morbid appetite for money" (*Uncoll. PP*, I, 123).

53. *LG 1855*, p. 47, "Song of Myself," *Inc. Ed.*, p. 65, §42, l. 17 et seq.

54. *Satires*, VIII, l. 84.

55. *LG 1855*, p. 34, "Song of Myself," *Inc. Ed.*, p. 50, §32, ll. 3, 8. See an earlier version of this passage in *Uncoll. PP*, II, 67–68.

56. *Inc. Ed.*, p. 570, variant reading of l. 8 of §32.

57. "Leaves of Grass," no. 10, *LG 1860*, p. 225 (8), "Myself and Mine," *Inc. Ed.*, p. 202, ll. 20–22.

58. ". . . philosophy speculates . . . ever regarding the eternal tendencies of all toward happiness never inconsistent with what is clear to the senses and the soul. For the eternal tendencies of all toward happiness make the only point of sane philosophy." (Preface to 1855 edition, *Inc. Ed.*, p. 498.)

59. See above, pp. 50–51.

60. *LG 1855*, p. 51, "Song of Myself," *Inc. Ed.*, p. 69, §45, l. 11. See also "Poem of the Road," *LG 1856*, pp. 234–235, "Song of the Open Road," *Inc. Ed.*, p. 130, §12, and "Poem of the Sayers of the Words of the Earth," *LG 1856*, p. 326, "A Song of the Rolling Earth," *Inc. Ed.*, p. 188, §1, l. 49.

61. "Chants Democratic," no. 8, *LG 1860*, p. 177 (4), "Song at Sunset," *Inc. Ed.*, p. 410, l. 20.

62. "Debris," *LG 1860*, p. 482, *Inc. Ed.*, p. 482, ll. 9–14. See also "Beautiful Women," *ibid.*, p. 234, which is a fragment of "Debris" that Whitman kept in later editions.

63. "Poem of Joys," *LG 1860*, p. 625 (25), "A Song of Joys," *Inc. Ed.*, p. 152, ll. 86–88.

64. We have found some ten of them in the Library of Congress. See these notes published by Bucke and which, he thought, dated back to 1855 or so: "A character — Ninety-four years old, keeps up with the times, reads the new literature, was a chaplain in the revolutionary army . . . hale and vigorous and sensible like a man of thirty. Was never sick." *CW*, VI, 62. Also, "Pythagoras was very beautiful and lived to a great age. He was of athletic tastes, a boxer, a dancer, wrestler, runner, etc. He delighted in music and perfumes — wore his beard long." *Ibid.*, p. 94.

65. *LG 1855*, p. 93, "Great Are the Myths," *Inc. Ed.*, p. 465, §1, ll. 9–10. In 1881 Whitman kept only the two lines referring to youth

and old age which he entitled "Youth, Day, Old Age and Night,"
Inc. Ed., p. 191.

66. Daniel Longaker, "Last Sickness and Death of Walt Whitman,"
In Re, p. 398.

67. "The Pilot in the Mist" (1885). *Inc. Ed.*, pp. 424–425.

68. *With WW in* C, II, 71–72. He then used a copy of *Epictetus'
Enchiridion* which still exists. On the fly-page he had written: "Walt
Whitman (sent me by my friend the translator, T. W. H. Rolleston
from Dresden, Saxony) 1881 — from 1881 to '88 have had this
little volume at hand or in my hand often all these years — have read
it over and over again." In one of his notebooks dating from 1868–70,
he had written: "Epictetus (Description of a wise man) . . ." *Uncoll.
PP*, II, 94. See also: "I guess I have a good deal of the feeling of
Epictetus and stoicism." Letter to J. W. Wallace, May 29, 1891, *SPL*,
pp. 1056–1057. On Whitman and stoicism, see C. E. Pulos, "Whitman and Epictetus — The Stoical Element in *Leaves of Grass*,"
JEGP, LV (January 1956), 75–84.

69. See below, Conclusion, n. 32.

70. "The Mystic Trumpeter" (1872), *Inc. Ed.*, p. 391, §7, ll. 9–10.

71. Preface to 1855 edition, *Inc. Ed.*, p. 498.

72. *LG 1855*, p. 29, "Song of Myself," *Inc. Ed.*, p. 44, §24, l. 28.
See also *ibid.*, p. 41, §21, l. 7; "Proto-Leaf," *LG 1860*, p. 17 (51),
"Starting from Paumanok," *Inc. Ed.*, p. 19, §13, l. 12; "Poem of You
Whoever You Are," *LG 1856*, p. 207, "To You," *Inc. Ed.*, p. 198, l.
20; "Chants Democratic," no. 13, *LG 1860*, p. 186 (3), "Laws for
Creation," *Inc. Ed.*, p. 324, ll. 7–11.

73. *LG 1855*, p. 53, "Song of Myself," *Inc. Ed.*, p. 73, §48, l. 3.
In his 1850–55 notebooks his pantheistic pride is sometimes even
more strongly expressed, as in the following passages:

If I walk with Jah in Heaven and he assume to be intrinsically
greater than I, it offends me, and I shall certainly withdraw from
Heaven — for the soul prefers freedom in the prairie or the
untrodden wood . . .

Uncoll. PP, II, 68.

Not even God . . . is so great to me as Myself is great to me. —
Who knows but I too shall in time be a God as pure and prodigious
as any of them?

Ibid., p. 83. In an article on Keats's "Hyperion" dating from 1851
(*Catalogue of the Trent Collection*, p. 72), he had underlined the
following passage in which he probably found an encouragement:

So much then for the pleasure of the Sublime; it is the pleasure
of superior natures, and akin to pride. As a proof, let us observe
that poets of the Sublime have been remarkable for pride.

74. Cf. Emerson: "The highest revelation is that God is in every man." Quoted by F. O. Matthiessen in *American Renaissance*, p. 8.

75. "Leaves of Grass," no. 1, *LG 1860*, p. 196 (4), "As I Ebb'd with the Ocean of Life," *Inc. Ed.*, p. 216, §2, ll. 1–7, and "Chants Democratic," no. 18, *LG 1860*, p. 191, "Me Imperturbe," *Inc. Ed.*, p. 9.

76. "A Backward Glance" (1888), *Inc. Ed.*, p. 532.

77. "Elias Hicks," *NB*, p. 135, *CP*, p. 486: In the higher structure of a human self, or of community, the Moral, the Religious, the Spiritual, is strictly analogous to the subtle vitalization and antiseptic play call'd Health in the physiologic structure. To person or State, the main verteber (or rather *the* verteber) is Morality.

IV. THE FUNDAMENTAL AESTHETICS

1. "Democratic Vistas," *CP*, pp. 244–245.

2. *Prose Works*, 1892, pp. 288–301, *CP*, pp. 295–309. This essay was first published in the *North American Review* in February 1881 under the title of "The Poetry of the Future."

3. *LG 1855*, p. v, *Inc. Ed.*, p. 492. See also the "Letter to R. W. Emerson," *LG 1856*, p. 346: "I am a man who has perfect faith."

4. "Democratic Vistas," *CP*, p. 250.

5. *Ibid.*, p. 254.

6. He used the word himself in the preface to the 1855 edition; see *Inc. Ed.*, p. 492.

7. "Death of Thomas Carlyle," *SD*, p. 168, *CP*, p. 168.

8. See Denis Saurat, *La religion de Victor Hugo* (Paris, 1929). This romantic conception in fact goes back a long way and is rooted in the occultist tradition; see Auguste Viatte, *Les Sources occultes du romantisme* (Paris, 1928). Whitman was familiar with the works of the English romantics and, above all, had encountered in George Sand's novels figures of inspired poets that had deeply struck him; see Esther Shephard, *Walt Whitman's Pose* (New York: Harcourt, Brace, 1938) and our criticism of her thesis in Vol. I, pp. 57–60. Another possible influence is that of a joint review of Christopher Wordsworth's *Memoirs of William Wordsworth* and of William Wordsworth's *Poetical Works,* which one D. W. W. published in 1851, probably in an American magazine. This review is now in the Berg Collection. Whitman has underlined, now in ink, now in pencil (which proves that he has read it several times and mused upon it) the following passages:

An age without its gifted inventor, without its lawgiver, without its poet, must live over the old life, walk by hearsay, and subsist on imitation. We have at least dumb consciousness that our well-being on this planet depends upon our insight into the nature of our existence, and we are always ready to ask help of him whose vision is clearer than our own. We welcome therefore the true seer. He is eyes for the world; he is the true keeper of keepers. [Cf. Preface to 1855 edition, *Inc. Ed.*, p. 492.]

Foremost among these is the true poet. He is an intuitive seer; something more than a seer. Novalis says: "The fresh gaze of a child is richer in significance than the forecasting of the most indubitable seer." The poet is the full-grown child.

The mere verse-maker — the artisan, working with imitative skill — is a kind of gypsey [sic] wanderer, homeless, friendless, and, to Apollo's household, worthless, while the true poet, the artist is at length housed in the affections, warmed in the bosom of love . . . An age of imitation never recognizes the inspired teacher who is true to man by being true to his own nature. Just so far as the spirit of the times is false will the true poet be neglected. The one who tacks to catch the popular breeze, may run with great rapidity — alas, not often heavenwards. When the multitude are repenting, woe to those who have received their favors, and joy to those who have raised heroic and prophetic voices of warning and guidance! Happy the age in which a strong, devout soul converses with the Spirit of the Universe in the hearing of men! Words of bitterness and jest may be thoughtlessly uttered, but many shall learn to worship . . . He is the eye of the universe giving expression to its otherwise boundless void . . . Every real poet . . . is necessarily metaphysical . . . He announces but does not prove, he combines, but does not analyse.

In all these sentences Whitman could recognize himself or find an encouragement.

9. See Emerson's essays on "The Transcendentalist" and "The Poet."

10. Preface to 1855 edition, *Inc. Ed.*, p. 492: "What the eyesight does to the rest, he does to the rest . . . he sees eternity in men and women . . ."

11. *Ibid.*, p. 495.

12. *Ibid.*, p. 491.

13. LG *1855*, p. 43, "Song of Myself," *Inc. Ed.*, p. 61, §38, ll. 5-11.

14. LG *1855*, pp. 57-58, "A Song for Occupations," *Inc. Ed.*, pp. 179-180, §1, especially ll. 24-26.

15. LG *1855*, pp. 51-52, "Song of Myself," *Inc. Ed.*, pp. 70-71, §46.

16. LG *1855*, p. 46, "Song of Myself," *Inc. Ed.*, pp. 64-65, §42.

17. *LG 1855*, p. 45, "Song of Myself," *Inc. Ed.*, p. 63, §40, ll. 17–19.

18. *LG 1855*, p. 45, "Song of Myself," *Inc. Ed.*, p. 63, §41, l. 7.

19. *Ibid.*, p. 63, §40, ll. 22–34. See also *LG 1855*, p. 71, "The Sleepers," *Inc. Ed.*, p. 356, §1, ll. 23–25.

20. "The great construction of the New Bible. Not to be diverted from the principal object — the main life work — the three hundred and sixty-five — It ought to be ready in 1859. (June '57)." *CW*, VI, 6 (14).

21. *Ibid.*, p. 4.

22. "To Him that was Crucified," *LG 1860*, p. 397, *Inc. Ed.*, pp. 322–323.

23. "So Long!" *LG 1860*, p. 451 (1), *Inc. Ed.*, p. 702, variant reading (after l. 1).

24. "The Mystic Trumpeter," *As a Strong Bird on Pinions Free*, 1872, p. 11, *Inc. Ed.*, pp. 391–392, §8, ll. 1, 4–5.

25. "Thou Mother with Thy Equal Brood," *As a Strong Bird* . . . , p. 5, *Inc. Ed.*, p. 382, §5, l. 39.

26. R. M. Bucke, *Walt Whitman* (Philadelphia: David McKay, 1883), pp. 183–185.

27. Preface to 1855 edition, *Inc. Ed.*, p. 505.

28. "Democratic Vistas," *CP*, p. 210.

29. *Ibid.*, pp. 211–212, 242–244.

30. He said so himself in 1888:

I think Literature — a new, superb, democratic literature — is to be the medicine and lever, and (with Art) the chief influence in modern civilization. I have myself not so much made a dead set at this theory, or attempted to present it directly, as admitted it to color and sometimes dominate what I had to say.

Preface to "Democratic Vistas" with other papers — English edition. *NB*, p. 96, *CP*, p. 447.

31. *WWW*, p. 37.

32. "So Long!" *LG 1860*, p. 454 (17), *Inc. Ed.*, p. 417, ll. 36, 39, 41.

33. "Chants Democratic," no. 16, *LG 1860*, p. 189, "Mediums," *Inc. Ed.*, p. 399.

34. *Catalogue of the Trent Collection*, p. 74.

35. "Leaves of Grass," no. 20, *LG 1860*, p. 239, "So Far and So Far, and On Toward the End," *Inc. Ed.*, p. 475, l. 2.

36. Preface to 1872 edition, *Inc. Ed.*, p. 507.

37. Preface to 1876 edition, *Inc. Ed.*, pp. 518–519.

38. "Prayer of Columbus," *Two Rivulets*, 1876, p. 23, *Inc. Ed.*, p. 353, l. 56.

39. Preface to 1876 edition, *Inc. Ed.*, pp. 518–519.

40. *LG 1881*, p. 368, *Inc. Ed.*, p. 403.
41. See "Faces" and "The Sleepers."
42. Preface to 1855 edition, *Inc. Ed.*, p. 501.
43. After Whitman's death, Thomas B. Harned published under the title of "Whitman and Physique" (*Conservator*, June 1896, pp. 68–70 — reprinted in *CW*, V, 261–274) all the manuscripts dealing with this subject which he found in the poet's papers, but William L. Finkel ("Sources of Walt Whitman's Manuscript Notes on Physique," *AL*, XXII, November 1950, 308–331) has proved that they were merely notes taken while reading and not personal statements as Harned believed. This discovery, however, detracts nothing from their importance, for whether Whitman wrote them himself or merely copied them, these manuscripts reveal the eager interest which he took in this subject and show that he adopted as his own all these borrowed ideas, as is proved by this passage from pages 9 and 10 of his *American Primer:*

> Drinking brandy, gin, beer, is generally fatal to the perfection of the voice; — meanness of mind the same; gluttony in eating, of course, the same; a thinned habit of body, or a rank habit of body — masturbation, inordinate going with women, rot the voice. Yet no man can have a great vocation who has no experience with women and no woman who has no experience with men. The final fiber and charm of the voice follows the chaste drench of love.

This last sentence shows that he did not preach moral asceticism, far from it. He felt moral purity to be indispensable to the artist, but condemned absolute chastity.
44. "Bathing — Cleanliness — Personal Beauty," *Brooklyn Eagle*, June 10, 1846, reprinted in *G of the F*, II, 201–207; see also "Art of Health," *ibid.*, pp. 199–201.
45. "Pugilism and Pugilists," *I Sit and Look Out*, pp. 105–106, and "Brooklyn Young Men — Athletic Exercises," *G of the F*, II, 207–209.
46. "He took occasion to inform us . . . of his bathing daily through the midwinter . . ." *The Journals of Bronson Alcott,* ed. and sel. by Odell Shepard (Boston, 1938), p. 289.
47. *Calamus,* p. 24.
48. See his letter to Hugo Fritsch of August 7, 1863, *SPL,* p. 917. He was not in favor of extreme solutions in these matters; see the article in the *Brooklyn Times* of June 29, 1858 (*I Sit and Look Out,* pp. 45–46), in which he made fun of vegetarians and water-drinkers. He also condemned prohibition (see *ibid.,* pp. 47–49).
49. In an article entitled "Personal Magnetism — How it may be augmented," now in the Trent Collection of Duke University, he had underlined the following passage:

A single act of gluttony or inebriety palsies for a time the perceptions, the judgment, the play of social feeling, the moral sense, the will, — every power that is necessary to success . . . One in this frame of body radiates no controlling influence, neither wins nor molds those about him. No matter what his constitutional capabilities, for the time he imparts nothing but receives — commiseration or contempt.

50. *CW*, VI, 211–212.

51. See above, n. 49.

52. "Poem of the Road," *LG 1856*, p. 233 "Song of the Open Road," *Inc. Ed.*, p. 129, §11, ll. 4–5.

53. Preface to 1876 edition, *Inc. Ed.*, p. 517.

54. Preface to 1855 edition, *Inc. Ed.*, p. 502.

55. *American Primer*, p. 2.

56. Unfortunately he was not always able to put into practice this other rule which he had formulated in 1855: "The poet shall not spend his time in unneeded work." Preface to 1855 edition, *Inc. Ed.*, p. 494. He nevertheless enjoyed long periods of inactivity which precisely coincided with times of intense poetic productivity: from 1859 to 1865 and then from 1873 to his death.

57. He used the word himself in 1891 in "Good-Bye My Fancy," but gave it the meaning of inspiration.

58. From a review of *Leaves of Grass* which Whitman wrote himself for the *American Phrenological Journal* and reprinted in "Leaves-Droppings," *LG 1856*, pp. 372–373.

59. "Poem of Many in One," *LG 1856*, p. 190, "By Blue Ontario's Shore," *Inc. Ed.*, p. 660, in the variant reading of §10, after l. 17.

60. "A Backward Glance O'er Travel'd Roads" (1888), *Inc. Ed.*, p. 524. See also "Says" (1860), *Inc. Ed.*, p. 481, §5, ll. 6–7.

61. See for instance "Thou Mother with Thy Equal Brood" (1872), *Inc. Ed.*, pp. 379–384. He uses "Columbia" in "Song of the Exposition," *ibid.*, p. 168, §4, l. 2, and "O Star of France," *ibid.*, p. 332, l. 36, etc.

62. *After all, not to create only*, 1871, "Song of the Exposition," *Inc. Ed.*, pp. 166–174.

63. Preface to 1876 edition, *Inc. Ed.*, p. 520, He had already spoken of it in more general terms, ten years before, in a letter about *Leaves of Grass* which he wanted O'Connor to copy and sign and send to Moncure D. Conway who was his agent for the forthcoming English edition of some of his poems (see *With WW in C*, I, 381–384, and *Coll. W*, I, 347–349). He praised in it the qualities which to his mind gave his own work its value and originality and would justify its publication in Great Britain. Among other things he wrote this:

The idea, however, which is this man's highest contribution, and which, compared even with the vastness of Biblical and Homeric poetry, still looms and towers, as athwart his fellow-giants of the Himalayas, the dim head of Kunchainjunga rises over the rest — is the idea of Totality . . . his talisman is *Ensemble*. This is the word that epitomizes the philosophy of Walt Whitman.

64. "Proto-Leaf," *LG 1860*, p. 16 (46), "Starting from Paumanok," *Inc. Ed.*, p. 19, §12, ll. 17–19.

65. "Chants Democratic," no. 13, *LG 1860*, p. 185 (2), "Laws for Creation," *Inc. Ed.*, p. 324, l. 4, and p. 696, first line of the variant reading.

66. "Poem of Joys," *LG 1860*, p. 268 (37), "A Song of Joys," *Inc. Ed.*, p. 149, §1, ll. 13–14.

67. Last two lines of "Intimations of Immortality from Recollections of Early Childhood."

68. Preface to 1855 edition, *Inc. Ed.*, p. 501.

69. *LG 1855*, p. 51, "Song of Myself," *Inc. Ed.*, p. 70, §45, l. 26. See also "Miracles," *ibid.*, p. 326, l. 16.

70. "Song of Myself," §§8–16 and 33–38 in particular.

71. "Poem of Joys," *LG 1860*, p. 267 (32), "A Song of Joys," *Inc. Ed.*, p. 153, ll. 112–114.

72. "Leaves of Grass," no. 15, *LG 1860*, p. 234 "Night on the Prairies," *Inc. Ed.*, p. 377, ll. 11–15.

73. See "The First Dandelion" (1888), *Inc. Ed.*, p. 423; "My Canary Bird," p. 422; "Broadway," p. 430; "A Font of Type," p. 421. There is a fine instance of broadening out to the infinite of a very humble scene in "Sparkles from the Wheel" (1871), *ibid.*, p. 327, l. 12.

74. "To the Sunset Breeze" (1890), *Inc. Ed.*, p. 449, ll. 9–11.

75. *N & F*, p. 79 (10).

76. See in particular *LG 1855*, p. 35, "Song of Myself," *Inc. Ed.*, p. 51, §33, ll. 1–7, and p. 52, ll. 81–82.

77. Preface to 1876 edition, *Inc. Ed.*, p. 520.

78. *Uncoll. PP*, II, 86. See also: "Astronomy was understood — with which no nation can be degraded nor any race of learned persons remain without great thoughts and poems." *CW*, VI, 105–106.

79. Except perhaps for Carlyle because of his historical sense.

80. See in particular "With Antecedents" (1860), *Inc. Ed.*, pp. 203–205, "Crossing Brooklyn Ferry" (1856), *ibid.*, p. 135, §3, ll. 1–2, and variant reading p. 606, and "Song of Myself" (1855), *ibid.*, p. 50, §31, p. 68–70, §§44–45.

81. *LG 1855*, p. 24, "Song of Myself," *Inc. Ed.*, p. 38, §16, l. 16.

82. "Old Chants" and "Long, long hence."

83. *LG 1855*, p. 46, "Song of Myself," *Inc. Ed.*, p. 64, §41, ll. 28–29. See also p. 50, §31, ll. 1–7 (*Uncoll. PP*, II, 70).

84. "Faith Poem," *LG 1856*, p. 265, "Assurances," *Inc. Ed.*, p. 373, l. 3.

85. *LG 1855*, p. 20, "Song of Myself," *Inc. Ed.*, p. 33, §13, l. 1–5. Cf. this recollection of Mrs. O'Connor:

He once went over to Georgetown, where coal barges were being unloaded at the Canal, and he told us that he watched for hours a negro at work who was naked to the waist, and the play of his muscles, as he loaded and unloaded the buckets of coal, was most fascinating; "No Greek statue would have been more superb," he said.

Ellen M. Calder (ex-O'Connor), "Personal Recollections of Walt Whitman," *AM*, IC (June 1907), p. 833.

86. "Poetry To-day in America," *SD*, p. 295, *CP*, pp. 301–302.

87. A quality which he called "truth" in "Great Are the Myths" (1855), *Inc. Ed.*, p. 466, §2, ll. 7–9. See also "Sun-Down Papers," no. 40, *Uncoll. PP*, I, 43.

88. Preface to 1855 edition, *Inc. Ed.*, p. 500. This passage was inserted with hardly any change into "By Blue Ontario's Shore" in 1856; see *Inc. Ed.*, p. 660, §10, among the variant readings, after l. 17, ll. 8–11.

89. "Sparkles from the Wheel," *Inc. Ed.*, p. 327, l. 12.

90. "Democratic Vistas," *SD*, pp. 253–254, *CP*, pp. 254–255, and "Poetry To-day in America," *SD*, pp. 297–298 and n, *CP*, pp. 304–305.

91. *LG 1855*, p. 27, "Song of Myself," *Inc. Ed.*, p. 42, §22, l. 14.

92. *LG 1855*, p. 53, "Song of Myself," *Inc. Ed.*, p. 73, §48, l. 4.

93. "Leaves of Grass," no. 23, *LG 1860*, p. 241, "Locations and Times," *Inc. Ed.*, p. 235.

94. This article, entitled "Imagination and Fact," is now in the Trent Collection at Duke University; see *Catalogue of the Trent Collection*, p. 73.

95. "Grand is the Seen," *Inc. Ed.*, p. 457, ll. 1, 4, 6.

96. "Poem of Many in One," *LG 1856*, pp. 188–189, "By Blue Ontario's Shore," *Inc. Ed.*, pp. 291–292, §10, ll. 3, 12.

97. "Wordsworth lacks sympathy with men and women — that does not pervade him enough — by a long shot." Written in the margin of an article entitled "Christopher under Canvas" (June 1849), now kept in the Trent Collection of Duke University.

98. "To a Common Prostitute" (1860), *Inc. Ed.*, p. 324. For the violent attacks to which this poem was subjected, see Vol. I, pp. 239–242.

99. "Continuities" (1888), *Inc. Ed.*, p. 432.

100. See W. S. Kennedy, *The Fight of a Book for the World,* pp. 174–175.

101. *LG 1856,* pp. 316–321, "Respondez," *Inc. Ed.,* pp. 469–472, and p. 706.

102. *Inc. Ed.,* p. 619, variant reading of §3, after l. 3 and ll. 33–38.

103. Manuscript notes now in the Library of Congress. See also: "Make no puns funny remarks Double entendres "witty" remarks ironies Sarcasms — only that which is simply earnest, meant, — harmless to any one's feelings — unadorned unvarnished nothing to excite a laugh . . ." *An 1855 Notebook Toward the Second Edition of Leaves of Grass,* Introduction and notes by Harold W. Blodgett (Southern Illinois University Press, 1959), p. 8.

104. Except for two pieces: "A Boston Ballad" and "To the States, To identify the 16th, 17th or 18th Presidentiad."

V. SEX LIFE

1. The phrase was used by Lord Alfred Douglas in the last line of the poem entitled "Two Loves." See Frank Harris, *Oscar Wilde — His Life and Confessions* (N.Y.: Covici, Friede, 1930), p. 409.

2. "Calamus," no. 10, *LG 1860,* pp. 356–357, "Recorders Ages Hence," *Inc. Ed.,* p. 102, ll. 1–2, 9.

3. "Calamus," no. 2, *LG 1860,* p. 342, "Scented Herbage of My Breast," *Inc. Ed.,* p. 95, l. 4.

4. *Ibid.,* p. 96, ll. 6–7.

5. "Calamus," no. 3, *LG 1860,* pp. 344, 346 (6–7), "Whoever You Are Holding Me Now in Hand," *Inc. Ed.,* p. 97, l. 4, p. 98, ll. 27–28, 31, 37–38.

6. "Calamus," no. 44, *LG 1860,* p. 377, "Here the Frailest Leaves of Me," *Inc. Ed.,* p. 109.

7. J. A. Symonds, *A Problem in Greek Ethics,* being an inquiry into the phenomenon of sexual inversion (London, 1883).

8. Letter to John Addington Symonds, August 19, 1890, *SPL,* p. 1052. It had been rumored for several years already that Whitman had illegitimate children and this amused him a great deal; see letter to W. S. Kennedy, October 4, 1887, *SPL,* p. 1048. He returned to the subject in a letter to R. M. Bucke, May 23, 1891: "I have two deceased children (young man and woman — illegitimate of course) that I much desired to bury here with me — but have ab't abandoned the plan on account of angry litigation and fuss generally, and disinterment from down South." *SPL,* p. 1056.

The full text of Whitman's reply to Symonds has not yet been published, but Symonds in a letter to Edward Carpenter (quoted by

Edward Naumburg, see below, n. 11) summed up one of the missing passages:

He rambles on about his being less "restrained" by the temperament and theory than I (J. A. S.) am. "I at certain moments let the spirit impulse rage its utmost, wildest, damnedest (I feel to do so sometimes in L of G and I do so)"

This last passage seems meant to qualify the first. But if it does so, it implies that these inferences are not so gratuitous, morbid and damnable as supposed.

On the Whitman-Symonds correspondence, see Edward Carpenter, *Some Friends of Walt Whitman: A Study in Sex-Psychology* (Publication no. 13 of the British Society for the Study of Sex Psychology, 1924).

9. See J. A. Symonds, *Walt Whitman: A Study* (London: George Routledge, 1893), p. 93, and *A Problem in Modern Ethics* (London, 1896), p. 125n and p. 130.

10. This is what Edward Carpenter said about it:

. . . he knew that the moment he said such a thing [that he was homosexual] he would have the whole American Press at his heels, snarling and slandering, and distorting his words in every possible way. Things are pretty bad here in this country; but in the States (in such matters) they are ten times worse . . .

Some Friends of Walt Whitman, p. 12.

11. See Edward Naumburg, "A Collector Looks at Whitman," *Princeton University Library Chronicle*, III (November 1941), 1–18, in which the author quotes a letter of H. B. Binns to Edward Carpenter which contains the following passage: "Traubel showed me a love letter from Ellen Eyre (? of New York) in 1862, and J. H. Johnston a photo of a young New York actress who had been "one of Whitman's sweethearts." Maynard says that Doyle admitted he knew a woman in Washington with whom Whitman had sex relations. This is all I could gather on our subject." This letter, however, consists mostly of gossip and does not prove anything.

On February 28, 1902, Traubel wrote to Carpenter: "During Walt's last sickness his grandson came to the house. I was not there at the time. When Walt mentioned the occurrence to me, I expressed my regrets that I had missed him. 'I wish I might see him!' 'God forbid.' " (*Ibid.*, p. 15.) This flat refusal following a missed opportunity sounds rather suspicious.

The letter of Binns to Carpenter contains another allusion to Whitman's illegitimate progeny: "Harned has a brief illiterate note written at Washington by someone who had called and missed Walt Whitman. It is dated April 1864 and is by W. E. Vandernack 'to his father.' I presume it is a 'manner of speech.' " Binns's supposition is correct.

There is in the Berg Collection a letter sent to Whitman by a young soldier bearing this name. He called Whitman "father" like many other young soldiers whom the "wound-dresser" visited in the hospitals.

Emory Holloway in *Free and Lonesome Heart: The Secret of Walt Whitman* (New York: Vantage Press, 1960) has tried to prove that Whitman had at least one illegitimate son, one John Whitman Wilder, born in 1868, but his contention has been refuted by C. Carroll Hollis ("The 'Big Secret' Unsolved," *Walt Whitman Review*, VI, June 1960, 36–37); see also the review of Holloway's book by Edward F. Grier in *AL*, XXXIII (March 1961), 85–86.

12. *Calamus*, p. 25.

13. See Roger M. Asselineau, "Walt Whitman, Child of Adam?" *MLQ*, X (March 1949), 91–95.

14. See *The Letters of Anne Gilchrist and Walt Whitman*, ed. by Thomas B. Harned (New York: Doubleday, Doran & Co., 1918).

15. Letter to William O'Connor, September 11, 1864, *Coll. W*, I, 242.

16. Eduard Bertz, "Walt Whitman, ein Characterbild," *Jahrbuch für sexuelle Zwischenstufen* (1905), pp. 156–287. He later developed his thesis in *Whitman Mysterien, eine Abrechnung mit Johannes Schlaf* (Berlin, 1907) and in *Der Yankee-Heiland: ein Beitrag zur modernen Religiongeschichte* (Dresden: Carl Reissner, 1906).

17. Mark Van Doren, "Walt Whitman Stranger," *American Mercury*, XXXV (July 1935), 277–285.

18. Edward Carpenter, *The Intermediate Sex* (New York and London: M. Kennerley, 1912) and *Homogenic Love and Its Place in a Free Society* (Manchester: Labour Press Society, 1894).

19. Edward Carpenter, *Days with Walt Whitman* (London: George Allen, 1906), pp. 137–152 ("Walt Whitman's Children"), and *Some Friends of Walt Whitman: A Study in Sex-Psychology*.

20. *Mercure de France* from April 1, 1913, to February 1, 1914.

21. Havelock Ellis, *Sexual Inversion* (Philadelphia: F. A. Davis Co., 1901) and Havelock Ellis, *The New Spirit* (London: W. Scott, 1890).

22. W. C. Rivers, *Walt Whitman's Anomaly* (London: George Allen, 1913).

23. When the truth became known there were even people who thought that Whitman should from then on be completely ignored; see for instance Charles F. Heartman, "The Untimeliness of the Walt Whitman Exhibition at the New York Public Library," *American Collector*, I (1925), 83–85.

24. *Uncoll. PP*, I, xlix, and II, 102.

25. Emory Holloway, *Whitman: An Interpretation in Narrative* (New York: A. A. Knopf, 1926) and *I Sit and Look Out*, ed. by

Emory Holloway and Vernolian Schwartz (New York: Columbia University Press, 1932), p. 104, n. 47, and p. 208, n. 11. Emory Holloway, however, has made some concessions to the advocates of the homosexuality theory in his last book: *Free and Lonesome Heart* (New York, Vantage Press, 1960).

26. Newton Arvin, *Whitman* (New York: Macmillan, 1938), p. 227.

27. Henry S. Canby, *Walt Whitman, An American* (Boston: Houghton Mifflin, 1943), pp. 186–187, 204–205.

28. Gay Wilson Allen, *Walt Whitman Handbook* (Chicago: Packard, 1946), Chapter I and *passim*; see also his *Solitary Singer* (New York: Macmillan, 1955), pp. 221 et seq. and 433–435.

29. Malcolm Cowley, "Walt Whitman: The Secret," *New Republic*, CXIV (April 8, 1946), 481–484. This article was reprinted as part of the introduction to *The Complete Poetry and Prose of Walt Whitman* (New York: Pellegrini & Cudahy, 1948), I, pp. 16 et seq.

30. In particular in the reviews of two books: *Marriage: Its History and Ceremonies* by L. N. Fowler (*Brooklyn Eagle*, April 2, 1847; *G of the F*, II, 304) and *Woman and Her Diseases from the Cradle to the Grave* by Edward H. Dixon (*Brooklyn Eagle*, March 4, 1847; *G of the F*, II, 305–306).

31. LG *1855*, p. 79, "I Sing the Body Electric," *Inc. Ed.*, p. 82, §5, ll. 6–12.

32. LG *1855*, p. 30, "Song of Myself," *Inc. Ed.*, p. 45, §24, ll. 31–47.

33. LG *1855*, p. 57, "A Song for Occupations," *Inc. Ed.*, p. 621.

34. LG *1855*, p. 19, "Song of Myself," *Inc. Ed.*, p. 32, §11.

35. LG *1855*, pp. 71–72, "The Sleepers," *Inc. Ed.*, pp. 356–357, §1, ll. 45–58.

36. See above, n. 29.

37. LG *1855*, pp. 15–16, "Song of Myself," *Inc. Ed.*, p. 27, §5.

38. LG *1855*, p. 72, "The Sleepers," *Inc. Ed.*, p. 683, variant reading of §1, ll. 1–7.

39. *Ibid.*, ll. 8–11. Jean Catel (*Walt Whitman: la Naissance du Poète*, Paris, Rieder, 1929, pp. 426–427) sees in this passage the mere description of a "fellatio," but this is a much too literal interpretation of the text.

40. *Ibid.*, l. 7.

41. "Bunch Poem," LG *1856*, pp. 310–311, "Spontaneous Me," *Inc. Ed.*, p. 89, ll. 21, 32–34.

42. "Sun-Down Poem," LG *1856*, p. 217, "Crossing Brooklyn Ferry," *Inc. Ed.*, p. 137, §6, l. 9.

43. *Ibid.*

44. *Ibid.*, ll. 15–17. In his open letter to Emerson he also wrote:

"Every day I go among the people of Manhattan Island, Brooklyn, and other cities, and among the young men to discover the spirit of them and to refresh myself . . ." *LG 1856,* p. 347.

45. See Vol. I, pp. 120–121.

46. Letter to M. D. Conway, November 1st, 1867, *SPL,* p. 964, *Coll. W,* I, 347.

47. *LG 1855,* p. 30, "Song of Myself," *Inc. Ed.,* p. 45, §24, l. 39.

48. "Calamus," no. 4, *LG 1860,* p. 348, "These I Singing in Spring," *Inc. Ed.,* p. 99, ll. 20–21, and the last two lines.

49. Quoted by Malcolm Cowley, "Walt Whitman: The Miracle," *New Republic,* CXIV (March 18, 1946), 388–389.

50. The word "comrade" which recurs so often in his verse after 1860 was hardly ever used in *Leaves of Grass* before that date. It occurred only three times in the 1855 version.

51. ". . . at most a very few," "Calamus," no. 3, *LG 1860,* p. 346 (7), "Whoever You Are Holding Me Now in Hand," *Inc. Ed.,* p. 98, l. 35. See also "Calamus," no. 2, *LG 1860,* pp. 342–344, "Scented Herbage of My Breast," *Inc. Ed.,* p. 96, l. 6, and the last two lines of "Roots and Leaves Themselves," *Inc. Ed.,* p. 104.

52. "Calamus," no. 1, *LG 1860,* p. 341, "In Paths Untrodden," *Inc. Ed.,* p. 95, l. 7.

53. See for instance the following fragments, all anterior to 1855:

> There five men, a group of sworn friends, stalwart, bearded, determined, work their way together through all the troubles and impediments of the world.

> Here and there couples or trios, young and old, clear-faced, and of perfect physique, walk with twined arms, in divine friendship, happy . . .

Pictures, pp. 13–14, 16.

A passage in one of his notebooks shows how tortured he was about the same time by the feeling that he was different from others: "Yet I know not why I should be sad. Around me are my brother men, merry and jovial . . . No dear one is in danger, and health, shelter and food are vouchsafed me." *Uncoll. PP,* II, 89. He did not know himself yet and could not understand the reason for his sadness. As early as 1854, though, he began taking down notes about young men; cf. *CW,* VI, 133–134, 142.

54. ". . . incredible dreams" ("Not Heaving from My Ribb'd Breast Only," *Inc. Ed.,* p. 100, l. 14). Does not this phrase show his own wonder at the monsters he discovered within himself?

55. See Vol. I, pp. 107–114.

56. On the shame which his abnormal desires caused him, see "Hours Continuing, Long, Sore and Heavy-Hearted," *Inc. Ed.,* p. 478,

ll. 6–7 ("Calamus," no. 9, *LG 1860*, p. 355). He sometimes wondered whether other men had ever felt as he did and then he resigned himself: "I am ashamed — but it is useless — I am what I am." However, he would not have confided this dreadful secret to his brother or his doctor; see "To You," *LG 1860*, p. 403, *Inc. Ed.*, p. 479.

57. "Calamus," no. 1, *LG 1860*, p. 341, "In Paths Untrodden," *Inc. Ed.*, p. 95, l. 10.

58. *Ibid.*, ll. 12, 14, 18.

59. *Ibid.*, l. 15. "This delicious Ninth-month in my forty-first year," he says, i.e., September 1859.

60. "Calamus," no. 15, *LG 1860*, p. 361, "Trickle Drops," *Inc. Ed.*, p. 105, l. 11.

61. "Calamus," no. 6, *LG 1860*, pp. 351–352, "Not Heaving from My Ribb'd Breast Only," *Inc. Ed.*, p. 100.

62. "Calamus," no. 18, *LG 1860*, p. 363, "City of Orgies," *Inc. Ed.*, p. 105.

63. "Calamus," no. 22, *LG 1860*, p. 366, "To a Stranger," *Inc. Ed.*, p. 106.

64. "Calamus," no. 41, *LG 1860*, p. 376, "Among the Multitude," *Inc. Ed.*, p. 112.

65. "Calamus," no. 23, *LG 1860*, p. 367, "This Moment Yearning and Thoughtful," *Inc. Ed.*, p. 107.

66. "Enfans d'Adam," no. 14, *LG 1860*, p. 314, "I Am He that Aches with Love," *Inc. Ed.*, p. 92.

67. "Calamus," no. 38, *LG 1860*, p. 375, "Fast-Anchor'd Eternal O Love," *Inc. Ed.*, p. 112, ll. 4–6.

68. "Not Heaving from My Ribb'd Breast Only," *Inc. Ed.*, p. 100, l. 9.

69. "Calamus," no. 39, *LG 1860*, p. 373, "Sometimes with One I Love," *Inc. Ed.*, p. 111.

70. "Calamus," no. 10, *LG 1860*, pp 356, 357, "Recorders Ages Hence," *Inc. Ed.*, p. 102, ll. 6, 9.

71. "Whoever You Are Holding Me Now in Hand," *Inc. Ed.*, p. 97, ll. 17–19.

72. "Enfans d'Adam," no. 8, *LG 1860*, pp. 310–311, "Native Moments," *Inc. Ed.*, p. 93, ll. 5, 7, 11. See also "Calamus," no. 11, *LG 1860*, pp. 357–358, "When I Heard at the Close of the Day," *Inc. Ed.*, p. 102, ll. 11–13.

73. Thomas Donaldson, *Walt Whitman, the Man* (New York: Harper, 1890).

74. Bertz calls him an "Edel-Uranist"; see W. C. Rivers, *Walt Whitman's Anomaly*, p. 66.

75. "The Untold Want," *Passage to India*, 1871, p. 118, *Inc. Ed.*, p. 415.

76. See J. A. Symonds, *A Problem of Modern Ethics,* p. 116n:
. . . it is curious to note what one of Casper-Liman's correspondents says about the morals of America:

Half a year after my return I went to North America to try my fortune. There the unnatural vice in question is more ordinary than it is here; and I was able to indulge my passions with less fear of punishment or persecution. The Americans' tastes in this matter resemble my own; and I discovered, in the United States, that I was immediately recognized as a member of the confraternity. (J. L. Casper and Carl Liman, *Handbuch der gerichtlichen Medizin,* Berlin: Hirschwald, 1899, I, 173.)

The special facilities offered by New York in this respect may have been one of the reasons why Whitman was so much attached to Manhattan. In a line of "Mannahatta" which he later suppressed he said:

The city of such young men, I swear I cannot live happy without, I often go, talk, walk, eat, drink, sleep with them!

Inc. Ed., p. 694, last line of the passage suppressed in 1881.

77. Another suspicious aspect of his temperament was his passionate love for his mother. All psychoanalysts are agreed that it frequently predisposes a man to homosexuality. Whitman expressed this love in particular in "There was a Child Went Forth," *Inc. Ed.,* p. 307, ll. 22–23, and in a variant reading of "On the Beach at Night Alone," *Inc. Ed.,* p. 641, l. 13 of the passage which originally followed l. 3.

See also what Mrs. Ellen Calder (ex-O'Connor) said in her "Personal Recollections of Walt Whitman," *AM,* IC (June 1907), p. 832: "So deep and instinctive was Walt's veneration of the mother that he did not relish any fun at her expense." According to her, he even objected to the phrase "leathery Frau Mamma" in Longfellow's Student's Song in "Hyperion."

78. See *Catalogue of the Trent Collection,* p. 15 (36). He had also thought of a poem entitled "Secrets" or "Secreta": "theme for an immense poem — collect'g in running list all the things done in secret." (*Ibid.*)

79. In a letter to Baudelaire, January 27, 1862.

80. "Calamus," no. 39, *LG 1860,* p. 375, "Sometimes with One I I Love," *Inc. Ed.,* p. 111, ll. 3–4.

81. "Proto-Leaf," *LG 1860,* p. 11 (22), "Starting from Paumanok," *Inc. Ed.,* p. 15, §6, ll. 21–24.

82. "When Lilacs Last in the Dooryard Bloom'd" (1865), *Inc. Ed.,* p. 277, §4, ll. 6–8.

83. "Song of the Universal," *Inc. Ed.,* pp. 192–193, §2, ll. 12–15.

84. See "Enfans d'Adam," no. 2, *LG 1860,* p. 288, "From Pent-up Aching Rivers," *Inc. Ed.,* p. 77, l. 4. Even before 1855 he pro-

claimed in *Pictures*, p. 27: "But here, (look you well,) see here the phallic choice of America, a full-sized man or woman . . ."

85. "Enfans d'Adam," no. 6, *LG 1860*, p. 308 (2), "One Hour to Madness and Joy," *Inc. Ed.*, p. 90, l. 4, and "Enfans d'Adam," no. 2, *LG 1860*, p. 289, "From Pent-up Aching Rivers," *Inc. Ed.*, p. 78, l. 26.

86. "Proto-Leaf," *LG 1860*, p. 13 (35), "Starting from Pauma-nok," *Inc. Ed.*, p. 17, §10, l. 10.

87. "Enfans d'Adam," no. 14, *LG 1860*, p. 314, "I Am He that Aches with Love," *Inc. Ed.*, p. 92.

88. "Calamus," no. 14, *LG 1860*, p. 360, "Not Heat Flames up and Consumes," *Inc. Ed.*, p. 104, ll. 8–9.

89. "Calamus," no. 7, *LG 1860*, p. 353, "Of the Terrible Doubt of Appearances," *Inc. Ed.*, p. 101, ll. 12–13.

90. "Calamus," no. 19, *LG 1860*, p. 364, "Behold this Swarthy Face," *Inc. Ed.*, p. 105.

91. "Calamus," no. 5, *LG 1860*, p. 351, "For You O Democracy," *Inc. Ed.*, pp. 98–99, ll. 1–4, 7–8.

92. See Vol. I, pp. 138–139.

93. See Vol. I, pp. 172–175.

94. Lewis Brown was one of Tom Sawyer's hospital friends; he was still under treatment in Washington when the letter was written.

95. Letter to Tom Sawyer, April 21, 1863, *Coll. W*, I, 93.

96. Letter to Tom Sawyer, April 26, 1863, *Coll. W*, I, 93.

97. Letter to Tom Sawyer, May 27, 1863, *Coll. W*, I, 107.

98. Letter to Tom Sawyer, November 18, 1863, *Coll. W*, I, 186.

99. Except perhaps for this passage: "Lew is so good, so affection-ate — when I came away he reached up his face, I put my arm around him [his neck — deleted] and we gave each other a long kiss half a minute long." Letter to Tom Sawyer, April 21, 1863, *Coll. W*, I, 91.

100. *Ibid.*, p. 92.

101. On this friendship, see *Calamus*, a series of letters written during the years 1868–1880 by Walt Whitman to a young friend (Peter Doyle), ed. with an introduction by R. M. Bucke (Boston: Laurens Maynard, 1897).
The first letters date from 1868, but Peter Doyle thought they had met for the first time in 1866 (p. 23).

102. See letter to Peter Doyle dated June 1883, *SPL*, p. 1044.

103. *Ibid.*

104. *Calamus*, p. 47.

105. *Calamus*, p. 27.

106. See above, n. 102.

107. There are 41 postcards sent by Whitman to Peter Doyle

between January 15 and December 31, 1875 in the Berg Collection.

108. *Calamus*, p. 88, or *SPL*, p. 991.

109. *With WW in C*, I, 311.

110. "Peter Doyle has also come on from Washington to spend a short time here and then return with me to Philadelphia." Letter to Mrs. Gilchrist dated September 1880, Niagara Falls, America. This letter is in the Whitman Collection of the University of Pennsylvania Library.

111. *Calamus*, pp. 78–79.

112. See the following letters to Peter Doyle: August 12, 1870, *SPL*, p. 991, September 6, 1870, *ibid.*, pp. 993–994, July 10, 1874, *ibid.*, p. 1020 (in which he used a Christian phraseology in order to adapt himself to Peter Doyle who was a Catholic), August 21, 1869, *ibid.*, pp. 984–985.

113. See Vol. I, pp. 184–189.

114. See letter to Peter Doyle, dated August 21, 1869, *SPL*, p. 985. He had made such proposals before — to Tom Sawyer, as we have seen, and to one Elijah Fox, a young soldier whom he had met in the hospitals; see his letter to Elijah Fox, November 21, 1863, *SPL*, p. 935. It is to be noted that Fox was married (*ibid.*, p. 936).

115. "Democratic Vistas," *SD*, p. 247, *CP*, p. 250.

116. "The Base of all Metaphysics," *LG 1871*, p. 130 (3), *Inc. Ed.*, p. 102, ll. 11–15.

117. Preface to 1876 edition, *Inc. Ed.*, p. 518n.

118. One of the notebooks of the Library of Congress bears the following indications: "Harry Stafford — New Rep. Printing Office — March '76 visit Kirkwood (White Horse) April 1 '76."

119. Quoted by Edward Naumburg, "A Collector Looks at Whitman," *Princeton University Library Chronicle*, III (November 1941), 12–13.

120. The first sentence is taken from a letter to Harry Stafford dated June 18, 1877, but Whitman added the second sentence the next day. The last sentence quoted was written by Whitman on the back of a letter to Stafford dated May 28, 1878 (or 1879). He underlined all the words. All these letters are now in the Berg Collection.

121. He wrote him for instance: "This little piece 'Will it Happen?' is real good — stick away at it, dear son — write little pieces of your thoughts, or what you see, off-hand *at the time* — (that *always* puts life into 'em) — Keep pegging away . . ." Letter to Harry Stafford, May 28, 1878 (or 1879).

122. See his letter to Harry Stafford dated January 27 (1881):

True religion (*the most beautiful thing in the whole world* and the best part of any man's or woman's, or boy's character) consists in *what one does* square and kind and generous and honorable all days *all the time,* — especially with his own folks and associates and the poor and illiterate and in devout meditation and silent thoughts of God and death — and not at all in what he *says* nor in Sunday or prayer meeting *gas* . . .

123. "Memorandum at a Venture," *SD,* pp. 302–305, *CP,* pp. 310–311.

124. "A Backward Glance O'er Travel'd Roads," *Inc. Ed.,* pp. 533–534.

125. "My 71st Year" (1889), *Inc. Ed.,* p. 445, l. 3.

126. "From Montauk Point" (1889), *Inc. Ed.,* p. 420.

VI. "THESE STATES"

1. Preface to 1855 edition, *Inc. Ed.,* p. 488.

2. *Ibid.* The passage was taken up again in 1856 in "By Blue Ontario's Shore," *Inc. Ed.,* p. 288, §5, ll. 14–17.

3. "Here the theme is creative and has vista," *ibid.,* p. 491.

4. *LG 1855,* p. 94, "Great Are the Myths," *Inc. Ed.,* p. 705, variant reading of §1, stanza 7. The passage was suppressed in 1867, perhaps because Whitman found it too arrogant in tone.

5. *LG 1855,* p. 94, "Great Are the Myths," *Inc. Ed.,* p. 466, §3, ll. 5–8. The poem was eliminated from the book after 1876, probably because it had ceased to represent the poet's thought.

6. In 1867, for instance, Secretary of State Seward declared: "I know that Nature designs that this whole continent shall be sooner or later within the magic circle of the American Union."

7. "Our Territory on the Pacific," *Brooklyn Eagle,* July 7, 1846, *G of the F,* I, 246–247. See also "Annexation" (June 6, 1846, *ibid.,* pp. 242–244, and "More Stars for the Spangled Banner," June 29, 1846), *ibid.,* pp. 244–246.

8. See *G of the F,* I, 33.

9. *Ibid.,* p. 244.

10. "Broad-Axe Poem," *LG 1856,* p. 160, "Song of the Broad-Axe," *Inc. Ed.,* p. 617, in the passage which originally followed §11 and was suppressed in 1867.

11. "Letter to Ralph Waldo Emerson," *LG 1856,* p. 354, in which he also prophesied: "Now America is a divine true sketch. There are Thirty-Two States sketched — the population thirty millions. In a few years, there will be a Hundred States, the population hundreds of millions, the freshest and freest of men."

12. "Calamus," no. 5, *LG 1860,* p. 350 (7–8), "States!" *Inc. Ed.,* p. 477, ll. 20, 24. In 1860, there were numerous allusions to Canada (or rather "Kanada," as Whitman spelled it to preserve the Indian flavor of the word); see for instance: "Starting from Paumanok,"

Inc. Ed., p. 21, §14, l. 35; "Our Old Feuillage," p. 144, l. 9, p. 148, l. 74; "On Journeys through the States," p. 8, l. 8; "Me Imperturbe," p. 9, l. 6; "To the East and to the West." p. 111, l. 3. In 1857, in an article in the *Brooklyn Times*, he had advocated an American intervention in Cuba; see *I Sit and Look Out*, p. 52.

13. "A Broadway Pageant," *Drum-Taps*, 1865, pp. 61–65 (but composed in 1860 as the subtitle indicates: "Reception Japanese Embassy, June 16, 1860"), *Inc. Ed.*, p. 208, §2, ll. 34–35.

14. "Democratic Vistas," *SD*, p. 247, *CP*, p. 250.

15. *Calamus*, p. 127.

16. "The Prairies and an Undeliver'd Speech," *SD*, p. 142, *CP*, p. 140.

17. "A Zollverein between the U. S. and Canada," *SD*, p. 163, *CP*, p. 163.

18. "Chants Democratic," no. 20, *LG 1860*, p. 192, "I Hear America Singing," *Inc. Ed.*, p. 545.

19. "So Long!" *LG 1860*, p. 451 (3), *Inc. Ed.*, p. 702 in the passage which originally followed l. 4.

20. "Years of the Unperform'd," *Drum-Taps*, 1865, p. 53, "Years of the Modern," *Inc. Ed.*, p. 405, l. 3.

21. "Flag of Stars, Thick-Sprinkled Bunting," *Drum-Taps*, 1865, p. 65, "Thick-Sprinkled Bunting," *Inc. Ed.*, p. 402, l. 6.

22. "Passage to India" (1871), *Inc. Ed.*, pp. 343–351. On the contrary, the bombast of "Thou Mother with Thy Equal Brood" recalls the grandiloquence of his patriotic utterances in 1855, but it must be borne in mind that this poem originally was mere occasional poetry (under the title of "As a Strong Bird on Pinions Free," 1872). Besides, a few passages have a very modest tone; for example, *Inc. Ed.*, p. 381, §4, ll. 6–11.

23. "Passage to India," *Inc. Ed.*, p. 346, §5, ll. 21–25.

24. His desire to transcend nationalism is particularly clear in the following fragment found among his papers and probably dating back to 1876:

> Perhaps the chief and final clue to the books of Poems, with their varied themes, intertwinings of prose [he referred to the 1876 *Leaves of Grass* and to *Two Rivulets*] is the determined attempt or resolution to put Democracy (we could say American Democracy, but the author himself never ceases to bring in other people, the British, the French, German, etc. and never loses sight of them and indeed of entire humanity) into an imaginative and poetical statement.

CW, VI, 13. The first germs of his internationalism appeared early; see *LG 1855*, p. 87, "Song of the Answerer," *Inc. Ed.*, p. 142, §1, ll. 44–47.

25. "Song for All Seas, All Ships," *Inc. Ed.*, pp. 222–223.

26. "Pioneers, O Pioneers!" *Drum-Taps*, 1865, pp. 25–30, *Inc. Ed.*, pp. 194–197.

27. "O Star of France" (1871), *Inc. Ed.*, pp. 331–332.

28. "A Christmas Greeting" (1889), Inc. Ed., p. 450.

29. "Poetry To-day in America," *SD*, p. 297, *CP*, p. 304.

30. "Notes Left Over," "Letter to ——, Dec. 20, '81," *SD*, p. 317, *CP*, pp. 325–326.

31. "One thought ever at the fore," *Inc. Ed.*, p. 460, ll. 2–3. This poem was published after Whitman's death.

32. As is shown by this passage in *Democratic Vistas*:

This is the American programme, not for classes, but for universal man, and is embodied in the compact of the Declaration of Independence, and, as it began and has now grown, with its amendments, the Federal Constitution . . .

SD, p. 243, *CP*, p. 246.

33. See "Democratic Vistas," *SD*, pp. 244–245, *CP*, pp. 247–248.

34. *With WW in C*, III, 132.

35. *LG 1856*, pp. 354–355.

36. *Uncoll. PP*, II, 222–321; see also "The Centenarian's Story," *Inc. Ed.*, pp. 250–254.

37. E. E. Hale, for instance, who wrote in the *North American Review* in January 1856:

Mr. Whitman leaves it a matter of doubt where he has been in this world, and where not . . . What he has once seen, he has seen forever — and thus there are in this curious book little thumb-nail sketches of life in the prairie, life in California, life at school, life in the nursery, — life indeed we know not where not, which as they are unfolded one after another, strike us as real . . . (*Imprints*, p. 6.)

Burroughs himself believed that Whitman had traveled through the West and Northwest of the United States for two years (see *Notes on Walt Whitman as Poet and Person*, 1867, p. 82) and so did Bucke (see his *Walt Whitman*, p. 17).

38. See "Apostroph" (1860), *Inc. Ed.*, p. 474, l. 43, "As the Time Draws Nigh," p. 405, ll. 3–4, and "Vocalism," p. 321, §1, l. 3. All these poems date back to 1860.

39. "The idea (illustrated by Kant) that it isn't those who travel the most that know the most, or think the deepest, widest, clearest, I even think that sometimes a life devoted to persistent travel is a squandered life. The knowingest people I have met have not been the gad-abouts." Manuscript fragment in the Trent Collection; see *Catalogue of the Trent Collection*, p. 36 (item 28).

40. "Longings for Home," _LG 1860_, pp. 389–390, "O Magnet South," _Inc. Ed._, p. 393, l. 3.

41. "I have wished to put the complete Union of the States in my songs without any preference or partiality whatever." "A Backward Glance o'er Travel'd Roads" (1888), _Inc. Ed._, p. 533.

42. On the place occupied by the West in the American mind of the time, see R. R. Hubach, "Walt Whitman and the West," a digest of a thesis . . . for the degree of Ph.D., University of Indiana, 1943.

43. "The West," _Brooklyn Eagle_, December 26, 1846, _Uncoll. PP_, I, 151–152.

44. "Where the great stretch of power must be wielded," _Brooklyn Eagle_, April 2, 1847, _G of the F_, I, 25.

45. "Excerpts from a traveller's note-book," _New Orleans Crescent_, March 5, 1848, _Uncoll. PP_, I, 185.

46. "Chants Democratic," no. 11, _LG 1860_, pp. 182–183, "Thoughts," _Inc. Ed._, p. 409, §2.

47. "Calamus," no. 25, _LG 1860_, p. 368, "The Prairie-Grass Dividing," _Inc. Ed._, pp. 107–108, ll. 4, 6, 9.

48. "Calamus," no. 30, _LG 1860_, p. 371, "A Promise to California," _Inc. Ed._, pp. 108–109.

49. "Poem of Wisconsin — Poem of Missouri — Poem of Texas — Poem of Lake Superior — Poem of the Rifle — for Western Edition." _CW_, VII, 19.

50. "Eighteen Sixty-One," _Drum-Taps_, 1865, p. 17, _Inc. Ed._, p. 239, ll. 9–11. (The idea was taken up again in "Virginia — the West," _Inc. Ed._, p. 249, ll. 5–8). See also "O Tan-Faced Prairie Boy," _Drum-Taps_, p. 56, _Inc. Ed._, p. 270.
In his prose works there are also numerous traces of his boundless admiration for Westerners: "Spiritual Characters," _SD_, p. 48, _CP_, p. 43; "Sherman's Army's Jubilation," _SD_, p. 69, _CP_, p. 65; "Western Soldiers," _SD_, pp. 73–74, _CP_, pp. 69–70.

51. "Pioneers! O Pioneers!" _Drum-Taps_, 1865, pp. 25–30, _Inc. Ed._, pp. 194–197.

52. "Calamus," no. 42, _LG 1860_, p. 377, "To a Western Boy," _Inc. Ed._, p. 111.

53. "From My Last Years," _Two Rivulets_, 1876, p. 30, _Inc. Ed._, p. 487.

54. "New Poetry," _Two Rivulets_, pp. 28–30.

55. See "Mississippi Valley Literature," _SD_, p. 152, _CP_, pp. 151–152, and letter to Charles W. Eldridge, July 19, 1872, _SPL_, p. 1009.

56. "The Prairies," _SD_, p. 141, _CP_, p. 140.

57. On his trip to the West, see _SD_, pp. 139–156, _CP_, pp. 137–156.

58. See "What Best I See in Thee" (1881), _Inc. Ed._, p. 403;

"Death of General Grant" (1885), pp. 428–429, and "A Kiss to the Bride" (Marriage of Nelly Grant, May 21, 1874), p. 460.

See also "The Prairies," *SD*, p. 141, *CP*, p. 140, and "The Silent General," *SD*, pp. 153–154, *CP*, pp. 153–154.

59. "Poem of the Propositions of Nakedness," *LG 1856*, pp. 316–321, "Respondez," *Inc. Ed.*, pp. 469–472.

60. William O'Connor, *The Good Gray Poet: A Vindication* (New York: Bunce and Huntington, 1866), p. 26.

61. See in particular, William Ellery Channing in his *Remarks on American Literature* (1830), Longfellow in an article published by the *North American Review* in 1832 and entitled "Defense of Poesy," Fenimore Cooper in his *Letter to His Countrymen* (1834), and Verplanck in "The American Scholar" (1836). The subject had been in the air for several years when Emerson treated it in his turn.

62. "The American Scholar," 1837.

63. *LG 1855*, p. 28, "Song of Myself," *Inc. Ed.*, p. 43, §23, l. 2.

64. Preface to 1855 edition, *Inc. Ed.*, p. 488, See also bottom of p. 489. This passage was transferred to "Poem of Many in One," *LG 1856*, pp. 182–183, "By Blue Ontario's Shore," *Inc. Ed.*, p. 288, §5, ll. 1–13.

65. "Independent American Literature," *Brooklyn Eagle*, February 10, 1847, *G of the F*, II, 237–241. See also "Home Literature," *Brooklyn Eagle*, July 11, 1846, *G of the F*, II, 244–245; "Why do theatres languish and how shall the American stage be resuscitated?" February 12, 1847, *ibid.*, pp. 314–316, and "A thought of ours about music in the United States," September 8, 1847, *ibid.*, p. 345. Apparently the problem obsessed him.

66. "Government," *Brooklyn Eagle*, July 26, 1847, *G of the F*, I, 51. See also this passage: ". . . while each babbling priest of the mummery of the past is babbling his alarm, the youthful Genius of the people passes swiftly over era after era of change and improvement . . ." *ibid.*, pp. 4–5.

67. *CW*, VI, 35–36.

68. *American Primer*, pp. 32–33.

69. *LG 1856*, pp. 347–348. He also said in the same passage: "That huge English flow, so sweet, so undeniable, has done incalculable good here and is to be spoken of for its own sake with generous praise and with gratitude."

70. "The Radicals in Council," *Brooklyn Times*, June 29, 1858, *I Sit and Look Out*, p. 46.

71. "Chants Democratic," no. 7, *LG 1860*, pp. 217–218, "With Antecedents," *Inc. Ed.*, p. 204, §2, ll. 13–14, and p. 205, §3, l. 3.

72. "Chants Democratic," no. 19, *LG 1860*, p. 192, "I was Look-

ing a Long While," *Inc. Ed.*, pp. 324-325, ll. 1-5, and variant readings p. 678.

73. Variant reading of §3 of "By Blue Ontario's Shore," *Inc. Ed.*, p. 657. On the bitterness of his attitude toward the European governments during the Civil War, see "Attitudes of foreign governments during the war," *SD*, pp. 64-65, *CP*, p. 61.

74. "Turn O Libertad," *Drum-Taps*, 1865, p. 70, *Inc. Ed.*, p. 274. We give here the original version. Ironically enough, this condemnation of the past contains a reminiscence: "the trailing glories of the past"; cf. Wordsworth's "Ode on Intimations of Immortality."

75. "Passage to India" (1869), *Inc. Ed.*, p. 343, §1, ll. 9, 10, 15.

76. *Ibid.*, §2, especially ll. 1-10.

77. "Thou Mother with Thy Equal Brood" (1872), *Inc. Ed.*, pp. 380-381, §4, ll. 1-3, 10-11. He had already paid homage to Asia in 1860 in "A Broadway Pageant," *Inc. Ed.*, pp. 207-209, §3, 4.

78. "Song of the Exposition" (1871), *Inc. Ed.*, p. 168, §5, ll. 1-2.

79. "Democratic Vistas," *SD*, p. 241 (2nd §) and 253 (2nd §), *CP*, p. 244 (2nd §) and 254-255.

80. "Poetry To-day in America," *SD*, p. 301, *CP*, p. 306.

81. "A Backward Glance o'er Travel'd Roads" (1888), *Inc. Ed.*, p. 529.

82. *Good-Bye My Fancy*, 1891, p. 34, *CP*, p. 505. See also the disillusioned tone of his comments on the impossibility of founding a specifically literary review in America because of the sordidly mercantile spirit of his contemporaries, in *With WW in C*, II, 125-126.

83. On his worship of the Union, see "Starting from Paumanok" (1860), *Inc. Ed.*, p. 15, §6, ll. 6-13, p. 549, after l. 7, p. 548, §3; "So Long!" (1860), p. 417, ll. 19-20; "Song of the Exposition" (1871), p. 172, §8, ll. 4-9, p. 174, §9, ll. 14-24; "Wandering at Morn" (1873), p. 334, etc.

In 1891, he still declared: ". . . one of my dearest objects in my poetic expression has been to combine these Forty-Four United States into One Identity, fused, equal, and independent." *Uncoll. PP*, II, 62.

VII. DEMOCRACY — "MYSELF" AND MAN "EN-MASSE"

1. Newton Arvin, *Whitman* (New York: Macmillan, 1938), pp. 271-272.

2. *LG 1855*, p. 29, "Song of Myself," *Inc. Ed.*, p. 44, §24, l. 10.

3. See Vol. I, pp. 158-159.

4. "Salut au Monde" (1856), *Inc. Ed.*, p. 44, §11, l. 8.

5. *LG 1855*, p. 25, "Song of Myself," *Inc. Ed.*, p. 40, §20, l. 9.

6. "Proto-Leaf," *LG 1860*, p. 11 (23), "Starting from Paumanok," *Inc. Ed.*, p. 15, §7, l. 2. ". . . art and part of the commonalty, likes

the cheap ways of laborers," he wrote of himself in a review of *Leaves of Grass* which he published in the *Brooklyn Times*; see "Leaves-Droppings," *LG 1856*, p. 360.

7. "Poem of Many in One," *LG 1856*, p. 196, "By Blue Ontario's Shore," *Inc. Ed.*, p. 296, §14, l. 11. See also in *CW*, VI, 145 (134) an undated manuscript fragment: "The noble soul steadily rejects any liberty of privilege or wealth that is not open on the same terms to every other man and every other woman on the face of the earth . . ."

8. *LG 1855*, p. 53, "Song of Myself," *Inc. Ed.*, p. 72, §47, ll. 24, 26.

9. "Poem of Many in One," *LG 1856*, p. 196, "By Blue Ontario's Shore," *Inc. Ed.*, p. 295, §14, l. 8.

10. "Blood-Money," *New York Tribune Supplement,* March 22, 1850, *SPL*, pp. 503–504.

11. "Resurgemus," *New York Tribune,* June 21, 1850, *Uncoll. PP*, I, 27–30, or *SPL*, pp. 505–506.

12. *LG 1855*, pp. 87–88, "Europe, the 72nd and 73rd Year of These States" (from 1860 on), *Inc. Ed.*, pp. 227–228.

13. *LG 1855*, p. 39, "Song of Myself," *Inc. Ed.*, p. 56, §33, ll. 124–135.

14. *LG 1855*, p. 29, "Song of Myself," *Inc. Ed.*, p. 43, §23, l. 20.

15. "Poem of Many in One," *LG 1856*, p. 196, "By Blue Ontario's Shore," *Inc. Ed.*, p. 295, §14, l. 7.

16. "Poem of Many in One," *LG 1856*, p. 198, "By Blue Ontario's Shore," *Inc. Ed.*, p. 297, §16, l. 11. Same Idea in "Democratic Vistas," *SD*, pp. 229–230, *CP*, p. 232 (3rd §). See also preface to 1876 edition, *Inc. Ed.*, p. 517n (4th §).

17. "Democratic Vistas," *SD*, pp. 213–214, *CP*, pp. 217–218.

18. "Democratic Vistas," *SD*, pp. 218–219, *CP*, p. 222.

19. "Starting from Paumanok," *Inc. Ed.*, p. 12, §1, l. 3.

20. *LG 1855*, p. 85, "Faces," *Inc. Ed.*, p. 386, §1, ll. 14–15. See also "Broadway," p. 430, l. 4 — this poem appeared only in 1888, but was probably a left-over dating back to a much earlier period like several other poems published by Whitman in his old age.

21. "Poem of Joys," *LG 1860*, p. 261 (14), "Song of Joys," *Inc. Ed.*, p. 610, the passage which originally followed l. 31.

22. *LG 1855*, p. 93, "Great Are the Myths," *Inc. Ed.*, p. 465, §1, l. 4.

23. In October 1856, Whitman had underlined — and therefore approved and adopted — the following passage in a review of *Democracy in America* by De Tocqueville:

A taste for freedom. Do not ask me to analyze that sublime taste; it can only be felt. It has a place in every great heart which God has prepared to receive it; it fills and inflames it. To try to explain it to those inferior minds who have never felt it is to waste time. A document now in the Trent Collection (*Catalogue*, p. 70). Whitman had also read J. S. Mill's essay "On Liberty"; he mentions it in the very first paragraph of "Democratic Vistas."

24. Preface to 1855 edition, *Inc. Ed.*, pp. 498–499.

25. See "Song of Prudence" (1856), *Inc. Ed.*, p. 314, l. 25. Milton uses the phrase in particular in "The Ready and Easy Way to Establish a Free Commonwealth."

26. Preface to 1855 edition, *Inc. Ed.*, p. 499. See also "Europe" (1855), *Inc. Ed.*, pp. 227–228, and "Starting from Paumanok" (1860), *ibid.*, pp. 12–13, §2.

27. *G of the F*, I, 3–4.

28. "Poem of Many in One," *LG 1856*, p. 198, "By Blue Ontario's Shore," *Inc. Ed.*, p. 297, §16, l. 9.

29. "Broad-Axe Poem," *LG 1856*, p. 148, "Song of the Broad-Axe," *Inc. Ed.*, p. 160, §5, ll. 10–12, and p. 165, §12, l. 4.

30. *LG 1856*, p. 357.

31. "Poem of Many in One," *LG 1856*, p. 181, "By Blue Ontario's Shore," *Inc. Ed.*, p. 287, §4, ll. 1–4.

32. "Broad-Axe Poem," *LG 1856*, p. 142, "Song of the Broad-Axe," *Inc. Ed.*, p. 157, §3, l. 15.

33. "Leaves of Grass," no. 10, *LG 1860*, p. 224 (4), "Myself and Mine," *Inc. Ed.*, p. 201, l. 12.

34. "Walt Whitman's Caution," *LG 1860*, p. 401, "To the States," *Inc. Ed.*, p. 8, l. 1.

35. "On the Duty of Civil Disobedience," *Aesthetic Papers*, 1849.

36. "Calamus," No. 24, *LG 1860*, p. 367, "I Hear It was Charged against Me," *Inc. Ed.*, p. 107.

37. "As I Lay with My Head in Your Lap Camerado," *Sequel to Drum-Taps*, 1865–66, p. 19, *Inc. Ed.*, p. 272, ll. 5–6.

38. Victor Hugo, *Hernani*, III, 4, l. 992.

39. "We Progress!" *Brooklyn Times*, November 7, 1857, *I Sit and Look Out*, p. 43.

40. "Democratic Vistas," *SD*, p. 221, *CP*, pp. 224–225. See also *SD*, pp. 219–220, *CP*, p. 223, where democracy is represented as a higher law which governs human communities just as physical laws govern the universe.

41. "Freedom," *Two Rivulets*, 1876, pp. 31–32, *SD*, pp. 336–337, *CP*, pp. 346–347.

42. The first symptoms of this evolution appeared very early. In 1846–47, he led a campaign against capital punishment in the *Brooklyn Eagle*: "Hurrah for Hanging!" March 23, 1846, *Uncoll. PP*, I, 108–110; "Orthodox but Sanguinary," September 9, 1846,

"Hurrah for choking human lives!" June 24, 1846; "The Law of Blood — Shall Russ be hung?" January 21, 1847; "The Law of Blood," June 30, 1847; "What the defenders of the gallows say and an answer thereto," November 10, 1847 (*G of the F*, I, 97–116). So, at that time, he sympathized with humanitarian reformers, but, ten years later, his views had changed. He was now in favor of capital punishment for murderers and was indignant that it was not applied more often: "The Death Penalty," *Brooklyn Times*, January 13, 1858, *I Sit and Look Out*, pp. 46–47.

43. "Washington's Monument" (February 1885), *Inc. Ed.*, p. 430, l. 13.

44. *LG 1855*, p. 26, "Song of Myself," *Inc. Ed.*, p. 40, §20, l. 13.

45. *LG 1855*, pp. 86–87, "Song of the Answerer," *Inc. Ed.*, p. 141, §1, ll. 34–44, 50–53. See also "Song of Myself," p. 64, §41, ll. 17–26.

46. *LG 1855*, p. 21, "Song of Myself," *Inc. Ed.*, p. 34, §14, l. 15.

47. *LG 1855*, p. 80, "I Sing the Body Electric," *Inc. Ed.*, p. 83, §6, ll. 17–20.

48. *LG 1856*, p. 350.

49. "Proto-Leaf," *LG 1860*, p. 14 (37), "Starting from Paumanok," *Inc. Ed.*, p. 17, §10, l. 16; "Apostroph," *LG 1860*, p. 105, *Inc. Ed.*, p. 473, l. 9; "Chants Democratic," no. 8, *LG 1860*, p. 176 (1), "Song at Sunset," *Inc. Ed.*, p. 140, l. 3; "Chants Democratic," no. 21, *LG 1860*, p. 194 (4), "As I Walk these Broad Majestic Days," *Inc. Ed.*, p. 404, l. 19; "Chants Democratic," no. 19, *LG 1860*, p. 192, "I Was Looking a Long While," *Inc. Ed.*, p. 325, ll. 7, 10; "Song of the Redwood Tree" (1876), *Inc. Ed.*, p. 176, §1, l. 56. There was a sudden blossoming of such terms in 1860.

50. "On, on the Same, Ye Jocund Twain" (1891), *Inc. Ed.*, p. 444, l. 9.

51. "Broad-Axe Poem," *LG 1856*, p. 147, "Song of the Broad-Axe," *Inc. Ed.*, p. 160, §4, ll. 15–16.

52. "Broad-Axe Poem," *LG 1856*, pp. 149–150, "Song of the Broad-Axe," *Inc. Ed.*, p. 161, §6, ll. 3–7.

53. "Poem of Many in One," *LG 1856*, p. 181, "By Blue Ontario's Shore," *Inc. Ed.*, p. 287, §3, l. 7.

54. See Gregory Paine, "The Literary Relations of Whitman and Carlyle with Especial Reference to their Contrasting Views on Democracy," *North Carolina University Philological Club, Studies in Philology*, XXXVI (July 1939), 550–563. The author points out in particular that when Whitman prepared for publication in book-form (in *Democratic Vistas*) the essay on Democracy which he had published in December 1867 in *Galaxy*, he suppressed three violent attacks on Carlyle, because he had realized in the interval that the

censures contained in *Shooting Niagara* were founded and that he himself had more than once experienced the same indignation, as he admitted in a note (see *SD*, p. 215, *CP*, p. 261, n. 5).

Cf. also Alice L. Cooke, "Whitman as a Critic: *Democratic Vistas* with special reference to Carlyle," *Walt Whitman Newsletter*, IV (June 1958). 87–90.

55. "Leaves of Grass," no. 10, *LG 1860*, p. 224 (4), "Myself and Mine," *Inc. Ed.*, p. 201, ll. 12–13.

56. "Thoughts," no. 7, *LG 1860*, p. 411, "Thought," *Inc. Ed.*, p. 234 (Of Obedience . . .). There is a severe criticism of *Heroes and Hero-Worship* in *With WW in C*, I, 285 and in "Carlyle from American points of view," *SD*, pp. 172–173, *CP*, p. 172.

57. "Song for All Seas, All Ships" (1876), *Inc. Ed.*, pp. 222–223.

58. "Passage to India" (1871), *Inc. Ed.*, p. 344, §2, ll. 21–25, and p. 346, §5, ll. 21–25.

59. See Vol. I, Chap. IV, pp. 94–95.

60. "National Uprising and Volunteering," *SD*, pp. 21–22, *CP*, pp. 16–17; "Three Young Men's Death" (William Alcott), *SD*, p. 107, *CP*, p. 104, and "Democratic Vistas," *SD*, pp. 217–218, *CP*, p. 221.

61. "Unnamed remains the bravest soldier," *SD*, p. 36, *CP*, pp. 31–32.

62. "A New Army Organization Fit for America," *SD*, p. 52, *CP*, p. 48. He had already protested against the organization of the army which he thought too feudal and not democratic enough in "Promotion from the Ranks," *Brooklyn Eagle*, July 14, 1846, *G of the F*, II, 213–214.

63. "Rulers Strictly out of the Masses," *Two Rivulets*, 1876, p. 30, *CP*, pp. 344–345.

64. "Years of the Modern" (1865), *Inc. Ed.*, p. 406, l. 15.

65. "Democratic Vistas," *SD*, pp. 218–219, *CP*, p. 222.

66. "Democratic Vistas," *SD*, p. 218, *CP*, pp. 221.

67. "Democracy in the New World," *SD*, p. 330, *CP*, p. 340. He had written almost the same sentence forty years before in the New York *Aurora*: "Human nature is the same, whether in a republic or despotism . . ." (*Walt Whitman of the New York Aurora*, p. 98). That he should thus have repeated himself at forty years' interval shows the constancy of his political convictions.

68. "An Interviewer's Item," *SD*, p. 153, *CP*, p. 152.

69. "A Backward Glance o'er Travel'd Roads" (1888), *Inc. Ed.*, pp. 532–533.

70. "Preface to 'Democratic Vistas' with Other Papers — English Edition" (1888), *CP*, p. 447n.

71. "The Dead Emperor" (1888), *Inc. Ed.*, p. 440.

72. O'Connor and Tucker in particular were furious; cf. *With WW in C*, I, 22.

73. *Ibid.*, p. 59.

74. See "Song of Myself" (1855), *Inc. Ed.*, p. 38, §16, ll. 13–14, and p. 57, §33, l. 141.

75. "Poem of the Road," *LG 1856*, p. 233, "Song of the Open Road," *Inc. Ed.*, p. 130, §12, l. 1.

76. "Calamus," no 19, *LG 1860*, p. 364, "Behold this Swarthy Face," *Inc. Ed.*, p. 105. See also "Calamus," no. 18, *LG 1860*, p. 363, "City of Orgies," *Inc. Ed.*, p. 105.

77. "Calamus," no. 5, *LG 1860*, pp. 349–351, "States," *Inc. Ed.*, pp. 476–477, ll. 14–15, 31–33. The greater part of this poem disappeared in 1867. Whitman kept only two fragments now entitled "For You O Democracy" and "Over the Carnage Rose Prophetic a Voice." The same idea was expressed in "Calamus," no. 30, *LG 1860*, p. 371, "A Promise to California," *Inc. Ed.*, pp. 108–109; "Calamus," no. 37, *LG 1860*, p. 142, "A Leaf for Hand in Hand," *Inc. Ed.*, p. 110; "Calamus," no. 34, *LG 1860*, p. 373, "I Dreamed in a Dream," *Inc. Ed.*, p. 110, and "Calamus," no. 35, *LG 1860*, p. 374, "To the East and to the West," *Inc. Ed.*, p. 111.

78. See Vol. I, Chapter VIII, pp. 221–222.

79. See "Song of Myself," *Inc. Ed.*, p. 70, §45, l. 31 (this line was added in 1867) and "Passage to India" (1871), p. 349, §8, l. 26.

80. On the feminist movement, see Floyd Dell, *Women as World Builders; Studies in Modern Feminism* (Chicago: Forbes, 1913). On Whitman's feminism, see Helen Abbott Michael, "Woman and Freedom in Whitman," *Poet-Lore*, IX (April–June 1897), 216–237 (very superficial); Mabel MacCoy Irwin, *Whitman, the Liberator of Woman* (New York, privately printed, 1905); Paul Jordan Smith, *The Soul of Woman; an Interpretation of the Philosophy of Feminism* (San Francisco: P. Elder, 1916) (on Whitman, pp. 48–50).

81. See Vol. I, pp. 292–293.

82. She had published *Woman in the Nineteenth Century* in 1845 and it had excited considerable interest.

83. "Women," *Brooklyn Eagle*, July 24, 1846, *G of the F*, II, 87–91.

84. *Uncoll. PP*, II, 71. This passage is strangely similar to the following lines by Tennyson: "For woman is not undeveloped man/ But diverse." (*The Princess*, VII, ll. 258–259).

85. *LG 1855*, p. iv B, "Preface to 1855 edition," *Inc. Ed.*, p. 491.

86. *LG 1855*, p. 26, "Song of Myself," *Inc. Ed.*, p. 41, §21, ll. 4–6. See also *LG 1855*, p. 58, "A Song for Occupations," *Inc. Ed.*, p. 180, §2, ll. 6–8; "Proto-Leaf," *LG 1860*, p. 15 (45), "Starting from Paumanok," *Inc. Ed.*, p. 18, §12, l. 10. See also this passage in

the open letter to Emerson which takes up again some of the ideas which he had expressed in 1846: "Women in These States approach the day of that organic equality with man, without which, I see, men cannot have organic equality among themselves. This empty dish, gallantry, will then be filled with something. This tepid wash, this diluted deferential love, as in songs, fiction, and so forth, is enough to make a man vomit . . .," *LG 1856*, p. 336.

87. "Poem of Women," *LG 1856*, pp. 100–102, "Unfolded out of the Folds," *Inc. Ed.*, pp. 327–328. See also *LG 1855*, p. 80, "I Sing the Body Electric," *Inc. Ed.*, p. 82, §5, ll. 15–20.

88. "Broad-Axe Poem," *LG 1856*, p. 149, "Song of the Broad-Axe," *Inc. Ed.*, p. 161, §5, ll. 19–20, 25. See also "Apostroph," *LG 1860*, p. 106, *Inc. Ed.*, p. 473, l. 27, and "Chants Democratic," no. 4, *LG 1860*, p. 164, "Our Old Feuillage," *Inc. Ed.*, p. 147, l. 63.

89. See "Democratic Vistas," *SD*, pp. 225–226, 234–236, *CP*, 229, 237–239. See also ". . . also words to answer the modern rapidly spreading faith of the vital equality of women with men, and that they are to be placed on an exact plane, politically, socially, and in business, with men." *American Primer*, p. 9.

90. "Democratic Vistas," *SD*, p. 212n, *CP*, p. 261, n. 3.

91. "With all thy gifts," *Two Rivulets*, 1876, p. 30, *Inc. Ed.*, p. 335.

92. "Democratic Vistas," *SD*, p. 225, *CP*, p. 229.

93. "Health among Females," *Brooklyn Times,* October 17, 1858, and "Female Health," *ibid.,* March 31, 1859, *I Sit and Look Out,* pp. 116–118.

94. "Democratic Vistas," *SD*, p. 212 and n, *CP*, pp. 215–216, 261, n. 3.

95. He was more particularly thinking of corsets against which Fowler had also protested. But he objected even to the use of make-up.

96. "The Women of the West," *SD*, p. 153, *CP*, p. 153.

97. "Pioneers! O Pioneers!" (1865), *Inc. Ed.*, p. 197, ll. 80–81.

98. "Democratic Vistas," *SD*, p. 212, *CP*, p. 216.

99. "The Radicals in Council," *Brooklyn Times*, June 29, 1858, *I Sit and Look Out*, pp. 45–46. On what he thought of marriage, see *ibid.,* pp. 111–113. He condemned free love in the course of his conversations with Horace Traubel; see *With WW in C*, III, 439.

100. "Free Academies at Public Cost," *Brooklyn Times,* July 9, 1857, and "Our Daugthers," *ibid.,* September 25, 1857, *I Sit and Look Out,* pp. 53–55.

101. "Song of the Redwood Tree" (1876), *Inc. Ed.*, p. 117, §1, l. 57.

102. *CW*, VI, 27. This fragment was dated 1876. Writing to Mary Costelloe, he warned her: "Don't invest thyself too heavily in

those reforms of women movements over there." (Mary Costelloe was the daughter of rich Philadelphia Quakers and was at the time staying in England.) Quoted by Rollo G. Silver, "For the Bright Particular Star,"*Colophon,* II (Winter 1937) 214.

103. "The Queen of England," *Brooklyn Eagle,* December 5, 1846, *G of the F,* II, 140–144.

104. "For Queen Victoria's Birthday" (May 24, 1890), *Good-Bye My Fancy, CP,* p. 28. One of the reasons why he admired Queen Victoria so much was, as he indicated in a footnote, the neutrality which she had imposed on her government during the Civil War. See also *With WW in C,* III, 205–206.

105. "Europe," *Inc. Ed.,* pp. 227–228, "A Boston Ballad," pp. 224–227.

106. "Great Are the Myths," *Inc. Ed.,* pp. 465–467.

107. "Poem of Many in One," *LG 1856,* pp. 180–201, "By Blue Ontario's Shore," *Inc. Ed.,* pp. 286–299.

108. *LG 1856,* pp. 121–139, "A Song for Occupations," *Inc. Ed.,* pp. 179–185.

109. *LG 1856* pp. 268–270, "To a Foil'd European Revolutionaire," *Inc. Ed.,* pp. 310–312.

110. *LG 1856,* pp. 346–358.

111. *LG 1860,* pp. 105–194, 391–403.

112. "Inscription," *LG 1867,* p. 5, "Small the Theme of my Chant," *Inc. Ed.,* p. 434. Whitman recast this poem in 1871 and gave it the form which it now has under the title of "One's Self I Sing."

113. See Vol. I, Chapter I, pp. 25, 38–43.

114. *LG 1855,* p. 47, "Song of Myself," *Inc. Ed.,* p. 65, §42, l. 23.

115. Reprinted in *WWW,* pp. 92–113; see also Edward F. Grier's critical edition, *The Eighteenth Presidency* (Lawrence: University of Kansas Press, 1956).

116. This passage in particular:

The churches are one vast lie; the people do not believe them, and they do not believe themselves; the priests are continually telling what they know well enough is not so, and keeping back what they know is so. The spectacle is a pitiful one. I think there can never be again upon the festive earth more bad-disordered persons deliberately taking seats as of late in These States, at the heads of the public tables — such corpses' eyes for judges — such a rascal and thief in the Presidency . . .

LG 1856, p. 352.

117. "By Blue Ontario's Shore," *Inc. Ed.,* p. 298, §1, ll. 7–8; the whole of §1 was added in 1867 as well as §2, ll. 14–16, §9, ll. 8–9,

§15, ll. 11–12, §18, ll. 14–16. All these passages are still put between parentheses.

118. *Ibid.*, §1, ll. 7–8, *Inc. Ed.*, p. 286.

119. See Vol. I, Chapter VII, pp. 199–200.

120. "Democratic Vistas," *SD*, p. 255, *CP*, pp. 256–257.

121. See above, n. 54.

122. *Galaxy*, December 1867, pp. 919–933, and May 1868, pp. 540–547. *Democratic Vistas* first appeared as a small paper-bound pamphlet of 84 pages in 1871.

123. "Democratic Vistas," *SD*, p. 213, *CP*, pp. 216–217.

124. See Gay W. Allen, *Walt Whitman Handbook*, p. 303, and Clifton J. Furness' review of Fausset's book on Whitman in *NEQ*, XV (September 1942), 557–560. See also W. Maxwell, "Some Personalist Elements in the Poetry of Whitman," *Personalist*, XII (July 1931), pp. 190–199 and Albert C. Knudson, *The Philosophy of Personalism* (New York: Abington Press, 1927).

125. "Democratic Vistas," *SD*, pp. 228, 232, *CP*, pp. 231, 234–235.

126. "Democratic Vistas," *SD*, p. 230, *CP*, p. 233.

127. "Democratic Vistas," *SD*, p. 213n, *CP*, p. 261, n. 4.

128. "Proto-Leaf," *LG 1860*, p. 15 (45), "Starting from Paumanok," *Inc. Ed.*, p. 18, §12, l. 9. See also "Apostroph" (1860), *ibid.*, p. 473, l. 25, and *LG 1855*, p. 47, "Song of Myself," *Inc. Ed.*, p. 66, §42, l. 30.

129. "Poem of Many in One," *LG 1856*, p. 197, "By Blue Ontario's Shore," *Inc. Ed.*, p. 296, §15, ll. 6–10. See also in the same poem, p. 287, §3, ll. 1–15 (*LG 1856*, p. 181), and "Poem of Salutation," *LG 1856*, p. 119, "Salut au Monde," *Inc. Ed.*, p. 122, §11, ll. 33–36.

130. *LG 1855*, p. 60, "A Song for Occupations," *Inc. Ed.*, p. 182, §4, ll. 1–5.

131. This manuscript is now in the Trent Collection of the Duke University Library. The most interesting comment added by Whitman is the following:

> Where Rousseau is yet undeveloped is, in not realizing that the *individual* [underlined on the original] man or woman is the head and ideal, and the State, City, Government, or what not, is a servant, subordinate — with nothing sacred about it — nothing in a Judge or Court either — But all the sacredness is in the individual, — and the other, at most, is but a reflection of the individual's.

FC, pp. 40–41.

132. "Democratic Vistas," *SD*, p. 230, *CP*, pp. 232–233.

133. "Democratic Vistas," *SD*, pp. 218–219, *CP*, p. 222.

134. "Democratic Vistas," *SD*, p. 214, *CP*, p. 218.

135. This quotation from Jefferson served as an epigraph to the *Democratic Review* for many years and Whitman had used it as a text for one of his editorials in the *New York Aurora* (March 16, 1842); see *Walt Whitman of the New York Aurora*, A collection of recently discovered writings by Joseph Jay Rubin and Charles H. Brown (State College, Pa.: Bald Eagle Press, 1950), pp. 90–91. On this point the transcendentalists thought as Jefferson did. "The less government we have the better," Emerson wrote in his essay on "Politics" (*Essays*, 2nd series, p. 206, vol. 3 of the *Complete Works*, Boston: Houghton Mifflin, 1884). Whitman used the quotation from Jefferson once more in the *Brooklyn Eagle* on July 26, 1847 (see *G of the F*, I, 52). He developed similar ideas in his editorial of January 2, 1847, (*ibid.*, p. 54). As a consequence of this principle, it is wrong to maintain, according to him, that it is the duty of a government to make its citizens happy, for everyone is the best judge of his own happiness (April 4, 1846, *ibid.*, p. 56). He also thought that it is not the business of a government to make people virtuous against their own wishes (March 18, 1846, *ibid.*, p. 59, and March 27, 1846, "Putting down immorality by stress of law," *ibid.*, p. 63). He expressed exactly the same idea in his old age, in 1888: "Salvation can't be legislated." (*With WW in C*, I, 234.)

136. "Once before the war, (Alas! I dare not say how many times the mood has come!) I, too, was fill'd with doubt and gloom." "Democratic Vistas," *SD*, p. 223, *CP*, p. 227.

137. *LG 1855*, p. 93, "Great Are the Myths," *Inc. Ed.*, p. 705, variant reading of §1.

138. "Proto-Leaf," *LG 1860*, p. 10 (20), "Starting from Paumanok," *Inc. Ed.*, p. 15, §6, ll. 8–9. See also "To the States" (1860), *Inc. Ed.*, p. 236, and these two lines entitled "Of the Democratic Party — '58, '59, '60":

> They are providing planks of platforms on which they shall stand —
> Of those planks it would be but retributive to make their coffins.

MS kept in the Trent Collection (*Catalogue*, p. 36, item 27). See also an editorial in the *Brooklyn Times*, July 8, 1857, entitled "The Dead Rabbit Democracy" (*I Sit and Look Out*, pp. 92–94). The preface to the 1855 edition was already very bitter; see for instance *Inc. Ed.*, bottom of p. 499.

139. "Democratic Vistas," *SD*, pp. 222–224, *CP*, pp. 225–227.

140. "Death of Thomas Carlyle," *SD*, p.169, *CP*, pp. 168–169.

141. "Democratic Vistas," *SD*, pp. 226–227, *CP*, p. 230.

142. See his editorial in the *Brooklyn Eagle*, December 31, 1847, in *G of the F*, II, 212–213. In his old age, on the contrary, he once

declared to Traubel: "I agree with Dr. Bucke that man is better than he was — is constantly growing better still." *With WW in C*, III, 5.

143. "Democratic Vistas," *SD*, p. 223 (2nd para.), p. 224 (4th para.), p. 255 (2nd para.), *CP*, p. 226 (2nd para.), pp. 227–228, 256–257. See also "Origins of Attempted Secession," *SD*, pp. 261–262, *CP*, pp. 267–268.

144. Preface to 1855 ed., *Inc. Ed.*, pp. 488–489.

145. "Democratic Vistas," *SD*, pp. 216–218, *CP*, pp. 219–221.

146. "Democratic Vistas," *SD*, pp. 223–224, *CP*, pp. 226–227. The same idea already occurred in "Thought," *LG 1860*, p. 286, "Thoughts," *Inc. Ed.*, p. 398.

147. "The Tramp and Strike Questions," *SD*, p. 329, *CP*, p. 339.

148. "The Sewing-Women of Brooklyn and New York," *Brooklyn Eagle*, January 29, 1847, *G of the F*, I, 148–151.

149. "Shutting of the Stores at 8 o'clock P.M. — Junior Clerks," December 4, 1847, and "Servants," September 16, 1846, *ibid.*, pp. 152–156.

150. "Cutting down those wages," October 30, 1846, *ibid.*, pp. 156–157. See also "A Working-Woman's Savings," June 17, 1847, and "Liberality, indeed!" May 20, 1847, *ibid.*, pp. 157–158.

151. *LG 1855*, p. 47, "Song of Myself," *Inc. Ed.*, p. 65, §42, ll. 20–21.

152. "Down Below," *Brooklyn Times*, July 12, 1858, *I Sit and Look Out*, pp. 82–83.

153. "(Unemployment)," *Brooklyn Times*, October 21, 1857, *ibid.*, p. 73.

154. "The Gas Question," *Brooklyn Times*, May 5, 1857, *ibid.*, pp. 126–127.

155. "Leaves of Grass," no. 17, *LG 1860*, p. 236, "I Sit and Look Out," *Inc. Ed.*, p. 232, 1st and last lines.

156. "Democratic Vistas," *SD*, p. 255, *CP*, pp. 256–257.

157. *WWW*, p. 229.

158. "Brother of All with Generous Hand," *Passage to India*, 1871, pp. 108–111, "Outlines for a Tomb," *Inc. Ed.*, pp. 319–320. In 1876, in order to give this poem a more general meaning, Whitman added this dedication: "To any Hospital or School-Founder, or Public Beneficiary, anywhere." And, in 1881, probably realizing that he had carried flattery a little too far, he suppressed the more offensive passages: see *Inc. Ed.*, pp. 673–674.

159. *Calamus, passim.*

160. Trent Collection.

161. "The Tramp and Strike Questions," *SD*, pp. 329–330, *CP*, pp. 339–340.

162. In "How to diminish pauperism," *Brooklyn Times,* Septem-

ber 24, 1858, *I Sit and Look Out*, pp. 82–84, the solutions which he recommended were neither novel nor advanced. He thought the unemployed should be sent to more favored parts of the country and those who refused to co-operate should be shut up in poor houses made as uncomfortable as possible in order to discourage the dissipated or indolent. One year before, though, he had declared himself in favor of helping the unemployed out of public funds: "(Unemployment)", *Brooklyn Times*, October 21, 1857, *I Sit and Look Out*, pp. 72–75.

163. As is shown by a passage which he did not publish: "I find a large class of our talkers and writers, probably the largest class, always taking for granted that plenty of active manufactures, plenty of money and foreign markets, and a demand for factories, stores for millions of employees, are the crowning result and triumph of a nation." *FC*, p. 67.

164. *With WW in C*, I, 42, 113, II, 187–188, 282, III, 344.

165. *American Renaissance*, p. 543.

166. *Whitman*, pp. 113–149.

167. It is true that the first English translation of *Das Kapital* appeared only in 1887 and the first American edition in 1890 (?). Marxism spread very slowly in the United States because of the indifference to theorizing of the early American socialists. See Bertram Wolfe, *Marx and America* (New York: John Day Co., 1934).

168. *With WW in C*, II, 151, 186.

169. Sidney Morse, "My Summer with Walt Whitman," *In Re*, pp. 379–380.

170. "The Sewing-Women," *Brooklyn Eagle*, January 29, 1847, *G of the F*, I, 151.

171. See above, n. 169.

172. He described it to Morse as "containing much that was about so and gratifying." See above, n. 169,

173. *With WW in C*, III, 315 (December 1888):

I asked: Do you see a way out? — I look forward to a world of small owners. I put in: Or may be to no owners at all. He asked: What do you mean by that? no owners at all? Do you mean common owners — owning things in common? I nodded: Yes, don't you think that would be best? He said: I don't know, I haven't thought it out: it sounds best, could it be best? could it be made to work? — Can it? — Don't you say so? He laughed. You've got me on the witness stand: you're like a lawyer! — Well — But answer me: don't you say so? Then he acquiesced: I have to believe it: if I don't believe that, I couldn't believe anything.

This conversation is an excellent example of how Traubel, by plying

Whitman with questions, tried to make him subscribe to his own opinions.

Whitman also declared himself in favor of a moderate form of capitalism in "Our Real Culmination," *SD*, p. 337, *CP*, pp. 347-348, and in "Living in Brooklyn," *Brooklyn Times*, May 13, 1858, *I Sit and Look Out*, p. 145.

174. In his notes on Rousseau's *Social Contract, FC*, p. 41.

175. "Advice to the Farmer," *Brooklyn Times*, June 10, 1858, *I Sit and Look Out*, pp. 164-165, in which he advised farmers never to leave their land for the city. Same idea in "Our Real Culmination" (*SD*, p. 337, *CP*, p. 347): "There is a subtle something in the common earth, crops, cattle, air, trees, etc., and in having to do at first hand with them . . . I must confess I want to see the agricultural occupation of America at first hand permanently broaden'd. Its gains are the only one on which God seems to smile. What others — what business, profit, wealth, without a taint? . . ."

176. "Chants Democratic," no. 21, *LG 1860*, p. 194, "As I Walk These Broad Majestic Days," *Inc. Ed.*, p. 404, ll. 17-21.

177. He wrote numerous articles on this subject: "What we thought at the Institute Fair this morning," *Brooklyn Eagle*, October 6, 1846, *G of the F*, II, 59-61; "What the Free-Traders Want," December 10, 1847, *ibid.*, pp. 65-67; "What is Best for Workmen," September 3, 1846, *ibid.*, pp. 67-69; "Do such energies require protection?" October 1, 1846, *ibid.*, pp. 69-70; "A Thought," July 10, 1846, *ibid.*, p. 70.

178. *LG 1855*, p. 95, "Great Are the Myths," *Inc. Ed.*, p. 705, variant reading of §3, 3rd stanza.

179. See "Broad-Axe Poem," *LG 1856*, p. 146-150, "Song of the Broad-Axe," *Inc. Ed.*, pp. 159-161, §§4-6, and also "Song of the Exposition" (1871), *Inc. Ed.*, p. 174, §9, ll. 20-24.

180. "Proto-Leaf," *LG 1860*, p. 12(28), "Starting from Paumanok," *Inc. Ed.*, p. 16, §8, l. 6, and §7, ll. 16-17.

181. "Democratic Vistas," *SD*, p. 209, *CP*, p. 213.

182. "Democratic Vistas," *SD*, pp. 255-256, *CP*, p. 257.

183. "Poetry To-day in America," *SD*, pp. 299-300, *CP*, pp. 305-306, and "Foundation Stages — The Others," *SD*, p. 331, *CP*, p. 341.

184. "Democratic Vistas," *SD*, pp. 237-238, *CP*, pp. 240-241.

185. "Politics," *Essays, 2nd Series*, vol. 3 of the *Complete Works* (Boston: Houghton, Mifflin, 1884), pp. 195-196.

186. See "Two Hours on the Minnesota," *SD*, p. 137, *CP* p. 135, and "The true test of civilization is not the census, nor the size of cities, nor the crops — no, but the kind of man the country turns out." ("Samples of My Common-Place Book Down at the Creek," *SD*, p. 183n, *CP*, p. 204, n. 17).

187. "A Backward Glance o'er Travel'd Roads" (1888), *Inc. Ed.*, p. 534. See H. A. Myers, "Walt Whitman's Conception of the Spiritual Democracy," *AL*, VI (November 1934), 239–253.

188. "Democratic Vistas," *SD*, pp. 233–234, *CP*, p. 236.

189. "Democratic Vistas," *SD*, p. 220, *CP*, p. 223.

190. "Sun-Down Poem," *LG 1856*, pp. 211–212, "Crossing Brooklyn Ferry," *Inc. Ed.*, p. 134, §2, ll. 1, 7.

191. Unanimism was found in 1909 by Jules Romains who claimed that the study of the collective souls of human groups should supersede the analysis of individual souls. He applied these principles in a collection of poems entitled *La Vie Unanime*. On Whitman's influence on the unanimists, see Fernand Baldensperger, "Walt Whitman and France," *Columbia University Quarterly*, XXI (October 1919), 307.

192. "Sun-Down Poem," *LG 1856*, pp. 211–222, "Crossing Brooklyn Ferry," *Inc. Ed.*, pp. 134–139.

193. "Poem of the Road," *LG 1856*, pp. 236–237, "Song of the Open Road" *Inc. Ed.*, p. 131, §13, ll. 17–23.

194. "A Broadway Pageant" (written in 1860), *Inc. Ed.*, p. 206, §1, ll. 9–20.

195. *Brooklyn Times*, September 22, 1857, *I Sit and Look Out*, pp. 71–72.

196. "Rise O Days from Your Fathomless Deeps," *Drum-Taps*, 1865, p. 36, §2, *Inc. Ed.*, p. 247, §2, l. 6.

197. "Bathed in War's Perfume," *Drum-Taps*, 1865, p. 43, *Inc. Ed.*, p. 483, l. 4.

198. "Spirit Whose Work is Done,"*Sequel to Drum-Taps*, 1865–66, p. 14, *Inc. Ed.*, p. 273, ll. 1, 4.

199. "Years of the Unperform'd," *Drum-Taps*, 1865, p. 54, "Years of the Modern," *Inc. Ed.*, p. 406, ll. 20–21.

200. "Chants Democratic," no. 4, *LG 1860*, p. 163, "Our Old Feuillage," *Inc. Ed.*, p. 146, l. 47.

201. "Poetry To-day in America," *SD*, p. 299n, *CP*, pp. 307–308, n. 4.

202. "The Sobbing of the Bells" (1881), *Inc. Ed.*, pp. 414–415.

203. "Broadway" (1888), *Inc. Ed.*, p. 430.

204. "A Backward Glance" (1888), *Inc. Ed.*, p. 523.

205. *Ibid.*, pp. 529, 533, 534.

VIII. DEMOCRACY AND RACIALISM — SLAVERY

1. See Marjory M. Moody, "The Evolution of Emerson as an Abolitionist," *AL*, XVII (March 1945) 1–21.

2. *With WW in C*, III, 91 (November 13, 1888). See also p. 5:

"I was anti-slavery always: the horror of slavery always had a strong hold on me . . ." In 1882, he had already declared in *Specimen Days* ("One of Two Index Items," *SD*, p. 202, *CP*, p. 207): "I was then quite an 'abolitionist' and advocate of the 'temperance' and 'anti-capital punishment' causes . . ."

But we have seen how, as regards the latter point, his opinion changed (see above, Chapter VII, n. 41) and how he had eventually ridiculed reformers and progressists in the *Brooklyn Times* (June 29, 1858), "The Radicals in Council"; see *I Sit and Look Out*, pp. 45–46.

3. "Some Diary Notes at Random — Negro Slaves in New York," *NB*, 1888, p. 76, *CP*, p. 428. Slavery was suppressed in the state of New York only in 1827. All the other Northern states had already banned it for several years.

4. "Franklin Evans," 1842, *Uncoll. PP*, II, 183–184.

5. "Black and White Slaves," *New York Aurora*, April 2, 1842; see J. J. Rubin and Charles H. Brown, *Walt Whitman of the New York Aurora*, pp. 126–127.

6. However, we know that at Smithtown, in his youth, he had taken part in debates on slavery and spoken against the following motion: "Is the system of slavery as it exists in the South right?" The same debating society had also discussed the following motion: "Is the present abolition excitement in this country likely to be injurious to the slave population, as well as attended with evil consequences to the nation at large?" The motion was carried by a vote of six against two. It is not known with which side Whitman voted; see Katherine Molinoff, *An Unpublished Whitman Manuscript: The Record of the Smithtown Debating Society, 1837–1838* (Brooklyn, 1941). It is probable that his opinions were already about the same as in 1846. His extreme indulgence for slavery in 1842 can probably be explained by his patriotism. He excused it because the Europeans condemned it.

7. "Slavers and the Slave Trade," March 18, 1846, *G of the F*, I, 187–191.

8. *Brooklyn Eagle*, December 5, 1846, *G of the F*, I, 192–193.

9. "Democratic Doctrine," *Brooklyn Eagle*, January 16, 1846, *G of the F*, I, 195–196. The phrase "dough-face" was used for the first time by John Randolph in 1809.

10. "The Opinions of Washington and Jefferson on an Important Point," *Brooklyn Eagle*, March 11, 1847, *G of the F*, I, 199–200.

11. "Slavery in New Territory," *Brooklyn Eagle*, February 17, 1847, *G of the F*, I, 198–199. See also "The most emphatic expression of opinion on an important subject ever given by the Empire State," February 3, 1847, *ibid.*, 197–198, "New States: Shall They be Slave or Free," April 22, 1847, *ibid.*, 200–202.

12. "Rights of Southern Freemen as well as Northern Freemen," April 27, 1847, *ibid.*, 203–208.

13. *Ibid.*

14. "American Workingmen versus Slavery," September 1, 1847, *ibid.*, 213–214.

15. *Ibid.*

16. "The next blessing to God's blessing — Shall it be jeopardized?" February 6, 1847, *ibid.*, 229–230. See also "What an idea!" February 24, 1847, *ibid.*, 234–235; "The Union now and forever!" February 26, 1847, *ibid.*, 235–238, and "Disunion," May 22, 1847, *ibid.*, 238–239.

17. "Real Question at Issue!" October 28, 1847, *ibid.*, 214, and "Some Reflections on the Past and for the Future," November 3, 1847, *ibid.*, 221–222.

18. See Vol. I, Chapter I, pp. 29–30.

19. See this passage, for instance: "But now, in the South, stands a little band, strong in chivalry, refinement and genius . . . We admire the chivalric bearing (sometimes a sort of imprudence) of these men. So we admire, as it is told in history, the dauntless conduct of kings and nobles arraigned for punishment before an outraged and too long-suffering people." *G of the F,* I, 212–213.

20. See Vol. I, Chapter I, pp. 38–40.

21. "Song for Certain Congressmen," *New York Evening Post,* March 2, 1850 (under the signature of "Paumanok"), later entitled "Dough-Face Song," *SD,* pp. 339–340, *CP,* pp. 349–351; "Blood-Money," *New York Evening Post,* April 30, 1850, also signed "Paumanok" and wrongly dated April 1843 in *SD,* pp. 372–373, *CP,* pp. 389–390; "The House of Friends," *New York Tribune,* June 14, 1850, *Uncoll. PP,* I, 25–27 (the version given in *SD,* pp. 373–374, *CP,* pp. 390–391, is somewhat shortened); "Resurgemus," *New York Tribune,* June 21, 1850, *Uncoll. PP,* I, 27–30 (this poem is the only one which Whitman included in *Leaves of Grass,* under the title of "Europe, the 72nd and 73rd Years of These States" which he used for the first time in 1860).

22. "Wounded in the House of Friends," ll. 4–7.

23. See *With WW in C,* II, 204. He even contributed a few articles to an abolitionist paper, the *National Era,* edited by Gamaliel Bailey: see Rollo G. Silver, "Whitman in 1850: Three Uncollected Articles," *AL,* XIX, 301–317 (January 1948); but only the beginning of the first of these articles shows Whitman's sympathy with the Barnburners. The rest of his contributions deal exclusively with artistic life in New York.

24. *WWW,* p. 74.

25. *WWW,* p. 76.

26. *WWW*, pp. 74, 80–81.

27. See ". . . laws for informers and blood-money are sweet to the people . . . ," preface to 1855 edition, *Inc. Ed.*, p. 499, and he cites among other good actions: "all furtherance of fugitives and of the escape of slaves," *ibid.*, p. 503. He incorporated this passage in "Song of Prudence" in 1856 (see *Inc. Ed.*, p. 671, the line which originally followed l. 23).

28. *LG 1855*, p. 87–88, "Europe," *Inc. Ed.*, pp. 227–228.

29. *LG 1855*, pp. 89–90, "A Boston Ballad," *Inc. Ed.*, pp. 225–227.

30. *LG 1855*, p. 39, "Song of Myself," *Inc. Ed.*, p. 56, §33, ll. 126–135.

31. *LG 1855*, pp. 80–81, "I Sing the Body Electric," *Inc. Ed.*, pp. 83–84, §7.

32. "Poem of Salutation," *LG 1856*, p. 106, "Salut au Monde," *Inc. Ed.*, p. 115, §3, l. 15.

33. "Poem of Salutation," *LG 1856*, p. 106, "Salut au Monde," *Inc. Ed.*, p. 599, §3, the line which originally followed l. 8.

34. *LG 1855*, p. 45, "Song of Myself," *Inc. Ed.*, p. 63, §40, ll. 17–18.

35. *LG 1855*, p. 19, "Song of Myself," *Inc. Ed.*, pp. 31–32, §10, ll. 23–32.

36. "Poem of Salutation," *LG 1856*, p. 117, "Salut au Monde," *Inc. Ed.*, p. 121, §11, l. 4. See also the 1855 preface: "Now he has passed that way see after him! there is not left any vestige of . . . the ignominy of a nativity or colour. . . , *Inc. Ed.*, p. 492.

37. *LG 1855*, p. 74, "The Sleepers," *Inc. Ed.*, p. 684, the section which originally followed §6. The theme of the grandeur and beauty of the South will be still more strongly emphasized in 1860; see "Apostroph," *Inc. Ed.*, p. 474, ll. 35–36, and "O Magnet South," pp. 393–394.

38. "Letter to R. W. Emerson," *LG 1856*, p. 355.

39. See *Uncoll. PP*, II, 69.

40. Preface to 1855 edition, *Inc. Ed.*, pp. 490–491. This passage was taken up again in 1856 in "By Blue Ontario's Shore," *Inc. Ed.*, p. 659, §6, variant reading of ll. 40–41.

41. "Abolition Convention," *Brooklyn Times*, May 14, 1857, *I Sit and Look Out*, p. 88. See also Edward Carpenter, "A Visit to Walt Whitman in 1877," *Progressive Review*, I, February 1897: "Many people came to me about slavery and 'wondered' that I was so quiet about it; but in truth, I felt that abolitionists were making noise enough, and that there were other things just as important which had to be attended to."

42. See "Down Below," *Brooklyn Times*, July 12, 1858, *I Sit and Look Out*, pp. 82–83.

43. "Chants Democratic," no. 4, *LG 1860*, p. 162, "Our Old Feuillage," *Inc. Ed.*, pp. 145–146, ll. 35–37.

44. "Says," *LG 1860*, p. 418, *Inc. Ed.*, p. 480 (3), l. 1.

45. *Ibid.* (4), l. 1.

46. "So Long!" *LG 1860*, p. 452 (7), *Inc. Ed.*, p. 703, l. 2, in the passage which originally followed l. 14.

47. See Sanborn's article in the *Springfield Republican*, April 19, 1876: "My first glimpse of Whitman was under such circumstances that I could not easily forget him. It was in April 1860, when I had been seized at night by the U.S. marshal, under an unlawful warrant from Washington . . . had been taken from him by the sheriff and carried before the Massachusetts Supreme Court on a writ of habeas corpus . . . A large number of friends gathered in the Court-Room in Boston to prevent this [i.e., his being seized by the bailiffs of Washington in defiance of the state authority, if discharged] by force if necessary . . . and among them came Whitman."

48. "I never enthused greatly over Brown." *With WW in C*, III, 206. See also II, 486.

49. *Drum-Taps*, 1865, p. 51, *Inc. Ed.*, p. 202, ll. 4–6.

50. See "Song of the Banner at Daybreak," *Drum-Taps*, pp. 9–16, *Inc. Ed.*, pp. 241–246, and also a poem composed several years later, "Delicate Cluster," *LG 1871*, p. 349, *Inc. Ed.*, p. 272. Whether in his lecture on the death of Lincoln (*SD*, pp. 306–315, *CP*, pp. 315–323) or in "This Dust Was Once the Man" (*Inc. Ed.*, p. 285), he never represents Lincoln otherwise than as the champion and savior of the Union. See also "Death of President Lincoln," *SD*, pp. 68–69, *CP*, p. 65.

51. See T.O. Mabbott and Rollo G. Silver, " 'Tis But Ten Years Since," *AL*, XV (March 1943), 51–62; it is a collection of fragments of articles published by Whitman in 1874 in the *Sunday Graphic* and which he did not include in his "Memoranda during the War" (1875). "By that War, exit Fire-Eaters — exit Abolitionists," he wrote in the manner of Carlyle (p. 53). On his attitude toward Lincoln, see "Small Memoranda — A Glint inside Lincoln's Cabinet," *NB*, 1888, p. 106, *CP*, pp. 457–458. According to Hugh I'Anson Fausset (*Walt Whitman, Poet of Democracy*, New Haven: Yale University Press, 1942, p. 198), Whitman understood Lincoln's true worth only after his death in spite of what he claims in *SD* ("The Stupor Passes. . . ," p. 25, *CP*, p. 20), though Whitman does not seem to have tried to distort facts in his reminiscences. Even if he was at first somewhat distrustful of Lincoln, like most of his contemporaries, he soon realized

the high-mindedness of the new President, as is shown by a letter to his mother dated March 19, 1863 (*SPL*, pp. 897–898).

52. T. O. Mabbott and Rollo G. Silver, " 'Tis But Ten Years Since," *AL*, XV (March 1943), 54.

53. "Proto-Leaf," *LG 1860*, p. 10 (20), "Starting from Paumanok," *Inc. Ed.*, p. 549, §6, the line which originally followed l. 7, but was dropped in 1867 because it was no longer valid, and "By Blue Ontario's Shore," *Inc. Ed.*, p. 290, §6, l. 40 (added in 1867).

54. George Whitman was also indifferent to this Proclamation; see his letter to his mother, September 30, 1862, in *FC*, p. 163.

55. *LG 1871*, p. 357, *Inc. Ed.*, p. 269.

56. *Pictures*, p. 22.

57. Clara Barrus, *Whitman and Burroughs: Comrades* (Boston: Houghton Mifflin, 1931), p. 335.

58. "The Lecture Season," *Brooklyn Times*, December 12, 1857, *I Sit and Look Out*, p. 52.

59. *Shooting Niagara, and After*, 1865. In 1849, Carlyle had also written a short essay entitled "The Nigger Question." His position was close to that of Whitman: "To me individually the Nigger's case was not the most pressing in the world, but among the least so!" *Critical and Miscellaneous Essays* (London: Chapman and Hall, 1891), VI, 34.

60. *Uncoll. PP*, II, 69.

61. ". . . when I meet black men or boys among my hospitals, I use them kindly, give them something, etc." "The Wound Dresser," *CW*, IV, 195. He also mentions a few wounded Negro soldiers in "Last of the War Cases," *NB*, 1888, p. 116, *CP*, p. 467.

62. Letter to his mother, June 6, 1868, *Letters Written by Walt Whitman to His Mother from 1866 to 1872*, p. 54.

63. "Paying the 1st U.S.C.T.," "Some War Memoranda," *NB*, p. 84, *CP*, pp. 436–437.

64. Letter to his mother, April 26, 1864, *SPL*, p. 942.

65. Letter to Peter Doyle, 1872, *Calamus*, p. 97.

66. See his letters to his mother of December 3, 1867, and April 2, 1868, in *Letters Written by Walt Whitman to His Mother from 1866 to 1872*, pp. 16, 42: ". . . the streets are jammed with darkies — I tell you when they do turn out they are thicker than crows in a cornfield . . ." — "Washington is filled with darkies — the men and children and wenches swarm in all directions (I am not sure but the North is like the man that won the elephant in a raffle) . . ."

67. *With WW in C*, I, 454.

68. See above, n. 1 of Chapter VIII.

69. "This chapter [he wrote in his notes on Rousseau's *Social Contract*] is to prove that the *right* of Slavery, either through cession,

victory, sparing life, or what not, is *null* . . . He says 'The words *Slavery* and *right* are contradictory, each excludes the other.' " *FC*, p. 38.

70. "After all I may have been tainted a bit, just a little bit with the New York feeling with regard to anti-slavery." Quoted by Newton Arvin, *Whitman*, p. 31.

IX. INDUSTRIAL CIVILIZATION

1. See *Camden's Compliments to Walt Whitman, May 31, 1889, Notes, Addresses, Telegrams*, ed. by Horace Traubel (Philadelphia: David McKay, 1889), pp. 64–65. On the industrialization of the United States during the nineteenth century, see Norman Ware, *The Industrial Worker, 1840–1860, The Reaction of American Society to the Advance of the Industrial Revolution* (Boston: Houghton Mifflin, 1924), and E. C. Kirkland, *A History of American Economic Life* (New York: Crofts, 1932). On Whitman and industry, see A. L. Cooke, "Whitman's Background in the Industrial Movement of His Time," *University of Texas Studies in English*, XV (July 1935), 79–91.

2. "Democratic Vistas," *SD*, p. 247, *CP*, p. 250.

3. Whitman was perfectly conscious of his originality in this respect as is shown by his declarations to a Boston journalist in 1881:

I have also accepted as a theme modern business life, the streets of cities, trade, expresses, the locomotive and the telegraph — I have portrayed all these. Orthodox poetry had rather turned up its nose at these things, and its stock poetry of the last sixty or seventy years has remained essentially the same — something very select, not to be jarred by the shock and vulgarity and rush of business life.

Quoted by Herbert Bergman, "Whitman on His Poetry and Some Poets — Two Uncollected Interviews," *American N & Q*, VIII (February 1950), 165.

4. On the bull which smokes, pants and roars,
   Man has ridden too early,

"La Maison du Berger," ll. 143–144. On the attitude of French romantic poets to industry, see E. M. Grant, *French Poetry and Modern Industry* (Cambridge, Mass.: Harvard University Press, 1927).

5. Sidney Lanier shared the prejudices of the European romantics and used such expressions as "the hell-coloured smoke of the factories" and "the terrible towns." See Van Wyck Brooks, *The Times of Melville and Whitman* (New York: E. P. Dutton, 1947), p. 362. As to Melville, he was just as backward as Cooper and Irving, as is shown by the passage from "Cock-a-doodle-doo" quoted by Brooks, p. 245. Occasionally, however, in spite of his love of the past, Cooper could be sensitive to the functional beauty of a plough or, like Whitman, of

an axe; see F. O. Matthiessen's *American Renaissance* (Oxford University Press, 1941), p. 145, n. 2.

6. *Walden*, 1854, Chapter IV, "Sounds" (Boston: Houghton, Mifflin, 1894), pp. 180–183.

7. "The Poet," *Essays — 2nd Series* (Boston: Houghton, Mifflin, 1899), p. 23. Whitman perhaps knew the passage. At any rate, he had felt encouraged by this quotation from Lessing which he had partly underlined in ink in an article on Hume's philosophy:

We cannot forbear noticing *that of all descriptions in the ancient poets, those of mechanical and agricultural labor are the most interesting and exquisitely wrought.* The idea of indignity or disgrace did not attach itself, in the sublime age of the epos, to mechanical labor. The stigma seems to be *feudal* [in italics in the text] and is certainly the disgrace of our time. Thank God we are approaching a new age when labor shall no longer be a disgrace, but shall be dignified as in heroic ages, by sages and poets, with the highest honors of humanity; *and in the day when toil is honored and men are free, when they have ceased to "love a lord", perhaps we shall have other heroes and poets, it may be, even greater than those of antiquity — but not while we are cursed with a servile literature and a more servile art.*

From a document kept in the Trent Collection of the Duke University Library (*Catalogue of the Trent Collection*, p. 71).

8. In particular in "The Adirondacs" (1858) where he celebrated the laying of the first transatlantic cable. But the setting of the poem was still essentially rural since Emerson described above all a vacation spent in the Adirondacks.

9. He had had an English predecessor, however, in Samuel Warren who in 1851, in *The Lily and the Bee*, had drawn up rhapsodical lists of all the wonders displayed in the Crystal Palace, without, however, successfully communicating his enthusiasm to the reader.

10. LG *1855*, pp. 62–63, "A Song for Occupations," *Inc. Ed.*, pp. 626–627.

11. LG *1855*, p. 63, *Inc. Ed.*, p. 625.

12. LG *1855*, p. 63, *Inc. Ed.*, p. 627.

13. LG *1855*, p. 32, "Song of Myself," *Inc. Ed.*, p. 47, §26, l. 12.

14. LG *1855*, p. 36, "Song of Myself," *Inc. Ed.*, p. 52, §33, l. 29.

15. Preface to 1855 edition, *Inc. Ed.*, pp. 490–491.

16. LG *1855*, p. 95, "Great Are the Myths," *Inc. Ed.*, p. 705, §3, the line which originally followed l. 2 of the third stanza.

17. Letter to R. W. Emerson, LG *1856*, pp. 354–355.

18. See above, n. 11.

19. "Broad-Axe Poem," LG *1856*, pp. 154–155, 160, "Song of the Broad-Axe," *Inc. Ed.*, p. 164, §9, ll. 25–27, and p. 165, §12, l. 4.

20. Letter to R. W. Emerson, *LG 1856*, p. 349.

21. "Apostroph," *LG 1860*, pp. 106–107, *Inc. Ed.*, p. 474, ll. 33, 46.

22. "Chants Democratic," no. 20, *LG 1860*, pp. 192–193, "I Hear America Singing," *Inc. Ed.*, p. 10.

23. "Poem of Joys," *LG 1860*, p. 263 (22), "A Song of Joys," *Inc. Ed.*, p. 151, ll. 62–64.

24. "Proto-Leaf," *LG 1860*, pp. 21–22 (63), "Starting from Paumanok," *Inc. Ed.*, p. 22, §18, ll. 1, 2, 7, 9, 11. See also "Apostroph" (1860), p. 473, l. 5, and "Chants Democratic," no. 4, *LG 1860*, p. 164, "Our Old Feuillage," *Inc. Ed.*, p. 147, l. 65.

25. "Year of Meteors" (1860), *Inc. Ed.*, pp. 202–203, ll. 7, 16.

26. "Song at Sunset," *Inc. Ed.*, p. 700, l. 45 — a correction made in 1881.

27. "So Long!" *LG 1860*, p. 453 (9), *Inc. Ed.*, p. 703, ll. 7–9, in the passage which originally followed l. 14.

28. "Song of the Exposition" (1871), *Inc. Ed.*, p. 169, §5, l. 10.

29. *Ibid.*, p. 168, §3, ll. 34–38.

30. *Ibid.*, p. 169, §5, ll. 1–11.

31. *Ibid.*, pp. 169–170, §5, ll. 27–37.

32. *Ibid.*, pp. 171–172, §7, ll. 38–40. He added "Hoosac tunnels, the Brooklyn Bridge" in 1876 and "Gothard" in 1881, which shows how careful he was to keep his poems up to date.

33. "Song of the Exposition" (1871), *Inc. Ed.*, p. 173, §8, ll. 30–40. That same year, he celebrated in "Passage to India" the completion of the Suez Canal and of the first transcontinental railway and the laying of the first transatlantic cables; see *Inc. Ed.*, p. 343, §1. In 1867, after the Civil War, he called up the new agricultural machines now used in the great plains of the West, "those crawling monsters"; see "The Return of the Heroes," *Inc. Ed.*, p. 305, §8, ll. 6–12.

34. "To a Locomotive in Winter," *Two Rivulets*, 1876, pp. 25–26, *Inc. Ed.*, pp. 392–393. That same year, he emphasized in the preface to this new collection of poems "the benefits of artificial progress and civilization," preface to 1876 edition, *Inc. Ed.*, p. 506. In France, Monet painted the Saint Lazare Station in 1877 and in Italy Carducci in his *Odi Barbare* devoted a poem to a locomotive: "Alla stazione in una mattina d'autunno" (1877). Emily Dickinson had also written a poem on this subject, "The Railway Train" (*Poems, 2nd Series*, Boston: Little Brown, 1923, p. 39). See also G. Ferris Cronkite, "Notes: Walt Whitman and the Locomotive," *American Quarterly*, VI (Summer 1954), 164–172.

35. "In the Sleeper," *SD*, pp. 139–140, *CP*, p. 138.

36. "Orange Buds by Mail from Florida," *NB*, 1888, p. 35, *Inc. Ed.*, pp. 438–439.

37. "Happiness and Raspberries," *SD*, p. 115, *CP*, p. 112.
38. "Steam-Power and Telegraphs, &c.," *SD*, p. 144, *CP*, pp. 142–143.
39. "Winter Sunshine," *Philadelphia Times*, January 26, 1879, p. 8, reprinted in *New Jersey Historical Society Proceedings*, LXVI, no. 4. As Whitman never reprinted this text himself, we quote two fragments:

> All boys and the young farmers like railroad life, I notice — want to be engineers, firemen, conductors. Then the swiftness, power, absolute *doing something* which it teaches! . . . it is doubtful to me if democracy (in its bases, stimulants, educings, indirections) has had anywhere else so precious and potent an aid. Not sentimental aid — not mere words in the style of the goody-goody mush of the average reformers . . . but strong, real, rank and practical, like Nature — doing just the thing that is needed without timid regard to nicety — with an opulence of power — just what is wanted for the case and conditions that need treatment . . .

40. "Song of the Exposition," *Inc. Ed.*, p. 166, §1, ll. 1–3 (1881), and 4–10 (1871).
41. "Years of the Unperform'd," *Drum-Taps*, 1865, pp. 53–54, "Years of the Modern," *Inc. Ed.*, p. 406, ll. 14–22.
42. "Song of the Exposition" (1871), *Inc. Ed.*, p. 170, §6, ll. 12–13.
43. "Ten Minutes in the Engine-Room of a Brooklyn Ferry-Boat," *Brooklyn Eagle*, January 10, 1848, *G of the F*, II, 210–211. The year before, he had triumphantly announced to his readers that his paper had bought a new press which was infinitely more powerful than its predecessor: "Our New Press," *Brooklyn Eagle*, April 19, 1847, *G of the F*, II, 227.
44. "Song of Myself," *Inc. Ed.*, p. 65, §42, ll. 22–24.
45. See Sigmund Freud, *Leonardo da Vinci, A Study in Psychosexuality*, trans. by A. A. Brill (New York: Random House, 1947).
46. One observer commented:

> At all times he was keenly inquisitive in matters that belonged to the river or boat. He had to have a reason for the actions of the pilot, engineer, fireman and even deckhands. Besides, he would learn the details of everything on board, from the knotted end of a bucket-rope to the construction of the engine. "Tell me all about it, boys," he would say, "for these are the real things I cannot get out of books." I am inclined to think that such inquisitiveness must always have been an industrious habit with him, for his writings abound with apt technicalities.

From an anonymous article entitled "Some Recollections of the Good

Gray Poet from One of the Old Roughs," *New York World*, June 4, 1882.

47. See above, n. 43.

48. See the following note found in Whitman's papers and now kept in the Berg Collection of the New York Public Library:

Iron works — There is a forge in the Adirondack Mountains . . . A forge would be a large rude building with from one to a dozen or more charcoal fires — on which the ore is thrown and melted — the iron runs down and settles at the bottom, like a bushel-basket-shaped lump — a "loup" or "loop" they call it — The men are around these fires with huge crow-bars — they have to tell the state of the melting by the "feel" of the ore or iron, with the crow-bars.

49. *Inc. Ed.*, p. 613.

50. "Porcelain Manufactories," *Brooklyn Times*, August 3, 1857, *I Sit and Look Out*, pp. 132–138. In 1862, he devoted the whole of one of his "Brooklyniana" to the industries of Brooklyn in the *Brooklyn Standard*; see *Uncoll. PP*, II, 249–252.

51. A note in pencil on a list of patents dated May 1857 now in the Trent Collection of the Duke University Library. He had also written on an article of the *New York Times* published in 1857: "Prophecy that soon the Atlantic will be sailed nearly altogether by *Iron Ships* and that there will be *Screw Propellers*."

52. In a letter dated June 20, 1857; see Rollo G. Silver, "Seven Letters of Walt Whitman," *AL*, VII (March 1935), p. 77, or *Coll. W*, I, 43.

53. This clipping is now in the Library of Congress.

54. "Porcelain Manufactories," *Brooklyn Times*, August 3, 1857, *I Sit and Look Out*, pp. 132–133. The word had been in use since 1845.

55. *LG 1855*, p. 62, "A Song for Occupations," *Inc. Ed.*, p. 627, l. 50.

56. "Plate-Glass Notes," in "Some Diary Notes at Random," *NB*, pp. 78–79, *CP*, pp. 430–431.

57. *American Primer*, pp. 23–24.

58. *LG 1855*, p. 47, "Song of Myself," *Inc. Ed.*, p. 65, §42, ll. 17–19, and preface to 1855 edition, *Inc. Ed.*, p. 491.

59. "Broad-Axe Poem," *LG 1856*, p. 150, "Song of the Broad-Axe," *Inc. Ed.*, p. 161, §6, l. 8.

60. *LG 1855*, p. 63, "A Song for Occupations," *Inc. Ed.*, p. 184, §5, l. 32.

61. "Broad-Axe Poem," *LG 1856*, pp. 146–148, "Song of the Broad-Axe," *Inc. Ed.*, pp. 159–161, §4, 5.

62. "Democratic Vistas," *SD*, p. 209, *CP*, p. 213.

63. "Democratic Vistas," *SD*, p. 239, *CP*, p. 242.
64. "Democratic Vistas," *SD*, p. 240, *CP*, pp. 242–243.
65. "Democratic Vistas," *SD*, p. 251, *CP*, pp. 252–253.
66. "Song of the Exposition" (1871), *Inc. Ed.*, p.174, §9, ll. 20–24. See also "Passage to India" (1871), p. 344, §2, ll. 16–25.
67. *Inc. Ed.*, p. 434.
68. "Warble for Lilac-Times," *Passage to India*, 1871, pp. 96–98, *Inc. Ed.*, pp. 318–319, and p. 672, the passage which originally followed l. 24, especially l. 2 of this passage.
69. "The Return of the Heroes" (1871), *Inc. Ed.*, p. 667, the beginning of the poem, which was dropped in 1881. In that year (see n. 68), Whitman seems to have suppressed all the passages which were too unfavorable to industry. But the following year, on the contrary (see n. 70) he sang in *SD* the praises of agriculture.
70. "Our Real Culmination," *SD*, p. 337, *CP*, pp. 347–348.

X. STYLE

1. See Bliss Perry, *Walt Whitman* (Boston: Houghton, Mifflin and Co., 1906), p. 276, n. 1.
2. *LG 1855*, p. 17, "Song of Myself," *Inc. Ed.*, p. 30, §8, ll. 1–2.
3. *LG 1855*, p. 93, "Great Are the Myths," *Inc. Ed.*, p. 465, §1, ll. 4, 7–8.
4. *LG 1855*, p. 55, "Song of Myself," *Inc. Ed.*, p. 75, §51, l. 9.
5. *LG 1855*, p. 90, "There Was a Child Went Forth," *Inc. Ed.*, p. 306, l. 12.
6. *LG 1855*, p. 55, "Song of Myself," *Inc. Ed.*, p. 75, §52, l. 1. An earlier draft of the passage (p. 583) shows that originally Whitman used a perfectly normal and homogeneous vocabulary and that the introduction of a slang word was therefore conscious and deliberate. When, on the contrary, he introduced a pretentious word into a simple context, he did so inadvertently.
7. "The mountains, rivers, forests and the elements that gird them round about would be only blank conditions of matter if the mind did not fling its own divinity around them." This sentence is from an article entitled "Imagination and Fact" which had appeared in *Graham's Magazine*. Whitman wrote in the margin: "This I think is one of the most indicative sentences I ever read." *CW*, VI, 53.
8. *LG 1855*, p. 16, "Song of Myself," *Inc. Ed.*, p. 28, §6, l. 3.
9. *LG 1855*, p. 27, "Song of Myself," *Inc. Ed.*, p. 41, §21. ll. 17, 18, 20.
10. See above Part I, Chapter IV, pp. 99–101.
11. *LG 1855*, p. 27, "Song of Myself," *Inc. Ed.*, p. 41, §20, l. 33.
12. *LG 1855*, p. 35, "Song of Myself," *Inc. Ed.*, p. 571, §32, variant reading of ll. 24–26.

13. *LG 1855*, p. 35, "Song of Myself," *Inc. Ed.*, p. 51, §33, ll. 5–6, and p. 55, ll. 91–92.

14. *LG 1855*, p. 56, "Song of Myself," *Inc. Ed.*, p. 76, §52, ll. 7–8.

15. *LG 1855*, p. 26, "Song of Myself," *Inc. Ed.*, p. 41, §20, l. 31.

16. *LG 1855*, p. 34, "Song of Myself," *Inc. Ed.*, p. 50, §31, ll. 1, 9.

17. *LG 1855*, p. 47, "Song of Myself," *Inc. Ed.*, p. 65, §42, l. 15.

18. *LG 1855*, p. 38, "Song of Myself," *Inc. Ed.*, p. 55, §33, l. 93.

19. *LG 1855*, "Song of Myself," *Inc. Ed.*, p. 28, §6, l. 8.

20. *LG 1855*, p. 59, "A Song for Occupations," *Inc. Ed.*, pp. 180–181, §2, ll. 17–18, 20–21.

21. *LG 1855*, p. 55, "Song of Myself," *Inc. Ed.*, p. 74, §50, ll. 4–5.

22. Preface to 1855 edition, *Inc. Ed.*, p. 491.

23. *LG 1856*, "Poem of the Sayers of the Words of the Earth," p. 329, "A Song of the Rolling Earth," *Inc. Ed.*, p. 190, §3, ll. 13–14. See *American Primer*, p. 21: ". . . in manners, poems, orations, music, friendship, authorship, what is not said is just as important as what is said, and holds just as much meaning."

24. *LG 1860*, "Chants Democratic," no. 13, p. 185 (2), "Laws for Creation," *Inc. Ed.*, p. 324, l. 5.

25. "The words I myself put primarily for the description of them (*Leaves of Grass*) as they stand at last, is the word Suggestiveness. I round and finish little if anything; and could not, consistently with my scheme. The reader will always have his or her part to do, just as much as I have mine." "A Backward Glance O'er Travel'd Roads," *Inc. Ed.*, p. 531.

26. *LG 1855*, p. 14, "Song of Myself," *Inc. Ed.*, p. 26, §3, l. 16.

27. "A great poem is no finish to a man or woman but rather a beginning." Preface to 1855 edition, *Inc. Ed.*, p. 505.

28. "After Trying a Certain Book," *SD*, p. 198, *CP*, p. 196.

29. Emerson had already used the word "indirection." See F. O. Matthiessen, *American Renaissance*, p. 57. But Whitman may have borrowed it from Shakespeare: see *Hamlet*, II, 1, l. 66: ". . . By indirections find directions out." As to the romantics, Whitman was quite aware of what he owed to them. In "Poetry To-Day in America" (*SD*, p. 289, *CP*, 301), he founds his principle of indirect expression on a quotation from Sainte-Beuve. On the other hand, he had underlined the following passages in an article on *The Princess* by Tennyson bearing the date of 1848: ". . . the highest art, which is chiefly dependent for its effect upon suggestion, is by no means universally appreciated, as mere skillful imitation is . . ." "A poet, by becoming openly didactic, would deprive his work of that essential quality of sug-

gestiveness by which activity on the part of the reader is absolutely demanded . . ."

In an article entitled "Thoughts on Reading," he had underlined the following passages, which seem to have exerted a certain influence on his thought: ". . . it is not the idleness with which we read, but the very intensity of labor which our reading calls forth, that does us good . . . *To think* ourselves into error, is far better than *to sleep* ourselves into truth . . ." (Cf. this passage in *Democratic Vistas, SD,* p. 257, *CP,* p. 258: "Books are to be call'd for, and supplied, on the assumption that the process of reading is not a half-sleep, but, in highest sense, an exercise, a gymnast's struggle . . .") "An author enriches us not so much by giving us his ideas as by unfolding in us the same powers that orginated in them. Reading, in short, if it be truly such, and not a mere imparted drowsiness, involves a development of the same activities, and voluntary reproduction of the same states of mind, of which the author was subject in writing." Articles listed in the *Catalogue of the Walt Whitman Collection in the Duke University Library* (1945), p. 78. The very fact that Whitman always kept these articles with him shows how deeply attached he was to the ideas which were developed in them and which he undeniably adopted. He had also underlined in an article from the *American Whig Review* for January 1846, entitled "A Socratic Dialogue on Phrenology," the following sentence: "We agreed, O Phidias, that it is impossible to speak otherwise than mystically and symbolically concerning the spirit of man." (*Catalogue* . . ., p. 75). The dates of two of these articles show that his thought had already taken this course nearly ten years before the first edition of *Leaves of Grass.* Even while he was writing conventional poems, he was already thinking of another form of art.

30. *LG 1855,* p. 15, "Song of Myself," *Inc. Ed.,* p. 554, §3, variant reading of ll. 23–24. The passage was later made even more indirect by the suppression of the word "God."

31. *FC,* p. 53.

32. The study of the evolution of Whitman's imagery would reveal nothing special. The drafts which preceded the 1855 text show the chaotic profusion of the original images, but, as early as the first edition, Whitman had to some extent succeeded in simplifying and controlling them. They were never again to be as luxuriant and confused (except in "Calamus" and "Children of Adam" where he purposely took refuge in obscurity in order to tone down the boldness of his subject). This process of clarification and simplification went on during all his career. As a result, at the end of his life, Whitman wrote only very short poems built round a single image. To the last, there-

fore, images persisted in his poetry, but they lost in power what they gained in clarity.

33. *LG 1855*, p. 20, "Song of Myself," *Inc. Ed.*, p. 34, §13, l. 15.

34. *LG 1855*, p. 39, "Song of Myself," *Inc. Ed.*, p. 56, §33, l. 136.

35. "Poem of Many in One," *LG 1856*, p. 181, "By Blue Ontario's Shore," *Inc. Ed.*, p. 287, §3, ll. 2–3.

36. "Leaves of Grass," no. 15, *LG 1860*, p. 234, "Night on the Prairies," *Inc. Ed.*, p. 377, l. 7.

37. "Great Are the Myths" (1855), *Inc. Ed.*, pp. 465–467, "Grand is the Seen" (1891), *Inc. Ed.*, p. 457.

38. Killis Campbell is of the same opinion; see his article on "The Evolution of Whitman as an Artist," *AL*, VI (November 1934), 254–263. See also Rebecca Coy, "A Study of Whitman's Diction," *University of Texas Studies in English*, XVI (July 1936), 115–124.

39. *American Renaissance*, p. 531.

40. See Vol. I, Chapter VII, pp. 196–198, and Chapter IX, pp. 239–240.

41. "By Blue Ontario's Shore," *Inc. Ed.*, p. 662, §12, the line which originally followed l. 17.

42. "The Sleepers," *Inc. Ed.*, p. 684, §7, the line which originally followed l. 3. The suppression was made in 1881.

43. Here is a list of some of these suppressions: "Song of Myself," *Inc. Ed.*, p. 562, §20, ll. 11–12; p. 572, §33, ll. 43, 46–47, 126; p. 573, §34, l. 11; p. 576, §39, ll. 7, 9; p. 578, §42, ll. 19–20; "I Sing the Body Electric," p. 586, l. 24. All these suppressions date back to 1856.

44. The dispersion in 1867 of "Chants Democratic" to which "Apostroph" served as an introduction in 1860 may have been another reason for suppressing this poem.

45. See for instance *Inc. Ed.*, p. 638, l. 128. The poem was violently criticized in the *Cincinnati Commercial* when it appeared: "The poem goes on in the same maudlin manner, for a hundred lines or more, in which the interjection 'O' is employed about five-and-thirty times." The critic then quoted the line: "O I fear it is henceforth chaos!" and treacherously added: "There is no doubt of it, we do assure you." Whitman printed this article in his *Leaves of Grass Imprints*, 1860, p. 59. He also suppressed numerous O's in "A Song of Joys"; see *Inc. Ed.*, pp. 610–611, the lines which originally followed ll. 6, 31, etc.

46. See for instance "Starting from Paumanok," *Inc. Ed.*, p. 551, §11, ll. 17, 19; p. 549, §5.

47. See for instance "A Song of the Rolling Earth," *Inc. Ed.*, p. 613, §3, l. 10, and §4, second stanza.

48. "By Blue Ontario's Shore," *Inc. Ed.*, p. 657, §2, l. 4.

49. *Ibid.*, p. 658, §4, l. 11. For similar changes, see "Passage to India," *ibid.*, p. 653, §15, l. 6, and §16, l. 1.

50. "A Song for Occupations," *Inc. Ed.*, p. 622, §1, l. 17.

51. *Ibid.*, p. 633, l. 15; a correction made in 1867.

52. "Year of Meteors," p. 634, l. 11.

53. *Ibid.*, p. 607, §9, the line which preceded l. 7 of "Terminus."

54. *Ibid.*, p. 607, §9, the line which followed ll. 5 and 7.

55. *Ibid.*, p. 561, §20, the line which followed l. 7 and p. 563, the line which followed l. 16.

56. "Song of the Exposition," *ibid.*, p. 619, §3, the line which followed l. 3.

57. See for instance "As I Ebb'd with the Ocean of Life," *Inc. Ed.*, p. 639, §3, l. 16 ("the wondrous murmuring" became "the murmuring" in 1871), and "When Lilacs Last in the Dooryard Bloom'd," p. 654, the line which followed l. 2 and contained the adjective "mystic" was suppressed in 1881. See also "Out of the Cradle Endlessly Rocking," *ibid.*, p. 637, l. 132.

58. "The Artilleryman's Vision," *Inc. Ed.*, p. 651, l. 2.

59. "As I Ebb'd with the Ocean of Life," *ibid.*, p. 639, §2, l. 11.

60. *Inc. Ed.*, p. 685, §3, l. 2, and §4, l. 7.

61. "Cavalry Crossing a Ford," *Inc. Ed.*, p. 649, l. 6. See also "Thou Mother with Thy Equal Brood," *ibid.*, pp. 379, and 691, §2, l. 10.

62. "Song of Myself," *Inc. Ed.*, p. 571, §33, l. 17.

63. "By Blue Ontario's Shore," *Inc. Ed.*, p. 666, §19, l. 3.

64. "Song of Myself," *Inc. Ed.*, p. 574, §35, l. 5.

65. "As I Ebb'd with the Ocean of Life," *Inc. Ed.*, pp. 216, 638–639, §1, ll 7 and 17.

66. *Inc. Ed.*, p. 545.

67. *Ibid.*, pp. 380, 691, §3, l. 12. See also "Out of the Cradle Endlessly Rocking," *ibid.*, pp. 215, 638, l. 182.

68. "Song of Myself," *Inc. Ed.*, p. 574, §35, *passim.* See also "Camps of Green," *ibid.*, p. 701, l. 21.

69. *LG 1855*, p. 77, "I Sing the Body Electric," *Inc. Ed.*, p. 584.

70. *Ibid.*, p. 589.

71. *Ibid.*, p. 594.

72. *Ibid.*, p. 641. This title was merely the first line in 1867.

73. *Ibid.*, p. 638. Title added in 1881.

74. *Ibid.*, p. 656. Title added in 1881.

75. *Ibid.*, p. 640. Title added in 1871. In 1881 he made an interesting change in l. 3. He had originally written in 1867:

> A bell through fog on a sea-coast dolefully ringing,
> An ocean-bell . . .

In 1881, he cut out "A bell," so that we now deal with a raw sensation gradually worked into a perception.

76. *Inc. Ed.,* p. 636. In 1860 the first line was "Out of the rocked cradle," but the rhythm was not smooth enough and it was only in 1871 that the line received its present shape.

77. *Inc. Ed.,* p. 630. Title added in 1881.

78. "A Broadway Pageant," *Inc. Ed.,* pp. 208, 636, §3, l. 2.

79. *Inc. Ed.,* pp. 325, 678, l. 10. The addition of "and ready" to "A Song of the Rolling Earth," *ibid.,* pp. 191, 631, §4, l. 10, had a similar effect.

80. *Inc. Ed.,* pp. 233, 645.

81. See for instance *Inc. Ed.,* p. 533, §1, l. 1; p. 559, §15, l. 66; p. 570, §32, l. 1; p. 571, §33, l. 1; p. 575, §38, l. 1; p. 581, §45, l. 31; p. 583, §50, l. 10.

82. One could go even further back, to the time when *Leaves of Grass* was gradually taking shape in Whitman's mind. *Pictures* (published by Emory Holloway in 1927) essentially consists of a series of vignettes, similar to the ones which are to be found in *Drum-Taps*. The same remark applies to the catalogues. One of the reasons why the later editions do not contain any is that Whitman cut them up, so to speak, and published them in the form of short poems.

83. This particular poem did not appear in *Drum-Taps,* but in the 1867, edition of *LG,* p. 214.

84. "A Backward Glance O'er Travel'd Roads," *Inc. Ed.,* p. 530.

85. See Poe's "The Philosophy of Composition": "Holding in view these considerations, as well as the degree of excitement which I deemed not above the popular, while not below the critical taste, I reached at once what I conceived the proper *length* for my intended poem — a length of about one hundred lines."

86. Preface to 1855 edition, *Inc. Ed.,* p. 530.

87. Letter to O'Connor, Jan. 6, 1865, *SPL,* p. 949. But that very year he wrote in "Shut not Your Doors to Me Proud Libraries" (*Inc. Ed.,* p. 545); "The words of my book nothing, the life of it everything" — which proves that even then he considered his message more important than his art.

88. *CW,* VI, 32–33. Unfortunately this fragment bears no date. The passages in italics are underlined on the original.

89. "Says," *LG 1860,* p. 420, *Inc. Ed.,* p. 481, §7, ll. 2–3.

90. "A Backward Glance O'er Travel'd Roads," *Inc. Ed.,* p. 527.

91. Preface Note to 2nd Annex (1891), *Inc. Ed.,* p. 537.

92. Preface to 1855 edition, *Inc. Ed.,* pp. 495–496.

93. *CW,* VI, 21. This fragment bears the date of 1871.

94. "Democratic Vistas,"*SD,* p. 252, *CP,* p. 253.

95. "An Egotistical Find," *SD,* p. 143, *CP,* p. 142. The same idea is expressed in "Spirit that Form'd This Scene" (1881), *Inc. Ed.,* p. 403.

96. "Democratic Vistas," *SD*, p. 253, *CP*, p. 254. That is why during all his life he meant to write poems capable of producing the same impression on the reader as natural sights. See "On Journeys through the States" (1860), *Inc. Ed.*, p. 8, ll. 6, 13–14, "As I Ebb'd with the Ocean the Crowd," (1860), p. 638, variant reading of the beginning of §1, "A Song of Joys" (1860), p. 149, ll. 4–6, and in 1885, taking up the image of the wave again: "Had I the Choice," p. 425, ll. 5–9. In 1856, he distinguished "real poems," that is, objects, from the poems written by poets which he called "pictures"; see "Spontaneous Me," *Inc. Ed.*, p. 88, l. 8, and also "A Song of the Rolling Earth" (1856), p. 186, §1, l. 1–14.

97. He returned repeatedly to this principle of the superiority of nature over art; see in particular: "New Senses — New Joys," *SD*, p. 143, *CP*, p. 142; "Art Features," *SD*, p. 145, *CP*, pp. 144–145: "Capes Eternity and Trinity," *SD*, p. 164, *CP*, pp. 164–165; "Final Confessions — Literary Tests," *SD*, p. 199, *CP*, pp. 196–197.

98. Preface to 1855 edition, *Inc. Ed.*, p. 493.

99. See *Coleridge's Shakespearean Criticism*, ed. by T. M. Raysor, 1930, I, 224, and *Biographia Literaria*, ed. by Shawcross, 1907, II, 109. Whitman had reviewed the *Biographia Literaria* in the *Brooklyn Eagle* on Dec. 4, 1847 (*G of the F*, II, 298–299). On the theory of organic unity, see James Benziger, "Organic Unity: Leibniz to Coleridge," *PMLA*, LXVI (March 1951), 24–28, and Gay W. Allen, *Walt Whitman Handbook*, pp. 218–219, 292–302, 409–422, 428–437.

100. *CW*, VI, 189.

101. See *Uncoll. PP* and *FC*, pp. 3–7.

102. See *N & F*, p. 93 (40), and "Poem of the Singers of the Words of Poems," *LG 1856*, p. 263, "A Song of the Answerer," *Inc. Ed.*, p. 143, §2, ll. 19–20.

103. See Oscar L. Triggs, "The Growth of Leaves of Grass," *CW*, VII, 125.

104. *N & F*, p. 38 (118). He differed from Bryant in this respect and noted the fact in one of his common-place books: "William Cullen Bryant surprised me once, relates a writer in a New York paper, by saying that prose was the natural language of composition, and he wonder'd how anybody came to write poetry." *SD*, p. 184n, *CP*, p. 204, n. 17.

105. On his methods of composition, see W. S. Kennedy, *Reminiscences of Walt Whitman* (London: Alexander Gardner, 1896), p. 24 — quoted by Furness, *WWW*, p. 118, n. 11. See also Sculley Bradley and John A. Stevenson, *Walt Whitman's Backward Glances* (Philadelphia: University of Pennsylvania Press, 1947), pp. 4, 12, 13.

106. Whitman used the image himself, "Life Mosaic of Native

Moments." He had at first thought of using it as a title for *Specimen Days*.

107. *With WW in* C, III, 84.

1. *American Primer*, pp. viii–ix.

2. Ezra Pound, *ABC of Reading* (New Haven: Yale University Press, 19–34), p. 181.

3. Preface to 1855 edition, *Inc. Ed.*, p. 488.

4. "Through Eight Years," SD, p. 20, CP, p. 15.

5. CW, VI, 35 (58).

6. *LG 1855*, p. 36, "Song of Myself," *Inc. Ed.*, p. 52, §33, l. 24.

7. *LG 1855*, pp. 55, 57, 64, 84, "Song of Myself," *Inc. Ed.*, p. 75, §51, l. 9, "A Song for Occupations," p. 179, §1, l. 13, and p. 185, §6, l. 5 (in the superlative), "Faces," p. 388, §4, l. 10.

8. *LG 1855*, p. 88, "Europe . . .," *Inc. Ed.*, p. 228, l. 38.

9. *LG 1855*, p. 89, "A Boston Ballad," *Inc. Ed.*, p. 225, l. 1.

10. *LG 1855*, p. 39, "Song of Myself," *Inc. Ed.*, p. 56, §33, l. 132.

11. *LG 1855*, p. 51, "Song of Myself," *Inc. Ed.*, p. 69, § 45, l. 9.

12. *LG 1855*, p. 83, "Faces," *Inc. Ed.*, p. 386, §2, l. 4.

13. *LG 1855*, pp. 36, 41, "Song of Myself," *Inc. Ed.*, p. 52, §33, l. 25, and p. 59, §35, l. 6.

14. *LG 1855*, pp. 16, 17, 46, 58, "Song of Myself," *Inc. Ed.*, p. 28, §6, l. 7, p. 29, §7, l. 3, p. 64, §41, l. 23 and "A Song for Occupations," p. 180, §8, l. 4.

15. "Poem of Salutation," *LG 1856*, p. 103, "Salut au Monde," *Inc. Ed.*, p. 114, §1, l. 7.

16. "Poem of the Road," *LG 1856*, p. 226, "Song of the Open Road," *Inc. Ed.*, p. 126, §5, l. 2.

17. "Broad-Axe Poem," *LG 1856*, p. 151, "Song of the Broad-Axe," *Inc. Ed.*, p. 162, §7, l. 6.

18. "Poem of Salutation," *LG 1856*, p. 107, "Salut au Monde," *Inc. Ed.*, p. 115, §4, l. 4.

19. He also added "nigh" a number of times: see "Sun-Down Poem," *LG 1856*, pp. 217–220, "Crossing Brooklyn Ferry," *Inc. Ed.*, p. 137, §6, l. 15, p. 138, §9, l. 9; "Poem of the Road," *LG 1856*, p. 230, "Song of the Open Road," *Inc. Ed.*, p. 127, §7, l. 4, and also "Poem of Joys," *LG 1860*, p. 264, "A Song of Joys," *Inc. Ed.*, p. 152, l. 91.

20. "Enfans d'Adam," no. 12, *LG 1860*, p. 313, "Ages and Ages Returning," *Inc. Ed.*, p. 91, ll. 3, 8.

21. "So Long!" *LG 1860*, p. 451 (2), *Inc. Ed.*, p. 416, l. 3.

22. True, there are two verbs in the second person singular in "A Song of Joys" (ll. 121, 127), but they were added in 1871.

23. "The Return of the Heroes," *Inc. Ed.*, p. 304, §7, l. 16.

24. "The City Dead-House," *Inc. Ed.*, p. 309, l. 16, and "To a Certain Civilian," p. 272, ll. 3, 4.

25. For instance in "A March in the Ranks . . .," *Inc. Ed.*, p. 258, l. 13.

26. "Starting from Paumanok," *Inc. Ed.*, p. 21, §16, l. 3.

27. "The Centenarian's Story," *Inc. Ed.*, p. 251, l. 29.

28. For instance in "A March in the Ranks," *Inc. Ed.*, p. 258, l. 6.

29. "Delicate Cluster," *Inc. Ed.*, p. 272, l. 5, and "The Return of the Heroes," p. 301, §2, l. 10.

30. For instance, "Lo, Victress on the Peaks," *Inc. Ed.*, p. 273.

31. "Ethiopia Saluting the Colors," *Inc. Ed.*, p. 269, l. 11.

32. "Song of Myself," *Inc. Ed.*, p. 54, §33, l. 76, and p. 572.

33. "Song of the Answerer," *Inc. Ed.*, p. 140, §1, l. 1, and p. 608; also "A Song for Occupations," p. 182, §4, l. 6, and p. 624. He also added a "lo" to "Faces," p. 386, §1, l. 1, and p. 692, and an "ere" to "Song of Myself," p. 72, §47, l. 29, and p. 582. Besides, he resorted to archaisms which he had already used in the preceding editions: "betwixt" in "Calvary Crossing a Ford," p. 254, l. 1 and "jocund" in "The Return of the Heroes," p. 304, §7, l. 17.

34. *Inc. Ed.*, p. 369.

35. "Prayer of Columbus," *Inc. Ed.*, p. 352, l. 24, etc.

36. "Song of the Exposition," *Inc. Ed.*, p. 172, §8, l. 2, etc.

37. "A Riddle Song, *Inc. Ed.*, p. 397, l. 25.

38. "Passage to India," *Inc. Ed.*, p. 343, §2, l. 5.

39. There are many examples of it in "Prayer of Columbus" and "Passage to India."

40. "Paumanok," *Inc. Ed.*, p. 420, l. 4.

41. "The Mystic Trumpeter," *Inc. Ed.*, p. 389, §1, l. 1.

42. "Thou Mother with Thy Equal Brood," *Inc. Ed.*, p. 380, §3, l. 6.

43. For instance in "Song of the Universal," *Inc. Ed.*, p. 194, §4, l. 22.

44. "Song of the Exposition," *Inc. Ed.*, p. 174, §9, l. 9.

45. "Proud Music of the Storm," *Inc. Ed.*, p. 341, §5, l. 10.

46. "The Mystic Trumpeter," *Inc. Ed.*, 391, §7, l. 1, etc.

47. "O Star of France," *Inc. Ed.*, p. 331, l. 4.

48. "Prayer of Columbus," *Inc. Ed.*, p. 352, l. 22.

49. "Death of General Grant," *Inc. Ed.*, p. 428, l. 2.

50. "Song of the Exposition," *Inc. Ed.*, p. 169, §5, l. 13.

51. "The Voice of the Rain," *Inc. Ed.*, p. 436, l. 6.

52. "Thou Mother with Thy Equal Brood," *Inc. Ed.*, p. 383, §6, l. 10.

53. "Song of the Exposition," *Inc. Ed.*, p. 168, §3, l. 30.

54. "Old Age's Lambent Peaks," *Inc. Ed.*, p. 441, l. 6.

55. "When the Full-Grown Poet Came," *Inc. Ed.*, p. 451, l. 2.

56. "By Blue Ontario's Shore," *Inc. Ed.*, p. 293, §11, l. 10; all this section was added in 1867.

57. Song of the Exposition," *Inc. Ed.*, p. 171, §7, l. 34.

58. "Wandering at Morn," *Inc. Ed.*, p. 334.

59. "A Kiss to the Bride," *Inc. Ed.*, p. 460, l. 2.

60. "A Twilight Song," *Inc. Ed.*, p. 451, l. 10.

61. "A Persian Lesson," *Inc. Ed.*, p. 454, l. 9.

62. "The Unexpress'd," *Inc. Ed.*, p. 456, l. 9.

63. "Eidólons," *Inc. Ed.*, p. 5, l. 21.

64. "Song of the Redwood-Tree," *Inc. Ed.*, p. 175, §1, l. 6.

65. "To Think of Time," *Inc. Ed.*, p. 366, §7, l. 15.

66. "Out of the Cradle . . .," *Inc. Ed.*, p. 215, l. 165, a line added in 1867.

67. *Ibid.*, l. 3. In this particular case, however, it was no artificial return to a dead tradition, for about the same time he wrote in one of his note-books at Timber Creek: "I should say indeed that those old dryad reminiscences are quite as true as any and profounder than most reminiscences we get . . . In the revealings of such light, such exceptional hour, such mood, one does not wonder at the old story fables, (indeed, why fables?) of people falling in love-sickness with trees." "The Lesson of a Tree," *SD*, p. 90, *CP*, p. 86.

68. "To a Locomotive in Winter," *Inc. Ed.*, p. 392, l. 14.

69. *Inc. Ed.*, p. 444.

70. It must be admitted that he also occasionally suppressed a few archaisms: "thereof" in "Starting from Paumanok," *Inc. Ed.*, p. 550, §7, l. 9, and "olden" in "Song of Myself," *ibid.*, p. 572, §33, l. 124; but these few suppressions seem to have been more or less accidental and nothing can be inferred from them.

71. See "A Word about Tennyon," *NB*, pp. 65–67, *CP*, pp. 417–419; "Death of Longfellow," *SD*, pp. 193–194, *CP*, pp. 191–192; "Edgar Poe's Significance," *SD*, pp. 156–158, *CP*, pp. 156–158.

72. On archaisms in Whitman's poetry, see Lois Ware, "Poetic Conventions in *Leaves of Grass*," *Studies in Philology*, XXVI (January 1929), 47–57, and above all Rebecca Coy, "A Study of Whitman's Diction," *University of Texas Studies in English*, XVI (July 1936), 115–124.

73. *American Primer*, p. 5.

74. *LG 1855*, p. 16, "Song of Myself," *Inc. Ed.*, p. 28, §5, l. 17.

75. *LG 1855*, p. 23, "Song of Myself," *Inc. Ed.*, p. 37, §15, l. 56.

76. *LG 1855*, p. 32, "Song of Myself," *Inc. Ed.*, p. 48, §27, l. 3.
77. *LG 1855*, p. 21, "Song of Myself," *Inc. Ed.*, p. 34, §14, l. 5.
78. *LG 1855*, p. 37, "Song of Myself," *Inc. Ed.*, p. 54, §33, l. 61.
79. *LG 1855*, p. 37, "Song of Myself," *Inc. Ed.*, p. 54, §33, l. 69.
80. *LG 1855*, p. 16, "Song of Myself," *Inc. Ed.*, p. 28, §6, l. 11.
81. *LG 1855*, p. 21, "Song of Myself," *Inc. Ed.*, p. 35, §15, l. 16.
82. A complete list of the Americanisms which occur in *Leaves of Grass* will be found in the article by Rebecca Coy mentioned above in n. 72. She has omitted only one: "faucet," which occurs in "The City Dead-House," *Inc. Ed.*, p. 308, l. 7.
83. *American Primer*, p. 6.
84. *LG 1855*, p. 90, "A Boston Ballad," *Inc. Ed.*, p. 227, l. 42.
85. *LG 1855*, p. 90, "A Boston Ballad," *Inc. Ed.*, p. 227, l. 42.
86. *LG 1855*, p. 52, "Song of Myself," *Inc. Ed.*, p. 71, §46, l. 15.
87. See above, n. 72.
88. "A Backward Glance O'er Travel'd Roads," *Inc. Ed.*, p. 524.
89. *Ibid.*, p. 529.
90. On this problem, see Stuart Close, "Whitman's Catalogues," *Conservator* (April 1897), Frederick Hier, "Walt Whitman's Mystic Catalogues," *Conservator* (May 1919), 39–42, Henry Alonso Myers, "Whitman's Consistency," *AL*, VIII (November 1936), 243–257, Mattie Swayne, "Whitman's Catalogue Rhetoric," *University of Texas Studies in English*, XXI (1941), 162–178, Detlev W. Schumann, "Enumerative Style in Whitman, Rilke Werfel," *MLQ*, III (June 1942), 171–183.
91. See above, Chapter IV, pp. 102–103.
92. *LG 1855*, p. 94, "Great Are the Myths," *Inc. Ed.*, p. 466, §3, ll. 1–3. See also "What Am I After All" (1860) p. 328.
93. "Song of the Banner at Daybreak," *Inc. Ed.*, p. 241, l. 9.
94. *American Primer*, pp. 16–17.
95. *Ibid.*, p. 6.
96. *Ibid.*, p. 8.
97. "A Song of the Rolling Earth" (1865), *Inc. Ed.*, p. 186, §1, ll. 3–4.
98. *Ibid.*, p. 190, §3, ll. 9–12.
99. *American Primer*, p. 1.
100. "Poem of the Sayers of the Words of the Earth," *LG 1856*, p. 322; this poem was latter entitled "A Song of the Rolling Earth."
101. On this point, as on many others, Whitman consciously or instinctively applied principles which had already been formulated by Emerson. See, for instance, "Bare lists of words are found suggestive to an imaginative and excited mind." "The Poet," *Essays, 2nd Series* (Vol. III of *Emerson's Complete Works*, Riverside Edition), p. 22.
102. He noted in *Specimen Days* in 1881: "Many [birds] I can-

not name; but I do not very particularly seek information. (You must not know too much, or be too precise or scientific about birds and trees and flowers and water-craft; a certain free margin, and even vagueness — perhaps ignorance, credulity — helps your enjoyment of these things, and of the sentiment of feather'd, wooded, river or marine Nature generally." "Birds — and a Caution," *SD*, p. 183, *CP*, p. 182.

103. *American Primer*, p. 3.

104. In an anonymous article on "The Vanity and Glory of Literature"; see *Catalogue of the Trent Collection*, p. 80.

105. *CW*, III, 258–159.

106. Trent Collection.

107. See above, Chapter IX, p. 200. On Whitman's love of words, see C. Carroll Hollis, "Names in Leaves of Grass," *Names*, V (September 1957), 129–156; "Whitman's Word-Game," *Walt Whitman Newsletter*, IV (March 1958), 74–76; John Bernbrock, "Whitman's Language Study: Work in Progress," *Walt Whitman Review*, VI (December 1960), 69–72.

Whitman himself has told how, after talking with an old whaleman, he corrected in 1860 an inaccuracy of which he had been guilty in 1855 in "Song of Myself" (*Inc. Ed.*, pp. 52, 571, §33, l. 33). See "The Whale (Talk with Mr. Maher, an old whaleman) . . . The cow has but one calf at a birth . . . " (*CW*, VI, 136–137) and *Philadelphia Press* (March 3, 1881): "In one of my descriptions of the vast spaces of the sea occurred the line, 'Where the she-whale swims with her calves and never forsakes them.' I submitted this to an old whaler, and, after hesitating a good deal, he told me that he had never seen a she-whale with more than one calf; that all whalers believed the whale had but one calf at a time. In the next edition of my volume, I changed the line to 'with her calf and never forsakes it.' "

108. *CW*, VII, 25.

109. "Slang in America," *NB*, p. 69, *CP*, pp. 420–421.

110. *Inc. Ed.*, p. 506.

111. "Slang in America," *NB*, pp. 68–72, *CP*, pp. 420–424.

112. See C. Carroll Hollis, "Whitman and William Swinton: A Co-operative Friendship," *AL*, XXX (January 1959), 425–449.

113. See "Democratic Vistas," *SD*, pp. 256–257, *CP*, p. 258.

114. See preceding chapter, p. 208.

115. See *Dictionary of American English* and C. Carroll Hollis, "Whitman and the American Idiom," *Quarterly Journal of Speech*, XLIII (December 1957), p. 411.

116. See Louise Pound, "Walt Whitman's Neologisms," *American Mercury*, IV (February 1925), 199–201.

117. *LG 1855*, p. 18, "Song of Myself," *Inc. Ed.*, p. 30, §8, l. 7.

118. *LG 1855*, p. 42, "Song of Myself," *Inc. Ed.*, p. 60, §36, l. 10.
119. *LG 1855*, p. 91, "There Was a Child Went Forth," *Inc. Ed.*, p. 306, l. 19.
120. One should also add "erysipalite," "The Sleepers" (1855), *Inc. Ed.*, p. 360, §7, l. 24.
121. *Inc. Ed.*, p. 9.
122. "Passage to India" (1869), *Inc. Ed.*, p. 343, §2, l. 2.
123. "Starting from Paumanok" (1860), *Inc. Ed.*, p. 14, §5, l. 11.
124. "The Return of the Heroes" (1867), *Inc. Ed.*, p. 302, §3, ll. 12, 13.
125. "When Lilacs Last . . . ," *Inc. Ed.*, p. 281, §14, l. 40.
126. "To a Foil'd European Revolutionaire," *Inc. Ed.*, p. 312, l. 28. This word was added in 1860.
127. "Song of the Exposition," *Inc. Ed.*, p. 173, §8, l. 45.
128. "Lo, Victress on the Peaks" (1856–1866), *Inc. Ed.*, p. 273.
129. "A Broadway Pageant" (1865), *Inc. Ed.*, p. 207, §2, l. 6.
130. "Starting from Paumanok" (1860), *Inc. Ed.*, p. 14, §5, l. 12.
131. "Song of the Exposition" (1871), *Inc. Ed.*, p. 171, §7, l. 24.
132. "Mediums" (1860), *Inc. Ed.*, p. 399, l. 7.
133. Title of an 1860 poem; see *Inc. Ed.*, p. 473.
134. "On the Same Picture," *Inc. Ed.*, p. 463, l. 3.
135. "Song of Prudence," *Inc. Ed.*, p. 314, l. 19. Whitman's use of "literat" dates back to 1867.
136. "Me Imperturbe" (1860), *Inc. Ed.*, p. 9; see C. Carroll Hollis, "Whitman and the American Idiom," *Quarterly Journal of Speech*, XLIII (December 1957), p. 413 B.
137. "Apostroph" (1860), *Inc. Ed.*, p. 474, l. 43.
138. "Ages and Ages Returning at Intervals" (1860), *Inc. Ed.*, p. 91, l. 6.
139. "Vocalism," *Inc. Ed.*, p. 674, §1, the line which originally preceded l. 1 and which was suppressed in 1881. It is probably the only neologism that Whitman ever rejected.
140. "A Hand-Mirror" (1860), *Inc. Ed.*, p. 228, l. 5.
141. "Omnes" in "Starting from Paumanok" (1860), *Inc. Ed.*, p. 15, §7, l. 4, "odium" in "When I Peruse the Conquer'd Fame" (1860), p. 108, l. 4, "trinitas" in "Passage to India" (1869), *Inc. Ed.*, p. 347, §5, l. 31, "mater" in "Apostroph" (1860), p. 473, l. 1.
142. "Americanos" in "Starting from Paumanok" (1860), *Inc. Ed.*, p. 13, §2, l. 18, §3, l. 1, "Libertad," *ibid.*, l. 2. The word is also to be found in "Apostroph" (1860), p. 474, l. 53, "A Broadway Pageant" (1860), p. 206, §5, p. 208, §3, l. 1, p. 209, §3, l. 16 and "As I Walk These Broad Majestic Days" (1860), p. 404, l. 19. According to T. O. Mabbott, "Walt Whitman's Use of 'Libertad,' " *N & Q*, CLXXIV (May 1921), 367–368, Whitman found this word on the

Mexican silver coins which were legal tender in the United States until 1857 and were quite common.

143. He had already used a few French words in the first two editions:

"amies" in "Song of Myself," *Inc. Ed.*, §22, l. 13; see also variant reading of §32, ll. 16, 17, p. 570. In 1855 he used the feminine form "amie" as if it were a masculine.

"chef-d'oeuvre" (mis-spelled or misprinted "chef-d'ouvre" in 1855, p. 34), in "Song of Myself," *Inc. Ed.*, p. 50, §31, l. 3.

"accouche," "accouchez" in "Song of the Rolling Earth," p. 187, §1, l. 28.

"accouchement" in "To Think of Time," p. 363, §2, l. 1.

"accoucheur" in "Song of Myself," p. 74, §49, l. 2.

"ennuyé" in "The Sleepers," p. 355, §1, l. 8.

"ennui" in "To You," p. 199, l. 47.

"douceur" in "The Sleepers," p. 356, §1, l. 34.

"en-masse" in "Song of Myself," p. 43, §23, l. 2.

"respondez" (either a combination of "répondez" and "to respond" or the archaic French form) in the poem which bore this title in 1856, *Inc. Ed.*, p. 469.

"delicatesse" in "By Blue Ontario's Shore," p. 287, §4, l. 12.

But it was after 1860 that such borrowings from the French multiplied:

"allons" in "Song of the Open Road," *Inc. Ed.*, p. 128, §9, l. 1, and *passim* throughout the poem.

"éclaircissement" in "A Thought of Columbus" (1891), p. 464, l. 17, and in "On, on the Same, Ye Jocund Twain," p. 444, l. 6.

"ennui" in "Song of Joys," p. 154, l. 136 (in a passage added in 1871), in "As I Sit Writing Here" (1888), p. 442, l. 3, and "Ah, Poverties, Wincings and Sulky Retreats" (1865), p. 398, l. 8.

"ensemble" in "Starting from Paumanok" (1860), p. 19, §12, l. 18, "Song of the Exposition" (1871), p. 169, §5, l. 14, "Song of the Universal" (1874), p. 194, §4, l. 18, "Thou Mother with Thy Equal Brood" (1872), p. 383, §6, l. 5.

"delicatesse" in "Spirit that Form'd this Scene" (1881), p. 403, l. 9.

"eclat" in "As I Walk These Broad Majestic Days" (1860), p. 404, l. 7.

"débouché" in "Last of Ebb, and Daylight Waning" (1885), p. 426, l. 12.

"habitan" (an incorrect form apparently deduced from the plural "habitans" which was then the standard plural; all words in *-nt* had their plural in *-ns*; this was the only spelling accepted by the *Diction-*

naire de l'Académie from 1798 to 1878) in "To a Historian," p. 3, l. 4 (1871 version).

"habitans" in "Our Old Feuillage" (1860), p. 144, l. 11.

"habitué" in "To a Historian" (1860), p. 542, l. 5, and "Song of the Open Road" (1860), p. 130, §12, l. 5.

"formules," *ibid.*, p. 129, §10, ll. 5, 6.

"soirée" in "City of Orgies" (1860), p. 105, l. 6.

"nonchalance" "A Song of Joys" (1860), p. 155, l. 150.

"aplomb" in "Song at Sunset" (1860), p. 410, l. 16.

"melange" in "Starting from Paumanok" (1860), p. 17, §10, l. 6.

"en-masse" in "Starting from Paumanok" (1860), p. 550, §7, variant reading of l. 2. The phrase was dropped in 1871 — but it subsisted in other contexts.

"ma femme," *ibid.*, p. 18, §12, l. 2. Also in "For You O Democracy" (1860), p. 99, l. 10, and "France" (1860), p. 201, l. 28.

"trottoirs" in "You Felons on Trial in Court" (1860), p. 323, l. 5, and "Mannahatta" (1860), p. 395, l. 17.

"fils" in "Apostroph" (1860), p. 473, l. 1.

"feuillage," *ibid.*, l. 21, and in "Our Old Feuillage" (1960) p. 144.

"Salut au Monde," p. 114; this title was first used in 1860.

"arriere" in "Our Old Feuillage" (1860), p. 377, l. 7.

"élève" in "To a Western Boy" (1860), p. 111, l. 1.

"chansonniers" in "France" (1860), p. 200, l. 22, and "The Centenarian's Story" (1865), p. 253, l. 96.

On all these borrowings from the French, see Louise Pound, "Walt Whitman and the French Language," *American Speech*, I (May 1926), 421–430. Between 1857 and 1859, Whitman published in the *Brooklyn Times* an article entitled "Appendant for Working People, Young Men and Women, and for Boys and Girls" (a title which reads somewhat like some of the titles he used in *Leaves of Grass* in 1856) in which he gave a long list of French words preceded by this note: "A few Foreign Words, mostly French, put down suggestively. Some of these are tip-top words, much needed in English — all have been more or less used in affected writings, but no more than one or two, if any have yet been admitted to the houses of the common people" (*New York Dissected*, pp. 61–65.) Thus his use of French words was not a matter of affectation: on the contrary, he wanted to popularize and acclimatize in English a number of new words which he considered particularly expressive.

144. See Esther Shephard, *Walt Whitman's Pose.*

145. A contributor to the *Critic* offered another explanation for all these borrowings: "He shows crudely the American way of incorporating into the language a handy or high-sounding word without elaborate examination of its original meaning, just as we absorb the

different nationalities that crowd over from Europe." *Essays from the "Critic"* Boston: James R. Osgood, 1882, pp. 182–183.

146. With one exception, however, for he remained faithful to "Libertad" which he used again in "Turn O Libertad" and "Lo, Victress on the Peaks" in 1865. On the contrary, he suppressed a few French words and phrases: "mon cher" which he replaced by "dear friend" in "To a Pupil," *Inc. Ed.*, pp. 327, 679, l. 6, and by "dear son" in "Starting from Paumanok," pp. 17, 550, §9, l. 4.

147. On his use of Italian words, see Louise Pound, "Walt Whitman and Italian Music," *American Mercury*, VI (September 1925), 58–63. He used the following Italian words in "Proud Music of the Storm": "cantabile" (p. 337, §2, l. 9), "Paradiso" (p. 338, §2, l. 35), "tutti" (§2, l. 39), "Italia" (p. 339, §3, l. 17), "soprani, tenori, bassi" (p. 341, §5, l. 8). He also used "Libertad" once more (p. 330, §3, l. 27) and resorted to a French word "chansons" (p. 339, §3, l. 16). In the same year he used a new French word "émigré" in "Song of the Exposition (p. 168, §3, l. 33) and "reservoir" in "Passage to India" (p. 349, §8, l. 24) and a few years later "ateliers" in "Eidólons" (1876) (p. 4, l. 15). New Latin words also appeared: "animus" in "Song of the Exposition" (p. 619 in the line which originally followed l. 32 in §3), "Victoria" in "Proud Music of the Storm" (p. 337, §1, l. 11) and "scenas" (with an English plural) in the preface to the 1872 edition (*Inc. Ed.*, p. 508). Before that, he had used only two Italian words: "bravuras" (with an English plural), *LG 1855*, p. 31, "Song of Myself," *Inc. Ed.*, p. 47, §26, l. 3, and "ambulanza," *LG 1855*, p. 40, "Song of Myself," *Inc. Ed.*, p. 57, §33, l. 157.

148. He could not read French, as he confessed to Traubel; see *With WW in C*, I, 119. It seems that he picked up some of his borrowings from the society reports of the New York *Aurora* in which French phrases were frequently used to give *ton*. Whitman was on the staff of the *Aurora* in 1842; see Joseph Jay Rubin and Charles H. Brown, *Walt Whitman of the New York Aurora* (State College, Pa.; Bald Eagle Press, 1950), p. 11. Whitman also picked up some French phrases during his stay in New Orleans, as is shown by the articles which he contributed to the *Crescent*.

149. "You Felons on Trial in Court" (1860), *Inc. Ed.*, p. 323, l. 7.

150. "Proud Music of the Storm" (1868), *Inc. Ed.*, p. 342, §6, l. 20.

151. "As I Walk These Broad Majestic Days" (1860), *Inc. Ed.*, p. 404, l. 20, and "Apostroph" (1860), p. 475, l. 63.

152. He used the word from 1867 on and inserted it in many poems instead of "comrade"; see "So Long!" *Inc. Ed.*, pp. 418, 704, l. 53, and "As I Lay with My Head on Your Lap Camerado" (1865).

153. "So Far and So Far, and On Toward the End" (1860), *Inc.*

Ed., p. 475, l. 10, and "To the States" (1860), p. 236, which bears the following subtitle: "To identify the 16th . . . Presidentiad."

154. See J. T. Trowbridge, *My Own Story*, pp. 393–394.

155. *American Primer*, pp. 18, 29–30, 32. See also "Brooklyniana," no. 13 (*Brooklyn Standard*, 1862), *Uncoll.* PP, II, 274–275, and *Diary in Canada*, p. 55, under the date of July 3, 1878.

156. *Ibid.*

157. *Ibid.* "Starting from Paumanok," *Inc. Ed.*, p. 12, §1, l. 1, and above all pp. 21–22, §16, ll. 5–9, where he filled two entire lines with the music of Indian names.

158. "Mannahatta" (1860), *Inc. Ed.*, p. 394.

159. "Mannahatta" (1888), *Inc. Ed.*, p. 420.

160. "Ynnondio" (1888), *Inc. Ed.*, pp. 432–433.

161. Figures given by F. O. Matthiessen in *American Renaissance*, p. 529. W. H. Trimble who had compiled a Concordance of *Leaves of Grass* did not succeed in getting it published. There exists one now: Edwin Harold Eby, *A Concordance of Walt Whitman's Leaves of Grass* (Seattle: University of Washington Press, 1955).

162. This does not mean that he did not write some very fine poetry after 1860. The beauty of a poem is not a function of the richness of the language used, as is shown by the example of Racine.

163. "Song of Myself," *Inc. Ed.*, pp. 65, 578, §42, l. 7.

164. "Song of the Universal" (1871), *Inc. Ed.*, pp. 192, 632, §2, l. 17.

165. "By Blue Ontario's Shore," *ibid.*, pp. 289, 658, §6, l. 8, p. 658, §8, l. 7, and "A Woman Waits for Me," pp. 86, 588, l. 5.

166. *American Primer*, p. 6.

167. "I Sing the Body Electric," *Inc. Ed.*, p. 585, §1, ll. 5–6.

168. "Facing West from California's Shore," *ibid.*, pp. 94, 590, l. 2.

169. *Inc. Ed.*, pp. 179, 622, §1, l. 24.

170. "To Think of Time," *ibid.*, p. 686, §4, l. 14. As early as 1856, he had corrected "eat" into "ate" in the same line.

171. "Ashes of Soldiers," *ibid.*, pp. 407, 698, l. 19.

172. "The Sleepers," *Inc. Ed.*, pp. 356, 683, §1, l. 23.

XII. PROSODY

1. "Music that is Music," *Brooklyn Eagle*, December 4, 1846, *G of the F*, II, 348.

2. *With WW in C*, I, 163.

3. "To Soar in Freedom and Fullness of Power," *Inc. Ed.*, p. 459. There is a slightly different version of this piece in the collection of

Charles Feinberg; see *An Exhibition of the Works of Walt Whitman* (Detroit, 1955), p. 43, item 126.

4. He sometimes invoked the authority and precedent of the Bible to justify his use of unrhymed verses; see "The Bible as Poetry" (1888), *NB*, p. 43, *CP*, p. 396.

5. He was the popular and then despised author of *Proverbial Philosophy*; see J. J. Rubin, "Tupper's Possible Influence on Whitman's Style," *Am. N & Q*, I (October 1941), 101–102.

6. Samuel Warren, *The Lily and the Bee* (1851). This book was extremely successful and went through several editions in the United States. For its possible influence on Whitman, see Bliss Perry, *Walt Whitman*, 1906, p. 92, and H. Traubel, "Bliss Perry not disingenuous," *Conservator* (March 1907), pp. 7–8. (Bliss Perry showed that in at least one edition of *The Lily and the Bee* the make-up of the book was quite similar to that of *Leaves of Grass*. Traubel had claimed that Samuel Warren had written in prose, but he had consulted a different edition.)

7. *With WW in C*, I, 163.

8. From 1881 on, which proves that he addressed himself more and more to the ear rather than to the eye, his punctuation became still more discreet. He changed semi-colons into mere commas and simply and solely suppressed a great number of commas.

9. Quoted by Jean Catel in *Rythme et Langage dans la Première Edition des "Leaves of Grass"* (Montpellier: Causse, Graille & Castelnau, 1930), p. 71.

10. *LG 1855*, p. 14.

11. "Poem of Walt Whitman, an American," *LG 1856*, p. 7. This punctuation remained the same in later editions; see "Song of Myself," *Inc. Ed.*, p. 25, §2, l. 22.

12. *LG 1855*, p. 58. The division into four separate verses dates back to 1867; it is not mentioned in the variant readings section of the *Inc. Ed.* which rarely records such changes. Other examples are to be found in "I Hear America Singing," p. 545, ll. 10–11, "Song of Myself," p. 579, §42, l. 41. These two corrections also date back to 1867.

13. Thus the long verse which originally followed l. 6 of §18 of "Starting from Paumanok" (*Inc. Ed.*, pp. 552–553) was dropped in 1867 and so was the line which originally followed l. 11 of §6 of "By Blue Ontario's Shore" (pp. 658–659) and the line which came after l. 21 in "Who Learns My Lesson Complete?" (p. 680). This process of simplification was carried on in 1881. In that year, he suppressed the lines which followed ll. 5 and 9 in "On the Beach at Night Alone" (p. 642) and in "Warble for Lilac-Time" the lines which came after ll. 7 and 21 (p. 672), etc.

14. "Starting from Paumanok," *Inc. Ed.*, p. 18, §12, and p. 551.

There are many such examples of lightening: "Song of the Answerer," p. 609, §2, ll. 13, 22 (simplified in 1867), "By Blue Ontario's Shore," p. 658, §5, l. 7, p. 659, §6, ll. 14, 18 (same year), "Unnamed Lands," p. 670, l. 25 (and l. 11 in 1881), "Who Learns My Lesson Complete?" p. 680, l. 21. Same kind of revisions in 1881: see "Warble for Lilac-Time," p. 672, ll. 2, 18, etc.

15. This punctuation was retained in the 1871 and 1876 editions.

16. "The Evolution of Whitman as an Artist," *AL*, VI (November 1934), 260.

17. See above, Chapter X, p. 217.

18. See Gay W. Allen, *Walt Whitman Handbook*, pp. 393–401.

19. See, besides Allen, *Walt Whitman Handbook*, pp. 401–409, Autrey Nell Wiley, "Reiterative Devices in *Leaves of Grass*," *AL*, I (May 1929), 161–170.

20. And that is why Karl Shapiro has written:

> . . . A comparative
> Study of Bible English and *Leaves of Grass*
> Does not, however, reveal kinship, as some
> Maintain . . .

Essay on Rime, copyright 1945 by Karl Shapiro (New York: Random House, 1957), ll. 376–379.

21. Jean Catel and Clifton J. Furness, for instance.

22. It appears that these notes had merely been copied by Whitman and were not original compositions; see William L. Finkel, "Walt Whitman's Manuscript Notes on Oratory," *AL*, XXII (March 1950), 29–53.

23. *WWW*, pp. 197–198.

24. Gay W. Allen, *Walt Whitman Handbook*, p. 399.

25. "The Fundamental Metrical Principle in Whitman's Poetry," *AL*, X (January 1939), 437–459. See also Gay W. Allen, *Walt Whitman Handbook*, pp. 409–417.

26. G. M. Hopkins once compared Whitman's technique with his own in a letter to Robert Bridges dated October 18, 1882; it is quoted in *The Poetry and Prose of Walt Whitman*, ed. by Louis Untermeyer (New York: Simon & Schuster, 1949), pp. 1010–1013.

27. "On voit par là la simplicité à la fois et l'immense variété de l'état de connaissance qui sera celui de l'âme séparée après la mort. L'organe essentiel en sera ce temps double de la conscience dont les figures en cette vie sont la respiration, le battement de coeur, l'aigu et le grave, les brèves et les longues, l'iambe fondamental de tout langage." Paul Claudel, *Art Poétique* (1907), Article V (*Oeuvre Poétique,* Paris: Gallimard, Bibliothèque de la Pléiade, pp. 203–203).

28. Herbert Bergman, "Whitman on His Poetry and Some Poets

— Two Uncollected Interviews," *Am. N & Q*, VIII (February 1950), 163–166.

29. "Poem of the Daily Work of the Workmen and Workwomen of These States," *LG 1856*, pp. 133–134, *Inc. Ed.*, p. 626.

30. During the war, he gave a regular rhythm to "Pioneers! O Pioneers!" as befitted a poem which called up a march forward, but the meter was trochaic rather than iambic in order to suggest speed and a restless urge.

31. These examples are given by Killis Campbell in "The Evolution of Whitman as an Artist," *AL*, VI (November 1934), 261.

32. "Beginning My Studies," *Inc. Ed.*, p. 7, l. 3 and p. 543.

33. "Starting from Paumanok," *Inc. Ed.*, p. 16, §7, ll. 13–14 and p. 550.

34. See for instance the corrections made in "Starting from Paumanok," p. 550, §10, ll. 14–15, p. 552, §14, l. 15, "The Return of the Heroes," p. 667, §5, l. 2, and as early as 1860 in "Song of Myself," p. 555, §4, l. 12, and §5, l. 6.

35. *Essay on Rime*, copyright 1945 by Karl Shapiro (New York: Random House, 1957), ll. 379–382.

36. J. T. Trowbridge, "Reminiscences of Walt Whitman," *AM*, LXXXIX (February 1902), 172–173.

37. *Inc. Ed.*, p. 273, l. 7.

38. *Inc. Ed.*, p. 444.

39. "Song of Myself," *Inc. Ed.*, p. 565, §24, l. 1. See also §13, l. 9, pp. 33 and 557; in 1881, he added part of a sentence containing an inversion to a passage which already contained several.

40. "A Glimpse," *Inc. Ed.*, pp. 109, and 596, l. 1. Sometimes, on the contrary, he eliminated inversions; see for instance "This Compost," p. 669, l. 6. But this happened rarely.

41. "Sun-Down Poem," *LG 1856*, p. 214, "Crossing Brooklyn Ferry," *Inc. Ed.*, p. 135, §3, l. 23.

42. "Thou Orb Aloft Full-Dazzling" (1881), *Inc. Ed.*, p. 385, ll. 3, 4.

43. "Last of Ebb and Daylight Waning" (1885), *Inc. Ed.*, p. 425, ll. 1, 2.

44. "With Husky Haughty Lips, O Sea!" (1883), *Inc. Ed.*, p. 428, ll. 13–17.

45. *Ibid.*, p. 214, ll. 130–142.

46. *Ibid.*, p. 214, ll. 130–142.

47. "To a Certain Civilian" (1865), *ibid.*, p. 272, ll. 1, 9. In the preface to the 1855 edition, he had already declared: "The poetic quality is not marshalled in rhyme or uniformity." *Inc. Ed.*, p. 493. But this was not new; as early as 1850, he had decided to do without rhyme:" . . . poetry exists independently of rhyme . . . ," "Letter to

the Editor of the *National Era* (Washington)," quoted by Rollo G. Silver, "Whitman in 1850: Three Uncollected Interviews," *AL*, XIX (January 1948), 314.

48. *Inc. Ed.*, pp. 269, 284. In each of the triplets which make up "Ethiopia Saluting the Colors," ll. 2 and 3 rhyme together and l. 1 contains an internal rhyme.

49. "The Singer in the Prison" (1869), *ibid.*, pp. 316–317.

50. *FC*, pp. 14–16.

51. "New Poetry," *Two Rivulets* (1876), pp. 28–29; this text was reprinted in *SD*, pp. 322–323, *CP*, pp. 332–333.

52. Besides the two poems which we have mentioned, there are a few rhymes here and there in *Leaves of Grass*, and first of all, curiously enough, in "Song of the Broad-Axe" *(Inc. Ed.*, p. 156, §1) which begins with three couplets and in which l. 4 even contains an internal rhyme. Such an arrangement was quite exceptional in 1856. "Turn O Libertad" (1865) (pp. 274–275) contains a few rhymes, but except for "past-caste," they are all mere repetitions. Sometimes, too, one encounters couplets, but they are based on poor rhymes and they seem more accidental than deliberate: for example, "By Blue Ontario's Shore," p. 286, §1, ll. 1, 2, 4, 6 (all this beginning was added in 1867), "Song of the Exposition" (1871), p. 167, §3, ll. 19–20, "Darest Thou Now O Soul" (1868), p. 369, ll. 5–6, "Thou Mother with Thy Equal Brood" (1872), p. 383, §6, ll. 20–21. Except for the first one, all these examples are borrowed from poems written during or after the Civil War.

53. Carl F. Strauch, "The Structure of Walt Whitman's 'Song of Myself,'" *English Journal*, XXVII (September 1938), 597–607.

54. About the same time, he tried to insert a sort of rudimentary burden into "By Blue Ontario's Shore," for in 1867 he added at the end of a number of paragraphs in this poem a few lines which all contain the word "Mother": see *Inc. Ed.*, p. 287, §2, ll. 14–16, p. 291, §9, ll. 8–10, p. 296, §15, ll. 11–12, p. 298, §18, ll. 14–16, p. 299, §20, ll. 5–8. It was in 1867 too that he added a burden to "For You O Democracy" *(Inc. Ed.*, pp. 98–99, 592).

55. *Inc. Ed.*, p. 240. The first line is probably a reminiscence of Tennyson.

56. *Ibid.*, p. 255.

57. *Ibid.*, p. 402. See also "Ashes of Soldiers" (1865), pp. 318–319, and "Joy, Shipmate, Joy!" (1871), p. 415.

58. *Inc. Ed.*, pp. 265–266.

59. *Ibid.*, p. 269.

60. *Ibid.*, pp. 194–197.

61. *Ibid.*, p. 402.

62. *Ibid.*, p. 284.

63. T. B. Harned has left manuscript notes of his conversations with Whitman which are now kept in the library of Bryn Mawr College.

64. The stanzas of "Eidólons" consist of four lines; in each stanza, ll. 1 and 4 are in general dimeters or trimeters, ll. 2 and 3 are of variable lengths. The last line of each stanza always contains the word "eidólons" and thus is a sort of embryonic burden.

65. True, one might already regard "By Blue Ontario's Shore" as a symphonic poem built on two main motifs, the poet as a child and the song of the mocking-bird, on which are later grafted two minor motifs mentioned in §1 — the moon and the sea. This poem was composed in 1868. So there was no solution of continuity in Whitman's development, no break between what he wrote before the Civil War and what he wrote afterwards. Malcolm Cowley is therefore wrong, it seems to us, when he schematizes and oversimplifies Whitman's artistic evolution by dividing it into three periods: 1855–1856, 1856–1860, and the postwar period (in his introduction to *The Complete Poetry of Walt Whitman,* 1948, pp. 32–39). The war had no direct influence on the development of Whitman's art; the new tendencies which appeared in *Drum-Taps* already existed, at least potentially, in the first three editions of *Leaves of Grass.* The "Song of the Banner at Daybreak" (probably composed as early as 1861 or 1862) in which a father, his son, and the star-spangled banner speak in turn, also, in a way, consists of the intertwining of several motifs, but the alternation imposed by the very form of the dialogue remains mechanical and rather rigid.

66. *Inc. Ed.,* p. 276, §1. An analysis of this poem from a musical point of view will be found in Calvin S. Brown, *Music and Literature, a Comparison of the Arts* (Athens, Georgia: University of Georgia Press, 1948), pp. 178–194, under the title of "The musical development of symbols: Whitman."

67. "Blow trumpeter . . . ," "Blow again trumpeter . . . ," *Inc. Ed.,* pp. 390–391.

68. *Inc. Ed.,* pp. 379–384.

69. Whitman did not only try to compete with music by borrowing some of its techniques, but he also celebrated it more and more fervently in "Song of Myself" (1855), §26, ll. 15–29, "That Music Always Round Me" (1860), "The Singer in the Prison" (1869), "Proud Music of the Storm" (1871), "Italian Music in Dakota" (1881), "The Dead Tenor" (1888). On Whitman's love of music, see Julia Spiegelman, "Walt Whitman and Music," *South Atlantic Quarterly,* XLI (April 1942), 167–176, A. L. Cooke, "Notes on Whitman's Musical Background," *NEQ,* XIX (June 1946), 224–235, Louise Pound, "Walt Whitman and Italian Music," *American Mercury,* VI

(September 1925), 58–63, Georgiana Pollak, "The Relationship of Music to *Leaves of Grass*," *College English*, XV (April 1954), 384–394, Charmenz S. Lenhart, *Musical Influences on American Poetry* (University of Georgia Press, 1956), pp. 161–209 ("Walt Whitman and Music in *Leaves of Grass*"), Sydney F. Krause, "Whitman, Music and 'Proud Music of the Storm,' " *PMLA*, LXXII (September 1957), 705–721, Thomas L. Brasher, "Whitman's Conversion to Opera," *Walt Whitman Newsletter*, IV (December 1958), 109–110.

In 1846 and 1847, Whitman often went to the opera in New York; see "Plays and Operas Too," *SD*, pp. 19–20, *CP*, pp. 14–15. In Washington, he attended concerts quite regularly (*Calamus*, p. 27). He seems to have been especially sensitive to vocal music and more particularly to Italian opera, but he was also fond of instrumental music, as is shown by the tribute which he paid to Beethoven in *Specimen Days* ("Beethoven's Septette," *SD*, p. 158, *CP*, p. 158). Besides the poems on music which we have listed, Whitman thought of writing another which he never finished; see *FC*, pp. 13–14.

70. T. O. Mabbott and Rollo G. Silver, *A Child's Reminiscence* (Seattle: University of Washington Bookstore, 1930) pp. 19–21.

71. Besides the books and articles already mentioned, the reader will find useful information in Norman Guthrie, "Walt Whitman as a Poetic Artist," *Conservator*, April 1898, pp. 22–24, May–June 1898, pp. 52–55 (he was the first critic to attempt to scan *Leaves of Grass*), Pasquale Jannacone, *La Poesia di Walt Whitman e l'Evoluzione delle Forme Ritmiche* (Turin: R. Frascato, 1898) (excellent pioneering work), Fred Newton Scott, "A Note on Walt Whitman's Prosody," *Conservator*, July–September 1910, pp. 70–72, 85–90, 102–104, Gay W. Allen, *American Prosody* (New York, 1935), pp. 217–242, and by the same author, "On the Trochaic Meter of "Pioneers! O Pioneers!" *AL*, XX (January 1949), 449–451, in answer to Edward G. Fletcher, "Pioneers! O Pioneers!" *AL*, XIX (November 1947), 259–261, John Erskine, "Whitman's Prosody," *Studies in Philology*, XX (July 1923), 336–344, Ruth M. Weeks, "Phrasal Prosody, with special reference to Whitman," *English Journal*, X (January 1921), 11–19.

CONCLUSION

1. "A Backward Glance O'er Travel'd Roads," *Inc. Ed.*, p. 531. Same idea in the 1876 preface: "Then probably *Passage to India*, and its cluster, are but freer vent and fuller expression to what, from the first, and so on throughout, more or less lurks in my writings, underneath every page, every line, everywhere," *Inc. Ed.*, p. 513n.

2. "Song of Myself" (1855), *ibid.*, pp. 51–66, §§33–42.

3. "Out of the Cradle Endlessly Rocking" (1856), *ibid.*, p. 210, l. 20.

4. Malcolm Cowley, "Whitman: The Poet," *New Republic*, October 20, 1947, pp. 27–30, reprinted as an introduction to *The Complete Poetry and Prose of Walt Whitman*, 1948.

5. "Shakespeare-Bacon's Cipher," *Inc. Ed.*, p. 447. He used an image of the same kind in 1855 in "Or I guess it [the grass] is a uniform hieroglyphic . . ." ("Song of Myself," *ibid.*, p. 28, §6, l. 8).

6. Preface to 1876 edition, *Inc. Ed.*, p. 513n.

7. Newton Arvin, *Whitman*, pp. 222–231.

8. "After Trying a Certain Book," *SD*, p. 198, *CP*, pp. 195–196.

9. "To the Man-of-War Bird"; see Gay W. Allen, "Walt Whitman and Jules Michelet," *Etudes Anglaises*, I (May 1937), 230–237.

10. He realized it very well himself; see "Preface-Note to 2nd Annex" (1891), *Inc. Ed.*, p. 537.

11. For instance, included in *November Boughs* (1888) was "Small the Theme of My Chant" which had already been included in the edition of 1867 (as he acknowledged it himself) and "Stronger Lessons" (which he had published before, though he omitted to mention it). On the other hand, "A Prairie Sunset" and "Mirages" very probably dated back to his trip to the West in 1879.

12. See "Scented Herbage of My Breast," *Inc. Ed.*, p. 95.

13. See "You Lingering Sparse Leaves of Me" (1888), *Inc. Ed.*, p. 439, and "Lingering Last Drops" (1891), p. 443.

14. *CW*, VI, 7–16.

15. See Lionel Trilling, "Sermon on a Text from Whitman," *Nation*, CLX (1945), 215–220.

16. *Uncoll. PP*, II, 66.

17. See "Song of Myself," *Inc. Ed.*, p. 75, §21, ll. 6–8 and "Great Are the Myths," p. 706, l. 4 of the third stanza which originally followed l. 2 of §4. See also the preface to 1876 edition, p. 518, end of the note.

18. *With WW in C*, II, 37.

19. "There is hardly a proposition in Emerson's poems or prose which you cannot find the opposite of in some other place." *CW*, VI, 160 (2).

20. "I mean Negative Capability, that is, when a man is capable of being in uncertainties, mysteries, doubts, without any irritable reaching after fact and reason." John Keats, letter to George and Thomas Keats, dated December 22, 1817. Whitman knew this principle which was set forth in an article which he had read on "Modern Poetry and Poets" (*Catalogue of the Trent Collection*, p. 74); he had even underlined the whole passage, p. 224.

21. He borrowed the word from an article on oratory in the

Christian Intelligencer (July 2, 1857): "May not the Grecian orator have intended to recommend in addition to an animated delivery, the study of that style which Aristotle has named the 'agonistic,' wherein we wrestle with an auditory." Quoted by William L. Finkel in "Walt Whitman's Notes on Oratory," *AL*, XXII (March 1950), 39, n. 35. He spoke himself of the seven or eight "struggles" which had preceded the different editions of his book in "A Backward Glance" (1888), *Inc. Ed.*, p. 522.

22. *Uncoll. PP*, II, 79; a passage from a notebook dating back to 1850–1855.

23. *Uncoll. PP*, II, 97.

24. *Good-Bye and Hail Walt Whitman*, 1892, pp. 8–9.

25. Robert Ingersoll, "Liberty in Literature," *In Re*, p. 280.

26. "As I Sit Writing Here" (1888), *Inc. Ed.*, p. 422

27. "Sounds of the Winter" (1891–1892), *ibid.*, p. 451, ll. 6–7.

28. "Of That Blithe Throat of Thine" (1884), *ibid.*, p. 430.

29. "True Conquerors" (1888), *ibid.*, p. 434.

30. Theodore Spencer thought he had the cold eyes of a cat or a fish:

> The photographs of Whitman show
> Eyes as cold as those of a cat,
> Eyes like a cold fish, glass eyes . . .

"Walt," in *An Acre of Seed* (Cambridge, Mass.: Harvard University Press, 1949), p. 11.

31. His indomitable will to endure and hope was accompanied by a stubborn will to create which made him devote every single hour of his life to his poetical works: "Never even for one brief hour abandoning my task . . . ," "L. of G.'s Purport," *Inc. Ed.*, p. 456, l. 8.

He was also fond of quoting this passage by Bulwer-Lytton: "All men are born with genius, but every man can acquire a purpose, and purpose is the marrow and backbone of genius — nay, I can scarcely distinguish the one from the other." Moreover, he said that a great orator is "fully occupied with his subject and with nothing else all the time." (Thomas B. Harned, "Whitman and Oratory," *CW*, V, 225, 258.)

32. Here is the complete text of the letter-head he used in 1891: "From the *Boston Eve'g Transcript*, May 7, '91: The Epictetus saying as given by Walt Whitman in his own quite dilapidated case, is, 'a little spark of soul dragging a great lummux [sic] of corpse-body clumsily to and fro around.' "

33. Edward Carpenter for instance; see "A Visit to Walt Whitman in 1877," *Progressive Review*, I (February 1897), 408.

34. See "Out from Behind this Mask" (1876), *Inc. Ed.*, p. 321, §1, ll. 5–7, and *With WW in C*, II, 256–257. See also Bliss Perry,

"Whitman under the Searchlight," *New York Times Book Review,*
December 25, 1921.

35. "The Old Bowery," *NB,* pp. 88–89, CP, pp. 440–441.

36. Joaquin Miller realized it: "Yea, lone, sad soul, thy heights
must be thy home . . ." in "to Walt Whitman — A poem," *Galaxy,*
January 1877, p. 29.

37. "Starting from Paumanok," *Inc. Ed.,* p. 12, §1, l. 14.

38. He was quite aware of his own inadaptation to society, as is
shown by the following remarks which he once made to Traubel:

You know there is a sense in which I want to be cosmopolitan:
then again a sense in which I make much of patriotism — of our
native stock, the American stock, ancestry, the United States . . .
That is the same old question, adjusting the individual to the mass
. . . Yes, the big problem — the only problem of them all.

With WW in C, III, 132.

39. See his "Ode to Walt Whitman."

40. Quoted by Rollo G. Silver, "Walt Whitman and Dickens," *AL,*
V (January 1934), 370–371.

GENERAL INDEX

References to pages in the bibliography are marked by a superior b.

INDEX OF POEMS AND PROSE-WRITINGS